GEORGE CANNING

GEORGE CANNING
by Lawrence

George
CANNING

Wendy Hinde

ST. MARTIN'S PRESS

NEW YORK

AFFILIATED PUBLISHERS: Macmillan & Company, Limited, London—
also at Bombay, Calcutta, Madras and Melbourne

Contents

Illustrations

Acknowledgements

I would like to thank the following for their kind permission to quote from manuscript material in their possession or care:— the Earl of Harewood (Harewood Mss); the City of Leeds (Stapleton Mss); the Trustees of the British Museum; and the Keeper of the Public Record Office. I am very grateful for the friendly co-operation I always received from Mr Collinson, the Leeds City archivist, and his staff at the Sheepscar Library where the Harewood and Stapleton manuscripts are kept. I would also like to thank the staff of the London Library for their invariable helpfulness. This book could never have been written without the London Library, with its comprehensive resources and generous lending policy. Finally, I would like to express my warm thanks to Patricia Norton for scrupulously going through the proofs, and to Sally Bicknell for the painstaking and meticulous care with which she has constructed the index.

G.C.

B

CHAPTER I

Childhood and Youth
1770-1793

George Canning was born in London, in the parish of Marylebone, some time between eight and nine o'clock on the morning of April 11, 1770. His father, announcing the birth to his brother a few hours later, wrote: 'He is a sturdy fellow and roars most lustily.'[1]

The Canning family originally came from the West country and during the fourteenth and fifteenth centuries various members distinguished themselves as merchants and civic dignitaries of Bristol. In the middle of the fifteenth century a certain Thomas Canynges moved to London where he became Sheriff and later Lord Mayor. Through his marriage to an heiress he acquired the estate of Foxcote in Warwickshire, which became the family home. In 1618 one of his descendants, George Canninge, emigrated to the English plantations in Ulster after being granted the manor of Garvagh in Derry by James I. The family remained Protestant, survived the troubles of the seventeenth century and eventually prospered in a modest way.[2]

Stratford Canning, the grandfather of George Canning, was stern, austere and so formidable that his children used to listen with terror to the creaking of his shoes as he walked about the house. He had three sons and disinherited two of them. George, the eldest, born in 1736, fell in love with a young lady of whom his father, for no apparent reason, violently disapproved. He did not marry her but was exiled to London all the same with a meagre annual allowance of £150 – perhaps because he had also disgraced himself in his father's eyes by writing verse and holding advanced views on civil and religious liberty. In London he read for the Bar and was actually called at the Middle Temple. But he was more interested in literary and political controversy than in getting on in his profession and he did not improve his prospects by becoming a violent partisan of Wilkes. He ran seriously into debt and was forced to appeal to his father, who refused to help him out unless he agreed to allow himself to be disinherited.

Undeterred by his bleak prospects, George Canning senior proceeded to woo and win a beautiful young Irish girl called Mary Ann Costello, who was living in the care of her maternal grandfather, Colonel

Guydickens, in Wigmore Street. Mary Ann came of a good family and had everything to recommend her except that she was penniless. But both she and Canning were too deeply in love – and perhaps too Irish in temperament – to let poverty stand in their way. They were married at Marylebone Church on May 21, 1768. Their first child, a girl, was born the following spring but did not survive more than a few months. Their son George was more robust, but his chances of being reared in anything but dire poverty were slim. The elder George Canning's allowance of £150 was quite inadequate to support a family. He tried without success to get an official appointment and was reduced to borrowing what he could from friends. A year after his son's birth he died, suddenly and unexpectedly, from an 'inflammation in his bowels.'

At the age of 24, Mary Ann Canning was left a widow with a baby son and, since her husband's allowance stopped at his death, without any means of support. She was also again pregnant. Among her own family she seems to have had no one to whom she could turn. On the Canning side there was her father-in-law in Ireland, and Stratford, her husband's youngest brother. Stratford had also been sent to London to fend for himself after making a marriage of which his father disapproved. He had gone into business and although not feckless like his eldest brother had a hard struggle during his first years in London. He managed all the same to send his sister-in-law small sums of money from time to time. But old Stratford Canning's anger against his eldest son was not softened by his death nor by the birth of a grandson. In reply to Mary Ann's appeal for help, he said he would allow her £40 a year so long as she remained in England. He enclosed a first instalment of £20 which she used to pay her husband's funeral expenses. On December 23, 1771, she gave birth to a second son. He lived for a few years but exactly when or why he died, or even what he was called, is not known. After his birth, Mary Ann made another appeal to her father-in-law. He replied that the £40 was for her children and he would increase it as they grew older, but he felt no obligation towards her. When she wrote a third time, more than two years after her husband's death, he did not even reply.[3]

At this point Mary Ann decided to try her fortune on the stage. It was a socially disastrous step but there was little else she could do to provide for herself and her children. The great Garrick was persuaded, with some difficulty, to see her and eventually decided to give her a part. She made her debut at Drury Lane in November 1773 in a drama called *Jane Shore* in which Garrick also played. She was beautiful and had a very attractive voice. But she was not much of an actress and did not manage to stay the course at Drury Lane, even in minor roles, for much more than a year. After that she was obliged to descend to the provincial theatre, often in the West country, where she was more successful. She also began to live with a well-known tragic actor called Samuel Reddish. Although extremely attractive to women, he was dissolute and disreputable. Mary Ann called herself Mrs Reddish and bore him several children, but there is no evidence that they were ever legally married.[4]

How long the liaison between Reddish and Mary Ann lasted is not known, but before it ended young George had been removed and placed in the care of his uncle, Stratford Canning. By this time Stratford was a prosperous merchant. He had apparently broken off all communication with his sister-in-law when she went on the stage, but was persuaded to take charge of her son by an actor called Moody who knew Reddish and was anxious to remove the boy from the influence of such an unsuitable pseudo-stepfather. At the same time George's grandfather in Ireland at last brought himself to make adequate provision for the boy's maintenance and education.

Thus at the age of eight young George Canning was transplanted from the impecunious and unstable background of a touring actor, which was the only one he could remember, to a comfortable, highly respectable middle-class home and a prep school called Hyde Abbey at Winchester. What the boy thought of his changed circumstances we do not know. He certainly came to enjoy his school and there is no reason to suppose that he was unhappy with his uncle, aunt and cousins in the holidays. But he never ceased to yearn for his mother who had loved him with a passionate, demonstrative love; nor did he forget his unknown father, whose memory his mother must have kept alive. The first letter to his mother which survives is dated November 19, 1780. It is a rather blotched epistle in which he tells her that when it came to his turn to learn a poem and recite it before the whole school, he had chosen a poem of his father's called: 'The Epistle from Lord William Russell to William Lord Cavendish.'[5] The elder George Canning was reputed to have been a very indifferent poet, but presumably the filial piety of a ten-year-old was not very discriminating.

When he was twelve George left Hyde Abbey and went to Eton. At first, very naturally, he was unhappy in his new surroundings, and his sense of insecurity and loneliness expressed itself in anxiety about his mother, whom he now had not seen for four years. To make matters worse he had not heard from her for some time. In one rather frantic letter towards the end of September 1782, he pleaded: '. . . do pray write dearest Mother for I am excessively uneasy I do assure you I am.'[6] A few weeks later, however, having made a good start by being placed at once in the fourth form, he decided that Eton was not such a bad place after all and began to write much more calmly and even complacently. 'As to my dislike to Eton School, I find it wears off as I grow more acquainted with the boys and as my station is pretty high I shall soon be able to be very easy here.'[7]

His five years at Eton were in fact very happy and successful. He made many good and some lifelong friends, in particular the brilliant but eccentric John Hookham Frere and Charles Ellis whose family fortune had been made in the West Indies and who became, and remained, the closest and dearest of all Canning's friends. He also enjoyed his studies with their strong bias towards the classics, although at the end of his fourth year he confessed to a friend that he had not always been as diligent as he might have been. His slacking, however, had not prevented him from coming out top of the school. His success entitled him to become a colleger, but he stoutly refused to give up the more prestigious and more comfortable status of 'commoner'.* From his point of view there were also practical disadvantages in going on the foundation to set against the financial saving and the possibility of a place at King's College, Cambridge. As a colleger, he would be obliged to stay at Eton until he was nineteen, whereas as a commoner he could leave at seventeen. He had already made up his mind to read for the Bar and the two years gained in starting on his career seemed well worth having.[8]

In the sixth form at Eton there were many opportunities for declaiming passages from the classics and it was there that Canning first discovered his flair for public speaking. In a letter to a friend, he wrote with obvious satisfaction of 'some very *oratorical* parts' in the passages he had been reciting. He meant, he added, 'parts very pleasant to speak, as being very fine turns etc.'[9] On public occasions at the school he was able to orate to a wider audience and on Election Day during his last term he received the honour of being chosen to speak last.

Public speaking was not the only field in which Canning had made something of a name for himself by the time he left school. During his last year he played a large part in the production of a weekly paper called the *Microcosm*. Purporting to be the work of a certain Gregory Griffin of the College of Eton (the Microcosmopolitan) it was in fact the work of Canning and three friends – John Hookham Frere, John

* His own words: the modern term is 'oppidan'.

Smith and Robert (Bobus) Smith. They took it in turns to be responsible for an entire number and wrote on whatever subject took their fancy. Canning described the project as 'very entertaining and amusing'.[10] One of his contributions was an essay on the art of swearing, another parodied literary criticism with a 'Critique on the Heroic Poem of the Knave of Hearts', and a third poked fun at the sentimental novels which were then very much in vogue. The periodical, which was printed and published by a bookseller in Windsor, enjoyed a much wider and more appreciative readership than most schoolboy efforts. By the tenth number, it was selling about 700 copies – enough to cover expenses if not to make the authors' fortunes. Eventually they sold the copyright for £50 and by 1825 five editions had been printed and sold.

The most eminent readers of the *Microcosm* were the King and Queen, who always took a great interest in the Eton boys and their activities. When Canning met them on the Terrace at Windsor just after the end of his last term, the King entered into what Canning condescendingly described as 'a tiresome enough but gracious conversation', asking him about his college, profession and future plans, while the Queen congratulated him and his colleagues on the *Microcosm* and told him that she was sorry 'to lose so pleasant a companion at breakfast'.[11] For many years afterwards, whenever the royal couple met Canning, they never failed to remind him of the *Microcosm*. Nine years later, when he went to Court soon after being made Under-Secretary of State at the Foreign Office, the King asked his chief, Lord Grenville, whether he had written much yet, adding, 'We all know he *can* write, my Lord, we remember the *Microcosm* at Eton.'[12]

By the time he left Eton at the age of seventeen, Canning had every reason to feel satisfied and some excuse for being self-satisfied. He had been successful and popular at school and he faced the future with a confident belief in his ability to make the most of it. The poverty and vicissitudes of his early life seemed to have left him unscarred. But in spite of all that he had gained in worldly terms over the past nine years, he still missed the emotional security of his mother's presence and love. Soon after he went to Eton, in February 1783, she became the wife of Richard Hunn, a silk mercer of Plymouth. But although now respectably married, she still had to earn her living on the stage, for Hunn, having failed to make much of a success of his trade, decided that he too would seek his fortune on the boards. Mrs Hunn was therefore still considered unfit for respectable society and George's uncle felt it his duty to tell him so. The twelve-year-old boy, who probably had no idea what his uncle was getting at, seems not to have been impressed. He sent warm good wishes to his mother's new husband and went on longing to see her and fretting when she did not write.[13]

When George was just fifteen, his uncle turned down an appeal from Mrs Hunn that she should be allowed to see her eldest son. He told the boy that there was too great a risk of his mind receiving a bias which might be prejudicial to him during the rest of his life and he must not see his mother until he had acquired 'a sufficient stock of proper sentiments'.[14] It seems unlikely that George managed to achieve this in less than a year, but for whatever reason he was at last allowed to visit his mother when she came to London the following February in search of work. It was the first time they had met for eight years. There is no record of George's immediate reactions, but to judge from his subsequent conduct, the meeting did nothing to shake his affection for his mother or lessen his anxiety for her welfare. In November 1786, the death of his grandmother, the elder Stratford Canning's widow, brought him under the terms of her husband's will a small estate in Ireland worth some £400 a year. It was sufficient for him to work and study 'as a gentleman', but not to provide for his mother as well. However, he persuaded his guardian to let him make her an annual allowance of £50; it would, he hoped, be enough to shield her from actual want.[15]

It is clear that Hetty Canning, Stratford's wife, never filled the emotional gap created for George by his separation from his mother. She was a very intelligent, high-spirited, kind-hearted and competent woman. Like her husband, she was a dedicated Whig, and both Fox and Sheridan were sufficiently attracted by her company to call frequently at her house in Putney. George Canning owed, and knew that he owed, a great deal to her. But for some reason – perhaps partly because of the Stratford Cannings' undisguised disapproval of his mother – she did not inspire him with any very strong or warm affection. Of her daughter, Bessy, he was very fond. She was eight years his junior and he treated her with the bantering affection of an elder brother. But among his Canning relatives, it was Stratford's sister Bess and her husband, the Reverend William Leigh, who meant most to George. From the age of thirteen he began to spend at least part of his Christmas holidays with them at their home in Norwich. In the summer of 1784 they took him to Lowestoft with them, and in his letter to his mother reporting his first sight of the sea, he added that he loved the Leighs very much.[16] After Stratford Canning's death in May

1787, George looked primarily to Mr Leigh for advice and guidance, although his uncle's business partner, Mr Borrowes, was made his legal guardian.

In the autumn of 1787 Canning went up to Christ Church. He chose Oxford, not because of any personal preference, but because his uncle Stratford had wanted him to go there. Among the Oxford colleges, however, Christ Church was very much his first choice. He went up full of good intentions to work hard and do everything he ought to do. He was still determined to make the law his profession, but beyond that the distant prospect of the House of Commons was beginning to lure him, even though he described it rather disparagingly as 'a field, open indeed, not so much for *solid pudding* as empty praise'.[17]

He did indeed work hard, but he also found time to be sociable, to play elaborate practical jokes and to make some lively and intelligent friends. It was now that he first met Robert Banks Jenkinson and began the lifelong relationship which after surviving more than its fair share of ups and downs ended with nearly five years of harmonious and fruitful co-operation as Prime Minister and Foreign Secretary. Jenkinson was the eldest son of the first Lord Hawkesbury, one of William Pitt's ministers. He was an extremely earnest young man with awkward manners. But Canning took to him at once and described him as 'very clever and very remarkably good-natured'.[18] Before long the two young men were leading members of a select debating society which met every Thursday evening in the rooms of one of its members. They devised a special coat of a rather uncommon shade of brown, with velvet cuffs and collar and the initials D., C., P. and F. entwined on the buttons. The initials stood for Demosthenes, Cicero, Pitt and Fox. Sometimes the members appeared in hall in their uniform and thoroughly enjoyed the curiosity it provoked.[19] When the club's activities began to leak out, the Dean of Christ Church, Dr Cyril Jackson, decided to give Canning a friendly warning that his prominence in the club would inevitably cause him to be suspected of political ambitions and this might well damage his prospects in the legal profession. Canning, who respected and liked the Dean, heeded his warning and resigned from the club.

His fellow debaters were furious, but as yet the fascination of politics did not blind Canning to more prudent considerations. Unlike many of his Oxford friends, he had his own way to make in the world; he had no family wealth or connections to hoist him into a ready-made political niche. 'I am already, God knows,' he wrote to an Oxford friend, 'too much inclined, both by my own sanguine wishes and the connections with which I am most intimate, and whom I above all others revere, to aim at the House of Commons, as the only path to the only desirable thing in this world, the gratification of ambition; while at the same time every tie of common sense, of fortune, of duty, draws me to the study of a profession. The former propensity I hope reflection, necessity, and the friendly advice and very marked attentions of the Dean, will enable me to overcome; and to the Law I look, as the profession which, in this country, holds out every enticement that can nerve the exertions and give vigour to the powers of a young man. The way, indeed, is long, toilsome and rugged; but it leads to honours solid and lasting; to independence without which no blessings of fortune, however profuse, no distinction of station, however splendid, can afford a liberal mind true satisfaction; to power, for which no task can be too hard, no labours too trying.'[20]

After making such an effort to be sensible and high-minded about his future, it was perhaps not surprising that Canning should face the prospect of his second year at Oxford in a thoroughly gloomy frame of mind. He was, moreover, cast down by the departure of so many of his friends, including Jenkinson. He was convinced that he was left with not more than five faces which he ever wished to see again. 'I begin to look forward,' he told Mr Leigh, 'with a sort of shuddering horror, to the dull days which are to pass over my head this next term in that dungeon Christ Church. Nothing but the kindness of our gaoler, the Dean, could make it tolerable.'[21]

In the event, his remaining years at Oxford were very happy. It turned out that the friends who had gone down were not irreplaceable. He made many new ones and some remained close friends for life. There was Lord Boringdon, who had a beautiful house at Saltram, overlooking Plymouth; Lord Morpeth, later the Earl of Carlisle, who played an important part in Canning's negotiations with the Lansdowne Whigs forty years later; Charles Moore, the son of the Archbishop of Canterbury; William Sturges Bourne, a great fusser, whom Canning loved to agitate with absurd stories and whom he once described as having 'a natural disposition to see in black rather than rose-colour'. Above all there was Lord Granville Leveson-Gower, son of the Marquess of Stafford and three years younger than Canning, for whom he formed a warm if rather bossy attachment.

The busy social round of an Oxford undergraduate did not divert

Canning altogether from his studies. In fact he turned himself into a first class classical scholar and at the end of his second year carried off both a college and a university prize for Latin verse. In his third year, to his great delight, Dr Jackson awarded him a studentship. From a financial point of view it was not worth much. 'Its greatest value in my eyes,' wrote Canning, 'is its having been given to me in such a manner as to become a testimony of the Dean's esteem and goodwill towards me.'[22] And since hard work was the only way in which he could show his appreciation of Dr Jackson's kindness, the studentship would also help, 'if anything can, to conquer a sort of lounging indolence which yet I fear I have but half got the better of. . .'[23] It was not a weakness that was to trouble him for long.

One of the advantages of the studentship was that it allowed Canning to live at Christ Church for almost nothing during the vacations. He took full advantage of this privilege during the short vacations, partly in order to economise and partly because he enjoyed the unaccustomed peace and quiet of his surroundings and the opportunity to get on with his work. He was very anxious to learn French and spent much time working away at it with the help of a French tutor. On New Year's Eve 1789 he told Leveson-Gower that he had spent a solitary Christmas at Christ Church and 'du Quesne and I every day make a most astounding progress in the French tongue'. He added that he had come to enjoy his solitude and was not sure whether he looked forward to the return of 'all you noisy riotous animals with any great impatience'.[24]

His long vacations were spent staying with friends and relations – as often as he could with the Leighs at Bath or Yarmouth or their new home, Ashbourne Hall, in Derbyshire, and not as often as he should with his aunt Hetty, who had moved to Wanstead soon after her husband's death. Through Mrs Canning's Whig friends he was introduced to Mrs Crewe, the famous Whig hostess, who took him up and gave him what seems to have been an open invitation to her country house near Chester. Canning very much enjoyed staying there because everybody was allowed to do exactly what they liked. Moreover it was an excellent free holiday, and more than once when he was obliged to economise he was glad to settle down quietly at Crewe Hall. In October 1790, he paid the first of many visits to Trentham, the vast country house of Leveson-Gower's parents. Apart from Crewe Hall, where he felt rather on home ground, it was his first visit to a big country house and at first he felt rather nervous at being in company that was both grand and almost entirely unknown to him. But after a few hours his shyness wore off and together with Leveson-Gower and Boringdon he ended the evening sitting up with Lord Stafford (who was Lord Privy Seal) and the Attorney-General 'talking, sometimes as wisely as if *we* had been veteran statesmen, like them, and sometimes as foolishly as if *they* had been young, like us.' He came away next morning 'very much delighted with all the people I had seen, and half in love with two or three of the Lady Levesons'[25]. His host and hostess, for their part, took equally quickly to him. Lady Stafford in particular grew very fond of him, partly for his own sake and partly because he had a habit of saying, with transparent sincerity, such nice things about her son.[26]

During the summer of 1790 he made an excursion with some friends to the Lakes, staying at Low Wood, by Windermere. He did not, however, share the passion felt by so many of his contemporaries for the beauties of nature and firmly told his mother not to expect any description of Windermere, Grasmere and so on, 'for though the romantic scenery which characterises them is very charming when seen, yet I do not think it very pleasant to describe it or very satisfactory to hear it described.'[27] No doubt the inevitable rain helped to put him off. His cousin Bessy was told that, 'it always rains, at least I guess so, as we were drenched every day regularly – and the people on the banks of Windermere told us that they had been drenched too, every day for two months before we arrived there.' Altogether, Canning's visit to the Lakes made him appreciate not the beauty of the scenery, but 'the comfort of a good bed, clean linen – and a cheering fire'.[28]

Canning's only serious worry throughout his Oxford years was his mother. Richard Hunn turned out to be no more successful on the stage than he had been in trade, and his wife's chances of success were not improved by advancing years and the production of five more children. But it was not only his mother's poverty which worried Canning. As he grew older and learnt more of the world and its ways, he became increasingly distressed by the way in which she earned her precarious livelihood. When he was a boy of fifteen he had been eager for the success of her latest 'theatrical campaign' and suggested that perhaps Exeter and Plymouth were not the best places in which to display her talents. 'I should not think,' he wrote with youthful superiority, 'the feelings of the people of Plymouth (being as I suppose they are so very conversant and intermixed with seafaring people) particularly alive to tender emotions, or sensible of the refined amusements of a theatre.'²⁹ Three years later, when his mother was playing at Chester, he was not too proud to ask Mrs Crewe to patronise her benefit night; but he could not bring himself to stay at Crewe Hall while his mother was so close because it would be too painful to feel obliged to go and see her on the stage.³⁰

He longed to rescue his mother from the theatre, but his own finances were none too sound* and he could not afford to raise her annual allowance, although in June 1791 he managed to send her a hundred guineas, all but ten of which were to be laid out for the benefit of his half-sister Mary Hunn. At the same time, he bluntly told his mother that if she stayed in the theatre she could not help but harm Mary and also himself once he had embarked on his legal career. 'My dear Mother,' he wrote, 'everything is surely to be considered, not so much as what it really is, as what the world *thinks* it to be. When I say everything, I mean only such things as concern neither religion nor morality (where all is fixed and settled beyond the wavering of worldly opinion) – such things as are in themselves indifferent or variable, and therefore take their colour from the light in which the world may please to view them. Among these are professions; and there is perhaps no subject on which public opinion decides more positively than on the respectability or *dis*respectability of different pursuits and occupations.' Admittedly, he added, 'the world is capricious and unjust – but it is peremptory – and to explain myself fully – need I do more than ask you – to what cause is Mr Sheridan's want of success and popularity to be attributed?'³¹ Whether or not Canning was correct in his diagnosis of Sheridan's problems, he was certainly right about the world's attitude to the stage and those connected with it. Inevitably, in spite of his generosity and his genuine affection, an element of self-interest was beginning to enter into his attitude towards his mother.

Perhaps the consciousness that he was about to grapple with the world himself helped to make Canning deliver this worldly lecture to his mother. It was June, 1791. He had just taken his degree and come down from Oxford and his mind was very full of his future. But before embarking on it he spent a couple of months in Holland and Brussels with his friend, Charles Moore. Canning described their stay in the Hague as 'most rational and improving'³² – which indeed it must have been since he spent much of his time continuing his protracted struggle with the French language. Most of the young men's company was

* In October 1792, Canning asked Mr Leigh to lend him £300 to pay off his debts in Oxford and London as the expected funds from Ireland had not arrived. (Harewood Mss. 12)

provided by the family and friends of the British ambassador, Lord Auckland, and their chief relaxation was visits to the 'french comedy'. Before going on to Brussels they took a short sightseeing trip to Leyden, Haarlem, Amsterdam and Utrecht. Like many other English travellers before and since, Canning had a sensitive nose for foreign smells; at the end of the trip he reported that only the Hague seemed to be free of the 'most noisome and unwholesome smells.'[33]

By the end of September he was back in England. Shortly afterwards he established himself in chambers in Paper Buildings, Lincoln's Inn, and settled down to his new studies. He spent the Christmas vacation at Christ Church in some rooms borrowed from Lord Holland, partly to economise and partly in order to make use of the college's excellent law library. But he was gradually becoming aware that the law was not enough. The possibility of entering politics, which until then he had allowed himself to consider only as a distant goal, was becoming something at which to aim in the much more immediate future. Possibly his early resolutions to concentrate on the law would have gone by the board anyway. But the tumultuous events set in motion by the French Revolution and the reactions to them in England must have sharply stimulated his interest in politics. Even more important, they forced him to examine the political outlook in which he had been brought up and make up his own mind whether it was adequate for the world in which he found himself.

Canning had imbibed the pure milk of Whiggism from the Stratford Cannings and their distinguished circle. With Sheridan in particular his relations had been so close that many people were under the impression that he was his ward. Sheridan and Fox had sympathised with his desire not to become a colleger at Eton and had helped to persuade his uncle to let him remain a commoner. It was with Sheridan that he stayed at the time of his uncle's death. And when he left Eton he confidently looked to him for help and advice. 'His advice and assistance,' he wrote, 'will, doubtless, be to me of every advantage, and will be always open to me.'[34] In May 1790, when Sheridan gave 'a grand supper and catch singing', he introduced his young friend to the Prince of Wales and Canning was immensely flattered to be honoured with a 'good deal' of the prince's conversation.[35] Fox and Mrs Armitstead (whom Fox later married) also treated Canning with great kindness. During his last term at Oxford he met 'Mr Fox and his lady' several times at different places between Oxford and London and 'paddled about with them and Lord Holland and other folks on the water and dined by the side of clear streams at Clifden on cold viands of the most exquisite flavour.'[36]

Personal regard for his Whig friends reinforced Canning's youthful idealism and during his years at Oxford he became known for his enthusiastically radical outlook. George III, in spite of his enthusiasm for the *Microcosm*, was reported to have said that Canning's republican principles had done great harm at Christ Church.[37] But from the little we know of them from Canning himself, they seem to have been too utopian and theoretical to be taken very seriously. Like many other liberal-minded Englishmen, he welcomed the outbreak of the French Revolution. He believed in 'the eternal and immutable principle' that every country should be allowed to choose its own form of government and he admitted to 'a sort of *speculative fondness* . . . for the idea of a *Representative Republic*; and a desire to ascertain, by the *experience* of a *neighbour*, without being at any of the risk or expense of the experiment at *home*, how far *such* a form of government would increase or diminish the freedom and happiness of a people.'[38]

This attitude of cool detachment was not common in the political party towards which Canning had been naturally gravitating. The Whigs in fact were deeply divided over the significance of the revolution in France. To Fox it was one of the most glorious events in the history of mankind; to the Irishman Edmund Burke it was a threat to the whole fabric of society. In his *Reflections on the Revolution in France*, published in November, 1790, Burke showed a very imperfect grasp of what lay behind the upheaval in France, but he expressed in moving and eloquent prose some of the educated Englishman's deepest feelings about his own society and system of government. With his appeal to traditional values, his condemnation of facile generalising about abstract rights and his solemn warning against the danger of heedlessly pulling up a people's past by the roots, he appealed to his countrymen's innate conservatism and practical common sense. He foresaw all the dangers that might – and indeed did – flow from the new system in France; he perceived that it did not abolish the exercise of uncontrolled absolute power, but placed it in other hands. He realised too – before most of his contemporaries – that sparks from the conflagration in France might fly across the Channel. 'Whenever our neighbour's house is on fire, it cannot be amiss for the engines to play a little on our own.' But Fox, with his extravagant praise of the new French institutions, seemed to be fanning the flames, rather than dousing them.

Fox tried to preserve his private friendship with Burke and to minimise their dispute by arguing that it was a purely theoretical difference. Burke's prophecies of disaster were ahead of public opinion, both inside and outside the Whig party, and Fox was able – for the time being – to keep the support of the party, but he lost Burke both as political ally and private friend. In his passionate way, Burke rejected all compromise and every olive branch and in May 1791 a paragraph in the *Morning Chronicle* formally announced his separation from the Whigs. Fox's victory, however, was more apparent than real. Many of the Whig aristocrats had supported him out of personal loyalty, but privately they deplored his uncritical admiration of the French Revolution and sympathised with Burke's appeal to order and tradition. They were alarmed by the spread of popular political clubs inspired by the writings of Tom Paine and the revolutionary upheaval in France. At the other extreme, some of the younger Whigs, affected in a different way by events across the Channel, were becoming increasingly exasperated by their elders' reluctance to contemplate really radical reform.

Unfortunately we know virtually nothing about Canning's reactions to the quarrel between Burke and Fox. He appears to have gone on regarding the French Revolution as an interesting experiment – for the French. But from a few stray comments made later it is clear that he greatly admired Burke; and the whole trend of his subsequent political thinking suggests that he was greatly attracted by his ideas. 'As to this country,' he wrote towards the end of 1792, ' – though I am not so enthusiastically attached to the beauties of its constitution, and still less so determinedly blind to its defects, as to believe it unimprovable – yet I *do* think it by much the best practical Government that the world has ever seen. . .' And, he added, 'I do think it almost impossible to begin improving now, without a risk of being hurried beyond all limits of prudence and happiness . . .'[39] But some of the Whigs seemed determined to do just that.

According to his own account, what finally provoked Canning's rejection of the Whigs was the formation of the Association of the Friends of the People by a group of radical young Whigs led by Charles Grey in April 1792. Their chief aim was to press for parliamentary reform. The Whigs had always been divided on this issue, and to raise it when popular agitation, partly political and partly economic, was creating considerable alarm could only deepen the divisions in the party and damage its standing in the country as a whole. The Friends had hoped to put themselves at the head of the reforming movement and make it respectable. But they were distrusted by the working class societies and attacked by the ministerial press as levellers and repub-

CANNING
by Hoppner

PITT
by Hoppner

GRENVILLE
by Hoppner

SPENCER PERCEVAL
by G. F. Joseph

licans. In Canning's view, they made it impossible for any man to agree any longer with the whole of the opposition and after trying to decide which part he agreed with, he decided to reject both.[40] He asked himself whether 'amidst a general change and division and confusion, I, who had never yet declared any choice, might not without question or control, without reproach from my own mind, or from any other person, choose for myself? I could find no good reason to the contrary.'[41]

We do not know whether, or how far, Canning's decision to sever any political connection which the world might suppose him to have with the Whigs was influenced by his irrepressible desire to enter politics himself. If it was, it was neither shameful nor surprising. Although he kept it very much to himself, it is clear that by the summer of 1792 he had lost the long battle against his political ambitions. And having decided that he wanted to become a politician sooner rather than later, it was natural that his disenchantment with Whig views and the damaging disarray in the Whig ranks should combine to make him turn towards the governing party. When it became public knowledge, some Whigs accused him of political apostasy and opportunism. But a young man of 22, whose only practical experience of politics had been undergraduate debating, could hardly be expected to allow his political views and prospects to be permanently governed by the friendships of his childhood and youth. At some stage the young usually weigh the wisdom of their elders and as often as not find it wanting. Canning in particular could never take the views of anyone, however distinguished, on trust; he had to work out his own opinions for himself.

Pitt was first made aware of Canning's wish to enter politics on the government side through some friend or intermediary – it is not clear exactly who or exactly when. But on July 26, 1792, Canning himself wrote to the prime minister to ask permission to call. He explained that although he was on terms of familiar friendship with some of the most eminent members of the opposition, he was not in any way committed to them politically. He also made it clear that although he wanted to enter Parliament, he lacked the financial resources to bring himself in.[42] Pitt replied two days later from his mother's home in Somerset, asking Canning to call in Downing Street on August 15 and expressing his satisfaction at the prospect of 'forming a personal acquaintance and connection with one whom I have long known by reputation, and whose talents I sincerely wish to see exerted for the benefit of the public.'[43]

In his account of his first meeting with Pitt, Canning gives no hint of the warm personal attachment that he came to feel for him. He merely remarked that 'he was at least as awkward as I' and took a long time to get down to business. Presumably to Pitt, the budding young politician was simply a promising recruit whom it would be worth while to try to filch from the opposition. But although he may have flattered Canning, he did not delude him with any false expectations of what he could do for him. Canning for his part made it clear that there were strict limits on what he would have done for him. He was deter-mined not to enter Parliament with any commitments to anyone except Pitt personally and the administration in general. Pitt explained that the amount of patronage directly at his disposal was tiny but that sometimes owners of seats were prepared to dispose of them simply at his recom-mendation. Canning replied that this would be acceptable so long as it was clear that he owed the seat to Pitt's recommendation and not to the owner's choice. He also expressed the hope that he would be allowed to make up his own mind on issues that were not of major importance to the government, like the Test Act on which he knew that he and the prime minister disagreed. Pitt accommodatingly replied that think-ing men could not always be expected to agree, especially on 'speculative subjects' and what he hoped for from Canning was 'a general good disposition towards Government'.[44]

There, for the time being, the matter rested. Pitt was prepared to try to bring Canning into Parliament on terms that were acceptable to the young man, but he could give no undertaking when this would be. Canning was probably relieved that his metamorphosis into a follower of Pitt should not burst on the world too suddenly. He could not help feeling rather nervous about the reception it would get, especially from his Whig friends. Sheridan was informed indirectly by a series of carefully dropped hints and passed the news on to Fox. Mrs Hetty Canning took her nephew's decision very badly and her unsuccessful efforts to argue him out of it imposed a new strain on their relationship. It was, however, more important to him that the Leighs should have thoroughly approved. So to a large extent must Mrs Crewe have done. She too sympathised with Burke's ideas and she was a close friend of the Duchess of Portland whose husband was beginning to be sadly torn between his loyalty to Fox and his fear of political disorder and social upheaval.

By the end of 1792 events at home and abroad were confirming Canning in the rightness of his choice and making it easier for him to justify it to his friends. The September massacres in Paris shocked

English people as no previous event in the Revolution had done. Canning was distressed that by 'those dreadful excesses' the French should have shown themselves unworthy of the liberty he had been so anxious for them to obtain. But – rather surprisingly – he was not yet completely disillusioned with the French 'experiment'. He strongly disapproved of the efforts of a continental coalition, led by the Duke of Brunswick (with his 'bloody blackguard *manifestoes*') to crush the French revolutionaries,[45] and rejoiced greatly in the duke's defeat at Valmy on September 20 – 'not only as a liberal politician would rejoice in the repulsion of any attack upon the political liberties of a nation – but also as Walker the philosopher would rejoice in the punishment of any boy at Eton who should have attempted to spoil his electrical experiments, by breaking one of his great cylindrical glasses.'[46]*

But Canning began to feel very differently when the French in their turn took to issuing manifestoes and invading other countries. By the end of the year they had not only proclaimed their readiness to help revolutionaries everywhere, but had invaded Belgium and occupied Savoy and Nice. Canning indignantly described their activities as 'a system of impudent, savage and profligate warfare, equal to the most tyrannous enterprises of the most despotic governments.'[47] In England the increase in radical agitation and the ostentatious fraternisation of the London Corresponding Society and the other political clubs with the French Convention made it seem as if revolutionary sparks might after all start a blaze across the Channel. Early in December, 1792, Canning wrote that the 'rapid progress of the French arms, and the wide diffusion of French principles, has given to a republican party here such strength and spirit that there is, in my opinion, nothing mischievous and desperate that may not be apprehended from them.'[48] He did not realise, any more than his elders, that bad harvests and economic distress were just as inflammatory as revolutionary slogans.

The execution of Louis XVI in January 1793 and the French declaration of war on England in the following month must have helped to complete Canning's disillusionment with the French revolutionary experiment. Even Pitt and his colleagues in the government, who had hitherto regarded the chaotic events in France with cool disdain, were forced to see that they could no longer stand aloof. The quickening tempo of events seems to have made Canning anxious to

---

* Presumably a reference to Adam Walker who lectured at Eton on the wonders of nature and science, made revolving lights and other mechanical contrivances and in Shelley's day created an uproar by prophesying that he would soon be coming down from town by steam. (*Shelley*, Edmund Blunden (1946) p. 36)

play a more active role. In February he made detailed inquiries from a friend about a seat in Staffordshire which he thought the influence of Lord Stafford might persuade the incumbent to resign in his favour. Nothing came of this, but shortly afterwards he learnt from Mrs Crewe that the Duke of Portland was prepared to offer him a seat. It was a tempting suggestion. Although the duke's views were still wavering and ambiguous, he had come out in favour of the war against France and he was not trying to stop his followers from copying Burke's example and supporting the government. It would be embarrassing personally for Canning to spurn Portland's offer; to accept it would at least get him into Parliament and he had no idea when Pitt would be able to do that. Yet turn it down he did. He had committed himself to Pitt and he would accept no obligation to any lesser man. 'I will go over in no man's train,' he wrote. 'If I join Pitt, I will go by myself.'[49] Moreover, if he entered Parliament as Portland's nominee, he would be classed as a Whig, and he knew that he did not want to be associated with – let alone perhaps be obliged to defend – the more radical members of the party. The accumulating difficulties at home and abroad only confirmed his profound disapproval of the activities of the Friends of the People.

Canning's loyalty to Pitt did not long go unrewarded. Towards the end of April 1793 he received 'the most unequivocal assurances of the anxious manner in which Mr Pitt has been and is looking out for the means of fulfilling his promise.'[50] Within two months Pitt's search was successful. Sir Richard Worsley, the member for Newtown in the Isle of Wight, was prepared to vacate his seat in return for a post in the government, and on June 21 Pitt informed Canning that he could be elected in his place 'exactly in the manner which will be agreeable to your wishes as you explained them in your letter and when I had the pleasure of seeing you.'[51] Within a week the accommodating voters of Newtown had done their duty and duly elected George Canning as their member of Parliament.

His delight was unbounded. '*I am come into Parliament*,' he wrote to a friend with triumphant underlining. He condescendingly described his constituents (whom he had never met) as 'a select, but not unrespectable set of people, who live on the sea-coast in the Isle of Wight at a small but convenient town called Newtown, and amuse themselves with catching fish.' But what really mattered was that 'the seat does not cost me one farthing nor put me under the slightest obligation to any one man, woman or child, Mr Pitt only excepted.'[52]

If there was anyone more overcome with delight than Canning, it was his mother; and before going to stay with the Leighs in Derbyshire, he felt obliged to go and see her in order to try to persuade her that a seat in Parliament was not exactly of the same order of dignity as a Sultanship of the Indies or equal in profit to £500,000 in 3 per cent Consols.[53] It may be doubted whether his persuasions really convinced either his mother or himself.

CHAPTER II

Member of Parliament
1794-1795

In the middle of January 1794 Canning returned to his rooms in Paper Buildings and presented himself in Lincoln's Inn Hall just in time to keep the new law term. He was still supposed to be preparing himself for a career at the Bar, and he went down at once to Westminster Hall in order to contradict the numerous rumours that he had already decided to abandon his legal career. It would have been both imprudent and presumptuous to assume at this stage that he would need no other occupation and means of support. But now that he had actually got a seat in Parliament, his heart was even less in the legal profession than in the days when the Dean of Christ Church had urged him not to try to combine the law and politics. On his first day back in London, having 'displayed my person to the best advantage in the Court of King's Bench'[1] in Westminster Hall, he went straight on to leave his card in Downing Street.

Pitt's response was to invite Canning to a dinner party at which the other guests included some of his closest political associates, including Lord Grenville, the Foreign Secretary, and Henry Dundas, the Secretary of State for War. Canning, who went in a state of euphoria, enjoyed himself exceedingly. Afterwards he reported to the Leighs that Pitt, at the head of his own table, was 'exactly what hits my taste – attentive without being troublesome – mixing in the conversation without attempting to lead it – laughing often and easily – and boyish enough if it should fall in his way, to discuss the history of Cock Robin.'[2] Before the holidays were over he had again been invited to dine at Downing Street as well as to dinner parties given by Grenville and Dundas.

Canning could not take his seat until Parliament reassembled on January 21. In the meantime he attended at Westminster Hall fairly regularly and amused himself like any other young man reading for the Bar. He usually dined at the lawyers' dining club, the Crown and Anchor, or at a new club for lawyers recently established in Carey Street. He often looked in at the play, at the Haymarket or Covent Garden, or spent the evening with a friend. Sometimes, but not very often, he had too much to drink. One evening he dined at the Free-mason's Tavern before going on to a party given by the Duchess of Gordon with whom he had struck up a 'violent acquaintance' when he met her the previous summer. Unfortunately, by eleven o'clock he had drunk so much madeira, port and excellent white burgundy that 'I was perfectly unfit to go to the Duchess of Gordon's, but unluckily was incapacitated also from perceiving my own unfitness.' So he went to the party and held forth for three hours until some kind person took him home and put him to bed. Next morning he woke up wondering what on earth he had been doing.[3]

Canning spent most of the Christmas holidays quietly at Oxford, trying to suppress his stage fright over his forthcoming parliamentary debut. He was uncomfortably aware that, before he was even launched on his political career, his desertion of his Whig friends had made him political enemies and exposed him to unkind comments. On the other hand, his hopes of solid support from the quarter where he would most like to get it were soon confirmed. Pitt, who was always interested in promising young recruits, had already seen enough of Canning to decide that he was worth taking trouble over. He may have lacked the political connections which assured his friend and contemporary, Robert Jenkinson, of a claim on Pitt's attention, but he was intelligent, witty, ebullient and charming (although rather naïve) in a way that Jenkinson never was. A few days before Parliament met, Pitt sent for Canning and had a long talk with him about the state of public affairs. He gave him a copy of the King's Speech and told him that if he had any questions or wanted to see any papers, he must send to him or call on him whenever he pleased. So Canning went home and got down to his homework; then he wrote to Pitt for various papers mentioned in the King's Speech, and they were all sent to him that evening. There was more 'reading, noting, composing, digesting and preparing',[4] another briefing from Pitt, and by Tuesday the 21st, he must have been much better informed than many a backbencher who had been in Parliament for years.

It was not an encouraging outlook. England had been at war with France for just on a year, and the military situation was rapidly worsen-ing. By the end of 1793 the British expeditionary force in the Low Countries, under the Duke of York, was stuck in front of Ostend, the Austrians and Prussians had retreated across the Rhine and the French republicans (with Napoleon Bonaparte commanding the artillery) had recaptured Toulon from the French royalists and allied forces under Admiral Hood, who had been occupying it since the previous August.

With Carnot successfully rallying the French to total war in defence of *la Patrie*, Pitt and Dundas had missed their chance of getting away with a short war limited to preserving Britain's security by expelling the French from the Low Countries. They had been fatally hampered by the over-caution, uncertain counsels and divided aims of their allies, as well as by their own military unpreparedness and failure to grasp what they were up against.

By the beginning of 1794, the revolutionaries in Paris had warded off the threat of foreign invasion, but they had become deeply involved in the horrible process of mutual destruction. There was no telling where it would end and the watchers across the Channel were not entirely without excuse for wondering whether something similar was not about to begin in their own country. There was much political, social and economic injustice in Britain, but in the early 1790s the reformers spoilt a good cause by their enthusiastic and sometimes rather childish attempts to identify their cause with that of the revolutionaries in France. By 1794 they had succeeded only too well. After a series of bad harvests, hunger was everywhere and famine never far away. But to the authorities, who had the poor and hungry with them always, and anyway believed that little could be done about them, a mob planting a Tree of Liberty in a park in Dundee was a much more alarming phenomenon than a mob rioting for bread. The danger of revolution was almost certainly very remote. And Fox, commenting on the trial of the Scottish reformer, Muir, had good reason to exclaim: 'Good God! that a man should be sent to Botany Bay for advising another to read Paine's book . . .'[5] But Fox himself, with his uninhibited pro-French sympathies, had helped to create the climate of fear in which Pitt could claim that there existed 'an enormous torrent of insurrection, which would sweep away all the barriers of government, law and religion.'[6]

Canning was to spend his life overcoming and then coming to terms with the powerful forces for change that were unloosed by the French Revolution. But when he first took his seat in Parliament it was not the state of the world or his own country that preoccupied him, but simply his exquisite and unsophisticated pleasure at finding himself a member of the House of Commons. He got up, he wrote in his journal, with 'I know not how many odd feelings about me and could not sit still for a moment till it was time to go down to the House.' When he got there, soon after three o'clock:

'I cannot describe to you with what emotions I felt myself walking about the floor which I had so often contemplated *in my youth* from the gallery, and wondered when I should have a right to tread upon it – I sat down too on the Treasury bench, just to see how it felt – and from that situation met the grinning countenances of half my acquaintances who were in the gallery – I was all in a flutter for some minutes – but however I bowed to the chair, and shook hands with the Speaker, and went through all the ceremonies down to that of paying my fees with the utmost decorum and propriety . . .'

The debate began at four o'clock and lasted for thirteen hours, which was not a minute too long for Canning. 'It was to me one of the highest entertainments that can be conceived. I had no notion that there had been such a difference, as I find there is, in the interest with which one hears a debate, when merely a spectator in the gallery, and that which one feels as a member, with the consciousness of having a right to join in it, if one pleases, and to give one's vote upon the decision.'[7]

Of course Canning was more than anxious to exercise his right to join in if he pleased. It even crossed his mind that he might do so on the first day, but Pitt, when appealed to, agreed that it would be a bit too presumptuous. Ten days later, however, when the Commons were due to discuss the granting of a subsidy to the King of Sardinia, Canning decided to take the plunge. For him, perhaps even more than for most M.P.s, it was a great emotional occasion – 'the most important day of my life' – on the outcome of which he felt that his whole political career depended. When he took his seat behind the Treasury bench, he whispered his intention to Pitt and was fortified by his approval. But he could not avoid an indescribable feeling of 'tumult' when at last, after both Fox and Grey had spoken, he found himself on his feet and heard his name spoken by the Speaker and echoed from all sides of the House.[8] He got into his stride quite quickly and went on confidently enough for about half an hour until he happened to observe several members of the opposition, as he thought, making fun of him. This, combined with the fact that he had run out of breath, reduced him to complete silence. Fortunately, Pitt and the other occupants of the Treasury bench realised what had happened and began to cheer him loudly; the rest of the House joined in, and thus safely launched again he sailed on 'happily and triumphantly' to the end.[9] When he sat down he was surrounded by people shaking his hand and congratulating him. Burke in particular praised him warmly. As soon as he could, he escaped upstairs to dine with some friends – 'and the bumpers of port wine that I swallowed – and the mutton chops that I devoured – and the sensations that I felt, are not to be described.'[10]

Canning wrote afterwards that when he got to the latter part of his speech, 'I know no pleasure (*sensual* pleasure I had almost said) equal to that which I experienced. I had complete possession of all that I meant to say, and of myself, and I saw my way clear before me.'[11] He was showing the beginnings of the superb speaker and debater that he later became. He began in the way that he meant to go on, speaking (like Pitt and Fox) without any notes, and deliberately waiting till several of the other side had spoken so as to make it clear from the start that he meant to be a good debater and not just a maker of set speeches. But his actual technique of speaking left, so he was told afterwards, much room for improvement. He spoke too rapidly and too loudly and his gestures were too violent and theatrical, so that the people sitting near him were at considerable risk. Lord Bayham, the son of Lord Camden, who was sitting next to him and holding his hat for him, did get a 'plaguey hard blow on the shoulder', while 'Pitt who was beneath me *sidled* a little out of the way and Dundas was obliged to *bob* to save his *wig* from confusion.'[12]

At this stage, what Canning said probably caused him less anxiety than the way he said it. He was Pitt's disciple and on almost every issue he had no intellectual doubts or political scruples about following the master's lead. Much of his speech was devoted to refuting the arguments of the opponents of the war. He said he would not have wanted to interfere with the French if they had kept their lunacy to themselves, if they had contented themselves with 'dressing up strumpets in oak leaves, and inventing nicknames for the calendar.' But he was convinced that they intended to try to impose their system on everybody else, and that if England had not gone to war the Commons would not be debating whether or not to subsidise the King of Sardinia, but how to raise a forced loan for the 'banditti of Paris.'

Already Canning showed the concentration, devoid of either sentiment or ideology, on his own country's interests that was to govern his views on foreign policy throughout his life. He referred to the criticism of the ministers for choosing to fight the French rather than the powers which had just partitioned Poland, which, it was argued, showed that they were fighting against freedom. He pointed out 'the obvious absurdity of going in search of distant dangers and overlooking that which knocked at our door.' He emphasised the disadvantage of fighting Austria, Russia and Prussia without an ally, compared with fighting France with these three great powers as allies. And he suggested that a war for Poland 'for the sake of the balance of power' would be far less popular than the present war with France 'for our own defence and preservation'.[13]

Not everyone admired Canning's maiden speech, but it was clearly a creditable beginning. He himself was perfectly satisfied. A few days later he wrote to the Leighs: '. . . I have succeeded to the utmost of my expectations (I thank God) – *hopes* and *wishes*, I ought to have said.' Then after telling them which papers gave the best accounts of his speech and urging them not to take the *Morning Chronicle* any more because it had treated him ill on purpose, he added that 'Dundas's eulogium was short but pithy – it was *"By God this will do."* '[14] Pitt did not say anything to him directly, but he said things about him, probably meaning them to be passed on, which – Canning told a friend – 'would make your blood curdle, your hair stand on end, and your silver turn black in your pocket.'[15]

It was all rather too much of a good thing. In the middle of February Canning fell seriously ill, worn out no doubt by the tremendous emotional and nervous energy which he had put into his maiden speech. During his illness he thought and dreamt about it night and day. Alarming rumours that he might not recover flew around the town, and when he did, all the ladies called to congratulate him. It was as a result of this illness that he decided to follow his doctor's advice and not go down to the House on an empty stomach. He realised that Pitt's habit of eating 'at least a fowl' and drinking 'I know not how much madeira' before he went down was not to be scorned so much as he had thought – so long as one took care not to drink enough to 'puzzle one's self,' and not eat so much that one had no appetite for dinner or supper after the debate.[16]

By the beginning of April, Canning had returned from convalescing at Wanstead and was back in his place in the House of Commons. He told the Leighs that 'this second entry into it was not without its palpitations and odd feelings. But how contented, and satisfied, and calm, compared with the anxious uncertain tumult of the first.' This letter, headed 'Committee Room of the House of Commons', began: 'This is the first letter I have ever written *on the spot*. I find they do not give one gilt paper to write upon, which is very shabby and democratic.'[17] The law, although not entirely abandoned, had clearly receded very much into the background. His main aim now was to establish his parliamentary reputation. Apart from his own energy and abilities, he had one great asset: his growing friendship with Pitt. He was often invited back to supper at Downing Street, after the House rose; he went to see the prime minister whenever he liked and Pitt gave generously of his time, advice and ideas without ever seeming bored.

But even with Pitt's support it was not an easy time for a young man to establish himself in Parliament. There was not enough for him to get his teeth into. Pitt enjoyed overwhelming support, for the country was felt to be in danger, both from foreign foes and domestic traitors, and serious disillusionment with the war had not yet set in. In July, 1794, the split in the Whig party was formalised when the Portland Whigs joined Pitt's ministry, with Portland himself becoming Home Secretary. Fox's dwindling band of supporters were not united among themselves and he himself would have preferred to retire to his library at St Anne's Hill. In March he wrote despondently to his nephew, Lord Holland, admitting that his party was weak both in numbers and weight, 'but though weak we are right and that must be our comfort.'[18]

A weak and dispirited opposition, however conscious of its own rightness, does not make for lively debate, and Canning had barely been in the Commons a month before he was complaining of the sluggishness of the opposition. He had other difficulties to contend with. Members were preoccupied with the war and its consequences at home and in Ireland and this increased their preference for listening only to ministers who knew what was going on and were responsible for government policy. Canning knew that he could not compete with Cabinet ministers like Dundas or Windham,* just as he knew it would be ungracious for a young man not to give way in debate to someone of the seniority and standing of Fox. Moreover at that time the standard of oratory in the Commons was particularly high. On an important occasion, Pitt, Fox, Burke and Sheridan – to mention only the most distinguished names – were all capable of sounding off for at least two hours. Even if M.P.s had an unquenchable appetite for oratory – which they had not – it was very hard for a newcomer, however gifted, to make an impact in such company. Canning, who was sensitive to atmosphere, willing to be guided by Pitt and, behind his gay and confident manner, desperately anxious to do the right thing, usually knew when it would be better not to try. Just before the Easter recess in 1794, Pitt introduced a bill to authorise the government to enlist French émigrés in the army. Canning briefed himself thoroughly on the subject and determined to catch the Speaker's eye. But when the debate came on, Fox, Dundas, Burke and Sheridan each delivered a

---

* William Windham (1750–1810) was a disciple of Burke who joined the government with the other Portland Whigs in July, 1794. He was made Secretary at War with a seat in the Cabinet.

two hour speech. Canning realised that 'four *long* speeches tire out an audience ten times more than a dozen shorter ones, which may take up a good deal more time eventually.' So he took Pitt's advice and held back, making 'a sort of vow never to exceed *an hour*, except on very particular occasions.'[19]

By the time the next parliamentary session opened on December 30, 1794, it was clear that Prussia was a broken reed and that the campaign to save the Low Countries had failed. Even the King, whose determination to fight on rarely faltered, recommended that the British army should be brought home. But Pitt was unshaken. After a long talk with him on November 22 Canning reported that the war was to be vigorously prosecuted with or without allies. He added, with the note of rather possessive affection that was beginning to creep into his references to Pitt, that he was 'just as I would have him'.[20] On December 25, before going down to Wanstead to eat his Christmas dinner, he called at Downing Street at Pitt's request and was shown the rough draft of the King's Speech. Again he found Pitt 'stout and undismayed'.[21] Three days later Canning was told by Pitt that the Address was to be moved by Sir Edward Knatchbull, but the name of the seconder had not yet been settled. When he got home that same night, however, he found a polite note from the prime minister asking him to second the Address. He had only one full day in which to prepare his speech, but in his surprise and excitement he could not help being even more worried by the awkwardness of having to speak in a dress coat.

It was not very unusual for Pitt to behave indecisively in such a matter. Nor was it uncommon for the honour of seconding the Address to be given to a comparatively inexperienced member. Pitt's interest in Canning had been steadily growing and this was an obvious way of enabling him to show what he could do. The speech which he hurriedly prepared was largely devoted to going over the arguments in favour of carrying on the war with all possible vigour in spite of the military reverses and although a new government had come to power in France after the overthrow of Robespierre the previous July.[22] He did not find it easy to get up, as it were in cold blood, without the benefit of any lively debate to warm up either himself or his audience and, moreover, with a difficult brief to present. But his nervousness left him as soon as he stood up, and the unemotional atmosphere perhaps helped him to remember not to talk too fast and too vehemently. But he told Mr

Leigh afterwards that he still 'caught myself dusting Dundas's wig with my handkerchief, and perceived that I had frightened him and Pitt to a considerable distance from each other that they might leave a space for my exertions between them.'[23]

By the end of his first eighteen months in the House of Commons Canning had gained a useful stock of parliamentary experience. He was acquiring the reputation for usefulness by which he set great store and which meant being able and willing to intervene in any sudden emergency as well as not shirking the 'piddling work in committees'. As early as May 1794, when Pitt was late for a debate on the suspension of *habeas corpus*, it was Canning who got up and made excuses for him and prevented Sheridan from adjourning the House. He discovered afterwards that it was not urgent business but a hearty dinner that had made Pitt late and he commented in his journal: 'I wished I had been with him at that ceremony, instead of *lying* for him in the House.'

What probably did most to establish Canning's reputation for usefulness was his conscientious determination to sit through the debates. At that time members were far from considering their attendance a duty, except on special occasions, and ministers were often in despair at the slackness of their supposed followers. So they were naturally well disposed towards keen young supporters who in a thin house were prepared to forego their dinner if a division was likely. Canning did not fail to support Pitt even when he found the subject under discussion tiresome or boring. There were only two occasions during his first two years in Parliament when he deliberately abstained from giving the government his vote. The first was in May 1794, when Sheridan introduced a motion in favour of political equality for Roman Catholics and Canning, who agreed with Sheridan in principle but thought it a mistake to raise the matter at that time, decided after a private talk with Pitt that he had better stay away from the debate altogether. The second occasion was in June 1795, when the Commons debated the campaign in the West Indies, which, after some initial successes in the spring of the previous year, had begun to go badly. Canning decided to abstain after discovering that the government intended to whitewash (as he thought) the responsible naval and military commanders.

Although such a conscientious politician, Canning had plenty of time to enjoy himself – and plenty of opportunity. He almost always had one social engagement each day, and usually several, and if he did lack a dinner invitation and did not feel like going to his club, he had plenty of friends at whose dinner table he could just turn up and be sure of a welcome. Soon after he made his maiden speech, Lady Stafford wrote to her son, Granville Leveson-Gower: 'We may expect soon to see him [Canning] very fat, if constant dinners can have that effect.'[24] Politics did not at that time play such havoc with the social round as they had done earlier in the century, and in any case Mrs Crewe counted herself a Portland Whig. Canning often went to her parties at her villa in Hampstead. Dr Burney met him there one day in June 1795, taking a turn in the garden with the other 'peripatetic-politicians' after the cold *déjeuner*. He had a knack of making himself agreeable in whatever kind of company he found himself. One day he dined with a former master of Winchester, who was a considerable scholar, and next day with Charles Ellis and some of his hunting friends. After Ellis's dinner he wrote in his journal: 'The conversation did not take exactly the same turn as yesterday's. But I like variety and can accommodate myself to it, and we did very well.'

Perhaps what Canning liked most in his social life at this time were invitations to stay with the Countess of Sutherland and her husband, Lord Gower, at their house on Wimbledon Common. Lady Sutherland, who was in her thirties, was beautiful, intelligent and charming. In a platonic sort of way Canning probably fell in love with her a little. During his first visit he told Mr Leigh: 'Lord Gower is very pleasant and well-informed. But Lady Sutherland is quite a *love*.'[25] Apart from the company, the house on Wimbledon Common was an ideal refuge from the rackety life of London. Lord Gower had added to it what in Canning's view no house should be without – 'a room of *all hours*, I mean one in which you may live morning, noon and night, full of maps and books and easy chairs, and *sofas* to *sit by* those one *likes*.'[26]

Another attraction of Wimbledon was the neighbours. Just across the common lived Dundas and his second wife, the former Lady Jane Hope. Dundas, known as 'the Thane', was a bluff, unpretentious, experienced politician who had fallen under the spell of the much younger Pitt and become one of his chief supporters. Although not a great talker himself, he presided over his table with a quiet good humour that encouraged his guests to talk. One of the most frequent of these was Pitt and sometimes Dundas would ask Lady Sutherland and her husband to dinner when Pitt was his guest and Canning theirs. After one of these occasions, in November 1794, Canning reported that the men had got on so well that they had sat over their bottles until it was almost time to go. Pitt had been in excellent spirits 'for even in these desperate times one is allowed to be very merry if one likes.' The most convivial dinner parties in fact were probably those given by Pitt himself. After one of them Canning respectfully noted that their host had consumed so much port that 'I think we left him a little unfit for business.'[27]

While Parliament was sitting Canning never went far from London, except for a visit to Oxford at the end of June 1794 to take his M.A. But when Parliament was in recess he was constantly on the move between the country houses of his friends or the homes of his relations. The longest visits were reserved for the Leighs at Ashbourne. But he also stayed with the Staffords at Trentham, the Carlisles at Castle Howard, the Malmesburys at Belmont on the way to Oxford and Charles Ellis at Wootton in Bedfordshire.

But the social round, however enjoyable, was only a part, and by no means the most important part, of Canning's life. He wanted above all to make his mark in public life and he did not want to be too long about it. When Parliament rose for the summer recess in 1795, he was twenty-five and he had sat in the Commons for eighteen months. Most people would reckon that he had made a promising start as a politician. He enjoyed the friendship and confidence of Pitt which at that time was the biggest political asset he could have. He was already being talked about, and whether this was done in a friendly or unfriendly spirit he realised that it was much better for a politician to be abused a little than not to be spoken of at all. Already in the spring of 1795 his name had been canvassed as a possible Lord of the Admiralty. There was in fact nothing in the story, but Canning was gratified that people should already be considering him a suitable candidate for an official vacancy. He argued to himself that it was better to have more time in which to earn his promotion than have the world say he had been given it before he deserved it. But he may not have been fully convinced by his own unexceptionable arguments.

By the summer of 1795 his connection with Lincoln's Inn had reached a stage at which he was having to think seriously whether or not he should be called to the Bar. He could no doubt have become an extremely successful barrister. But he could not help wanting to put all his eggs into the political basket. He realised that to do this he must have some financial provision, but he was particular about how he got it. Although Canning quickly got used to being abused in the rough and tumble of politics, when it came to his own personal conduct he was extremely sensitive about the world's opinion – perhaps because he lacked the self-assured aristocratic background of most of his friends. He felt that since everyone knew that he needed to follow some profession, it would be discreditable to give up the law for 'an office of mere income and idleness' – in other words, for a sinecure. He must have a post with work attached to it so as to show that 'if I received public money, I meant to do public duty.'[28] Moreover, it was not through sinecures that he would acquire the knowledge and experience that would qualify him for the more important political posts; and it was after all power and responsibility, not financial security, that he really wanted.

With all these thoughts in his head, Canning decided to consult Pitt about his political future. When he bewailed the frustrations of his parliamentary career, Pitt was sympathetic and suggested that the best remedy was office. Canning of course was delighted with this reply and revealed that the post he would most like to aim for was Chief Secretary for Ireland, the Lord-Lieutenant's right-hand man in Dublin. Pitt thought this a perfectly proper ambition, but explained that he could not easily provide him with a stepping-stone because there were so few 'efficient working offices'; the Under-Secretaries of State and two Commissioners of the India Board were about all, and even these were not necessarily at the prime minister's disposal.[29]

Pitt, however, was better than his word. By the time Parliament had reassembled on October 29, he had persuaded one of the Under-Secretaries at the Foreign Office, called Aust, to let Canning have his job as soon as he himself could be found another. All Canning had to do – and for him it was quite a lot – was to possess himself in patience until Aust was provided for.

It made no difference to Canning that the government he was about to join was facing difficulties so severe and an unpopularity so intense that if anyone else had been at its head it might well have fallen. Increasingly severe economic distress had created what all the theoretical delights of political liberty had not been able to achieve a few years earlier: a deep and widespread movement of popular unrest, directed against the authorities in general and Pitt in particular. During the summer the windows of Pitt's house in Downing Street were smashed and there were bread riots in Birmingham, Coventry, Nottingham and Sussex. The demands for bread were coupled with demands for peace in the belief that the first would follow from the second. And the radical reformers climbed on to the popular bandwagon by adding a demand for cheap food to their demands for peace, annual parliaments and manhood suffrage. Two days before Parliament met, a huge mass meeting of the London Corresponding Society in Islington approved an address which virtually recommended a resort to civil war if necessary. On his way to and from the opening of Parliament, the King had to run the gauntlet of a huge hostile crowd. Stones and dirt were hurled at his coach and a missile from an air gun pierced one of its windows.

Inside the House of Commons, Pitt's situation did not seem so critical. The domestic unrest together with the alarming possibility, now beginning to take shape in men's minds, of a French invasion of England or Ireland, made the Commons rally behind him. Even Wilberforce, with his pronounced pacifist views, rallied to Pitt. 'Wilberforce,' reported Canning triumphantly, 'and his conscientious followers, the Effusion-of-human-blood party, all came back to us – and thus at the end of three years of unsuccessful war, here is Pitt stronger and gaining strength.'[30]

Pitt immediately took steps to increase the bread supply. More controversially, the government decided to arm itself with stronger repressive powers. More mass protest meetings in London had increased its fears, although there had been no disorder. If the ministers had been able to rely on a proper police force they might have felt calmer and the Treasonable Practices and Seditious Meetings Bills, introduced into Parliament on November 10, might have been less repressive. Canning, however, had no doubts or scruples. In the debate on the bills on November 12 he insisted that Fox and Sheridan were wrong in claiming that there was no connection between the Islington mass meeting on October 27 and the outrage against the King two days later. He was also very anxious to speak in the debate on the third reading of the Treason Bill on December 16 and spent all the morning preparing his speech. 'I am come down full of speech and wound up to the utmost pitch of anxiety to give my speech vent,' he wrote to Mr Leigh from Pitt's house.[31] That day, however, his luck was against him and he had to let his speech remain bottled up inside him.

But the time was fast approaching when he would get a new and absorbing outlet for his energies. By early December a new post had been found for Aust and Canning's appointment as his successor was announced. According to his complacent report, the opposition were very cross about it and affected to pity Aust for being turned out to make room for a young gentleman who dined with Pitt daily but had never been behind a desk in office in his life.[32] In fact Aust was perfectly happy with the provision that had been made for him – and so, it is needless to add, was Canning with his.

CHAPTER III

Early days at the Foreign Office
1796-1797

'Manifold are the mysteries of office,' wrote Canning on Christmas Eve, 1795, '. . . it is very pleasant to get behind the scenes and see things and persons in their undress and explore the mechanism and machinery by which the actions of the great Pantomime are guided . . .'[1] But Canning was never a backroom boy, and he took an equally naïve delight in his new consequence and consideration in the eyes of the world. He wished, indeed, that the consequence could have been greater. At that time one could hardly be said to have arrived in the political world until one had been clearly recognisable, even in a horribly distorted form, in one of Mr Gillray's savagely critical cartoons. But this dubious honour still eluded Canning. Gillray's latest political cartoon was displayed in the window of Mrs Humphrey's print shop; called 'The Death of the Great Wolf', it was a parody of Benjamin West's painting of the death of Wolfe, and it portrayed Pitt as a hero dying in the moment of (political) victory surrounded by his lieutenants. Canning anxiously examined it in the hope of finding someone resembling himself – but without success. In another respect, however, he could feel that he had satisfactorily gone up in the world. He had moved out of his old chambers in Paper Buildings and was now installed at 4 Charles Street, St James's Square. He described it as 'a very pretty, small snug comfortable house,' and to look after him he had three servants (a housemaid, a cook and a bootman) as well as his valet, Fleming.[2]

By the time Canning officially began work at the Foreign Office on January 5, 1796, he had already been well briefed by his new chief during a visit to Dropmore, Lord Grenville's country house. Grenville, a cousin of Pitt's, was an intelligent, able and industrious administrator, but he had the reputation of being cold and unfeeling. He could marshal arguments and pieces of paper with skill and effect, but – as he himself once confessed – he could not manage men. When Canning first met Grenville at Pitt's house late in 1793, he was agreeably surprised to find that he was much less reserved than he had been led to expect and was shy rather than haughty. This charitable view was not entirely due

43

to the rose-tinted spectacles which Canning was wearing on that occasion. Several years later Lord Minto wrote. that 'nothing can be pleasanter than the Grenville family at home. Lady Grenville is beautiful and nice and pleasant in all ways ... Lord Grenville is entirely different in his family from the notion which his general manners have perhaps naturally given of him to the world.'³ Later, however, when Grenville and Pitt no longer saw eye to eye on the issue of peace and war, and Canning was torn between his loyalty to Pitt and his duty to Grenville, he tended to adopt a less friendly, more impatient, attitude to the Foreign Secretary. All too soon it became more a bore than a pleasant duty to have to go down to Dropmore.

When Canning went to work under Grenville, the Foreign Office as we know it today was still very much in its infancy. It was only in 1782 that it had been properly constituted as a separate department under one Secretary of State; and it was only in 1793 that it had moved into two leased houses in Downing Street on the site it has occupied ever since. Grenville's staff consisted of two Under-Secretaries and eleven clerks, as well as various officials, like the Keeper and two Deputy Keepers of state papers, who were shared with the two other Secretaries of State – for home affairs and for war. In 1795 the salaries of the two Under-Secretaries were fixed at £1,500 a year (raised four years later to £2,000) but their duties were still pretty elastic. The work was divided into a northern and a southern department with an Under-Secretary in charge of each. In practice, the amount and kind of work each did usually depended on who was most in the confidence of the Foreign Secretary. There was no fixed rule about whether either or both of the Under-Secretaries should be Members of Parliament. Canning was; his colleague, George Hammond, was not. Hammond, seven years older than Canning, had already spent four years as the first British minister to Washington; an American who met him there described him as 'an exceedingly good man'.⁴ Canning's first impressions of him were equally enthusiastic. He reported that Hammond 'appears one of the pleasantest and quietest-tempered as well as confessedly one of the ablest men of business in this country.'⁵ Their friendship was cemented by their shared political outlook. Hammond contributed articles to the *Anti-Jacobin* and later to the *Quarterly Review*.

By the time Canning started work at the Foreign Office, the hopes and calculations which had accompanied Britain's entry into the war three years earlier had faded or been proved false. France's ability to wage war had not been destroyed by her revolutionary excesses. Pitt had not succeeded in his primary war aim of safeguarding England's security by preserving the Low Countries from French aggression and occupation. By the end of 1795, the Austrian Netherlands (Belgium) had been incorporated into France, and the United Provinces had been turned into a French satellite state, the Batavian republic. In addition, the whole of the left bank of the Rhine had been annexed to France; so, farther south, had Savoy and Nice.

Nor had Pitt succeeded on the diplomatic front in maintaining a strong anti-French coalition. Prussia had been too preoccupied with Russia's designs on Poland – and in making sure of her share of the loot – to concentrate on the dangers of French aggression in western Europe. In May 1795, she had made peace with France. Other countries followed suit and by the end of the year Austria was England's only major military ally. To set against these military and diplomatic failures, and the severe discontent and distress at home, there was the occupation of Corsica and, farther afield, the capture of French and Dutch possessions in the West Indies, the Cape of Good Hope, Ceylon and India. These might help the expansion of British trade and they might prove useful counters at the bargaining table, but they could not hold back the French armies in Europe.

In these inauspicious circumstances, even the hard-liners, in particular Grenville and the King, were reluctantly and with grave misgivings, prepared to consider peace if it could be had on sufficiently advantageous terms. But it could not. The tentative overtures which Pitt made through William Wickham, the British envoy at Berne, came to an abrupt end on March 26 when the French Directory announced in uncompromising and undiplomatic terms that it would not consider surrendering any of the territories that had been incorporated into France. It also implied that England would have to give up all her colonial conquests. Nothing could have been better calculated to stiffen sagging English morale. Even Fox admitted that it would not do, while Grenville wrote cheerfully to Wickham that the Directory had 'in fact played our game better than we could have hoped.'[6]

For the moment Grenville was free to concentrate on weaving a diplomatic web against the French. It was a more congenial task, but scarcely easier or more fruitful than trying to make peace. What were the Austrians up to? English agents on the Continent were constantly reporting rumours that they meant to settle separately with France. But when invited early in 1796 to make a joint declaration with the British of their willingness to seek peace, the Austrians hung back.

They were angry with Pitt for his tardy response to their urgent appeals for more money to finance their spring campaign. But it was becoming increasingly hard to raise money in London for unsatisfactory foreign allies – Austria alone had had a loan of £3,000,000 the previous year – and in any case was it wise to go on subsidising an ally who looked like coming to terms with France? By the beginning of May, however, Pitt was managing to pay the Austrians a small monthly subsidy without revealing the fact to Parliament; he hoped to satisfy the Austrians without upsetting Parliament or the public.

If it was difficult to keep the Austrians in the war, it was even more difficult to bring the Prussians back into it. Grenville thought up a plan to tempt them with the offer of the Westphalian provinces and the Austrian Netherlands, while Austria would be compensated with Bavaria which she had always wanted. Although Grenville's plan made no provision for the displaced Elector of Bavaria, Pitt accepted it as the only way he could see of ending the war in Europe without enhancing the power of France. But George III, who never forgot that he was Elector of Hanover, told Grenville indignantly that his scheme was both immoral and unjustifiable.

Perhaps more to the point were the discouraging reports from Berlin of Prussia's fixed determination to stay out of the war. Even worse were the reports of Bonaparte's military successes in Italy; by the middle of May 1796, he had knocked Sardinia out of the war, defeated an Austrian army at Lodi and entered Milan in triumph. On June 26, Lord Cornwallis, then a member of the Cabinet, wrote to a correspondent in India: 'Nothing can in my opinion be more gloomy than the prospect of things here; we have neither an army nor specie and can barely say that we have an ally.'[7] By July, Grenville was desperately dusting over his plan for a Bavarian-Belgian exchange. Pitt and the Cabinet pessimistically agreed that anything was worth trying, the King's objections were with difficulty overcome and George Hammond was sent off to Berlin to try to entice the Prussians back into the fight. It was a fruitless mission. The Prussians seemed to be merely embarrassed by Hammond's guarded proposals. After nearly a month he realised that he was getting nowhere and came home. Nobody in Berlin told him that just before his arrival Prussia had secretly signed a treaty of neutrality with France.

As far as Canning was concerned, no news of military defeat, or back-sliding ally, or diplomatic failure could dampen his pleasure in at last having a real job of work to do. He was in charge of the southern department – that is, France, Spain, Portugal, Austria, Flanders, Switzerland, Italy and Turkey. So, since the war was wholly in his part of the world, he had the most to do; and when Hammond was away in Berlin for well over two months Canning was delighted to have everything to do. All the despatches from British envoys abroad passed first through the hands of one or other of the Under-Secretaries, and because of the irregular arrival of the mails from abroad, the amount of work varied greatly. Some ten days after he started work, Canning wrote to Leveson-Gower: 'The winds and waves have conspired to keep back all the mails and messengers of the Continent until I came into office – and they have come pouring in upon me this week in such quantities as the *oldest clerk in the office* does not *remember* to have witnessed before.' The other day he had gone home about six o'clock after a hard day's work, but hardly had he finished his dinner than an Austrian courier arrived at his house 'with a mountain of papers which he had been three months collecting throughout the whole terraqueous globe . . .' It had taken him until two o'clock in the morning to deal with them all, and he was hardly up in the morning before a whole lot more despatches poured in.[8] Sometimes the rush of work was caused by the preparation of a batch of despatches for an outgoing messenger. On one occasion he drafted despatches right through the day until three o'clock the next morning.[9]

He would not have wished it otherwise, even though he had to sacrifice his long summer holiday and largely abandon his busy social life. There was a mass exodus from London of the political and fashionable world as soon as Parliament rose for the summer recess. That summer Canning stayed behind. If the sudden arrival of some despatches forced him to work late at the office, he would go home to eat a solitary dinner and read Miss Burney's latest novel *Camilla* which he thought rather poor. He was completely absorbed in his work. 'I wonder,' he soliloquised in a letter to Boringdon in the middle of August, 'what sort of times those must have been when there were no armies to watch, no conflicts to apprehend, and when Europe had no fate depending. I fancy a summer passed in Downing Street must have been a very different thing at such a period; and that I should hardly have gone on, as I have now done, to the middle of August, I will not say without missing, or regretting the society which I have lost, certainly without any distressing impatience of my solitude.'[10]

In fact, his solitude was not all that complete. He had made himself more accessible to his friends by taking up riding. 'I am become,' he told Boringdon, 'a most vehement and pertinacious horseman, and excepting that my bay mare starts, and my black gelding stumbles a little and that my groom is just at this minute laid up, and has been so for these three weeks, with a hurt which he got against the pummel of the saddle, I do not know any gentleman, for a young beginner, that is more handsomely mounted and has his cavalry in better order.'[11] Canning might mock at himself but his friends were impressed. 'You never saw,' wrote George Ellis (Charles's cousin), 'such boots and leather breeches. Jenky, [Jenkinson] after exhibiting so long at reviews on a live horse, is not at all to be compared with him.'[12]

Canning's new equestrian skill made it possible for him to spend the night anywhere within twenty miles of Downing Street, whenever the office was reasonably quiet. One place he visited quite frequently at this time was the home, near Beckenham, of the distinguished diplomat, Lord Auckland. In one of his letters to Mr Leigh, Canning described a typical Sunday spent at Eden Farm. 'It was a whole holiday – spent entirely in the country – in riding, and rambling about with Lord Auckland, the Chancellor and Pitt all the morning – and in playing all sorts of tricks, frolics and fooleries, with the same persons and with the addition and assistance of all the Edens [Auckland's family] from dinner-time to bed-time.'[13] Sometimes Canning's peripatetic arrangements were quite elaborate. He would plan to spend several consecutive nights out of London with different friends, and Fleming would take his baggage from house to house in his chaise while Canning and his groom rode to and from London.

But the most important advantage to Canning of his new mobility was that it enabled him to see more of Pitt, who spent a lot of time at Holwood, his house near Bromley. Quite often, especially when Grenville was not about, he was able to finish his work in time to get down to Holwood by four or five o'clock. He usually found Pitt alone, and 'I think,' he told Boringdon, 'I have never left him without liking him better than before. I could not love or admire him more, even if I had no obligations to him; though in that case, I should give a freer, because less suspicious testimony of the claims which I think he has to be both loved and admired.'[14] Canning's attitude towards Pitt was still one of uncomplicated affection and hero-worship. What Pitt thought about Canning we do not know. But he would hardly have treated him as he did if he had not liked him and enjoyed his company.

A new Parliament was elected during the summer of 1796, and on May

26 Canning was returned for Wendover. The seat cost him nothing more than a day of noise and bustle and dining and drinking. It belonged to a personal friend of Pitt's, who was content to let his nominee have it without anything in exchange. This made it more secure than Newtown which Sir Richard Worsley would only surrender in return for an appointment abroad and this was not easy to arrange except on a temporary basis.

When the new Parliament met, on October 6, the King's Speech announced that the government had decided to try again for peace. Canning ecstatically reported that Pitt had made a speech 'which for eloquence, for wisdom, and for effect, equalled anything that I have ever heard or ever read – all this was of itself a scene of sufficient exultation to the country, particularly to *his* friends, and not least to one who loves him so well as I do.'[15] Canning's elation was all the greater because it had been decided to entrust the peace mission to Lord Malmesbury, an experienced diplomat whom he knew well and whom he had persuaded to take Granville Leveson-Gower with him. Canning, who was always delighted if he could promote the interest of his friends, wrote happily: 'This will be rare news for Lady Stafford.'[16]

Just before Parliament met, George Ellis reported that Canning had been working 'shockingly' hard, but was in 'high health and beauty'.[17] Lord Malmesbury's peace mission was to make him work even harder. On one occasion towards the middle of November, after he had spent nearly twenty-four hours at a stretch toiling at despatches and letters for Malmesbury, he was told that such a spell of work was not remembered in the office. 'So I am very proud of it and very well after it.'[18] For the first time he was closely and intimately involved in a major diplomatic negotiation; and his friendship for Malmesbury and his two aides (Leveson-Gower and George Ellis) made him all the more anxious that it should succeed.

If Canning had been more experienced and less enthusiastic, he might have realised that there was very little that he – or, for that matter, Pitt – could do to save the mission from failure. Neither side felt there was much chance of achieving peace but each thought, for different reasons, that they ought to go through the motions of trying. Pitt had been encouraged by reports that the moderates in Paris, and most of the French people, wanted peace. The French were indeed discouraged by the Austrian Archduke Charles's victories in the Rhineland and worried by the news that Catherine of Russia, having finished mopping up Poland, was now thinking of intervening in the war against them. Catherine had in fact offered to send 60,000 troops to help the Austrians; the offer had reached the British Cabinet early in September just after it had decided to try again for peace. But Catherine demanded such a high price in subsidies in return for her troops that Grenville and Pitt thought it best to press on with the peace talks in the hope that the threat of Russian intervention would make the French more amenable. The King thought the proposed negotiations were neither timely nor dignified. The Austrians too, elated by Archduke Charles's victories and by Catherine's apparent change of heart, thought this was no time for peace feelers. Their unco-operative attitude tied Grenville's hands and may have made him appear less anxious for peace than he probably was. Britain was committed not to make a separate peace without Austria, and Grenville's reluctance to break that commitment, as the French pressed him to do, did not make things any easier for Malmesbury in Paris. Nor was he helped by Grenville's refusal to give him any room for manœuvre in case he was led into some sacrifice of British interests.

Malmesbury sailed from Dover on October 18 and arrived in Paris five days later. Burke commented sourly that it was no wonder the journey had taken so long for Malmesbury went all the way on his knees. In fact, he was well received along the way and when he got to Paris even the French officials gave him a reasonably civil reception. But Malmesbury confessed to Grenville soon after his arrival that he had 'the feeling of an unsteady head on the edge of a high precipice'.[19] He kept his head all right but his chief gave him very little opportunity of showing how well he could use it. His dependence on instructions from London was sufficiently well known to be the subject of a derisory Cruikshank cartoon. Canning's loyalty to Grenville was strained to breaking-point by Malmesbury's plight. On November 7 he wrote indignantly to Granville Leveson-Gower: 'Look at the Instructions that are sent to him (the Lion)* today – and see how he is tied and bound up at both ends, mane and tail, no stirring, his claws pared and teeth drawn . . .'[20] In his letters to Malmesbury he urged him to be bolder in dealing on his own initiative with some of the more offensive parts of the Directory's communications and assured him that if he did he could count on Pitt's support and approval.

On one occasion, when Grenville asked him to draft some instructions for the mission, Canning gave Malmesbury very much of a free

---

* Malmesbury was called 'the Lion' by his friends because a foreign newspaper had once described him as *'un lion blanc'* because of his fine eyes and profusion of white hair.

hand; he showed this despatch to Pitt but not to Grenville. The much more experienced Malmesbury wrote to him soothingly: 'I would have roared too soon, and without effect, if I had begun to roar sooner.'[21] But to Grenville he wrote firmly that if he were not allowed to produce detailed proposals and given broad and flexible instructions, he might as well be recalled, or eventually he would have to recall himself. Grenville's instructions, when they did arrive more than a fortnight later, insisted uncompromisingly that Belgium must be removed from French control. His proposals were rejected and on December 19 Malmesbury was told by his hosts to depart within forty-eight hours. The French attitude had been stiffened by news of the sudden death of Catherine the Great and of Bonaparte's successful offensive in Italy. The Austrians' attitude was correspondingly weakened and at the end of the year they belatedly made up their minds to join the British in seeking peace. But by that time Malmesbury was back in London and Pitt had won an overwhelming vote of confidence when he asked the Commons for their support in carrying on the war.

Before many weeks were past, however, disasters began to crowd in thick and fast upon Pitt and his colleagues. The financial crisis which had been threatening for months past finally broke in February, 1797, and on the 26th the Bank of England was ordered to suspend cash payments. Rumours abounded of landings by French invasion forces. The naval mutiny at Spithead was followed by a more dangerous mutiny by the North Sea fleet at the Nore. There was an army mutiny at Woolwich and Ireland was on the verge of insurrection. Abroad, the French armies continued their victorious course in Italy and on April 7 the Austrian commander was forced to sign an armistice with Bonaparte. When Wilberforce announced his engagement in May, it was considered a sign of his confidence in God that he should decide to get married at such a troubled time.

Canning also did not worry too much about the troubled times. The day before the cash payments were suspended, he wrote buoyantly to Mr Leigh that in London 'every little noise makes the monied people quake, and infects all those who are not upon their guard with a thousand foolish apprehensions.'[22] Twelve hundred sheepstealing Frenchmen were said to have landed in Wales. But, concluded Canning cheerfully, 'there is nothing but a Bank Director that cannot be got the better of in these times.'[23] In May he seized on a slightly comic phrase used by Windham (who always tended to take a gloomy and alarmist view of the situation) and sent him the following verse missive:

'Windham! when e'er thy fervent mind
Some thought, uncommon, just, refined,
In happiest phrase expresses;
Thy vulgar audience stare and gape,
And shout, and chuckle, at the *scrape*
Of "Negative Successes."

Oh tell me! does today's event
Serve to illustrate what you meant?
Or will the soldiers riot?
Oh! if the Guards have not rebell'd,
And if the naval fray is quell'd
If Portsmouth yet is quiet;

Come, Windham! celebrate with me
This day of joy and jubilee,
This day of *no* disaster!
Our Government is *not* o'erturned –
Huzza! – Our Fleet has *not* been burn'd,
Our Army's *not* our master.'[24]

By the end of May, however, even the normally optimistic Pitt could not share Canning's cheerful outlook. Early in April, when it was becoming clear that the Austrians would have to come to terms with France, Pitt and Grenville had sent Hammond to Vienna to try to arrange a joint Anglo-Austrian peace negotiation with the French – thus once more leaving Canning, to his immense satisfaction, with all to do at the office. Hammond arrived at Vienna at the end of April only to find that the Austrians had already signed peace preliminaries at Leoben. To make matters worse, they refused to reveal the terms of the Leoben agreement – which suggested that they had something to hide – and declared that they intended to repudiate their debts to Britain. Although Pitt and Grenville were at one in condemning the financial perfidy of Austria, when it came to deciding how to play their admittedly weak diplomatic hand, they were soon at odds. At the beginning of June, a peace overture was despatched to Paris, much to the disgust of the King who commented bitterly to Grenville on the tame state of mind of Parliament.[25] Grenville considered the French reply so insolent that he wanted the search for peace to be abandoned forthwith. Pitt, however, thought otherwise. The division between the two men was reflected in the Cabinet and it was only after protracted discussions that a decision to negotiate was reached.

Pitt was by now so anxious for peace that he was prepared to swallow his pride and surrender most of Britain's colonial conquests and abandon the British demand that Belgium should be removed from French control. Grenville, on the other hand, had more than his fair share of pride and when the Cabinet decision went against him he told the King that he only refrained from resigning because of the gravity of the national crisis – the naval mutiny at the Nore had still not been settled. The King was sympathetic and, sure of his royal master's support, Grenville saw no reason to modify his disapproval of the negotiations of which he was supposed to be in charge. Not surprisingly, Canning enthusiastically supported Pitt's attitude. Once again, and to a much greater extent than the year before, he found himself forced to choose between his duty to Grenville and his devotion to Pitt. It was not difficult for him to make up his mind.

Lord Malmesbury was again chosen to lead the peace mission, which this time met the French delegates at Lille, and Canning laboured mightily to make sure that at any rate it would not fail for lack of preparation. On July 1, the day after Malmesbury set out, he wrote to Mr Leigh: 'Day and night for three days together have I been at my desk with my clerks around me, working and superintending work without any intermission, except for about two hours each day for dinner and of about six for sleep. But it is such a comfort to hear that there never was so much done in the office in so short a space of time and never so well done (so they will tell me) and to have it agreed on all hands that I ought to go out of town and take care of myself for a few days – all this repays one's labours – and the last part,' he concluded wryly, 'would be better still if Lord Grenville did not hook on to it an exhortation to me to come to Dropmore for relaxation . . .'[26] A fortnight later he was again writing in an equally complacent strain about how hard he had been working on the Malmesbury mission, 'and with how tired a hand and head, but with how clear and satisfied a conscience, did I then retire to my bed! – more especially as the last three or four hours of my work were perfectly voluntary, being employed about private letters to Lord M. and G. Ellis – to put them more fully in possession of all that is thought, felt and expected here about their negotiation, its conduct and its issue.'[27]

The outcome was in fact failure. Although Malmesbury was received with much greater courtesy than on his previous visit, the demands put forward by the French were so unacceptable that by July 20 the talks seemed to be hopelessly deadlocked. Malmesbury, however, discovered that the counsels of the French were just as divided as those of the English, and that the outcome of his mission really depended on whether the peace or the war party came out on top in the struggle for power then going on in Paris. As week followed week, no fresh instructions reached the French delegates at Lille. Malmesbury told Grenville on August 14 that the French themselves seemed to think the delay unreasonable and tried 'to make up by personal attentions and civilities the deficiency in their ministerial communications.'[28] Malmesbury too had his troubles with his superiors; he had to work hard to prevent Grenville from using the French delays and intransigence as an excuse to break off the talks. He was wholeheartedly abetted by Canning who on one occasion explained to Malmesbury that he and Pitt had thought it best not to suggest any official commendation of his conciliatory conduct in case this inflamed Grenville's warlike spirit.

Malmesbury felt that there was a real possibility of agreement provided the extremists did not seize power in Paris; and by the end of August he was feeling thoroughly put out by the dilemma in which he was placed by the different attitudes of 'the Minister under *whose orders I am bound to act*' [Grenville] and 'the Minister *with whom I wish to act*' [Pitt] – as he put it with much angry underlining in a letter to Canning. If, he added, 'I am only to remain here, *in order to break off the negotiation creditably, and not to terminate it successfully,* I then instead of resigning my opinion, must resign my office.'[29] In the end, it was the warlike spirit in Paris, not London, that ruined the peace talks. On September 5 Malmesbury noted in his diary news of a great commotion in Paris; it was the coup of the 18th Fructidor in which the two moderate Directors were overthrown with the help of one of Bonaparte's generals. The pro-peace French negotiators at Lille were replaced, and the extreme demands of their successors left Malmesbury with no alternative but to go home. By September 20 he was back in London. Canning, temporarily forgetting the obstructive attitude of his chief, angrily declared that 'nothing but that cursed revolution at Paris, and the sanguinary, insolent, implacable and ignorant arrogance of the triumvirate'[30] could have prevented them from making peace.

Canning's anger was understandable. He had been deeply involved in the peace talks, and by the time they broke down his anxiety for their success had involved him in a web of secrecy and dissimulation. One perfectly straightforward reason for secrecy was the newspaper leaks of which neither Canning nor Grenville could trace the source, although Canning suspected indiscretions on the King's part. Grenville wrote to Malmesbury on July 20, pointing out how important it was to prevent any public speculation on the progress of the talks, not only because of the political consequences, but also because it promoted so much financial speculation.[31]* The day before, Grenville himself had persuaded the Cabinet to agree not to discuss the negotiations with anyone outside. Canning uncharitably thought that his aim was to 'tie up Pitt's tongue alone' because Grenville suspected the prime minister of seeking outside support against his opponents in the Cabinet and of wanting to sound out public opinion through the newspapers as to how far he could go in making concessions for peace.[32] It was also decided that all despatches from Lille should be opened and answered only by Canning or Hammond, and that only copies made by Hammond, whose handwriting was virtually illegible, should be circulated to the less important members of the Cabinet.

An additional reason for secrecy arose when Maret, the most reasonable and influential of the three French negotiators, opened a secret negotiation with George Ellis through an intermediary called Pein. If anything about this secret negotiation within a negotiation leaked out, the careers, and even the lives, of Maret and Pein would be in danger from the extremists in Paris. So Malmesbury was told to write one despatch suitable for the whole Cabinet and to report on the Pein-Ellis talks in a separate despatch that only Pitt and Grenville would see. But this was not all. Before Grenville was shown the reports of the Pein-Ellis talks, they were carefully edited to remove any passages likely to incense him still further against the French. In the end, Canning was the only person in London, apart from Pitt, who knew every detail of the negotiations. He must have been hard put to it to remember what could be told to whom. It was not a very estimable situation for a young Under-Secretary to find himself in. But it was not of Canning's choosing and he more than once complained of the difficulty of his situation. Since, however, he believed that Pitt was right and Grenville wrong, and since he had Pitt's approval of, and connivance in, everything he did to keep Grenville in the dark, it would perhaps be unreasonable to expect him to have acted otherwise.

And in spite of all the worry and hard work, he enjoyed himself very much. For the second year running he had to stay in London when most of his friends were off to the country. 'Not a day,' he wrote on

* Canning himself was reported to be stock-jobbing during the negotiation. He traced the report to Mr Perry of the *Morning Chronicle*, and then sent him a 'civil message' that he would prosecute him if he printed what he had said.

July 24, 'but some person drops off, and narrows my range of dinners and evening society.'[33] If he was actually expecting a messenger from Lille, he stayed conscientiously at his post. But in general he had more leisure than he had had since coming into office. He was glad when Grenville settled down at Dropmore so that he 'does not trouble me by coming up to town one day, and going out the next, and keeping me in constant doubt as to the possibility of executing my own plans according to my own fancy.'[34] One of his occupations that summer was sitting for his portrait to Hoppner; he thought the artist's second attempt was ten times more like him – or at least he hoped so 'for this is ten times a better-looking fellow than the other.' He was also busy furnishing and fitting out the house in Spring Gardens to which he had moved earlier in the year. Altogether it had cost him rather more than £800 – 'but then I have money, so what need I care?'[35]

Whenever possible Canning made weekend excursions – to his aunt at Wanstead, to Dundas at Wimbledon, to Lord Auckland at Eden Farm, and of course to Holwood. Towards the end of July he told Mr Leigh that Pitt was about to settle at his country house 'where I shall go as soon and as often as I can, and Lord Grenville settles himself if possible more than ever at Dropmore where I shall go as seldom as I can, for it is dull and disagreeable.'[36] A few days later he described how he had had to cancel a dinner at Holland House because of the arrival of a messenger with despatches from Lille, but instead had much enjoyed a very snug dinner at home with Pitt and the young man who had brought the despatches from Lille. 'It is impossible to describe to you,' he added, with his usual unabashed and rather naïve enthusiasm, 'how pleasant, simple and unaffected Pitt is in private society. I like him best of all with very few indeed – and best of all perhaps quite *tête-à-tête* – as we were on Sunday last at Holwood – where we rode all the morning – dined and walked all the evening together, and talked over all sorts of matters, public and personal, foreign and domestic.'[37]*

Perhaps inevitably, the Lille negotiations drew Canning still closer to Pitt and alienated him still further from Grenville. During the winding up of the mission after Malmesbury's return to England there was a great deal of discussion over whether or not to publish part of Malmesbury's correspondence. Malmesbury, backed by Canning, urged that nothing should be published which might endanger the friendly Maret or his colleagues. Grenville, on the other hand, wanted to publish everything that strengthened the British case regardless of the

* There is no hint in Canning's letter of the ill-health from which Pitt apparently suffered that summer.

consequences for others. In the end, nothing was published, but the incident left Canning feeling still more out of sorts with his chief. He even talked of resigning from the Foreign Office, and taking a place at the India Board. Malmesbury, according to his own account, dissuaded him and it was not until nearly eighteen months later that Canning made the transfer. But after the failure of the Lille mission he seems to have lost much of his enthusiasm for the Foreign Office. Two years later he was still referring to 'the *disagreeableness* which I experienced during my Under-SecyP. with Lord Grenville.'[38] In so far as the 'disagreeableness' was due to twinges of conscience, the feeling was no discredit to him and in the end it inflicted no lasting damage on his friendly personal relations with Lord Grenville.

CHAPTER IV

The Anti-Jacobin
1797-1799

'The negotiation at Lille,' wrote Fox's nephew, Lord Holland, 'exposed the unreasonable pretensions and preposterous conduct of the French in a light which reconciled the country to the continuance of the war.'[1] But Canning, now thoroughly disillusioned about the prospects of getting a satisfactory peace, felt that more ought to be done to expose the present rulers of France. By October 1797, he was actively considering plans for a weekly paper that would deride and refute the ideas of the Jacobins, present the government's point of view on the issues of the day and expose the misinformation and misinterpretation which filled the opposition newspapers. On October 19, he wrote to George Ellis from Walmer to tell him that he and Pitt had been discussing plans for a new paper 'which is to be full of sound reasoning, good principles, and good jokes and to set the mind of the people right upon every subject.' Canning's naturally robust self-confidence became unassailable when backed by Pitt's approval. He went on to tell Ellis that he and Pitt had decided provisionally that a secret committee to run the paper should meet every Sunday at dinner at Pitt's, and they had gone over nine or ten names of possible members. 'Pitt,' he added, 'enters into it with all the spirit and earnestness you could desire.'[2]

The weekly dinners at Pitt's did not materialise but the proposed paper did. It was called the *Anti-Jacobin* or *Weekly Review*. William Gifford, whose 'mild spirit' was once commended by Lady Holland, was appointed editor. In his youth he had been a cabin boy and a shoemaker's apprentice before being sent up to Oxford. In 1797 he was nearly 40 years old and principally known as the author of some satiric poems. Twelve years later, he became the first editor of the *Quarterly Review*, another journal in which Canning was keenly interested. According to the painter, Hoppner, who about this time was painting Canning's portrait, the *Anti-Jacobin* was printed on Sundays on the press of the *Sun* newspaper. It was published by the bookseller, Wright, who was paid a guinea a week for his pains.[3] Canning and his friends, in particular Frere and George Ellis, rented a vacant house next door to Wright's shop at 169 Piccadilly, and set up their editorial headquarters on the first floor. A hole was knocked in the wall between the two houses so that the Anti-Jacobinists could get to their office through Number 169. The advantage of this arrangement was that as Wright's shop was a well-known meeting place for supporters of the ministry, Gifford, Canning and other contributors could go to and fro without attracting any particular notice.

Or so they hoped. But in fact the anonymity of the chief contributors to the *Anti-Jacobin* was soon a very ill-kept secret. The first issue was published on November 20 and only five days later the painter Farington noted in his diary that it was supported by the Treasury and that Canning and his Eton friends wrote for it.[4] On January 17, 1798, the *Morning Chronicle* published a poem entitled, 'Epistle to the Editors of the *Anti-Jacobin*,' which mentioned several of the most important contributors by name – Canning, Ellis, Hammond and Morpeth – and ended with the scathing exhortation: 'Proceed – be more opprobrious if you can; Proceed – be more abusive ev'ry hour: To be more stupid is beyond your power.'* The Anti-Jacobinists, who had not the faintest idea who the author was, published in their next issue a rather cross reply in verse, in which they said that they asked for nothing more than 'Censure, cloth'd in vapid verse like thine.' If they had known that the author was William Lamb, the future Lord Melbourne, then a youth of nineteen, they would no doubt have been even more incensed.

The *Anti-Jacobin* appeared every Monday during the parliamentary session of 1797–8. It was a time when Britain's fortunes in the war against France were at a very low ebb. Apart from Portugal, the country was now without continental allies (Austria made peace with France in October); throughout the winter there were serious fears of an invasion by Bonaparte's 'Army of England' stationed across the Channel at Boulogne. In May rebellion broke out in Ireland. At home Pitt wrestled with the financial difficulties that were hamstringing his efforts to weld together another continental coalition. Only the navy, which in October soundly defeated the Dutch fleet at Camperdown, provided a gleam of encouragement. On the other hand, this grave crisis brought the British people their second wind in the long struggle

* The reference to Canning was as follows:
  Who e'er ye are, all hail! – whether the skill
  Of youthful CANNING guides the ranc'rous quill;
  With powers mechanic far above his age,
  Adapts the paragraph and fills the page;
  Measures the column, mends what e'er's amiss,
  Rejects THAT letter, and accepts of THIS;

against France. There no longer seemed any choice but to fight to the bitter end. Fox and his friends, who continued to argue against the war as if the events of the past ten years had never been, were losing touch with the real feeling in the country.

So Canning and his friends, who in the *Anti-Jacobin* were appealing directly to their countrymen's sense of patriotism, were pushing against a door that was already swinging open. The energy, skill and buoyant wit that they brought to their journalistic enterprise would probably have ensured its success anyway; but the fact that they caught the tide of public opinion at the turn, and expressed pungently and clearly what many people were vaguely thinking, must have contributed to their success. In general they argued their case on a superficial and largely polemical level, without seriously trying to consider why the ideas of the French Revolution had strongly attracted certain sections of English society. They were content to defend the country as it was, and for their purposes, at that particular time, patriotism was enough.

The principles of what might be called patriotic conservatism, by which the authors of the *Anti-Jacobin* proposed to be guided, were set out by Canning in the first issue.[5] He confessed, with mock humility, that he and his friends 'avow ourselves to be *partial* to the COUNTRY *in which we live*, notwithstanding the daily panegyrics which we read and hear on the superior virtues and endowments of its rival and hostile neighbours. We are *prejudiced* in favour of *her* Establishments, civil and religious; though without claiming for either that ideal perfection, which modern philosophy professes to discover in the more luminous systems which are arising on all sides of us.'

The most effective attacks on 'Jacobinical' ideas are found in some of the poetry published in the *Anti-Jacobin*. A typical example, called 'The Friend of Humanity and the Knife-Grinder,' was a parody of a poem by Southey and was meant to illustrate the Jacobin theory of eternal warfare between the rich and the poor, in other words, of class warfare.[6] According to Frere, he and Canning composed the poem in half an hour. 'It is really a capital thing,' he wrote, 'though I say it that should not say it.'[7] This poem was the subject of a Gillray cartoon published separately. The *Anti-Jacobin* was not illustrated but Canning was anxious to increase the paper's impact by getting the cartoonist to publish plates illustrating themes from the paper. A pension was procured for Gillray, and it has been estimated that the link established between him and Canning and Frere while the *Anti-Jacobin* was coming out was responsible in varying degrees for about twenty plates.[8]

Canning's most serious, vehement and effective onslaught in verse on what he believed to be the false values propagated by the French Revolution was reserved for a long poem, 'New Morality'*, in the last issue of the *Anti-Jacobin*.[9] Some of his most famous lines in this poem were part of an attack on 'French philanthropy' which he described as glowing with a vague love of all mankind but destroying every patriotic impulse. He described any Englishman unfortunate enough to become infected by this kind of philanthropy as a 'pedant prig' who 'disowns a Briton's part, And plucks the name of England from his heart.' Such a man cannot confine his feelings to one small island.

> No – through th' extended globe his feelings run
> As broad and general as th' unbounded sun!
> No narrow bigot *he*; – his reason'd view
> Thy interests, England, ranks with thine, Peru!
> France at our doors, *he* sees no danger nigh,
> But heaves for Turkey's woes the impartial sigh;
> A steady patriot of the world alone,
> The friend of every country – but his own.

In another passage in 'New Morality' Canning emphatically summed up one of the *Anti-Jacobin*'s favourite themes – the unsettling effect of Jacobin ideas on generally accepted ideas of right and wrong. He came down strongly on those who hesitate to take a firm stand against what they know to be wrong because they are endlessly worrying about men's motives and about being sure to see all sides of a question. He condemned

> CANDOUR – which spares its foes; – nor e'er descends
> With bigot zeal to combat for its friends.
> CANDOUR – which loves in see-saw strain to tell
> Of *acting foolishly*, but *meaning well*:
> Too nice to praise by wholesale, or to blame,
> Convinced that *all* men's *motives* are the same;
> And finds, with keen discriminating sight,
> BLACK's not *so* black; – nor WHITE *so very* white.
> . . . . .
> Give me th' avow'd, th' erect, the manly foe;
> Bold I can meet – perhaps may turn his blow;
> But of all plagues, good Heav'n, thy wrath can send,
> Save, save, oh! save me from the *Candid Friend*!

* The first 70 lines and a shorter section in the middle were written by Frere, according to his own account given to his nephews. (See the *Works of J. H. Frere*, Vol. II (1874))

By no means all the poems in the *Anti-Jacobin* were written with such a serious intention as was 'New Morality'. Many were light-hearted efforts designed principally, as was stated in the first number, to amuse the readers. And if amusement could be combined with a little instructive debunking of political opponents, or Bonaparte, or even of other people's verse, so much the better. 'The Progress of Man', for which Canning was almost entirely responsible, was an amusing and perhaps rather unkind take-off of a pretentious didactic poem called 'Progress of Civil Society', written by Richard Payne Knight.* It was published in three instalments and made fun not only of Mr Knight but of some of the Jacobins' more dotty ideas on social institutions like marriage.[10] His light-hearted attitude comes out in a letter to George Ellis on February 27, 1798, the day after the second instalment was published. He had not, he said, meant to write the second part so soon, but he had been provoked by the way people were saying that Mr Knight had been hardly treated. 'At present the poem rests on a good footing – as it is prepared (you see) to be the vehicle of whatever nonsense one may have in one's head, without plan, or subject.'[11]

Many of the *Anti-Jacobin* poems were probably equally unpremeditated *jeux d'esprit*. There seems to have been little exclusive pride of authorship among Canning and his close friends. They would leave their poetic efforts lying about in their own rooms or in the paper's editorial office, and apparently anyone was free to make changes or additions as he saw fit. There were also unsolicited contributions from outside, some of which had to be handled with considerable tact. On one occasion, Canning had to write a letter of apology to Lord Carlisle for not publishing his 'Ode upon the Duke of N[orfolk]'. 'His rage,' Canning told George Ellis, 'at its omission has been more comical than I can describe.' The rejected ode was eventually published in the *Sun*. 'And worse it is than I thought it possible for anyone to write. But having rejected it on the score of its humour and of the choice of the subject, it will not be possible without affronting him for ever to adopt anything at all to the *same purpose*. Of the *same merit*,' concluded Canning crushingly. 'I trust nothing will be to be found.'[12]

* Richard Payne Knight, an eminent classical scholar and archæologist, was not successful as a poet. When his 'Progress of Civil Society' was published in 1796, Horace Walpole told a friend that he was 'offended and disgusted by Mr Knight's new, insolent and self-conceited poem.' He enclosed a parody on two lines of the poem 'which will show you that his poem is seen in its true light by a young man of allowed parts, Mr Canning, whom I never saw.' Thus Canning must first have considered parodying the poem directly after it was published. (*Poetry of A-J.*, p. 106)

The *Anti-Jacobin* made its name by its poetry, but in fact the greater part of each issue was made up of much more solid fare. At that time, even the pro-government newspapers were not very reliable; while the opposition ones were thoroughly inaccurate and tendentious. Admittedly, reliable news was hard to come by, especially from the Continent. In effect, the *Anti-Jacobin* tried to do the job that in a modern war would be the responsibility of a ministry of information; it presented the official version of the news and defended the government's policies. There were some very solid defences of the government's financial policies – three of them by Pitt himself – which at that time were very unpopular because of sharp increases in taxation. There were articles comparing the treatment of British prisoners-of-war in France with that of French prisoners in England, justifying the government's interpretation of the rights of neutral shipping, and so on. There was a weekly bulletin of whatever news had filtered through from the Continent. And each week there was a section devoted to exposing and refuting the 'Lies', 'Misrepresentations' and 'Mistakes' perpetrated by the opposition newspapers. According to the prospectus, this section, which was largely produced by Mr Gifford, was to be the most important part of the paper. Whether or not it lived up to these expectations, it was certainly one of the liveliest sections. The opposition papers, with their patently inaccurate reporting and sloppy editing, often laid themselves wide open to ridicule, while their tendentious reporting often provoked the gentlemen of the *Anti-Jacobin* to transports of righteous (and highly abusive) indignation.

In fact, it was the opposition journalists, rather than the politicians, who had most cause to resent the *Anti-Jacobin*. While the former were roundly abused, the latter were made fun of – which, however, they may have felt was just as bad. Much of the mockery was at a fairly schoolboy level; none of it approached the offensiveness and savagery of some of the cartoonists, particularly Gillray. Indeed, Canning's anxiety to prevent the *Anti-Jacobin* from going in for personal abuse and caricature always complicated the paper's relations with Gillray.* By the standards of the time, the *Anti-Jacobin* was all good, clean – and fairly mild – fun. In any case, Canning and his friends, realising that

* In 1800 Wright commissioned Gillray to produce the illustrations for a special edition of the poetry of the *Anti-Jacobin*, which he proposed to publish. Canning and Frere, although not allowed to see Gillray's designs, strongly suspected that they would be full of personal caricature. Eventually Canning persuaded Gillray to suppress them, compensating him with £150 in banknotes. (See Draper Hill. *Mr Gillray*, p. 88ff)

Pitt's backing for their paper was no secret, were always conscious of their obligation not to embarrass him. On one occasion there were long discussions as to whether an 'Ode to Lord Moira' could be published without disagreeable consequences for Pitt. The prime minister at first agreed to its publication and then changed his mind.* The ode, based on a proposal made to Moira by some disgruntled M.P.s that he should head a new ministry excluding both Pitt and Fox, not only made fun of Moira but also touched on a particularly sensitive political topic.

On the whole, however, Pitt gave the *Anti-Jacobin* his willing, even enthusiastic, support. Canning tried to cash in on his interest by getting articles out of him, and space for a hoped-for contribution from the prime minister was often kept open till the last possible minute. But Pitt apparently tended to promise more than he could fulfil. On February 6, he wrote to Canning: 'I contributed about a fifth of one of the finest mornings possible in hopes of being in time for the *Anti-Jacobin*'; but he did not regret being too late because 'there seems to have been abundance of material without it and a *leading* paper which is better than anything which could have appeared at this moment.'[13] (The leading article in the issue of February 5 dealt with the dismissal of the Whig Duke of Norfolk as Lord Lieutenant of the West Riding after his toast to the sovereignty of the people.) Again, on May 21 Pitt sent Canning a disarming apology for his failure to come up to scratch. 'I lounged over a book all the evening,' he wrote, 'meaning to be early and diligent this morning, which has unluckily ended in finding Lord Auckland here before my breakfast. This leaves me no chance of sending you anything in time. I hope you have not counted on me enough to make the failure inconvenient.'[14] Apart from the inconveniently early arrival of Lord Auckland, Pitt was after all prime minister, with a great deal to do and a great need of relaxation.

There seems to be no evidence for the story that the *Anti-Jacobin* ceased publication because Pitt found it embarrassing. It stopped at the end of the parliamentary session as it had always said it would. According to Frere, Canning 'felt that the office of a weekly journalist was derogatory to the position he held in society and in the official world – accordingly, as soon as he found he had succeeded in giving a wrench to public opinion he closed the publication with the poem of "New Morality".'[15] This sounds plausible. Canning may well have decided that the roles of aspiring politician and successful journalist could not be combined for too long without detriment to the first.

* The ode was inserted in later editions of the *Anti-Jacobin*, Vol. I, pp. 380/2. January 22, 1798.

How much of a wrench the *Anti-Jacobin* did in fact give to public opinion, cannot of course be known. In its last issue on July 9, it indulged in some ingenious, if rather dubious, calculations about the extent of its influence. It multiplied by seven (the average size of a family) its regular weekly sale of 2,500 copies, thus arriving at a readership of 17,500. But, knowing that many of its readers lent their copies to their poorer neighbours, it added on a further 32,500, thus making a grand total of 50,000 readers, which it complacently described as a 'most respectable minority of the readers of the whole Kingdom'. The paper then went on to calculate, even more ingeniously, that if an average of twelve lies, misrepresentations and mistakes were exposed in each issue, a total of 420 had been dealt with in the course of the 35 issues. If this figure is brought up to 500, to take account of 'bye-blows and odd refutations in notes, etc.' and multiplied by the total of readers, 'the total of twenty-five millions will represent the aggregate of false-hood which we have sent out of the world.' On this typically audacious note the curtain was rung down on the *Anti-Jacobin*.

'Never,' wrote Canning on September 5, 1798, 'no never in the history of the world was there a victory at once so brilliant in itself and so important in its consequence.'[16] He was referring to Nelson's defeat of the French fleet at the Battle of the Nile on August 1, 1798, news of which arrived in London just over a month later. He was understand-ably, if exaggeratedly, elated. Nelson's victory effectively scotched Bonaparte's plans for eastern conquests to which he had turned when he realised that the invasion of England was for the moment impractic-able; it re-established the Royal Navy in the Mediterranean; and it encouraged the indecisive Tsar, Paul I, to take up arms in support of the Austrians, who in May 1798 had again been attacked by France. With Bonaparte locked up in Egypt, and with the rebellion in Ireland crushed, Pitt and Grenville were beginning to feel optimistic about what might be achieved by a new continental coalition.

Canning, of course, shared the anxiety of his seniors to strike at the French while they were at a disadvantage. He also shared Pitt's growing feeling that Britain's long-term security demanded a satisfactory and stable settlement of Europe. And as he no longer had the columns of the *Anti-Jacobin* in which to express himself, he was all the more anxious to do so in the House of Commons. His chance came on December 11 when the Whig spokesman, George Tierney, introduced a motion requesting that the King's ministers should not enter into any engagement which might prevent or impede peace negotiations. The insular and isolationist tone of his speech gave Canning the opportunity he needed to present what might be called a more European outlook.

In typical *Anti-Jacobin* vein, he began by mocking that 'large and liberal system of ethics' according to which one should consider what is good, not for one's own country, but for the whole human race. 'I for my part,' he said, 'still conceive it to be the paramount duty of a British member of parliament to consider what is good for Great Britain.' He then went on to argue against the wisdom of making a separate peace (which was what Tierney's motion seemed to imply) unless we were absolutely forced to, and explained to the House that in his view Britain's involvement in Europe was both necessary and inevitable. He argued that the most complete and desirable end to the war would be the deliverance of Europe and he could not understand how anyone could look at the map of Europe and not understand what he meant by that phrase.

'I do not envy that man's feelings, who can behold the sufferings of Switzerland, and who derives from that sight no idea of what is meant by the deliverance of Europe. I do not envy the feelings of that man, who can look without emotion at Italy – plundered, insulted, trampled upon, exhausted, covered with ridicule, and horror, and devastation – who can look at all this, and be at a loss to guess what is meant by the deliverance of Europe? As little do I envy the feelings of that man, who can view the peoples of the Netherlands driven into insurrection, and struggling for their freedom against the heavy hand of a merciless tyranny, without entertaining any suspicion of what may be the sense of the word deliverance. Does such a man contemplate Holland groaning under arbitrary oppressions and exactions? Does he turn his eyes to Spain trembling at the nod of a foreign master? And does the word deliverance still sound unintelligibly in his ear? Has he heard of the rescue and salvation of Naples, by the appearance and the triumphs of the British fleet? Does he know that the monarchy of Naples maintains its existence at the sword's point? And is his understanding, and is his heart, still impenetrable to the sense and meaning of the deliverance of Europe?'

Canning scornfully demolished the argument that no British objects would be gained by continuing the war. Why, he asked, did everyone wonder what effect Nelson's victory at the Nile would have on the continental powers? Was it cold speculation or idle curiosity? 'No. It sprang from the instantaneous, and almost instinctive conviction that . . . we *have* an interest in the liberties of the Continent; that *our* "assurance is doubly sure" when those around us are preserved from destruction; that *we* can be but precariously safe, so long as there is no safety for *the rest of Europe.*' He ended his speech by asking the House what it thought the country ought to do in the present situation. ' "Hoard up your safety for your own use," says the motion of the honourable gentleman, "Lend a portion of it to other nations, that it may be returned to you tenfold, in the preservation and security of the world", is the dictate of a larger, and I think, a sounder policy.'[17]

In a sense, of course, Canning was tilting at a windmill. Tierney's motion was easily negatived. Although the Commons were suspicious of foreign entanglements if only because they hated to see good English guineas transferred to the coffers of unreliable foreigners, at this stage in the war they did not want to let Pitt down. It was not from the Commons that he could expect real trouble in his efforts to build up a second coalition, but from the procrastination, indecision, financial exigency and mutual suspicions of Vienna, St Petersburg and Berlin.

By the following spring, however, Canning had ceased to be officially concerned with Grenville's painstaking diplomatic labours. He handed over his post at the Foreign Office to Frere, and on March 20, 1799, kissed the King's hand on his appointment as a Commissioner of the Board of Control for India.

The Board had been set up under Pitt's India Act of 1784 to oversee, and to an increasing degree control, the activities of the East India Company. Originally the Commissioners all had to be privy councillors, but in 1793 it was decided to appoint two additional members who were to be salaried and need not be privy councillors. The government was getting more and more involved in the company's increasingly complicated financial, commercial and administrative problems. Although Dundas, who was President of the Board of Control, already had an exacting job as Secretary of State for War, he gave a good deal of his time and attention to Indian affairs and privately thought they were a full-time job.[18]

Canning, however, took a rather relaxed attitude towards his new work. On April 16, he wrote from his new office: 'Here I am immersed in papers, of which I do not yet comprehend three words in succession; but I shall get at their meaning by degrees and at my leisure. No such hard work here as at my former office. No attendance but when I like it, when there are interesting letters received from India (as is now the case) or to be sent out there.'[19] It seems that the ordinary members of the Board could make very much what they liked of their post. Canning chose not to make too much of it, perhaps because he wanted more leisure for other pursuits or perhaps because he was not really very interested. Like many of his contemporaries, he was never greatly attracted by the challenge of India.

Ireland was a different matter. An Irishman by birth, Canning was always deeply interested in its problems, and after the rebellion of 1798 they seemed more intractable than ever. Although brought up in England, as a young M.P. he became well briefed on Irish attitudes and affairs through his membership of the Irish Club. The club's members were mostly Irish merchants living in London who met once a fortnight in each other's houses, talked, played whist and had supper. Canning's early political ambitions had centred on becoming Chief Secretary for Ireland – a post of great responsibility and formidable difficulty. When he first met Pitt he told him frankly that his Irish sympathies made him favour a more rapid advance towards full emancipation for Roman Catholics than Pitt himself thought expedient.* But in 1795 he had no difficulty in warmly supporting Pitt's decision to force the resignation of Lord Fitzwilliam, a Portland Whig, who went to Ireland as Lord Lieutenant and within three weeks threw Dublin into turmoil by revealing his pro-Catholic sympathies too precipitately. However strong the Catholic case, Canning did not believe in pressing it when the government was already grappling with a foreign war and domestic unrest.

But if the English Cabinet had hoped to put the Irish problem on ice until the end of the war with France, the rebellion of 1798 forced it to think again. While the rebels were gradually being brought under control, Pitt came round to the view that the only way to give Ireland social and political stability and make it a loyal ally in the fight against France, was to create a legislative union between the two countries. Once this was achieved, the Irish Catholics could be given full civil and political equality with the Protestants, and a major source of discontent removed without any political danger; for while the Catholics would be in a large majority in a purely Irish parliament, in a parliament of the two kingdoms they would be in a permanent minority. Pitt clearly regarded union and emancipation as two parts of the same policy. Some of his colleagues thought he ought to bring them both in at once. But because there was so much bitter opposition to emancipation –

* In 1793 Pitt had in fact managed to give the Irish Catholics the vote on the same basis as the Protestants.

from the King, from some members of the Cabinet, from many Irish Protestants – he preferred a step-by-step approach. Even so, the first attempt to bring in union alone, in January 1799, failed; not unnaturally, the Irish parliament jibbed at voting itself out of existence. Pitt, however, determined to try again and this time to ensure success by buying, in one way or another, the acquiescence of the Irish borough-mongers and politicians. 'I despise and hate myself every hour,' wrote Lord Cornwallis, the Lord Lieutenant, 'for engaging in such dirty work . . .'[20] But the dirty work did the trick. In June 1800, the Irish parliament agreed to its own demise. A month earlier, the Act of Union had been passed by large majorities at Westminster.

In all this Canning was not officially or directly involved, although he contributed – not, it seems, very effectively – to the debates on union in the English parliament. But although it was not apparent at the time, the Irish crisis of 1799–1800 had a significant effect on his career. Pitt never gave a specific commitment that emancipation would follow union, but this was widely believed to be his intention. On October 23, 1799, Canning told Windham that the High Protestant party wanted to make it a fundamental article of the union that nothing further should be done for the Catholics. 'This,' wrote Canning, 'to be absolutely rejected and the whole question reserved, and with a full determination to do what is right upon it at a proper season.'[21] But when, early in 1801, the proper season seemed to have arrived, the King, as might have been foreseen, would have none of it. Pitt felt obliged to resign, and so did Canning. After Pitt's death, Canning felt committed to the cause of Catholic emancipation for the rest of his career, however unpopular this made him with the King and some of his fellow Tories; if it was not exactly a political albatross round his neck, it was certainly not an asset.

Another issue to which Canning gave a good deal of time and attention was the abolition of the slave trade. It was just as controversial as Catholic emancipation but less of a political liability. When Canning first became an M.P., the parliamentary campaign for abolition had already been under way for six years. With Wilberforce at its head, it was backed by the biggest guns in the House of Commons – Pitt, Fox and Burke – and supported by a mass of harrowing evidence produced by a Privy Council inquiry. There seemed to be every reason for success. But year after year the fear of change – sharply stimulated by events across the Channel – and the profound eighteenth century respect for the rights of property, proved stronger than the dictates of humanity. It was an issue that cut across friendships, loyalties and voting habits.

Some of Canning's closest friends were anti-abolition. Charles Ellis, the closest of all, in effect headed the West Indian party in the Commons. Granville Leveson-Gower and Jenkinson were also opposed to abolition.

Canning's own attitude to the slave trade was always commendably downright but at first curiously unrealistic. He felt that the case for abolition was so obvious and had been discussed so exhaustively that there was nothing left to argue about. Although he would always give his vote for abolition, he did not see much point in getting up and speaking for it. But this uncharacteristically passive attitude did not last long. By 1798 he had come to realise that the slave traders were very far from admitting that they had no case to argue, and that he ought to support a cause in which he believed so strongly with his voice as well as his vote. So when Wilberforce introduced his annual abolition motion on April 3, 1798, Canning supported it. The motion was lost as usual, but a concession proposed by Canning – that the West Indian traders should bring no new land into cultivation – was accepted; and Wilberforce told him that this would go further to abolish the trade than any measure yet adopted. This was being over-optimistic since Canning's resolution did not have the force of law. But Wilberforce was presumably anxious to encourage a promising young recruit.

When Wilberforce yet again introduced his abolition motion on March 1, 1799, the wit, irony and passion with which Canning attacked the slave traders' arguments added a refreshingly novel touch to the debate. He declared that it was useless for M.P.s to try to shuffle off their responsibilities on to the backs of the colonial assemblies because it was quite plain that the colonials had no intention of doing away with the slave trade. Characteristically, he pounced joyfully on to some of the more eccentric speeches that often seemed to be a feature of slave trade debates. One anti-abolitionist had argued that slavery was not so bad after all and that many ancient philosophers had been slaves. Another professed to be horrified by Wilberforce's remark that some parts of Africa were quite civilised and even had books, because books had produced the French Revolution and done a lot of mischief in the world. Canning mockingly compared the two arguments: ' "Export the natives of Africa," said the honourable gentleman, "lest they become *literati* at home." "Bring them away," said the honourable baronet, "that they may become philosophers in the West Indies." '[22] But Canning, like greater men before him, might have spared his breath for all the impression he made on the anti-abolitionists.

THE ANTI-JACOBIN 1797-1799

Wilberforce's motion for immediate abolition was as usual defeated, and he did not try again for five years. That summer, however, Canning, with all the enthusiasm of a new recruit to a good cause, found it hard to let the matter drop. He toyed with the idea of himself bringing in a compromise bill which he hoped might unite the abolitionists and the moderate 'West Indians' who were against immediate and total abolition. But, realising that the most effective step would be to get Pitt to put all the weight of his authority behind a bill of his own, he concentrated on trying to persuade him to do so. 'The poor slave trade question,' he wrote to Mr Leigh, 'has been long enough left to individual fancy and feelings. It is high time . . . to bring forward some definite measure upon it with all the strength of *Government*.'[23] He pointed out to Pitt himself that some government supporters opposed the slave trade motions simply in order to enjoy the luxury of demonstrating their independence; and that the only way to stop this was to make abolition a government question. By early June he thought he had won his point. On the 5th Pitt gave notice that he would bring in a bill early the next session. Canning, therefore, put off his own slave trade motion. 'I have,' he wrote rather pompously to Mr Leigh, 'discharged my conscience, and I trust he will discharge his.'[24] But Pitt did not fulfil Canning's hopes. With so much else to worry about he had every excuse not to. Canning's reaction to Pitt's failure to keep his promise is not known. Perhaps by then he also had too much else to worry about.

CHAPTER V

Courtship and Marriage
1799-1800

In the late summer of 1799, for the first time in his life, Canning fell suddenly and overwhelmingly in love; and throughout the following winter and spring his energies were concentrated almost exclusively on the problem of overcoming the formidable obstacles to his marriage. In August he went down to Walmer to stay with Dundas and his wife who had been lent the castle by Pitt. The other guests included Pitt and Miss Joan Scott, a girl of about twenty-two with a large fortune. She was the daughter of General John Scott of Balcomie in Fife. When Canning first met her, both her parents and one of her sisters were dead and her closest relative was her eldest sister, Henrietta, who was married to Lord Titchfield, son of the Duke of Portland. The only thing Canning could remember having heard about her was that she was always about to be married or was turning down offers of marriage. So he made up his mind to avoid her in order to prevent his own name from being linked with hers. Throughout his stay at Walmer he studiously kept to his resolution, carefully avoiding sitting next to her at dinner and only narrowly managing not to behave with obvious discourtesy to a fellow guest.

It was all in vain. When the time came for him to leave, he was hopelessly in love. He himself could only account for his having done the exact opposite of what he had intended by suggesting that he had tried too hard. Perhaps, he wrote to Granville Leveson-Gower on August 22, it was just because of having her so constantly in his thoughts as something to be avoided that made him gradually aware of 'her beauty and good sense and quiet interesting manners.' However that may be, when his chaise was at the door, and only Miss Scott and the Dundases were left, Canning felt such an overwhelming reluctance to leave them that he somehow contrived to get Dundas to ask him to stay on for another day.

But he made little use of the time gained. 'I question,' he wrote to Leveson-Gower, 'whether in any of the most populous days at Walmer I had less intercourse with her than on this day when we were left almost entirely to each other.' Next morning, after hanging about as

long as he decently could in the hope of getting five minutes alone with
Miss Scott – but without the least idea what use he would make of
those minutes if he got them – he said goodbye and departed; 'and
when I got to Dover was fool enough to feel proud of a victory I
fancied I had obtained over myself.' But this triumph was short-lived.
That very evening when he happened to meet Leveson-Gower's sister,
Lady Susan Ryder, who was a friend of Miss Scott, he felt an irresistible
compulsion to tell her all; and immediately forgetting all his resolutions
not to get involved, he begged Lady Susan to try to find out what Miss
Scott thought of him.[1]

While waiting for Lady Susan's report, Canning hurried off to
Holwood to tell Pitt what had happened to him. Much to his amazement, he found that his news came as no surprise. The supposedly
preoccupied statesman, who was thought to have a mind above such
things, and anyway to be hopelessly inexperienced in them, had
observed for himself what was going on. According to what Frere
wrote much later, Pitt was extremely anxious that Canning should
make a good marriage, believing that this was the one thing he needed
to give him the position he must have if he were to lead a party.[2] When
Canning first confided in him, Pitt had already virtually cast himself in
the role of matchmaker. He confidently assured Canning that he would
get a favourable report from Lady Susan and proceeded to tell him
'how he had observed a certain manner and attention towards me (on
the part of Miss Scott), and how he had observed my shunning it, and
a great deal more such observation as you perhaps would not have
expected him to have made, as perhaps you may not think very much
to be relied upon when he has made it.'[3] Pitt was sure that Dundas
would be in favour of the match, and had craftily mentioned to him
before he left Walmer that he thought of bringing Canning back with
him, in the hope that this would lead Dundas to mention whether he
had noticed anything. Dundas, however, had merely politely answered
that he would be glad to see Canning again.*

Contrary to Pitt's optimistic expectations, Lady Susan's report was
not particularly encouraging, and she advised Canning not to go back
to Walmer. Canning, however, took courage from the fact that Joan
had neither expressed any personal dislike of him nor suggested that
she was attached to anyone else. He also felt that he might not easily

---

* Maybe Dundas had other things on his mind. While Canning was falling in
love, he was anxiously waiting for news of the fate of a British expeditionary force
which was battling against exceptionally heavy gales in the Channel on its way to
try to liberate the Dutch Netherlands and restore the Prince of Orange.

get another opportunity to see her, and that she might well pass the next six months in the company of people who thought poorly of him. 'I do not know,' he wrote to Lady Susan, 'that I shall gain by her better knowledge of me; but at least I would have her know me without disguise.'[4] Pitt too thought that Canning should not retire from the field, and went on ahead to Walmer to spy out the land. On August 26, Canning wrote to the Leighs to tell them that he had fallen in love. He added that he would set out again for Walmer the next day unless he got a letter from Pitt stopping him. 'What the event will be Heaven knows; but such an anxiety I have never felt before.'[5]

In the event, Canning had no reason to regret his temerity, although he still had plenty of reason to fear the final outcome of his suit. He managed to get Joan to himself one day and without actually proposing made his feelings pretty plain. She suggested that the fancy of a fortnight would soon pass away and hoped they might just remain good friends. But she did also say that she would tell her brother-in-law, which in Canning's view suggested that at least she took him seriously. And he noted with satisfaction that her manner towards him became more unreserved and confident. She revealed that she found him quite different from what she had expected. His public reputation, he told the Leighs, 'had taught her to be afraid of me, and to expect to be wearied and oppressed by constant endeavours at shining in conversation, by unmerciful raillery and I know not what – and that she had never been more surprised, etc.'[6] The surprise was mutual, and for Canning it must have been, if painful, rather salutary. However, at Walmer he was buoyed up by his friends' encouragement. Lady Jane Dundas thought Joan was coming round, while Dundas told Pitt, who told Canning, that he thought so too. 'As for Pitt,' Canning told the Leighs, 'it is our first topic every morning, and our last before we go to bed, but after everybody else is gone, every night.'[7]

The last day of Joan's visit was rather a disaster. Canning naturally wanted to have another *tête-à-tête* with her before she went. But unfortunately Mrs Crewe, the Duke of Portland and Lady Mary Bentinck came over from Dover and stayed the whole day. Canning was in despair and by the end of the day feared that Mrs Crewe not only suspected that he wanted to get rid of her, but also guessed why. 'We went on as well as we could,' he wrote afterwards, 'though I fairly confess not without infinite vexation – And then to make bad worse, towards evening Mrs C. began to form her little suspicions and to desire to communicate them to me. I listened, but would make no confidence.'[8] Still, in spite of the frustration of Joan's last day, Canning felt – although he knew it seemed vain and presumptuous to say so – that if the decision depended only on her, all would be well.

But it did not depend only on Joan. She regarded Lord Titchfield as *in loco parentis* and however much she may have been attracted by Canning, she was not yet sufficiently involved to defy her brother-in-law's objections. And Canning was the first to acknowledge that there were objections. In the first place his social background was inferior to Joan's. He had too much self-confidence to let this give him an inferiority complex, but he was sensitive about his mother's career as an actress. He discovered that rumours of this had reached the Titchfields and increased their dislike of the match. Eventually Canning wrote fully to Lord Titchfield (as he told Mr Leigh) 'upon the whole subject of family connections, incumbrances, etc. It was a painful task – but Pitt was firmly persuaded that the doubts started by L. and Ly. T. had originated chiefly from having heard something confusedly and indistinctly about my mother – and he thought it necessary that this should be all set right and that I should do it myself by letter.'[9] It was clearly good advice, although one cannot tell how big a part Canning's background played in the Titchfields' continued opposition to the match.

A more formidable objection was the fact that Joan was an heiress, while Canning had no fortune of his own. 'I cannot bear,' he wrote after his first meeting with Joan, 'to be the creature of my wife's [fortune]; and though I might, and do, flatter myself that I want not any such accession of fortune to carry me in due time as high as I am ambitious of going; yet there is a danger, which I cannot but see and have not the courage to despise, of being supposed to rise on a foundation not of my own laying.'[10] If his political fortunes were more firmly established – as he hoped they might be a year hence – it would not be so easy to misinterpret his motives for marrying an heiress. Joan herself had told Lady Susan that she expected her husband to bring at least a competency to be added to her fortune and had pointed out that a political career was rather a hazardous way of securing this. Canning, who had discovered that she liked living in the country, was afraid that in any case she might not like being married to a man in public life. If that were so, there was, he told Lady Susan, nothing to be done. 'My hopes and desires, and taste and turn of mind are bent, I fear, irrecoverably to public objects.' And he would want his wife, not only to share his political anxieties, but also to be his most faithful adviser and confidential friend. 'I am much mistaken if in describing this character I have not described exactly what her mind is capable of realising,

75

though I cannot presume to judge how far her inclinations might lead her to approve it.'[11] Considering that Canning wrote this after his first stay with Joan at Walmer, it shows a remarkably perceptive insight into the sort of person she was. If that was the kind of wife he wanted, he made his application in the right quarter. But before it was accepted, he needed plenty of patience and persistence as well as perception.

For as soon as Joan was removed from the warmly pro-Canning atmosphere of Walmer she again fell under the influence of her relations and docilely wrote to Lady Jane asking her to advise Canning not to press the matter any further. Canning received the news with equanimity. Titchfield after all, he wrote condescendingly to Lady Susan, had only done his duty. '. . . I am sure I have no reason to complain that he offers the same objections which I have so repeatedly stated myself.'[12] So long as Joan did not definitely turn him down, he would not give up. Pitt also agreed that all was not yet lost. He wrote to Canning on September 18 to tell him that he and Lady Jane agreed that 'there is nothing in what she had received which ought in any degree to be discouraging as to the final result.' Though, added Pitt with tactful understatement, 'it will require more patience than on such an occasion it is pleasant to exercise.'[13]

Throughout that winter Joan was tucked away with her relations at Welbeck, the Duke of Portland's country seat, and there was precious little that Canning could do to further his suit. But he did enlist the services of a friend, the Reverend John Sneyd, who lived not very far from Welbeck and who happened to be a friend of Titchfield's. He begged him to go over to Welbeck and plead his cause. 'You must make him [Titchfield] like me,' he wrote urgently, 'and make him think it altogether a good and desirable thing. Will you? There's a good Sneyd. She knows you and likes you very much, and will hear and make Td hear what you have to say.'[14] In due course Sneyd did go over to Welbeck and at the end of November Canning was staying with the Leighs at Ashbourne waiting to hear from him – '. . . even this useless and imperfect sort of communication,' he wrote to Leveson-Gower, 'gives me a degree of comfort . . . and makes me look forward to Sneyd's arrival here on Monday with a kind of foolish satisfaction which I cannot describe to you.'[15] But all that Sneyd brought with him from Welbeck was the news that Titchfield almost certainly would not go up to London in the New Year, in which case Joan would go by herself and stay with Lady Jane Dundas. Since she was friendly to his cause, Canning made the most of this crumb of comfort.

By the beginning of February, 1800, Joan was installed with Lady Jane at Wimbledon. Canning was in the thick of the parliamentary fray. On the 3rd he made a major contribution to the Commons' debate on the government's rejection of Bonaparte's peace offer. Pitt, he reported afterwards, was 'satisfied and happy in my success'; *The Times* was benevolently approving; and the King, at his levee, two days later, received him with the 'most marked kindness.'[16] None of this, however, diverted him from his preoccupation with Joan. He wrote at once for permission to visit her, assuring her that he had no intention of being tiresome or importunate. Although he was as good as his word, the world at large very quickly suspected that something was going on. By the middle of February he was having to call on newspaper editors to stop them from publishing reports of his engagement. By early March, the Queen was asking Lady Jane about the affair at her Drawing Room. And when Canning accompanied the Dundases and Joan to the play, he was embarrassed to find that their box was just where the King and Queen could spy right into it, 'so we had the full gaze of inquiry upon us from them.'[17]

Joan, removed from the influence of her relations, seems to have succumbed very quickly to Canning's restrained and gentlemanly siege. As early as mid-February she put his head into a complete whirl by declaring, after seeing the newspaper reports of their engagement, that it only made her vain to be pointed out as the object of his choice. By the middle of March he had very little doubt of her wishes – provided her family could be brought round. By the middle of April he and Joan were discussing his political prospects, and on the 18th he wrote rhapsodically to the Leighs that he found her 'not only the most lovely and delightful companion for private life, but one of the most judicious and confidential of friends and advisers in whatever may be the future occupations of my public station.'[18]

About two days later Joan fell dangerously ill – according to Canning, as a result of neglecting a cold. Her illness caused him intense anxiety, but at least it helped to bring matters to a head. She was moved to Dundas's house in Somerset Place so as to be near the best doctors, and for more than a fortnight Canning hovered miserably outside her sickroom. On May 2 he reported to the Leighs that she still had a low fever and was 'so refractory' about taking her medicines. Two days later, he reported a change for the better and next day he was allowed for the first time to see her for a few minutes – 'they are minutes never to be forgotten while I live.' Next day he saw her for a whole half-hour – 'I can write no more,' he told the Leighs, '. . . for my head is quite bewildered with pleasure and I do not know how to sit still, or what to do, or where to go – Yes, I must go to Somerset Place.'[19]

At this point the Titchfields, who had not changed their minds about the match at all, arrived in town. They proposed to remove Joan to their own London house as soon as possible and then carry her off to the seaside to convalesce. Canning was in despair and strongly urged Joan to make her position plain before she was moved. She was still so weak that she had to be carried from her bed to a couch. But although in no state to stand up to anyone, she was by this time sufficiently deeply committed to Canning to face a showdown with her brother-in-law – and get the better of him.

Titchfield, having been worsted, acknowledged his defeat in the handsomest possible way. He immediately called on Canning and frankly announced himself to be 'the bearer of a message from *her*, announcing her final *yes*.' Canning replied 'as well as I could – which was not very distinctly,' and the two men shook hands.[20] Not long afterwards, when Canning wrote to announce his engagement to a friend, he said he had no quarrel with Titchfield for having thought him a bad match; 'and I am firmly persuaded that he is disposed to find me, and to prove to me, a good brother-in-law.'[21]

Canning and Joan were married on July 8, 1800, at 7.30 in the evening. Three hours before the ceremony, Canning tried, with unusual incoherence, to describe his feelings in a letter to Mrs Leigh. 'I believe,' he wrote, 'the feeling is something like that of going to be executed. It is strange, and wild, and tumultuous, and though I am happier than ever man was, yet it is an awful feeling and full of seriousness and deep and quick-succeeding reflections.'[22] Then he went off to dine with Pitt, Frere, who was best man, and Mr Leigh, who was to officiate. According to Frere's account, on the way to the church a man happened to peer into the coach, 'recognised Pitt and saw Mr Leigh, who was in full canonicals, sitting opposite to him. The fellow exclaimed, "What Billy Pitt! and with a parson too!" I said, "He thinks you are going to Tyburn to be hanged privately," which was rather impudent of me; but Pitt was too much absorbed, I believe, in thinking of the marriage, to be angry.' If he had not seen it for himself, Frere would not have believed that Pitt could have been so moved. When the ceremony was over, he was so nervous that he could not sign the register, and Canning had to whisper to Frere to go ahead and sign himself.[23]

In a letter to Lady Stafford, Canning described his engagement as 'the event the most essential to my happiness that has ever yet occurred in the course of my life.'[24] If he could have re-read that sentence towards the end of his life, he would still have felt that it was abundantly true. It is not easy to make out what kind of a person Joan Scott was at the time she married Canning, or indeed afterwards. She seems to have been content to remain in the background and never aspired, as she might have done, to become a great society hostess. Many of his letters to her have survived, but not hers to him. A year after their marriage, Auckland reported to Arthur Wellesley, then in India, that Canning had married 'a pretty woman with a large fortune and of very pleasing manners.'[25] Charles Ellis and his wife liked her 'extremely'. But apart from these scraps, Canning's friends and contemporaries do not seem to have had much to say to each other about the girl he married. She must have been intelligent because all his life he discussed public affairs and his private concerns exhaustively with her. She must also have been a woman of character. If to the outside world she seemed a rather self-effacing figure, in her own home she was certainly not a cipher. She was neither overwhelmed by her husband's personality, nor extinguished by his overwhelming, intense and lifelong devotion. Partly, but not entirely, through his own fault, his public life turned out to be chequered and often frustrating. Without his wife, and the stability and love she gave him, he might have let it go even more awry.

But all that lay in the future. When Canning became engaged, his public as well as his private life seemed set on a fair and steady course. Pitt, realising how much it meant to Canning that his marriage to Joan should not seem too unequal from a worldly point of view, took the opportunity presented by a routine political reshuffle to make the office of Joint Paymaster-General vacant for him. The post was not of much importance, but it was a step on the political ladder and it brought with it a house which Canning described as admirable. It also brought him into the Privy Council. He had, so he told Mr Leigh, always determined to be a Privy Councillor *'at thirty'*.[26] After he had been sworn in on May 28, he wrote jubilantly to the Leighs that he was 'just returned home as Right Honbl as you could desire.'[27] Lady Holland, noting in her journal Canning's political promotion and Miss Scott's 'immense fortune', commented rather sourly (and ungrammatically): 'If ever a man was born with a silver spoon in his mouth, surely it was him.'[28]

With Canning happily married, financially secure and launched on a political career, this is perhaps a good point at which to take stock of him – his character, personality, tastes, ambitions and personal relationships.

The portrait of him by Hoppner, painted about two or three years before his marriage and now hanging in the Provost's Lodge at Eton College, shows a good-looking young man with an alert and amused expression. The nearest we have to a contemporary description of Canning as a young man was written by his cousin, Stratford, towards the end of his long life. He describes in his memoirs his first recollections of his cousin when George was 25 and he himself a young boy just going up to Eton. 'His features, alternately expressive of deep thought and lively wit, his mild yet penetrating eyes, his full but rather scornful lip, the handsome contour of his thin and slightly freckled face, are still before me. His dark well-shorn chin bore witness to the colour of his hair, which before he wore powder, a raven might have envied.'[29] Making allowances for the mellow and rather beatific haze through which the old ambassador would have seen his famous cousin, this is not a bad description of Hoppner's portrait.

To the outside world, Canning seemed a lively, amusing young man with a flair for writing witty verses. Few doubted that he was exceptionally able, but some felt he was superficial and lacked steadiness. His friends sometimes found him rather quick-tempered. His most damaging fault was his inability to suffer fools either gladly or silently; and many who were not fools, either in their own estimation or in most other people's, had reason to resent his sarcastic comments. Canning mocked and abused other people, either because he disliked them or thought them stupid, without apparently realising that his remarks might not be received in the light-hearted spirit in which he himself made them.

Those who make unkind comments about other people are liable to do more damage to themselves than to anyone else, and Canning was no exception. Lady Stafford, who was genuinely fond of him, saw this clearly; and in November, 1798, she suggested to her son, Granville Leveson-Gower, that he might drop a hint to his friend that he should give up a habit which was making him many enemies – 'I mean,' she wrote, 'that of talking in a contemptible way of those he does not like – calling them fools, etc. etc.'[30] Canning himself was not unaware of his failing, but he never quite managed to overcome it. Indeed, a habit which had grown upon him when he was young and seemed to have the whole world at his feet, was not likely to be eradicated after he had become embittered by political setbacks and frustrations.

Even if Canning had always behaved in an unexceptionally innocuous way, Pitt's obvious partiality for him would still have made him mistrusted and envied, at any rate in the small circle of Westminster politicians. Wilberforce referred in his diary more than once to the sad envy that prevailed against Canning in the Commons and thought that Pitt ought not to have encouraged him so much. Malmesbury, too, who knew Canning very well, wrote a year after Pitt's death that Canning's mind 'would have taken a better bend' if he had been allowed to ripen slowly instead of being forced in the hot-house of Pitt's partiality.[31] Yet as far as office was concerned, Canning did not progress as fast as his aristocratic contemporaries, and without Pitt's helping hand, it would have been much more difficult for him to get started in politics at all. Canning, for his part, must have increased the pangs of jealousy that Pitt's friendship aroused by the uninhibited way in which he expressed his own affection. Most people treated Pitt with great respect and deference, however long they had known him and however great their own political or social consequence. Canning, on the other hand, shocked people by treating him with easy familiarity. During his second year in Parliament he was told that he had even been observed to touch Pitt on the shoulder when he wanted to attract his attention. Canning, who by nature had what he himself described as 'something of a *caressing* manner', was amazed that this should cause offence. Already he felt he had penetrated behind Pitt's aloof and reserved exterior and could confidently assert that he did not belong to the class of men with whom one would not think of shaking hands or exchanging any kind of 'corporal civility'. On the contrary, Pitt was a 'very hearty, *salutation-giving, shake handy* sort of person,' and therefore it seemed perfectly natural to Canning to take him by the arm or touch his shoulder just as he would anyone else he liked.[32]

For if Canning was good at making enemies, he was even better at making friends - and keeping them. The young man, whose public reputation - as he was dismayed to discover from Joan Scott - was of an alarmingly brilliant and unmerciful conversationalist, could in fact be unusually sensitive about other people's feelings. Kindness came naturally to him, and he was thoughtful and considerate even to those who were not personal friends. He would take his Foreign Office clerks home to dinner with him when he was working them particularly hard and go to a lot of trouble to provide for the relations of a messenger drowned on the cross-Channel passage. Those to whom he was personally attached always found him ready to involve himself sympathetically in their affairs. He dispensed a great deal of talk, advice and comfort to Jenkinson whose father was stubbornly opposed to his marriage to Lady Louisa Hervey and master-minded a most careful and ingenious plan designed to reconcile Lord Hawkesbury. Unfortunately the plan was a bit too clever and hopelessly misfired. (In the end the King took it upon himself to complete the protracted softening-up of the obstinate father.)

Realising that he was not so well placed as some of his wealthier and better-connected friends to do a good turn, he was always particularly pleased when he could. When Granville Leveson-Gower, who was on Malmesbury's staff at Lille, came over to London to report on the negotiations, Canning took him to have several long talks with Pitt. He was extremely pleased at having been able to make his friend better known to the prime minister. 'And I confess,' he wrote to Mr Leigh, 'I *do* like to *confer* kindnesses, and do good, when according to the usual tenour of worldly affairs, I might rather be supposed to have expected to *receive* advantage.' In the days when he might have badly needed some help to get started in the world, the Staffords had made their anxiety to help him so clear that it was particularly pleasant for him to be able to 'repay them in the quarter where I know *their* feelings and wishes are wrapped up, instead of having had to call upon them for any purpose of my own.'[33] A year later, after Leveson-Gower had been persuaded with some difficulty to make his maiden speech in the Commons, Canning from his place on the Treasury bench at once sent Lady Stafford a note telling her that her son had acquitted himself excellently and adding the congratulations of Pitt who was watching him write the note.[34] In November 1799, Lady Stafford wrote to Canning, expressing her own and her husband's appreciation of the 'kind interest' he always took in their son's affairs. 'Indeed,' she added, 'your unremitting friendship for my beloved Granville, and your particular attention to my Lord, have made you very dear to me.'[35] Perhaps because his own enjoyment of normal parental affection had been cut off so early, his kindness and good nature were often particularly apparent when his older friends were worried about their children*.

Among the group of close friends of his own age, Canning was the

* In May 1805, when Lady Bessborough told William Lamb in the passage behind her box at Drury Lane that he could marry her daughter, Caroline, he threw his arms round her and kissed her. She looked up and saw Canning gazing at them in amazement. Unable to bear his 'mortifying conjectures' she rushed after him and told him the news. He was so kind and delighted and took such trouble to remove her fears about Lamb, whom he praised 'extremely', that she could not resist pressing his hand to her lips. (Granville Leveson-Gower II, p. 68)

natural and undisputed leader. When he decided to give up the *Anti-Jacobin*, no one else apparently thought of going on without him. When, at the end of 1794, Lord Boringdon became what Canning rather condescendingly called 'one of those who have got their heads puzzled about peace', it was Canning who undertook successfully to convince him that he could not detest opposition and wish well to Pitt if he refused to vote for Pitt's war policy.[36] Charles Ellis once said that although he himself was an M.P. he was not really interested in politics; but he liked Parliament because it gave him an occupation and a position and, above all, because it allowed him to be of service and support to those he loved – and he meant to Canning. Lady Holland alleged in 1798 that Canning exercised a despotic sway over his friends and controlled not only their votes but also their opinions, conduct and social life. Lady Holland is neither a very reliable, nor a very impartial witness; and she may well have been irritated by the private jokes, unintelligible to two-thirds of the company, which she accused Canning and his friends of perpetrating.[37] Canning undoubtedly did influence his friends in all sorts of ways. But they do not seem to have either resented his influence or found it despotic. Those who were in the Commons took it for granted that they should follow his lead, so that it soon began to look as if he were collecting round him a little party of his own – which was not considered an entirely respectable thing to do. But there is no reason to suppose that this came about, as Lady Holland suggests, from Canning's 'love of intrigue and management'.

Beyond his circle of friends from Eton and Oxford days, Canning's life, before his marriage, included three sets of family relations – the Leighs, Hetty Canning with her family, and his mother with hers. Of these, the least closely related, Mr Leigh, was the closest, most intimate and most valued friend. It was to him and his wife that Canning most readily confided his plans and his feelings, more as if they were contemporaries than members of an older generation; and it was to their home in Derbyshire that he liked best to go when he had a holiday. It was a relationship that was so central to Canning's life, and which he took so much for granted, that he never felt the need to comment on it.

With his other aunt, Mrs Hetty Canning, his relations did not really mellow as he grew older. Although she was genuinely devoted to him in her own way, she found it very hard to forgive or forget his desertion of the Whig faith in which he had been brought up. So his visits to Wanstead were not all that frequent and tended to be a little tense and even quarrelsome. But his difference with his aunt never made him neglect his cousins, particularly the two younger boys. Canning used to invite Willy, who was then at a school at Hackney, up to town, stuff him with food and get him into the gallery of the House of Commons to listen to the debates. In the summer of 1795 he took his aunt's youngest son, Stratford, familiarly known as Stratty, to Eton, introduced him to the Provost and the Lower Master and did his best to launch him smoothly on his school career. Some dozen years later he also started Stratford off on the diplomatic career in which he was to become one of the most famous of British ambassadors.

But if his Aunt Hetty was rather a trial to Canning, his mother became a far worse one. When he began his political career in London, she had numerous other children by Samuel Reddish and by Richard Hunn. By this time her marriage with Hunn was breaking down and she had retired from the stage. Being an enterprising and resourceful woman, she was trying to make her fortune with an eye ointment which she had invented. Not surprisingly, as soon as Canning was established as a young M.P. in London, the elder Reddish boys, who were beginning to have to make their way in the world, began to descend on him in the hope that he would give them a helping hand. He did his best for them. When Samuel Reddish, an army sergeant, was given an unenviable posting to Botany Bay, Canning tried to hasten his promotion. Charles Reddish, who was thoroughly unstable, a victim of unpleasant fits and given to lying, was a much more tiresome problem. Canning, however, fitted him out with a complete wardrobe from amongst his own old clothes, lectured him severely on the folly of his violent passion for the stage and got him at least two jobs neither of which he stuck to. Eventually, towards the end of 1796, Canning in despair got him taken on as a 'guinea-pig' in an East Indiaman. Two years later he was back being a terrible plague to his relations. In the end, Canning obtained a cadetship in Bengal for him in the frank hope that he would never see him again. He was also faced with the unpaid school bills of William, another half-brother. The schoolmaster, a Yorkshire clergyman, wrote to him to complain that his mother owed him £28.3.2. and was trying to pay with cartloads of her eye ointment which no one would buy.* Canning tried to appease him with a £10 note.[38] To his half-sister, Mary, to whom he wrote affectionate brotherly letters, he seems to have been genuinely attached. When she got married he secured a place in the Customs worth £300 a year for her husband, Richard Thompson, and later became godfather to their eldest son.

* When Canning tried it his eye became very inflamed and sore.

Canning coped good-naturedly and more or less philosophically with his half-brothers and sisters. But his relations with his mother became increasingly difficult. Naturally she was anxious to see as much as she could of this son who was turning out so well, but Canning himself knew only too well – as he had tried to tell her when he came down from Oxford – that to have a mother who had been an actress (and not even a successful one) and whose private life had at one time been distinctly disreputable, was both a political and a social liability. Already in the spring of 1795 he refused an invitation to stay with Boringdon at Saltram, which was inconveniently near Plymouth, because of the danger that his mother might get to know he was there and decide to pay him a visit – which 'would be rather inconvenient and distressing'.[39] So he made up his mind that while he would continue to fulfil his filial duty – write his weekly letters, visit her in her own home whenever he could and make sure she was amply provided for – he would not allow her to jeopardise his career.

To be ashamed to acknowledge one's own mother is neither comfortable nor estimable, but to Canning's contemporaries it was the obvious and sensible thing for him to do. Pitt, far from disapproving, was willing to go to some trouble to help him make discreet provision for her. When Canning asked him, early in 1798, whether a pension could be paid his mother on his death, if he died before she did, Pitt pointed out that this would mean linking his name publicly with his mother's, and suggested instead that Mrs Hunn should simply be given a pension at once which need not be connected with her son at all. Canning thought this might turn out rather awkward for Pitt if any questions were asked; moreover he was unwilling to accept any separate provision for his mother while he himself was getting an official salary. They eventually agreed that whenever Canning was out of office he should get a pension large enough to support his mother during his life and provide for her in the event of his death by means of an insurance. Canning, although satisfied, was torn by the conflicting pulls of his conscience. He wanted the plan to be shelved for a time until he had given more public service, which would make the arrangement look better. On the other hand, he doubted whether he was right to sacrifice his mother's security to his own reputation.[40] It is not clear whether the arrangement had been made by the time Canning went out of office early in 1801. In any case, by that time his financial position had been transformed by his marriage to Joan Scott.

But the problem of ensuring Mrs Hunn's financial security was nothing compared with the problem of keeping her at a discreet distance. With the complete breakdown of her marriage,* she had no compelling reason for staying in the West country, and the idea of settling as close as possible to her increasingly well-known son naturally became more and more attractive. In January 1798, Canning gave way to the extent of renting for her a pleasant furnished house at Totteridge. But the arrangement was not a success. His mother was always badgering him for more of his time than he was prepared to give her and even hinted that she might move to London. This, however, he would not have, and the upshot was that she agreed to go back to Devonshire. But it was not until the following June that she actually went, and not before Canning had been forced to have some very unpleasant scenes with her.

After the failure of the Totteridge experiment, Mrs Hunn established herself at Bath. But Canning's marriage and the arrival of grandchildren, naturally made her all the more anxious to be close at hand. Although Joan wrote once to her mother-in-law, Canning made it clear that she was to be kept at a distance. Mrs Hunn, however, was a persistent woman, and early in 1802 Canning was again very much vexed by her threats to settle in London. It was not until well over two years later that she was at last allowed to see her daughter-in-law and grandchildren. To Canning's immense relief, the meeting passed off very well. But two months later Mrs Hunn was again raising the old question of living in London. In the summer of 1805, she did in fact appear there, and in order to induce her to go away again, Joan brought the children up from South Hill, the Cannings' home near Bracknell, especially to see her. After that, Mrs Hunn seems to have accepted defeat. However relieved he may have felt, Canning can hardly have felt proud of his victory.[41]

Conceivably, Canning's rather unhappy and complicated relationship with his mother may have had something to do with his tendency as a young man to form warm but quite platonic friendships with older women like Mrs Crewe and Lady Sutherland. However that may be, until he met Joan Scott, when he was nearly thirty, he showed little disposition for any serious emotional involvement with a woman, whether as wife or mistress. Early in 1798 he thought he had fallen in love. We do not know the name of the girl, but she must have been known to Mrs Leigh, because he wrote her a long letter, enumerating the qualities he would like to find in his wife and asking her to probe

* Canning helped to negotiate the separation agreement between his mother and Mr Hunn, and then secured a government post for Hunn.

the girl's feelings for him.[42]* Nothing came of this. Next year, however, he nearly became involved in an affair which might have had serious consequences but from which he was providentially saved by falling in love with Joan Scott. A good deal of mystery surrounds the incident, but there is enough circumstantial evidence to suggest that the person involved was the Princess of Wales. At this time she was living at Montague House, Blackheath, making a desperate and rather pathetic attempt to console herself for the lost splendours of Carlton House. She had not yet forfeited, through her indiscreet and foolish conduct, the respect and sympathy of all those who thought that the Prince had treated her badly. Many prominent people, including Pitt, Dundas, Windham and Eldon, the Lord Chancellor, made regular pilgrimages to Blackheath to keep the Princess company at her dinner table and to amuse her with party games afterwards.

Canning was first introduced to the Princess on June 18, 1799, when he and Frere were invited to meet her at Lord Palmerston's house at Sheen. 'It seems,' he wrote to Mr Leigh, 'she has a great curiosity to be gratified with a sight of us. I hope we shall answer her expectations.'[43] Canning, at any rate, found the Princess fully up to his; four days later, he was writing enthusiastically to Mrs Leigh about how much he admired her.[44] It rather looks as if the Princess, who about this time was beginning to worry her friends by her indiscretion, admired him too. At any rate he seems to have become a regular visitor at Blackheath, and some time in August – presumably before he went down to Walmer – he told Granville Leveson-Gower in a hurried note that he had just come back from a visit to someone unnamed in the letter but evidently known to Leveson-Gower. 'The keeper left us for a few minutes and the thing is too clear to be doubted. What am I to do? I am perfectly bewildered.'[45] Shortly afterwards, when he wrote again to his friend from Walmer to tell him about Joan Scott, he referred to his affair with a married lady and how if he had not fallen in love with Miss Scott, he might not have resisted a passion which was quite different from what he now felt and which must have been dangerous, perhaps ruinous, both to him and the lady. He hoped that if he could keep out of her way for two or three months and then confess his engagement to Miss Scott, she would be able to rejoice with him at their mutual escape.[46] If it was the Princess of Wales who had made unmistakable advances to Canning, he might well have felt tempted and flattered by the prospect of becoming her lover; he must also have

* He considered a fortune of comparatively little importance – 'or not so much as it would be to a man of landed property – or of any property at all.'

realised that such an affair could easily have unpleasant consequences. The following February Canning discovered that Mrs Crewe had inadvertently told the Princess about his feeling for Joan Scott. So he decided that he had better confide in her himself. Afterwards he told the Leighs that his account 'was received – it is impossible to say *how* kindly! Never, never shall I forget or cease to be grateful for the generous, amiable, disinterested affection, which was shown on that occasion.'[47] It is hard to see why the Princess should have had such a special interest in Canning's love affairs, or why he should have been so excessively grateful at her kind reception of his news, unless she herself had in effect made a pass at him. Another crumb of evidence is provided by a sentence in a letter from Pitt, written about two months after Canning's wedding, in which he told him that he must not let the Princess think that he shirked meeting her.[48] Why should Canning have thought of avoiding her unless he feared that his marriage might have embarrassed their relationship? In fact it seems to have led to a steady friendship between them. The Princess visited the Cannings at South Hill and became godmother to their eldest son.

Six years later, when the 'delicate investigation' into the Princess's conduct was undertaken, Canning's name was on the list of her supposed lovers. No evidence was ever produced to substantiate this. If he had wanted to hide anything about his relations with the Princess from Joan, it is hardly likely that he would have invited her to South Hill. But Canning's friendship with Caroline, however innocent, was to prove politically expensive. It made him feel obliged to resign from the Cabinet in 1820 when she was put on trial, a step which George IV interpreted as evidence of a former guilty relationship with his wife. For several years after becoming Foreign Secretary in 1822 Canning had to battle against the King's bitter hostility.

Canning's chief claim to fame rests on this second stint as Foreign Secretary from 1822 to 1827. But twenty years earlier, it was far from clear to him or anyone else that diplomacy was the field where he most wanted, or would be most likely, to shine. The one thing he was quite clear about was that he wanted a career in politics and public affairs. Neither a legal nor a military* career attracted him. Although he was

---

* Unlike most of his contemporaries, including Pitt, he was not even interested in participating in the military preparations against a possible French invasion. In 1794, when Jenkinson tried to persuade him to become a captain in his regiment of fencible cavalry, Canning wrote in his Journal: 'But I do not find the military

an excellent classical scholar, enjoyed writing verse and took a lively interest in the literature of his day, literary pursuits by themselves would never have satisfied him. He was not interested in acquiring worldly wealth so long as he had enough to meet his responsibilities and live like a gentleman. He never yearned to establish himself as a landed proprietor, in spite of the influence and prestige this would bring. In any case he would have been dreadfully bored to live in the country most of the time. When he visited country houses he went to see his friends, not to enjoy country pursuits – he firmly opted out of hunting – nor to admire the beauties of nature. He was never, he once wrote, an enthusiastic judge or admirer of hills, vales, woods and water for their own sakes. 'They must be *well tenanted* to make me look at them with delight.'[49] It was in people, not in places or things, that he was primarily interested.

By the time he was thirty Canning's commitment to a political career was complete. He was fortunate in that as yet there was no contradiction or tension between his political beliefs, his political ambitions and his personal affections. There is no reason to assume that his beliefs were chosen and tailored to further his ambitions. The dominating political issue of the day was the French Revolution and Canning was genuinely convinced – as his part in producing the *Anti-Jacobin* showed – that both its principles and its armies must be decisively defeated. He had no sympathy for the Whigs' rather starry-eyed approach to the Revolution, still less for their defeatist attitude towards the war. And he accepted the repressive measures adopted by Pitt's government to deal with domestic unrest as part of the inevitable price to be paid for preserving the country's institutions and liberties. Possibly, he might have found it rather more difficult to fit into the political establishment had he not been presented with a grand, simplifying issue to which all lesser issues had to give way, at any rate for the time being.

He had no use for notions of democratic equality and he did not believe that parliamentary reform would give the country better or more efficient government. There is no evidence that he was any more aware than most of his contemporaries of the grave economic and social problems that were being created by the industrial revolution. But there are indications that he was more actively aware than most that politics was not only about power, but also about people, their

---

disposition sufficiently strong within me. And so I have only bargained *not* to *laugh* at him about it.'

problems, needs and feelings. Although he seems to have accepted the rather exclusive and aristocratic circle in which he found himself as easily and casually as it, on the whole, accepted him, he did not feel himself bound by its rather circumscribed outlook. Some of his aristocratic lady friends, whom he like to instruct in his views, thought that his conversation was sometimes positively Jacobinical. He was capable of opposing a bill to curb bull-baiting on the grounds that it was a poor man's sport. He knew it was cruel 'but so is hare-hunting, so is shooting, so is angling – and I do not like to see all the amusements of the rich held sacred, nay guarded by laws, however cruel, and those which are peculiar to the lower orders of the people alone exposed to all the moral severity of legislation.'[50]* To suggest that it would be unfair to deprive the poor man of his cruel sport so long as the rich man continued to enjoy his, was a novel attitude.

After listening to Canning holding forth at a dinner party, Lady Bessborough once decided that he was like the French – 'determined to give liberty to all mankind, whether they will or no. I shall certainly draw him in the two characters of Don Quixote and a schoolmaster.'[51] Canning certainly had a dash of the schoolmaster in him, and as his political career became less smooth, his behaviour sometimes seemed to be distinctly quixotic. But at the time of his marriage he was essentially an ambitious young politician who, having made sure of private happiness, was anxiously considering his political future. He knew that his comparative youth need not necessarily stop him from holding one of the senior posts in the government. Lord Castlereagh, who was his own age, had since 1798 been Chief Secretary in Dublin. Lord Grenville had been Speaker and Home Secretary by the time he was thirty. Addington had been made Speaker just after he was thirty. Canning admitted in a letter to Boringdon in November 1799, that he should feel a 'little impatient' if he were obliged to be the one person who had to advance step by step so that he only fulfilled his ambition 'in a green old age'.[52]

Yet his approach to the problem of promotion was cautious. He was aware that he was not the most popular young man in the House of Commons; and however hard he found it to mend his approach to individuals he did not like or respect, he was unwilling to fly in the face of public opinion at Westminster and beyond by appearing to grasp too greedily at political advancement. Towards the end of 1799 it became known that Dundas, feeling over-worked and disgruntled

---

* That was in April, 1800. A year later he changed his mind after discovering just how cruel bull-baiting really was.

with the opposition inside the Cabinet to his war plans, wanted to give up his most important post as Secretary of State for War. Canning would have preferred, from his own point of view, that Dundas should give up his less important post of Treasurer of the Navy, because he himself might aspire to that without causing surprise or envy and it would pave the way to something more important a few years later. In a letter to a friend discussing the problem he wrote: 'Do you fear shocking the public? I do. Pitt? I do not.'[53]

Pitt, indeed, seems to have had no hesitation about pushing Canning forward, and naturally was much less bothered about what people might think. He may well have had reasons of his own, apart from his affection for Canning. In the autumn of 1800, his political situation was not easy. The members of the Cabinet were at loggerheads about how best to pursue the war, and Pitt had reason to believe that he no longer had the undivided confidence of the King. Although Canning no longer automatically agreed with him about the conduct of the war, Pitt may have felt that the political advancement of a protégé who was both basically loyal and exceptionally able would strengthen his own position. It is not clear exactly what he offered Canning during some long talks together at Holwood in the late summer of 1800. All we can assume is that the post was prestigious but without administrative responsibility. Canning was at first 'overpowered' and accepted, but on second thoughts changed his mind. In a long and rather agonised letter to Pitt on September 10, he explained why he could not bring himself 'to consider an office of mere emolument, which giving neither the means to form nor the right to declare any opinion upon the measures of government, would yet bind one implicitly to the acts of persons in whose judgment and talents (without meaning anything unkind to them) one may fairly say one does not have implicit confidence ... Any office which might afford the opportunity of *being useful* to the country would be a different thing. But I have never been accustomed to look to public employment with a less enlarged view; and, *non hoc pollicitus*, I do not think it would now become me to do so.'[54]

The tone may have been unnecessarily lofty, but Canning's desire to use his talents actively and for the public good was perfectly genuine. His over-readiness not to trust the judgment or talents of his prospective colleagues was a less creditable outcome of his restless confidence in his own ability; it was to prove a serious liability when he became Foreign Secretary seven years later. A further consideration which he did not mention to Pitt but which might have helped to sway his decision was his reluctance to be shunted off into a position of prestige but no power, where he might be considered out of the running for the really important vacancies if and when they came up.

Whatever the mixture of motives behind Canning's decision, it was a significant sign of his growing independence that he should have insisted on opposing Pitt's wishes. Not much more than two years earlier he had written to Pitt: '. . . I think and trust that you feel perfectly confident that whatever my first thoughts or desires may be upon a subject, I can ultimately have no opinion and no wish but yours.'[55] That was no longer true. But Canning's personal devotion to Pitt was as strong as ever, and to be forced to differ from him gave him nothing but pain and anxiety. 'Most truly I can say,' he wrote at the end of his letter of September 10, 'that I never in my life have struggled so hard to be sure I was making a right decision.' It was barely two months since his marriage, and yet he was harping on his dread lest his opportunities for seeing Pitt 'comfortably' should be lessened. Although Pitt replied very kindly, Canning could not leave the subject alone, although it would have become him far more to worry about Pitt's over-tiredness or Bonaparte's military successes. In November, he wrote again to ask Pitt whether there had not been a 'sensible estrangement' between them since the beginning of the summer? And if so, what was the cause? Or had he just 'imagined a vain thing?' Pitt replied at once, with commendable patience, that he had indeed imagined 'altogether a vain thing.'[56]

By the New Year of 1801 Canning was in a happier and more settled frame of mind. Joan was expecting a baby and after spending the Christmas holiday at Welbeck, they returned to London in the middle of January to await her confinement. On the 17th, Canning wrote very cheerfully to Frere that he was 'highly pleased' to be settled and hoped not to move again 'till we are by one more numerous than at present.' Altogether, he was 'in perfect good humour.'[57] It was not to last long. Early in February Pitt, finding the King implacably opposed to the policy of Catholic emancipation to which he himself felt committed, handed in his resignation. Canning, much against Pitt's advice, decided that he must resign too. Next day, he wrote to a friend: 'I resign *because Pitt* resigns. And that is all.'[58]

Nothing was ever quite the same again for Canning after he took this decision. It was not just that it caused a setback to his political career. It also imposed a severe strain on his relationship with Pitt from which it probably never completely recovered until the months just before Pitt's death five years later. Thanks largely to Pitt's forbearance and patience, there was no open quarrel, rarely even any actual estrangement. But it was a deeply embittering experience for Canning. Unfortunately he vented his bitterness, not on Pitt, who would have forgiven him, but by revealing his less attractive qualities to the political world at large – which was only too ready to make the most, or rather the worst, of them.

CHAPTER VI

'The Pilot that weathered the Storm'
1801-1802

'I will do what I think right, do others what they will. I will do what I think right *by Pitt*, even against his own professed opinion and earnest persuasion. I know not what may come of it – perhaps that I may be a private gentleman for the rest of my life – I cannot help it.'[1] Thus wrote a rather hysterical Canning on February 7, the day after he and Pitt had dined together and tried hard but fruitlessly to argue each other into a different course of action. Pitt was determined to go out – so Canning was determined to go too. Pitt was convinced that Catholic emancipation was essential if Ireland was to be tranquillised and that he was morally – if not in so many words – committed to bring it about. The King said he would rather beg his bread from door to door than – as he believed – break his coronation oath. Pitt believed that he had no right to force the King to act against his conscience, and with a divided Cabinet and Commons behind him, he would hardly have been able to anyway. He therefore felt bound to resign. But he did not feel bound to join the Whigs in 'systematic opposition' nor did he feel that anyone else need resign with him. On the contrary, with the war going from bad to worse, and with a serious food shortage causing grave distress at home, he thought that he and his colleagues should give the new prime minister their full support.

Pitt's position was quite proper and reasonable. His chief mistake, as he himself later admitted, was that he had not done enough to prepare the King's mind for Catholic emancipation. But after being continuously in power for seventeen years he had become almost an institution. It was hard to believe that he really meant to step down, especially as Henry Addington, whom the King had asked to take over, seemed an almost ludicrously inadequate successor. Addington, son of Chatham's doctor, was a friend of the younger Pitt. He had been a successful Speaker, he was sensible and moderate and he was easy to get on with. But he was also dull and humdrum, too obviously middle class and slightly comic. When the change of government was announced, the newspapers thought it was all just a 'juggle'. All kinds of jokes about the new ministry went the rounds of the London drawing-rooms, and Lady Malmesbury was reflecting a widespread view when she reported to a friend in Scotland that it was merely a temporary 'lath and plaster edifice.'[2]

Canning should have known better. He realised the importance of the Catholic issue, and he of all men should have understood the workings of Pitt's mind and whether or not he meant what he said. It was silly of him to claim that he knew what was better for Pitt than Pitt did himself. If he insisted on resigning too because he was equally committed on the Catholic question, that was understandable, although as a junior member of the ministry, outside the Cabinet, it would not have been considered improper of him to stay on, especially if it were at Pitt's express wish. But if he felt it was right for him to resign on this issue, how much more right was it for Pitt, and how little good reason had Canning for trying to dissuade him. It is not clear, however, from Canning's voluminous but not very clear comments on the crisis, that the Catholic issue was the most important factor in his decision. In a letter on February 14 he wrote: 'My story is a very short one – Pitt resigns, no matter for what reason, and I feel it right to follow him out of office.'[3] It was the man, not the measure, that Canning seems to have been really concerned about. He admitted that most of his colleagues thought it right to stay on, and confessed that it was 'not at all good fun going out of office . . . and out of the best house in London . . . and to have a Mr Wollup or Lord Glenbubby come into all my compots instead of me. I never liked anything less, but I think I should have liked myself less, if I could have allowed myself to be prevailed upon by Pitt's arguments and entreaties . . .'[4] If he really believed that Pitt was the only man fit to be prime minister, he might not unreasonably argue that he could not serve under anyone else, especially not under anyone so obviously second-rate as Addington. Moreover it appears that, like some others, he genuinely believed – until Pitt later disabused him – that Addington had tried too eagerly to make use of the King's conscientious scruples to push Pitt out of office. But it is difficult to avoid the conclusion that what really moved him was quite simply extravagant loyalty to Pitt and unreasonable resentment against his successor. Between the two emotions he lost his head.

Much more eminent people than Canning also felt that they could not remain in office. Four of the most important members of the Cabinet – Dundas,* Grenville, Windham and Earl Spencer, the First Lord of the Admiralty – all resigned because of their commitment to

* Dundas told the King he could no longer walk the streets as a gentleman if he abandoned Catholic emancipation.

Catholic emancipation. So did Cornwallis, the Lord Lieutenant in Dublin, and Castlereagh, his Chief Secretary. George Rose, Charles Long and Granville Leveson-Gower resigned from minor offices. Rose openly admitted that his principal motive was his personal attachment to Pitt. Altogether, the resignations left Addington with a pretty mediocre team. And although the King, a large part of the Commons and many people outside were not sorry to have an ordinary sort of man at the head of affairs for a change, it was not easy for Addington to fill the vacancies in his administration.

He pursued his task against a running barrage of ridicule from Canning and his friends, who in their turn were abused by Addington's friends. There was a good deal of rather childish bickering; those who stayed in office said they were sacrificing themselves to their attachment to Pitt, while those who had resigned commented that it was an odd sort of sacrifice that involved hanging on to lucrative offices. Pitt tried to restrain Canning but not apparently very successfully. Lady Stafford, who with her husband was watching the troubled London scene from the comparative detachment of Bath, wrote gravely to her son that they had heard many reports that Canning had been talking very contemptuously of the new government. Leveson-Gower immediately sent his mother a long and stout defence of his friend.[5] If his explanation satisfied Lady Stafford at all, it was not for long. A fortnight later she wrote again to her son to tell him that one of their visitors had read out part of a letter describing the very unpleasant state of London society, with everyone divided into violent parties, and none more violent than Mr Canning's party, which included Mrs Canning, Mr and Mrs Ellis, Lord Granville Leveson-Gower, Lord Boringdon and Mr Sturges. Fortunately, she added ominously, Lord Stafford had not caught his son's name when the list was read out.[6]

Pitt might have restrained Canning more effectively if he had felt equal to seeing him personally. But he told him on February 15 that although 'it would be a real relief and comfort to me to talk with you (as we have been always used to do) on every thought in either of our minds . . . I will fairly own that while I have as much to go through in each day as I am equal to, I wish to be spared discussion on subjects where so many feelings are interested and on which (in some views) it is most painful to dwell with those one loves best.'[7] He indeed had plenty to worry about. In the middle of February the King caught a bad feverish cold. By the 23rd he was a very sick man, mentally as well as physically. The Prince of Wales foresaw the need for a regency, while his Whig friends thought they glimpsed the prospect of office at last. Meanwhile, Addington was left with his ministry half-formed and no way of properly completing it until there was a functioning head of state again. 'This is the strangest state of things,' wrote Canning, 'which a country ever experienced. Who is in, or who out – or where the Government will at last settle, nobody knows or even guesses. One thing I know, that I am *in* till Pitt is *out*, though I have had a battle to fight on that question with my successor-designate, Lord Glenbervie.'[8]

Canning of course hoped that the King's illness would stop Pitt from resigning after all. He hoped it even more after the King's recovery, for Pitt, learning that the King had blamed him for his illness, sent him a promise that he would not raise the Catholic question again during his reign. Most of Pitt's friends felt that there was now no reason why he should not return to power. Dundas worked out a plan for a strong new ministry that would include Addington as Home Secretary and some of his friends in minor posts. Pitt seemed to be tempted, but was unwilling to make the first move himself, and Addington, understandably, did not see why he should either. Malmesbury, lamenting the extreme folly of letting the country go to ruin because two men were either too proud or too weak to come to a right understanding, persuaded Canning to send Pitt a passionate appeal to withdraw his resignation. In the end, however, Pitt came to realise more clearly than his over-enthusiastic friends that it would be quite wrong for him to supplant Addington now.

Canning had to admit defeat. But, overcome by disappointment, chagrin and jealous fears that Addington now enjoyed more of Pitt's confidence than he did, he again could not leave well alone. Eventually Pitt persuaded him to admit that Addington had not behaved badly, and to send him written assurances that he would support him, not only from a sense of public duty, but also out of personal esteem and goodwill. It sounded well, and no doubt at the time Canning meant well. He accepted Pitt's argument that the new government must be supported in order to keep out the Whigs, and on March 25, when Pitt made a brilliant speech in the Commons in support of the new ministry, Canning was sitting with him on the third row behind the Treasury bench.

But he remained ill at ease. And it cannot have helped his uneasy frame of mind to know – as he must have done – that his reputation, both personal and political, had not been improved by his performance over the past two months. Some people criticised him for not doing what Pitt wanted him to do. Others – ironically – abused him for his evil influence over Pitt and blamed him for everything that had gone wrong. Most people agreed that he had been altogether too busy and forward throughout the whole affair. Too many people had been the butt of his ridicule, his satirical verses and cutting epigrams. And even those who were spared thought poorly of him, however much they might privately enjoy passing on his cracks about Pitt being to Addington as London was to Paddington. It was an age of crude and cruel mockery and the cartoonists were far more savagely critical of Addington and his team than was Canning. But then that was their job. Somehow, by his manner, his persistence, his skill, his sheer cheek, Canning had overstepped the mark of what was permissible between fellow politicians. And although he had many devoted friends, he had no reserves of popularity and goodwill to draw on; too many people were jealous of Pitt's partiality for him, or were alienated by his careless assumption of superiority and were glad of an excuse to think and speak ill of him.

Meanwhile there were other things to think about. On April 25 Joan gave birth to a boy. She was seriously ill afterwards, but the baby, according to Canning, was 'a fine large handsome boy, in the highest possible health and spirits . . .'[9] There was no sign then of the chronic ill-health which in a few years was to give Canning and Joan so much anxiety and eventually cause the early death of this much-loved eldest son. In the middle of June, when Joan was at last well enough to leave London, the family moved to South Hill, a house in Windsor forest, near Bracknell, 28 miles from London and nine from Windsor. Disgusted – for the time being – with politics, uncertain even whether he could bear to attend Parliament after the summer recess, Canning decided to try to settle down to domesticity and the life of a country gentleman.

At first he succeeded pretty well. The day after arriving at his new home he reported enthusiastically on the 'most prosperous and beautiful condition' of his new property, which included a 200-acre farm. 'Our house too is all that a house can be without furniture.'[10] On a closer, less euphoric inspection, the farm was found in fact to be in a distinctly run-down state, which Canning energetically set himself to remedy. His letters became full of enthusiastic references to manure, cows and sheep and the vicissitudes of his hay harvest. '*Here*, literally speaking,' he wrote in mid-August, 'our talk is of barley; and of the hay which I have got in, and of the wheat which is cutting – and of the bees which are swarming, and one of which stung me this morning, an article not mentioned in the 4th Georgick.'[11]* As he saw his harvest gathered in, he began to make complicated financial calculations by which, he told Frere, 'I have the satisfaction of proving to myself that I shall lose about £100 annually by my farm (supposing it to prosper as it is now doing with every help of fine weather and high prices) in addition to the interest on the purchase money.'[12]

The expensiveness of his new hobby, however, did not deter him from planning all sorts of costly improvements to the house and garden. A new kitchen was to be built on. The entrance to the house was to be changed from south to north, the old entrance hall turned into a bookroom and a conservatory built all along the south front between the two bow windows, with a 'beautiful arboretum, or shrubbery, flowering and feathery quite down to the water' in front of it. The conservatory, Canning told Frere, was 'to be a thing to be admired far and near'; and Frere, who at the time was British envoy in Lisbon, was commissioned to send some orange trees which would set off the conservatory to the best advantage. Frere was indeed bombarded with instructions and reminders about the orange trees; they were to be sent 'with a little mould to the root of each, matted carefully' and were to come in a King's ship in charge of the captain so as to avoid any trouble with the Customs. Later in the year when it looked as if Frere was coming home and would therefore be able to escort the orange trees himself, Canning's instructions became still more demanding; Frere was to bring 'great abundance' of them and they were not to be just cuttings but 'good large stumps'.[13]

Another and much greater source of pleasure and interest was Canning's baby son, referred to in his letters as 'little gee'. He is grown 'prodigiously', Canning told Mr Leigh on July 6, 'and enjoys being nursed by me – though that is no wonder, as to say the truth, I do it with surprising dexterity.'[14] When the baby was about three months old, he told Frere that Joan and the nurses might be too full of his praises. 'But to give you a cool and candid and considered opinion of him myself, I do honestly think that he is one of the finest boys, if not the very finest, that ever was seen: plump, good-humoured, lively, full of health and vigour and spirits – having blue eyes which I am assured are to turn to the exact colour of mine and Joan's – having been innoculated with the cow pox, when he was but three weeks old, and

* The bee-sting made a great impression. Next day he wrote to Mr Leigh that for a long time he had been 'all over in bumps with gnat-bites,' but had not bargained for a very painful bee-sting on the right cheek, 'or I should never have gone like a ninny to see them hived.' (Harewood Mss. 15. August 11, 1801)

having had the disease very favourably, and now being busy in teething as fast as he can; a surprising child, in short; and promising, for his years – or weeks rather, beyond what it would be prudent for me to announce to a world naturally bent upon depreciating extraordinary merit.'[15] This infant prodigy was called Charles George. He should have been just Charles because his godmother was Caroline, Princess of Wales. But the Princess, knowing that Joan wanted him to be called after his father, decreed that he should be called George. So, as Canning explained to his diplomat friend in Lisbon, 'he drops his Charles as you do your Hookham – never signing it but to despatches nor allowing it to be printed except in the red book.'[16]

No one realised better than Canning himself that he had a great deal to make him happy and that indeed he was happy. 'But the thought will obtrude itself now and then,' he confessed to Frere in the middle of the summer, 'that I am not where I should be – *non hoc pollicitus.*'[17] Unlike so many of his more aristocratic contemporaries, he did not regard politics as a rather tiresome duty from which one escaped as quickly as one decently could to a country estate or library. To him, the life of a country gentleman was really only a form of retirement. He was, he felt, prematurely on the shelf, and his bitterness escaped in the repeated references in his letters to his complete ignorance of what was going on in Downing Street, in London and on the Continent. Moreover, he could not rid himself of the feeling that something had gone wrong between him and Pitt; combined with his frustration at being out of office, this produced a mixture which, if not exactly explosive, was quite enough to throw him off his balance again. The novel pleasures and interests of being a proud father and a busy farmer did not stop him from brooding on his supposed wrongs, and on July 12 he wrote Frere a long, rambling, rather incoherent letter, full of dashes and underlinings, in which he alleged that Pitt had done 'scrupulously and magnanimously *right* by everyone *but* me.'[18]

Canning however was really no more capable of throwing away his friendship for Pitt than he was of abandoning his wife and child, and he was extremely lucky to be able to try Pitt's patience so far and get away with it. By the end of August he had more or less recovered his equilibrium. He was comforted by two days alone with Pitt at Holwood and Pitt was invited over to South Hill for little George's christening. At the end of September, Canning was assuring Frere (in response presumably to a letter of remonstrance) that 'I do love him,[Pitt] and reverence him as I should a Father – but,' he added characteristically, 'a Father should not sacrifice me, with my good will. Most heartily I forgive him. But he has to answer to himself, and to the country for much mischief that he has done and much that is still to do . . .'[19] It was one thing to love and forgive Pitt (however stoutly Pitt disclaimed the need for any forgiveness) but quite another to change one's views and pretend that Pitt had been right after all.

With friendship restored and a veil more or less drawn over the past, Pitt and Canning still did not see eye to eye about the future. Pitt could hardly be expected to serve under Addington himself (although there were rumours that he might) but he felt committed to giving him his full support. One way of doing so would be to persuade one of the new prime minister's bitterest critics (who was also known to be a fervent Pittite) that he had been wrong and ought to join him. Moreover, the new ministry could do with someone of Canning's ability and debating power. Pitt's persuasions caused Canning considerable distress. 'I do not like,' he wrote to Mr Leigh, ' – far from it – what I am asked to do – and yet I cannot summon resolution enough to give a direct negative to what *he* has so much at heart. It is a very painful perplexity – and disquiets and agitates me as much almost as the transactions of last winter. I really do not know how I am to decide.'[20] At one point he decided that he really could not bear to be out of office much longer. But in the end he stood firm, fortified by the advice of Granville Leveson-Gower and Sturges Bourne who, although they knew that they would be offered places if Canning went back, advised him not to. In the middle of September, Pitt wrote accepting his refusal with his usual kindness and good grace.

Canning's motives for resisting the strong pull of ambition were mixed. For one thing, although he was prepared to judge Addington's personal qualities and behaviour more charitably than in the past, he still thought him woefully inadequate as prime minister; nor did he think much of the rest of Addington's team and to bring himself to serve with men he despised went very much against the grain. Moreover, he could hardly expect to be given more than a subordinate post in which, in his view, he would have the worst of both worlds – he would be identified with the government's policies without having any effective means of influencing them.

But probably the strongest, and certainly the most creditable, of his reasons for staying out of office was his conviction that having made such a parade of his disapproval of the Addington ministry, it really would not do to turn round now and accept a place in it. It would be too easy for people to accuse him of making an unprincipled snatch after power and position. More than most men who longed for both as much as he did, Canning was genuinely scrupulous about how he got them. 'My road,' he wrote to Boringdon that autumn, 'must be through *character* to power; that I may take this road and miss the end is very possible; nay, that by acting as I think right, I may not, as surely as I expect it, get even to my second stage – *character* – is very possible also; but that I cannot help; I will try no other course.'[21] He was sincere. He was also sadly prophetic; for in doing what he thought right, he too often missed out – in the eyes of the world – on character.

Canning's strict standards of political honesty and political obligation caused him much perplexity that autumn when he had to make up his mind about the preliminary peace treaty signed on October 1 by Jenkinson (now Lord Hawkesbury), the new Foreign Secretary. The case for trying to come to terms with Bonaparte was a strong one. England's continental allies had all been knocked out of the struggle. At home people were thoroughly weary of the war; bread was scarce and dear; in parts of the country there was ugly unrest; and the exchequer was alarmingly depleted. People did not yet realise the full extent of Bonaparte's ambitions or his readiness to regard treaties as scraps of paper. It could be, and was, argued that the French guarantees of the independence of Holland, Switzerland and northern Italy, which were incorporated in the Franco-Austrian Treaty of Lunéville in February 1801, represented a continental settlement that would satisfactorily guarantee Britain's security. And even if the peace did not last, a breathing space was badly needed. Addington and Hawkesbury were prepared to pay a high price for one. They agreed to relinquish all Britain's overseas conquests, except Ceylon and Trinidad, and to hand Malta, captured from the French a year previously, back to the Knights of St John. In return, France promised to withdraw her troops from Naples, central Italy and the Papal States – not a very impressive concession since they could so easily march back again.

Whatever Pitt's private feelings about the peace treaty, he put a brave face on it in public. On the day the preliminaries were signed he wrote to Canning that the terms were 'as satisfactory as I expected, and though not in *every* point exactly what I would have wished, are certainly honourable and I think on the whole very advantageous.'[22] He stuck doggedly to this line – although to Grenville he described the terms as only 'reasonably' advantageous – and his strong support plus the popular enthusiasm for the peace helped Addington to weather the angry disapproval of the treaty's critics. Grenville and Dundas, while recognising in principle that peace was necessary, were convinced that Addington had gravely compromised Britain's future security by giving back so many overseas bases, particularly Malta and Cape Town, and that he might, if he had tried hard enough, have struck a better bargain with Bonaparte. Britain's negotiating position might have been worse; her naval supremacy was unbroken and only a few months earlier had been spectacularly demonstrated by Nelson at the Battle of Copenhagen. Moreover, the new young Tsar, Alexander I, who had succeeded his murdered father in March, was clearly much less willing than Paul I had been to support Bonaparte's anti-British schemes. Grenville wrote piteously to Dundas, stressing his reluctance to harass the King's government but asking whether it was not too much to expect him to say, contrary to his own convictions, that 'the measures in which I bore a share have reduced the country to the desperate necessity of purchasing a short interval of repose by the sacrifice of those points on which our security in a new contest may principally depend?'23 Dundas solved the problem by simply staying at home in Scotland. But Grenville in the end felt he must stand up and be counted among the parliamentary opponents of the peace terms.

Canning was faced with very much the same dilemma. When he first read the peace terms, he was astonished and dismayed, and like many other people, he was sickened by the excessive popular enthusiasm for the peace.* There is no reason to suppose that his reactions were not as genuine as anybody else's. But unfortunately he laid his own motives open to suspicion because he could not resist the temptation to mix personal attacks on Addington with his criticism of the peace treaty. It was unfair of him to suggest that Addington had accepted the peace primarily to boost his own popularity and power. But it was equally unfair of others to insinuate that Canning condemned the peace terms not out of conviction but because he wished to attack Addington.

The problem of deciding what action his convictions obliged him to take was complicated for Canning by his personal devotion to Pitt. Because of his intense anxiety not to hurt him personally or harm him politically, he made up his mind not to vote against the treaty. If he voted for it, he argued, it would be plain that he was deferring to Pitt's judgment 'because I could not do otherwise without hurting his feelings and perhaps his character, and without forfeiting my own character for consistency, having put my former conduct (in refusing

* When General Lauriston, Bonaparte's aide-de-camp, arrived in London with the ratification of the preliminaries, the mob greeted him with loud cheers and insisted on dragging his coach through several streets.

to make part of the new government) on the ground of exclusive attachment to him.'[24] All the same, the thought of voting for the treaty was dreadfully distasteful and – since he genuinely disapproved of it – perhaps not altogether honourable. In his perplexity, he wrote to Pitt for his advice. The reply was a friendly suggestion that he should stay away altogether.[25] It must have been the reply Canning had hoped to get.

He could not emancipate himself from his personal attachment to Pitt, but he could now afford to make himself politically independent by giving up the seat he owed to Pitt's goodwill and buying one for himself. With Pitt's approval he began to look for one that would cause him the minimum of trouble either before or after an election. In the middle of November 1801 he was negotiating for one which was being offered for 4,000 guineas. It is not clear whether he got it, but by the time of the general election the following summer he had procured for himself a safe seat at Tralee – which was 'among the rottenest of Irish boroughs.'[26]

Early in November 1801 Canning told Frere that he was going to rest on his oars for the remainder of the present parliament. He was of course temperamentally incapable of doing anything of the sort. He could not even keep away from the House of Commons, let alone refrain from plotting and planning with his friends. He was after all intending to launch forth for the first time on an independent political course, although not at all certain where exactly that course should lead him. He hoped that 'a temperate and mitigated opposition in Parliament, in which one should judge and act fairly upon *measures* as they arose, contending, however, uniformly all the while and upon every occasion that the *man* was utterly the fool he is, and that it is mischief and madness to trust the country in his hands – might do a great deal of good, and presents a highly respectable line of conduct, not to say a very amusing one – for the opposition to a fool, *quaetenus* fool, would be a new and hitherto unexhausted ground.'[27] In this long and involved sentence Canning reveals how, even when sitting quietly writing to Frere, he could not prevent his rancour against Addington from swamping his sensibly moderate intentions. How, Frere might have asked himself, could his friend maintain a temperate and selective opposition in the Commons if he was determined at the same time, and all the time, to proclaim the prime minister an unmitigated fool?

In fact, Canning could not behave consistently because he had been

104

forced into a political course which did not come naturally to him. However much he expounded to himself, to Joan and to his friends, the advantages of political independence, what he really wanted was to be able to work hand-in-glove with Pitt again – but not at the sacrifice of his own convictions. 'I would risk my life,' he wrote on November 22, 'to be assured of being able to act always *with* P in a manner satisfactory to my own feelings and sense of what is right, rather than have to seek that object in separation from him.'[28] For the next two and a half years he concentrated all his energies on persuading Pitt that it was his duty to oppose, overthrow and finally take over from Addington. What Canning wanted so passionately eventually came to pass – not, however, because of his eloquence and powers of persuasion but because of Addington's inadequacy and the renewal of the war with France.

With that 'damn Peace' out of the way, Canning felt there was no practical point of discord between him and Pitt and he quickly began to recover his equanimity and optimism. He began to treat Pitt as if he were an obstinate friend who had got into bad habits and worse company and needed to be argued, ever so gently and tactfully, into acknowledging the error of his ways. After several long talks with him in London towards the end of November 1801, he felt reasonably encouraged. But by the beginning of the New Year he was plunged into depression, and on January 3 told Leveson-Gower with extreme and quite unbalanced bitterness that the prime minister and his friends might 'do with him [Pitt] what they will; and they are right to break him in by degrees to bear all their caprices – to keep him out of confidence, and without an invitation to dinner, now and then for a week or ten days, during which he frets and fancies that he can break off all connection with them . . . and then with the string they have to his leg, to pull him back again, give him a bit to eat, and show him half a dog's ear of a despatch from Ld Cornwallis.* With this discipline he is become as tame as a chaplain . . . And yet this is the mind that governed the world and might have saved it. I am heartily ashamed of him – and I am heartily ashamed of myself for having written so much about him.'[29]

Intense anxiety about Joan added to Canning's distraught state. At the end of January she had a miscarriage and was extremely ill. Canning sat up with her and grew thin with worry and fatigue. But by the

* Cornwallis was in charge of the definitive peace talks at Amiens.

middle of February she was on the mend and Canning, who could not refrain from plotting and planning Addington's downfall, again felt able to dash up occasionally to London for a night. In his calmer moments he realised that his intemperate hostility to Addington would not do either himself or his cause any good. But when Pitt, on a visit to South Hill, expressed the hope that Canning's opposition would not be 'savage and personal' but 'liberal', he flatly replied that the only possible opposition to a government so completely devoid of talent was one of 'contempt and derision, of the whip rather than the sword.'[30]

He simply could not overcome his irritation at Pitt's blandly magnanimous attitude towards Addington. Nor could he rid himself of the feeling that Addington unworthily, and without acknowledgment, made use of Pitt's experience and reputation, particularly when preparing the budget. He accused Addington of squeezing Pitt like an orange and only keeping him in his hand or pocket in order to pelt him at the opposition; he added, furiously mixing his metaphors, that Pitt would finally 'be swept off the stage and left in the kennel.'[31] This was most unfair on Addington, who was in fact a competent financier who had done his homework and had his own ideas, however much he might talk them over with Pitt. But for Canning all sense of fairness or proportion was swamped by his conviction that Pitt was fatally undermining his own reputation.

Pitt's refusal to use the peace treaty, finally signed at Amiens on March 27, 1802, even as a light weapon against Addington did not help to lift Canning's gloom about Pitt's (and therefore his own) prospects. During the six months since the preliminaries had been signed, Bonaparte's behaviour had not been reassuring. He had 'accepted' the presidency of the Cisalpine republic; he had sent a French fleet to reconquer St Domingo from the Negroes; he had made even sympathetic English visitors wonder whether he was not after all a dangerous and ambitious dictator. So the news of the treaty, unlike the news of the preliminaries six months earlier, was received without much enthusiasm in London. In the House of Commons the treaty was overwhelmingly approved by 276 votes to 20. It looked like a crushing defeat for Addington's opponents, but the vote did not really reflect the widespread misgivings over the peace. Minto told his wife that 'we seem to have had everybody for us in opinion, and everybody against us in votes.'[32]

In Canning's view, the best way to help Pitt return to power was to drive as wide a wedge as possible between him and Addington. Pitt, however, understandably tended to find Canning's efforts in this direction more an embarrassment than a help. This was especially true of Canning's Trinidad motion, a long and dearly cherished ploy which for months helped him to keep depression at bay. As so often, his motives were mixed and not all of them were as unworthy or blatantly partisan as his confessed desire to 'worry the Dr like a pole-cat.'[33]* Ever since Trinidad had been captured from Spain in 1796, the West Indian planters had been badgering the government for the unrestricted right to buy land on this fertile and uncultivated island. Now that British possession was confirmed by the peace settlement, the pressure from the powerful West Indian lobby in London increased, and neither Addington's character nor his convictions equipped him to resist it so well as Pitt had done. Those who had fought unsuccessfully for years to get the slave trade abolished feared that Addington would give way to the planters and that the cultivation of Trinidad would lead to a big increase in the importation of slaves from Africa. They wanted the government at least to promise that it would grant land in Trinidad only to those planters who would undertake to cultivate it with slaves who were already in the West Indies.

Canning, as his past record showed, would almost certainly have taken up the question anyway on humanitarian grounds. But the possibility that it might lead to a showdown between Pitt and Addington added a wicked zest to his activity. He had an impeccably respectable ally in Wilberforce, who was also energetically bestirring himself. Pitt could hardly object, but realising what Canning was up to, he remonstrated privately with Addington and urged delay on Canning. But Canning would not delay for long. On May 27, he asked in the Commons that all grants of land in Trinidad should be forbidden until Parliament had had time to consider how the future of the island should be regulated. It was a moderate request and the speech that accompanied it was moderate too. It was also constructive. He suggested that Trinidad should be developed as a strong military post and naval station for the protection of Britain's other West Indian islands; and that an effort should be made to settle it with people who would stay there for good – ex-soldiers, free blacks and creoles. He wanted the thousand or so native Indians whom the Spaniards, 'by some unaccountable oversight', had failed to exterminate to be protected and helped. He argued that European labour could raise at any rate vegetables and cattle, if not sugar, in the West Indies, and suggested that Trinidad should be used to test the theory – then in dispute between

* Addington was nicknamed 'the Doctor' after his father.

the colonists and the anti-slave traders – that better methods of cultivation would lessen the need for slave labour.[34]

When Addington began his reply he was distinctly critical of Canning's motion and it looked as if his speech would spark off a debate in which Pitt would feel obliged to oppose the government. But half-way through his speech he suddenly veered right round and ended by promising all and more than he had been asked. Canning was obliged to take Pitt's advice and accept Addington's pledges. Once again the partisan fighter took over from the sober politician. 'The Dr bitched it (*comme l'on dit*),' he wrote to Mr Leigh, 'and promised me more than I wanted without a contest.' Mr Leigh, presumably, was better pleased to read Canning's calculation (made it is not clear on what basis) that if Addington kept his word, he (Canning) had saved about 750,000 lives.[35]

A more orthodox way of preparing the ground for Pitt's return to office was to organise demonstrations of parliamentary or, better still, popular support for him. Some time in April Sir Henry Mildmay, a country gentleman M.P., told Canning he thought it would be a proper sign of regard for Pitt to have a public dinner on his birthday, May 28 – after all, Fox's friends had one on his. Canning thought it a splendid idea but pointed out that it would have a better start if it did not appear to originate among Pitt's friends. So he asked someone he knew in the City to set the idea going and on April 22 was able to report to Leveson-Gower that it had taken so 'prodigiously' that it seemed to originate in 'the spontaneous attachment of the citizens'.[36] About a dozen of the most important men in the City agreed to act as stewards and everyone approached in the Commons was most enthusiastic. The only person carefully left in the dark was Pitt himself. Canning did not expect him to attend and was afraid that he might try to get the dinner called off. 'As for poor P.,' he wrote to Frere on April 26, 'he will be all astonishment at the fuss made about himself.' He had called in at South Hill a week earlier on his way to Bath and had told Canning that Addington was now immovable. Canning agreed that he (Pitt) had at last cut his own throat, but added that he still hoped there was enough left of him for his friends to make use of against the Doctor without his consent – 'and please God we will try.' Pitt, mystified, asked for this cryptic pronouncement to be elucidated, but Canning thought it best to leave him in a state of bewilderment.[37]

The dinner, when it was finally held in the Merchant Taylors' Hall, was a tremendous success. According to *The Times*, 975 persons were present; according to Canning, they were 'the flower of every rank and description of persons in London'. Addington was not among them. Hawkesbury was, but rather oddly retired to a private room for his dinner – thus demonstrating the awkwardness now felt by those who liked to consider themselves Pitt's friends but were members of Addington's ministry. The high spot of the dinner came when Mr Charles Dignum, a well-known tenor from Drury Lane, sang a song with words in fact written by Canning but allegedly by a certain Claude Sprott Esq.* The last verse went:

> And oh! if again the rude whirlwind should rise,
>   The dawnings of peace should fresh darkness deform,
> The regrets of the good and the fears of the wise
>   Shall turn to the Pilot that weathered the Storm.†

No one doubted whom the song was addressed to – indeed, Pitt was addressed by name in one verse – and after it had been repeated and the last verse called for yet again, Lord Spencer got up and proposed a toast to the 'Pilot that Weathered the Storm.' Canning was observed to applaud and encore the song with great vigour – only later discovering to his embarrassment that its real authorship was widely known. *The Times*, having announced that the song was attributed to Mr Canning's muse, added condescendingly that 'the poetry possesses great merit.' Some people, however, even among Pitt's supporters, found the proceedings, with all the toasting and the hammerings on the table and the rapping with hands, feet and knives, too much of a good thing. Lord Minto wrote rather sourly to his wife: 'This measure will be talked of for a few days and then forgot. It is, in fact, Canning's, and is in his style.'[38] Canning however was delighted with the enthusiasm shown for Pitt and he found Pitt himself surprisingly moved by what he had heard about the dinner. 'Whether it will rouse Pitt to stir for himself I do not know,' he wrote, 'but his friends have done *their* part.'[39]

Yet there was not really very much that Pitt's friends could do for him that summer. In the country as a whole, Addington was still popular and he had no reason to be displeased with the outcome of the general election. Moreover, Pitt was not at all well and in no state to bestir himself, however much he may have begun to feel dissatisfied with

---

* The name was dreamed up by Canning.
† In Canning's original copy the last two lines went:
>   'While we turn to thy hopeless retirement our eyes
>   We shall long for the Pilot that weathered the Storm.'

Addington's performance and his exasperatingly self-confident manner. Not for the first or last time, he felt unable to cope with his most enthusiastic friend, and just after the birthday dinner declined an offer from Canning to go and stay with him at Walmer. Canning was extremely indignant, decided that Pitt was chained to Addington for life and settled down sulkily at South Hill. He relieved his feelings by writing some pretty poor verse about the prime minister. More sensibly, he looked after Joan, who had recently again been very ill after nearly having another miscarriage, and entertained various visitors, some of whom were more congenial than others. George Ellis brought his new wife and in a letter to Frere written during their visit, Canning described himself watching 'poor Joan suffering under the duty of entertaining' the Ellises. 'Not but I am very glad,' he wrote, 'to see G.E. – and I do not mind *She* G.E. – but *Shes* in general do I think – and Joan is of all Shes the shyest!'[40]

Such diversions however could not satisfy Canning for long. His conviction that he was right to oppose Addington did not console him for the setback to his political career.* He was also very worried by the strain he knew he was putting on his relationship with Pitt. When he heard that Pitt was going to Bath for an extended stay in the early autumn, he could not bear the thought of not seeing him for many months and suggested a meeting in London. Pitt came to South Hill instead and invited Canning back to Walmer for three days of quiet private discussion. In the middle of September, Canning took his whole household to Walmer for a lengthy visit of more than five weeks. Pitt lent them a cottage in the grounds – 'just eleven persons in a house no bigger than a medicine chest.' They found Pitt very ill indeed – on one day his life was thought to be in danger – and for some weeks he was quite unfit to discuss politics. Pitt's convalescence brought out the best in Canning. He wrote rather touchingly to Frere from Walmer, describing how he had kept off all painful and perplexing topics and tried to make Pitt feel at his ease – 'as if I had no political notions to trouble him with.' He added that 'I have, or rather *We* have (for Joan is a great help to me in this, as in everything else, and loves poor P. and has always taken his part in the worst times) been in the way to pay him little attentions, which though nothing in themselves, he has appeared not to dislike at our hands.'[41]

* Castlereagh was made President of the Board of Control in July. Shortly before, Canning alleged in a letter to Frere that Castlereagh was intriguing for office. He added, balefully, that if he had any difficulties over the peace treaty 'he has overcome them manfully – *I* could not.' (Festing, pp. 82/3)

But as soon as Pitt was better, he and Canning once more began to mull over the political situation together. Pitt admitted that he had been mistaken about the extent of Bonaparte's ambitions and that Addington's inability to stand up to him firmly probably made a renewal of the war inevitable. He regretted that he could take no initiative himself, but conceded that if Addington voluntarily resigned he would feel released from all obligation to him.

This was enough for Canning. If Addington would not resign of his own accord – which seemed unlikely – then he must be pushed. So, without saying anything to Pitt, who by this time was taking the cure at Bath, Canning and a few of his closest friends (Granville Leveson-Gower, Morpeth and Sturges Bourne) decided that when Parliament met they would at once give notice that if the government was not strengthened within a fortnight they would move that an Address should be made to the King. Canning confided the plan to Malmesbury and between them they drafted a letter designed to prepare – and perhaps soften up – the prime minister. It was hoped to get plenty of imposing signatures, but unfortunately all that was forthcoming was plenty of non-committal sympathy. Canning, realising that it would not do to send the letter signed mainly by his own friends, decided to send it without any signatures at all. Malmesbury, who had gone down to Bath where he was trying to keep out of Pitt's way for fear he should inadvertently let the cat out of the bag, wrote to Canning that an unsigned letter might produce a greater effect 'by leaving Mr A's imagination to suppose the signatures were more numerous and more *tremendous* than those you are sure of.'

But in fact all was already lost. On November 17 Canning suddenly turned up at Malmesbury's house in Bath. Having discovered that the plot had been accidentally revealed to Pitt, he had travelled down through the night in order to put the best face he could on what he had been up to. He had already seen Pitt who, although as kind and tolerant as ever, had very firmly placed his veto on the plot. It was indeed a silly business.[42] The conspirators should have had the sense to stop as soon as it was clear that they were not going to get an overwhelmingly impressive collection of signatures for their letter. Canning, moreover, should have remembered that Pitt, who was very sensitive about the King's feelings, doubted whether it was right for Parliament to try to force him to change his ministers.

Canning and his friends were not the only people who were getting at Pitt to drop Addington, and when Bonaparte marched his troops into Switzerland in October 1802, Addington's ineffective remonstrances provided his domestic critics with a persuasive argument to try out on Pitt. Lord Grenville wrote indignantly on November 16 condemning the prime minister's 'ostentatious display of impotent resentment.' He felt that not to stand up to Bonaparte now would be virtually to admit his claim that Britain was not concerned with continental affairs and 'penned up as we should be in this fold, we could hope for no aid from others when it is our turn to be driven to the slaughter house.'[43] This gloomy forecast of things to come was reinforced by George Rose, who took full advantage of being also in Bath to descend on Pitt day after day to point out how foolish the ministers had been over Switzerland.

When Parliament met in the middle of November, Canning carried his pro-Pitt campaign on to the floor of the House of Commons. One of those who heard him speak on the first night of the debate on the Address thought he made incomparably the best speech of the night and that his defence of Pitt's ministry was 'one of the best things, either argumentatively as to matter, or critically as to manner and style' that he could ever remember.[44] Unfortunately Canning was provoked into intervening again on the following night and some people thought that on that occasion he was indiscreet. Pitt, who had to rely on the newspapers and the reports of well-meaning friends, was upset.* He told Malmesbury that their private friendship gave Canning no right to assert opinions in his, Pitt's, name. Canning wrote at length to both Pitt and Malmesbury denying that he had been guilty of any imprudence. He told Malmesbury that after Hawkesbury's speech on the second day he felt 'so warmly, from gathering indignation during the whole course of the debate, as well as from this particular outrage, that I congratulate myself now upon having put into what I said no *greater* degree of violence.'[45]

But however self-righteously he might defend himself, Canning could not bear to upset Pitt. In spite of the independence which his Irish borough was supposed to give him he was determined not to offend again. He wrote twice to Rose to find out what Pitt thought of the government's plans for strengthening the navy; and when he got back the unhelpful message that Pitt knew too little to form an opinion, he played safe and lamely approved the naval estimates. He too was feeling sore and huffily assured Rose that he was far from presuming to ask, or still less take for granted that he knew, Mr Pitt's opinions.[46] A few days later he wrote again lamenting 'the *fetters* in which *we* act from dread of misrepresentation to Mr P.'[47]

* It is not clear from the parliamentary report exactly how Canning offended.

But Canning could not hold himself back for long. In the debate on the army estimates on December 8, Sheridan made a brilliant and witty speech, supporting Addington and denying that Pitt was the only man who could save the country. It was too much for Canning, in spite of his unshaken personal regard for Sheridan. In a long and passionate reply he criticised in detail the government's conduct of foreign policy, justified his own political record and made an impassioned plea that the House should recognise and accept the greatness both of the country and of the man who ought to be at the helm. He took issue with those (like Wilberforce) who argued that we could safely shut ourselves up in our island. 'Let us consider the state of the world as it is, not as we fancy it ought to be. Let us not seek to hide from our own eyes . . . the real, imminent and awful danger which threatens us . . .' He also took issue with those who argued that the country could choose between greatness and happiness. 'The choice is not in our power. We have . . . no refuge in littleness. We must maintain ourselves what we are, or cease to have a political existence worth preserving.' If forced to give his opinion, he would say, in spite of his personal attachment to Pitt, that he did think the government ought to be in the fittest hands and he would not pretend not to know where 'that fitness most eminently resides.' He thought that members ought to speak out openly on this matter. 'Away with the cant of "measures, not men", the idle supposition that it is the harness and not the horses that draw the chariot along.' In times of danger and difficulty, said Canning, kingdoms rise and fall to the extent that they are upheld 'not by well-meant endeavours . . . but by commanding, over-awing talents.' He denied that Pitt had either prompted what he was saying, or was directing the government from behind the scenes, or was intriguing to get back into office. On the contrary, since his resignation Pitt had tried his hardest not to attract followers or support. But, added Canning triumphantly, 'retreat and withdraw as much as he will, he must not hope to efface the memory of his past services from the gratitude of his country; he cannot withdraw himself from the following of a nation; he must endure the attachment of a people whom he has saved.'[48]

Next day Canning wrote down as accurately as he could remember what he had said about Pitt and sent it off to Malmesbury in Bath with instructions to show it to Pitt. He told Malmesbury that Granville Leveson-Gower and Sturges Bourne 'who are discretion and prudence personified' had assured him that he had said nothing amiss and others had told him that he had only made a just and called-for defence of Pitt. A few days later, Pitt called on Malmesbury and asked him to let

Canning know that he was perfectly satisfied with his speech and had heard from others that it was very good.[49] For once, a letter from Bath must have given Canning undiluted pleasure and satisfaction.

But as the Christmas recess approached there was little else in the political scene to give Canning – or, indeed, anyone else – much satisfaction. No one had a good word to say for the new House of Commons. Canning described it as very 'flat', Tierney as 'more loose and unsettled, if possible, than the last', and Minto assured his wife that nothing could be 'more unhinged' than the political world. In the circumstances, however, it was hardly surprising if M.P.s, many of whom were newly elected, were thoroughly confused. The warlike Grenville and Windham, Pitt's former colleagues, sat on the same side of the House as the 'old' opposition led by Fox who believed in peace at almost any price. Canning sat with his small group of friends on the highest seats behind the Treasury bench, but made no secret of his burning desire to turn out those who were sitting on it, while from the opposition side, Fox and Sheridan, with varying degrees of openness, were sticking up for Addington, although Fox thought the present ministers '*dreadfully* foolish' and felt quite frightened at the thought of having anything to do with them.[50] And while all this was going on, it was gradually dawning on both Parliament and the general public that 'the right honourable gentleman now unfortunately absent' (in Bath) had withdrawn his active support from the government. Creevey, that most partisan of Whigs, saw that Fox was coming to be the government's main ally and that if he could not himself become prime minister, he might at least be able to prevent Addington from being turned out.

That was exactly what Canning was beginning to fear too. In his more distraught moments he went so far as to fear that if Pitt did not return to power, Fox would instead. That was in fact most unlikely, if only because of the King's strong dislike of him. Indeed, Fox's support for the government was a mixed blessing for Addington, because it was likely to turn the King against him, especially as he seemed to welcome the Whig leader's support. In the meantime, however, Addington was jogging along quite nicely. His budget had been well received. The Commons, in spite of their confusion, were still giving him their support, and Malmesbury reported from Bath that Pitt felt he had no justification for intervening. 'Sooner or later,' replied Canning, 'he *must* act or the country is gone.'[51]

CHAPTER VII

Manœuvrings at Westminster and Boulogne 1803-1806

It was more than fifteen months before Pitt brought himself to act. In the meantime he reduced his would-be supporters to a state of extreme exasperation by his – as it seemed to them – havering, hair-splitting indecisiveness. Grenville fulminated to Pitt about 'personal delicacies which a *very strict* conscience would perhaps not allow to influence even a vote upon a turnpike bill . . .';[1] while Canning, unable to cut the umbilical cord which tied him to Pitt and appalled at the thought of genuinely acting independently of him, oscillated wildly between unjustified optimism and equally unfounded despair.

Pitt was maddeningly indecisive. But the situation seemed more complex to him than to his friends, and he may well sometimes have felt (as he was said to have remarked) that nobody did his cause so much disservice as Lord Grenville in the House of Lords, except Mr Canning in the House of Commons.[2] He was clearly becoming more and more convinced of Addington's inadequacy and the two men's personal relations grew strained. But Pitt was inhibited from active opposition by his promise to Addington, by his fear of upsetting the King, and by his reluctance to do anything which might look like factious opposition to the government at a time of national crisis. Addington still commanded big majorities in the Commons and enjoyed the firm support of the King. And even if Parliament was becoming dubious about him, the opposition, although individually brilliant, was collectively neither strong nor united. To most M.P.s the only acceptable alternative to Addington was Pitt, and so long as he either stayed away altogether or refused to give any clear lead, Addington remained the best prime minister available.

So the New Year of 1803 found Canning and Grenville working hand-in-glove to prevail on Pitt to give a lead. Pitt was unwary enough to come up to London. By this time he had got over his irritation at Canning's parliamentary indiscretions and the two were back on their old intimate footing. Pitt was indignant about Addington's budget speech which he believed to be misleading and both Canning and Grenville tried hard to persuade him to commit himself to open opposition. But in the end Pitt went back to Walmer with nothing definite decided. He stayed there until nearly the end of March, contending with another attack of gout, seeing few people and saying little to those he saw. Canning felt cut off from him and consequently was extremely vexed. He bombarded him with immensely long letters (one was fifteen pages long) full of admonition and advice,* to which Pitt replied either not at all or briefly and dryly.

But at least Pitt's friends could console themselves with his refusal to be enticed back into a fresh understanding with Addington. The prime minister, evidently worried by Pitt's growing aloofness, had invited him down to his house in Richmond Park in January, but failed to make any definite bid for his support. Towards the end of March, Addington made fresh overtures, proposing that Pitt should be prime minister, but not that the government should be completely reconstructed. Pitt however insisted on a full-scale takeover. The King, annoyed that he had not been consulted about the negotiations beforehand, thought it was a foolish business from beginning to end. But Canning thought it had all turned out for the best; he was convinced that the next time Addington would have to make an unconditional surrender which would be much better than a 'little, beggarly, sneaking arrangement of conditions and compromises.'[3]

Probably the main reason why Addington wanted to bring Pitt into the government was his realisation that war could not be long postponed. Bonaparte's aspirations to turn the Mediterranean into a French lake by reconquering Egypt had become known; he was greatly enlarging the French navy; he had tried to browbeat Whitworth, the British ambassador, and demanded the instant evacuation of Malta. This last he had a right to do under the terms of the Treaty of Amiens. But Addington felt he could not surrender Malta until the limits of French ambitions were firmly fixed. Early in March, he called out the militia, asked Parliament to vote 10,000 additional men for the navy and sent Whitworth tough new instructions. Eventually, on May 18 he declared war. If there was surprise in France, there was little in England. Although the country's defences were sadly run down, few people (apart from the Foxites) disagreed with Addington's decision; but many doubted whether he was the right man to lead the country in time of war.

* Malmesbury, who tried to dissuade Canning from sending the letters, described one of them as 'too admonitory and too fault-finding for even Pitt's very good-humoured mind to bear.' (Malmesbury, *Diaries*, IV, p. 168, February 7, 1803)

The declaration of war brought Pitt back to the House of Commons for the first time since the previous summer. Many people hoped it would bring him back to Downing Street as well. Canning, optimistically assuming that Pitt would take over forthwith, forgot all the differences and difficulties of recent months and hurried round to see him in York Place. 'I confess,' he told Joan, 'the moment that we met (though I was naughty enough in my heart) I felt that there was nothing to do but to shake hands cordially.'[4] But he soon made the disappointing discovery that Pitt was caught in a state of perplexed paralysis between what he badly wanted and what he felt was expedient, honourable and patriotic for him to do to get it. Canning, himself something of an obsessional expert in the intricate analysis of his own and other people's political motives, for once saw the issue clearly and simply; and with uncharacteristic patience and forbearance, he tried to get Pitt to see that now, with war just declared and men's minds full of patriotic fervour, was the ideal moment to declare himself. But Pitt worried about provoking a political crisis before supplies had been voted for the war; he feared to turn the King against him or even send him mad; he was concerned lest a violent outbreak of party strife might make it impossible to form a really broadly-based government. Canning tried hard to set these fears and worries at rest, but without success; and in the end he concluded pityingly that 'poor P' had not 'nerves' either to act against the government himself or give his direct approval to any opposition.

But on May 23, when Parliament debated the breakdown of the negotiations with France, 'poor P' did not do so badly after all. Canning, carried away by the applause and enthusiasm, described the speech as magnificent – 'full of vigour and spirit. Stout for the war and for the country. For ministers not a word. Nothing against them directly. But the impression of even abstinence from praise is enough.'[5] Canning was not the only one to notice Pitt's significant silence about the government and to conclude that it implied disapproval. To him and his friends this seemed the moment for the vote of censure which they had been mulling over for some weeks, and they agreed that on June 3 Colonel Patten should introduce a motion censuring the government's conduct of relations with France. Pitt, however, said he could not vote for it. Canning gloomily reported to Joan that ' "poor Mr P" is become "naughty Mr P" again.' But he thought he could understand his motives – Pitt hoped that if he came to Addington's aid, the King would not feel that he was forcing himself back and would of his own accord invite him to take over. 'A refinement,' commented Canning, 'which like all other refinements in politics will probably end in disappointment.'[6]

Canning turned out to be quite right. Against his advice, Pitt attended the House on June 3, made a non-committal speech and proposed that the House should pass to the previous question. Canning got up, pointed out with some emotion that this was the first time he had felt compelled to differ from his right honourable friend and declared that as he thought the censure motion completely justified, he was bound to vote for it. The government too, for different reasons, did not want to shelve Patten's motion; it would look too much like an implied admission of guilt. So in the division on Pitt's proposal a massive but ill-assorted crowd – Addington's, Grenville's, Fox's and Canning's friends and supporters – streamed into the lobby and Pitt found himself left in a minority of 58, against 335.* Pitt and most of his friends then left the House and, in the second division on Patten's motion, Canning found himself in a still smaller minority – 36 against 275.

It looked like a famous victory for Addington. The King was delighted at the defeat of 'faction'[7] and Lord Minto thought that only a great disaster could now displace Addington.[8] The prime minister himself may have felt that it was a not inconsiderable disaster to have Pitt separate himself so unmistakably from the government. For Canning this at any rate was a cause for rejoicing. He hoped moreover that the smallness of the minority in the first division would give Pitt a salutary shock and make him see 'that to have a hearty following, he must take an intelligible line of conduct.'[9] Pitt was indeed shocked to discover how much his support in the Commons had shrunk,† and he confessed to Canning that he was now heartily sorry for his part in the Patten debate.

In the autumn of 1803 the Addington government faced its most severe test. Across the Channel the French were assembling an army and fleet of boats and it was confidently assumed that they meant to launch an invasion whenever the winds and tides allowed. The belief that only England now stood between Napoleon and his dreams of world

* Canning reported to Joan that as they went into the lobby, Castlereagh whispered unhappily to him: 'Little did I ever think to see P. in so small a minority, and myself one of the majority against him.'

† After the Patten debate Canning reckoned that, making allowances for some double votes, Pitt could count on about 80 supporters; this included both those who would not vote with him to save Addington and 'those whom he can persuade to do anything.'

domination created an extraordinary outburst of popular patriotic fervour. Throughout the country, from Cumberland to Kent, preparations to repel the invaders were busily afoot. Addington, too, made his preparations and remained calm and confident.* But there was a growing feeling that neither he nor his colleagues were equal to the emergency. Even Wilberforce, the most pacific and kind-hearted of men, who liked Addington personally, bewailed the government's lethargy in face of the threat of invasion.[10]

The government's handling of the Volunteers perhaps did more than anything else to damage it in popular estimation. Its appeal for more Volunteers met with an immediate and overwhelming response. But since it failed to provide either weapons to arm them with or instructors to train them, the flood of enthusiastic amateurs soon became more of a liability than an asset. The government's reaction was first to discourage further recruiting and then to stop it altogether in some counties. Both the would-be recruits and the local authorities reacted with perplexed indignation to the authorities' changing attitudes and contradictory instructions. Wordsworth, who had rushed to join the Grasmere Volunteers as soon as he got back from his wedding tour in Scotland, reported that although in his own parish almost all the men had turned out, in Keswick they were sadly remiss, having been 'thwarted by the orders and counter-orders of the Ministry and their servants'.[11]

Few doubted that if only Pitt would give a clear lead, Parliament and people would support him. But he still hesitated, arguing that although he should attack specific measures which he thought bad, he ought not to oppose the government systematically. Canning had no patience at all for what he called 'Pitt's new theory of opposition – the suggesting good measures to a foolish Ministry, and goading them to carry them into effect.' He hoped that, after the government's blunders, 'the good old way of turning them out and then bringing in your measures yourself, will probably now be thought (as I have always presumed to think it) rather better for the country.'[12]

At times that autumn Canning seriously contemplated throwing up his political career in disgust. And to add to his disillusionment, when the time came towards the end of November for the new parliamentary session to begin, Pitt seemed to think it more important to remain at Walmer to fight the invader who had still failed to put in an appearance, rather than take his place in the front of the parliamentary battle. On

* Plans were made for the King and Addington to go to Chelmsford if the French landed in Essex, and to Dartford if they landed in Kent; the Queen was to go to Worcester and the Privy Council remain in London.

November 15, he told Canning that he must stay on the coast until about the 10th or 12th of December by which time the weather would force the enemy to postpone his invasion plans.[13]* On receiving this letter, Canning blew off steam in a furiously indignant letter to Granville Leveson-Gower. With his characteristic disdain for all amateur soldiering, he railed at Pitt for 'this idle display of shabby patriotism, magnanimously preferring the duty of a drum-boy to that of a member of parliament.' More perceptively, he went on to say that it was nonsense for Pitt to pretend that he did not want Addington turned out. But, he added in a final indignant flight of fancy, if he let yet another opportunity slip, 'he may bid adieu to all hopes of success, and instead of turning out the Doctor in Parlt, be content for the rest of his life to turn out his own toes upon the Cinque port parade.'[14]

Canning confessed to Leveson-Gower that he was ashamed to feel such anger, and to Pitt himself he managed to write mildly enough. Perhaps it was Pitt's refusal to help him out of his political predicament that made him so incensed. He felt unable to follow his advice to abstain from 'harassing opposition,' but he felt equally unable to act independently unless he was first set at liberty to do so. And Pitt never gave him – so he claimed – 'a fair, unreserved, and *unmistakable* and *unwithdrawable* power and commission' to act as he pleased.[15] Even if he had been given it, he would probably have preferred to pretend he had not. He was bound to Pitt by emotional as well as political ties. 'I know,' he wrote to him on December 3, 'and have always known that I am – I would be – either yours or nothing.'[16] And in order to avoid any impossible choices, he stayed away from Parliament altogether until after the Christmas recess.

Early in January 1804 Lord Grenville made a last attempt to persuade Pitt to join forces with him in order to force Addington out. Pitt agreed with almost everything Grenville said, but would not do what he asked. It was not that he was reluctant to return to office. But he was genuinely afraid of making a weak government even weaker without managing to turn it out altogether. To the exasperated Grenville, however, Pitt's explanations were just so many 'middle lines, and

* Lord Hobart wrote to Wellesley (in India) on December 12 that according to reports from France the troops were not too keen on invading and 'it is said that at this season of the year they do not anticipate the probability of being drowned without sensations that are not quite comfortable.' (Wellesley Papers, I, pp. 169/o)

managements, and delicacies *ou l'on se perd*.'[17] So he decided to look elsewhere and sent his brother Thomas to sound out Fox.

At first Fox listened reluctantly. It was not that he, who had been the most dedicated champion of peace, had any objection in principle to co-operating with the most extreme advocates of war. The Whigs no longer opposed the war in principle, only the way it was conducted and Fox would have agreed with Windham, the most fervent warrior of all, who said he did not see why men who had disagreed once should have to go on disagreeing for ever. But regular opposition would be terribly inconvenient; he would have to stay in London and interrupt the writing of his history of James II's reign* – and most likely for no good reason, since Fox saw clearly that if Addington were overthrown, it would probably be Pitt, not himself, who would benefit. Still, the prospect of helping to ditch the Doctor – as the current fashionable phrase went – was very attractive; so was Grenville's determination that the next administration should be formed on the broadest possible basis. Fox therefore agreed to co-operate with Grenville in the strictly limited aim of turning out Addington without any precise commitment about what should happen next.

No one could have been a more delighted or approving observer of the growing Grenville-Fox entente than Canning. But in his view, of course, the arrangement was incomplete without Pitt, and he did not hesitate to tell him so, repeatedly and at length, in interviews, in letters and even in verse. A long, impassioned poem, appealing to Pitt to take office again, ended:

> Enough. In Truth's, in Friendship's sacred names,
> Accept the Verse which indignation frames;
> Accept, O Pitt! – But if the powerless strain
> With Truth's clear voice, and Friendship's, plead in vain,
> If still, to oppose less prompt than to endure,
> Thy sufferance sanctions ills thy act might cure;
> Then what remains – but this presumptuous pray'r
> That bounteous Heav'n – whose wonderworking care
> Hath bless'd for many an age, this favour'd shore –
> For our deliverance work one wonder more,
> With partial pow'r reversing Fate's decrees
> To keep an Empire safe, in hands like these?[18]

---

* On January 1, Fox wrote to a friend, 'Yesterday and not before died James, Duke of Monmouth etc. It will be well if the historian has not made as bungling a piece of work with him as the hangman.' (Loren Reid, *Charles James Fox* p. 398)

Pitt would not change his mind, but he wrote kindly and gracefully to thank Canning for the poem – 'I can hardly say whether I was most delighted with the poetry, or Lady Hester* with the politics.'¹⁹ He was aware of the strain he was putting on 'my eager and ardent young friends' (Canning and Granville Leveson-Gower). He knew that his refusal to grasp at office would keep them out of office too. For Canning had flatly assured him (and Grenville) that he would never join an administration from which Pitt was excluded or oppose one to which Pitt belonged. In the middle of February, Pitt told Malmesbury that Canning, finding he could not make him change his mind, 'half staggered by his friendship for him, and half disapproving all he did, knew no longer what to say, but had gone down to Mrs Canning, where he now was.'²⁰ It was a perceptive description of Canning's frame of mind.

Pitt may not always, as Fox complained, have known his own mind, but in the last resort he was guided, not by the advice of his friends, but by his own political judgment. And Parliament had not been long reassembled after the Christmas recess before it became clear that the Addington administration really was dying– not from any one crippling blow, but from general debility and lack of the will to live. The independent country gentlemen in the Commons were beginning to desert it; and Pitt learned that most of the members of the Cabinet only refrained from resigning out of loyalty to Addington. He began to criticise the details of the government's defence measures and on March 15 introduced what was clearly a hostile motion on the state of the navy. Supported by Pittites, Foxites and Grenvillites, the motion was lost by 130 votes to 201. Pitt was disappointed, but Canning was quite satisfied. He had expected no wonders and thought that 130 would form 'a sufficient nucleus round which detached stuff may gather,' especially if Pitt now abandoned his 'fine theories' for 'more mortal views'. Although Canning himself would have liked to get up and 'maul' Addington, he had refrained for fear he should be blamed for losing Pitt some votes.²¹ Pitt understood and praised his forbearance.

Towards the end of March, Pitt voted with the government on the final reading of the Volunteer Consolidation Bill. Such a doughty champion of the Volunteer system could hardly have done less. But it was the last support he gave to Addington. By this time too Fox's dislike of 'the Doctor and his crew' had overcome his reluctance to inconvenience himself. Canning, who had been seen walking arm-in-

* Lady Hester Stanhope, Pitt's niece, who was living with him at the time.

arm with Fox down Pall Mall, did all he could to promote co-operation between the two great rivals. And Fox, although still rather rude about Pitt ('a sad stick')[22] in his letters, was surprisingly considerate about his susceptibilities when discussing the tactics to be used against Addington. Altogether it was 'a very strange jumble of men and parties'.[23]

Presumably Canning knew that Pitt had made up his mind in principle to act but he still persevered in his self-appointed role as Pitt's goad. Although Joan, at South Hill, was waiting the imminent arrival of another baby,* he felt obliged to rush down to Walmer on April 11 because there were some points on which Pitt must urgently make up his mind. 'He seems,' reported Canning to Joan, 'in perfectly good heart indeed – but shudders a little at the brink, just as I suppose George does at the edge of the tub of cold water. He must *in.*'[24] With his mind thus turned to his family, Canning added distractedly, 'Pray, pray, pray little thing, do not come before Saturday.'

By April 16 Joan had produced a daughter, Harriet, and Canning, who could not keep away from London for long, was anxiously looking out for every post to tell him 'that she and little thing are doing well.'[25] On that same day Pitt came up from Walmer to oppose the third reading of the Irish Militia Bill. The government's majority sank to 21. It was not a fair test as many people had not yet returned from their Easter holiday, but Addington knew it was a portent and sent a message to Pitt asking his advice. Pitt curtly replied that he could only deal directly with the King's emissary. On April 23 Fox introduced what amounted to a censure motion. The government defeated it by only 52 votes. Two days later Pitt launched a strong attack on the whole of the government's defence policy, and what Canning scornfully called 'the majority for Mine Goose' sank to 37. On that occasion he abandoned his prudent efforts not to let his 'violence' spoil Pitt's cause and at 2 o'clock in the morning let off a short, sharp, impromptu broadside at Addington because of his comprehensive condemnation of Pitt's defence proposals. His speech, he told Joan, was 'of great effect (though I say it – but if I did not – who would say it for me to my own love, I wonder – and she to be down there in the country knowing nothing – for my *modesty*'s sake? – No no – not she).' Addington's fury at his speech, added Canning complacently, was 'inconceivable'.[26]

There were a few more days of doubt and contradictory reports until on April 30 Eldon, the Lord Chancellor, called on Pitt at the King's request, told him of Addington's resignation and asked him to

---

* A second son, William Pitt Canning, had been born in December, 1802.

submit a new administration. On the same day, Addington introduced the budget, but no one tried to discuss it and the House quietly adjourned. Next day Canning wrote to Joan: 'Yes, they are *out* sure enough. And this is all that I have to tell my own dear.'[27]

What Canning had to tell Joan over the next ten days was a sad anticlimax to all the hopes and effort that had gone before. Pitt's attempt to form the broadest possible administration foundered on the obstinate prejudices of the King and the equally obstinate sense of loyalty of Fox's friends and allies. Pitt himself had felt doubtful about the King's attitude all along, and some time before Addington resigned he had taken the precaution of sending Canning to warn Fox that although he wanted a strong and comprehensive government as much as anyone, he would not press it upon the King against his wishes. As Pitt had feared, the King was implacably opposed to Fox's inclusion in the Cabinet. Fox accepted the situation with good-humoured resignation and advised his friends to join the new government without him. But out of personal loyalty to him they would not. Grenville too decided that he was pledged to Fox and told Pitt that he could not join a government formed upon a 'principle of exclusion.' Pitt was pleased with Fox's realistic good sense and thoroughly displeased with the scruples of 'that proud man', his cousin Grenville.[28] These setbacks only stiffened his resolve. But as he had to make do with his own personal friends (in particular, Melville*) and members of the old ministry,† his Cabinet was both narrowly based and not especially distinguished either for talent or debating ability.

Canning was in despair at the 'shabby narrow Gvt' which Pitt was forming. He thought that Pitt ought to have tried much harder to overcome the King's opposition to Fox. (So did other people, both at the time and even more two years later when the King acquiesced at once in Fox's inclusion in Grenville's Ministry of all the Talents.) But there must also have been a strong element of personal disappointment in Canning's distracted indignation about the new government. If Pitt had been able to call on all the talents of the Foxites and Grenvillites, he would have been content to serve outside the Cabinet. But it was terribly galling to be supplanted by contemporaries like Hawkesbury

* Henry Dundas who had accepted a peerage from Addington in 1802.
† Pitt retained six members of Addington's Cabinet – Westmorland, Portland, Eldon, Castlereagh, Chatham and Hawkesbury (moved from the Foreign to the Home department).

and Castlereagh whose abilities he firmly believed to be inferior to his own but who enjoyed, as he did not, the advantages of inherited pull and influential connections. When he wrote to Joan about 'the poor Cabinet – stuffed – such people . . .' and assured her he would not now join it for any consideration, he was indulging himself with sour grapes.[29] But plenty of other people were equally disapproving, if not for quite such personal reasons, at the new arrangements. 'No class of people, I believe,' wrote the moderate Whig, J. W. Ward, 'is more dissatisfied than Mr P's real friends. They find it hard to leave him, and perhaps at the head of so singular a gang still harder to support him.'[30]

It is not clear why Canning was not included in the Cabinet. There is no reason to suppose that he had fallen out of favour because of the violence of his opposition to Addington. Pitt understood and appreciated his efforts to restrain himself. But those who knew him less well might have been surprised to learn that he had tried to curb himself at all. His skill in cutting criticism and mocking polemic had not helped his reputation either as a person or a politician and Pitt may have feared that his presence in the Cabinet would prove more of a liability than an asset.

However that may be, on May 12 Canning received a very kind, gentle and friendly letter from Pitt asking him to accept either the Secretaryship at War or the Treasurership of the Navy if he could do so without violence to his feelings. Pitt added that he did not want Canning to accept the offer simply on his account, but to have him in either post 'would contribute very greatly to my personal satisfaction in every view, and in none more than from the persuasion that your being there is the best thing for yourself.'[31] Fortunately Canning managed to realise this too. Next day he accepted the post of Treasurer of the Navy and immediately wrote to Joan to assure her that 'I am quite, quite persuaded that I have done well and wisely in accepting it.' But only a very bitterly disappointed man would have felt it necessary to explain and justify at such length to his wife (and himself) a decision which, as he admitted, had delighted all his friends; '. . . so far from a slight or degradation, the appointment will be considered by everybody as a complete triumph to me . . . I am quite thoroughly persuaded my own best love, that if I had held out in my refusal, and still more if I had held out on the ground of *Cabinet* – all the world would have cried out against me and that P. and I should have been separated for ever.'[32] And so on. What helped him most to swallow the bitter pill of being supplanted by men he found so uncongenial that he could hardly bear to sit on the Treasury bench with them was the argument that if he had stayed out he would have deserted Pitt just when Pitt needed him most.

The office of Treasurer of the Navy, which Canning said he found himself filling in spite of himself, was in fact considered a plum among the minor offices. It carried a salary of £4,000 and a house went with the job. Melville had held it from 1782 to 1801 (together with much more important Cabinet posts); he was succeeded by Dudley Ryder* and Canning's immediate predecessor was Addington's brother-in-law, Charles Bragge. Pitt thought it was in some respects a more desirable office than Secretary at War and equally fit to be held with a seat in the Cabinet.† The function of the office was to obtain from the Treasury the funds voted for the navy and distribute them to the various departments. Until 1785 the Treasurer held his balances on his private account, but since then all money voted for the navy had been paid into the Bank of England and credited to the Treasurer. He delegated most of his duties to the Paymaster of the Navy, but the fact that the post could contain traps for the careless or unwary Treasurer was dramatically demonstrated in the following year when Melville was impeached after Alexander Trotter, who had been Paymaster when he was Treasurer, had been accused of the misuse of naval funds. Canning, of course, was not to know about this when he took over and it is interesting and rather ironic to find him telling Joan that he was glad to have such an experienced man as Mr Trotter as his deputy. 'I find I should have been sadly at a loss without such a person to help me, and should have got perhaps into money scrapes from my own carelessness and the ignorance of a new man under me.'

There was more for the Treasurer to do than Canning had thought. 'I remember,' he told Joan, 'Ryder used to talk of having a great to do in his office, and I used to laugh, imagining it to be only his fidgety disposition – but he was right.' He also found that there seemed to be 'many things wrong to be set right.'[33] It is not clear whether he was referring to the financial arrangements of the office, or to the alarming shortage of ships and naval supplies caused by the misguided economies of the last government. Melville, whom Pitt had persuaded to become

* Succeeded his father as Baron Harrowby in 1803. Created first Earl of Harrowby in 1809.
† Pitt to Windham in April 1800. Secretary at War did not usually carry Cabinet rank, but it did when held by Windham from 1794 to 1801.

First Lord of the Admiralty,* described the state of the navy as 'deplorable' and abandoned his usual long summer holiday in Scotland in order to try to improve it. Canning, however, as Treasurer, can hardly have had much to do with that. His main job was still to support in the Commons Pitt's measures for waging the war more energetically and effectively.

While the long political crisis had dragged on throughout the spring and early summer, the war – even the threat of invasion – had receded to the back of men's minds. Lord Sheffield reported to a friend in the middle of May that while he was in London the enemy was never thought of and if he had come he would only be asked which way he meant to vote.[34] In fact, the immediate danger of invasion was less than it had been because Napoleon had come to realise that his navy must secure at any rate temporary control of the Channel while the invasion flotilla was crossing. But he was still building up and training his 'Army of England' at Boulogne, and Pitt's first priority was to make sure that it got a warm reception if and when it landed on the English coast. On June 5 he introduced an Additional Forces Bill with the aim of strengthening the regular army and preventing the best men from being drained away into the reserve forces or the militia. The general aim was sensible and widely approved – in spite of Sheridan's lamentations about the danger of a standing army. But the details were open to criticism and the Foxites and Grenvillites, apparently forgetting that only the King's prejudice and their own choice had prevented Pitt from bringing them into his government, turned round and joined forces with the ousted Addingtonians in violently attacking his measures. The majority for the second reading was only 40. A week later, in a snap division in a thin House, Pitt was actually in a minority. In a further division that same night, his majority sank to 28. The opposition thought they might defeat the bill, and so did Pitt. The decisive debate came on June 18, on the second reading of the amendments, in a House more crowded than anyone could ever remember. When the Commons finally divided past four o'clock the following morning, Pitt found himself with a majority of 42. In such a full House, and after so much effort, it was not a very creditable or inspiring result for the government. But it was enough. The opposition did not try to mount any further major challenge before the summer recess. Pitt had a breather in which to try to consolidate his position.

---

* In September, Thomas Grenville maliciously described Melville as 'learning the conduct of the navy by studying the manœuvres of the bathing machines at Worthing.' (Dropmore, VII, p. 230)

Canning, characteristically, made the best of Pitt's small majority. Before he went to bed after the debate he sent Joan a scrap of a letter to tell her that 'our division is *quite decisive* . . . to the infinite disappointment of the Opposition.' He added, with his usual lack of false modesty, 'I spoke exactly as I intended – only *better*.'[35] Lord Minto thought that Canning made a clever speech, but was 'indiscreet as he generally is'.[36] Minto's criticism was not unjustified. Instead of sticking to the matter in hand, Canning had launched into an attack on the previous government and criticised some of its members. As a result the speakers who followed him, particularly Sheridan, Fox and Pitt, were to some extent deflected from the country's defences to general political polemic. Moreover personal attacks on members tended to be frowned upon in the Commons and often proved counter-productive; on that night at least one member is known to have actually switched his vote because of Canning's attack on Addington. Once again his partisan style of debating had harmed him.

It very nearly damaged Pitt's Cabinet as well. Hawkesbury's record as Foreign Secretary (which indeed had not been very distinguished) had been one of the subjects of Canning's disparaging comments, and after the debate Addington optimistically predicted that he did not think Hawkesbury and Canning could remain in office together – 'at least they could not were I the wearer of H's beard.'[37] Hawkesbury seemed to be of the same opinion. When Canning called on him next morning because of a paragraph in *The Times* suggesting that one or other would have to resign, he found him in a state of extreme agitation. Canning, who had been accustomed to 'quiz' Hawkesbury ever since they had been up at Oxford together, was genuinely surprised to find him so upset. 'I cannot tell you,' he wrote to Joan, 'how sorry I am for this.'[38] When Hawkesbury hinted at resignation, Canning tried to dissuade him and declared that if anyone resigned it must be he. But Hawkesbury had in fact already resigned, and it needed all Pitt's tact and patience (helped by a contrite Canning) to get him to change his mind.

Unfortunately that was not the end of the affair. The following winter rumours began to circulate to the effect that Canning had humbly apologised to Hawkesbury for his speech of June 18. When the rumours reached Canning, he was furious, complained to Pitt and insisted, through the mediation of Lord Morpeth, on a written denial of the rumour from Hawkesbury. It was also put about that Pitt had offered to dismiss Canning and that Hawkesbury had magnanimously declined the offer. This rumour continued to circulate in London drawing-rooms for months and Canning could get little satisfaction from Pitt's prevaricating attitude about it. He did not press the point because, unlike the matter of the alleged apology, it was not a 'point of honour'. But although others thought he had come well out of the affair,* the feeling that Pitt had treated him badly continued to rankle and made him all the more sensitive about his comparatively lowly position in the government.

Towards the end of November, he thought he saw an opportunity of moving up, at any rate temporarily. Lord Harrowby, the Foreign Secretary, was known to be in poor health and it was believed that he would have to resign. The names of possible successors were being canvassed and among them was Canning's. He must have had a shrewd idea of what was being said, and when he discovered from Hammond that Pitt had settled nothing except that the new appointment should be on a temporary basis, he soon persuaded himself that he ought to try to advance his own cause. On November 21, he told Joan that as Pitt might think he would not like to be offered the post on a temporary basis, it was 'a duty to let him know that I would, but I shall not press the point as one that I am anxious about or making it a request at all.' [39] While Canning was still making up his mind to put this transparent proposition to Pitt, Harrowby fell from top to bottom of a flight of stairs and concussed himself so badly that it was clear he would not be fit for work for several months, if ever again. One morning a week later Canning screwed himself up to make his suggestion to Pitt. He could hardly have put it more modestly, for he was willing to take on the duties of Foreign Secretary on a temporary basis without either the title or the salary and without insisting on a seat in the Cabinet. Although Pitt said there were great difficulties, he received the suggestion very well and Lady Hester Stanhope reported that she had never seen him look so happy as after Canning's visit. But time passed and nothing more was said. Finally, at the end of December, Canning, to his bitter disappointment, learnt that Lord Mulgrave had been appointed in place of Harrowby who had insisted on resigning for good.† Canning thought this might be the reason why he had been passed over, but he never had any explanation from Pitt.

With his usual hopefulness that what he wanted was in fact going to

---

* One tribute came from Thomas Grenville, a reasonably objective observer, who when discussing the Hawkesbury affair praised Canning 'extremely' to Lady Bessborough and told her 'he thought highly of him both as to talents and high honour and integrity.' (Leveson-Gower, II, p. 4)

† Harrowby remained in the Cabinet as minister without portfolio.

happen, he may have imagined that the thing was more 'on' than it really was. There was in fact a perfectly good reason why Mulgrave should have been preferred to him. But unfortunately it was a reason that was bound to make his disappointment infinitely harder to bear. Pitt, alarmed by his parliamentary weakness and egged on by the King, had for most of December been negotiating, through Hawkesbury, with Addington who had a large and loyal following in the Commons.* An agreement was not easy to arrange because Addington insisted that six of his friends and relations should be found places too, including a seat in the Cabinet for Lord Hobart (who had just become Earl of Buckinghamshire). Pitt did not think Hobart was much use, but was prepared to give him a suitable seat in the Cabinet as part of the price for Addington's support. Harrowby's insistence on resigning allowed him to move Mulgrave to the Foreign Office, thus leaving vacant for Hobart the sinecure seat of Chancellor of the Duchy of Lancaster. Addington himself was to replace the Duke of Portland as Lord President of the Council. Canning knew nothing of these negotiations, only that it was intended to offer Addington a peerage† and a pension which he thought was reasonable. It was not until the bargain between Pitt and Addington was finally signed and sealed that he learnt about it.

His immediate reaction was to offer Pitt his resignation. It was quite a proper reaction, even from an extremely angry and bitter man. His disapproval of Addington as a minister was so strong and so well known that no one would have been surprised if he preferred not to serve in the same government with him. On New Year's Day 1805, he unburdened himself in a long letter to Lady Hester and begged her to persuade Pitt that it would be 'personally discreditable' to him to remain in the government. He felt humiliated by the fact that Addington was a minister 'and I am – nothing. I cannot help it,' he went on, 'I cannot face the House of Commons or walk the streets in this state of things, as I am.' He was deeply distressed by Pitt's failure to tell him what was going on. Only too well aware, however, of what his critics said about him, Canning begged Lady Hester to note the moderation of his letter. 'If I am not mistaken, there is not one expression of anger, resentment, irritation, or extravagance, nor, I am sure, a witty one (which is the next crime in degree) throughout the whole.'[40]

* According to George Rose, who was something of an expert on the voting habits of M.P.s, Addington had about 68 followers in the Commons in 1804. (Rose, II, p. 219)
† Addington received the title of Viscount Sidmouth.

After reading this outburst Pitt told Canning that he had been meaning to write to him for the past ten days and now he hardly knew how to write at all. He urged him to come and see him instead.[41] Canning had had a bad fall from his horse the previous October and had told Lady Hester a week earlier that he was in no state to come up to London because of his 'everlasting leg.' But he answered Pitt's summons, in spite of his leg. It was not a happy meeting. Pitt told him plainly that his resignation would mean a permanent breach between them because it would seem to cast a slur on his own conduct. He offered to send Canning to Dublin as Secretary for Ireland, but Canning felt this would now look too much as if he were being got out of the way.[42]* Eventually he agreed to remain. When it came to the pinch, however angry he was with Pitt, nothing could be worse than to be parted from him. 'I am resolved,' he wrote to Mr Leigh, 'to "sink or swim" with Pitt, though he has tied himself to such sinking company. God forgive him.'[43]

Canning had to put up with the government's new recruits, but his open disapproval cast a shadow on his relations with Pitt. Instead of being completely in his confidence, he felt that he was usually the last to hear of any event. He felt uncomfortable and unhappy, but he did not turn sulky and refuse to pull his weight in the Commons. In fact he would have spoken more often if he had got the chance, hoping no doubt in this way to demonstrate his worth to Pitt. His opportunity came early in April. Just as Pitt seemed to be beginning to re-establish his old mastery over the Commons, a blow fell which deeply divided his government and supporters, nearly forced him out of office and caused him acute personal distress.

In February the commission set up during Addington's ministry to inquire into abuses in the Navy Board published its tenth report. It dealt with the office of Treasurer of the Navy and revealed that while Melville had been Treasurer, his Paymaster, Mr Trotter, had transferred naval funds to his private account at Coutts's bank and speculated with them. Melville admitted before the commission that he had agreed to these transfers, although apparently unaware of their extent. His excuse was that he thought the arrangement would facilitate the more efficient payment of small sums. What was not clear from the com-

---

* On January 7, Thomas Grenville wrote: 'Some people fancy Canning is to go to Ireland to soften to him the asperity of these domestic arrangements.' (Dropmore, VII, p. 249)

mission's report was whether Melville himself had personally profited from Trotter's speculations. But he had certainly been guilty of gross carelessness and negligence. Pitt clearly could not hush the matter up, especially as he had been prime minister at the time. In any case the opposition would not let him. To them, this was a heaven-sent opportunity to get at Pitt through one of his oldest and closest colleagues.

On April 8 Whitbread introduced in the Commons a series of resolutions one of which, without actually charging Melville with personal corruption, accused him of 'a gross violation of the law and a high breach of duty.' Pitt agreed that the matter was grave, but argued that the report should be referred to a select committee of the House for further investigation before the Commons attempted to pass judgment. He was warmly supported by Canning who, as the present Treasurer, had an official interest in the affair in addition to his political and personal loyalties.* But even Pitt, whose personal incorruptibility was unquestioned, could not sway the House that night. A number of his friends went away because they would not vote against him and could not bring themselves to vote for him. The worst blow was delivered by Wilberforce who had prayed for divine guidance before the debate. His quiet but downright condemnation of Melville was believed to have swayed as many as 40 votes.[44]

When the House divided at 4 o'clock in the morning, the votes were found to be equal – 216-216. The Speaker, upon whom fell the invidious duty of giving the casting vote, turned white as a sheet and sat in silence for some minutes before voting in favour of the motion. The opposition let out a great cry of triumph. Pitt for once lost his proud impassivity. He put on his hat and jammed it over his face to hide the tears of distress and mortification trickling down his cheeks, while his friends gathered closely round him with linked arms to shield him from the stares and jeers of his enemies.[45]

Melville resigned at once. But the opposition was not satisfied. Two days later Whitbread moved an Address to the King for the removal of Melville from all his offices and from the royal councils for ever. As soon as Whitbread sat down, Canning started up and bitterly attacked the opposition for wanting to heap this fresh humiliation on a man whose political career was already in ruins. He was tremendously – and genuinely – angry. Next day he wrote to Mr Leigh: 'The trampling on the fallen I could not bear and the House was fair enough to side with

* Canning dismissed Trotter immediately after the debate, but refused to dismiss Mr Wilson who sometimes deputised for Trotter, on the grounds of insufficient evidence. He was severely attacked later in the Commons for sticking by Wilson.

me.'[46] Whitbread was indeed forced to withdraw his motion at the end of a long debate. But the House's mood may have been influenced less by Canning's indignant outburst than by the pledge wrung out of Pitt that Melville would not be allowed to return to power.

Pitt could not and would not desert Melville but he was on weak ground. Sidmouth was doubtful, some of his followers even more so, and Wilberforce's troublesome conscience would help to thin the government's ranks. To make matters worse, just as Parliament reassembled after the Easter recess, Sidmouth resigned in a huff because Pitt would not appoint any of his candidates to Melville's vacant seat in the Cabinet. Pitt talked Sidmouth round, but only at the cost of letting him feel that he and his friends could do virtually what they pleased. Canning's indignation at Sidmouth's behaviour was boundless although he could not help rejoicing at the opportunities ahead of showing Pitt how his real friends behaved in a time of crisis. 'Here we are,' he wrote to Mr Leigh, *'in* the struggle, and the first thing to think of is not how we came there – but how we are to get through it.'[47]

At first the outlook seemed not too bad and by June 11, when Whitbread moved the impeachment of Melville, Pitt was optimistically expecting the motion to be easily thrown out. So it was, but an amendment moved by an Addingtonian, Nathaniel Bond, to substitute for impeachment a criminal prosecution, was then carried by nine votes.* Pitt, who looked miserably ill and tired, surprised his friends by not speaking. But Canning observed him gnawing his lips with rage at the vituperative attacks of the Addingtonians on Melville. According to one observer, Canning went out of his way to widen the breach that was rapidly opening up between them and Pitt.[48] Feeling as he did, he could hardly have been expected to do otherwise. 'Scoundrels!' he wrote afterwards. 'It *was* a comfort to tell them what I thought of them; and it *was* a pleasure to see that the House in general felt with me.'[49] But most of his speech was a stout and sober defence of Melville's personal honesty. Lady Bessborough wrote afterwards that only Canning had done well in the debate. 'He in true, manly honesty and courage stood forth alone, in defiance of public opinion, in defence of the friend he thought wronged.'[50] Although Lady Bessborough had a very soft spot for Canning, her tribute was not altogether unfounded.

One important consequence of the debate of June 11 was the resignation of Sidmouth on July 5. After listening to the unnecessarily bitter attacks of Bond and Hiley Addington on Melville, Pitt could not bring himself to grant the political promotion which Sidmouth

---

* On June 25 the Commons agreed to an impeachment after all.

demanded for them. Even the King could not bring about a reconciliation. Pitt realised that he ought to use the opportunity provided
by Sidmouth's departure to bring some vigorous new blood into his
second-rate ministry. His plan was to fill the vacancies left by the
Addingtonians at once on a temporary basis and prepare to offer Fox
and Grenville six places in the Cabinet later. Canning, delighted with
the way things seemed to be going, stayed on in London to encourage
and advise Pitt. On July 17 he reported to Joan that he had had dinner
with him and 'a great deal of very good, useful, comfortable talk. I
urged, and he promised, expedition in making overtures.'[51] Two days
later he wrote to say he had been to Putney again, had had two hours
of good talk and thought he saw a way through some of the difficulties
of making an overture to Fox. Towards the end of the month, he tore
himself away to join Joan and the children in a cottage by the sea in
Hampshire, all the more ready to enjoy his family and the delights of
sea-bathing* because light seemed to be breaking at last over the
political scene, and above all because, as he had reported to Joan,
'nothing ever was more cordial and comfortable than P.' And after all,
he had added, with a condescension that was both ridiculous and
endearing, 'when I cease to be angry, I find that I have a kindness for
him greater than I had suspected.'[52]

In the few months that remained before Pitt finally succumbed to
over-work and ill-health nothing again came to cloud his friendship
and affection for Canning. But their plans for a government of national
unity to meet the threat of Napoleon's apparently insatiable ambition
were soon disappointed. In the middle of September Pitt went to
Weymouth, where the royal family were spending their summer holiday,
and after pointing out his own poor state of health pressed on the King
the urgent necessity of strengthening the government. But he met with
an uncompromising refusal. The King would apparently have preferred to risk civil war rather than have anything to do with the
opposition. Pitt might have brought him round by threatening to
resign; but to force the King in this way was against his ideas of
constitutional propriety. In any case there would have been no point
because there seems to have been no real chance of agreement between
Pitt and the opposition. Although Fox had hinted in the Commons

* On August 2 Canning wrote to Mrs Leigh from Christchurch in Hampshire to
say he had no news but 'how very well we all are, and how our bathing becomes us
(there are no awnings) . . .' (Harewood Mss. 15)

that he himself was prepared to stand down, he was determined, if he were approached, to insist on a completely new government without Pitt at its head. But Pitt, stymied by the King's veto, never did approach him. Instead he began to consider ways of strengthening his Cabinet from among his own supporters.

At the end of October he invited Canning to dine with him *à deux*. It was a particularly welcome invitation because Canning, bitterly disappointed by the King's intransigence, was going through one of his periodic bouts of disillusionment with politics. The night before, he told Joan (who was at South Hill) he had come home from a large dinner party feeling 'very cross, and thought of getting out of politics altogether, and living, nice, with dear and little things, and coming to town no more.' So when he found himself alone with Pitt for the evening he seized the chance of getting everything off his chest. Out it all poured, the accumulated frustrations and grievances of the past eighteen months, even the still-rankling 'mortification' of the Hawkesbury affair. He told Pitt that he was content with his present post so long as there was a possibility of some of the opposition being brought into the Cabinet. But now that this could no longer be hoped for, he could not bear to go on as a junior member of an administration in which men he knew to be much less able than himself held responsible Cabinet posts. He would prefer to retire from politics altogether.

When Pitt could get a word in edgeways – for Canning, once started, had allowed no interruption to his tale of woe – he quietly said he had never had any doubt but that Canning must be in the Cabinet before Parliament met in the New Year, and suggested that he should join it while retaining his present post as Treasurer of the Navy. If Canning insisted on being given the Board of Control,* Pitt said he would not deny him. But if he would be satisfied with his present office, Pitt would like to offer the India Board to Charles Yorke† whom he was also anxious to have in the Cabinet.[53]

It was a tempting offer. But Canning had decided that it would only be worth while to stay in politics if he could have an 'efficient' post – that is, one with departmental responsibilities – and that was still virtually denied him. On the other hand, to be in Pitt's Cabinet at all would be a great step forward. Pitt told him – perhaps stretching a

---

* Castlereagh had been promoted to be Secretary of State for War after Sidmouth's resignation in July, but had not yet been replaced in his old post of President of the Board of Control.

† Charles Yorke (1764–1834) had been first Secretary at War and then Home Secretary in Addington's ministry.

point in order to win him over – that what mattered was membership of the Cabinet, not what particular office a man held in it. He would at least have access to all the information at the Cabinet's disposal and be able to take his full share in shaping and deciding government policies. This was a particularly important point for Canning. His forceful personality, close relationship with Pitt and aggressive debating style had made him more of a target for the opposition's hostility than his political weight as a junior minister really warranted. And it was typical of his restless impatience at being confined to the outer corridors of power that he was continually irked by having to defend measures which he had had no part in formulating.

In the end, although no definite decision was taken, Canning did have the grace to admit to Joan that he no longer had any right to grumble and be glum. Before the week was out, however, he was full of doubts as to whether, for Pitt's sake, he ought to accept his offer, in case it caused adverse comment about Pitt's favouritism. He told Pitt that he could not take advantage of his kindness and fairness 'at the hazard of your ease and advantage.'[54] But Pitt was reassuring and by November 21 Canning was able to tell Joan that before Parliament reassembled on January 7 he would be a member of the Cabinet. '*I am to be*,' he wrote to her. 'Nothing could be more considerate, open and good-natured.'[55] In the event it was to be another eighteen months before he sat at the Cabinet table and by then Pitt was no longer there to preside over it.

Pitt's last months were absorbed by the tragic drama of the third coalition which throughout the summer he had spent so much of his slender reserves of energy on trying to create. It had been a thankless and uphill task because although the great continental powers – Russia, Austria and Prussia – were insatiable in their demands for British gold, there was no real unity of purpose or aim between them and Britain. It was Napoleon's seizure of an Italian crown and annexation of the Genoese Republic that finally shocked the Russians and Austrians into taking the field against him. Before the end of August the French army, which had been waiting all the year at Boulogne for a chance to invade England, was wheeled round and marched across Europe to attack the Austrian and Russian armies. On October 20, the day before the Battle of Trafalgar, Napoleon inflicted a heavy defeat on the Austrian army at Ulm on the Danube. In England the news of Napoleon's victory was outshone by the glory and the tragedy of Trafalgar. Canning, in his capacity of Treasurer of the Navy, had gone down to Portsmouth to bid goodbye to Nelson a few hours before he sailed on what was to be his last voyage. When the news of Trafalgar reached England, he remembered with pride how Nelson had shaken his hand on board the *Victory* and explained all his plans to him.[56] Pitt, deeply distressed though he was by Nelson's death, felt a surge of his old optimism. He was convinced, he told Canning on November 7, that Europe would be saved before the end of the year.[57]

But although Nelson's great victory had finally confined Napoleon's ambitions to the Continent, it could have little direct effect on France's military dominance of Europe. Pitt understood the vital importance of achieving a military success on the Continent as soon as possible. But he under-estimated the danger of launching an operation while an essential ingredient of success was still missing. His plan was that Prussia should be persuaded to join the third coalition, that British forces should open a second front in northern Europe and that the allied forces should then drive the French out of northern Europe, including Hanover and perhaps even Holland. By the end of October the first British troops were on their way to the Elbe, and by the end of the year the British expeditionary force was 60,000 strong. Many, especially among the opposition, heard of the transports' departure with incredulity and dismay. Buckingham exclaimed to his brother, Grenville: 'What madness is this if the Ministers are not sure of Prussian co-operation.'[58] Unfortunately the ministers were not at all sure. The Prussian government, wooed by both sides, was torn between the competing attractions of generous British subsidies, the Prussian king's friendship for Tsar Alexander and the temptation to do a deal with Napoleon. What the Prussians wanted above all was Hanover, the English king's patrimony, which no British government could dream of bartering away. On the other hand, Hanover had been invaded by Napoleon's troops and was his to offer.

Canning was among those who were extremely dubious of the wisdom of the north German expedition. He also feared that the failure of an attempt to liberate Hanover really might lead to the government's overthrow. At the end of November, he wrote a long letter to Pitt arguing that if Prussia were to be offered Hanover by France, she would take it, and any British troops in Hanover would either have to withdraw or maintain themselves by force. He urged that it would be much more sensible to send an expeditionary force to Walcheren, since all the enemy forces were for the moment withdrawn from the coasts of Belgium and Holland.[59] It was typical of Canning's independence and confidence in his own judgment that he should have so freely criticised the plans of a Cabinet which he very much hoped would invite him to join it within a matter of weeks.*

In any case, although neither Pitt nor Canning could know this, the issue was by then almost decided. Before the Prussians had finally made up their minds, Napoleon's sword made it up for them. On December 2 he inflicted a crushing defeat on the Russian and Austrian armies at Austerlitz. Pitt's last attempt to curb France's military power through a continental coalition was wrecked beyond repair. Alexander was forced to agree to withdraw the remains of his armies behind his own frontiers, while on Boxing Day the Austrians had to sign humiliating peace terms at Pressburg. By the end of the year, Frederick William of Prussia had decided to accept Napoleon's offer to cede him Hanover. A few days before Pitt's death on January 23, 1806, his colleagues ordered the withdrawal of all the British troops in northern Germany.

But before the rumours of these disasters began to percolate through to England, Pitt's health broke down once again. For the last time he went down to Bath to see what the waters could do for him, and there in the middle of December Canning joined him. He found Pitt, in the grip of a bad attack of gout, anxiously awaiting some definite news from the Continent, and he hit on a way of distracting him by getting him to criticise some verses he had written on Ulm and Trafalgar. It seems to have been a happy thought. On December 16 Canning reported to Joan that they had been reading his verses over and over and Pitt was extremely delighted with them. 'I really think,' he added, 'they seem to have been quite a comfort to him in his gout. *Serious business* is not very good for him but criticism is a harmless recreation.' Next day they went over the poem again to Pitt's 'increased delight.' Canning confided to Joan that it really was 'a great comfort to have happened to contribute so much to his amusement.' He added that Pitt's criticism had improved the poem a great deal. 'It is now very good I hope.' A few days later he reported that Pitt's gout was getting better. 'But, I think,' he added, 'he is weak beyond what he ought to be and business quite overpowers him. I am glad to stay with him this one day more.'[60] All his life he must have been glad he had spent that week in Bath. After Pitt's death he told Granville Leveson-Gower that it had been passed 'in habits of confidence and free discussion more like the old times at Holwood than any that have been passed since.'[61]

* Holland Rose (*Pitt and the Great War*, p. 547) suggests that Pitt may have feared the effect of Canning's 'sharp though friendly' criticism of the Hanover expedition inside the Cabinet and this led him to put off bringing him in.

Canning was back at South Hill in time to spend Christmas with his family. He had left Pitt slowly recovering and still completely unaware of the magnitude of the disaster that had struck the allied cause a few weeks earlier. On December 29 the first definite reports reached London of an armistice between Napoleon and Austria. Two days later Canning wrote from London to tell Pitt, who was still at Bath, that he had not been able to collect anything to disprove the armistice reports. He went on to argue with desperate hopefulness that even now the game might not be entirely up, that Russia might not withdraw and that Prussia might yet rally round. But he did not really believe it. He told Pitt he must go back to South Hill next day. 'I hate to walk the streets in such ill news.'[62]

As the New Year came in and the ill news was confirmed, a feeling of gloom and despondency settled on the country. Lord Auckland, who was staying at Blenheim, wrote to Lord Grenville about the momentous and menacing events which seemed to involve 'not only the well-being but the very existence of the British Empire.' As he looked at the pictures and tapestries around him, he could not help wishing for a new John, Duke of Marlborough.[63] But all too many of Auckland's fellow politicians were yearning not for a new military genius, but for a chance to destroy the statesman whom they were only too delighted to blame for the country's plight. But that chance was denied them. Canning was only one among many who believed that the news of Austerlitz, when translated from a rumour into an incontrovertible fact, was the final blow that killed Pitt.

Early in January, still stricken by gout, Pitt decided to make his way back to his home in Putney. Canning suggested that it would be better if he came to South Hill, which was not so close to the bustle and business of London, and Pitt seems to have been pleased with the idea. On January 9, Canning wrote again to Pitt pressing him to come and telling him that he was writing to his doctor, Sir Walter Farquhar, 'to enter into a solemn engagement with him not to talk with you or (so far as I can help it) allow you to talk upon interesting subjects, till you are fitter for it than you represent yourself to be. You shall have south rooms entirely to yourself and see as much or as little of us as you please.' And in an anxious effusion of hospitality, he assured Pitt that there would be room for Lady Hester and Sir Walter – or Sturges or Castlereagh or Huskisson or anyone else he might like to see if he was fit enough. He added in a postscript, 'I need not tell you how anxiously Mrs C joins in my request.'[64]

But in the end Pitt went straight to Putney. On January 13 a messenger from Lady Hester arrived at South Hill to ask Canning to come at once because Pitt was very ill. Canning got to Putney that same evening and saw Pitt for about ten minutes the next morning. It was their last meeting and Canning scribbled in his diary afterwards: 'The change since Bath dreadful! and his appearance such as I shall never forget. He was very very kind, and seemed to have something on his mind that he wished to say to me but could not.'[65] Pitt spoke a little of his own condition and showed more optimism than Canning suspected he really felt. He asked Canning to stay in the house and said he would send for him again in the evening so that they could have a little more talk. But he never did send for him and Canning wondered afterwards whether Pitt, suspecting that it was their last meeting, had deliberately tried to spare him the pain of leavetaking.

During the last week of his life, Pitt saw no one except his doctors, his immediate family and his old friend, the Bishop of Lincoln. Canning waited about miserably in London, making the most of every scrap of encouraging news from Putney. At last, in the evening of January 22, he received a despairing note from Lady Hester. He set off at once for Putney and on the way met Castlereagh, who told him that Pitt was already dead. When Canning got to Putney he found that Castlereagh had been misinformed: Pitt was still just alive but was not expected to last more than a few hours. Canning went back to London about 10 o'clock, convinced at last that Pitt was dying. Next morning, a few hours after Pitt had died but before the news had actually reached him, Canning sat down to tell Joan what had happened. 'God bless my own best love, and dearest little dears,' he ended. 'This is the saddest letter I ever had to write to her. Poor dear Pitt – how all his good now lives in his heart, and all his bad (and how little he had of that! never surely man so little) fades away! God bless him. He is a loss not to be repaired.'[66]

Charles Ellis was reported to have described Canning's state, immediately after Pitt's death, as 'dreadful; he could not cry or speak; he had been sanguine enough to hope to the very last, and the blow came unbroke upon him.'[67] It was the first time he had lost someone so close to him and, like many others in a similar position, he had not really believed that such a thing could happen to him. He was not, however, so overcome that he could not think of those who had even more cause than he had to mourn Pitt; he took Lady Hester and her youngest brother, James Stanhope, away to South Hill, there to be cared for and comforted by Joan and himself.

Pitt was buried in Westminster Abbey on February 22. During the funeral service Canning managed at first to maintain his composure, but when they were standing round the actual burial place, he could hardly control himself. Afterwards he wrote to Joan: 'It is all over, dearest love, I have seen poor Pitt laid in his grave, and I feel somehow, a feeling of loneliness and dismay which I have never felt half so strongly before. I wish I had been able to get into my chaise and go down to shelter myself with my own dear love at South Hill. But that may not be. How dreary, nevertheless, all society and all politics appear at this moment.'[68] He knew that the world of politics would go on and because it was inextricably part of his nature, he would go on playing his part in it. But it was never again to be quite the same.

CHAPTER VIII

Politics without Pitt
1806-1807

After Pitt's death Canning never acknowledged any other political
master; he was no longer bound to anyone by any overwhelming sense
of obligation and personal devotion; he was free to make his own way
by whatever means seemed to him both appropriate and honourable.
He may have dimly realised that if Pitt had lived, sooner or later, he
would have had to emerge from his shadow or risk becoming politically
stunted. With Pitt gone, he knew that it was essential for him to build
up a solid reputation of his own. 'I must not,' he told Joan, 'be again
the child of favour, either in truth or in the opinion of the world, or
with any show of plausibility represented so by enemies.' He realised
that he himself was not yet ready for leadership and his immediate aim
was to make himself as considerable as he could in the House of
Commons.[1] He already had the nucleus of a small political following.
At the time of Addington's fall in April, 1804, he could count on a
fairly firm group of his own of about a dozen. Whether, nearly two
years later, the number was smaller or larger is not clear. In any case,
what really mattered then, and for more than three and a half years to
come, was the struggle for the leadership of the whole group of
politicians known as 'Mr Pitt's friends'.

Common devotion to a dead leader, however sincere, is not likely to
prove a cohesive force for long, especially when the leader leaves
behind him no obvious successor. There were in fact too many possible
heirs – Castlereagh, Hawkesbury, Spencer Perceval* and Canning to
name the most obvious – all roughly the same age and with about the
same qualifications and none of them aware of any good reason why
he should defer to any of the others. They wanted, in principle, to try
to stick together, partly because of a shared feeling that they ought to
try to carry on where Pitt had left off, partly because there was no
important political or personal reason for their separation and partly
because of their mutual indignation at being excluded from Lord
Grenville's new ministry. The new administration, although mislead-

* Spencer Perceval (1762–1812) had been Attorney-General first under Addington
and then in Pitt's second ministry.

ingly known as the Ministry of all the Talents, was in fact predominantly Whig. With surprisingly little trouble, Grenville had persuaded the King to accept Fox as Foreign Secretary; he had brought in Sidmouth, partly as a sop to the King and partly because he could provide useful support in the Commons; but he had left the Pittites out in the cold.* They regarded their total exclusion as a deliberate slight on Pitt's memory and Canning had nothing bad enough to say about a ministry that included none of Pitt's friends and so many of his enemies. According to Lady Bessborough, however, Fox had felt that 'it would be coarseness bordering on brutality' to invite any of Pitt's friends to join his most inveterate opponent before their dead leader was even laid in his grave. He felt this particularly with regard to Canning, but hoped in due course to win over him and other Pittites.[2]

If Fox really said this, his delicacy was wasted on those it was meant to propitiate, and like most companions in misfortune, they simply drew closer together. When Castlereagh and Perceval called on Canning on February 8, they agreed without difficulty that they should all co-operate to defend the memory and measures of Mr Pitt. More surprisingly, Canning's visitors also agreed with him that Grenville – in spite of their disapproval of his recent effort at Cabinet-making – was the only fit man to lead the government if he could be weaned away from Fox and Sidmouth. Understandably, the question of who should lead the party (if such it can be called) in the Commons was not discussed. Later Canning told George Rose that he would not accept the leadership of either Castlereagh or Hawkesbury (especially not of the latter) but was less hostile to Perceval or Charles Yorke – perhaps because he did not regard them as serious rivals. He suggested that a peer should be asked to put himself at the head of a combination of Pitt's friends in order to give it weight and substance. He thought of several possibilities and actually wrote to Viscount Lowther, asking him to undertake this thankless duty. Lowther, however, was non-committal; he preferred hunting to speaking in the House of Lords.

If no suitable peer could be found, Canning thought the next best thing would be to carry on 'a vigorous opposition, looking to Ld Grenville *at the same time* as the person really at the head of the party.'[3] 'Vigorous' opposition sounded more respectable than 'factious' or 'systematic' opposition, but the distinction was not easy to grasp. To go hammer and tongs for the government of the man whom you really regarded as your leader seemed to add a note of inconsistency to the

* He did invite Lord Bathurst, who had been Master of the Mint outside the Cabinet, to stay on, but Bathurst flatly refused.

prevailing confusion of thought on the proper aims and function of the opposition. During Pitt's long ascendancy, the Whig opposition had been limited to a rather ineffective watchdog role. In the fluid political situation after his death, the opposition could play a more positive part. But few of Pitt's friends grasped this as quickly as Canning did. They wanted the Talents to be turned out. But like most contemporary politicians, they still felt an instinctive reluctance to oppose the King's government, especially when it was new to office. The result was that they found it almost as difficult to agree on tactics as on a leader.

On the other hand, the Talents themselves were hardly a happy crew. Both Grenville and Fox wished they could dispense with Sidmouth and his importunate friends. But not many people thought they could make their own alliance stick, and while the Pittites were trying to detach Grenville, the Foxites were busily seeking recruits from among Pitt's friends. Everybody praised the virtues of moderation but few managed to practise it; and those who loftily proclaimed their intention of not getting mixed up in all the political caballing could not refrain from adding to the general uncertainty by assiduously passing on every scrap of political gossip that came their way.

Canning, who had no pretensions to detachment and only the flimsiest to moderation, made very little effort to disguise his hostility to the government. He was no longer inhibited (as during Addington's ministry) by fear of Pitt's disapproval; nor apparently was he troubled for long by doubts about the propriety of regularly opposing the King's ministers, especially when the country was at war. Like some of the other Pittites, he began to hold political dinners as a means of recruiting support in the Commons. On March 10 he held one at White's 'as a trial of what could be done in that way towards getting people together – and it answered pretty well.' There were about a dozen guests, mostly Canning's personal following. A fortnight later, he collected a rather larger gathering, 'but the dinner was so bad and the wines so execrable, that it is as much as one's health is worth to dine there again.' Another disadvantage of White's was that only members of the club could attend the dinners. Canning decided to move elsewhere after the Easter holiday, and by the beginning of June he was able to report to Joan that a dinner at the Thatched House had gone off 'prodigiously well'. There had been nearly a hundred people present, most of them 'names that will tell,' and the Duke of Cumberland had dropped in during the evening. According to Canning, there had been 'nothing factious, but everything so provokingly and pointedly loyal as to amount precisely to the same thing.'⁴ Appearances still had to be kept up, but as one onlooker observed, the 'cloven hoof' of systematic opposition was visible all the same.⁵

In Parliament, the government itself soon provided a tempting target. Sidmouth wanted to have one of his own particular friends to keep him company in the Cabinet and in order to accommodate him Grenville decided to make Ellenborough, the Lord Chief Justice, a member of the Cabinet. If not exactly unconstitutional (as the opposition tried to argue) this was certainly improper and inexpedient and on March 3 an opposition motion on the subject gave rise to a lively debate. Although the motion was overwhelmingly defeated, Canning professed himself 'quite, quite satisfied' with the debate. Perhaps he might have felt less satisfied if he himself had not made a particularly good speech. Some people, he told Joan, were saying it was his best, 'but that I do not think – for there was very little variety and no ornament in it; and no declaration and no personal politics in it; and without some or all of these ingredients a speech cannot be one's very best. It was all hard, dry, plain, straightforward argument and so temperate and quiet, it would have done you good to hear it.'⁶ Stimulated perhaps by Joan's criticism, he was trying hard to correct the faults in his debating style, in particular his tendency to become too heated and melodramatic. After another debate that session he told Joan that his speech had been praised and had been 'without any of my usual faults, for I hardly ever went out of a conversation tone, and pace, and instead of falling hard upon Fox (as he complains I did last week) I was all mildness, to Grey all kindness too which was exceedingly pretty.'⁷ He was learning that a quieter style of speaking could be just as effective and was less likely to antagonise his listeners.

Although Canning told Rose at the end of the session that he had done very little to canvass the support of individual members, he certainly did his best to keep up the morale of the Pittites. 'I should have been glad to escape speaking,' he wrote to Joan after one of the stormy debates on the government's many recruiting measures* early in May, 'but it was impossible to do so without letting Fox close the debate saucily, and so I spoke. Nothing,' he added, 'would put our friends so much out of heart, as having reason to suppose that Fox might at any time put his paw upon the debate and extinguish us.'⁸ Other leading Pittites also attacked the government energetically. Both

* The government's new recruiting plans were controversial, even among its supporters. To the Pittites they were damned because they did away with Pitt's system of recruitment.

Perceval and Castlereagh in fact rose to their feet a good deal more often than Canning did. Sheridan was reduced to suggesting that ministers should share the burden of listening to the opposition's interminable speeches by attending the House in relays.[9]

The session dragged on until towards the end of July, although by then only the most dedicated had resisted the temptation to escape from the heat and discomfort of a London summer.* When Parliament at last rose, many of the Pittites were feeling in a rather defeatist frame of mind. They had, it is true, managed at least to shelve their leadership problem by persuading the Duke of Portland to become their titular head. The duke, a sick, modest and well-meaning man, said he thought the effort would kill him, but 'he did not know how a man could wear out the fag end of his life better than in performing so high a duty.'[10] But his self-sacrifice did not help to resolve the power struggle among the Pittites in the Commons; and their activities still suffered from poor co-ordination and lack of organisation. All the same, they had often had the best of the government in debate, although they had not yet solved the problem of getting their debating strength properly reflected in their voting strength.

Canning did not share the pessimism of some of his colleagues, and he was certainly right to suspect that Grenville did not feel at all secure. The unexpected acquittal of Lord Melville, whose impeachment had been grinding on for several months, did nothing to bolster either the government's self-confidence or its prestige, especially as five Cabinet ministers had voted against acquittal. Moreover Fox's efforts to make peace with Napoleon had petered out; the war, which the politicians sometimes seemed to overlook in their preoccupation with their own discords, was clearly not going to go away. Finally, Fox's health looked like breaking down completely. Before the end of the session, Grenville had decided that he would not, if he could help it, face a further bout of parliamentary warfare without some additional strength.

But before Grenville had actually put out any feelers to the Pittites, they had themselves embarked on what can only be described as an intrigue with the King. It was enveloped in the deepest secrecy and its

* On July 14 Canning, replying to a letter from Mrs Leigh in which she had described the warm saltwater baths at Yarmouth, wrote: 'I can tell you that the sweat and vapour bath of the House of Commons is full as moist, tho' not quite so cleansing, in this weather.' (Harewood, 21)

details still remain obscure. But it seems that on June 10, after a long discussion, Canning, Castlereagh, Hawkesbury, Eldon and Pitt's elder brother, the Earl of Chatham, decided that they were prepared to take over the government if called upon, but that it would be more respectful to the King to leave him to choose the right moment. They could defend such a highly dubious and irregular step by arguing that the King did not like his present ministers (which was largely true) and they merely wanted to let him know that they were willing to rescue him from them. The problem was to establish any kind of secret contact since the King was rarely alone and was surrounded by spies and busybodies. Eventually an emissary (possibly Hawkesbury*) was sent to Windsor to try to obtain a secret interview. A few days later he brought word from the King that he would like to receive a written communication. A letter was duly despatched to Windsor and by July 5 the King had sent back a message expressing great satisfaction at its contents: he added that although a private interview was impossible at present, he would try to contrive one as soon as possible.[11] As far as is known, the meeting never was contrived.

Grenville's first tentative approach to Canning was made through Lord Wellesley (Arthur Wellesley's eldest brother) on July 1. Canning at once consulted Perceval, Castlereagh and Hawkesbury. They decided to play their hand with a self-confidence that Canning at any rate genuinely felt. They were willing to serve under Grenville but would only consider an offer made to them as a group and with the King's sanction and authority. In other words, Grenville must go to the King and ask permission to form a completely new government. Wellesley told Grenville that he was inclined to think that Canning spoke 'with sincerity and fairness, and with an extensive knowledge of the House of Commons and of parties generally.'[12] Grenville's difficulty was that if he were to meet the Pittites' claims fully he would have to drop a considerable part of his present team, and little as he liked the Addingtonians, he felt himself bound in honour to stick by them. The person he really wanted was Canning himself, partly because of his ability (especially his debating talent) and partly because he had known and liked him personally for many years. Early in August he got in touch with him again and made what Canning described as 'a more direct and pressing personal offer, and such a one as, if personal objects alone were in question, must have come up to any the most exaggerated wishes and pretensions of *mine*; coupled with an intimation of a readi-

* On June 20 Canning told Joan he had been busy settling the details of 'H's instructions for his mission with him and C.' (Harewood Mss. 21)

ness to consider the fair wishes and pretensions of *others* . . .'[13] Bu
Grenville made it clear that he was not prepared to treat with the
Pittites as a body.

Canning found Grenville's attitude both unintelligible and un
reasonable. How could the prime minister expect to take in some new
recruits if he was not prepared to dismiss anyone? How could he expec
the Pittites to 'give up the principle upon which we have hitherto
professed to stand, that of a union among all, of whatever description
who love and revere Mr Pitt's memory, to take our seats humbly and
contentedly between Addington who betrayed, and Windham who
reviled, him; – and this, because forsooth, Lord G's connections . . . are
to be considered incapable of dissolution?'[14] How could he himsel
possibly have the face to tell his friends that they must abandon thei
claims just because he had been offered a seat in the Cabinet and one
or two other offices for his friends? It would be the most discreditable
situation 'into which any man was ever misguided enough to pu
himself by an inconsiderate precipitancy of ambition.'[15]

Canning's attitude was personally honourable and politically sensible
But to the Whigs it was as unintelligible as theirs was to him – especially
when they remembered how poorly he used to think of Hawkesbury
Grey expressed his amazement to Lady Bessborough that Canning
should sacrifice himself and the country for the sake of Hawkesbury
and Castlereagh. He assured her that he would much rather have had
the Pittites – at least some of them – than the Addingtonians, but now
the Pittites 'all cling together, bad and good, and for the sake of one or
two worth having we must take all their riff-raff, and by it offend more
people than we gain . . .'[16]

Grenville would not have the 'riff-raff' but he went on repeatedly
trying to get Canning. By early September he had enlarged his definite
offer of a Cabinet seat for him to include a law office for Perceval and a
minor office for whoever Canning cared to name. But Canning still felt
that these terms amounted to taking office at the expense of character
and holding it without power. He gave his final refusal to Wellesley on
September 11. Next morning Wellesley came back and asked him to
draw up a list of his minimum demands. Canning replied that the
Pittites must have five seats in the Cabinet, and he drew up a list of all
those who ought to be asked to agree to their own exclusion from
office. As might have been expected, Wellesley came back next day with
a polite refusal.[17]

On the same day Fox died, thus depriving the Talents of their most brilliant, commanding and able personality. His death* made it all the more necessary for Grenville to strengthen his government, but without making the task any easier. As soon as Sidmouth realised that Fox was really dying, he buttonholed Grenville and made it clear that if Canning were brought into the ministry, he and his friends would go out. And even those of the Talents who had no personal objection to Canning or the other Pittites were determined that any redistribution of offices should be confined to their own friends and relations. So Grey (now Viscount Howick) became the new Foreign Secretary and leader of the Commons, while Grenville's brother, Thomas Grenville, and Fox's nephew, Lord Holland, were brought into the Cabinet.

These appointments can hardly have surprised the Pittites. What did surprise and shock them – especially those who had been secretly in touch with the King – was the announcement in the middle of October that Grenville had been granted a dissolution, although the existing Parliament still had three years to run.* The Talents had failed in their bid to make peace with Napoleon, they were worried by their unpopularity and they felt the need of an unequivocal sign of royal favour. Moreover, they had apparently begun to suspect that something was going on between the King and the opposition. They demanded the dissolution as a matter of urgency and the King reluctantly decided that it was his duty to agree. But he showed his disapproval by refusing to make his customary contribution of £12,000 from the Privy Purse for his government's election fund. Eldon's summing up of the matter was probably fair and certainly compassionate. 'His [the King's] language led one to hope better things; and, in charity, I would suppose from it that his heart does not go with his act. But his years, his want of sight, the domestic falsehood and treachery which surround him, and some feeling . . . of resentment at our having deserted him on Mr Pitt's death . . . have conspired to make him do an act unjust to himself.'[18]

The unexpected dissolution caught a good many members of the opposition on the hop, without having had a chance to make their usual preparations for securing a seat in the new Parliament. Canning was one of these; he found that his Irish borough would not again be available. After several unsuccessful attempts to secure a seat elsewhere,

* Although Canning had conceived an unfortunate animosity for Fox after Pitt's death, when Fox himself died he wrote a warm and generous tribute to him in a letter to Lady Bessborough. She thought it would have delighted Fox – but then, she added, if Fox were alive Canning 'would not have spoken of him so; and there is the misery.' (Leveson-Gower, II, p. 214)

* A government could usually strengthen its parliamentary position through a general election.

he eventually got himself returned for his old seat of Newtown in the Isle of Wight. But whereas in 1793 the seat had been given him as a favour to Pitt, in 1806 he had to pay heavily for it. One consolation, however, was that the government, having apparently made rather a mess of its own electioneering arrangements, did not benefit as much as it had hoped to do.

While Canning was still trying to adjust his political behaviour to the changes produced by Pitt's death, he and Joan were obliged to undertake a major change in their domestic arrangements. It was caused by their growing anxiety over the health of their eldest son, George. 'Little gee' was a fine, healthy baby but by the time he was four the Cannings were beginning to be worried by a lameness in one of his legs. They took him to several of the leading surgeons who each produced a different diagnosis. One said it was a strain, another a weakness, a third, who was the most famous surgeon in London, diagnosed a 'gathering' (which in Canning's opinion it certainly was not) and a fourth frankly confessed that he could not tell but felt sure the boy would grow out of it. But he did not, in spite of a course of treatment which was as painful for the patient to undergo as it was distressing for the parents to watch.[19]

Early in 1806 the Cannings decided to sell South Hill and in April moved into a house in Berkeley Square. The reason for this decision is not clear, but it may have been partly or largely because they wanted to be near the best doctors for George's sake. South Hill proved unexpectedly difficult to sell and that summer was still being used as a country home by the Cannings. Sometime during the late summer, when the children were at South Hill without either of their parents (a very rare occurrence) George had a fall which damaged his lame leg so badly that he was unable to walk at all.

It was this disaster, which none of the doctors or surgeons they knew seemed to have any idea how to cope with, that made the Cannings decide to move their base from London to Hinckley, a small country town in Leicestershire, nearly a hundred miles from London. Hinckley was the home of a Mr Chesher whose fame as a healer of lameness in children had spread as far as London. The eldest son of Lord and Lady Holland, born in 1802, who had a diseased hip, was taken as a small boy to consult Mr Chesher whom his mother described as 'a famous mechanician for instruments; he measured the limb and gave us hopes that he could contrive an instrument to assist his walking.'[20] But the

Cannings evidently felt that it was necessary to put their son under the close and constant care of Mr Chesher. And since there was no question of Joan being parted from any of her children, she, William and Harriet (commonly known as Toddles) all went into exile with little George.

Canning took his family up to Hinckley towards the middle of January 1807. His first impressions of Mr Chesher were extremely good, but of Hinckley itself they could hardly have been worse. On January 13 he reported to Mr Leigh from the Bull's Head that they were in 'the vilest inn, in the nastiest town, in the dirtiest country, that imagination can conceive.'

Two weeks later, just before he himself went back to London, he wrote more cheerfully. They had found somewhere to live and 'we are got quite reconciled to our miserable two-roomed house, and white-washed walls and a thousand other inconveniences.' It was a far cry from the spaciousness of South Hill or the elegant dinner parties in Berkeley Square,* but the Cannings were buoyed up by the hope that something was at last being done for George. 'But now we complain not at all,' he wrote, 'and if poor little Gee does but get well we shall not grudge the time we spend here – though it must be very, very long I am afraid.' By the middle of February they had found a 'fine hand-some' house, with a garden, right in the middle of Hinckley within easy reach of Mr Chesher. They took it for six months and later, when George was rather better, moved to a house in the country a few miles outside the town.[21] As far as comfort and convenience were concerned, the exile gradually became more tolerable, at any rate for Joan. But nothing could be done about the long months of separation, especially after Canning became Foreign Secretary. And even Mr Chesher could not really do very much for George.

When the new Parliament met in the middle of December, the Pittites had done little to solve their problems of tactics, co-ordination or leadership. Many backbench opponents of the Talents stayed away, hoping that the government would fall, but too timid themselves to help give it a push. They should realise, complained Spencer Perceval, that unless they helped to overthrow the government, it would not get overthrown.[22] Canning was equally convinced that the opposition

* On October 1, 1806, the painter, Farington, noted in his diary that Lord Thomond, with whom he was staying, had 'passed a pleasant day at Mr. Canning's – carp, turtle etc., hock, claret, madeira. The turtle was dressed *too high* and His Lordship suffered inconvenience from it.' (Diary, IV, p. 21)

ought to go in for 'vigorous' opposition, and both he and Perceval stoutly put their precepts into practice on the floor of the House of Commons. But the debating vigour of the opposition leaders did not make up either for the timidity or the lax attendance of their rank and file.

The government, on the other hand, scored a striking psychological success by at last securing the passage of a bill for the abolition of the slave trade. Grenville did what Pitt had never felt able to do – he made abolition a government measure. He began with what had hitherto been the insurmountable hurdle and successfully pushed the bill through the Lords. Then about 4 o'clock in the morning of February 24, 1807, the bill triumphantly received its second reading in the Commons by the overwhelming majority of 283 to 16. Wilberforce, who was as surprised as anyone at the size of the majority, attributed it to the direct intervention of Providence. Canning, who had tried unsuccessfully to get Pitt to make abolition a government measure, commented ruefully that the vote showed 'what a Government *can* do if it pleases.'[23]

The slave trade was of course a special case, which had always cut across normal party lines. Its abolition did not change the basic political realities. Canning was very much torn between his loyalty to his fellow Pittites and his strong desire for office and early in January he seemed to succumb to the second. He told Perceval he felt that the opposition had been dissolved by the dissolution of Parliament and that each of its members was now free to follow his own line.[24] His subsequent conduct suggests that he did not believe wholeheartedly in this theory himself. In any case it was not as unprincipled as some of his contemporaries thought. He now genuinely believed that the King was not really interested in changing his administration and that even if he was, the Pittites were not strong enough to form a new one. So he did not agree with people like Castlereagh, Perceval, Hawkesbury and Eldon, who by now wanted to try to overthrow Grenville completely. Nor was he by any means the only Pittite to favour a compromise with Grenville and to feel that once they had established a foothold in the ministry, they could gradually enlarge it and bring in more of their friends.

In addition to these arguments there was also for Canning himself the flattering and tempting knowledge that Grenville would still like to have him. Early in February, the Bishop of Lincoln, Pitt's old friend and tutor, called on him to tell him so. The bishop also said that he knew the Whigs were worried about the probability that Howick would soon be translated to the Lords by the death of his father, Earl Grey; and that they had their eye on Canning as a possible successor to Howick as leader of the Commons.[25] Such an offer would have been almost irresistibly tempting, but when Canning and Grenville met early in March at Mrs Crewe's villa in Hampstead nothing was said about the leadership of the Commons. Grenville merely offered Canning the Chancellorship of the Exchequer, to which he replied that he would prefer the Admiralty or one of the Secretaryships of State. Canning also insisted that any arrangement reached must look like a junction between the government and Pitt's friends and must have the approval of Lord Lowther and the Duke of Richmond who between them would probably be able to win over the rest of the Pittites. Privately, he told Joan afterwards that he definitely did not think that the Admiralty, plus some appointments and a few minor offices, was good enough.[26] In any case, for obvious reasons, Canning did not wish to join the Cabinet until the business of the Princess of Wales was settled.*

Before the negotiations had gone any further, Grenville suddenly had more pressing things to think about. The day before his meeting with Canning, a bill to allow all Roman Catholic subjects to hold commissions in the army was given its first reading in the Commons. Hopefully designed to stave off a crisis in Ireland, where the Catholics had been giving alarming signs of discontent, it precipitated a major crisis in London between the King and his ministers. The drafting of the offending bill was clumsy and the scope of its concessions to the Catholics obscure, even at first to the ministers themselves. Mismanagement was piled on misunderstanding. Grenville and Howick were less than frank with the King, who in his turn, either by accident or design, left them very much in the dark about his own reactions. At some point, however, he realised that the bill presented to Parliament contained wider concessions than those he thought he had reluctantly given his consent to a few weeks earlier. Once again he felt, as he had done six years before with Pitt, that Grenville was asking him to break his coronation oath; once again he refused to give way.

On March 11 Sidmouth tried to resign. He was an inflexible anti-

---

* The 'Delicate Investigation' held the previous summer had acquitted the Princess of the charge of having had an illegitimate child but had censured her for frivolous conduct. The King had gone back on an intimation that he was ready to receive her at Court and Caroline had retaliated by threatening to appeal to public opinion by publishing the full details of the Delicate Investigation. By early March Perceval had the documents printed and ready to be published if the Princess's demands were rejected. But the fall of the Talents brought her friends to power and they managed with some difficulty to persuade the King to receive her again.

Catholic and he had already enraged his Whig colleagues by making it his business to impress on the King the full scope of the Catholic Bill. But he had a second reason for resigning. He would not sit in the Cabinet with Canning, and by this time Grenville had told him that Canning must be brought in as soon as possible so that he could take over from Howick when old Lord Grey died. Grenville persuaded Sidmouth to refrain from rocking the boat openly, at any rate for the time being. But the boat was sinking anyway. On March 15 the Cabinet decided to give up the bill. It was not a unanimous decision and the government would almost certainly have fallen apart anyway. But the ministers' refusal to meet the King's demand that they would not raise the matter again gave him an excuse to dismiss them himself.

Most people, whatever their party, felt that the Talents had only themselves to blame for their downfall. Canning commented that it was 'just like one of poor Ld G's *pigheadedness* to create the obstacle which is to stand in his own way.'[27] Certainly no prime minister ever had less reason to blame his political opponents for his fall. Perceval and Canning in particular tried hard to promote a settlement. Perceval eloquently urged Sidmouth* to act as intermediary between the King and the rest of the Cabinet, while Canning tried his powers of persuasion on Grenville. 'Never,' he wrote to Joan, 'I will venture to say, were ministers treated so fairly by their (presumptive) successors, and I am glad to hear that they so feel it, and that with respect to *me*, at least, they express it loudly.'[28] His motives were not quite as high-minded as they seemed, because he believed that his own political advancement lay through an alliance with Grenville. On the other hand, in spite of his waverings, he did not want to leave the other leading Pittites in the lurch. He had tried hard to persuade Grenville that if he would give way over the Catholic Bill and replace Sidmouth and his followers by Pittites, a stronger and more homogeneous ministry could be formed.[29]† But Grenville had preferred to contrive his own downfall in his own way.

On March 19, the King summoned Eldon and Hawkesbury to Windsor and on their advice asked the Duke of Portland to form a new govern-

* Sidmouth, having unsuccessfully tried to resign, tried, with equal lack of success, to establish contact with the opposition through Perceval. (Gray, *Spencer Perceval*, pp. 73/4)

† Canning argued that since his and Grenville's parties were really one and the same, the government would be formed of only two parties, their own and the Whigs, and theirs would be the strongest.

ment. The King himself would have liked to have had Pitt's elder brother, but Chatham felt (quite rightly) that he was not up to it. Nor, for different reasons, was Portland, who only accepted out of a sense of duty and loyalty to the King. As leader of the group of Whigs who went over to Pitt in 1794, he had never particularly impressed his followers, and by this time he was very much an invalid, dependent on regular doses of laudanum to keep going at all. He had a nervous horror of opening his mouth in public and while premier never once spoke in the Lords.* He rarely attended at the Treasury either.

So Portland's Cabinet, unlike Pitt's, was very much a ministry of departments with no active co-ordinating head. But eight of the eleven members had served in Pitt's last Cabinet.† One of the newcomers was Lord Bathurst, who took the posts of President of the Board of Trade and Master of the Mint. The other two were Perceval and Canning. There was no argument over their promotion, but some doubts over which office each should hold. In the case of Perceval, who had twelve children and no private means, the trouble was financial. Portland wanted him to be Chancellor of the Exchequer and leader of the Commons. This meant sacrificing a steady and lucrative income from the Bar (in 1804 it had amounted to nearly £10,000) for an office worth less than £3,700. The difficulty was eventually overcome by giving Perceval a sinecure – the Chancellorship of the Duchy of Lancaster – for life. Canning had rather supposed that either he or Castlereagh would have the lead in the Commons; but Perceval, unpretentious and likeable, was an acceptable compromise. Moreover Perceval's colleagues were relieved that someone was willing to take on the unpopular and still rather ill-defined and non-prestigious post of Chancellor of the Exchequer.

At first Canning had had his eye on the War Office for himself, but on second thoughts rather favoured the Admiralty, which was 'snug to

---

* In December 1792, Portland agreed with his followers to get up in the Lords and declare their opposition to Fox's line. But he sat through the debate 'as fixed as the lady in Comus, enchanted . . . like her without uttering a syllable . . . He was kept down by mere nerves and the horror of public speaking, and he was as unhappy and miserable afterwards as we are angry.' (Minto, II, p. 95)

† Six returned to the offices they had held at Pitt's death: Earl of Westmorland (Lord Privy Seal); Lord Eldon (Lord Chancellor); Lord Hawkesbury (Home Secretary); Lord Castlereagh (Secretary for War and Colonies); Earl of Chatham (Master General of the Ordnance); Earl Camden (Lord President of the Council); Lord Mulgrave was transferred from the Foreign Office to the Admiralty; and the Duke of Portland, who had been a Minister without Portfolio in January 1806, became First Lord of the Treasury.

itself', whereas the War Office had 'to do with the D. of York'.[30] His favourite for Foreign Secretary was Lord Wellesley, with whom he had struck up a warm political friendship. To have him at the Foreign Office was, he told Joan on March 22, 'of the utmost importance for the well-doing of the Government – and for *my* personal weight and consequence in the Cabinet.' It would be, he added, 'the greatest imaginable stroke that could be struck.'[31] In retrospect it is not easy to see why. Wellesley had served as Governor-General of India from 1797 until he was recalled in 1805 after quarrelling with his directors in London. He was an able man whose ideas on Britain's role in the east could be described as sensibly statesmanlike or foolishly grandiose according to taste. He was better at rising to an extraordinary occasion than dealing with humdrum day-to-day business. He was also exceedingly vain and arrogant and in India had insisted on maintaining such pomp and ceremony that the King was once heard to remark that when he came home his head would be quite turned and there would be no enduring him.[32]* In 1807 he was anxious to make his mark on the political stage. Presumably, Canning, with his vigour, charm and obviously outstanding ability, seemed a suitable ally. Canning, for his part, must have taken Wellesley at, or near, his own high estimation of himself and apparently felt rather dazzled at the prospect of having such an impressive ally in the Cabinet.

But it was not to be. Wellesley's financial administration in India was under attack in the House of Commons. Nobody – not even that stickler for propriety, the King – seemed to think that this need stop Wellesley from entering the Cabinet. But Wellesley himself was troubled by doubts; sometimes he got the better of them and sometimes he did not. In the end the doubts won. 'Poor Wellesley!' wrote Canning to Joan on March 25. 'After a painful struggle of three days, during which he decided three different ways, he ended yesterday at 5 o'clock (just as the D. of P. was going to the King with the arrangement) in a positive refusal.' Canning concluded philosophically that 'in such a state of nerves, it is quite as well that he has not this situation to encounter.'[33]

Portland at once suggested to Canning that he might like to swap the Admiralty for the Foreign Office. That evening Canning was not sure. But next morning, after getting a letter from Joan and having a

* On the same occasion the King also said that when it was pointed out to Wellesley that he was exacting more from those around him than the King did, his Lordship replied: 'Then the King is wrong; but that is no reason why I should improperly relax also.' (Rose Diaries and Correspondence, 11, p. 165)

talk with Malmesbury, he made up his mind to take the Foreign Office. The duke took him at once to see the King who kept him for 'a very long audience, in the course of which I hope I did away some of the ill impression I *know* he had conceived against me.'[34] Then he went on to take possession of his new domain, and there, in his room at the Foreign Office, he wrote that evening to Mr Leigh: 'It is true I went to bed last night First Lord of the Admiralty; but I changed at about noon this morning into a Foreign Secretary of State.'[35] In one way it was perhaps just as well he did. The Admiralty might be snug, but it was also cabined and confined and not very influential. On the other hand, not even the Foreign Office could satisfy Canning's restless energy for long, and in it he was well-placed to act as his colleagues' goad and critic. The consequences for him were to be little short of disastrous.

Portland completed his Cabinet by appointing Lord Mulgrave to the Admiralty which Canning was to have had. Mulgrave, a great patron of artists, was quite an able man, but like several of his colleagues (notably Chatham) he too easily subsided into indolence. The Cabinet as a whole could be divided into the useful sheep and the more or less useless goats. The first category comprised Castlereagh, Perceval and Canning in the Commons, and Hawkesbury and Eldon in the Lords. But in spite of some outstanding individual ability, the ministry as a whole did not look very durable. Nor did it feel it. 'The battle which we shall have to fight,' wrote Perceval to Harrowby, 'will be a very hard one, and between ourselves, I think with the present Parliament quite desperate.'[36] Perceval had particular reason for feeling depressed because the day before the Commons had passed, by a majority of 93, an address condemning his grant of the Duchy of Lancaster for life. It was not an auspicious beginning.

The opposition had little doubt that they could soon turn the ministers out and staged a trial of strength for April 9 on a motion introduced by Mr Thomas Brand. The motion had been carefully vetted by the leading Whigs and amounted to a condemnation of the change of government and of the King's attempt to tie the hands of his ministers permanently on the Catholic issue. The debate raged right through the night. Perceval claimed that the proposed concessions to the Catholics would have dangerously undermined the established church. Not all his colleagues – certainly not Canning nor Castlereagh – could agree with that. But they could all righteously rally to the defence of the Crown. Canning, who summed up for the government,

declared that it was the first occasion since the time of Charles I that a
sovereign had been brought to the bar of Parliament. He warmly –
some thought fulsomely – praised the King and ended with an unmistakable hint that the government was prepared if necessary to ask
for another dissolution.[37]

When the House at last divided at 6 o'clock in the morning, the
government was found to have a majority of 32. Presumably the
ministers' pose as the defenders of the King gained them the votes of a
good many independents, about 200 of whom had sat on the fence and
not voted at all since their election the previous year. How many,
especially among those who had so recently bought their own seats,
were swayed by Canning's threat of a dissolution, it is impossible to
say. The opposition, which had confidently expected to win, was loud
in its condemnation of his 'gross expedients' and 'unconstitutional
menace'. Even Malmesbury thought that Canning had used the threat
of dissolution too imperiously.[38] Naturally the Whigs were annoyed.
It was one thing for them to appeal to the country against the King,
and quite another for the King (in effect) to appeal to the country
against them.

In any case, even without Brand's motion, a dissolution had been
under consideration. Canning had been in favour of one as soon as the
Talents fell. It would certainly follow rather shockingly (and expen-
sively) close on the previous one, but logically there was no reason
why the new ministers should penalise themselves just because their
predecessors had stayed the course for such an unusually short time.
Moreover, for the time being, public opinion seemed to be on their
side. On April 24 Portland asked for an immediate dissolution. The
King at once agreed, hoping that the dissolution would 'be productive
of every advantage expected of it'.[39]

The King's hopes were not disappointed. To a considerable extent
the election was fought over his quarrel with his late ministers, although
the man in the street, constantly meeting the emotive slogan 'No
Popery', may have felt that the defence of the established church was
the main issue. The Whigs' counter-slogan was 'No Corruption', and
they did their best to blacken the reputation of their opponents, both
individually and collectively. But the feeling of the country had turned
against the Whigs who – so it seemed – had presumptuously tried to
set themselves up against the 'good old King'. And they only made
matters worse by making so little effort to hide their anger and disappointment at being dismissed from office.

The extent to which the Whigs had dished themselves could not really be seen until the two sides had fought an engagement on the floor of the House of Commons. The new Parliament met on June 22 and the debate on the Address took place four days later. Once again the Whigs rehearsed their grievances at length. Charges and counter-charges of corruption (a fashionable issue) were hurled to and fro. When the House at last divided, the opposition, which had been confidently reckoning on more than 200 votes, found itself with only 155, while the government was almost equally surprised to find itself with a whopping majority of 195. 'Our division is beyond all expectations,' wrote Canning triumphantly later that day.[40] Nor was it a flash in the pan. Four days later, the opposition mustered only 149, and in a third division early in July, only 136. For the rest of the short session it never again managed to get as many as 100 votes.

But if the opposition's performance was not impressive, neither was that of the ministers. Perceval, overburdened by the unfamiliar duties of his new office and by domestic worries, was well below his usual form. So was Castlereagh, who was in poor health; on one occasion he was too exhausted by 8 o'clock in the evening to introduce his new army recruiting bill and after the end of the session, one observer thought he seemed very ill.[41] Only Canning was doing justice to himself, and Perceval more than once paid generous tribute to his debating skill in his reports to the King. On July 18 Boringdon wrote in a letter to Granville Leveson-Gower that 'in the Commons, it is clear *consensu omnium* that Canning is beyond comparison the first man on his side of the House.' As an intimate friend, Boringdon may not have been a very reliable witness; in any case, the competition was not severe. But there is a ring of probability about his description of Canning as having quite lost his 'little irritation in difficult circumstances ... There is no idle lamentation, no finding fault, no despondency, no blustering – but a quiet and calm determination to see everything as it really is, and to act for the interests of the country without fear, and certainly without dishonour.'[42] As Foreign Secretary, at a time of grave and deepening crisis in the struggle against Napoleon, Canning was more stretched, with more work and more responsibility, than ever before. It was the kind of situation in which he throve and which brought out the best in him.

CHAPTER IX

The Bombardment of Copenhagen
1807-1808

By the time Parliament rose in the middle of August, Canning was well established at the Foreign Office. He had dealt, not without exasperation, with his importunate friends who descended on him in search of a share of the spoils of office. Frere, in particular, was troublesome. He wanted to be Surveyor-General of Woods and Forests, spurned the Pay Office and ended with neither. His visit, wrote Canning to Joan, 'has quite unhinged me for the whole day. Nobody,' he added ruefully, 'has behaved quite as they ought to do but Boringdon.'[1]

Within his own office it was easier. His old friend and colleague, George Hammond, who had retired when the Talents took over, came back as one Under-Secretary, and he offered the other to Lord Fitzharris, son of another old friend, Malmesbury. Fitzharris accepted, but found he had taken on more than he could manage and within five months had resigned. His recollections of his taskmaster, however, were entirely happy. 'I found him,' he wrote, 'a most kind-hearted and agreeable man to act under, never saw him discomposed, and ever viewed with astonishment the labour he bestowed on his duties, and the rapidity and ability with which he executed them.'[2] Fitzharris's successor was Charles Bagot, eleven years younger than Canning, but a member of his circle. Bagot's father-in-law, Wellesley-Pole, with whom Canning discussed the appointment, reported that Canning's conversation 'was altogether held in such a spirit of kindness and fairness that it has quite charmed me.' Canning said frankly that Bagot would have to give his whole mind to the job and be prepared for 'fagging without cessation or relaxation'. He would also need to be well versed in French (which Canning was not*) and might find it necessary to resign his

* Canning was twitted for his poor French when he first took office. In one current skit he was told to:
> 'Brush up your very best jokes, I pray:
> And though you can't speak any French they say,
> Why, as for that matter,
> Fitzharris can chatter,
> And you can keep out of the way.'

seat in the Commons.[3] Bagot did resign his seat, and he satisfied Canning so well, both by his capacity for hard work and the soundness of his advice, that he stayed the course until his chief's resignation in the autumn of 1809.

When the Portland ministry took over in the spring of 1807 the situation abroad could hardly have looked blacker. Nothing seemed able to stop Napoleon from subjugating and rearranging Europe in any way he pleased. Spain was his subservient ally. His influence was paramount throughout Italy. In February 1806, he placed one brother, Joseph, on the Neapolitan throne, and a few months later another, Louis, on the Dutch throne. Austerlitz had knocked Austria out of the war and forced her to sign a humiliating peace. Early in 1806 Prussia, with Napoleon's permission, had occupied and annexed Hanover. In July the Confederation of the Rhine, including Bavaria, Württemberg, Baden, and a number of other German states, was set up under French protection. In the autumn the King of Prussia, alarmed by Napoleon's tightening grip on Germany and afraid that he would bargain away Hanover in a peace settlement with Britain, suddenly mobilised his armies and demanded that the French should withdraw west of the Rhine. Napoleon's response was to advance rapidly into Germany and crush the Prussians and their Saxon allies at Jena and Auerstadt. Before the end of October 1806, Napoleon had entered Berlin while Frederick William III retreated into East Prussia with what troops he had left. Napoleon pressed on across the Vistula in order to settle accounts with Russia, the only major continental power still defying him. But in February 1807, at Eylau in East Prussia, the Russian and Prussian armies fought him to a bloody and inconclusive halt.

Meanwhile Britain had remained on the sidelines. The Talents had concentrated on trying to make peace with Napoleon. They thought it absurd even to think of sending troops to help the Russians and the Prussians and preferred to confine their warlike activities to the periphery of the struggle – an attempt to recapture Naples, which failed in spite of Sir John Stuart's gallant victory over the French at Maida, a naval demonstration against the Turks, the occupation of part of Egypt, and an expedition to faraway South America to capture new markets and sources of bullion. A plausible case could be made out for most of the operations. But their effect on the European heart of the struggle was negligible. They could not even help to extract tolerable peace terms from the French.

By the autumn of 1806, however, Grenville still hoped that peace might be achieved and he tended to regard Prussia's sudden defiance of Napoleon as a tiresome and unnecessary complication. The battle of Jena removed one obstacle to an Anglo-Prussian understanding because it forced the Prussians to agree to abandon their claim to Hanover. On the other hand, their ability to resist Napoleon now seemed so doubtful that Grenville was all the more reluctant to send them financial aid. He remembered the vast sums which Pitt had poured out to finance ineffective anti-French coalitions as well as the sorry list of unsuccessful British military interventions on the Continent. Even when Tsar Alexander was left as the only major obstacle in Napoleon's path, Grenville's response to his urgent demands for men, money and munitions was neither generous nor enthusiastic. A consignment of British arms was promised. But the Russians were told that a British expeditionary force was out of the question, and instead of the loan of £6 million for which they had asked, they were fobbed off with an immediate shipment of £500,000. Probably nothing the Talents could have done during the winter of 1806–7 would have seriously impeded Napoleon. But their aloof attitude helped to confirm a widespread feeling on the Continent that the British were selfish and unreliable allies.

Both Canning and Castlereagh were convinced that tolerable peace terms were not to be had from Napoleon and they realised that the most likely outcome of Grenville's policies was Britain's complete isolation. Canning's first concern was to assure the European powers that his country had no intention of opting out of the continental struggle, and to send them as much help as possible as soon as possible. He sent the Prussians £100,000 at once to tide them over until a new subsidy treaty could be concluded, and by May 1807 a large consignment of artillery, muskets, cartridges and flints were on their way to the Baltic. He immediately replaced Lord Douglas, the British Minister at St Petersburg, whose only achievement had been to madden Alexander by his tactlessness, by Granville Leveson-Gower who had already served in St Petersburg. He was instructed to give the Tsar the strongest possible assurances of British support and tactfully explain the limitations on the amount of financial aid Britain could provide. The Austrians were sent a special mission led by the Earl of Pembroke. He was told not to try to bribe Austria back into the war with offers of subsidies, but to indicate that as soon as she was 'unequivocally committed against France and embarked in the common cause . . . His Majesty will not then be backward to consider the necessities of his ally.'[4]

That sentence epitomises Canning's policy. Any country that would throw itself wholeheartedly into the struggle against Napoleon was Britain's ally and would be given as much help as possible. No longer, as in the early days of the war, was it a case of Britain in effect hiring troops from the continental powers for use in a quarrel which they might not necessarily consider theirs too. Now Russia and Prussia were fighting for their own independence and territory, while the Austrians were looking for a chance to regain what they had already lost of both. Three years earlier, when Pitt was trying to construct the third coalition, he also offered financial aid to any country prepared to fight France. But his subsidy treaties were complicated and unrealistic. When the Prussian envoy consulted Canning about a new subsidy treaty in June 1807, he was astonished to be offered £1,000,000, in three instalments, in return for a simple pledge that Prussia would throw all her resources into the war.[5] And even before the treaty was signed, arrangements for the payment of the first instalment had been set in train.

While Canning was trying to boost the sagging morale of the Russians and their allies and potential allies, grave news arrived from the Mediterranean. During the previous summer, Napoleon's envoy at Constantinople, General Sebastiani, had managed to stir up the Porte against the Russians with such success that in August the Sultan, in defiance of his treaty obligations, dismissed the pro-Russian hospodars (governors) of the Ottoman principalities on the Danube – Moldavia and Wallachia.* The Tsar immediately marched an army into the Principalities. The British had no more wish to have French influence paramount at the Porte than they had to see Russia extend her territory at the expense of the weak and sprawling Ottoman empire. Nor, above all at that particular moment, did they want to see the Russian military effort against Napoleon in northern Europe weakened by a lengthy diversion of troops to the Danube. So in November the Talents sent a naval force to Constantinople under the command of Admiral Duckworth. Its object was to back up the efforts of Charles Arbuthnot, the British envoy, to get rid of Sebastiani, and to mediate between the Turks and Russians. Arbuthnot himself was convinced that a display of naval strength within sight of the Seraglio would do the trick. He might have been right. But at the end of February 1807, Duckworth was forced to beat a hazardous retreat through the Dardanelles, taking Arbuthnot with him.

* Now part of Rumania.

The failure of Duckworth's expedition, Britain's sole attempt to do something for the Russians, made a lamentable impression in St Petersburg and Vienna. It was made worse by the news that 6,000 British troops had left Sicily for Egypt and on March 20 had captured and occupied Alexandria. General Henry Fox, the British commander in Sicily, had only been obeying orders, although he disapproved of them. He had been told that if Duckworth's mission failed, he was to occupy Alexandria in order to deter the French from trying to gain a new foothold in Egypt. There was in fact no sign of any immediate threat to Egypt from the French, and the main effect of the expedition was to confirm the opinion of all too many foreigners, including Alexander, that British policy was incurably devious and selfish.

By the time the disastrous news from the Dardanelles reached London on April 18, 1807, it was Canning and Castlereagh who had to cope with it. They learned that Sebastiani, far from being dislodged from the Porte, was more influential than ever, and that their own country as well as Russia was now in effect at war with the Turks. They had no wish to hasten the disintegration of the Ottoman empire by making war on it. Nor did they want, any more than their predecessors, to see Russia helping herself to slices of Ottoman territory. Above all, the folly of diverting large Russian forces from Napoleon's threatening armies in northern Europe was even more obvious than six months earlier. Canning therefore decided to try to retrieve the situation by sending Sir Arthur Paget, a young but experienced diplomat, to the Porte with instructions to make peace and to help the Russians do the same. By this time the Tsar had realised the imprudence of getting involved in a Turkish war and had sent an emissary, Count Pozzo di Borgo, to try to patch things up. Canning told Paget to assure Pozzo that Britain had no interest in the Turkish question except as Russia's ally. She did not regard her recent conquests in Egypt as a permanent acquisition but as a means of bringing pressure on the Turks.[6] At the same time, Paget was to stamp tactfully but very firmly on any Russian attempt to infringe the territorial integrity of the Ottoman empire.

When Paget arrived off Tenedos on July 28, he found that Pozzo di Borgo had already been there for more than two months without making any progress; instead of sending a plenipotentiary to him, the Turks had sent their fleet to attack the Russian garrison on Tenedos. The Turks could ignore the successful sea blockade of Constantinople imposed by the British and Russian navies, because the city was being satisfactorily supplied overland by caravan. Above all, news of Napoleon's victory over the Russians at Friedland on June 14 had reached the Porte and done 'enormous mischief'. Paget wrote gloomily to Canning that only a 'complete drubbing' of the Turks in a naval battle would make them see reason.[7] He could not help but feel that his mission had failed even before it had started.

While Paget was on his long journey to Constantinople, Castlereagh and Canning were working hard to strengthen the crucial military and diplomatic front in northern Europe. The difficulty was to find any spare troops; Castlereagh reckoned that only 12,000 could be released immediately from the defence of Britain. The Russian and Prussian envoys in London pressed for a landing between the Elbe and the Weser which they believed might spark off risings against the French all over Germany. The British were not in principle opposed to this, but thought it too risky and difficult with the small force at present available. They preferred to send it to the Baltic port of Stralsund in Swedish Pomerania, and with the help of the King of Sweden mount an attack on the French in East Prussia which would relieve the pressure on Russia's western frontiers. Gustavus Adolphus IV had indeed asked repeatedly that a British force should be sent to Stralsund. It was vital to keep him on the right side and Stralsund was one of the few ports through which English merchants could still trade with the Continent. So while Castlereagh energetically prepared the expedition, Canning negotiated with the Swedes for a combined operation against the French. Agreement was reached by the middle of June and by the end of the month, George III's German legion, under the command of Lord Cathcart, had sailed for the Baltic.

But it was all far too late. On June 22, Napoleon decisively defeated the Russians at Friedland. The French victory paralysed Alexander's will to resist. He immediately signed an armistice and three days later met Napoleon on a raft in the River Niemen near Tilsit, while the French and Russian armies looked on from either bank. 'The two Emperors have shaken hands,' said the Russian Commander-in-Chief, General Bennigsen, that night; 'Europe has cause to tremble.'[8] They not only shook hands. They walked and talked and ate together; they pored over maps together. The Tsar behaved as if he had fallen completely under Napoleon's spell; and on July 7 he signed and sealed his capitulation in the Treaty of Tilsit.

No news of Friedland reached Canning until June 30. Until then he had been hopefully sending Granville Leveson-Gower, by then on his way to St Petersburg, any items of news he thought might help to

convince Alexander of Britain's determination to fight. Even when
news of the lost battle reached him, he did not realise how calamitous
the consequences would be. He immediately told Leveson-Gower to
assure the Tsar that Britain would never abandon him if he went on
fighting, but that if peace was inevitable, she would stand by Russia in
the negotiations.[9]

Leveson-Gower, however, was stuck at Memel, unable to get on to
Tilsit and in no position to influence or encourage the Tsar. On June
26 Colin Mackenzie, a British soldier of fortune who had served with
the Russians, arrived in Memel and told him, on the authority of
General Bennigsen, that the two emperors were planning to sign a
treaty of alliance. Leveson-Gower immediately sent the news off to
London. His despatch arrived in the middle of July, by which time *The
Times* had confidently announced the signature of peace preliminaries
and begun to sound off with backs-to-the-wall articles. 'We are not,' it
proclaimed on July 11, 'at his [Bonaparte's] feet, if the Continent is;
nor shall we, surely, sink into humility, since we have never partaken
of disgrace.'

But Canning was still not wholly convinced. The 'disgusting
details' in French press reports about the two emperors' constant
meetings were so far beyond 'all reasonable belief' that he hoped the
reports of the peace preliminaries might also be false. He told Leveson-
Gower that if there were peace talks, he must go on demanding a place
for Britain at them. But he still hoped, on the basis of reports from
Vienna, that the Austrians might at last be shocked into joint military
action with the Russians against Napoleon.[10] Hopelessly out-of-date
with his information, and genuinely shocked by Alexander's humiliating self-abnegation before the man who to most Englishmen was still
only a Corsican upstart called Bonaparte, Canning found it hard to
believe that Alexander might have played his allies false. But on July
23, he read in a despatch from Leveson-Gower, dated July 2, that 'from
every account . . . it appears that Bonaparte has obtained complete
possession of the mind of the Emperor Alexander.'[11] By the end of the
month he learnt that a Franco-Russian treaty had definitely been signed.
Reality had broken in at last and the Portland government's foreign
policy lay in ruins.

Leveson-Gower did not yet know the terms of the Treaty of Tilsit,
but on August 8 Canning read in a French newspaper all that the two
emperors chose to make public of their arrangements. Prussia was to
lose all her territory west of the Elbe as well as her share of Poland
which was to be turned into a grand duchy under French protection.

The Tsar agreed to recognise Napoleon's brothers as kings of Naples, Holland and Westphalia. He also undertook to cease hostilities against the Turks and accept French mediation with the Porte. Napoleon, for his part, agreed to accept Russian mediation with Britain provided she accepted the offer within a month of the ratification of the treaty on July 9. What was not revealed was that Alexander had promised to go to war with Britain and close his ports to her if she refused mediation; that Napoleon had agreed to let the Tsar pick a quarrel with Sweden so that he could annex Finland; that Alexander had agreed to hand over the Ionian Islands to France and generally leave her a free hand in the Mediterranean; that he was to be allowed to annex the Danubian Principalities and that between them France and Russia would expel Turkey from all Europe, except Constantinople.

For Canning, what he read in the French newspaper and all that it implied was bad enough. He was furious about the mediation offer, of which the Russians had not bothered to inform the British ambassador and which expired the day after Canning more or less accidentally learnt of it. 'The British nation,' he wrote indignantly to Leveson-Gower on August 12, 'is not yet reduced to such a state as that HM should suffer a circle to be drawn around him.' It was essential to have a frank and full explanation of the Russian emperor's attitude. 'What confidence could be placed,' asked Canning, 'in the impartiality of a mediation of which the first public act had been an unqualified submission to one party and an ungenerous concealment from the other?'[12] He had trusted in Alexander's good faith up to the last possible minute. Now that his trust had been proved false he felt that there was no limit to the treachery of which the Tsar might not be capable.

Even before he had read the text of the treaty, Canning assumed that it would contain secret articles, and he instructed Leveson-Gower on August 4 to insist on being told what they were. When he did read the treaty, he felt confirmed in his assumption, because it was silent about so many subjects that the two emperors could hardly have failed to discuss and dispose of in their lengthy conferences. Leveson-Gower from the first had had little doubt that the treaty would include the 'spoliation' of Turkey. And when Canning instructed Sir Arthur Paget on August 14 to make peace at once with the Porte without bothering any more about Russian interests, he told him to warn the Turks that the British government had received the most positive information of a secret Franco-Russian agreement to expel them from Europe.[13] What this information was based on is not clear. But it was soon obvious that the Russians had at any rate agreed to give way to the French in the Mediterranean. On August 17, *The Times* published a report that the Russian troops at Cattaro and Castel Nuovo on the Dalmatian coast had been ordered to hand over to the French and embark for home. If this was a specimen of the secret treaty of Tilsit, commented *The Times* with lofty foresight, then the next step would be the transfer of the Ionian islands to the French. In fact, the cession of the islands to France had been officially announced in Corfu on August 10 and the first French troops landed there ten days later.

Of even greater importance than the fate of the Ottoman empire was where England now stood with France and Russia. Leveson-Gower's reports from St Petersburg, where he eventually arrived on July 22, were thoroughly gloomy. Alexander had 'completely thrown himself into the hands of Bonaparte' and had been heard extolling the wisdom and liberality of the French system of government. Napoleon had apparently told the Tsar that he meant to close the ports of Denmark, Portugal and Austria to British ships, and Leveson-Gower feared that if peace were not made, Britain would find herself at war with the whole Continent. A fortnight later he wrote even more gloomily to say that everything he had seen or heard since his arrival at the capital had confirmed his impression that the Russians were expecting a break with Britain. The Tsar, for example, had gone to Cronstadt and inquired 'with peculiar earnestness' about the state of the fortifications – as if he was expecting a British naval attack.[14] Leveson-Gower's reports made Canning still more dubious about the Russian offer of mediation, even supposing it was still open. If the Tsar was so completely in Napoleon's pocket, he clearly could not act as an impartial mediator. In any case, it was essential that Britain should first know whether the two emperors had made any secret agreements which affected her interests. But on this the British ambassador could extract nothing at all from the Russians. On the whole, Canning was inclined to think that if there were to be any peace negotiations, they had better be directly with the French.

But was Napoleon interested in a negotiated peace with England? Or did he want to reduce her to a state in which he could simply impose his own terms? If that was his objective, he might well try to force neutral Denmark to close the Baltic to British ships, if necessary through the occupation of Zealand by French troops. Access to the Baltic was vitally important to Britain, not only for commercial reasons – important though these were – but because of the scope it gave British seapower to influence the struggle against France and help Britain's Swedish and (before Tilsit) Russian allies. Denmark's survival as an independent power seemed increasingly unlikely, especially after Prussia had been knocked out of the war in December 1806. Canning's predecessor, Lord Howick, had been aware that Denmark might be next on Napoleon's list, or at least might, under a spurious cloak of neutrality, be forced into anti-British measures.* He had offered a secret defensive alliance between Britain, Sweden and Denmark (which was rejected) and told the British envoy in Copenhagen that Britain could in no circumstances tolerate the Danish navy falling into French hands.

By midsummer, 1807, Canning was even more anxious than Howick had been about Danish neutrality; it would never do to let the Stralsund expedition get bottled up in the Baltic. Moreover, like many other people in London, he suspected that the Danes were not friendly to Britain, and might even be definitely hostile. They had said little when Napoleon instituted his continental blockade from Berlin in November 1806; but when the British retaliated the following January with their Order-in-Council, they protested loudly. The British were more impressed by the contrast in the Danes' reactions than by the simple explanation that whereas the French decree could do them little harm, the British counter-move could do them a great deal. Just before the Talents fell, they upset the Danes still more by instituting a blockade of the Elbe, and one of Canning's first tasks at the Foreign Office was to deal with the angry complaints of the Danish chargé d'affaires. His concessions failed to mollify the Danish diplomat whose attitude became so unpleasant that in the end Canning asked for his recall. Although he did not say so, privately he was convinced that the Dane's behaviour was not just a personal failing but reflected the attitude of his government.[15] Early in July his suspicions were increased when he received a letter from Lord Pembroke, who had stopped off in Copenhagen on his way to Vienna, advising him not to trust the Danes, whose fleet was nearly ready to put to sea – presumably with hostile intent against the British navy. This information was in fact incorrect, but at the time, it seemed to fit into the general pattern of Danish hostility that was being pieced together in London.†

It may have been that the Danes were not so much pro-French as simply determined to preserve their neutrality. But what really mattered were the intentions of Napoleon. And the reports, rumours, and

* In the parliamentary debates on the bombardment of Copenhagen, Howick tried to minimise the concern which as Foreign Secretary he had shown over the danger from Denmark.

† After its capture by the British, it took six weeks to get the Danish fleet ready for sea.

intelligent guesses that were coming in from British diplomats and merchants in northern Europe made Canning fear the worst. By the middle of July, it looked very much as if the French intended to march into Holstein and make the Danes line up openly against England; according to some reports the Danes had actually given the French permission to occupy Holstein.

In London the Cabinet decided that something must be done. On July 14 Mulgrave got the King's permission to send a naval force of twenty to twenty-two ships to the Kattegat to watch the Danish navy and carry out whatever 'prompt and vigorous operations' seemed necessary.[16] On the 17th Castlereagh wrote to the King clearly indicating that the 'measures of precaution' contemplated by the Cabinet in the Baltic might include the use of land as well as naval forces if there was a rupture with Denmark and it seemed necessary to get hold of her fleet.[17] A Cabinet meeting next day decided to send Francis Jackson, who had been British envoy in Berlin from 1802 to 1806, on a secret mission to Copenhagen to try to secure peaceful possession of the Danish fleet.[18]* But the use of force was also apparently contemplated. On the same day, the Admiralty issued orders for more than fifty ships to prepare for sea to undertake a 'particular service' under Admiral Gambier;[19] the naval force contemplated by Mulgrave only four days earlier no longer seemed large enough. And next day Castlereagh sent instructions to Lord Cathcart at Stralsund to embark with his troops for the Sound where he would receive reinforcements.[20]

On the same day, July 19, the Cabinet considered the King's reply to Castlereagh's letter of the 17th. It expressed only qualified approval and contained a warning that ministers ought to proceed 'with temper and caution' and avoid any 'violent step' that might force Denmark and Russia into France's arms.[21] Somewhat perturbed by these royal doubts, the Cabinet sent Portland down to Windsor on what seems to have been a moderately successful attempt to resolve them. It is fairly clear that by this time the Cabinet was convinced that steps must be taken to prevent Napoleon from bringing the Danes willingly or unwillingly into the war. They had no definite proof that this was his intention. Taken separately, the various reports of his hostile plans from Altona,

* Canning sent post-haste for Jackson on the 17th. The diplomat, who was staying 80 miles away in the country, was roused in the middle of the night and reached Downing Street about midday on the 18th. Canning, whom he saw before the Cabinet meeting, seemed very worried and perplexed by the ominous reports from Copenhagen and Altona. Jackson was told of his assignment directly after the meeting. (G. Jackson, *Diaries and Letters*, Vol. II, pp. 187/8)

Hamburg, Copenhagen and elsewhere might not seem much to go by. Cumulatively, however, they must have seemed to add up to an impressive body of circumstantial evidence. At any rate, it was sufficiently impressive to convince such sober and cautious characters as Spencer Perceval, Castlereagh, Hawkesbury, Portland – indeed all the ministers. There is no hint that this Cabinet, which two years later was to be so reft by dissension, was on this occasion anything but completely united.

Traditionally, Canning is supposed to have persuaded the Cabinet to take action against the Danes after receiving information direct from Tilsit about the secret articles in the treaty signed by the two emperors. Various ideas have been put forward about the source of this information, and what exactly it was. Neither Canning nor any other minister ever claimed to have any written information about the secret articles; if they had, they could have firmly established their case by publishing it. All they claimed to have was private information 'that there were secret engagements in the Treaty of Tilsit to employ the navies of Denmark and Portugal against this country.' When Lord Hawkesbury stated this in the House of Lords the following January, he flatly refused to reveal his source, hinting broadly that to do so would endanger the life of someone on the Continent who was friendly to Britain. This seems to rule out the most picturesque theory according to which Colin Mackenzie managed to get on the raft in the Niemen in disguise and overheard Napoleon discussing his plans with the Tsar. Mackenzie was safely back in England by about July 23.

Who in fact the friendly foreigner was is not known and probably never will be. Nor is it known for certain when his report reached the Cabinet. What we do know is that during the night of July 21 to 22, Canning received intelligence directly from Tilsit which 'appears to rest on good authority' that Napoleon had proposed to Alexander the formation of a maritime league against Britain of which Denmark and Portugal would certainly be members.[22] It was presumably this message that Spencer Perceval was referring to in a memorandum* that he composed to explain the government's case for sending an expedition to Copenhagen. He wrote that 'the intelligence from so many and such various sources' that Napoleon intended to force Denmark into war against Britain could not be doubted. 'Nay, the fact that he has openly avowed such intention in an interview with the E[mperor] of R[ussia]

* The memorandum was undated, but according to Perceval's latest biographer, Mr Denis Gray (p. 165), internal evidence suggests it was written on or before July 22.

is brought to this country in such a way as it cannot be doubted. Under such circumstances,' added Perceval, 'it would be madness, it would be idiotic . . . to wait for an overt act.'[23]

If this was the secret private information direct from Tilsit which the ministers afterwards used to justify their action, they had in fact virtually taken their decision before it reached them. By July 19 they had only the vaguest ideas about what had been going on at Tilsit. It seems to have been primarily the reports from northern Europe about Napoleon's intentions with regard to Denmark and the Danish fleet that made the Cabinet resolve to act. The mysterious messenger from Tilsit confirmed and justified their resolution.

The expedition to Copenhagen, once decided on, was prepared with unusual speed and efficiency. A military force about 25,000 strong was assembled and the first contingent of troops and ships sailed on July 30. Francis Jackson set off next day. Canning had instructed him that his one essential aim was to secure possession of the Danish navy. But realising that this was a harsh and unacceptable demand to make to an apparently inoffensive neutral, he tried to sugar the pill. The fleet was to be received as a 'sacred deposit' and a convention signed for its return at the end of the war. The Danes were offered a treaty of alliance and mutual defence, the protection of twenty-one British warships and a subsidy for however many troops they kept on active service. Canning, moreover, had urged that the naval and military force sent to back up Jackson's demands should be impressively large so as to make it as easy as possible for the Danes to give way; a plea of *force majeure* might also help to avert Napoleon's wrath.

Once the expedition had sailed, those responsible for sending it could only wait hopefully for the best. Canning wrote to Joan on July 31, 'The anxious interval between this day and the hearing the result of his [Jackson's] expedition will be long and painful indeed. Long, I mean, in *feeling*. In fact it will be about a fortnight or three weeks . . . I think we have made success almost certain. I am sure if we succeed we do a most essential service to the country. But the measure is a bold one and if it fails – why we must be impeached I suppose – and dearest dear will have a box at the trial.'[24] Next day, he wrote again very cheerfully to say that he had received a letter in the House the previous night which gave an 'account of the French being *actually* about to do that act of hostility, the possibility of which formed the groundwork of my Baltic plan. My fear was that the French might *not* be the aggressors – and then ours would have appeared a strong measure, fully justifiable I think and absolutely necessary, but without apparent necessity or justification. Now the aggression will justify us fully . . . I am therefore quite easy as to the morality and political wisdom of our plan.' If this letter was based on more than unfounded rumour, it is difficult to see what it can have contained. On July 31 Napoleon did in fact instruct Talleyrand to tell the Danes to prepare for war against Britain if they did not want Holstein to be invaded and occupied by Bernadotte. But Canning obviously cannot have learned of this from a letter received on the same day. True or false, however, the letter was good for his morale. 'Now for the execution,' he went on in his letter to Joan, 'and I confess to my own love, I wake an hour or two earlier than I ought to do, thinking of this execution. I could not sleep after asses' milk today, though I was not in bed till ½ p.2.'[25]

He was to have a good many more restless nights; it was six weeks before news of the Danish capitulation reached London. August 14 was to have been the day on which military operations were to begin if Jackson's negotiation was getting nowhere. On that day, Canning wrote to Joan: 'I woke at asses' milk time with the noise of disembarkation in my head. But perhaps force may not be necessary.'[26] There were reports in the newspapers about Jackson's movements, but no despatches from him arrived at the Foreign Office. On the 22nd Canning wrote to Boringdon: 'Nothing yet. It is very extraordinary, and very, very anxious.'[27] On August 25, he wrote to tell Granville Leveson-Gower that there was still no news. 'The suspense is, as you may well imagine, agitating and painful in the extreme; but I have an undiminished confidence as to the result, either by force or by treaty. The latter however is so infinitely preferable to the former that the doubt whether it has been successful is of itself almost as anxious as if the whole depended on it alone.'[28]

Canning can have had little genuine hope that force could be avoided, and the knowledge that the 'poor old K' still had his doubts did not make him any easier. One day towards the end of the month when he was discussing the expedition with the King, he could not help remarking that he feared his majesty was still shocked by the 'immorality' of the measure. 'Yes – yes – I have not altered my opinion,' replied the King. 'It is a very immoral act. So immoral that I won't ask who originated it. I have determined not to ask that question.' But, added Canning when describing the scene to Joan, 'all this in the most perfect good humour, laughing even at his own difficulties – but determined honestly to declare his opinion.'[29]

Gradually the news of what had happened trickled in. Brooke Taylor, the new British envoy to Denmark,* had arrived at Copenhagen on August 2, but as neither the Danish foreign minister, Count Joachim Bernstorff, nor the Prince Royal would see him, he withdrew to the fleet on August 11. Francis Jackson did not fare much better. He arrived at Kiel on August 6 and had a series of explosive and unsuccessful interviews with the Prince Royal and the Danish premier, Count Christian Bernstorff. Jackson was very complacent afterwards about his performance, but in fact he seems to have handled his admittedly difficult brief with unnecessary clumsiness. He concentrated on his main objective – possession of the Danish fleet – and immediately rammed that bitter pill down the Danes' throats without first thickly coating it with the sugar that Canning had provided. But not even the most accomplished diplomat could have disguised from the Danes the fact that they were being asked to give up not only their fleet but also their cherished neutrality and enter the war on what seemed to be the weaker side. That the diplomat's demands were backed by an over-whelming display of force did not make them, as Canning had hoped, any easier to accept; it only made the Danes feel outraged and insulted. Like Canning, they did not yet realise how completely the Tsar had put himself under Napoleon's thumb and they counted on him using his influence to restrain the French. They did not yet know that Napoleon had already told their envoy in Paris that they must come into the war on his side.

On August 15 Jackson, who had himself never believed in the success of his mission, threw in his hand and retired to the impressive British armada by then assembled in the Sound. Next day, Cathcart's advance guard, under the command of Sir Arthur Wellesley, disembarked at Wibeck, between Copenhagen and Elsinore. The British issued a proclamation demanding the deposit (not surrender) of the Danish fleet. The Danes replied with what amounted to a declaration of war. Cathcart advanced on Copenhagen and invested the city. But the Danes showed no sign of giving way and after they had turned down a second offer of an amicable settlement, a naval bombardment of the city was begun on September 2. It went on for three days and nights until at 7 o'clock on the evening of the 5th the Danes asked for a truce. In a letter written the following evening, a naval officer described the bombardment as 'the most tremendous sight that can be well conceived, but the night before last much surpassed all the rest,

---

* Canning, rather unfairly, did not think much of his predecessor, Benjamin Garlike, and decided to replace him in the middle of July.

particularly when the largest church caught fire, and the spire (which was a remarkably beautiful one) fell in.' He added that he could not tell how much damage had been done, but the town was still burning furiously.[30] It was later estimated that the death-roll was about 2,000, that more than 300 houses and trading premises were completely destroyed and that about a third of all the buildings in the city were damaged.

The capitulation was signed on September 7. The Danes agreed to give up their fleet* and naval stores and in return the British agreed to leave Copenhagen and the island of Zealand within six weeks. The news did not reach Canning until September 16. In his relief and excitement all he could think of was that the Danish fleet was safe in British hands. 'Did I not tell you we would save Plumstead from bombardment?' he scrawled jubilantly to Mr Leigh. 'A fig for Col. Craufurd. That was not our expedition† – nor was Egypt, nor Constantinople but this was.'[31] A week later he wrote: 'Nothing ever was more brilliant, more salutary or more effectual than the success [at Copenhagen].'[32] Perceval expressed equal, if more sober, approval. *The Times* admitted that Copenhagen must have suffered severely, but warmly emphasised Cathcart's efforts to avoid and then shorten the bombardment. Two days later it declared that the seizure of the Danish fleet was 'a bare act of self-preservation,' and pointed out how short the voyage was between Denmark and Ireland or north-east Scotland.[33] And in his *Political Register* Cobbett asserted that it was 'vile mockery' and 'mere party cavilling' to suggest that Denmark could have preserved her neutrality.[34] Even Wilberforce decided that the expedition could be justified on grounds of self-defence.[35] And Thomas Grenville confessed to his brother, Lord Grenville, that he could not help feeling 'that in their [the government's] situation we should very probably have given the same order without being able to publish to Parliament the grounds on which we had believed in the hostile mind of Denmark.'[36]

But most of the opposition reacted to the news from Copenhagen with shocked, and sometimes extravagant, hostility. Lord Erskine was said to have declared that 'if hell did not exist before, Providence would create it now to punish ministers for that d——able measure.'[37] There was much lamentation in the opposition press about the stain on the national character. To some extent the lamentation was sincere.

* It consisted of 18 sail of the line, 15 frigates and 31 smaller ships. (Malmesbury, *Letters*, II, p. 45)

† A reference to the Talents' unsuccessful efforts to capture and hold Buenos Aires. Craufurd was in fact a Brigadier-General by this time.

The rules of war, the 'law of nations', the rights of neutrals, were taken seriously. The bombardment of towns and civilian populations whether from sea or land was not an acceptable method of warfare, and people, whatever their politics, were genuinely shocked by the reports of death and destruction at Copenhagen. When the complacent Francis Jackson got back to London, he was surprised to find 'a disposition to commiserate the Danes.'[38]

But inevitably there was also a strong element of party politics in the opposition's attacks. In 1806, when it was feared (wrongly, as it turned out) that the French were about to invade Portugal, the Talents had mounted very much the same kind of operation with the primary aim of making sure that the Portuguese navy did not fall into French hands. Canning read out the Talents' instructions to Lord St Vincent in the Commons on February 3, 1808, adding ironically that the 'only shyness' felt in producing them earlier had been that they would 'place him and his colleagues in the situation of convicted plagiarists.'[39] Thomas Grenville was well aware that the opposition's record exposed it to counter-attack if it condemned the Copenhagen expedition. Windham, on the other hand, managed to convince himself that the behaviour of the previous Cabinet (of which he was a member) towards Portugal was 'not within a thousand degrees so exceptionable' as the Danish business.[40]

The opposition was perhaps on safer, if equally controversial, ground when it claimed that the Copenhagen expedition had been not merely immoral and unprincipled but unnecessary. It complained of the government's failure to produce convincing evidence to support its case. The ministers had no conclusive evidence to offer, only a strong presumptive case; and any government fighting a war must try to foresee and forestall the enemy's moves. Canning and his colleagues may have thought the Danes to be more anti-British than they really were; but they were justified in believing that Napoleon meant to force them to help him defeat the English and they were right to assume that Denmark was too weak to defend her neutrality. Unfortunately, the only 'positive information' that they claimed came from the unidentified messenger from Tilsit. In the parliamentary post-mortem on Copenhagen, they did not in fact make much play with this. But their tight-lipped refusal to reveal the source of their secret information made it easier for the opposition to accuse them of taking an unprincipled leap in the dark. When the government published a state paper setting forth its strong presumptive case for the Copenhagen expedition, *The Times* rather percipiently commented that the only weak thing about it was its reference to 'positive information'.[41]

But when the Cabinet planned the Copenhagen expedition, they made a tragic miscalculation on one point: the reaction of the Danes. Canning, who tried to make the demand for the Danish fleet, if not acceptable, at least tolerable, seems to have wavered between a feeling that nothing could do this and a desperate hope that force would not be necessary. But if a resort to force had to be made, it was assumed that it would be brief, only moderately nasty and soon forgotten. It was a sadly over-optimistic assumption.

Although the Cabinet believed that the Danish declaration of war was only a temporary ebullition of violent resentment, they quickly realised the potential danger of Cathcart's undertaking to evacuate Zealand within six weeks. The Danish fleet was safe, but the Danes were still vulnerable to French pressure – indeed, deprived of their fleet, they were even more vulnerable. When the British troops left Zealand, they would almost certainly be succeeded by French as well as Danish troops, and the Swedes would find themselves directly menaced by Napoleon. The King of Sweden realised this and offered to send 30,000 troops to help the British keep the island. Moreover, Canning realised that the Tsar's reaction was likely to be extremely unfavourable, if, by abandoning Zealand, the British helped the French to gain a foothold in Sweden and eventually establish an army along Russia's vulnerable northern frontier. Three days after the news of the Danish capitulation reached London, he suggested to Castlereagh that he should leave it open to Cathcart to hang on to the island if he could.[42] Castlereagh agreed and delicately explained to Cathcart that the Danish declaration of war had somewhat changed the Cabinet's views, and 'as far as it can be done consistently with the engagements entered into, we are desirous of converting our present position in Zealand into an instrument for keeping the French out of it.' More specifically, Cathcart was to seize on any infringement of the terms of the capitulation by the Danes as an excuse for not carrying out his side of the bargain.[43]

But the Danes failed to oblige. And Castlereagh and Canning, whose unprincipled and dishonourable conduct was being daily denounced in the opposition press, did not feel able to flout the convention signed by their commanders on the spot. Instead, they hit upon the ingenious expedient of letting the evacuation go forward, as honour demanded, but ordering Cathcart to reoccupy the island immediately. This extraordinary manœuvre was seriously considered by the Cabinet and might have been approved if the military, in particular Sir Arthur Wellesley who arrived back in England on September 30, had not so firmly opposed it. Wellesley also brought back such a distressing account of the conduct of the British troops in Zealand that Canning felt this in itself was a strong argument against keeping the island – for 'it is morally certain that the whole population of the country must detest and abhor the English after the outrages which have been committed there.'[44]

According to the report of an eyewitness, Canning was reduced to a state of 'great indecision, embarrassment and annoyance' by this setback to his plans.[45] But after havering for a week, the Cabinet decided that it could not ignore the strong opposition of both naval and military officers and instead would try to protect Sweden by stationing a force in Scania.* In the circumstances it must have been rather galling for the ministers to be attacked and mocked by the Whig leader, George Ponsonby, for evacuating Zealand and being so 'shabby' in their 'iniquities'.

But Canning still did not despair of retrieving the situation by diplomatic means. He sent a professional diplomat, Anthony Merry, to Copenhagen to offer the Danes the option of a neutrality guaranteed by England, Russia and Sweden, or a defensive alliance with England. Merry – described by Malmesbury as a 'very worthy but nervous man' – set off at the beginning of October with instructions that could hardly have been more conciliatory. But the Danes refused to have anything to do with him and he was obliged to come home with his proposals still in his pocket. It was seven years before Britain and Denmark were again at peace.

It can be argued that the Cabinet might have avoided turning a neutral into an enemy and still achieved their main purpose, if they had been content to send a naval and military force to the Baltic but taken no overt action unless the French invaded Denmark and the Danes asked for help. But British aid might have then arrived too late; if the French waited to strike until the Baltic was in the grip of winter, it might not have arrived at all. Moreover, Canning – rightly or wrongly – feared that the Danes would not resist a French invasion. Altogether, at the time, a cautious policy seemed more risky than a bold one.

All this time, in spite of Leveson-Gower's gloomy warnings, the

* This offer was turned down by the Swedish king.

British government had been assuming that the Tsar's hobnobbing with Napoleon was only a temporary aberration. Canning hopefully reckoned that the Copenhagen expedition would '*stun* Russia into her senses again',[46] and at first it looked as if he might be right. That dashing soldier, Sir Robert Wilson, arrived in London from St Petersburg about September 19, having made the journey in the record time of sixteen days. He had seen the Tsar just before he left and had found him markedly conciliatory. Alexander admitted that since the British had thought fit to send an expedition to Copenhagen, he was anxious about their intentions farther up the Baltic and assured Wilson that he wished to remain on friendly terms with England.[47]* Sir Robert had the reputation of being rather credulous and over-sanguine; as the King delicately warned Canning, any report 'from a person of so lively an imagination' must be treated with caution.[48] Granville, however, had sent a similar report. Moreover Canning knew that the Tsar must also be worried about what the British might do to the Russian fleet which Napoleon had ordered out of the Mediterranean and which was now making the long and hazardous voyage home. It might well be obliged to winter somewhere on the way and there was much anxious speculation in Downing Street about how to treat it if it took shelter in a British port.

But even if, through fear or any other motive, Alexander was having a change of heart towards England, the mystery of the secret articles that he was supposed to have signed at Tilsit remained unsolved. Canning still suspected that the two emperors had come to a general understanding hostile to England. And his suspicions were heightened after he learnt from two different sources that Alexander had confessed to some of his advisers that he had privately made some verbal agreements with Napoleon (in addition to the written secret articles) and had even left it to the French emperor to draft a memorandum of their conversation on his return to Paris. On September 27 he sent Leveson-Gower urgent instructions to find out the truth of these reports.[49]

But by the time this despatch reached St Petersburg, the moment for diplomatic pressure was past. Early in November, a French officer arrived in the Russian capital from Paris. He brought with him a peremptory demand from Napoleon that the Tsar should immediately

---

* On August 13, Canning did in fact authorise Leveson-Gower to ask Gambier to make a naval demonstration off Cronstadt, if he suspected the Russians of hostile intentions. But he was very pleased that the ambassador did not find this necessary because he much preferred to rely on '*managing* the Emperor's personal feelings.' (F.O. 65/70 and P.R.O. 30/29 8/4)

carry out his secret undertaking to break with Britain. A few days later, Alexander obediently did what he was told. Leveson-Gower immediately demanded his passport and set off for home.

The Russian declaration of war became known in London on December 2; it was brought, perhaps rather appropriately, by Sir Robert Wilson. The King declared that it was 'couched in language so gross and insulting that . . . it must have been framed by those who write for the Paris *Moniteur* and transcribed word for word at Petersburg.'[50] Canning for his part must have felt that he now knew all he needed to know about the secret treaty of Tilsit. Two days later, he wrote to Boringdon: 'The Peace of Tilsit you see is come out. We did not want any more *case* for Copenhagen; but if we had, this gives it us.'[51]

The case for Copenhagen was also strengthened by news from the other end of Europe. Prince John of Portugal, who ruled as regent for his mad mother, Queen Maria, was a weak and wavering man, whose chief hope was that the storm sweeping through Europe would somehow pass him by. But it was hardly likely that Portugal, an ally and an important trading partner of Britain, would be allowed to opt out of Napoleon's plans for the total exclusion of the British from the Continent. Within a fortnight of signing the Treaty of Tilsit, he began to threaten the Portuguese ambassador in Paris; and on August 12 he sent a formal ultimatum to Lisbon, demanding that the Portuguese should close their ports to British ships, seize all British subjects and property on their territory and issue a declaration of war against England. The news reached Canning on August 26, while he was anxiously waiting for news from Copenhagen. 'We have more work upon our hands,' he wrote to Joan, 'Lisbon *ought* to be another Copenhagen. Would our fleet and army were come back and ready to start again! Never was a time of so much anxiety.'[52]

The government, however, put on a bold front; and for the next three months the Portuguese Prince Regent tried to make up his mind whether he had more to fear from Napoleon or the British fleet. At first he assured the imperious British ambassador, Lord Strangford, that he would flee to Brazil rather than sequestrate any British property. In the circumstances, this would suit the British very well. A transatlantic migration by the House of Braganza would boost the development of its vast Brazilian colony, and provide the new and expanding markets urgently needed by the English merchants now largely shut out from Europe. Moreover, if the Portuguese fleet escorted its royal family across the Atlantic, it would conveniently remove itself from French control without any invidious bullying from the British. But the Prince Regent was far too timid and indecisive to stick to such a bold decision. It was clear to the British ambassador that he 'viewed with horror' the prospect of going to Brazil. The inconvenience and fatigue of going, commented Strangford scathingly, were much more within the range of his understanding that the importance and bene-fits.[53]

And so, in London, Lisbon and Paris, the three contestants in the game that would decide Portugal's future made their moves and counter-moves, each usually quite ignorant of the latest ploy of either of his opponents. On October 20, the Prince Regent, in a desperate attempt to propitiate Napoleon, formally declared war on England. He could not know that on the same day Napoleon declared war on him and that a French army was already on the march towards Lisbon. Two days later, Canning, knowing nothing of either of these declarations of war, signed a secret convention with the Portuguese envoy in London. It stipulated that if the Portuguese closed their ports to the British, a British force would occupy Madeira; and if the Prince Regent decided to flee to Brazil with his fleet, the British would provide naval and military help. This convention was sent off to Strangford, accom-panied by a voluminous despatch in which Canning painted a glowing picture of the bright future that awaited the Portuguese royal family in Brazil and declared with the utmost firmness that England would and could defy the whole of Europe rather than truckle under to Napoleon.

But by the time this stirring despatch reached Strangford on November 2, he was beginning to feel very dubious about the Prince Regent's intentions. Portuguese ports had been closed to British ships, the coastal batteries were being prepared and manned against the British navy, and the Prince Regent continued to haver over whether he and his fleet should flee from the advancing French. Reports of the Portuguese backsliding reached Canning, who immediately sent Strangford several urgent despatches, insisting that the Portuguese fleet must be got away; if persuasion would not work, then Sir Sidney Smith, who was on his way with six ships of the line, must back persuasion with a strict blockade of the Tagus, and if the worst came to the worst, the Portuguese ships must be captured 'by a bold and sudden attack'.[54]

Strangford was quite ready to take a high line. So was Smith when he arrived in the Tagus on November 16. By that time, the Portuguese, terrified by reports of Napoleon's anger, had ordered the detention of all British subjects and property. They were also importunately beseeching Strangford to be gone, although stormy weather made this extremely hazardous. So pressing, however, did the Portuguese foreign minister become that on the 18th Strangford set off in a fishing boat; it was not a very dignified exit, but at least it emphasised the 'precipitancy and indecency' of the Portuguese government's behaviour.[55] After a dangerous passage, he eventually caught up with Sir Sidney Smith whom bad weather had driven some way from the mouth of the Tagus, and established his new headquarters on the admiral's flagship.

Neither Strangford nor Smith had any intention of sailing tamely away, but before Smith seized the Portuguese ships by force, Strangford decided to make one more personal appeal to the Prince Regent. By now time was running out. Marshal Junot, making a rather leisurely progress through Spain, had received peremptory orders from Napoleon at all costs to get to Lisbon before the British forestalled him. Junot obeyed, undeterred by torrential rain, impossibly bad roads, a wild and inhospitable country and the hardships of his starving troops. By the night of November 28, when Strangford, after another long and stormy passage, landed once more at Lisbon, Junot and the ragged remnants of his army had almost reached their goal. Strangford found the city 'in a state of sullen discontent' with armed men roaming the streets. All the Portuguese royal family had already embarked, except for the Prince Regent, who, although in principle determined to flee, still could not make up his mind actually to go. Strangford sought him out, and after terrifying him with 'dark and gloomy descriptions of the state of Lisbon' and directing 'all his fears to a French army and all his hopes to a British fleet', eventually persuaded him to flee.[56]*

On November 29, the Portuguese fleet – twelve warships and about twenty-six smaller vessels – with fourteen members of the Portuguese royal family, their hangers-on and their belongings on board, began the long voyage to Brazil. The escorting British squadron gave them a 21-gun salute while Strangford, determined to prevent any royal second thoughts, stayed on the Prince Regent's ship until it was safely across the bar of the Tagus. The Russian Mediterranean fleet, which a few

---

* Strangford was accused, rightly or wrongly, by Lord Holland and by the historian Charles Napier of exaggerating the importance of his own part in persuading the Prince Regent to go.

weeks earlier had taken refuge from the winter storms in the Tagus, was a passive spectator of the whole operation.

Next day, while the Portuguese fleet was still within sight of the shore, Junot and 1,500 exhausted men entered Lisbon. They met with no resistance, but the object of their terrible forced march had escaped them by a few hours. According to Sir Sidney Smith, if the Portuguese fleet had delayed its departure by only two hours, the bad weather would have prevented it from getting away at all.[57]

When the news reached London, Canning reacted with characteristic exuberance. 'Huzza! Huzza! Huzza!' he wrote on December 19. 'We have saved the Portuguese royal family, and the Portuguese navy and the merchantmen and they were all on the 5th off Madeira under convoy of a British squadron steering with a fair wind for the Brazils. Denmark was saucy and we were obliged to *take her* fleet. Portugal had confidence, and we have rescued hers.'[58]

Shortly before Strangford successfully completed his mission at Lisbon, Sir Arthur Paget arrived back in England. As he had himself foreseen, his mission to the Porte had not been a success. Canning's despatch of August 14, informing Paget of the Treaty of Tilsit and instructing him to make a separate peace with the Turks, did not reach him until October 1. He had learned about Tilsit some five weeks earlier when a Russian officer arrived with instructions to the Russian admiral to break off hostilities against the Turks and return home at once, taking Pozzo di Borgo with him. Paget realised that all he could do now was make the best terms he could with the Turks. It was a thankless and exasperating task. The Porte had not yet recovered from a recent palace revolution; the new Sultan was young and inexperienced, his ministers were ignorant and incompetent and all were mortally terrified of offending Napoleon or the Russians. It was also an extremely uncomfortable task; Paget tossed about in a British warship off the Dardanelles, buffeted by the autumn gales, with one secretary in one ship, one in another, his interpreter in a third, and his servants and belongings in a fourth. His rare conferences with Ismail Pasha, the Porte's representative, were held in the Castle of Europe at the mouth of the Dardanelles. By early October he was convinced his cause was lost. On the 7th he told the Turks that if they did not agree to receive him in Constantinople within twelve days, he would depart. The Turks allowed the ultimatum to expire, but told Paget that they would negotiate a formal peace after they had concluded their delicate negotiations with the Russians, and in the meantime would not consider themselves actually at war with Britain. This communication, commented Paget acidly in his despatch to Canning, 'strongly marks the pitiful feelings and conduct of those who made it.'[59] More informally, he told his father that he had had a cruel time and felt he had done little more than learn to eat with his fingers.[60]*

Paget's failure at Constantinople and Junot's occupation of Lisbon left Britain without any European toehold apart from what might be provided by the termagant Queen of Sicily and the half-mad King of Sweden. Canning's energetic efforts to promote and encourage resistance to the French in Europe had been defeated partly by the mesmeric effect of Napoleon's power, prestige and personality and partly by the eccentricities of the rulers with whom the British had to deal. The Royal Navy controlled the seas but, militarily, the British had been thrust on to the defensive and their situation was made all the more hazardous by the obscurity enveloping Napoleon's intentions. The Cabinet in London had no idea whether he would strike next in the Mediterranean or the Baltic or even conceivably against the British Isles. The complicated orders issued by Castlereagh in an effort both to guard against all eventualities, and take account of the slowness of communications, led to a somewhat confused and wasteful deployment of military resources already stretched to the limit. But in the circumstances it was a case of risking a muddle by trying too hard, or a setback by attempting too little.

In the winter of 1807–8 neither Napoleon nor the British could deal any really damaging blow at each other by military means because neither could get at the other. Napoleon therefore determined to bring the British to heel by intensified economic warfare. Ever since the outbreak of war in 1793, the French had been trying to damage British commerce, at first with little success. But after Jena and Tilsit, which gave Napoleon control of virtually the whole Continent, he was much better placed to shut British exports, including colonial exports, out of Europe and deny Britain vital imports of corn and timber. In November 1806, he had issued his Berlin decrees, declaring Britain to be in a state of blockade. The following January, the British government had

* Paget's successor, Robert Adair, had a more successful but scarcely less frustrating mission to Constantinople. He arrived off Tenedos towards the end of September 1808, and after much procrastination on the part of the Turks, signed the Peace of the Dardanelles the following January.

replied with an Order-in-Council forbidding all trade between French or French-controlled ports, but not interfering with direct colonial or American trade with France. This turned out to be an unsatisfactory compromise which annoyed the neutrals much more than it inconvenienced the French. By the autumn of 1807 English warehouses were filling up with unsold manufactured goods and colonial products, neutral shipowners were swarming in to take advantage of the situation and English merchants and shipowners were complaining bitterly to the government about their predicament.

The Cabinet was much exercised both by the ethics and the practical difficulties of economic warfare. Canning himself had no specific responsibility, but he played his part in the lively debates and industrious circulation of memoranda within the Cabinet. The difficulty was that if Britain used her seapower to retaliate against Napoleon's attempt to destroy her trade, the first to suffer would be the neutrals and in particular the United States. Canning naturally regarded the problem from the point of view of a Foreign Secretary who would have to pacify the irate neutrals; he had already had difficulty in damping down an explosion of anger by the touchy Americans after one of their frigates, the USS *Chesapeake*, had been boarded by the Royal Navy in search of deserters. Supported by Portland, who pointed out that the British were already sufficiently unpopular on the Continent, Canning argued in favour of concentrating counter-measures on France and French-occupied territory rather than on all those who, whether voluntarily or involuntarily, were supporting Napoleon's 'continental system'. But another group in the Cabinet, led by Castlereagh and Hawkesbury, pressed for British retaliation to be as tough and extensive as possible.

On the whole, the extremists had their way. Under Orders-in-Council issued in November 1807, all ports from which the British flag was excluded were declared to be in a state of blockade, and with a few exceptions no neutral ship could visit them without first calling at a British port and paying a duty on the reshipment of its cargo. If the neutrals wanted to trade with Europe, they could, but only subject to British control and at a profit to the British exchequer. Napoleon's reply was to order the capture and confiscation of all neutral ships which submitted to a British search or called at a British port.[61] Henceforth, whatever the unfortunate neutrals did, they were bound to get into trouble with either the British or the French. In December the United States retaliated by banning trade with both belligerents. This brought international trade largely to a standstill. British exports to the Continent dropped sharply and discontent grew among northern cotton workers and others thrown out of work by the slump.*

Not surprisingly, as 1807 drew to an end, the longing of many ordinary people for an end to the war began to make itself heard; and when Parliament met in the New Year, petitions for peace from Bolton, Oldham and Manchester (the latter with 50,000 signatures) were laid on the table of the House of Commons.[62] Inside the Cabinet, however, there was no sign of defeatism. So long as Napoleon remained paramount throughout Europe, England would have to settle for a peace that, in Canning's vivid words, 'would sanction and settle some dozen green and tottering usurpations, and leave Bonaparte to begin anew.' He argued that it might be in Napoleon's interest to strike a balance from time to time with his conquests, but that 'our interest is that *till* there can be a final settlement that shall last, everything should remain as unsettled as possible; that no usurper should feel sure of acknowledgment; no people confident in their new masters; no kingdom sure of its existence; no spoliator sure of his spoil; and even the plundered not acquiescent in their losses:'[63] One of the most effective criticisms of the Copenhagen expedition was that it had turned the Danes into bitter enemies. Canning boldly met this criticism head on and argued that since – let it be frankly acknowledged – we were hated throughout Europe, we could wage an all-out maritime war against France without worrying any more about whom we were going to upset in the process.

This defiant attitude was typical of those in authority. In the middle of November, the Austrian ambassador, Prince Starhemberg, inquired whether the government was ready to treat for peace. The King was outraged; he thought that the overture was as insulting to England as it was disgraceful to Austria, and he trusted that every Englishman's blood would boil when he heard of it.[64] Starhemberg had indeed made no attempt to disguise the fact that he was acting on peremptory instructions from Paris, not Vienna, and Canning felt he could go no further than give a formal assurance that Britain was ready to negotiate for peace 'on a basis of perfect equality'. But that was something

* Relations between Britain and the United States remained uneasy for the rest of Canning's term as Foreign Secretary, although William Pinckney, the American minister in London, acknowledged the 'candid and temperate behaviour' of both Canning and Perceval. During 1808, talks between Canning and Pinckney on the mutual withdrawal of trade restrictions made little progress; and next year, Canning had to disavow and recall Henry Erskine, the over-enthusiastic British minister in Washington, for flagrantly exceeding his instructions. (Gray, *Spencer Perceval* p. 451)

Starhemberg had no authority to offer. Instead, on New Year's Day, 1808, he demanded that plenipotentiaries should be immediately sent to Paris to treat for peace. Canning replied that he would not send anyone to a hostile capital but as soon as the bases of peace talks had been satisfactorily settled, he would send negotiators to an agreed meeting place. Napoleon did not pursue the matter any further and before the end of the month Austria, as well as Russia and Prussia, was formally at war with England.

It is not clear why Napoleon bothered to make this phoney peace offensive. At more or less the same time, he was sending his troops into Portugal, plotting a takeover in Madrid, planning an attack on the British in Sicily and urging his brother Louis, King of Holland, to attack British commerce. Possibly he had been misinformed about the morale of the British government. Or he may have wanted to convince his reluctant Austrian and Russian allies that the British were incurably bellicose.

If Napoleon convinced anyone of this, it was not Metternich, but Samuel Whitbread and the group of Whigs who thought like him. On February 29, Whitbread launched a blistering and immensely long attack on the government for failing to make use of Russian and Austrian good offices to explore the possibilities of ending the war.[65] Canning was the special object of his wrath. He sneered at the 'smartness and satire so conspicuous' in the Foreign Secretary's despatches and condemned his 'utter insufficiency to guide us through the dangers and difficulties which surround us in this crisis of our fate.' Canning and his colleagues were not impressed by Whitbread's sound and fury. Perceval laconically reported to the King that the debate was 'far from interesting' apart from the 'curious' circumstance that George Ponsonby, now the official leader of the Whigs in the Commons, had opposed one of the resolutions introduced by his fellow Whig.[66]

The opposition, in fact, was virtually leaderless and very much at odds. The much-feared disaster of Howick's elevation to the Lords had duly struck in November 1807 on the death of his father Lord Grey. Ponsonby, the new opposition leader in the Commons, was an unpopular compromise choice. A rather scruffy-looking Irish country gentleman, he was quite able, but completely lacked the art of managing men. Grey blamed Ponsonby's mismanagement rather than Whitbread's views for the opposition's gratuitous display of disunity on February 29. At the same time he and most of the prominent Whigs profoundly disapproved of Whitbread's intemperate opposition to the war, which they felt could only encourage the enemy. They were responsible enough to set their faces 'decidedly and strenuously'[67] against trying to take advantage of the demand for peace that had arisen among the impoverished northern cotton workers.

But that was as far as their sense of responsibility took them. In private they reviled and sneered at ministers, sometimes with an almost pathological extravagance. In public they mercilessly attacked them, not for waging war, but for the way they waged it. The Orders-in-Council were given a rough and stormy passage through the Commons and the Copenhagen expedition was repeatedly attacked with an exuberance of moral fervour and sympathy for poor little Denmark. But however much the Whigs might huff and puff, the fact remained that the government had successfully outsmarted Napoleon, and most M.P.s felt that it deserved their patriotic support for doing so.

The Whigs, aware of the shakiness of their position, did not at first attempt a direct vote of censure on the Copenhagen expedition. Instead, on February 3, 1808, Ponsonby tried to embarrass ministers by demanding the production of all the information sent by the British envoy at Copenhagen on the strength and preparedness of the Danish fleet.[68] Canning, in reply, spoke for nearly three hours, making a speech which Palmerston described as 'so powerful that it gave a decisive turn to the debate.'[69] Grey conceded that what he had heard of the speech was 'eloquent and powerful,' but added that he had never heard such 'audacious misrepresentation' and even 'positive falsehood'.[70] What angered Grey and the other Whigs was that Canning had quoted extracts from the despatches exchanged between Garlike and Grey, then Foreign Secretary, at the end of 1806. They claimed that the extracts were garbled and by being given out of context gave a false impression of both men's views. Unfortunately Hansard does not reveal whether this claim was justified. But the Whigs pushed it vigorously through debates on two similar motions introduced by Whitbread and Sheridan.[71] Like Ponsonby's original motion, both were heavily defeated. Eventually, on March 21, the opposition attempted a direct motion of censure on Copenhagen. It was roundly defeated by 224 votes to 64 after Canning had wound up the debate in a speech described as 'very witty, very eloquent and very able'.[72]

But support for the Copenhagen expedition did not necessarily imply approval of Canning's method of defending it. He was very conscious of the importance of not being drawn into revealing the source of his secret information about what took place at Tilsit, and his extreme caution on this point may have made him unnecessarily evasive on others. He stoutly denied that he had been guilty of any misrepresentation and insisted that the responsible minister must be the sole judge of what confidential information could be safely revealed.[73] He was convinced, he wrote to Portland on February 23, that 'the full and free discretionary use of official information is essential to the situation of a minister; and that any attempt to draw a line between different modes of exercising that discretion must be attended with as much mischief as difficulty.' And why, he added, cannot a minister give the source of his information and state the actual words rather than the substance of a document?[74] Logically, and in principle, there was no reason why he should not. But Canning had given the opposition a good stick to beat him with and his reputation of being too clever by half probably made it all the more effective. Moreover, there was no obvious reason why the Grey-Garlike exchanges should not be published in full, and on February 26[75] Canning did at last produce them in order, he said, to protect his personal reputation. It might have been better if he had done so sooner rather than later.*

But the government's worst troubles arose over domestic issues. On most of these ministers were either divided among themselves, or uncomfortably hard-pressed in Parliament, or both.

Irish and Roman Catholic questions were especially troublesome. The Cabinet was sharply divided between the *red-hot* Protestants' (as Arthur Wellesley called them[76]), led by Perceval and supported by the King, and moderates like Castlereagh and Canning who understood and accepted Wellesley's warning that if the French landed, the Irish would rebel. Perceval, who usually showed such moderation and good sense, could only see the intractable and explosive affairs of Ireland through an opaque haze of religious bigotry. When at the end of April some Irish M.P.s proposed an increase in the grant for Maynooth, the training college for Irish Roman Catholic priests, Perceval opposed them with such striking intolerance that the government's majority sank to 35. To make matters worse, when the opposition insisted on bringing up the Maynooth affair a second time, it transpired that Dr Duigenan, the Irish Advocate-General, who was notorious as the hottest of the red-hot Protestants, had just been made an Irish privy councillor; at the end of that debate, the government's majority sank to 24.

---

* Garlike claimed that excisions made in his despatches before they were published still misrepresented his views and he began an angry correspondence with Canning. But a comparison of the despatches as published in Hansard with the originals in the Public Record Office reveals only a very few cuts which cannot possibly be said to have the effect of misrepresenting Garlike's views.

GEORGE CANNING

Canning was conspicuous by his absence from both the Maynooth debates, and Castlereagh stayed away from the second. And when the opposition pressed their advantage by moving a vote of censure against Duigenan's appointment (which Windham described as a red flag held out to the Irish Catholics), it was left to Arthur Wellesley, who was Chief Secretary for Ireland,* to make the best of a bad job; not even a stream of humiliating taunts at their 'spell-bound' state could make any minister utter, although Whitbread claimed that he could easily tell from Canning's expression that he was just as impatient of his own silence as was the rest of the House.[77] The loss of the censure motion by 67 votes did not disguise the government's discomfiture. Next day Arthur Wellesley rather indignantly reported that the ministers, finding themselves in a 'confounded scrape', had decided that silence was the best way out of it.[78]

As far as Canning was concerned, that was certainly true. He strongly disapproved of Perceval's attitude towards Maynooth and he was dismayed by Duigenan's appointment of which he had had no previous knowledge. Taken together, the two events appeared to portray the government in a luridly anti-Catholic light. This, of course, was true of only part of it. For men like Canning and Castlereagh, who in principle were strongly in favour of Catholic emancipation, but believed that it was impracticable in the present state of public and royal opinion, the only tolerable course was to be as neutral and unprovocative as possible whenever the Whigs insisted – as they regularly did – on raising the issue. It was an inglorious and embarrassing line of conduct, and when Grattan presented a petition in favour of Catholic emancipation on May 25, it was generally agreed that the opposition had come best out of the debate, although the petition was rejected by the large majority of 153. Canning, whose speech was an extremely conciliatory plea for restraint, was described by Whitbread (with obvious satisfaction) as having made 'a most contemptible and miserable figure'.[79] Canning himself privately deplored the way in which the government had been put on the defensive by the Maynooth and Duigenan affairs which 'hung about our necks and weighed us down in the debate'.[80]

Canning may have exaggerated. But his implied reproach to his ultra-Protestant colleagues was an ominous reflection of the growing disunity inside the Cabinet. With an amiable invalid as prime minister,

* He had insisted on taking part in the Copenhagen expedition, but when it was over the Lord-Lieutenant of Ireland, the Duke of Richmond, insisted on having him back as Chief Secretary.

this was largely inevitable; there was no one to cope with the clashes of temperament and personality or reconcile the genuine differences of opinion. The opposition, of course, always made the most of every sign of disagreement they thought they could detect in the Cabinet. But Arthur Wellesley, who was not an alarmist, was convinced that 'unless the ministers draw better together, particularly on the subject of Ireland . . . they will not only be unable to hold their offices, but they will entirely ruin the King's affairs.'[81]

By the time Parliament rose for the recess, early in July, 1808, sheer exhaustion may have helped to fray the relations at any rate of those members of the government who sat in the Commons. It had been a particularly gruelling and acrimonious session, with debates going on night after night until five, six or even later the next morning. Everyone, according to Tierney, was sincerely thankful when it was over. The members on both sides, he wrote, 'seem to be tired of one another, and the public tired of us all. Never was there within the same space of time so much debating and so little interest excited.'[82]

No one can have been more thankful when the session ended than the ministers themselves, especially those with heavy administrative responsibilities. When ten or twelve hours of each day were spent in the House, there was not much time for everything else, even if sleep was given a low priority. The main burden of the parliamentary warfare fell on Perceval as leader of the House. But Castlereagh and Canning had the main administrative responsibility for carrying on the struggle against Napoleon.*

During the first half of 1808, this was a depressing and frustrating task. In the New Year, French troops, allegedly on their way to Portugal, spread out over more and more of northern Spain. In March Murat entered Madrid. Almost at the same time, Charles IV, terrified by the popular fury against his favourite, Godoy, abdicated in favour of his son, Ferdinand. In April, Napoleon summoned Charles, his queen and the new king, Ferdinand VII, to Bayonne, bullied them into surrendering all their royal rights and promoted his brother, Joseph, from the throne of Naples to that of Spain. The Cabinet in London became seriously worried lest Napoleon's next step should be to extend his control indirectly over the Spanish colonies in South America, and

* When Canning escaped to Hinckley for a few days during the Easter recess, he told the King that he had not had a chance to see his family since the previous November. (*Later Corresp. of George III*, V, p. 66, April 19, 1808)

Castlereagh busied himself with plans, and even actual preparations, for military expeditions to various parts of South America. Fortunately, none of these rather doubtful expeditions actually got under way. Only one military expedition was launched at this time. It went to Sweden and it was a disastrous failure.

Gustavus IV of Sweden was mentally unbalanced, eccentric and extremely difficult to deal with. He made extortionate demands for money but gave poor value (so it seemed in London) for what he got. On the other hand, he was Britain's only remaining ally on the continent of Europe, and although he felt he had been left in the lurch by Cathcart's removal from Stralsund to Copenhagen, he remained stoutly, almost embarrassingly, loyal. Towards the end of 1807, the Russians sent him repeated warnings that if he wanted to keep Finland, he had better join forces with them to exclude the British from the Baltic. Gustavus turned a deaf ear and instead applied to his British allies for more subsidies. Early in February 1808, Edward Thornton, the British envoy in Stockholm, signed a new subsidy treaty. Less than a fortnight later, Russian troops crossed the Finnish border, and shortly afterwards, Denmark too declared war on Sweden.

From this point on, Canning and Castlereagh were gradually pushed into an enterprise of whose aims and end they had only the foggiest notion. Canning realised that it would be much better for everyone if Gustavus made what terms he could with the Russians. But if he insisted on taking them on, then prudence and common sense must give way to the imperative obligation to help an ally with his back to the wall. Eventually, on April 17, alarmed by reports of the rapid Russian advance into Finland, the Cabinet reluctantly decided to send 10,000 troops to Gothenburg under the command of Sir John Moore.[83] Canning made it quite clear, both to Thornton and to Count Adlerberg, the Swedish envoy in London, that the British force was only to be used for limited defensive operations along the coast, where it could keep in touch with the fleet, and that the government reserved the right to withdraw it if it were needed elsewhere. A few days after Adlerberg had agreed to these terms, he received despatches from Stockholm in which Gustavus emphasised that the only use he had for British troops was to help him capture Zealand from the Danes. Determined not to risk delaying, or even stopping, the departure of Moore's expedition, the envoy decided to say nothing of this to Canning.[84]

Moore was given no precise instructions about his mission. He was to defer as much as possible to the wishes of the King of Sweden without actually putting himself under his command; and he was to

Promis'd Horrors of the French INVASION. — or — Forcible Reasons for negociating a Regicide PEACE. Vide. The Authority of Edmund Burke.

PROMISED HORRORS OF THE FRENCH INVASION, OR FORCIBLE REASONS FOR NEGOCIATING A REGICIDE PEACE.
Vide. The Authority of Edmund Burke

Canning's first public appearance in a cartoon. He and his friend Jenkinson are hanging from a lamp-post outside White's

[Gillray, October 1796]

CASTLEREAGH AND CANNING (OPPOSITE)
Both portraits painted by Sir Thomas Lawrence

BRITISH TARS TOWING THE DANISH FLEET INTO HARBOUR

Canning holds the tow-ropes of the Danish fleet while Castlereagh and Hawkesbury wear the *Billy Pitt*

decide for himself what exactly he should do with his 10,000 men. Three days after his arrival off Gothenburg on May 17, he wrote in his diary that he did not see any useful way in which he could employ such a small force limited to operations along the coast.[85] Indeed he did not see how the Swedes, with or without British help, could be saved from their encircling foes unless they made a much greater effort. Finland was by now lost beyond hope of recovery; a Swedish spring offensive in Norway was getting nowhere; and Zealand was so strongly defended that Moore was convinced it would be folly to try to take it. Gustavus, for his part, objected strongly to the limitations he found had been placed on the use of the British force and for once expressed his objections so lucidly and reasonably that Moore felt obliged to send the King's letter back to London with a request for further instructions. Castlereagh's reply was painstaking, but of little use; it was, commented Moore tartly, 'upon the whole sufficiently inexplicit and contradictory'.[86]

By this time it was nearly the middle of June and the British troops, refused (contrary to Adlerberg's assurances) permission to land, remained cooped up in their transports. Moore decided to go to Stockholm himself to try to reach an understanding with Gustavus. When he protested at the King's refusal to allow his troops to land, Gustavus replied that he had no use for them in Sweden, had never asked for them and would never allow them in.[87] Eventually, Moore declared that he had no alternative but to obey the orders he had received from London to withdraw his troops altogether if they were not allowed to land. Gustavus thereupon placed him under open arrest. Moore escaped disguised as a peasant, rejoined the fleet at Gothenburg and on July 3 he and his luckless expeditionary force began the return voyage to England.

A fiasco tends to cause more bad feeling than a defeat, and the abortive expedition to Sweden was no exception. It is very difficult to blame Moore, who behaved like a sensible and realistic soldier with impossibly difficult orders. But neither is it easy to blame the ministers in London. It would have been extremely difficult for them to ignore the plight of the King of Sweden. They tried to limit the risks by carefully defining the conditions on which the troops could be used. They tried to guard against their own ignorance of a very fluid military situation by leaving a great deal to Moore's judgment. Even Arthur Wellesley thought they could do nothing else and told Castlereagh that he could safely confide in Moore's discretion. Unfortunately, however, to enthusiastic but ill-informed ministers in London, Moore's realism looked all too much like defeatism; and instead of assuming that he had done his best, they seem to have indulged in a vague feeling that he had let them down. In fact it was the instability and unpredictability of the Swedish king that had let them down. There was also a failure in communication between the two governments over the limited uses to which the British force could be put which added to Moore's difficulties with Gustavus; and for this the two diplomats, Adlerberg and Thornton, must have been largely responsible. In the normal course of events there would probably have been an inquiry into the whole affair. But by the time Moore and his men arrived back in England, Sweden had come to seem an insignificant sideshow by comparison with the stirring events at the other end of Europe.

CHAPTER X

False Dawn in the Peninsula
1808-1809

On June 8, 1808, two emissaries from Spain arrived in London. They came from Asturias, the small and rather remote northern province, which had been the first to rise in revolt after the French had brutally put down a popular rising in Madrid. They had left their provincial capital, Oviedo, on May 26, embarked at Gijon in an open boat, been picked up by a British privateer and landed at Falmouth.[1] Within a few weeks, they were followed by deputies from Galicia and Andalusia. They vied with each other in the size of their requests for money and munitions; and neither they nor their English hosts thought it at all odd that they should have turned for help to a country with which they were supposed to be at war.

The English, in fact, gave themselves up to an orgy of wild enthusiasm for the Spaniards and their cause. The Spanish deputies were wined and dined by Cabinet ministers and City dignitaries; they were fêted and lionised by fashionable society, Whig as well as Tory. 'Every head and heart,' wrote Wilberforce, 'are full of schemes and sympathies for the poor Spaniards.'[2] Some of the arms captured from the Spanish armada more than 200 years earlier were taken out of the Tower and shipped off to Spain. Some people even wanted to volunteer to fight there, including Lord Louvaine who, as Auckland disapprovingly pointed out, was 'a Lord of the Treasury, not a military man, with three children, and Lady Louvaine in an increasing way.'[3]* Cobbett, in his *Political Register*, declared: 'This is the *only* fair opportunity that has offered for checking the progress of Napoleon.'[4] Other journalistic comment was not so restrained. If the Spanish patriots maintained their independence, announced the *Edinburgh Review*, they would have struck a blow for liberty throughout the world, 'and who shall then ever presume to cry down popular rights, or to tell us that the people have nothing to do with the laws but to obey them – with the taxes, but to pay them – and with the blunders of their rulers, but to suffer them.'[5] Even the officials in the Ordnance Department became infected by the

---

* Actually, in the Portland Ministry Louvaine was a Commissioner of the Board of Control.

general euphoria, and Canning rather stuffily took it upon himself to suggest to Chatham that to list supplies as for the 'Patriots of Spain' was 'too like the *Morning Chronicle* for the sobriety of official correspondence,' and that 'Spaniards' or 'Spanish nation' would be more appropriate.[6]

But Canning was really just as excited as everyone else. Although he had no sympathy with the views of the *Edinburgh Review*, a popular rising had much to recommend it. What with the half-mad King of Sweden, the vacillating Prince Regent of Portugal, the obstreperous Queen of Sicily and the obstinate Prince Royal of Denmark, the crowned heads of Europe and their royal relations had proved an uncommonly difficult set of people to rescue from French domination. The Spaniards, like everyone else, may have assumed that the British were universal and inexhaustible providers of hard cash; but at least they seemed anxious to fight and die for their own cause. Throughout the length and breadth of Spain they sprang to arms by what looked like a sort of process of spontaneous combustion. It was hardly surprising that men like Canning and Castlereagh, desperately worried by their failure to gain even a toehold on the Continent, and almost completely ignorant of conditions inside Spain, should have greeted the Spanish revolt with over-optimistic enthusiasm.

On June 15, Sheridan, by agreement with Canning, raised the question of aid for Spain in the Commons. He had meant to make a speech that would 'electrify the country', but unfortunately got so drunk first that when he spoke, he was (according to Wilberforce) 'like a man catching through a thick medium at the objects before him'.[7] However, it was not a bad effort, even for a sober man. He pleaded that the British should now make up their minds to stand up for the salvation of Europe and not rest content with 'filching sugar islands'. And he pointed out that hitherto 'Bonaparte has had to contend against princes without dignity and ministers without wisdom. He has fought against countries in which the people have been indifferent to his success; he has yet to learn what it is to fight against a country in which the people are animated with one spirit to resist him.'[8] Canning came straight to the Commons from a dinner for the Asturian delegates in his own house where he had had to leave Sir Arthur Wellesley to stand in for him as host. He assured the House that the government was anxious to give all practical aid to the Spaniards and would not be put off by the nominal state of war existing between the two countries. 'We shall proceed,' he declared, 'upon the principle, that any nation of Europe that starts up with a determination to oppose a Power which, whether professing insidious peace, or declaring open war, is the common enemy of all nations . . . becomes instantly our essential ally.'[9]

In other words, England would always help those who tried to help themselves. Canning willingly made himself available to the Spanish deputies in London, and equally willingly passed on their demands to his colleagues. The Asturian and Galician deputies, he wrote to Castlereagh on August 5, had been to see him that day and were loudly crying out for artillery and cavalry. What could be done to help them? Could Castlereagh let him know his views before the next Cabinet meeting?[10] Both Canning and Castlereagh nagged at Chatham to get things moving in the Ordnance Department. Apparently their efforts were not without success, for by November Chatham was able to report that at least 160,000 muskets had already been sent, and 30,000 to 40,000 more would follow within a month. But with the best will in the world, the government could not meet all the Spaniards' demands for money, although what could be spared was sent without delay. By early July, Charles Stuart was on his way to Corunna with £200,000 in Spanish dollars for the Galician junta. By the end of the summer, more than £1,000,000 in silver had been sent to the five main juntas and more was promised as soon as a supreme junta for the whole of Spain had been formed.[11]

For Canning was not so far gone in his enthusiasm for the Spanish cause that he did not realise the vital importance of getting the Galicians, Asturians, Andalusians and the rest to pool their efforts. The fiercely independent provincialism of the Spaniards had been invaluable in getting the revolt started because each provincial centre was quite ready to act on its own initiative. But when it came to the long haul against Napoleon's huge armies, a united, central direction was obviously essential. Canning urged Stuart again and again to do all he could to promote unity.* He himself tackled the Spanish deputies in London. But local jealousies, fears and ambitions made it a slow and disillusioning task.

Nor did it prove easy to help the Spaniards in the most effective way of all – with trained British troops. By the early summer of 1808 the improved method of recruiting introduced by Castlereagh had already begun to bear fruit, and with the fading away of Napoleon's invasion threat it was no longer necessary to keep such a large force in England. Encouraged by the Venezuelan patriot, General Miranda, Castlereagh

---

* There were also two British Consuls subordinate to Stuart; Hunter at Gijon and Duff at Cadiz.

was assembling a force of 9,000 men at Cork for service in South America. But within a few days of learning about the revolt in Madrid at the beginning of May, the Cabinet had decided to send this force to Spain itself, and early in June appointed Sir Arthur Wellesley to command it. The Asturian deputies, however, declared that they could throw the French out themselves and all they wanted from the English was money and arms. They insisted that it would be much better if all the available British troops were sent to Portugal, where they could stir the Portuguese into revolt and prevent Junot from marching on the rear of their own army in Galicia.

Early in June the Portuguese rose of their own accord. The revolt began in Oporto and before the end of the month had spread throughout the whole country. It was now clear where the force assembled at Cork should go and on July 12 Wellesley set sail for Corunna, on his way to the Tagus where he expected to be reinforced by some 5,000 men under General Spencer, who had been afloat off southern Spain for most of the past two months. Three days after Wellesley left Cork, Castlereagh wrote to tell him that he was to be reinforced by a further 15,000 men, including Moore and his troops who had just got back from Sweden; and this combined force of some 30,000 men was to be put under the supreme command of the Governor of Gibraltar, Sir Hew Dalrymple (who had only once seen active service some fifteen years earlier) with Sir Harry Burrard (a friend of the Duke of York) as his second-in-command. Wellesley received the news of his supersession at Mondego Bay, a hundred miles north of Lisbon, on July 30. Fortunately Castlereagh did not tell him to mark time until his new superiors caught up with him.

The reasons behind the appointments of Dalrymple and Burrard will always be a matter of controversy. Castlereagh had a strong preference for Wellesley; he knew him, thought very highly of him, and frequently consulted him on military matters. Moore was equally able, but he had made himself unpopular with the Cabinet by his undisguised disapproval of its plans both in Sicily* and in Sweden. On the other hand, neither Dalrymple nor Burrard had anything except their seniority to justify placing them over either Moore or Wellesley, both of whom were indisputably more able and experienced. Seniority, however, counted for a great deal with the Commander-in-Chief, the

---

* Moore had been deputy to General Fox, the British commander in Sicily, in 1807 when Maria-Carolina, the Queen of Sicily, was agitating for an attempt to recapture Naples. The British government agreed, but both Fox and Moore thought the operation was not feasible and stalled on their instructions.

Duke of York, and after Wellesley's original force had been just about doubled, he strongly opposed allowing so junior a general to remain in command.

What is not clear is whether the duke insisted on Dalrymple (rather than Moore, who was eight years older than Wellesley) or whether Castlereagh put him in because he thought that was the best way of bringing Wellesley forward. It may be significant that he made Dalrymple's appointment temporary and annoyed him by unmistakably indicating that he was to make the greatest possible use of Wellesley. Moore, for his part, was convinced that Dalrymple's appointment had been deliberately engineered by his enemies in the Cabinet and he complained bitterly to Castlereagh about his 'unhandsome treatment.' This outburst must have helped to confirm his reputation (however unfair) of being a difficult and 'violent' man to deal with. Castlereagh, indeed, was so incensed that he told the King about the quarrel and wrote Moore a letter which he apparently hoped would provoke him into resigning.

What part Canning played in all this is obscure. It has been alleged since – but not apparently by Moore at the time – that he was really the prime mover in the anti-Moore movement in the Cabinet.[12] Apart from the fact that Moore had undoubtedly put his back up, this seems to rest on nothing firmer than the assumption that Canning was less of a gentleman and more capable of skulduggery than was Castlereagh. But in any case if Castlereagh and Canning were able to choose between two more or less equally able generals, it was not discreditable in them to prefer the one they felt they could work with best. But if they could not have Wellesley, it was very misguided to pass over Moore and settle, whether deliberately or under pressure from the Horse Guards, for two elderly second-rate men. Those responsible did not have to wait long to find this out.

On August 21, Wellesley, who had landed at Mondego Bay and was making his way steadily south towards Lisbon, was attacked by Marshal Junot at Vimeiro. The French army was soundly defeated, but Burrard, who had caught up Wellesley by sea the day before, would not allow him to pursue the French and turn their defeat into a rout. Early next day, Dalrymple also turned up; he rejected Wellesley's proposals for an immediate advance and a few hours later agreed to a French request for an armistice. In the circumstances it was the best thing to do and Wellesley himself advised it. Since the opportunity to go after the French when they were on the run had been thrown away, it was sensible to try to get them out of Portugal without further bloodshed.

But as a negotiator Dalrymple was no match for the French General Kellerman and in the agreement which became known as the Convention of Cintra* he conceded far more than he need have done to the defeated French. All the French troops were to be carried back to the west coast of France in English ships; they were free to re-enter the war immediately;† and under article 5 they could take away with them not only all their arms and equipment, but also their 'private property' which included huge quantities of valuables looted from the Portuguese. There were also two political articles, protecting French subjects living in Portugal and Portuguese who had gone over to the French, which should never have been included in a military convention without previous consultation with the Portuguese government.‡

The news of Wellesley's victory at Vimeiro arrived in London late on September 1. By a happy coincidence, it was brought to Canning's house while he was entertaining the Duke of Portland and the Spanish deputies to dinner. 'Our claret,' wrote Canning's secretary pompously, 'was the better flavoured by this intelligence.'[13]

It was an exciting climax to several weeks of exhilarating news from the Peninsula. The French general, Dupont, had capitulated at Baylen, with nearly 18,000 men; Wellesley had landed at Mondego Bay; Joseph Bonaparte had retreated from Madrid eleven days after taking possession of his new capital; the people of Saragossa had successfully repulsed a besieging French army. Popular excitement in England steadily mounted, and the government basked in the reflected glory of the Spanish people's exploits. A Radical meeting at the Mermaid tavern, Hackney, even passed a vote of thanks to the King and his Tory ministers for helping Spain to show how Europe could be rescued from despotism.[14] When the good news of Vimeiro arrived, it was

* The armistice signed on August 22 was then transformed into a convention which became known as the Convention of Cintra because Sir Hew's despatch announcing it was dated from that place.

† Wordsworth thought this was an 'absurdity' as 'glaring' as if a captured French force invading England had been taken from Yorkshire and set ashore in Sussex (*The Convention of Cintra*, Ed. R. J. White, p. 142)

‡ Junot, however, did not manage to secure the release of the Russian fleet, which had been blockaded in the Tagus for nearly a year. Under a separate agreement between Admiral Cotton and Admiral Siniavin, the Russian ships were surrendered 'in deposit' until six months after the conclusion of peace between Russia and England, while their officers and crews were at once transported back to Russia.

spread far and wide by garlanded mail coaches. *The Times*, with starry-eyed optimism, opined that the 'immense mass of most gratifying intelligence brought from all parts of Spain', in addition to Wellesley's victory, encouraged the strongest hopes 'not only of the liberation of Spain itself, which may indeed be considered as in a great degree effected, but of the final dissolution of the Continental tyranny and the overthrow of the Tyrant.'[15] Cobbett was almost equally optimistic. He praised the government for its foresight and vigour and concluded that Vimeiro was far more important than Trafalgar because it had at last removed the fear that French troops were invincible.[16]

But on September 4, nearly a week before Cobbett penned these gratifying remarks, the Portuguese envoy in London, M. de Souza, appeared at the Foreign Office and indignantly showed Canning a letter he had received from the Bishop of Oporto denouncing the original armistice concluded on August 22. An appalled Canning at once sent the news to the King, who said he could hardly bring himself to believe it.[17] Nor could anyone else. Portland begged Castlereagh to relieve him as soon as possible 'from this cruel distress, and to solve this incomprehensible enigma.'[18] Castlereagh sent an almost incoherently angry letter to his half-brother, General Charles Stewart (who was with Dalrymple), at the end of which he flatly declared: 'In short, it is a base forgery somewhere, and nothing can induce me to believe it genuine.'[19]

For eleven days, owing to Dalrymple's extraordinary dilatoriness in reporting what he had done, the ministers were able to hush up de Souza's allegations and cherish their illusions. On September 8, Canning felt sufficiently at ease to set off for a holiday with his family at Hinckley. But on the 15th Dalrymple's despatches arrived. Next day the terms of the Convention of Cintra were published in an extraordinary *Gazette*. The over-inflated bubble of popular expectation suddenly burst and the disappointment was as overwhelming as the previous optimism had been exaggerated. Church bells were tolled. Some newspapers appeared with the report of the convention outlined in black. On the 19th *The Times* burst forth in its best denunciatory vein: 'A curse, a deep curse, wring the heart and wither the hand that were base enough to devise and execute this cruel injury to their country's peace and honour.' And three days later the *Courier* witheringly remarked that while it was not uncommon for a vanquished army to be seized with panic, 'here the panic seems to have seized the *victorious* after the victory.' Wordsworth tramped many miles to address a public protest meeting and later wrote a turgidly eloquent pamphlet against the convention. The wags declared that humiliation must now be spelled 'hewmiliation'. Spencer Perceval's sister-in-law, Lady Arden, thought it almost looked as if none of the generals understood French. 'If it rests with you Spencer,' she added, 'another time do order these generals to draw up their treaties in English. It may prevent another such disaster.'[20] The generals, indeed, including Wellesley, became the most unpopular men in the country. And the ministers who had appointed them were as indignant as everyone else. But, unlike everyone else, they had to consider very carefully how much they could give way to their feelings. It was to prove a thorny and divisive problem.

At Hinckley the first news of Cintra was brought by the guard of the mail coach on Friday, September 16. But his version was so garbled that the good people of Hinckley drew the most optimistic conclusions and began to ring the church bells and rejoice in the streets. Two hours later, a letter from Perceval, brought by special messenger, told Canning the truth. He poured out his anger and disappointment in a stream of letters to his colleagues. To Chatham he described the convention as 'both disgraceful and disastrous in the highest degree.'[21] To Bathurst, he wrote that parts of it were 'so utterly, manifestly, shamefully unjust, that I hope and believe the Portuguese people will rise against it.'[22] He was most incensed by the article allowing the French to remove their 'property'. 'It makes one sick with shame to think of it,' he wrote to Perceval. What property, he asked, could the French have but plunder? And would not this article, if carried out, put the British government in the wrong with the Portuguese? Moreover, since we were pledged to protect Portuguese collaborators, any traitor could buy looted plate from a French soldier before the rightful owner's eyes, 'and the traitor's sideboard will display it ever after with the British army as the guarantee of the transaction! And we went there as allies!'[23] To Castlereagh Canning wrote that he would rather break the whole agreement than let the French carry off their plunder. He insisted that the government must make clear its attitude to the convention, for throughout this 'new and dreadful war' it was going to stand 'as a sort of landmark for the guidance of future commanders, a terror to our allies, and an encouragement to our enemies.'[24]

Under the spur of disappointment and indignation, Canning's quick mind raced ahead to conclusions that were sometimes more devastatingly logical than strictly realistic. But his colleagues were impressed by his vehemence. Originally they had decided to accept the *fait accompli*, while strongly insisting that Dalrymple must somehow prevent the French from making off with loot disguised as private property. A despatch to that effect was actually sent off. Next day, however, Castlereagh seems to have realised that Canning would not like it and, moreover, would be furious that it had gone without his approval. So he went round to the Admiralty and got Mulgrave to telegraph to Plymouth to stop the messenger. The same evening Castlereagh told Perceval that he had held back his despatch because he felt 'a good understanding among ourselves' was more important than a few hours' delay. 'I am sure that I do not wonder,' he wrote, 'that Canning, in his turn, should have the hot as well as the cold fit of this desperate ague which has visited us all so lamentably; but I quite agree with you that we ought to deal with the past, now that it is irrevocable, only as it bears upon our future means of rendering service . . . I quite agree with you that we can only justify ourselves to Spain by *increased* and *accelerated* exertion . . .'[25]

Unfortunately Canning was incapable of adopting such a cool and sensible attitude. He thought that the despatch finally sent to Dalrymple after his return to London, although stiffer than the original one, was still far too mild. He simply could not understand why generals should be treated any different from diplomats. Is it to be understood, he asked, that although the King can disavow an accredited envoy, 'he cannot undo a convention, however ruinous and discreditable, if signed by a man who has a sword by his side?'[26] Why, he fulminated in another letter, should a 'pen in an armed hand' be held so much more sacred than a minister's?[27]

But if the government could not undo the generals' work, at least, argued Canning, it must proclaim its strong disapproval of it. The Cabinet agreed without much difficulty that Dalrymple should be immediately recalled. The trouble arose over Wellesley, who in Canning's (and Chatham's) eyes was equally guilty. It was, after all, Wellesley who, at Dalrymple's request, had put his name to the original armistice, although he had not negotiated it nor even read through the final draft. He had signed, partly because he was in favour of an armistice, partly because his commanding officer told him to and partly, it seems, because he did not want to make trouble. It was not a very clever thing to have done, as he himself realised afterwards.[28]*

---

* Lord Auckland commented: 'It will not, however, be easy to persuade even the weakest and most credulous minds, that either the articles of war, or the principles of military subordination require an officer to sign a convention dictated by a beaten enemy *because* his superior officer orders him to sign it . . .'
'Auckland to Grenville, September 29.
Dropmore IX, p. 220'

To Canning, it was both incomprehensible and unforgivable. He had not the slightest idea how the military mind worked.* Moreover he himself would never have dreamed of taking the line of least resistance about anything. He had nothing against Wellesley personally – indeed had supported Castlereagh's efforts to bring him forward. But Wellesley's exceptional part in the overthrow of Napoleon still lay in the future. In the autumn of 1808, he was a young general with a brilliant Indian record and a growing reputation as a political manager in Dublin. He had just won a famous victory in Portugal and then (so it seemed) thrown it all away in a convention whose baleful consequences, Canning believed, would seriously threaten the Spaniards' military effort and redound to Britain's political discredit throughout Europe.

In fact, Canning was wrong to make Wellesley any more than nominally responsible for the convention; and although it did indeed infuriate the Portuguese and the Spaniards, he was mistaken in foreseeing such very dire political consequences. Castlereagh, on the other hand, was right in his hunch that in Wellesley lay the best hope of winning the Spanish war and that at all costs his reputation and his career must be protected.[29] Wellesley, however, did not have public opinion or the Press on his side. He was an easy target, not only because he had signed the armistice but also because he was a politician and came from an influential family who it was assumed would try to shield him. And scattered among the attacks on Wellesley were broad hints that the ministers who had appointed him, in particular the Secretary for War, should bear their share of the blame.

Castlereagh, much to his credit, stuck to his guns, and a majority of the Cabinet supported him. By September 26 they had agreed that Dalrymple alone should be made responsible for the convention and that if public opinion forced an inquiry, Wellesley should somehow be protected. Canning carried his opposition to the convention to the point of sending the King a long memorandum on his reasons for disagreeing with his colleagues; he did not suggest that the French troops should not be transported back to France, but he argued that the King should repudiate those provisions which were unjust to the Portuguese and not within the competence of a military commander.[30]

By the end of October, the Cabinet decided it could not avoid a

* Wellesley pointed out, in the debate on Cintra in the Commons on February 21, 1809, that whereas if a civilian materially differed from his superior, he ought to resign, it was the duty of a military officer to obey his commander. (Parly. Debs. XII, 936)

court of inquiry. The court's report, published on December 22, concluded that there was no need to take any further proceedings against the three generals. But in arriving at this conclusion it resorted to so much beating about the bush that the government asked the seven members of the court to give a definite opinion on the armistice of August 22 and the subsequent convention. The armistice was approved by six to one, but only four votes were given for the terms of the controversial convention. Wellesley, whose defence of himself before the court was completely convincing, came well out of the inquiry. Dalrymple, on the other hand, received a rebuke for accepting the political articles of the convention. Neither he nor Burrard was ever employed on active service again.

When the opposition attacked the convention the following February, Canning, who wound up the debate, somehow managed to combine a clear restatement of his own reservations about the convention with general support for his colleagues and the generals.[31] Perhaps it was his manner which led an admittedly hostile witness to describe his speech as 'a reproof both to ministers and generals.'[32] It was indeed becoming increasingly clear that the malicious Whig gossip about dissensions in the Cabinet was well-founded. During the summer of 1808 Canning and Castlereagh had disagreed with Perceval over Irish and Catholic policy. By the end of the year Canning was disagreeing with Castlereagh over matters closely affecting his own department. If he had been a cooler and more detached person, he would have realised that he was making too much of a fuss. But his emotional involvement in what he was doing was complete.* He was goaded by intense disappointment at the outcome of the Portuguese expedition, and (probably) by nagging frustration at having to play second fiddle to Perceval in the House of Commons. If the war had taken a turn for the better, all might have been smoothed out. But the year ahead was to bring only tragedy and disappointment.

At the end of 1808, however, the British government and the British people were still buoyed up by ill-founded expectations of what could be achieved in Spain. By the end of the previous August the Spanish armies had pushed the French back across the Ebro. Misled by the

---

* In a letter to Portland on October 19, 1808, he described his struggles to draft a despatch to Frere in Spain which would not offend either his own or his colleagues ' ideas and feelings; he had struggled with himself night and day before he could bring himself to sign the draft he had sent Portland. (Harewood, 32)

over-enthusiastic reports of Castlereagh's military agents in Spain as well as by the extravagant over-confidence of the Spaniards themselves, the ministers in London cherished the hope that the French could be pushed back across the Pyrenees before Napoleon could come to their rescue with his Grand Army. They decided to give the Spaniards what help they could as promptly as possible. By the beginning of September a force of 14,000 infantry under the command of Sir David Baird was ready to be sent to Corunna. Within a week of hearing the news of Cintra, the Cabinet decided that this force plus a large part of the British troops in Portugal should be put under the command of Sir John Moore with orders to link up in northern Spain and co-operate with the Spaniards in expelling the French from their country. Whatever the ministers' reservations about Moore – and Canning still had plenty – they had to turn to him now. On October 6, news of his new command was brought to him at Lisbon, where for some five weeks he had been the depressed spectator of Dalrymple's and Burrard's incompetent efforts to run the army.

Two weeks later, messengers from Napoleon and the Tsar arrived in London with an offer of peace talks. At the end of September Napoleon had summoned Alexander and various lesser royalties to a carefully stage-managed conference at Erfurt. Aware of a growing restlessness at Vienna and among the peoples of Germany, he had decided to make quite sure that the Tsar would loyally guard his rear before he set out to deal with the Spaniards. The proposal for peace talks was full of high-minded sentiments. The King, however, thought it 'insidious' and 'probably only intended to produce paragraphs in the *Moniteur*.'[33] His ministers agreed with him and decided to take the line that although they were certainly ready to negotiate for a general peace, it must be clearly understood first that England's allies included Spain, as well as Sweden, Sicily and Portugal. Napoleon was furious at the 'insolent' tone, no less than the content, of Canning's answer* and replied with a flat refusal to admit the Spanish 'insurgents' to the negotiations. Canning's final riposte, dated December 9, declared indignantly that his government could not agree to Spain's exclusion 'without acquiescing in an usurpation which has no parallel in the history of the world.'[34]

While this propaganda battle was being waged, Napoleon was hurrying down from France to crush the Spanish 'insurgents' and Sir

* The Note included a sarcastic reference to the failure of Napoleon's Continental System. In the separate reply to the Tsar, however, Canning contented himself with a touch of polite irony.

John Moore was marching up into Spain from Lisbon to aid them. By the time Moore arrived at Salamanca in the middle of November, Napoleon had taken over command of his heavily reinforced armies in northern Spain and the Spanish forces were rapidly melting away under his hammer blows. Moore was met with despairing reports of Spanish defeats and importunate appeals from the Supreme Junta and the British envoy, John Hookham Frere, to stop the rot. He was obliged to wait while Baird's force and his own artillery under General Hope caught up with him, and while he waited he tried to decide where his duty lay. Was it to go forward and risk his comparatively small army in a desperate effort to rouse and rally the Spaniards? Or was it to put the safety of his army first and retire back into Portugal? On November 28 he wrote in his diary: 'We had no business here as things are, but, being here, it would never do to abandon the Spaniards without a struggle.'[35]

That night, however, Moore learnt that the last of the Spanish armies had been decisively defeated at Tudela. He immediately decided that he must retreat into Portugal and send Baird back to Corunna. A week later, he countermanded the order to retreat after hearing that the people of Madrid had risen against Napoleon. Perhaps the example of Madrid would spread and something could be done after all. He was not strong enough to relieve the capital, but Hope and the artillery had now reached him and if he could join up with Baird and strike eastwards at the French lines of communication he might force Napoleon to break off his southward drive and turn back to protect his lifeline; southern Spain would at any rate get a respite.

A few days later Moore heard that Madrid had capitulated after all. But he did not change his mind again, and while marching northward to link up with Baird, he learned from captured despatches that Soult, unaware how close the British were, was about to make a westward swing into the province of Leon. Moore realised that this was his chance to win a morale-raising victory. He hurried forward and on December 20 at last linked up with Sir David Baird. Next day British cavalry, under Lord Paget, routed some of Soult's cavalry at Sahagun. The attack on Soult's main position at Saldana was planned for Christmas Day. On the 23rd, Moore reported to Frere that the movement he was about to make was 'of the most dangerous kind.' But, he added, 'I wish it to be apparent to the whole world . . . that we have done everything in our power in support of the Spanish cause . . .'[36]

That same evening Moore heard that Napoleon, having discovered that the British were not, as he had thought, retreating into Portugal, had turned round, recrossed the Guadarramas and was hot on his trail. Aware that he had already 'risked infinitely too much,' Moore again felt that he had no choice but to retreat, this time to Corunna.[37] It was a retreat of horrifying hardship, through barren and desolate country, in the depths of winter, with little food and less shelter; discipline and morale disintegrated; about 5,000 were killed or captured. On January 11, 1809, the remains of Moore's army limped into Corunna. Three days later the transports that were to take them home sailed into the harbour. Moore indignantly rejected the suggestion of some of his officers that he should ask Soult for a negotiated evacuation. Soon after midday on the 16th, just as the troops were about to embark, the French attacked. They were thrown back in disorder, but Moore himself was fatally wounded. When he was buried on the ramparts above Corunna early the following morning, his army, packed into the transports in the harbour below, was ready to sail for home.

Before he died, Moore had the satisfaction of knowing that his army had redeemed its humiliating retreat by a decisive victory. He also knew that his brief campaign in Spain had not been pointless. He had prevented Napoleon from fulfilling his boast to plant his eagles on the ramparts of Lisbon and had forced him to postpone his grandiose plans to mop up southern Spain and push on across the straits of Gibraltar into North Africa. As he lay dying, he whispered the hope that the people of England would be satisfied and would do him justice.[38]

Unfortunately, a great many did not. The rejoicing over the British victories at Sahagun and Corunna was swamped in shocked dismay at the appearance of the haggard, ragged, wounded soldiers who were landed at most of the ports on the south coast from Falmouth round to Dover. The British were not accustomed to such a close confrontation with the brutalities of war. Moreover, apart from the suffering of the troops, what was most obviously apparent at the time was not the disruption that Moore had caused to Napoleon's plans, but the fact that the British army had been chased ignominiously into the sea. To most people, it seemed an unmitigated disaster, the brutal pricking of all the extravagant hopes that had been created by the Spanish people's revolt. No one could tell at that time that Spain was to prove the ulcer that would gradually drain away Napoleon's strength and ultimately destroy him.

Every disaster must have its scapegoat, and Moore's heroic death did not spare him from being cast in that role. His long delay at Salamanca, his apparent indecisiveness, his precipitate retreat to Corunna which caused such suffering to his troops – all encouraged the arm-chair generals in the press and elsewhere to point the finger of blame at him. For obvious reasons, the Whigs preferred to blame the ministers and on February 24, Ponsonby demanded an inquiry into the course and conduct of the campaign in Spain. His speech, strewed with inaccuracies and contradictory advice, showed little grasp of military realities in Spain, and neither he nor his colleagues seem to have mounted such an effective attack on the government as they had three days earlier when debating the Cintra Convention. Castlereagh gave a solid and sensible exposition of the course of the campaign, and Canning contributed what Perceval described in his report to the King as 'one of the best, most eloquent and commanding speeches that was ever heard.'[39] He described Moore's advance to Sahagun as the act of a statesman, no less than a soldier, because of its immediate effect on Napoleon's advance into Spain; he insisted that the spirit of the Spanish people was still unsubdued; he claimed that although we had been forced to leave Spain, we had left with 'fresh laurels blooming upon our brows,' and he denounced the defeatist view that Napoleon was irresistible and must be submitted to as if he were a 'divine infliction.' Napoleon's fortune, concluded Canning, 'no doubt had been augmented; but still it was fortune, not fate; and therefore not to be considered unchangeable and fixed.'[40]*

A favourite target of the opposition during its Spanish post-mortem was John Hookham Frere, who had taken up his post as diplomatic representative with the Supreme Junta early in November, 1808. No doubt the fact that Frere was an old and intimate friend of Canning's added a particular zest to this line of attack. On the face of it Frere was not ill-qualified for the post, since he had already been British envoy in both Lisbon and Madrid and was passionately pro-Spanish. But he was hopeless as 'a man of business', and he lacked sound judgment. Moreover, he was extremely self-opinionated and had a haughty and pompous manner. For some reason, Canning chose to overlook failings which were obvious to everyone else and of which he himself was by no means unaware. He wanted to send someone who he felt sure would do his best for the Spanish cause and perhaps did not foresee what a menace misdirected enthusiasm could be.

* Unfortunately, while Canning was speaking, an almost irresistible rival attraction was provided by the spectacle of Drury Lane Theatre going up in flames. The light from the blaze shone strongly through the windows of the House of Commons and lit up the river, the bridge, Lambeth Palace and all the surrounding buildings. (*Later Corresp. of George III*, V, p. 210. Perceval to the King, February 25, 1808)

It was not until after the debate on February 24 that the opposition really began to go for Frere. They pressed Canning to publish the correspondence between Moore and Frere while Moore was at Salamanca. For more than six weeks Canning stubbornly refused. When he at last gave way, under pressure from Moore's family as well as the Whigs, the opposition alleged that Frere's 'folly, ignorance and presumption' – as Grey described it in the Lords – had been responsible for Moore's decision on December 5/6 to countermand his retreat into Portugal. It was true that on the 5th he did receive a passionate appeal from Frere to support the popular rising in Madrid. But Moore had received news about Madrid from other sources as well; it is unlikely that a letter from Frere, for whom he had no respect, was the determining factor and there is no conclusive evidence that it was.

But Frere had certainly laid himself open to severe criticism. He had completely ignored Moore's responsibility to his own army; he had tried to instruct him on military policy which was none of his business; he had expressed himself in a way that can only be described as thoroughly offensive; and, finally, he was even prepared to appeal over Moore's head to the senior officers under his command if his advice was rejected.[41] Neither Liverpool in the Lords, nor Canning in the Commons, made any attempt to defend those parts of Frere's conduct that were clearly indefensible.* When the Spanish campaign (and Frere's part in it) were debated for the last time in the Commons on May 9, Canning had already sent Frere a stiff rebuke for the tone of his letters to Moore and for his attempted interference in military policy.[42] But he still strongly denied that Frere had had any influence on Moore's military decisions. Privately, Canning felt more sympathy for Frere than he allowed to appear in public. He did his best to reconcile private friendship with public duty, but public opinion was too much against Frere for him either to be kept in Spain or immediately given another post. On May 1, Canning told him that he was to be replaced by Lord Wellesley.[43]†

On the other hand, for Moore Canning felt much less sympathy than appeared in his public utterances. His attitude towards him was

* According to Lord Holland, when Canning was compelled to criticise Frere in the Commons, he did so 'with much emotion in manner.' (Holland *Further Memoirs*, p. 25)

† The following August, Canning wrote to Wellesley asking him to assure Frere that he entirely approved his conduct ('though the tone of some of his language was indefensible') but because of the general situation in London and his own position, it had been impossible for him to carry Frere through 'with a higher hand'. (Harewood, 34)

strongly coloured by his previous experience of him in Sicily and Sweden. Moore's invariably cautious and critical attitude towards his instructions (however justified) gave the impression that he lacked the essential will to make a success of any mission with which he was entrusted. He went to Spain strongly suspecting that the Spanish armies, which were so enthusiastically extolled in London, would turn out to be broken reeds. When he discovered he was right, he did not hesitate to say so. Frere did pass on and back up his complaints. But in his letters to Canning he always took a far rosier view of the situation than Moore did.

Canning for his part, whatever his private misgivings, was not guilty at the time of failing to give Moore the strongest possible diplomatic backing. On December 9, 1808, unaware that Moore had already changed his mind about retreating into Portugal, he instructed Frere to deny most strenuously that a retreat meant that the British were going to abandon the Spaniards altogether. The British army would certainly come back, but when it did it must get a better deal from the Spanish authorities. It must not, wrote Canning, be split up among the various Spanish armies, but must be kept together under its own commanders and it must operate on some definite settled plan. 'It will decline no difficulty, it will shrink from no danger, when through that difficulty and danger the commander is enabled to see his way to some definite purpose.' But the British army must never again be left 'in the heart of Spain without one word of information, except such as they [Moore and Baird] could pick up from common rumour, of the events passing around them.' Before Moore returned, the Spaniards must clearly explain to him how they intend to carry on the war. 'The part assigned to the British army in the combined operation must be settled with Sir J. Moore, and he will be found not unambitious of that in which he may be opposed most directly to the enemy.'[44] Even Moore, who had little use for ministerial despatches, could hardly have complained of that one.*

But three weeks later Canning was writing privately to Portland about Moore in the most scathingly critical terms. 'If there ever was a man formed to kill a cause that he was sent to save, it is Sir John Moore.' He thought that Moore might have saved Madrid if he had tried. But if he now made the loss of the capital an excuse for doing

* In a second despatch of the same date, Canning pointed out that the Spaniards had so far failed to supply the British troops properly. This *must* be remedied because it put the British, who were dependent on local goodwill, at a great disadvantage to the French, who were prepared to live ruthlessly off the country. (FO 72/60)

nothing further, and the Cabinet agreed, it would surrender the cause of Spain and it would be too late in three months' time to say it had acted on Moore's judgment – 'a judgment so manifestly, so deplorably, biassed as his is, it is our duty not to act on implicitly – but to suspect, examine, and if necessary, peremptorily to reverse it.' He did not doubt Moore's military skill and personal courage and was sorry to write so warmly, 'But I confess my blood boils when I think of what has been lost for want of a little enterprise, of a little heart . . .' It is clear from this letter that Canning had been pressing for Moore's recall; and in a further letter next day, after again reverting to Moore's 'thorough determination to despair of the cause of Spain', he urged that Lord Moira should be sent out to replace him.[45]

It was of course nonsense to suggest that a general on active service should let his heart rule his head. Whether Moore might have shown more enterprise and determination is something that military historians have argued over from that day to this. Moore's journal and letters suggest that in order to satisfy opinion at home and carry out his orders to help the Spanish people he felt that he risked more than was militarily justifiable. Canning in any case was not a fit judge because he was too emotionally involved in the Spanish cause, too much influenced by Frere's reports and too predisposed to be critical of Moore. He was an incorrigible arm-chair general simply because he could not refrain from forming very definite views about any problem in which he was deeply interested, however many hundreds of miles he was from the scene of action and however ill-equipped with the necessary information.

How seriously Canning pressed his demand for Moore's recall we do not know. Nor do we know how true is the allegation that, after Corunna, he urged that the blame for the disaster should be shifted on to the dead general. There is no direct evidence for this. But in public he never said more than was strictly necessary by way of tribute to Moore. And in a letter to Portland written on March 24, he complained that the government had lost popularity by managing to make itself seem responsible for the Convention of Cintra and the unfortunate outcome of the Spanish campaign.[46] If Canning was sufficiently distraught to press for Moore's recall in the middle of a military operation, conceivably he might also have lost his head enough to want to blame him when the campaign ended badly – although if he did he must have forgotten that the government had already endorsed the dead general's decisions and publicly acclaimed his success in thwarting Napoleon's plans. Whatever his enemies might say, Canning was by nature a decent and honourable man, both in his public and his private life. But although he could rise splendidly to an opportunity, he never learnt to make the best of a disappointment. Clearly, he was badly unhinged by the twin disappointments of Cintra and Corunna; and if he did press a shabby course on his colleagues after Corunna, his state of mind may explain (but not excuse) his behaviour.

Nothing, of course, was said by the soldiers back from Corunna about their own wild looting which had so shocked Moore. But they had plenty of tales to tell about the Spaniards' cowardice, apathy and heartless refusal to give them food and shelter. The tales grew in the telling and there was a strong revulsion of popular feeling against the Spanish cause. Many people felt it would be useless to try a third time to stop the Peninsula from falling under Napoleon's control.

Canning fully shared the popular disillusionment with the Spaniards, although for obvious reasons he tried in the Commons to smother their deficiencies under a flood of eloquence about their patriotic cause. From Downing Street, the strength of anti-French feeling among ordinary Spaniards, noted by many observers on the spot, was not nearly so apparent as the incompetence of their generals and the inexperience, inefficiency and divisions of their political leaders. The members of the central junta seemed to be more interested in awarding each other titles or discussing constitutional niceties than in organising their country for war or helping the allied troops who had come to help them. Moreover, although their demands for money were insatiable, they stubbornly refused to open the trade of their South American colonies to British merchants. (The Portuguese, by contrast, opened their Brazilian markets at once.)

A further grievance against the Spaniards arose over Cadiz. When the Cabinet heard that Moore was retreating to Corunna, it decided to send 4,000 men immediately to Cadiz so that the British army would at least have a secure base in southern Spain from which to continue operations against the French. But the Spaniards flatly refused to let any British troops into the port; they were convinced that if once the British got a foothold in Cadiz, the city would go the way of Gibraltar. The British government had no choice but to accept the rebuff. Canning told Frere not to *reproach* the Spaniards but merely to point out that the British government could not risk another Corunna, and without a fortified place to fall back on, it could not commit its troops to the heart of Spain, nor 'fritter' them away among the various Spanish forces. 'If,' he added, 'the Spaniards do not desire our assistance, we have no desire to press it on them.'[47]*

Canning could afford to adopt this tone of dignified huffiness because in the spring of 1809 the horizons of the war seemed to be opening out. In central Europe the steadily growing resentment against Napoleonic domination had been fanned by the popular rising in Spain. At the end of March an emissary from the Austrian government, Count Walmoden, arrived in London. Unfortunately the Austrians were more short of money than of manpower, and the British no longer had it to give on the scale necessary to finance a really effective Austrian war effort. They had had to scrape the barrel in order to supply the Spaniards with hard cash, and Napoleon's continental system had temporarily undermined British credit in Europe. Before the end of April, however, Walmoden was on his way back to Vienna with a treaty of friendship, a firm offer of some immediate financial aid and a virtual promise of more to come later.†

About the same time an emissary of the German nationalists (or some of them) also turned up in London. He was a rather shady character called Ludwig Kleist, who introduced himself as the agent of the central insurrectionary committee in Berlin and claimed that the whole of northern Germany between the Rhine and the Elbe was on the point of rising against the French. It was a dazzling prospect to set before the British Cabinet, only marred by the unofficial, clandestine character which the vacillations and timidity of the Prussian king had forced the German nationalists to adopt. However anxious Canning was to strike a blow at Napoleon, he hesitated to use a weapon that might later be turned against the Prussian monarchy. He was, however, greatly attracted by what Kleist told him, and sent him back with a token sum of money and a promise to send supplies of arms, ammunition and clothing to Heligoland.‡ He also sent a British agent with Kleist with instructions to find out all he could about the German

* Eventually some British troops were allowed into Cadiz to help in its defence.

† Canning thought up an ingenious plan to raise between £3,000,000 and £4,000,000 by offering British 5% Exchequer Bills for sale in Vienna, the proceeds to go directly to the Austrian government. The British government would pay interest to the purchasers twice a year and redeem the bills at the end of the war. But the Austrian finance minister thought the agrarian economy of his country made the scheme impractical. (Scherwig, *Guineas and Gunpowder*, pp. 210/12)

‡ The British had seized Heligoland from Denmark in 1807, and used it as a depot from which to smuggle English goods into Scandinavia and Germany.

insurgents and in particular whether they enjoyed the approval of the King of Prussia. If they did not, they could expect no further British help.

Before Kleist even got back to Germany, two premature and ill-organised attempts at revolt broke out in Westphalia and in Prussia. Both were quickly crushed and there was no further sign of any spontaneous German rising against Napoleon. The Austrian government also began hostilities against the French without waiting to hear what help it could expect from Britain. The Archduke Charles's preliminary offensive into Bavaria was quickly driven back and on May 13 Napoleon entered Vienna. But a week later, at Aspern just outside Vienna, the Austrians managed to inflict a reverse on Napoleon and it was not until some six weeks later, July 5–6, that he decisively defeated the main Habsburg armies at Wagram.

News of these disasters did not percolate through to London in time to prevent the Cabinet from spending a great deal of time and thought on trying to decide how Britain's limited military manpower could be most effectively deployed in support of what was hoped would prove a continent-wide revolt against Napoleon. Should it be in the Peninsula? Or north Germany? Or against the Scheldt? Or even, as Stadion strongly urged, should the British in Sicily make a diversion in southern Italy? Early in March, Arthur Wellesley sent Castlereagh a memorandum arguing that with 20,000 troops and a reconstituted Portuguese army, Portugal could and should be defended, whatever happened in Spain. By the end of the month Castlereagh had persuaded his colleagues to accept Wellesley's plan and put him in charge. Canning was always urging the Cabinet to do something about Portugal and there is no evidence that he opposed Wellesley's plan.

But the government, buoyed up by optimistic misinformation about the situation in Germany, saw no reason why the Peninsula should be the only, or even the main, theatre of operations. News of the disastrous abortive risings in Germany does not seem to have reached London until well on into July. On June 9, Canning wrote one of his needling letters to Chatham, excitedly urging him to send some arms to northern Germany where he had heard there was a strong move in favour of a rising *with the consent and co-operation of the King of Prussia.* He even suggested – apparently quite seriously – that the local militia in England should be made to surrender their arms to supply the more pressing needs of the Germans.[48] A month later he heard that a revolt was just about to break out in Hanover and besought Chatham to send some muskets immediately to Heligoland.[49] The despatch of a British expeditionary force to northern Germany was seriously considered. On June 11 Castlereagh told Arthur Wellesley that the news of the Austrian victory at Aspern had just arrived and this so much improved the prospects of 'something being done against the enemy in the North' that the government was anxious for whatever transport equipment he could spare.[50] (This was just after Wellesley had triumphantly chased the French out of Portugal and was preparing to pursue them into Spain.) At the end of June, within a few days of yet again urging Chatham to find some arms for the Spaniards, Canning instructed Lord Wellesley, who was about to set off for Spain, to tell the Spanish authorities that for the time being priority would be given to the war in Germany.[51]

But the ministers could not forget their unhappy memories of previous expeditions to Germany. Moreover, the King of Prussia remained unforthcoming and they were reluctant to act without being sure of the support of his troops. In the end, a prey to doubts, uncertainties and conflicting demands on their resources, they went on hesitating until it was too late anyway.

There remained the possibility of an expedition up the Scheldt. It was a much canvassed project that had never actually been put to the test. Napoleon himself had once described the river as a loaded pistol pointed at the head of England and was constantly worried lest the English might knock it out of his hand. The advice of the military and naval pundits against such an attempt was heavily discouraging. But the ministers were desperate to do something to take the strain off the Austrians, especially after hearing of Archduke Charles's success at Aspern. At last, on June 21, 'not disguising from themselves the general difficulties of the enterprise but deeply impressed with its importance,' they recommended it to the King. Although, as the King pointed out, the information on which it was based was unhappily so imperfect,[52] its objects were alarmingly ambitious: to occupy the island of Walcheren, destroy the arsenals and dockyards at Flushing and Antwerp and destroy or capture all enemy shipping.

The government chose Lord Chatham to lead the expedition. He had the advantage of a prestigious name, but his indolence was notorious. To have any chance of success, the attack on the Scheldt would have to be swift and secret. It was neither. Chatham, as usual, took his time, and the newspapers saw no reason to ignore such an interesting news item. On July 21 news of Wagram reached London, by way of a British warship which had fished copies of the official French bulletin out of the sea. The expedition went ahead all the same. Castlereagh, Canning and Perceval went down to Deal to watch its departure, and on July 28 it sailed at last.

It was a most formidable expedition – nearly 40,000 troops, 35 ships of the line, 23 frigates and nearly 200 smaller vessels. But it lacked good weather, good intelligence and good luck. Moreover, the naval commander, Sir Richard Strachan, was not up to the job and was soon in open disagreement with Chatham. Walcheren was eventually occupied and Flushing laboriously besieged and captured. But the French had plenty of time to reinforce the defences of Antwerp and more and more British troops went down with a fever from which – if they did not die – their recovery was very slow. By the end of August Chatham was forced to abandon any hope of attacking Antwerp. On September 2 the Cabinet decided to withdraw the main part of the expeditionary force. The garrison left behind to hold Walcheren lingered on, incapacitated and decimated by disease, until November. It should of course have been withdrawn much earlier, but by early September the Portland Cabinet was in the final stages of disintegration and its members had no attention for anything except the fascinating process of their own political dissolution.

The process had been started the previous Easter by Canning. Since he had become Foreign Secretary he had worked with passionate zeal to turn back the tide of Napoleonic conquest and at the end of two years there seemed to be precious little to show for his efforts. He found it only too easy to blame his colleagues, especially after the Cintra Convention which (to his lasting indignation) they had nearly approved in his absence, and Moore's campaign which he had only very reluctantly agreed to. He did not like the way in which Castlereagh managed the War Department and was irked by the crossed wires sometimes produced in Spanish affairs where military and political issues were so closely entwined. He felt that Perceval was too conciliatory towards the opposition in his management of the Commons – a judgment with which a good many other people agreed. And some of the other ministers were not, in his opinion, up to the job: Westmorland and Camden he described as 'useless lumber'.[53]

During the early part of 1809 the government was shaken and the Commons almost totally preoccupied by a scandal concerning the sale of army commissions by the Duke of York's former mistress, Mary

Ann Clarke. Canning managed to keep his grumbles to himself until the parliamentary inquiry into the affair was safely out of the way. It was finally settled on March 18 when the duke resigned as Commander-in-Chief. Two days earlier the Commons had acquitted him of corruption, while regretting his association with Mrs Clarke. But the hullabaloo against the duke, both inside and outside Parliament, threatened the government which had espoused his cause. Canning had agreed with the original rather misguided decision to hold a public parliamentary inquiry. But disagreement with the Cabinet's handling of the later stages of the affair became yet another grievance against his colleagues.[54]

Six days after the Duke of York's resignation Canning unburdened himself in a long letter to the Duke of Portland.* He pointed out how little the government was doing to repair the damage to its popularity caused by Cintra and Corunna, complained of a spirit of compromise that prevented decisive action and declared that he felt it his duty 'fairly to avow to your Grace, *that the Government as at present constituted does not appear to me equal to the great task which it has to perform.*' Canning named no names, but simply stated that if the defects ('wherever they lie') were not remedied, he must insist on resigning.[55] Portland's reaction to this ultimatum was to invite Canning to his country home at Bulstrode to talk things over. During several days of discussions, Canning became more specific: Castlereagh must be removed from the War Department (but not from the Cabinet) or he himself would resign. Portland was apparently sufficiently impressed by Canning's complaints (and the difficulty of meeting them without mortally offending Castlereagh) to offer his own resignation. The King rejected it out of hand, without even giving the duke a chance to explain himself. Portland then confided in his friend, Lord Bathurst, who undertook to tackle Canning and try to persuade him to keep quiet at least until the end of the parliamentary session.

It was an unfortunate moment to attack Castlereagh because he was already under fire from the opposition for misuse of Indian patronage when President of the Board of Control four years earlier. Castlereagh admitted that he had been imprudent and guilty of a technical offence. But there was no question of anything worse, and if the Commons had not been so compulsively preoccupied with smelling out corruption, the incident might well have been passed over. On April 25, however, the opposition attempted to censure Castlereagh's conduct. Canning dutifully took his share in defending his colleague, but Thomas

* The letter was not actually sent until April 4.

Grenville described his speech as 'most feeble and washy'.[56] In the end, the attack was defeated, not indeed without difficulty, but not by such a small majority that Castlereagh felt obliged to resign voluntarily. He expressed himself privately as 'perfectly satisfied with the result'.[57] Canning, on the other hand, thought that Castlereagh should have resigned after the debate, if not before. In his opinion, the whole affair now hung like a dead weight on the Cabinet, adding to Castlereagh's unpopularity and making it both more necessary and more difficult to remove him.[58]

Three days after the patronage debate, Portland confided his difficulties to Castlereagh's uncle, Lord Camden, at the same time swearing him to secrecy. Camden agreed that it would be best to move his nephew from the War Department, if it could be done without hurting his feelings too much. But neither Camden, Bathurst, nor the old duke could think up a satisfactory way of carrying out this delicate operation. Canning sympathised with their scruples, but not to the extent of letting the whole issue lapse indefinitely. On May 5 he again threatened to resign.[59] Portland, much embarrassed, begged Canning to wait until he had spoken to the King. At the next levee Portland again handed in his own resignation. This time the King asked for an explanation and when he had been given it said that he himself would consider what ought to be done. But he took his time, and after a fortnight's suspense, Canning's small stock of patience was exhausted. On May 25 he called on Portland and told him that he definitely meant to resign at the next levee. He seemed more determined than ever to carry out his threat. 'If it cannot be prevented,' lamented the duke to Eldon (who by then had also been brought into the secret), 'I see nothing but ruin to the country and to Europe, and so I told him most plainly and distinctly.'[60]

Portland might perhaps have stood a better chance of keeping Canning if he had not been so obviously anxious not to lose him. On May 31 Canning insisted on explaining his views on the conduct of the War Department to the King and offered his own resignation. The King refused to accept it, but a few days later, suggested that the political side of the War Department's responsibilities should be handed over to the Foreign Office, leaving the colonies in Castlereagh's charge and offering him in addition the Board of Control which happened to be vacant.* It was a well-meaning plan, but hardly likely to be well

---

* The Board of Control had become vacant in April when Mr Robert Dundas was appointed to succeed Sir Arthur Wellesley as Irish Secretary.

received by Castlereagh. Canning agreed to it very reluctantly, largely out of deference to the King's feelings, and on June 18 pressed Portland to get on with the new arrangements. Three days later the duke assured him that he would. He also told Canning that on the King's instructions he had told Camden to break the news to Castlereagh; but he did not apparently stipulate when Camden was to carry out this invidious chore.[61]

All this time Castlereagh, in happy ignorance of the threat hanging over him, had been busily organising the Walcheren expedition which the Cabinet finally approved on June 21. It hardly seemed sensible, or fair to Castlereagh, to swap horses in mid-stream, and before Canning had learnt that the King insisted that the present Secretary for War should remain in charge, he had suggested to Portland that there would be 'something peculiarly and unnecessarily harsh' in taking the Walcheren expedition out of Castlereagh's hands, especially as it was thought likely to be a success.[62] But he was less pleased to learn that Castlereagh was to be kept in ignorance of what was hanging over him until after the expedition. Since the revelation would almost certainly have precipitated Castlereagh's resignation, there was a case for delay. But Canning sent Portland an angry protest and next day made yet another unsuccessful attempt to resign.[63] Portland tried to mollify him by assuring him that he did not mean Camden to wait until the 'issue' of the expedition was known, but only until after it had sailed, which should be within the next fortnight.[64] After thinking it over for a week, however, Camden told Portland that he really could not bring himself to be the bearer of such ill tidings to his nephew.

So the King's plan was quietly allowed to lapse, unmourned by anyone except perhaps its author. By this time Perceval, Chatham, Harrowby and Liverpool* had also been told what was going on – which left only Mulgrave, Westmorland and Castlereagh himself completely in the dark. Liverpool was huffed at not being told before. But he told Canning that he realised the concealment from Castlereagh was not his fault, and he told the King that if the government had to make a choice between Castlereagh and Canning, it would have to choose the latter because it would fall without him.[65] Liverpool also offered to resign himself if it would be any help. So did Bathurst and Camden. Various rearrangements were discussed and discarded, while all those in the know grew more and more uncomfortable at finding themselves virtually plotting against Castlereagh behind his back.

* Robert Banks Jenkinson, Lord Hawkesbury, had become 2nd Earl of Liverpool on the death of his father in December, 1808.

According to Harrowby, Portland was 'heartily sick' of the concealment. Harrowby himself felt that Castlereagh must soon smell a rat 'which may lead him to ask some home questions and the situation in which some of us stand towards him is too painful to be very long endured.'[66]

At last Portland decided that the best plan would be to accept Camden's offer to resign as Lord President of the Council, offer this post to Castlereagh with a peerage and replace him by Lord Wellesley. It seemed unlikely that Castlereagh would have found this acceptable and Perceval said he could not support this plan until he knew Castlereagh's reactions.[67] But the King agreed, although he disliked Wellesley, and for Canning, who was still keen to bring his friend into the Cabinet, the plan had obvious attractions. Wellesley should have been on his way to replace Frere in Spain, but he had fallen sick and there had also been a little difficulty over his wish to take his mistress with him instead of his wife.* It was apparently contemplated that he should still go on his mission but would soon be recalled to higher things and in the meantime Canning would temporarily look after the War Department.[68]

But the King still insisted that Castlereagh should be kept in the dark. For a week Canning argued and protested. Finally on July 18 he sent Portland a formal request that it should be remembered 'whenever hereafter this concealment shall be alleged (as I doubt not it will) *against me*, as an act of injustice towards Lord Castlereagh, that it did not originate in my suggestion – that so far from desiring it, I conceived, however erroneously, Lord Camden to be the sure channel of communication to Lord Castlereagh, and that up to a very late period, I believed such communication to have been actually made.'[69]

The old duke accepted all the blame for the concealment and did his best to end it. As soon as the Walcheren expedition had actually sailed (on July 28) he began to urge Camden to say something to Castlereagh. But Camden could not face it. Moreover, once his offer to resign had actually been accepted, he began to wish he had never made it. On August 6, Portland told the King that Camden's reluctance was so great that he 'did not think it either right or useful to urge him to get the better of it.' In despair, Portland had at last arrived at the conclusion that he himself was the right person to speak to Castlereagh and that he had better do so before either the success or the failure of the Wal-

* Canning, who had been appealed to by Lady Wellesley, had to persuade Wellesley to forgo his mistress. Afterwards he said the interview had passed off very well. (*Later Corres. of George III*, V, p. 268 n1)

cheren expedition made a change at the War Department still more embarrassing.[70] Unfortunately a few days later, before he had been able to carry out his laudable intention, the duke was struck down with an epileptic fit while on his way from London to Bulstrode.

From then on, the question of replacing Castlereagh became inextricably involved with the larger question of the succession to Portland. Rather unexpectedly, the duke recovered for the time being. But the King gloomily realised that he could not decently go on brushing aside Portland's resignations, and at the next levee he told Liverpool and Bathurst that they ought to be thinking about a new prime minister. The competition was not keen. Chatham's name, if not his abilities, would have made him a strong contender if it were not increasingly obvious that he was about to become a failed military commander. Harrowby was a possibility, but he peremptorily refused to let his name be put forward. Bathurst was another possibility. Even Canning did not think that Wellesley would do, while Liverpool, who less than three years later was to begin his fifteen year stint as prime minister, does not seem to have been considered at all. In the Commons the only possibilities were Perceval and Canning.

Perceval's first reaction to the new crisis was that with so many members of the Cabinet of equal, or nearly equal, importance, the post of prime minister was 'very far from desirable' and he himself certainly did not wish to be a candidate.[71] On the other hand, with the Walcheren expedition steadily heading towards disaster and an unexploded time bomb under Castlereagh, the government could not afford the luxury of a protracted leadership struggle. But at any rate the general reshuffle, which would follow naturally from the appointment of a new prime minister, would be the least unpleasant way that anyone had yet thought up of dislodging Castlereagh from the War Department. With this consoling thought, Perceval decided, on August 28, to try to sound out Canning.

At first Canning was reluctant to be drawn into a discussion. But after Perceval had fairly cornered him at a levee, he sent him a letter explaining his position with a frankness which would have been brutal if it had not been so cordially polite. He said that he had for some time been convinced 'that a *Minister* – and that Minister in the *House of Commons* – is indispensable to the well-carrying-on of the King's Government in these times.' Such a minister, wrote Canning, would obviously have to be either Perceval or himself. 'I am not so presumptuous as to expect that you should acquiesce in that choice falling on me. On the other hand, I hope and trust that you will not consider it as any want of esteem and kindness on my part towards you personally (than which I do assure you nothing could be more entirely foreign to my real feelings) if I should not think it possible to remain in office under the change which would necessarily be produced in my situation by the appointment of a first Minister in the House of Commons – even in your person.'[72] Nothing could be more explicit. Nor could Perceval's reply, written on the same day. He admitted, with engaging modesty, that he had never supposed that Canning would agree to his being prime minister. But it was clear that whereas if he became prime minister, this would not affect the Foreign Secretaryship, if Canning became prime minister, he would supersede Perceval as Chancellor of the Exchequer and leader of the House. 'This (I mean my actual supersession),' he wrote, 'would be the thing that I should feel principally painful; and, I cannot disguise from you, that I should certainly feel it so.' Perceval's solution, therefore, was to find a third person whose appointment as prime minister would 'leave us where we were.'[73]

Next day Perceval called on Canning and assured him that if it were only a question of his own feelings, and not of his reputation, he would be quite willing to serve under Canning, perhaps as Home Secretary. 'This,' wrote Canning to his wife afterwards, 'I own, I could not bear. It would *hurt me for* him. It would be a great humiliation.' His solution was that Perceval should accept a peerage and become Lord President of the Council. But Perceval said he could not possibly afford to go to the Lords. This was a difficulty Canning had not foreseen and he admitted that it was most formidable. 'Nothing,' he added in his letter to Joan, 'could be more candid, more manly, more modest and more kind than Perceval's whole behaviour.'[74]

At this point bad news from the Peninsula and Holland reached London: Viscount Wellington had had to retreat across the Tagus and Chatham had decided to admit defeat and return to London without attacking Antwerp. Canning immediately wrote to Portland reminding him of the King's promise to replace Castlereagh by Wellesley and urging that it should be carried out at once.[75] Portland took no action except to consult Perceval and various other members of the Cabinet. No one could see the point of gratuitously upsetting Castlereagh when it would soon be possible to move him in the course of a general reshuffle without any unpleasantness. The main thing was to get Portland replaced as prime minister. And after Perceval had tactfully pointed out to the duke the advantages that would flow from his immediate resignation, he did make up his mind to go out in order to 'prevent the explosion that threatens us.'

Before going to see the King, Portland sent for Canning and told him that if he insisted on Castlereagh's immediate resignation, other members of the Cabinet would resign too; so he himself intended to resign so that Castlereagh could be moved to another post in the new Cabinet. Canning agreed not to break up the ministry by insisting on the immediate replacement of Castlereagh by Wellesley, but indicated that if the duke went out of office he would have to go with him. Next day, September 7, Canning's unexplained absence from a Cabinet meeting at which Foreign Office business was to be discussed caused Castlereagh to ask his uncle so many awkward questions afterwards over the dinner table that Camden was eventually obliged to tell him a nearly complete, but softened, version of the whole story. Although Castlereagh received it (according to Camden) 'firmly and reasonably', next day he too told the King that he must resign.[76]*

Thus by September 8 the ministry was in complete disarray and it was becoming increasingly clear that the crisis could only be solved by some understanding between Perceval and Canning. Their cordial personal relations were becoming strained by misunderstandings over what each thought the other was committed to, as well as by Canning's annoyance at the way in which Portland's resignation had been sprung on him. Perceval, anxiously aware that the ministry might not stand without Canning, still hoped that he would agree to the appointment of some innocuous peer as prime minister. At the same time, he began to canvass for support and to collect round him what was to all intents and purposes an anti-Canningite party.

Meanwhile on September 12 Canning wrote to Portland, formally explaining his position very much as he had already explained it to Perceval. He supposed that the 'easiest arrangement' would be to make Perceval prime minister, in which case the 'ordinary feelings of human nature' would oblige him to resign; but he did not in so many words offer his resignation.[77] Next day Canning was received by the King and in the course of a very long exposition of his point of view virtually offered himself as an alternative if a government formed by Perceval did not manage to survive.[78] It seems that he left the royal presence

---

* When Castlereagh sat to Lawrence for his portrait on the 7th, the painter thought him extremely depressed and more than once observed him to wipe his eyes. Lawrence thought the depression was due to bad news from the Continent, but it may have been due to suspicions raised at that day's Cabinet meeting. (Farington, V, 224/5)

genuinely believing that the King might prefer him to Perceval and that in any case, if he did go out of office, it would be 'without quarrelling with Knobbs [the King] and that was the grand point of all'.[79] In fact he had badly overplayed his hand. The King indignantly reported to Perceval that Canning's conversation had been 'the most extraordinary he ever heard'. Instead of merely saying that he would consider forming a government and would consult with others – 'as you or any other person would have said' – he had indicated that he was fully prepared to undertake it if Perceval failed. The King's reaction to this unbecoming forwardness was to tell Perceval flatly that he did not believe any of Canning's colleagues would serve under him.[80]

From then on Canning could do little more than watch and wait hopefully, while Perceval continued to canvass assiduously for support and the rump of the Cabinet held protracted meetings in an attempt to find a way out of the crisis that would not involve either surrendering to Canning or appealing for help to the Whigs. Canning saw no member of the Cabinet except Portland, who was extremely offended by Perceval's failure to tell him what was going on although technically he was still head of the government. On the 15th Canning confessed to Joan that the suspense was 'most certainly very nervous'. He knew only that there were 'constant meetings and co-jobberations' at Perceval's house, but he now rather expected that he would go out.[81] Next day his old friend, George Rose, who was Treasurer of the Navy, called on him and bluntly told him he was behaving badly and ought to accept Harrowby or Bathurst as prime minister. Three days later, Rose returned to tell Canning that he would not resign with him because he could not agree to his breaking up the government for 'motives of personal ambition'.* According to Rose, Canning was 'a good deal affected';[82] according to Canning, Rose was in tears.

But in the less censorious company of the old Duke of Portland, Canning could still hang on to his illusions, although most people thought he was as good as out of politics. In a letter to Chatham he maintained (which was formally true) that he was still 'not wholly *out*, yet not altogether *in* office',[83] and on the 19th actually attended a Cabinet meeting in order to present the draft of a despatch to Lord Wellesley. He and Portland were most indignant when they heard that Perceval and his colleagues wanted the King to approach Grey and Grenville. As late as the 20th Canning authorised Portland to assure the King that he thought he still had a good chance of forming a government without any help from the Whigs.[84] It was all castles in the air and

* Rose was also under strong pressure from his family not to resign.

it hardly needed the shock of Castlereagh's challenge to blow them away.

On September 15 Canning reported to Joan that Castlereagh had disappeared 'as thro' a trap-door'. In fact he was brooding over his wrongs and gradually learning the full story of the summer's goings-on. At last on September 19 he challenged Canning to a duel. He admitted that Canning was entitled to demand his removal from the War Department, but by concealing his purpose so long, he had damaged Castlereagh's honour and reputation.[85] The challenge was so strongly worded that Canning felt he had no choice but to accept it at once without trying to explain that the concealment had been neither his fault nor his intention. Moreover a few days earlier he had heard (and laughed at) a report that Castlereagh had been advised to call him out; if his challenger's intention was no secret, any attempt at explanation or deferment would speedily become public and be misconstrued as cowardice.[86] It was left to his second, Charles Ellis, and Henry Wellesley to spend the evening before the duel trying to convince Castlereagh's second, Lord Yarmouth, that the challenge was unjustified. Yarmouth reported all they had said but Castlereagh was unmoved.

Canning spent the evening before the duel making his Will and writing to Joan who was at Hinckley with the children. For all he knew it might be the last letter he would ever send her. 'If anything happens to me, dearest love, be comforted with the assurance that I could do no otherwise than I have done . . . I am conscious of having acted for what I thought best for my country; with *no more* mixture of selfish motives than the impatience of misconduct in others and of discredit to one's self, and the anxious and confident hope of being able to do good, and the desire of being placed in a situation to do it, naturally and laudably inspire.' He added the rather touching hope that '*the sort of widowhood*' in which Joan had been living for the past three years at Hinckley might make her miss him less than if they had been constantly together. Then, after discussing the characters and prospects of his three children, he explained the state of his finances and asked Joan, to whom he left everything, either to give his mother £2,000, or preferably allow her £300 a year. Finally, he made his farewell. 'There would be no end to taking leave and of saying how dearly I have loved you. I hope I have made you sensible of this, dearest, dearest, Joan. I hope I have been kind and good and affectionate towards you. I hope I have made you happy. If you have been a happy wife – and if I leave you a happy mother and a proud widow, I am content. Adieu. Adieu.'[87] It is to be hoped that Joan did not receive this letter before learning that Canning need never have written it.

The duel took place at 6 o'clock next morning on Putney Heath. Yarmouth drove Castlereagh to the meeting place in his curricle and on the way they discussed Catalani, a fashionable opera singer, and Castlereagh hummed snatches from her songs. At the scene of the duel, Yarmouth and Ellis, agreeing that they had no wish to make the business any more 'desperate' than necessary, fixed the distance at twelve paces, the longest for which there was any precedent. After making a last effort to avert the duel, Ellis gave Canning his pistol and said to Yarmouth: 'I must cock it for him for I cannot trust him to do it himself. He has never fired a pistol in his life.'

The first shots were fired and neither man was hit. Castlereagh rejected Yarmouth's suggestion that he had gone far enough, and Canning declared that as he had come to give his opponent satisfaction it was for him to say when he had had enough. When the two opponents took aim a second time, Canning missed again, but Castlereagh's bullet passed straight through the fleshy part of Canning's left thigh. Ellis immediately ran up to him and began to help him walk away. But after a few steps Canning stopped and said: 'But perhaps I ought to remain.' Then he added more loudly, 'Are you sure we have done?' Yarmouth emphatically assured him they had, and then Castlereagh came up, took his other arm and together with Ellis helped him to walk to Yarmouth's house nearby, where Mr Home, the surgeon, was waiting.[88]

Within a few hours, Canning was back in his own house, lying on a sofa, with no fever and very little pain. His secretary, Ross, set off for Hinckley at once to summon Joan while Canning himself wrote little notes to his relations, including his mother, and his closest friends to assure them that he was quite all right. In his letter to Mr and Mrs Leigh, he told them that if neither of them had had a ball through the fleshy part of their thigh, 'you can hardly conceive how slight a matter it is – provided (that is) that it passes through quite clean, carrying only a little bit of your nankeen breeches so big **O** with it – and comes out on the other side, without turning to the right or to the left to any of the arteries, and bones, etc., the which lie thereabouts. If you have a mind to try the experiment, I would recommend Lord Castlereagh as the operator.'[89]

The news that two of the King's ministers had actually fought a duel inevitably caused a great deal of shocked discussion. Most people, even those who sympathised with Castlereagh's political grievances, thought he was not justified in issuing a challenge, and certainly not to Canning. Perceval, who had tried to prevent the duel by producing copies of letters between Canning and Portland which showed that Canning had opposed the concealment, thought that Castlereagh had 'misconceived the case very much'.[90] Eldon was uneasy about the whole affair and thought all those in the know were 'more or less blameable'.[91] Lord Holland commented that Castlereagh's conduct 'seemed dictated by a thirst of vengeance rather than a sense of wounded honour.'[92] Wilberforce, shocked that Castlereagh should have 'chewed the cud of his resentment for twelve days', described the challenge as 'a cold-blooded measure of deliberate revenge'.[93] William Brodrick, a member of the Treasury Board, who was by no means friendly to Canning, concluded after reading all the relevant documents, that Castlereagh had more reason to complain of Portland and Camden 'who have erred from good nature and weakness' than of Canning.[94]

On October 4 the King accepted the unanimous advice of the rump of the Portland Cabinet and asked Perceval to form a government. By that time Canning was sufficiently recovered to be wheeled out in his garden. By the 11th he was well enough to attend the levee to take his formal leave as Foreign Secretary. Although the King had been extremely annoyed about the duel, he received Canning very graciously, expressed great regret at his resignation, brought up the subject of the duel himself and, with rather engaging curiosity, 'began to enter into all the particulars of that event. The situation of the wound (which he made me point out to him on his own royal thigh), the time when I received the challenge, when Charles Ellis heard of it, how I held my pistol, etc. etc., confessing all along great abhorrence of the custom of duelling, but admitting in the most unqualified manner that I had no option.'[95]

But the duel was only the sudden violent culmination of a political crisis that had been smouldering on for six months. It brought the whole affair into the open. There was public self-justification and private recrimination. The Press had a field-day and the rights and wrongs of the crisis were exhaustively discussed in letters and over polite dinner tables. The general verdict was very much against Canning. The self-justificatory statement over which he took immense care and trouble was on the whole badly received and even his friends thought he would have done better to keep quiet.* As Lord Holland put it: '. . . no explanation of Mr Canning could do away with the impression in the world that he had acted unfairly and treacherously by his colleague.'[96] What looked like Canning's treachery was largely the result of a royal veto combined with the havering and misplaced kind-heartedness of the Duke of Portland and the moral cowardice of Camden. But whatever the reason, it was certainly grossly unfair to let Castlereagh go on carrying out the duties of an important office without telling him that he was shortly to be moved out of it.

No one, however, seems to have seriously argued that Castlereagh ought to stay where he was, although he was able and conscientious, although the inauspicious opening of the Peninsular war was largely due to factors beyond his control, and although everyone – even Canning – agreed that he had worked extremely hard on the pre-liminary organisation of the Walcheren expedition. But there was evidently something about him that made him seem expendable. 'I certainly do not think,' wrote the Duke of Richmond from Dublin, 'Lord Castlereagh quite the properest person for his situation and am at a loss to say who is the best . . . I know Castlereagh is so unpopular that most things he does will be disapproved of.'[97]

That, perhaps, was Castlereagh's trouble. No one quite knew why – perhaps it was his inflexibly cold and reserved manner – but his unpopularity could easily turn him into a political liability. And his unfortunate involvement in cases of corruption had not improved his standing in a House of Commons that was still in the grip of 'Wardle-mania'.† He was not thought – even by his uncle Camden – worth keeping at the expense of losing Canning. According to Castlereagh, the King assured him that his removal from the War Department was never suggested upon any other ground, 'except the apprehension of breaking up of the Government by Canning's secession in the House of Commons'.[98]

At first, when his mind was filled with angry ruminations on the failure of the Peninsular campaign, Canning probably genuinely felt that a new man at the War Department would lead to the more efficient prosecution of the war. He had always been aware of the danger of

---

* Canning was hampered in his self-defence by his desire to avoid involving the King and by his determination to be as considerate as possible to Portland whom by mid-October he knew to be dying. The duke died on October 30 after an operation for the stone.

† Gwyllym Wardle was the M.P. who first raised the case of the Duke of York and Mary Ann Clarke.

trying to push himself up the ladder too fast, and in the spring, when Portland's resignation was first mooted, he had said he would be willing to serve under Chatham. But by the autumn when Portland really did resign (and Chatham was out of the running) he seems to have decided that the time had come for him to make a bid for the premiership himself. He had some reason to suppose he might get it. He must have been aware that most political observers, from the King down, believed that without his support, no Tory ministry could long survive. And although he knew that the King had a long-standing prejudice against him because of his support for Catholic emancipation, he had worked hard to win his confidence and apparently with considerable success. Above all, Canning seems to have had a now or never feeling. When he was trying to justify his conduct to George Rose, he pointed out that Harrowby and Bathurst were not much older than he was (they were in fact both eight years older) and if he let either of them become prime minister he 'would give up the lead in administration almost for ever.'[99]

Canning's failure to produce any other convincing reason for his resignation suggests that a bid for power was the real reason. He never explained why he could not accept Perceval's well-meaning plan to merge Castlereagh's move in a general reshuffle under Portland's successor. Nor did he ever explain the nature of the new difficulties which he alleged had been created by the duke's retirement and which made it necessary for him to resign too. There was a tell-tale lack of consistency about the reasons he gave then and later for his own resignation. And although he knew perfectly well that the old duke had no choice but to retire and nurse his many ailments, he was quite unreasonably censorious about the part that Perceval had played in persuading him to make up his mind. The fact was that Canning knew he had pushed his luck too far and in his anger and disappointment it was easier to blame anyone rather than himself.

He may also have been thrown off balance by the discovery that Perceval really was a rival for the premiership. Perceval complained that Canning, however he tried 'to gild and decorate the ornament . . . meant only to put an extinguisher on my head in the shape of a coronet . . .'[100] But Perceval, whom one observer described as having the 'best-regulated ambition' he had ever seen, had never before given the impression that he wanted the premiership – rather the contrary – and Canning may have genuinely believed that he would be perfectly satisfied with a sufficiently prestigious Cabinet post plus financial security.

Nobody thought of blaming Perceval for canvassing for support, even among Canning's friends, or for refusing to serve under Canning. But Canning's refusal to give way to Perceval was condemned as a shocking example of his arrogance and ambition. The King told Bathurst that he was anxious to keep Canning because he was 'essential' to the government, but if he had to choose between him and Perceval, he would choose the latter who was 'the most straightforward man he had almost ever known.'[101] Rightly or wrongly, Canning was always denied that compliment; his obvious brilliance made him distrusted. Eldon angrily described him as 'vanity in human form. Nothing will serve him but being what he will never be permitted to be.'[102] His colleagues were anxious to make use of his abilities, but not to have him placed over them. He was more of a professional than any of them and they eyed him with the grudging respect and wary suspicion with which amateurs tend to regard professionals. The extraordinary tale of that summer's negotiations over Castlereagh only served to feed their suspicions and lessen their respect. A man who could secure a promise from the prime minister that one of them should be moved by a certain time without telling the victim was a danger to all of them. Spencer Perceval seemed a much safer bet.

Lord Malmesbury, who had studied the workings of Canning's mind for years, believed that his principles had been and might still be 'right'. But he saw too much restless ambition and arrogance in him not to fear that his principles might suffer and his abilities become a curse instead of a blessing to his country.[103] Canning however was always more of a curse to himself than to anyone else. 'It is very vexatious,' wrote one observer towards the end of that year, 'that a man of such excellent abilities should have damaged himself so much.'[104] Canning had to make, and get over, another disastrous miscalculation and pass altogether seven years in the political wilderness before he again found himself with a seat at the Cabinet table. By that time he was content with a much lowlier place than would have satisfied him before disappointment and the passage of time gave him some of the patience and political wisdom he had lacked in the days of his soaring ambition.

CHAPTER XI

Into the Wilderness
1809-1812

While Canning was pursuing his calamitous course through one of the major political crises of his career, he was also involved in buying and moving into the house which was to be his home for most of the rest of his life. It was at Old Brompton, in those days a pleasant village among orchards and market gardens in what was considered a particularly salubrious neighbourhood. The house, which stood in six acres of grounds surrounded by trees, was within thirty minutes' walk of Hyde Park Corner, but (according to Canning) felt as if it were fifty miles in the country. It had been built by Maria, Duchess of Gloucester, who called it Oxford Lodge. After she had died there in 1807, her daughter, Princess Sophia, renamed it Gloucester Lodge. Canning bought it in the spring of 1809 and early in August moved there from the house he had been renting in Bruton Street. He soon discovered that out at Old Brompton, the post and the papers were tiresomely irregular, but during Joan's absence at Hinckley, he threw himself with enthusiasm into the task of supervising the gradual redecoration of the interior. The drawing-room, he told her in one letter, was to be 'a sort of drabbish, brownish, salmonish – in short the very prettiest colour of my own inventing that ever was seen.'

Canning's real reason for buying a house at Brompton was that he hoped that his eldest son would soon be well enough to be moved down from Hinckley, but feared that it would not suit him to be in the middle of London. By this time, George was sufficiently recovered to be able to walk across the room with the help of an 'instrument' on his leg. But in the end it was decided that he was not well enough to leave Mr Chesher's care, and towards the end of 1810 the Hinckley exile looked so little like coming to an end that the Cannings moved to a nicer house on the outskirts of the town on the road to Northampton. It was another four years before they saw the last of Hinckley. In the meantime, Canning sometimes joined his family there during the parliamentary recess and occasionally Joan left the boys in the care of tutors at Hinckley and came up to Gloucester Lodge with Harriet.

The long separations from his children were perhaps more painful to Canning than they would have been to many of his contemporaries. His perceptive affection for them was revealed in his farewell letter to Joan the night before his duel. 'I should have liked,' he wrote, 'to see my poor little George.' And he went on to discuss him in a way that threw a good deal of light on his own character. 'He is a good little boy – and an extraordinary one, I think. His feelings are too sensitive for public life even if (which God grant) his health should admit of his being anything else than a sedentary scholar. He may be a scholar I hope – and it will be for his happiness to be so if his lameness continues – but lame or not, do not breed him a statesman. He would feel, and fret, and lament, and hate, and despise – as much as his father; and those sentiments altogether make life troublesome – and the opportunity of doing good – and the means, are comparatively so few – that the chance of success is not worth the anxiety of the contest. If George can imbibe a strong taste for reading and (what Hinckley will have contributed to produce) moderation of wants and desires, he will have enough to live a quiet life – without ambition – and so he may be happy – and in a moderate degree useful. I could almost wish him to be a clergyman; but not unless he wished it too.'

William, who was nearly eighteen months younger than George, was altogether different. He was a difficult child who lacked his brother's sweetness of disposition. Canning told Joan that he did not know what to say about him and then went on to analyse his character with an insight and humanity unusual in a parent of his generation. 'I am afraid he is unamiable. But then he certainly is not loved like his brother and sister; and it is sometimes hard to say in such cases which is cause and which effect. George's health and Harriet's exquisite delightfulness have *perhaps* been in his way; and may *perhaps* have made him selfish and singular. I know my own dearest love's good sense too well to think that she wants any warning upon this subject; but let her be sure, before she decides on William's character, that kind – distinguishingly kind – treatment might not change his nature altogether.' Finally, there was Harriet – 'dear, dear little Toddles' – now five years old. About her Canning had nothing to say except to urge Joan to let her think of him as if he were just absent and to love him always, as – he added, with unusual diffidence – 'she appeared to do when last I saw her.'[1]

When Canning acquired Gloucester Lodge in the spring of 1809, he might reasonably suppose that he was set on a political course which, although at times it might be stormy, would also be increasingly successful. But when he returned there at the beginning of 1810, after spending Christmas at Hinckley, his future was far more uncertain. He was out of office; his painstaking efforts to justify himself seemed to have fallen largely on stony ground; he had been violently attacked in the press; and his political stock had fallen uncomfortably low. There had even been a few defections among his personal following of about a dozen M.P.s who were more or less formally committed to vote as he wished.* And apart from the regular 'Canningites' there had been some sad disappointments. Melville's son, Robert Dundas, who controlled the important 'Scotch legion' in the Commons, had eventually decided to take the War Department. Another political friend, Charles Long, had (like George Rose) changed his mind about resigning and decided to continue as a junior minister under Perceval. Above all, to his immense disgust, Canning had been deserted by Lord Wellesley,† whom he had believed to be his staunch political ally, but who, from his exile in Seville, accepted with alacrity Perceval's offer of the Foreign Office. 'I shall not flinch,' he wrote pompously to his brother Wellesley-Pole, 'from the traces now that I am in harness'; and he added the hope that he might be able to do some good although the country was in a lamentable state.[2]

As it turned out, Wellesley proved an unconscionably bad Foreign Secretary. He quarrelled with most of his colleagues and was excessively lazy, reducing the Foreign Office, according to one shocked diplomat, to a state of incredible confusion; 'procrastination and indecision are the order of the day.'[3] But at the time, his readiness to join the new government seemed an unmitigated blessing to poor Perceval, who had to labour for two months and put up with many snubs and disappointments before he managed to scrape together a very mediocre team. Canning and Castlereagh were, of course, both out of the running – for

* Young Lord Fitzharris left him after painful heartsearchings under strong pressure from his father, Lord Malmesbury, who both disapproved of Canning's public conduct and was privately huffed because of his supposed neglect in recent years. But at the end of 1809 Canning invited himself for the night to Malmesbury's home and successfully cleared up all personal misunderstandings.

† Lord Wellesley, who felt genuine respect and affection for Canning, might have stuck by him if he had not received the entirely mistaken impression that he had prevented him from being chosen as Portland's successor. 'If the Cabinet,' wrote Canning to him in extreme exasperation, 'had advised the King, and the King had approved the advice, to make you First Minister, in God's name why are you not so?' Eventually, after his return to London, Wellesley was convinced of his mistake. (BM. Add. Mss. 37295)

the time being at any rate. Sidmouth, as Perceval tactlessly told him, was too unpopular, and two of Sidmouth's friends refused out of loyalty to their chief. Sidmouth commented acidly: 'Mr Perceval is a *very* little man.'⁴ Perceval was certainly not that and it is doubtful whether anyone else could have done much better. As he pointed out to old Lord Melville, Pitt's party had lost its cohesion. 'The magic of that name is in a great degree dissolved, and the principle on which we must most rely to keep us together, and give us the assistance of floating strength, is the public sentiment of loyalty and attachment to the King.'⁵ Unfortunately loyalty to the old King did not prevent all sorts of difficulties being made about joining a ministry whose chances of survival seemed so slim. Perceval was given six refusals of the unpopular post of Chancellor of the Exchequer before he made up his mind to soldier on in it himself. It was largely his own plucky determination plus the divisions and ineffectiveness of the opposition that saw the government safely through its first stormy parliamentary session.

Canning approached the new session with an uncharacteristic mixture of caution and indecision. His future clearly lay in playing a part – preferably the leading part – in the attempt to reunite 'Pitt's friends'. Two days after Parliament reassembled on January 23 he told Joan that he saw his way less clearly than ever before. He assured her, however, that he was not dispirited and felt sure that somehow, some time, things would come right for him although he certainly could not see how.⁶ On the 27th, his report to Hinckley was just as puzzled. The government had won the vote on the Address by 96 votes, but the opposition had alienated much potential support by the violence of its attack; and on the 26th, the government failed by nine votes to defeat an opposition motion for an inquiry into the Scheldt expedition. Canning felt the government could hardly survive. But if the King were to send for him, or for Wellesley and him, he did not see how he could decently take over from Perceval so long as the opposition was in full cry over the Scheldt expedition for which he accepted his full share of responsibility. (He had spoken against the inquiry.) 'In short, if any superior power could say to me, "choose what you will," I hardly know how my choice would be made.' So the best thing was to go on quietly and make 'as few more enemies' as possible.⁷

That at least was clear to Canning – he had made too many political enemies. He seemed conscious of this when he rose to speak in the debate on the Address. He 'let off' – as Creevey described it – 'one of his regular compositions, with all the rhetorical flourishes that used to set his audience in a roar.'[8] But this time the atmosphere was wrong; his reception was cool and he could not raise a single cheer. A few days later, after he had spoken in favour of a vote of thanks to Wellington for his success at Talavera, he told Joan that he was not dissatisfied with his reception. 'But yet I cannot disguise from myself that pity works for Castgh. and that many well disposed people look upon me with a sort of a half-reproachful eye, as the cause of the ruin of the Govt.'[9] Less than a week later, however, he was feeling distinctly smug. 'I am satisfied,' he wrote, 'that my conduct since the beginning of this session has been marked by the most unusual prudence, and it has been more successful than if it had been more bustling and brilliant and offensive.'[10]

So it went on, while the Commons' inquiry into the Scheldt expedition dragged on throughout the whole of February and half March, and Canning brooded on his political prospects with alternate despair and elation. In the end the Commons refused to censure the policy of sending the expedition and even – although by only 21 votes – to condemn the tragic delay in evacuating Walcheren in spite of the fever epidemic. Canning spoke at length in defence of the decision to send the expedition in the first place and declared that although he had no personal responsibility for the delay in bringing the troops home, he would not censure the government for it. He told Joan afterwards he felt there would have been 'something very ungenerous' in voting against the government over the evacuation immediately after he personally had been cleared by the Commons' first vote – 'not to mention,' he added honestly, 'that in my conscience I *do* believe the distracted state of the Gvt might have something to do with the delay and mismanagement of the evacuation.'[11] And no one knew better than he who had been primarily responsible for the government's distraction.

No sooner had the government got over the hump of the Scheldt inquiry than it was faced with an alarming new crisis, this time largely of its own making. In February, a Mr Gale Jones, secretary of a radical society, had been committed to Newgate by the Commons for allegedly libelling their proceedings. When the Radical leader, Sir Francis Burdett, wrote an open letter denouncing the Commons' arbitrary use of their privileges, he too found himself in hot water. Three days later, on March 27, Mr Lethbridge, a member for Somerset, introduced a motion declaring that Burdett had been guilty of violating the privileges of the House. Burdett was already something of a popular hero because of his reforming views, and many people, including Canning, felt it would be most unwise to make a martyr of him. But Perceval was determined to show that he was not afraid of Burdett or his followers, and after Lethbridge's motion had been accepted by a huge majority on April 5, he arranged that a resolution should be introduced for Burdett's committal to the Tower. After an all-night debate the proposal was accepted by only 38 votes. Canning, after much havering, voted for the Tower on the rather inadequate grounds that he did not want to be misrepresented as 'all timidity', while Perceval was 'all stoutness'. Afterwards he found that many members who shared his doubts of the wisdom of pushing the matter so far wished he had given them a lead.[12]

If he had, he might just conceivably have saved London from four days of mob violence. Sir Francis evaded his would-be captors with cool effrontery and challenged the legality of their action, while the authorities behaved with remarkable ineptitude. Meanwhile the mob went on the rampage; barricades were thrown up in Piccadilly, where Sir Francis lived, prominent politicians who had spoken against him had their windows smashed and eventually the army had to be called in.

Canning hoped he was safe out at Brompton, but when he heard that the mob had been to Bruton Street inquiring for his present address, he prudently asked the Home Secretary for an armed guard. It was not until the 9th that the Serjeant-at-Arms managed to arrest Burdett and lodge him safely in the Tower.*

Somehow or other, the government had survived both the Burdett riots and the Walcheren inquiry. But neither friend nor foe thought it could go on as it was for long. And so for the next six months, while Wellington was grimly retreating from the Portuguese frontier to the lines of Torres Vedras outside Lisbon, the politicians in London occupied themselves with their own absorbing political manœuvres. Their aim was to strengthen the government, but as everybody's likes and dislikes, prejudices and pretensions had to be carefully considered, it was very hard to achieve. Canning would have brought the biggest access of strength, but after all that had happened the previous summer, Perceval and most of his colleagues were very reluctant to apply to him for help, and certainly to him alone. Wellesley, who was so anxious

---

* Burdett and Gale Jones were eventually released on June 21 after the end of the parliamentary session.

to bring in Canning that he was prepared to let him have the Foreign Office, suggested that his inclusion might be more acceptable if Castlereagh and Sidmouth were invited at the same time. This proposal was accepted by the Cabinet but was still-born because Sidmouth, who was approached first, flatly refused to serve with Canning. 'We have nothing for it,' wrote Wellesley-Pole philosophically on April 28, 'but to stick to the vessel until she sinks, which I expect she will do very speedily.'[13] Robert Dundas took the same gloomy view but hinted that he might leave the ship before she actually sank.

Several attempts were made during the early summer to persuade Sidmouth to change his mind, but without success. No one seriously supposed that Castlereagh would consider coming in with Canning alone. But Wellesley flatly rejected any plan that excluded Canning and began to argue that as Sidmouth was so obstinate, they ought at least to try a joint approach to Castlereagh and Canning. After a long discussion at a Cabinet dinner on July 26 the ministers at last agreed to do so. Wellesley afterwards reported to Canning that there followed an even more protracted and 'violent' debate across the dinner table over precisely what joint offer should be made.[14] Wellesley was prepared to give up the Foreign Office and Liverpool the War Department, so that Castlereagh and Canning could both have their old offices back. But it was feared they might start quarrelling again and in any case no one was keen on having Castlereagh once more in charge of the War Department. On the other hand, everyone except Wellesley felt that to let Canning alone have his old job back would be indelicate and unfair to Castlereagh. Several ministers helpfully offered their own resignations and eventually it was decided that Castlereagh and Canning should be jointly offered the Home Office and the Admiralty and asked to decide between themselves who should have which. It took Perceval some three weeks and much anxious thought to set forth the offer in an immensely long and exceedingly tactful letter to Castlereagh. It took Castlereagh only a day to send back a curt rejection.

Castlereagh's refusal, which surprised nobody but Wellesley, virtually cancelled out the offer to Canning. Too many members of the Cabinet distrusted him too much to bring him in on his own. Canning never seems to have made any personal objections to serving with anyone and was very indignant when his own admission seemed to depend on Sidmouth's whim. He was apparently reconciled to serving under Perceval and had set his heart on getting back the Foreign Office. In a letter to Joan he tried to put a brave face on things by making out that it was a relief not to be faced with an offer which it would have been prudent and advantageous for him to accept. 'Just as if I had made up my mind that I *ought* to take a dose of nasty physick – but should be glad if, from no fault of mine, the bottle fell down and broke before I took it.'[15]

But he could not help wanting and trying to get back his old job. Nearly a month later, towards the end of September, he formally assured both Perceval and Wellesley that he would still accept the Foreign Office and only the Foreign Office. But that post had never been offered him. At a time when a willingness to resign was admired, and any signs of ambition or over-readiness to serve were suspect, it did not do to aim too high. It was a lesson that Canning was very slow to learn.

So Perceval and his colleagues prepared to make do as best they could on their own. 'We must make the best battle we can,' wrote Mulgrave in heroic vein to Perceval, 'and if necessary "die in the last ditch."' [16] In fact the government's plight was not really as desperate as its fluctuating and uncertain majorities in the Commons suggested. It enjoyed the King's firm and undeviating support; and to most of the independent M.P.s it was at least preferable to the Whigs – the only obvious alternative – with their disagreeable quarrels, suspect ideas and unpatriotic attitude towards the war.

But before the year was out, the government had been struck by a blow that everyone, whatever their political views, assumed would prove fatal. The old King, overcome with grief by the death of his daughter, Princess Amelia, after a long and particularly harrowing illness, lapsed once more into insanity. The first symptoms appeared towards the end of October, about a week before the princess died. Parliament met on November 1 and was thrice adjourned, while the King hovered between violence and lucidity and Perceval tried to decide whether he could rely on the doctors' optimistic hopes for a speedy recovery, or must take steps to set up a regency. And no one doubted that, once Regent, the Prince of Wales would bring in his friends the Whigs.

By the middle of December, it was clear that a regency could not be avoided, and on December 20 Perceval introduced resolutions modelled on those drawn up by Pitt during the similar crisis of 1788–9. In the hope that the King might yet recover, the Regent's powers were for a period to be limited; in particular, he was not to be allowed to appoint to offices or peerages. The limitations were hotly contested by the opposition in the Commons. But respect for Perceval's character and steadiness, loyalty to the old King and mistrust of his son, combined to carry the day for the government. By the middle of January 1811, Perceval's regency resolutions had been accepted by both Houses of Parliament, and by the end of the month the bill modelled on them had also passed through all its stages.

Some weeks before Perceval introduced his resolutions, Canning had made up his mind what line he would take. In a letter to Granville Leveson-Gower on November 26, he wrote that if a regency could not possibly be avoided, the King's right to resume his authority if he recovered should be fully safeguarded, but in the meantime the Regent should not be limited in his authority as he was to have been in 1788–9. 'A strong executive government,' he wrote, 'is in my mind, absolutely essential . . . We cannot *afford now* to run the risk – which was no risk *then* [1788] – of exhibiting the executive authority in a state of curtailment – in which, if it fails of the power to do its duty, we all fail with it.'[17]

It seemed a perfectly respectable position. In 1788 the French Revolution had not begun to erupt, the spectre of social upheaval was scarcely visible, England was at peace and had no intention of going to war. Much had changed in twenty-three years, and Canning was much too intelligent to suppose that devotion to Pitt's memory demanded that he should slavishly copy his example in vastly different circumstances. Yet many people were apparently genuinely shocked by his opposition to proposals based on the precedent set by Pitt. His apostasy was underlined and his personal embarrassment increased by the inevitable harking back during the regency debates to the similar debates twenty-three years earlier. On one occasion he was stung into one of the bursts of eloquence for which he had become famous. Sir Samuel Romilly, the distinguished Whig lawyer and reformer, had made a sneeringly critical reference to Pitt which Wilberforce had immediately got up and answered with a glowing tribute to his dead friend. Next day some slighting references by Sheridan to Pitt, coming on top of Romilly's remarks, were too much for Canning who, in the words of one witness, 'burst out with one of the most exuberant and magnificent flowing invectives against Romilly for his attack on Pitt the night before . . . that ever could be heard anywhere. It seemed to electrify the House, and kindled an indignation against Romilly which actually thundered . . . I am obliged to allow that from Fox or from Pitt I never heard anything equal to this forcible declamation.'[18]*

* According to the same observer, Romilly listened to Canning with 'cold self-

It was his ability to dominate the Commons in this way which made politicians on both sides of the House anxious to have his support. During the regency debates, when the Whigs were confidently assuming that they would soon be called on to form a government, one of their several causes of dissension was whether or not they should try to win over Canning. Grenville, who had always remained on friendly personal terms with him, was very anxious to have him. Even the Prince of Wales, who disliked Canning because of his friendship for the Princess of Wales, more or less recommended to Grenville that he should try to form a coalition with him. Grey, on the other hand, who had thoroughly disliked him ever since the Copenhagen debates, as well as most of the old Foxites, distrusted him and felt they would lose more than they would gain by an alliance with him.

It was widely assumed, by the opposition and most other people, that if invited to join a Whig ministry, Canning would not refuse, and there were many rumours about what post he would get. Why otherwise was he opposing a restricted regency? But the truth seems to have been that Canning believed that was the right thing to do. He realised that his motives would be misinterpreted and told Granville Leveson-Gower on November 26 that he did not want to make his views known before he must because he would appear to be courting the Regent. It was not, he said, that he was indifferent to office, but he believed that his differences with the Whigs (particularly over the Peninsular war) went too deep. 'Nevertheless,' he added, 'I think it right that if they are to be the new ministers, they should inherit the full power of the Crown; and I wish to do my best to give it them – if I am to fight them afterwards. This is the whole of my creed.'[19]

The Prince Regent, however, decided not to send for the Whigs after all. He was annoyed by the arrogance of the Whig grandees, Grey and Grenville, who took it for granted that he would give them power and lectured him on his duty. (Lord Holland commented that unfortunately 'the passion for pen and ink was strong upon Lord Grenville during the whole of that session.'[20]) Moreover some of the reports of the King's condition were quite encouraging, and if he did recover and found the Whigs in office, he would be furious.

Afterwards, Canning told his mother that he was relieved he had not actually been invited to join a Whig ministry. 'I *could not* have accepted

---

possession' and dissipated much of the effect of his attack by adroitly pointing out that he had taken 24 hours to make it. Canning in fact had felt he could not add anything to what Wilberforce had said the night before.

because I believe the course of public counsels, in such an arrangement, would have been directly contrary to my opinions.'[21] In other words, he would not have ratted on his principles for the sake of office, but it would have been very painful deliberately to turn it down. Unfortunately, it was always his hankering after office, not his adherence to what he thought right, that struck those around him. His apparent desertion of Pitt and of Perceval, coming on top of his behaviour to Castlereagh which was still disapprovingly remembered, caused his stock to fall very low. Comparisons between him and Perceval were on everybody's lips, and always to Perceval's advantage. The prime minister had certainly grown in stature and skill and thoroughly deserved his bouquets. Canning, on the other hand, did not deserve all his brickbats.

Meanwhile, the struggle against Napoleon was still to be won. From London, in the early spring of 1811, the outlook in the Peninsula looked doubtful. Wellington and his army had spent the winter behind the lines of Torres Vedras outside Lisbon, while the pursuing French, although desperately short of supplies, sat out the winter behind their own lines thirty miles away. Retreat and a waiting game did not go down well at home, especially at a time of growing commercial, economic and social distress. But the government stuck stoutly by Wellington. So did Canning. When the army estimates were debated on March 4, he made an eloquent defence of Wellington's Peninsular campaign. He added that as he himself shared the responsibility for sending Wellington back to Portugal nearly two years earlier, he was bound to make his position plain while the issue of the campaign was still in doubt.[22] Next day the starving French began their long and harrowing retreat back into Spain. By April 10 they were across the frontier, and on the 26th Canning seconded the Commons' vote of thanks to Wellington for the liberation of Portugal.

Unlike the military outlook, the domestic situation did not brighten as the year advanced. The long years of Napoleon's continental blockade were having their effect. The volume of British exports dropped sharply. Manufacturers went bankrupt and cotton operatives, thrown out of work, took to machine-smashing. A Commons' committee appointed to inquire into the industrial distress reported that there were 'insuperable objections' to all the proposed remedies; few disagreed with this depressing conclusion. But the report of another committee on the country's monetary difficulties gave rise to a week of argument and speechifying, most of it highly involved and largely unintelligible. The committee concluded that the depreciation of paper money was due to the inflationary over-issue of notes by the Bank of England and that the remedy was to resume cash payments which had been suspended since 1797. The government opposed a remedy that was likely to hamper its war effort and eventually it was rejected. Canning was no financial expert and on the last day of the debate frankly admitted that 'the details of this intricate and perplexing subject are as little agreeable to my taste, or habits, as to those of any person in the House.' But on this, as on everything else, he had to make up his own mind, and in an extremely able speech he suggested that Parliament ought to accept the bullionist theory but not put it into practice for the time being.[23] Francis Horner, the chairman of the bullion committee, wrote afterwards: 'The best speech was Canning's, which astounded everybody by the knowledge he showed of the subject.'[24]

Canning put the homework he had done on the country's monetary problems to private as well as public use. Like many other people at the time, he thought it was better to invest in land rather than hang on to a depreciating paper currency, and that summer he and Joan bought an estate at Long Sutton in Lincolnshire, valued at £26,000. They made several expeditions from Hinckley to survey their new acquisition, to make arrangements for having it farmed and to see if there were any other possible bargains to be picked up. Canning told Bagot that by the following Lady Day he hoped not to have 'a £ in the world, for which my children shall be obliged to receive as creditors of the State any pieces of paper that the State may think proper to give them.'[25] It did not work out quite like that; nor did the estate at Long Sutton prove a profitable investment. At the time, however, Canning was full of uncritical enthusiasm for his acres of wheat which he described as the finest ever seen.

But although he might enjoy playing the landowner, Canning could not refrain from endlessly speculating and corresponding about his political future. The outlook was indeed extremely obscure – and not only for Canning. By the time Parliament reassembled early in January 1812, it seemed most unlikely that the old King would ever rule again. But what the Regent would do when the restrictions on his freedom of action lapsed on February 18 was a mystery – as much, it seems, to the Regent himself as to the politicians. It was assumed that he would get rid of his present ministers who before Christmas had not made

themselves any more congenial to him by successfully opposing his
financial demands. But the Whigs were not as sure as they had been a
year earlier that he would turn to them, or that if he did, his terms
would be acceptable. In 1811 they had rejected his suggestion that they
should try to join forces with Canning. But a year later most of them –
Whitbread being the chief exception – seemed to have come round to
the view that an alliance with Canning would strengthen their bargaining position with the Regent. So when he came up to London for the
opening of Parliament he found himself being tempted with offers of
high office in the ministry which the Whigs hoped they would be asked
to form. But feeling sure that he would fall out with them over the
Peninsular war, he did not respond.

A much more attractive possibility was that Lord Wellesley might
be asked to form a broadly-based government of moderates and some
of the Regent's friends like Lord Moira. Wellesley had reduced the
Foreign Office to chaos and his Cabinet colleagues to extreme exasperation, but in spite of these achievements his political standing was still
considerable. He himself, at any rate, thought he had, or ought to
have, a great future and throughout the winter he had been busily
promoting it. He had cultivated the Regent for all he was worth,
apparently with some success, and early in the New Year, offered to
resign, whenever convenient, from a ministry in which he said he no
longer had any confidence. He seems to have really believed – and made
Canning believe – that he was well on the way to becoming Perceval's
successor.

But although the Regent did not like his present ministers, he was
becoming reconciled to them. Like them (but unlike the Whigs) he
was not defeatist about the war and his ideas on the Irish problem had
become a good deal more cautious. Moreover, he could not ignore
Perceval's growing strength and stature in the Commons. On the other
hand, he was reluctant to turn his back on his Whig friends. So in the
end he opted for a compromise and on February 13 invited Grey and
Grenville to join a coalition with his present ministers. Predictably,
however, the Whig lords were not content with only half of the cake
and returned a dignified refusal. Wellesley thereupon supposed that
his moment had come. But unfortunately for him his manœuvres
reached the ears of his Cabinet colleagues who indignantly decided
that either he or they must go. Faced with this ultimatum, the Regent
told Wellesley that he would accept his resignation. It was better, after
all, to try for a quiet life with the devil he knew.

Wellesley and Canning, who felt they had been led up the garden path by the Regent, were furious with him. But there was worse to come. The vacant Foreign Office, which Canning proprietorially referred to as 'my office', was given to his great rival, Castlereagh; and Perceval, who naturally enough wanted to make his government as strong as possible, also found places for the despised Sidmouth and several of his friends. Canning was the only important survivor among 'Pitt's friends' to be left out in the cold. Not surprisingly, the most frequent epithet applied to his conduct at this time by contemporaries was 'violent'. 'Flesh and blood cannot stand this,' wrote Robert Ward, a Tory M.P., on March 1, 'and therefore he [Canning] is at length, though with all the forms and phrases of Rt Hon friend, in determined opposition.'[26]

But it was opposition with a difference. The day after Perceval had been finally confirmed in office, the Whigs sent an emissary round to sound out Canning. He rejected the overture, politely, but firmly. Three days later he told Joan that his course was becoming plainer. 'I think I see my way to a mode of conduct in Parlt which will give me all the aid of Opptn co-operation without pledging me to them . . . a concert like that of Pitt and Fox against Addington.' He had been assured that the opposition would not take a line over the war that would distress him, and that he and Wellesley would still be free to form a government if the Regent asked them.[27] In short, co-operation without commitment was to be the order of the day.

At first the plan seemed to be working well. On February 27 an independent member, Sir Thomas Turton, introduced a motion for a Committee of the House on the state of the nation. The opposition decided to turn the debate into a trial of strength with the government, and there was much interest in how Canning would vote. He said that he agreed with Perceval on most matters, especially the war in Spain, but on the question of Ireland disagreed with him so strongly that he would vote with the opposition.[28] Canning himself described his speech as 'very *judicious* and very very temperate'. The opposition speakers too were carefully moderate. Whitbread, usually a violent opponent of the war, pointed out to Tierney afterwards that he had not 'put *his little toe* upon the Peninsula'.[29] The motion was of course lost, but Canning's decision to take fifteen followers into the opposition lobby helped to make the government's majority smaller than Perceval had predicted it would be.

A few days later, however, the perils of trying to combine opposition with consistency were revealed with painful clearness. On March 3 the up-and-coming young Whig barrister, Henry Brougham, introduced a motion for an inquiry into the effect of the Orders-in-Council and the licence trade arising out of them on the commerce and industry of the country. The Orders were widely blamed for the country's economic distress and there was growing popular pressure for their repeal. Brougham's original motion had simply asked for the repeal of the Orders. Canning had let him know that as one of the principal champions of the Orders in the Portland government, he could not possibly support this; but he could vote for a motion which simply asked for an inquiry into the system of trade by licences. The motion was duly amended, but inevitably the debate still revolved round the merits or otherwise of the Orders-in-Council. Canning, who was struggling with a heavy cold, failed to make clear to others the distinction which satisfied his own conscience.[30] Wilberforce thought that for the first time he showed a 'plain opposition front'[31] and the contemptuous reactions which his speech aroused on all sides were, commented Robert Ward, 'no bad comment on the fair feeling of the times, which will not tolerate apostasy, however set off by the splendour of abilities or the powers of eloquence.'[32]

Canning himself seems to have realised that he had done badly and the elation with which he had embarked on his system of co-operation with the opposition was succeeded by a mood of black depression. The Whigs, he felt, would try to overcome their unpopularity by pushing projects for parliamentary reform which he could not support. As for Wellesley, who had seemed such a valuable ally, he was now only a tie and a burden.[33] More than once at this time Canning thought of giving up politics altogether, selling Gloucester Lodge and settling in Devonshire, where young George's precarious health might be improved by sea bathing and the mild climate. There seemed no future for him at Westminster, where Perceval's ascendancy was more firmly established than ever – 'and why he should not be Minister for 20 years like Sir Robert Walpole I cannot pretend to say.'[34] Some two months after Canning wrote this, Perceval was dead.

About five o'clock on the afternoon of May 11, 1812, Spencer Perceval was shot through the heart as he was entering the lobby of the House of Commons. His assailant was a commercial agent called John Bellingham, who had been ruined by the Franco-British economic war and had decided to revenge himself in this crazy way for the government's refusal to give him compensation. Perhaps no other politician would have been so sincerely mourned by all who knew him, whatever their political views. When the Commons met next day, 'in most faces,' wrote the Speaker, 'there was an agony of tears; and neither Lord Castlereagh, Ponsonby, Whitbread nor Canning could give a dry utterance to their sentiments.'[35] Since the beginning of the regency, Canning and Perceval had been estranged, on Canning's side with considerable bitterness. But all that was forgotten in the shock of Perceval's murder. 'In truth,' wrote Canning some days later, 'he was a man with whom one could not be personally at variance; and our rivalry had been a rivalry of circumstances which neither of us could command – not of choice, still less of enmity.'[36]

But while Perceval's friends and colleagues mourned his death, throughout the country the starving mobs rejoiced savagely. In London, 'Rescue Bellingham or die' was scrawled on walls; the mob cheered him loudly on the way to Newgate, shouted 'Burdett for ever' and reviled the soldiers as murderers. When the news of Perceval's assassination reached Nottingham, the mob paraded through the streets with drums and colours, cheering and rejoicing. On May 16 Wilberforce described the state of the West Riding manufacturing districts as 'dreadful – next to rebellion, smouldering rebellion.'[37] For months past the activities of the Luddites and rumours of risings had been causing increasing alarm. Early in April, Grey told Grenville that according to his brother the secrecy and organisation of the frame-breaking round Leeds suggested 'a superior and concealed direction'.[38] Although there was not a shred of evidence that Bellingham had acted on anyone's behalf but his own, there was a widespread fear among the better-off classes that Perceval's murder was the prelude to full-scale revolution.

Yet in this atmosphere of crisis and panic, with troops and militia being continually marched hither and thither to put down disturbances, it still took the politicians and the Regent well over three weeks to agree on a new government. A sense of urgency was not lacking; but it was not strong enough to override the personal rivalries and political differences that divided the leading politicians on both sides of the House. Nor was the Regent capable of giving them a strong lead. Altogether it seemed unlikely that the Perceval government without Perceval could survive for long.

That at any rate was the gloomy view of its surviving members. They told the Regent, however, that they would try to carry on if they could count on his backing, and then looked around for additional means of support. On May 17, Liverpool, as acting premier, called on both Canning and Wellesley and invited each of them to join the government. Next day both turned the invitation down. Canning's refusal was based on the 'loss of personal and public character' which he would sustain if he joined a government known to be hostile to his own views on the Catholic question; the government, he argued, would be weakened, not strengthened, if he joined it.[39] It was a perfectly genuine and reasonable ground for refusal. But it seems likely that a further obstacle was Liverpool's decision, which he mentioned to Canning, to make Castlereagh leader of the House of Commons as well as Foreign Secretary. The old rivalry was cropping up again, and Canning was not the only one to feel that he could not be expected to allow two of the plums to go to a man who was widely considered his inferior both as a speaker and an administrator. 'Surely,' wrote Thomas Grenville (who was no admirer of Canning) when he heard of it, 'Liverpool is gone as mad as Bellingham to entertain such a notion.'[40] And Grey, who positively disliked Canning, thought that quite apart from the Catholic question, the proposal made to Canning 'was one which he could not accept without absolute disgrace.'[41]

Meanwhile, Liverpool and his colleagues, having made their gesture to Wellesley and Canning, were apparently prepared to soldier on without any new recruits except for Nicholas Vansittart (an Addingtonian) who on May 20 was appointed to replace Perceval as Chancellor of the Exchequer. But any dawning self-confidence on the government's part was rudely shattered on May 21 when Mr Stuart-Wortley, usually a government supporter, introduced and carried by four votes a motion praying the Regent to take steps 'to form a strong and efficient Administration.' Liverpool resigned next day and the Regent, determined not to throw himself on the mercy of the Whig lords, turned to Wellesley. He did not instruct him to form a new ministry, but merely to explore the possibilities and report back.

Wellesley's first step was to consult Canning, who replied that in his view anyone, whatever his 'party connection', should be considered eligible for the new ministry if he was prepared to work for an immediate settlement of the Catholic question and wage the Peninsular war with vigour. On this basis, and with Wellesley's approval, Canning went hopefully round to Liverpool's house on May 23 to sound him out.[42] It was a fruitless visit, for Wellesley's cause was already lost. The day before, the *Morning Chronicle* had published a statement by him on his reasons for his resignation the previous February which contained some extraordinarily offensive comments on Perceval's abilities. Whether or not Wellesley himself was responsible for the publication – and there seems some doubt about this – the damage was done.

Perceval's former colleagues were shocked and furious; all their old dislike of Wellesley boiled up anew and they flatly refused to serve with him.[43] 'Nothing,' wrote the Duke of Richmond from Dublin when he heard what had happened, 'can go on well where Lord Wellesley has anything to do. How that man has lowered himself. After his publications [criticising Perceval] he is not fit to be one of the committee to regulate Whyte's.'[44]

The Regent, however, remained as reluctant to confirm Liverpool and his colleagues in office as he was to let the Whigs form a ministry. For several days he brooded over the problem, working himself up into such a state of irritation that Liverpool in alarm sent post-haste for the Duke of York to come and pacify his brother. But all the duke achieved was to get himself roundly snubbed for tactlessly advising the Regent to send for the Whigs. It was Lord Moira, an independent Whig, who did most to persuade the Regent that Grey and Grenville could not be ignored. On May 29, Moira reported to Wellesley that he had had 'a sharp skirmish with HRH about Lord Grey,' but hoped that Wellesley would in the end be allowed to approach the opposition.[45] On June 1, the Regent at last agreed to commission Wellesley to form a government.

Wellesley at once approached Grey and Grenville with an offer of four or five places in a Cabinet which, at the Regent's request, should also include Canning, Moira and Lord Erskine, another of the Regent's friends who had been Lord Chancellor in the Ministry of all the Talents.[46] Two days later Grey and Grenville turned down this offer; the reasons they gave were grandiloquent but unconvincing. Whitbread thought the offer was 'pretty impudent',[47] but Richmond felt that if the Whigs wanted 'to do good, it [the offer] ought to have satisfied them, but, as their object is power, it will not.'[48] The Whigs, however, believed that they could only do good if they secured power on terms that would give them the whip hand over a prince whom they had come to distrust as much as he distrusted them.

Wellesley was not given a second chance to form a government. The Regent turned to Moira instead, and for the next few days the outlook seemed to get progressively brighter – not least for Canning. There was no agreement between him and Wellesley that neither would accept office without the other. And the Regent had let it be known that he hoped Canning and Huskisson (who had resigned as a Secretary of the Treasury with Canning in 1809) would help 'to protect him against the opposition'.[49] Canning, of course, was delighted to oblige and Moira at once began to confer with him. In the early stages of the crisis, Moira, with his Whiggish sympathies, had been anxious to bring in Grey and Grenville. But he was disgusted by their rejection of Wellesley's offer and their thoroughly unsatisfactory response to his own efforts to renew negotiations with them convinced him that they were impossible to deal with.[50]

Instead he sent for Canning and Huskisson and began to put together a ministry without the Whigs. At first he was confident of success, encouraged by promises of zealous support from Liverpool and Eldon, although they preferred not to take office immediately.* According to a friend, however, Moira was a brave soldier, but 'the greatest political coward in the world.'[51] Just when a bold and confident assumption of power might have won him the support of a Parliament that by now was thoroughly sick of the long crisis, he lost his nerve. On June 8, while Grenville was writing to Buckingham that he believed everything was settled,[52] Moira was in fact telling the Regent that he must give up. On the same day the Regent also gave up and sent for the acting prime minister. The old firm found itself in business again and Liverpool began the long premiership that was to last until his fatal illness fifteen years later.

Towards the end of the crisis, Canning had hopes of reaching the summit of his ambition. But once again he was disappointed. The call for help from Carlton House never came and Canning never got a chance to discover whether he could do better than the egregious Wellesley or the pusillanimous Moira. He had the consolation of not having made any new enemies nor earned any more brickbats. But the same thought must have struck him as occurred to Wilberforce when he went down to the Commons on June 8 and discovered to his surprise that Liverpool was forming a government. 'How striking is Canning's example,' wrote Wilberforce in his diary. 'Had he fairly joined Perceval on the Duke of Portland's death, as Perceval offered, he would now have been the acknowledged head, and supported as such.'[53]

Before Parliament rose for the summer recess, Canning enjoyed a parliamentary success on what was perhaps the most controversial issue of the day: Catholic emancipation. The Catholics had by now

* Both Liverpool and Eldon had huffily let it be known that they would give the government their 'handsome' support, if only someone would have the courtesy to ask them for it. Moira agreed that this 'little point of honour' must be gratified and arranged that he and Canning should call on Liverpool. (Roberts, p. 415)

arrived at an unsatisfactory half-way house between rigid repression and full political and civil equality with the Protestants. They had the vote, but they could not sit in Parliament themselves. They could hold the lower posts in government and the professions, but not the higher ones. In England, where they were only a small minority, their plight was not a popular issue; among the general public, whether educated or not, anti-Catholic prejudices still ran deep and strong. But year after year the endemic unrest across the Irish Sea forced the Catholic issue on the attention of the Parliament at Westminster where those who feared for the peace and stability of Ireland if the Catholic claims were not met were opposed by those who feared for the safety of the constitution and the Protestant establishment if they were. It was the one question on which the Whigs were more or less united, and their loyalty to the Catholic cause had helped to keep them out of office. The Tories, on the other hand, were so disunited over this issue that Liverpool (a staunch anti-Catholic) felt obliged to allow it to become an open question on which ministers could vote as they chose.

With the establishment of the regency, the Irish Catholics began to hope for better days. In the past the Regent had committed himself more than once to their cause. But to the anger and consternation of the Irish Catholics and their friends in England, he showed a marked reluctance to honour his commitments. During 1811 the moderate Irish Catholics inadvertently helped to push the Regent into the Protestant camp by trying to organise themselves on a representative basis in a way that looked suspiciously like an embryo Catholic parliament. Their activities were declared illegal and firmly stamped on. Early in 1812 agrarian disturbances in various parts of the country added to the general atmosphere of frustration and unrest. Although a more or less simmering Ireland was something that the English had learned to live with, the less bigoted among them were coming to realise that the Irish might boil over again as they had done in 1798, and that emancipation would be preferable to revolt, civil war and even secession.

For Canning, the establishment of the regency removed the obstacle which ever since 1801 had prevented him from pressing the Catholics' claims. Like Pitt, he had determined to respect the prejudice and convictions of George III, so long as he lived or remained in his right mind. But now that the old King was believed to be incurably mad, he was anxious to move cautiously ahead. On April 24 he supported a motion introduced by the famous Irish orator, Henry Grattan, for a committee to inquire into the laws affecting the Catholics. He spoke at the end of a long two-day debate, and after he had sat down Grattan said he had nothing to add to a speech which had 'so eloquently answered every argument against the motion.' Predictably, the motion was lost by 85 votes, but the pro-Catholic minority of 215 was exceptionally large.[54]

Canning was encouraged to go on trying. On June 22 he moved that early in the next session the House should consider the laws affecting the Catholics with a view to a final settlement. In his introductory speech he made a moderate and conciliatory appeal to reason and common sense. Conservative by temperament, he realised that change was sometimes necessary. To reconcile 'the dread of innovation' with 'the expediency of timely reformation or concession' was, he told the House, 'almost the whole art of practical policy'. He pointed out that the Catholics had been penalised and persecuted, not for their religious tenets, but because they were believed to be actual or potential traitors. But the system of repression had already been recognised as unsuccessful, unnecessary and morally indefensible. The process of dismantling it had already begun, and the question before the House was simply how much further this process should be carried. Canning said that to oppose any concessions at all was at least consistent. But those who argued that the concessions made so far were safe but that any more would be dangerous, must prove their case.[55]

In the debate that followed, two Cabinet ministers, Castlereagh and Vansittart, spoke in favour of the motion. To Canning's surprise, it was triumphantly carried by 235 votes to 106. A similar motion, introduced by Wellesley in the Lords, was lost by only one vote. Few of the emancipationists – certainly not Canning – doubted that they were on the threshold of final victory. Few would have believed anyone who told them that they were more than fifteen years out in their reckoning.

At this point, just as Canning seemed to be recovering some of the ground he had lost three years earlier, he made the most disastrous political miscalculation of his whole career. He was offered a great deal, but once again he decided it was not enough and once again he lost everything. But this time it was ten years, not three, before a comparable opportunity came his way.

The government badly needed strengthening in the Commons. As a parliamentary performer, Castlereagh was not impressive. Just after the Catholic debate he had been forced to give way to Brougham's relentless pressure for the repeal of the Orders-in-Council. (The repeal, however, came too late to prevent the Americans from declaring war.) Apart from Castlereagh, the only senior ministers on the Treasury bench were Vansittart, who was no debater, and Bragge-Bathurst, Chancellor of the Duchy of Lancaster, who was only there because his brother-in-law Sidmouth insisted that he should be. Canning was, as Wilberforce said, 'inimitable in wit and sarcasm.'[56] He was the obvious recruit and Liverpool was extremely anxious to get him. So too was the Regent in spite of Canning's pro-Catholic views. One possible obstacle was Castlereagh, but he turned out to be anxious for a reconciliation. When Liverpool hinted as much to Canning, he promptly called on Castlereagh, who received him very cordially and begged that the past should be forgotten.[57]

Castlereagh went further. He offered to let Canning have the Foreign Office. Many years later Canning described this as 'perhaps the handsomest offer that was ever made to an individual',[58] and there is no reason to suppose that he did not think so at the time. But Castlereagh made it clear that if he gave up the Foreign Office he must keep the leadership of the House of Commons which had come to him after Perceval's death. It was Canning's reluctance to accept this which eventually caused the negotiation to break down.

Fundamentally, both men felt it would be humiliating to accept the superiority of the other. Castlereagh told Canning that if he did not already hold the lead he would not set himself up in competition with him, but he could not bring himself to step down.[59] Canning assured Charles Arbuthnot, a Joint Secretary at the Treasury, that he certainly did want to join the government, but if the price was to accept Castlereagh's supremacy in the Commons, it 'would cost me a bitter pang – *not* from any personal feeling towards C. upon my honour, but from a sense of humiliation – hard to endure and I *think* unnecessary to be proposed to me.'[60] There was also the belief common to politicians then and now that the world thought no better of a man than he did of himself; 'it is the feeling,' he told Liverpool on July 19, 'not only of my friends, but of every man whom I have consulted, that neither my public character and reputation (the only means through which a man can be useful in high office) nor the interests of the Prince Regent's service well understood, will allow of my consenting to enter the Government on the condition of acting under Lord Castlereagh in the House of Commons.' He was, however, quite ready 'to act cordially with him on a footing of perfect equality . . .' and suggested as a possible compromise that the management of the general business of the Commons should be given to Vansittart and that he and Castlereagh should hold the two Secretaryships of State. He even offered to take the Home Department himself although it was an office that had never attracted him.[61] This plan of course assumed that Sidmouth would be willing to give up the Home Department – a pretty large assumption, even though he had by now not only overcome his reluctance to serve in the same Cabinet with Canning but was anxious for a reconciliation.* Liverpool's reply was a painstaking attempt to persuade Canning that whoever had the lead in the Commons was not necessarily superior to the other ministers; he himself preferred to call it the 'management of the business' of the Commons rather than the 'lead'.[62] But Canning was hard to convince, and Castlereagh, having unfortunately 'taken it into his head that there was an intention to run him down', was not very accommodating.[63] By July 24, Arbuthnot reported that 'the anxiety had completely exhausted Liverpool.'[64]

Next day, however, Canning produced a new plan, with himself as Foreign Secretary and Castlereagh as Chancellor, and a distribution of responsibility for the Commons' business which he thought would ensure equality between them. Castlereagh's reactions were not entirely negative although he still insisted on having what he called the general management of the Commons' business and categorically refused to accept the principle of equality on which Canning set such store; he was convinced, he wrote, that some one person must be responsible for the Commons' business.[65] Liverpool read this letter to Canning on the 27th, but he managed to slur over Castlereagh's rejection of the principle of equality. In his well-meaning way, Liverpool felt that the two rivals were much more likely to work cordially together if their roles were not too precisely defined, and that if necessary he himself could act as friendly arbiter between them.[66] Canning was sufficiently satisfied to draft an agreement with Liverpool which conceded to Castlereagh the 'general management' of the Commons' business while preserving (at least in Canning's view) an equality of status between him and Castlereagh.[67] He and Liverpool parted in the belief that agreement was virtually in the bag.

* That August Sidmouth took the initiative in bringing about a reconciliation. One day when Canning called at the Home Department on business, Sidmouth asked to see him alone. According to Canning's account, Sidmouth held out both his hands and with an appearance of great sincerity and feeling said he had long been anxious to end the unpleasant personal relationship between them. 'I need not tell you,' wrote Canning to Granville Leveson-Gower, 'that I took both the poor Doctor's hands, and shook and squeezed them with perfect cordiality. He really moved me; considering, too, that it may be *at least* a question whether he be not the party that has a right to complain.'

But on the way home, Canning called on Huskisson who told him that the version of Castlereagh's letter which had been quoted to him was much less satisfactory than Canning seemed to suppose. Canning, in alarm, immediately asked to see the letter for himself, and as soon as he had read it he decided that any compromise was out of the question. The letter, he angrily told Huskisson, gave Castlereagh the right to say that 'I knew I was acting *under* him; that I knew he had refused to acquiesce in a principle of equality between us.'[68] There was, he told Liverpool when returning the offending letter, nothing more to be done 'to reconcile *my* claim of equality with his of pre-eminence.'[69]

Some people thought he had jumped to the wrong conclusion. Charles Arbuthnot, who had been closely involved, told Lady Bessborough despondently that he was not surprised that Canning had not liked some of Castlereagh's expressions, but Castlereagh was famous for not expressing himself clearly and both he himself and Liverpool understood that the arrangement was to be on a basis of 'perfect equality'.[70] The Regent too was reported as thinking that Canning should have shown more mercy to 'the blundering expressions of so puzzled a writer as Lord Castlereagh'.[71] But neither an explanatory letter from Castlereagh, nor repeated expressions of regret from Liverpool, nor a visit from the Duke of Cumberland on behalf of the Regent, could make Canning change his mind.

So the House of Commons was deprived of what Thomas Grenville maliciously described as the 'fine sport' of watching Castlereagh and Canning decide each day who should have the lead – whatever exactly that might mean.[72] In any case, it seems doubtful whether Castlereagh was really prepared to give up what he meant by it, however ingeniously well-meaning intermediaries might argue to the contrary. He may well have felt that if he was to keep his end up with Canning after letting him have the Foreign Office, he needed to keep the leadership of the Commons. But did Canning really feel that the lead was all that important? If he did, how could he have proposed that it could be given to a second-rater like Vansittart, or even quietly shelved? During the Portland administration, he had not taken it as a personal affront that Perceval should have the lead, however much he might grumble about his performance. And when Castlereagh generously offered to let him return to the Foreign Office, it was he, not Canning, who raised the question of the leadership of the Commons. Once raised, it was not so much Canning himself as his friends who insisted on blowing it up into a major issue. 'For my own part,' wrote Canning to Huskisson on

July 16, 'as you know this is a point upon which I feel infinitely less than is felt by others for me.'[73] Two days later, Huskisson, writing to Melville, referred to 'this much agitated point of the *Lead* raised into importance only by its having been so much agitated'. He assured Melville that Canning did not claim it for himself and only objected to Castlereagh's claim 'in deference to the judgment of others and to what his friends think due to his public character.'[74]

There is no evidence that Canning himself – whatever his friends may have thought – deliberately calculated that if he played hard to get he would do better in the end. Wilberforce, indeed, who was eminently fair, thought that considering his 'real superiority' his terms were not exorbitant.[75] He was certainly tremendously keen to get back into the government as quickly as possible; years later he said that at this time he would have given ten years of his life for two in office.[76] But somehow he let himself be persuaded that it would not do for him to acknowledge Castlereagh as leader of the House of Commons. The Regent thought he was over-punctilious, touchy and took 'as much courting as a woman and more than most'.[77] Touchiness was a failing to which most of the politicians of the day were susceptible, and Canning, who was self-made and lacked the aristocratic background of most of his friends, was more vulnerable than most. But with the war at such a crucial stage, it was hardly the time to stand on his dignity; Napoleon was marching on Moscow and the outcome of Wellington's Peninsular struggle was still undecided. Moreover even from his own point of view, it was a mistake to relegate himself to the political wilderness, although of course he could not have foreseen that the long war would come to a victorious end within two years and that whoever was then Foreign Secretary would have a major role in shaping the postwar settlement.

Having taken his stand, Canning's first uneasy reaction was to justify it, however unconvincingly. In a long letter to Wilberforce, whose advice he had sought throughout the negotiations, he denied that the lead in the Commons was only a 'feather' and that it did not matter whose hands it was in. He argued that whoever held it was the government's representative and was responsible for all that was said or done in the government's name in the House of Commons.[78] And to Granville Leveson-Gower he declared that he felt 'a strong conviction that I have had a great escape and that, if I had been taken at my word, I should by this time have been repenting of my bargain.'[79]

Five months later, he was not nearly so sure. Writing to his mother to explain that he could not help one of her protégés, he regretted that

being out of office deprived him of the chance of helping people. He
sometimes felt, he wrote, that 'I have decided too proudly, and that the
various opportunities of doing acts of kindness which I lose, *might* have
been balanced against the loss of personal character – and yet can that
be right? Or is it not safer and wiser and honester to do what *is* right
and leave the consequences to Heaven?'[80] Before long he could not
even console himself with the feeling that he had done right.

CHAPTER XII

Member for Liverpool:
Ambassador to Lisbon
1812-1816

In the autumn of 1812 Lord Liverpool decided to hold a general
election. If he could not strengthen his ministerial team, he might at
least hope to strengthen his majority in the Commons, especially as
the harvest was good and the Peninsular war was at last going well.
Liverpool's hopes were justified; the government was reckoned to have
won more than forty extra seats. On the whole the election was a
routine affair, but for Canning it was the most momentous and exciting
of his whole career. For the first time he took part in what in those days
passed for a popular contest.

The invitation to stand for Liverpool in the Tory interest came from
a leading merchant, Mr John Gladstone. (His son, William Ewart, aged
three, watched the election junketings from a window.) At first
Canning was not particularly attracted. He was in one of his moods of
depression when politics had lost their savour. 'I have indeed no violent
desire to be in Parliament again at all,' he wrote to Leveson-Gower on
September 17.[1] He knew nothing of the excitement of the hustings.
He already had a safe seat and Liverpool, although predominantly Tory,
was certainly not safe. He was afraid he might find himself having to
foot a large part of the bill and he knew not a single Liverpudlian. On
September 28, he told Huskisson that he had been 'fighting off'
Liverpool.[2] But Gladstone and his friends were persuasive; they wanted
their city to be represented in Parliament by the greatest Tory orator of
the day. They assured Canning that they could get him in and that he
would not have to find a single penny himself. In the end he accepted;
after all, to sit in the Commons for Liverpool would also be a feather
in his cap.

Liverpool returned two members to Parliament and was nominally
an open borough with a popular franchise. But out of a population of
100,000 only about 3,000 had the vote; and as they were mostly working
men and the voting was not secret, they could be subjected to strong
pressure from their employers. A Liverpool election in fact was not so

much a popular contest, although it had all the trappings of one, as a struggle between rival groups of Liverpool merchants. Canning's chief opponent was Henry Brougham, the Whig lawyer, whom Lord Holland described as being always feared, sometimes admired, but not liked by the House of Commons.[3] Brougham was a powerful speaker and his campaign against the Orders-in-Council had made him very popular among the Liverpool merchants whose prosperity had been severely damaged by the effect of the Orders on trade and on relations with America. On the other hand, his opposition to the slave trade and to slavery was a mark against him in a city which for a time had done extremely well out of the trade. Canning, of course, had also been a stout champion of abolition. He had also been a strong advocate of the Orders-in-Council as a weapon against Napoleon, although in the end he had supported their repeal in the hope that it would help to improve relations with America and relieve the distress in England. His pro-Catholic views were a further disadvantage; he described the Catholic question as a 'bugbear of tremendous size throughout all these counties'.[4]

Polling began in Liverpool on October 8 and went on for eight days. The other candidates were Thomas Creevey, the Whig diarist, and the sitting Tory member, General Gascoyne. (A fifth candidate, General Tarleton, dropped out on the third day.) Brougham spent three days canvassing before the poll opened. But Canning's carriage broke down three times on the way and he only arrived on the evening of the 7th, too late for what should have been his triumphal entry into the city. Liverpool elections had a reputation for violence; the year before, Romilly had refused to consider standing there for that reason. But although there was fighting between rival mobs in which two men were killed and several injured, the 1812 election was reckoned to be comparatively peaceful.

It was, however, pretty tough going for the candidates. Each day they had to attend at the polling station between ten and five and say a few well-chosen words to each voter. When the poll closed, there were rival processions ending up with speeches by the candidates. Creevey described how each party moved off, 'the one after the other with his friends, his band of music, his profusion of beautiful flags and his followers'.[5] The evenings were spent, until the small hours, visiting the numerous clubs and benefit societies throughout the city. Brougham estimated that he made 160 speeches during the election[6] and Canning must have made almost as many. His speeches were always printed and circulated by his committee and were apparently read with great interest. *The Times* reporter thought that this would certainly help to increase his vote, 'for when these speeches are read in families and social parties, the ladies, who are very zealous for Mr Canning, and to whom he never omits to pay court, always exert their influence with an increased energy and effect in his favour.'[7]

The candidates were unusually polite to each other. Brougham declared in his opening speech that he did not intend to make any personal attacks, and Canning followed suit. Creevey described how after he had made a speech on the first day of the poll, which was received with great applause, 'Canning instantly put his hand out to shake with me, and we have been cracking jokes all day, particularly upon an old cobbler who voted for him and me . . .' Three days later, Creevey wrote, '. . . We are all as amiable as ever we can be, there is not a particle of bad blood.'[8] It seems that Canning and Brougham managed to have a number of private chats and at the end of the contest had a much better understanding and opinion of each other than when it started.

Although Canning maintained a small lead throughout the polling, it was a hard fought contest. At the close of poll on the 10th, he was 31 ahead of Brougham, who was 5 ahead of Gascoyne, who in his turn was 8 ahead of Creevey. By the evening of the 12th, Brougham was still in second place. By the next evening Canning was 34 ahead of Brougham and Creevey had won the third place from Gascoyne by two votes. At this point the Tories suggested that Brougham and Canning should join forces, but Brougham preferred to fight it out. By the evening of the 15th, Gascoyne had moved into second place and was 171 votes ahead of Brougham. Creevey reported to his wife that evening that he and Brougham 'are fairly done – beat to mummy; but we are to take the chance of some miracle taking place in our favour during the night and are not to strike until eleven or twelve or one tomorrow.'[9] No miracle occurred and at noon next day the two Whigs conceded victory to their opponents. Brougham afterwards ascribed his defeat to his anti-slave trade activities and to the large-scale bribery which Canning's backers were prepared to employ. But he acknowledged that Canning himself had 'conducted the contest fairly and honourably'.[10]*

In his victory speech, Canning handsomely complimented his

* The final voting was: Canning 1,631; Gascoyne, 1,532; Brougham, 1,131; Creevey, 1,068. Canning was also returned for Petersfield, where his cousin Colonel George Canning took his place, and Sligo, where a politician with no Canningite connections was elected in his place. (George IV, I, footnote pp. 169/0)

opponents. Then, according to *The Times* report, he 'jumped off the table, and running up to Mr Brougham, in the most feeling and expressive manner shook hands with him most heartily, and also with Mr Creevey.' Next day he was carried round the town for three hours and then spoke from a window to a crowd of at least 10,000. 'I am this moment returned,' he wrote to Wellesley, 'from a triumphal chairing round the town, and have not steadiness of hands or head to do more than send you this general report of myself.'[11]

Canning stayed on in Liverpool for about another ten days, being fêted by the wealthy Tory merchants. His cousin, Stratford Canning, who was with him, thought that these dinners, with all the turtle and punch, were far more of a hazard to health than any riotous assaults in the streets.[12] When they moved on to Manchester, their host was a wealthy manufacturer who kept them at the dinner table from six to twelve on the sabbath (because no other form of amusement was allowed) and gave them only port to drink because in his opinion it would have been unpatriotic to drink claret.

At a grand entertainment given for him at Manchester Town Hall Canning made a speech in which he referred to the fact that Manchester was the largest unrepresented town in the kingdom. But far from lamenting this, he went on to argue that apart perhaps from a few minor changes in the method of choosing M.P.s, no reform was necessary because the evil complained of did not exist. In Canning's view, the House of Commons could not be changed without destroying the balance of the constitution, and he asked his audience never to forget that England had flourished under her present constitution and become the envy of the world. Whatever his audience thought of this, William Cobbett was outraged. 'Mr Canning,' he wrote indignantly in his *Political Register*, 'is perhaps the most impudent man, and he has, perhaps, more of what is called *brass* than any other man that ever yet addressed a public meeting; yet he never did, that I remember, utter before anything so impudent, so insulting to the public as this.'[13]

If he read them, Canning would probably have been unmoved by Cobbett's strictures. He had had an intoxicating few weeks. His supporters were so pleased with him that they told him he could sit as their member for as long as he pleased. He in fact remained a member for Liverpool through three more elections until in 1823 pressure of work at the Foreign Office forced him to seek a less demanding constituency.* For he was expected to work hard at safeguarding and

* He would have dearly liked to represent Oxford. But his championship of the Catholic cause had made him very unpopular in his old university, and when the

promoting the Liverpudlians' interests. His supporters even agreed to help him do so by paying the rent of an office and the salary of a clerk in London.

After it was all over Canning told his mother that he did not complain at all about all the bustle of the election, 'for it certainly has been gratifying, and glorious beyond my most sanguine dreams of *popular* ambition. I may have looked to be a Minister – but I hardly ever thought that it would have fallen in my way to come in so close contact with so large a portion of the people, and to be so received.'[14]* All his life his aim had been to achieve fame and distinction in the House of Commons. Suddenly his horizons were widened and he realised how exhilarating and valuable it could be to appeal to a wider audience outside the rather rarefied atmosphere of Westminster. The experience did not convert him to parliamentary reform, but he never forgot it.

Canning's triumph in Liverpool may have cheered him up, but it could not hide the fact that when the new Parliament met on November 24, 1812, his political fortunes were at a low ebb. The Treasury bench in the Commons was still weak in debating power and the government was still anxious to secure Canning's assistance. But after its success in the election it could face the prospect of doing without it with greater equanimity. He remained in a loose, rather uneasy, alliance with Wellesley; Peel commented with a good deal of truth that Wellesley was 'a sort of appendage to Mr Canning – incumbrance, perhaps the latter would say.'[15] There were rumours that he had thrown in his lot with the opposition. He himself told the Speaker that he had declined an overture from the Whigs;[16] but since several leading Whigs heartily disliked him, it is unlikely to have been a very pressing one.

Canning still believed that his political future – if he still had one – lay with the Tory party and that the policy of neutrality which he had been trying to pursue for the past three years was still the one most likely to bring him out of the wilderness. He realised only too well, he told Wellesley, how difficult it was to keep one's balance between the two parties, but he was convinced that 'in retreating from the Ministry to

seat fell vacant in 1817, it went, much to Canning's disappointment, to Robert Peel, a staunch Protestant.

* Castlereagh, on the other hand, once said that as between popularity and unpopularity, the latter was 'the more convenient and gentlemanlike'.

fall over into the Opposition would be to lose entirely the vantage ground which we occupy in public opinion, and to identify ourselves with a lost cause.'[17] His aim was to discredit the present administration and present the Pittites with an alternative leadership. But since on the whole he agreed with the government's policy, it was not easy for him to attack it without damaging the reputation for political consistency by which he set great store. All he could do was to suggest that it might perhaps have made a greater effort to support Wellington in the Peninsula, and attack it for the system of 'mitigated and half afraid hostility' with which it carried on the war against the United States.[18] But when Whitbread tried to make political capital out of the Princess of Wales's complaints against her husband, Canning used all his influence to damp down discussion of the Princess's affairs in the Commons; as one of her oldest friends in England, although no longer one of her close advisers, he could hardly do anything else. Nor in the lengthy debates on the renewal of the East India Company's Charter, could he avoid supporting the government's proposal that the company should lose its monopoly of trade with India; his Liverpudlian constituents had great expectations of the benefits they would derive from this concession.

But it was the Catholic question, which fell outside the ordinary scope of party warfare, which really engaged Canning's energy and emotions this session. 'I am *very* anxious,' he wrote on May 1, 1813, 'to carry the Catholic Bill. My persuasion is that it is more for the strength and peace of the Empire than any measure in my memory – the Union with Ireland not excepted.'[19] The general public also thought it was important. When Henry Grattan, the veteran champion of Catholic rights, was due to propose that the Commons should consider the Catholic claims, there was such a crowd of people waiting to get into the gallery that constables had to be called to clear a way for M.P.s to get into the House.[20] Grattan introduced his bill on April 30; its aim was to lift all the remaining civil and military disabilities from the Catholics. Canning felt that more could be done to disarm the bill's critics and when it was read a second time he added some amendments designed to give the Crown, on the recommendation of a commission, a right of veto over the appointment of Catholic bishops.[21] A similar veto had been proposed some years earlier and had been badly received by the Irish Catholics. Canning tried to devise something that would be acceptable to them while still convincing the Protestants of the loyalty of the Catholic hierarchy. 'My task,' he wrote, 'has been to reconcile conflicting opinions and to reason down unreasonable pretensions and prejudices on both sides.'[22] His efforts, however, met the fate of so many compromises – they were heartily disliked by both sides.

But it was an amendment proposed by the Speaker that decided the fate of the bill. On May 24, after arguing that its object was to give the Catholics political ascendancy, not religious freedom, he proposed that the first clause, which gave them the right to sit and vote in either House of Parliament, should be struck out. Castlereagh and Canning both emphasised that this was the heart of the matter, and Canning declared that if it was thrown out he would wash his hands of the rest of the bill. The clause was lost by four votes in one of the largest divisions ever recorded. It might easily have gone the other way if gout and other maladies had not happened to strike some of the pro-Catholics that night. The bill was abandoned but Canning managed to remain optimistic. He maintained that 'a great, a prodigious advance has been made,' and next year the bill must be carried.[23]

Canning was said to have cut a great figure during the Catholic debates. But displays of oratory, however exhilarating at the time, were no substitute for office which gave one the chance to 'do some good' and stamp one's imprint on the country's history. By the time Parliament rose for the summer recess on July 22, 1813, Canning's earlier optimism had been replaced by such a strong sense of political failure that he decided to disband what he used to call 'my little Senate'.

Although he had lost a few followers in the dark days after his duel with Castlereagh, Canning may still have had the largest personal following in the Commons; it included Charles Ellis, Granville Leveson-Gower, William Sturges Bourne and William Huskisson. During 1810 the Canningites could muster a maximum of a dozen as well as a few 'occasional conformists'. It was not very many, but in a close-run division it could make quite a difference. The Canningites were the most tightly disciplined of the 'floating parties' in the Commons. Perceval once expressed astonishment at the slavery exacted by Canning from his followers.[24] There was, indeed, to judge from Canning's own accounts, something rather feudal in his relationship with his followers. In January, 1810, he told Joan that his cousin Colonel George Canning, had taken him aside in the House 'to say that he was glad of this opportunity to make his profession to me of intire (*sic*) and constant attachment . . .' while William Taylor had explained that he meant his letter to be a vow of allegiance. 'He was ready to vote as I pleased.' Some weeks later Canning told Joan that Lord Binning had called on him 'to make his profession of faith and following, reserving only the question about Lord Chatham against whom he cannot vote for private reasons, Lady Binning being Lady C's intimate friend, I believe connection. For the rest he vows to follow me, in or out, implicitly.'[25] Those who made these professions were expected to stick to them, and they usually did, except on the rare occasions when Canning set them free to vote as they pleased.

By the time Parliament was dissolved in September 1812, the number of Canningites had increased to at least fifteen. But the election was something of a disaster for them. They could no longer count on government support and in some cases were opposed by government candidates; altogether six found themselves without a seat in the new Parliament.* Canning deeply regretted their plight for which he knew he was largely responsible. 'It is not pleasant to reflect,' he wrote on September 27, foreseeing what would happen, 'that a point of honour (if it be one) of mine is the occasion of such martyrdom.'[26]

The following July, Canning's growing feeling that he had become more of a liability than an asset to his political associates was confirmed by a visit from Wellesley-Pole, the politically aspiring brother of Lord Wellesley and Wellington. Wellesley-Pole was not a Canningite, but as a member of his elder brother's little party, he was connected with Canning. He felt the connection now did him no good and wanted to be free of it. Canning, in a touchy and despondent frame of mind, reacted by finally making up his mind to break his connection with Wellesley, and set all his own party free. 'The call upon me,' he wrote to Huskisson, '(for such in effect it was) to be no longer an impediment in *his* [Wellesley-Pole's] way, afforded a fair and obvious opportunity of saying that I would be no longer in *any* body's way.'[27]

Canning's followers seem to have been more surprised than pleased by their unsolicited liberation. John W. Ward (later the first Earl of Dudley), who received his 'dismissal from his master's service' on July 20, had only abandoned the Whigs for Canning the previous summer. He unburdened himself whimsically to E. J. Littleton, another recent Canningite: 'I was travelling along the road in the most agreeable manner with some chosen friends, when suddenly the coach pulls up and desires me and the other passengers to step out. Accordingly I had nothing for it but to sit patiently on the bank till the ministerial "Bang-up" came by; and I advise you to accept of the same convey-

---

* But with three new recruits Canning still had a party of twelve in the new Parliament, apart from those sympathetic, but less closely allied, to him.

ance.' Charles Ellis's loyal reaction was to minimise the importance of what Canning had done and to declare that he saw no reason why they should not all still be as great friends as ever.[28]

Outsiders, on the other hand, were puzzled and intrigued by what the Whig barrister, Francis Horner, called this 'singular political event'. Horner could not make out whether it was 'a deep measure, or the sudden fit of some ill-humour, and whether Canning, in reducing his establishment, thus abruptly points towards Govt or Opposition.'[29] His outright enemies hinted that he had only made himself smaller (like the weasel) in order to creep into office more easily.[30] Others, less malicious, lamented the discredit which Canning's action had thrown on all 'party connection'; a party, to be respectable, must be founded on public principle and should not be dissoluble simply at the whim of its leader.[31]

About a week after Canning had dissolved his party, Lord Melville told him that the prime minister and some of his colleagues had been trying to find a way of bringing him into the Cabinet.[32] Melville himself had been willing to let Canning have the Admiralty, but Lord Buckinghamshire, an Addingtonian distinguished chiefly for his single-minded determination to achieve and keep high office, had refused to let him have the Board of Control instead.[33] No one, in short, was willing to make room for Canning and there was no obvious reason why any one of them should change his mind. On the Continent, Wellington was remorselessly driving the French out of Spain, while in Germany the allied armies were gradually tightening the net round Napoleon. Why should any member of the Cabinet want to give up his share of the praise and responsibility for the victorious peace that now really did seem to be just round the corner? As he prepared to join his family on holiday at Seaford, Canning wrote bitterly to Leveson-Gower: 'I am afraid no possible combination of circumstances can place me again where I stood in July last year; and it is of no use to reflect where I might have been now had the "tide" of that time been "taken at the flood".'[34]

Canning spent about a month at Seaford, staying with Joan, Harriet and the baby Charles (commonly known as Carlo), who had been born the previous December, in a house belonging to Charles Ellis. Most watering-places were too crowded and fashionable for Canning's taste, but he liked Seaford 'where we are so utterly to ourselves, that we never hear of an arrival except of a wheat-ear, or of the little Speaker, who rode over here from Eastbourne yesterday to pay me a visit.'[35]

Later, Canning rambled off westwards by himself to visit his mother in Bath and stay with various friends on the way. By the time he rejoined Joan at Hinckley he had had plenty of time and leisure to forget his own admonitions not to rake over the past. His reflections were so painful that he could not bring himself to attend the opening of Parliament on November 4, although he put in a brief appearance later that month. Nor could he stop himself from feeling extremely sore with those whose advice he had so misguidedly taken. On October 22 he wrote to Leveson-Gower from Hinckley to confess that he was reluctant to see him in the immediate future. In time, he wrote, he might become altogether indifferent to the consequences of the fateful decision he took in July 1812. 'But *at present* – while they are in their flush and vigour; while the station in Europe and in history, which I have thrown away, is full before my eyes; while I am alive to the sense of conscious ridicule (to say nothing of the sense of public duty) as having refused the management of the mightiest scheme of politics which this country ever engaged in . . . from a miserable point of etiquette – one absolutely unintelligible (so I have almost uniformly found it) at a distance of more than six miles from Palace Yard – I really think I am much better at home, than with those with whom it would be equally painful to talk or to be silent on such subjects.'[36] But his bitterness kept spilling over into his letters. Some weeks later he was brought a letter from Prince Czartoryski, the Russian foreign minister, who evidently believed he was back at the Foreign Office. The prince, commented Canning to Leveson-Gower, was 'probably not aware (and I daresay could not easily be made to understand) that it would have been disgraceful to undertake the conduct of a great confederacy, and to stamp one's name upon the settlement of Europe, unless one had at the same time the privilege of making a daily motion in the House of Commons "That this House do now adjourn." '[37]

By the time Parliament met, Wellington had invaded France and Napoleon had been decisively defeated at Leipzig. No one rejoiced more wholeheartedly than Canning at the prospect of a victorious peace; it was after all the vindication of all he had said and done in the dark years when many people argued that Napoleon was unbeatable, and it moved him to one of those stirring oratorical set-pieces which the Commons so much admired.[38] But there was a bitter side to his rejoicing. 'It is singular is it not?' he wrote to his mother, 'that the success of my politics should be the surest guarantee of my exclusion from office – but so it is.'³⁹ The government, he felt, would not need his help now.

Canning's mood could swing quickly from despair to elation, but now the feeling that his political career was finished persisted. Not even several weeks of being fêted in Liverpool, in the New Year of 1814, could restore his morale. He played a reasonably active part in the rest of the parliamentary session, but his heart was not in it. In June he described himself to Leveson-Gower as having 'in my utterly extinct state, neither means nor disposition to meddle in anything of politics ever more.'⁴⁰

As his public prospects faded, Canning began to be increasingly preoccupied by his great private worry – the health of his eldest son. In June 1813, he told his mother that the boy, who was 'all patience, resignation and good sense', was never out of their thoughts.⁴¹ George, who was now twelve, had been getting worse rather than better. He was not well enough to join the rest of the family at Seaford and had to be left behind at Hinckley with his brother William for company. In September Canning wondered whether it might still be possible to bring him to Seaford to see what sea air and bathing (then a very fashionable specific for all kinds of complaints) would do for him. But when he returned to Hinckley he realised that it was out of the question. Joan did not like to leave the boy and Canning did not like to leave her more than was absolutely necessary. By February 1814, it seemed possible that the Cannings would have to reconcile themselves to settling indefinitely at Hinckley. The alternative was to try to restore George's health in a warmer climate abroad. By the spring of 1814, with the Allies in Paris and Napoleon on his way to Elba, there was nothing against it, provided George could stand the journey.

In the middle of June Canning learned that he might, if he liked, go on his travels in a more exalted role than that of a private Member of Parliament. Lord Liverpool, presumably hearing that he intended to go abroad, suggested that he should undertake an embassy. Canning's reaction was that his followers, who – as he was only too well aware – had lost more than they had gained by their loyalty to him, must be provided for as well. Liverpool had no objection. Although his government was a good deal stronger than it had been two years earlier, he was still anxious to bring Canning into his Cabinet (and an embassy was a convenient half-way house) and to prevent his friends from slipping into the arms of the Whigs; Huskisson, for one, had been actively opposing the Chancellor of the Exchequer's measures. Liverpool was also probably moved by a genuine desire to do something for one of his oldest friends. Their friendship had been chequered but when Canning wrote to thank Liverpool, he did so 'not from politician to politician, but with the genuine warmth of old Christ Church feelings . . .'[42]

Liverpool's first idea had been that Canning should go to Madrid. Spain was in fact the country that Canning most wanted to see. But the climate of Madrid would be most unsuitable for George, who would have to be exiled to somewhere on the Mediterranean coast. In any case, Henry Wellesley, who was then ambassador in Madrid, showed not the slightest sign of wanting to move. The Prince Regent of Portugal, however, who had fled from Napoleon to Brazil in 1807, was confidently believed to be about to return. It was appropriate that a special embassy should be sent to welcome him back and what better choice to lead it than the man who had done so much to urge and expedite his flight?

The offer which Liverpool made Canning through Charles Ellis was very tempting. He was willing, reported Ellis, to leave nothing undone to raise the Lisbon embassy into 'a great, splendid, anomalous situation wholly out of the line of ordinary missions'. But Canning was more interested in his son's health and in providing for loyal political friends than in his personal pomp and circumstance. He made out a list of about a dozen names with suggestions of what might be a suitable provision for each.[43] Liverpool responded generously. Huskisson, the most important politically and the most deserving because he had twice (in 1809 and 1812) turned his back on office for Canning's sake, was made First Commissioner of Woods and Forests. (Canning would have preferred him to have been made either Treasurer of the Navy or Master of the Mint.) Granville Leveson-Gower was promised a viscounty and Boringdon an earldom; others, like Sturges Bourne, were accommodated with a minor office or a baronetcy.[44] The only part of the arrangement about which Canning had serious doubts was his own embassy. He feared – rightly as it turned out – that his enemies would make capital out of it. Liverpool, however, wanted to have this clear evidence of Canning's support for his administration, and it was finally agreed that he would lead an embassy to Lisbon if it could be definitely established that the Portuguese Prince Regent was about to return. In any case, he was determined to go abroad before the winter for the sake of his son's health.

On August 26 Liverpool told Canning that the Portuguese Regent had definitely asked for a British squadron to escort him back to Europe. Canning was then on a round of visits in the north-west and it was not until his return to London in the second half of September that he finally decided to undertake the embassy. It was doubtful up to the last moment whether George would be fit to travel. But early in October he arrived safely at Gloucester Lodge, accompanied by his mother and none the worse for his two-day journey. 'You may judge,' wrote Canning to Leveson-Gower, 'what Mrs Canning's anxiety must have been, but the delight of having got him with her, and having (we trust) taken leave of Hinckley for ever, overbalances it all . . .'[45]

Canning and his family sailed from Portsmouth in H.M.S. *Leviathan* early in November. Their departure coincided with the reassembly of Parliament, and during the debate on the Address Whitbread scathingly attacked Canning's embassy as an expensive and pointless 'job'. Leveson-Gower told his wife afterwards that Charles Ellis, an infrequent speaker, defended his friend 'with so much good feeling, so perfect a manner, and such evident affection for him he defended, that the whole House seemed pleased with him for it, and Tierney complimented him upon it . . .'[46] It was a foretaste of many similar attacks. Probably more important to Canning at the moment was the marked improvement that even the short voyage from Portsmouth to Plymouth had had on his son's health. It was proof, he hoped, that sea air really would do him some good.

'The Bay of Biscay,' wrote Canning, 'is no down bed in November.'[47] Their passage was so rough that when the Cannings reached Lisbon at the end of November, they were met by a report that they had been blown up in a storm. Canning was able to reassure his friends and relations that the only disaster (apart from seasickness) had been the loss of his hat in a storm, and that 'was blown *off*, not *up*'. But as soon as they landed, disaster did strike Canning in the shape of a severe attack of gout. It was the second serious visitation of 'that respectable complaint' that he had had, and he attributed it entirely to his imprudence in leaving off a flannel under-waistcoat.[48] It was not until Christmas Eve that he was well enough to present his credentials to the Council of Regency and play his part in the accompanying ceremony and speechifying. 'You must not suppose,' he wrote rather sheepishly to Liverpool, 'or let Bathurst suppose, that I do not see how very quizzable all this reciprocation of flummery is – but it is the way to deal with them.'[49]

He certainly needed all his diplomatic tact and skill. The strains and stresses of years of war had thoroughly soured Anglo-Portuguese relations. Wellington and the British ambassador, Sir Charles Stuart, used to complain constantly about how the Portuguese wasted and misused the subsidies and supplies sent from Britain, while the Portuguese resented their dependence on the British whose behaviour, they felt, was both high-handed and selfish. When Canning arrived in Lisbon the struggle against Napoleon was assumed to be over and the Council of Regency felt much more free to express its resentment. It says a good deal for Canning's personal charm that within a few weeks he had the most hostile member of the council coming regularly to dine at his house and play whist, 'which luckily I play so ill,' he told Liverpool, 'as to be sure of losing – which of course contributes to his good humour.'[50]

There were domestic as well as official worries. The place the Cannings moved into on their arrival was described by Canning as 'a vile, inconvenient, fireless, small, dirty house'.[51] But it was extremely difficult to find anything better. Eventually the problem was solved by the Duke of Wellington, who sent permission for them to occupy the suite of rooms in one of the royal palaces which he had been given by an officially grateful nation. Canning regarded it as a temporary arrangement but in fact he never managed to find anywhere else. The suite, overlooking the Tagus, was very grand but rather short of domestic conveniences. The Cannings greatly deplored the lack of proper fireplaces, but at least there were stoves, with pipes running out of the windows. When they first arrived, the evenings tended to turn very cold, and the family were much preoccupied with 'precautions against cold-catching'.[52] But by the end of February, the weather was warm and sunny and they were making full use of the permission they had been given to walk (and play) in the large and beautiful garden of the adjoining convent.

Like all the English who had to set up house in Portugal at this time, Canning was appalled by the cost of living. London, he reckoned, was not two-thirds as dear to live in as Lisbon. He was particularly anxious to keep down his expenses because he knew that his political enemies were on the watch for any apparent sign of extravagance. After what had already been said about his embassy in the Commons, he did not like to suggest that it would be sensible for the government to buy and do up a house as a permanent embassy.[53] He and Joan entertained a good deal, but not, he felt, as much as they ought because of the expense. In the middle of May they gave a huge dinner in honour of the

Portuguese Prince Regent's birthday, and it was not till then that they unpacked the set of new plate which Canning had unsuccessfully tried to stop being sent out from England. He was incensed by reports in a London paper that his wife never went out in her chair without two running footmen. In fact there was neither chair nor footman in their establishment. They rode out each day on horseback attended by one English groom. The Lisbon streets were so steep and rough that they had found it impossible to go out to dinner in their English barouche; so they were forced to invest in a second- or third-hand Portuguese buggy, which Canning described as 'anything but sumptuous'; it reminded him of 'the picture of a post chaise in a harlequin farce'.[54]

As Wellington's apartments were not suitable for the transaction of official business, the small house where the Cannings had first stayed was kept on for this purpose; in any case, Canning did not think it would be quite suitable to put the King's Arms up on a Portuguese royal palace. Here he conscientiously carried out his routine duties and tried to put some order into the embassy archives. He dealt with the problems of British merchants. He sorted out the difficulties that British ships got into over the Lisbon port regulations. He made arrangements for looking after some of the Duke of Wellington's correspondence which had been salvaged from the sea after the ship carrying it back to England had been sunk at the mouth of the Tagus. He worried over whether the importation of Portuguese bibles by a missionary society was contrary to the 1810 Anglo-Portuguese treaty, and rather thought it was. He tried to dispose of surplus military stores. Above all, he tried to sort out the utter confusion into which the two countries' financial relations had been allowed to fall.[55] (This Herculean task was not completed until 1822.)

Throughout most of his first three months in Lisbon, Canning expected to wake up any morning to find a British squadron, with the Portuguese Prince Regent on board, anchored in the Tagus. But on April 9, 1815, a despatch from London announced that the government had reason to believe that the Portuguese ruler had decided to stay where he was. This removed the motive for Canning's mission and he immediately sent Castlereagh his resignation.

In the meantime, Napoleon had escaped from Elba and entered Paris in triumph, Wellington had set up his headquarters in Belgium and the allied armies were assembling. War was about to break out once more in Europe and no one at the time supposed that it would all be over by mid-summer. Canning believed that these developments made it more unlikely that the Portuguese Prince Regent would hurry back to Europe.

They also quite changed his own position, which he expected to keep until his resignation was accepted and his successor appointed. In time of war Lisbon should be a not uninteresting or unimportant post. In fact it turned out to be extremely frustrating.

The news of Napoleon's escape and entry into Paris created great consternation in Lisbon. It also increased the general resentment against Britain as if – as Canning remarked with surprise – she had connived at Napoleon's escape. Wellington's urgent request that 12,000 to 14,000 Portuguese troops should be sent at once to Flanders was not well received. The members of the Council of Regency were reluctant to send so many troops so far away on their own authority. There were also demands from Rio to send troops there. And they disliked the feeling that the imperious British were ordering them around again. Canning sympathised with their susceptibilities and was annoyed to discover that the British government had not waited for the agreement of the Portuguese authorities before despatching transports to take their troops to Flanders. By April 10 one of them had actually arrived in the Tagus after what Canning indignantly described as 'a most unfortunately short passage', and to make matters worse, the captain had made no secret of why he had come.[56]

The question of the Portuguese contribution to the war effort was still not settled by the time Waterloo was fought and won. But long before then, Canning's good nature was exhausted. Even the most routine matters were referred to Rio and it was six months before an answer arrived. He told Liverpool at the end of April that he thought a special mission should be sent to Rio to try to persuade the Portuguese Prince Regent either to make up his mind to come back to Europe or to take steps to make his Lisbon government more effective.[57]

Canning seems to have had no wish to try to extract any personal advantage out of the crisis. For the time being, his political ambitions were dormant, and he was unmoved by letters from friends who lamented his absence from the battles in the House of Commons. 'My "abdication" took place in 1812,' he wrote on April 15. 'I felt it so then, and never for a moment since, not even in the first success of Liverpool, have altered that opinion. Bonaparte, to be sure, has shown that abdications are not always final – but I see nothing in the state of affairs ... which tempts me to imitate his example, and to land at Falmouth by surprise.'[58]

He was happier and more relaxed than he had been for years, or would ever be again. In spite of the tiresomeness of the Council of Regency, he liked being ambassador. He appreciated the southern climate. He enjoyed being with his family and seeing more of them than he had done for years. And, of course, he was overjoyed at the marked improvement in George's health. He made up his mind that, if the government wanted him to stay on for a while as ambassador, he would gladly agree. If it did not, he would stay anyway until the following spring.

With the end of Napoleon's Hundred Days, the government in London saw no further point in keeping Canning at Lisbon. On July 14, 1815, he heard that his resignation had been accepted and that the Lisbon embassy was to be cut down to a minimum, with a chargé d'affaires at its head. Canning seems to have been quite happy to relapse into domesticity. At the end of June he took George to Caldas, where there were some famous warm baths. Caldas was even hotter than Lisbon in the summer months. Fortunately, the heat agreed with George. But it was too much for Joan and the younger children, and Canning installed them in a secluded villa among streams and orange gardens at Collares, near Cintra. Charles Ellis and his family, whose arrival in May had greatly delighted the Cannings, were living in a second villa only some 200 yards away. Canning described Collares and Cintra as 'cool as a grotto and beautiful beyond anything I ever saw, except perhaps the Lakes.' (He added that when he was visiting the Lakes the previous summer, Southey had told him that he thought them more beautiful than anything he had ever seen except Cintra.)[59] At the end of August, George was considered to have had as much of the Caldas waters, both internally and externally, as was good for him in one season, and his father fetched him to rejoin the rest of the family at Collares.

By now Canning had handed over his official responsibilities to one of his staff. He was free to do what he liked, and he decided on a wandering life. In the spring, he would take his family to France. He himself would go on to England for a few months to do his duty by his neglected Liverpudlian constituents. Then he would return to his family, take George to some baths at Barèges, and in the autumn – 'God knows where.' The end of the war had made it possible for him to travel and see places he had always wanted to see; it had not made it any easier for him to make a political comeback.

When Canning handed over the ciphers and correspondence to his successor in the Lisbon embassy, he might have expected that the persistent criticism of his appointment would die away. But at a time when the Commons were much preoccupied with 'jobs' and government extravagance, it was too sharp a weapon to be lightly discarded. It could be turned against both Canning and the government, and for months the opposition press kept returning to the charge. Canning made it a rule to ignore Press attacks – but he was nonetheless irked by them.

At length, in May 1817, a young Whig M.P., Mr J. G. Lambton, (later first Earl of Durham) tabled a motion censuring Canning's appointment to the Lisbon embassy in 1814 as an unjustifiable waste of public money. The opposition did not pull its punches. Lambton attributed the Lisbon mission to 'the lowest species of political barter and intrigue' while Sir Francis Burdett described it as the grossest job he had ever witnessed. Canning defended himself and the government with a sincerity, lucidity and, at times, barely concealed indignation that made a great impression on the House.[60] After he sat down, the opposition were quite unable to make an effective comeback, and they did not even try very hard. One of their opponents described them as never having made so contemptible a figure,[61] and they lost their motion by 96 votes to 270. When his mother wrote to congratulate him on his success, Canning replied: 'I *never* reply to calumnies; they wear themselves out, or I live them down; and it was a piece of good fortune beyond my hopes that the calumnies of the last year should be brought to the test of parliamentary refutation.'[62]*

At the end of his speech, Canning replied to Burdett's sneering allegation that it had been discreditable and dishonourable of him to accept an office from Castlereagh with whom he had quarrelled so violently. Wellesley-Pole thought that he handled this delicate issue so well that it must be set at rest for ever; 'he put the whole of the question beautifully, forcibly and most successfully.'[63] Canning revealed that five years earlier Castlereagh had offered to relinquish the Foreign Office to him. Whether or not he was right or wrong to refuse that generous offer, it had healed the breach between them. Henceforward the 'paltry distinction' of whether he was serving 'under' or 'with' his noble friend had not given him the slightest uneasiness; for 'in whatever station a man may be called upon to serve his sovereign and his country, there is among statesmen, co-operating honestly for the public good, a real substantive equality which no mere official arrangement

* But the calumnies persisted all the same. Ten years later, on the day after Canning's death, *The Times* described 'the overpaid and unnecessary embassy to Lisbon' as 'the real blot on Mr Canning's political emblazonment'.

can either create or destroy . . . in a free country like ours, it is for the man to dignify the office, not for the office to dignify the man.'[64]

These were remarkable words to come from a man who five years earlier had wrecked his political career by insisting that a certain 'official arrangement' was essential to maintain his reputation and 'public character'. But he had learnt his lesson; and when he made this speech, he had already acknowledged his mistake in the most public possible way by accepting one of the lowest-ranking places in Lord Liverpool's Cabinet.

CHAPTER XIII

England's Discontents
1816-1820

Early in February, 1816, the Earl of Buckinghamshire, President of the Board of Control, died from an injury received in a riding accident. Shortly afterwards Lord Liverpool wrote to offer Canning the vacant seat in the Cabinet.[1] Canning received the letter during an excursion in the country near Torres Vedras. He sat down to compose his acceptance on March 6 while staying at the monastery of Alcobaça, but got no further than writing the date. He thought that perhaps the air of the monastery did not agree with the discussion of such worldly matters; or perhaps he was distracted by 'the incessant attentions of the monks, and the enormousness of their good cheer'.[2] He did not suggest that he was held up by indecision. On the contrary, this seems to have been one of the less painful and difficult decisions of his political career – perhaps it was a help to have to make up his mind in an atmosphere so different from the rather frenetic, hothouse atmosphere of Westminster.

Of course he had his doubts. He was being offered the India Board which barely rated as a regular Cabinet post and was far below his former pretensions. But when he finally managed to write to Liverpool two days later, he assured him that his doubts did not concern the actual post he was offered, but whether he was ready to take office at all. It would, he said, have been 'infinitely more agreeable' to him not to have been faced with such a choice just yet.[3] There seems no reason to doubt his sincerity. His political past was still painful and he had managed to switch his attention to other things. He knew, however, that the fascination of Rome and Naples and Florence would pall. Sooner or later, he would succumb to the greater fascination of Westminster. Yet he was too restless and ambitious to settle down as a backbencher who from time to time enlivened the Commons with a display of oratorical fireworks; and he realised by now that he was in no position to pick and choose either the time or the manner of his return to office. The Board of Control was, as it were, an unexpected gift horse, and it was both good sense and good manners not to look it in the mouth.

When he wrote to Canning in February, Liverpool skated rather lightly over the fact that the government was under heavy pressure in the Commons. A month later, its request to keep the highly unpopular income tax was defeated by 37 votes – the ministers had hoped for a majority of 40 – and on March 21 Liverpool gloomily told the Regent's equerry that 'the Government certainly hangs by a thread'.[4] But Canning was not deterred when a fuller picture of the government's troubles reached him about the middle of March. On the contrary, he told Huskisson that 'the knowledge of their [the ministers'] difficulties tends (if anything could) rather to reconcile me to the course which I decided to take . . .' It also made him anxious to hurry home so that no one could accuse him of shirking the fray.[5]

By the end of May, Canning was back in England, having first established the family in a house at Bordeaux so that Joan could take George to try the waters at Barèges. Canning's first duty was to visit his mother at Bath. His second, since he was about to take office under the Crown, was to secure his re-election at Liverpool. In spite of nearly two years' absenteeism and his opponents' efforts to discredit his Lisbon embassy he was returned with an increased majority; and, according to his own report, his chairing afterwards 'outdid all former outdoings in magnificence and concourse of attendance'.[6] By the time he was re-established at Gloucester Lodge at the end of June, the battle in the Commons had fizzled out and Parliament had risen for the summer recess.

At the beginning of October, having spent the rest of the summer mastering the intricacies of the Board of Control, Canning fetched Joan from Bordeaux and for six weeks they settled down to explore and enjoy Paris. It was Canning's first visit and it was a great success, although he would have preferred to spend more time on sightseeing and less on the social round. His wife, he wrote to Lord Morley, had seen more of the Paris world in a month than of the London world since she was married. 'For my own part,' he added, 'I would not run the evening rounds in London, which I cannot avoid here, for any consideration, whether of pleasure or of politics.'[7] Still, it was extremely gratifying to be so well received by king, princes, ministers and everyone else in the capital of the ex-enemy. 'I have been much amused,' he wrote to the Leighs, 'and delighted and interested here. Indeed, I must have been hard to please if I had not been satisfied with my reception. We have wanted nothing, but a *little* quiet. That however was not to be had. So we have gone with the stream – and have seen everybody – and all – of all parties – equally civil to us.'[8] For several

years he had been trying to reconcile himself to political failure; he had
swallowed his pride and accepted one of the lowliest seats in the Cabinet.
His reception in Paris must have been a welcome boost to his morale
for which too many parties were a small price to pay.

The country to which the Cannings returned at the beginning of
December 1816 was a disturbed and troubled place, although those
who divided their lives between spacious country houses and elegant
London drawing-rooms knew little of it – unless the mob happened to
break their windows in mistake for those of an unpopular politician.
To the problems of economic and social adjustment arising out of the
industrial revolution were now added the strains created by the difficult
transition from war to peace. When the government stopped its
wartime spending, there was a sudden and drastic drop in the demand
for British manufactures. At the same time, the soldiers and sailors
returning from the war were demobilised as quickly as possible and
thrown on to the labour market. Less work was to be had and more
men were looking for it. Ironworks, mills and factories closed down,
while the unemployed hung about, sullenly or angrily, outside the
barred gates. With the end of the wartime boom in agriculture, there
was unemployment and cruel poverty on the land as well. Most of those
suffering from economic distress tried to find a remedy by peaceful and
orderly means. But inevitably some desperate men resorted to various
forms of violence. It did not help them but it was a time-honoured
remedy and there seemed to be none other open to them. In 1816 barns
were burnt, agricultural machinery was smashed and there were bread
riots at many places in East Anglia. There was an outbreak of machine-
smashing at Nottingham, serious rioting by the unemployed at
Birmingham and plundering of food shops at Dundee.

In addition to the unrest, whether passive or violent, caused by
economic distress, there was agitation for political reform. The leading
members of the movement were a mixed collection who tended to
disagree about what they wanted and how far they were prepared to
go to get it. They included the wealthy aristocrat, Sir Francis Burdett,
who did not always seem to have the courage of his convictions;
William Cobbett, whose *Political Register* carried the gospel of peaceful
petitioning throughout the land: the veteran Radical, Major Cartwright,
who in 1813 had tirelessly toured the industrial midlands and north of
England, founding Hampden Clubs through which the demand for
parliamentary reform could be peacefully organised; and Henry

(Orator) Hunt, the vain and flashy demagogue in the white topper, whose speechifying made many of the working class see the point of parliamentary reform, but whose style and personality created deep distrust among the better-educated.

Only the lunatic fringe of the political reformers advocated violence. Most of the leaders wanted to work through the pressure of public opinion demonstrated at mass meetings and by petitioning Parliament. The economic distress helped them to mobilise public opinion. Rioting and violence, urged Cobbett again and again, would help nobody; only a reformed Parliament, genuinely representative of all the people of England, could redress their wrongs.

On December 2, 1816, just after Canning had got back to London, Orator Hunt summoned a mass meeting in Spa Fields to protest against the Regent's refusal to receive a petition in favour of the extreme Radical programme, which included male suffrage and annual parliaments. But before Hunt got to the meeting, it was taken over by a few fanatics who persuaded the mob to make a crazy attempt to seize the Tower. It all fizzled out quickly and ignominiously, but it was enough to make a nervous government still more nervous. Canning himself thought the mischief was much less than it might have been. But he still felt that 'salutary measures of suppression' were necessary. 'It is a cruel necessity – but we must not let London be pulled down about the ears of the well-affected.'[9]

Before these 'salutary measures' could be put before Parliament, a huge meeting of political reformers was held at the Crown and Anchor tavern in London. It was attended by Hampden Club delegates from all over England. Burdett thought it prudent to stay away, but Cartwright, Cobbett and Hunt were there. There was some warm discussion on the pros and cons of universal, as opposed to household, suffrage, but in the end resolutions in favour of universal suffrage and annual parliaments were triumphantly passed. And when Parliament reassembled on January 28, 1817, Hunt, attended by a huge cheering crowd, arrived in Old Palace Yard with a petition in favour of parliamentary reform. On the same day, as the Regent was driving home after making his Speech from the Throne, a stone or a bullet (it was never decided which) pierced the window of his coach. Rightly or wrongly, it was assumed that the 'Pop-gun Plot' was an attempt on the Regent's life. A few days later secret committees of both Houses of Parliament were set up to examine the mass of evidence of supposedly seditious activities collected by government spies and informers all over the kingdom. The committees' reports were alarming, not to say blood-curdling, and the government reacted with shocked severity. It asked Parliament to suspend *habeas corpus*, and by the end of March a bill to prevent seditious meetings had also become law.

Both at the time, and by historians since, the Liverpool government has been severely criticised for its rather panic-stricken resort to repressive measures, culminating in the notorious Six Acts passed two and a half years later after the tragedy of Peterloo. In fact, the government's actual use of the weapons with which it provided itself can easily be exaggerated, just as the ministers themselves almost certainly exaggerated the dangers against which they had to guard. But even the mild and moderate Wilberforce, who was on the Commons' secret committee, was sufficiently impressed by the evidence produced to feel that measures to preserve the public peace were 'absolutely needed if we would not incur the danger of bloodshed and conflagration.'[10]

Lord Sidmouth, the Home Secretary, can be criticised for not choosing and using his agents – the most notorious was known as 'Oliver the Spy' – with more care, and the authorities were almost certainly wrong to suspect any nationwide revolutionary conspiracy. But in the spring of 1817 plenty of reports of unrest and wild talk were still coming in. Early in March, a hunger march of unemployed weavers (known as the March of the Blanketeers) was organised from Manchester to London. The marchers' intentions were entirely peaceable, but many were arrested before they got to Stockport; only one man got to London. In June a group of Derbyshire farm labourers began to march on Nottingham. They were dispersed by heavy rain and a few dragoons, but their pathetic effort was described as a 'revolution'.

It was an explosive situation, and perhaps all the more so now that the respectable law-abiding political reformers, like Cobbett and Samuel Bamford, had been discredited by the extremists and could no longer try to direct economic distress into legitimate political channels. In March Cobbett fled to America. In the same month Bamford was arrested, removed to London and taken before the Privy Council whose members he discovered to be far less disagreeable than he had imagined.[11]* Sidmouth and Castlereagh were indeed not the monsters depicted by Shelley in his *Masque of Anarchy*. They were men of their generation, who did not begin to understand the new economic and social forces at work in England and simply believed it was their duty to prevent a repetition in their own country of the upheavals which had shaken France.

* Bamford was released at the end of April. He described Sidmouth's manner as 'affable and much more encouraging to freedom of speech than I had imagined.'

Canning was also a man of his time. He lamented, no doubt sincerely, the poverty and distress that sometimes drove men to violence. But the poor had always been there. For the time being, there might be more of them and their plight might be worse, because of the dislocation caused by the long war. But Canning accepted the orthodox contemporary view that neither Parliament nor any other human agency could remove poverty and social distress. Only time and providence could do that. In January 1817, he told the Commons that he felt sure the country would overcome its present troubles and that 'a new course of happiness and prosperity may presently open upon us.'[12] But eighteen months later he wrote less confidently to his mother: 'How many weeks, or months or years it will take to set the world to rights, after the checks that everything in it . . . received during the last twenty-five years, is more than I can venture to predict. But all is yet out of joint . . . It is so all over Europe – but how much more wonderful that it should be so in this country, blessed and gifted as it is above all others – wonderful, but mortifying in a still greater degree.'[13]

Canning's sense of mortification, however naïve it may seem today, was the emotional expression of his profound conviction that the 'constitution', or system of government, established in England was essentially sound and satisfactory in all its parts. Like most of his contemporaries, whatever their political views, he believed that the hope of the future lay in restoring an ideal past. When he dramatically begged the Commons to 'let the venerable fabric, which has sheltered us for so many ages, and stood unshaken through so many storms, still remain unimpaired and holy,'[14] he was not just indulging his taste for oratory. He really meant it. He did not try to maintain that the political system was incapable of improvement; he admitted that modifications might be necessary in the light of changing circumstances. He was in favour of abolishing sinecures, not because he thought it wrong in principle that the Crown should have some tangible means of rewarding its deserving servants, but because the award of sinecure offices had become an inappropriate and extremely unpopular way of doing so.[15] In 1810, he supported Romilly's unsuccessful attempt to abolish the death penalty for thefts of up to 40/–, on the grounds that it was not necessary to keep very severe laws on the statute book for ever, and that juries would be more likely to convict if they knew they were not sending a man to the gallows for a trivial offence.[16] He conceded that the Poor Laws were an immensely important subject that Parliament ought to investigate; but he insisted that the government ought not to interfere hastily or prematurely in 'a question growing out of the usage of centuries, interwoven with the habits and deeply rooted in the prejudices of different classes of the people.'[17] Similarly, he supported Catholic emancipation because he believed it was necessary to preserve the constitution from increasingly damaging strains.

In short, Canning supported any change that improved or helped to preserve the existing system. Parliamentary reform did not come into this category. Like most of the leading men of his day, he stuck doggedly to Burke's view of Parliament as a 'deliberative' assembly, the members of which represented the interests of the whole nation and not just of their own constituents (if they had any). It did not matter, therefore, if Old Sarum sent a member to Westminster while Manchester did not, so long as all the various interests in the country – the 'landed', the 'commercial' and so on – were represented. Canning argued that there was no body of men in the country whose claims were not discussed with patience, skill and knowledge in the Commons, and he could not see by what better process this assembly could be chosen.[18] If there were only one way of electing members of Parliament, it would be more difficult to get a wide variety of interests represented there. Why, he once asked, should it be presumed that a man was not fit to sit in the House of Commons simply because he lacked the nerve to face the storm of the hustings?[19]

He defended pocket boroughs because they had brought many talented men into Parliament. Early in 1817, Francis Horner, a distinguished Whig, died. Mr Horner had sat for the pocket borough of St Mawes; so, some years earlier, had the late William Windham. After paying tribute to Horner in the Commons, Canning could not resist pointing out how well the theoretically defective constitution worked in practice. 'A system of representation cannot be wholly vicious, and altogether inadequate to its purposes which sends to this House a succession of such men as those whom we have now in our remembrance, here to develop the talents with which God has endowed them, and to attain that eminence in the view of their country, from which they may be one day called to aid her counsels, and to sustain her greatness and her glory.'[20] That, of course, in a nutshell was how Canning had envisaged his own career. It had not worked out quite as he had hoped, but without the help of a pocket borough, it could never even have started.

Canning believed that the delicate balance between the three parts of the constitution (the monarchy and the two Houses of Parliament) which allowed each part to be checked and controlled by the others, was now as satisfactory as human wisdom could make it; he feared that if one part were tampered with the whole would be deranged and ultimately destroyed. This was the basis of his stubborn opposition to even the most moderate and tentative proposals for parliamentary reform. To admit that the House of Commons could not properly carry out its duties was to open the way to changes that would upset the delicate constitutional mechanism, and must logically end by introducing the dangerous subversive principle of universal suffrage. He was, therefore, 'decidedly for opposing a system which must end in national destruction.'[21]

If such language seems extravagant today, it did not to most of those who heard it. The men who ruled England in the years after Waterloo, whether in Whitehall, or Westminster or the provinces, were talking and thinking in terms of an age that was fast vanishing. They could not, or would not, grasp the fact that new 'interests' had arisen which were not represented in Parliament. They might have done so more quickly if they had believed that the hungry could be fed and the poor provided with jobs by the intervention of Parliament. But they did not; and therefore to argue that the country's distress could be cured by a reform of Parliament was, they believed, to foster a dishonest delusion.* This seemed so self-evident to those in authority that it was only too easy for them to draw the conclusion that a minority of wicked men were deliberately trying to use the prevailing distress as a weapon with which to overthrow the constitution. Canning, who was level-headed enough when his own career was not involved, certainly thought so. This emerges, not only from what he said in the Commons, when he might have been tempted to exaggerate, but in his private correspondence as well. He could have no possible motive for alarming his mother – rather the opposite – but in a letter written to her in December, 1816, he referred to the mischief done 'in consequence of the instigations of those wicked and hard-hearted wretches who are stimulating indigence to madness and crime'.[22] The following March, he told her that he hoped the worst was over, 'but we have been within an inch of the precipice, and folly as well as villainy was at work to push us over it.'[23] In January 1818, he reported that things were much improved, 'but there is yet mischief enough lurking, and poisoning in secret.'[24]

* Thomas Grenville wrote on January 20, 1817, that he would not 'be party to the dishonest delusion that a reform of Parliament will give work to the poor and bread to the hungry.' (Dropmore, X, p. 421)

The great mass of the people, Canning always maintained, were perfectly sound and loyal. And it was the imperative need to protect them from this secret poison that justified the suspension of *habeas corpus* and the government's use of distinctly dubious agents to discover what was going on – although when he defended this latter practice, Canning specifically exempted the use of *agents provocateurs*.[25] In the Commons he vehemently denied that the Seditious Meetings Bill was directed against the great mass of the people; on the contrary, he said he voted for it on their behalf to protect them against those who would delude them.[26] The main criticism against Canning and his colleagues is not that they tried in a rather ham-fisted and amateurish way to protect the country against the activities of what they genuinely believed to be a subversive minority, but that they completely failed to grasp the importance of removing the political grievances of the basically loyal majority.

Canning, of course, had no direct responsibility for the government's policies for dealing with the domestic unrest, beyond his general responsibility as a member of the Cabinet. But he played a major part in defending them in the Commons. In a sense this was not as onerous as it might have been. Although individual Whigs, like Brougham, attacked the government with great vigour, the opposition as a whole seemed to have shot its bolt in the 1816 session, when it made the most of a popular issue – financial retrenchment – and severely frightened the government with it. When Canning resumed his seat in the Commons the following January, the disturbed state of the country was in the forefront of everybody's minds; the opposition was divided over whether or not to support the government, while the independent members – those who were conscientious enough to attend the debates – were strongly inclined to rally behind it as the guardian of law and order. Moreover, the ministry was not wholly occupied in smelling out subversive plots; government expenditure was substantially reduced and the number of sinecures was drastically pruned.

Early in the session, the radical weaver, Samuel Bamford, up in London for the great meeting at the Crown and Anchor, decided to watch a Commons' debate. Like many others, he found it a disillusioning experience. But he admitted that there were a few striking exceptions among the collection of the 'most ordinary-looking men' he had ever seen. 'Canning, with his smooth, bare and capacious forehead, sat there, a spirit beaming in his looks like that of the leopard waiting to spring upon its prey. Castlereagh, with his handsome but immovable features – Burdett, with his head carried back and held high as in defiance – and Brougham, with his Arab soul ready to rush forth and challenge war to all comers.'[27]

When Parliament rose in July 1817, Canning told a friend that the history of the session was 'also pretty nearly my own, for I have almost lived in the H. of Comms.'[28]; and to his mother he wrote that he never remembered a session 'which continued so teasing to its very end'.[29] He himself ended it in fine style. On the final day of the session, Brougham launched a violent onslaught on the government in general and a vindictive personal attack on Castlereagh in particular. Canning wound up the debate with an eloquent defence of Castlereagh, which was loudly cheered, followed by a brilliantly mocking attack on the rest of Brougham's speech, which provoked a great deal of mirth and applause.[30]

Canning's critics complained that when he found a good joke he harped on it till it was threadbare. The sharpness of his sarcasm in debate also still caused offence,* although in private society he was described as 'bland, courteous and yielding'.[31] In his mastery of the House, however, he was still pre-eminent among his colleagues on the Treasury bench and rivalled only by Brougham among the opposition. Yet although success in the House of Commons had always been among his dearest ambitions, it was not enough. He might be a better speaker than Castlereagh, but Castlereagh was the leader of the House; he was responsible for the business of the Commons and he intervened much more frequently than Canning in the debates. Canning could not forget that he had failed to get to the top, either in Parliament or the Cabinet, and he could see no reason now why he should ever do so. In November 1817, he wrote to his wife, who had been ill, expressing the wish that her aches and pains could be transferred to him – 'who could be well spared . . . and who am living on – a sort of postscript – after the real volume of my life is closed.'[32] Little more than a year after he had decided that it would not do to turn down Liverpool's offer to bring him into the Cabinet, he was toying with the idea of cutting his losses and beginning a new life in India – presumably as Governor-General. He told Joan that he believed India might suit their son George (as well as himself) better than England ever could, 'but there

* The best-known example at this time concerned a professional agitator called Ogden, who when he was released from prison, claimed that the weight of his chains had given him a rupture. He had in fact admitted to Sidmouth that he had had the complaint when he entered prison and was cured of it there. Early in the 1818 session, Canning ridiculed the efforts of the imprisoned agitators to pose as martyrs and rather unfortunately referred to Ogden as the 'revered and ruptured Ogden'.

are difficulties every way and I am cured of planning – and leave everything to time and chance for the future.'[33]

The parliamentary session of 1818 was considerably less stormy than the preceding one. Helped by a good harvest in 1817, the situation in the country also seemed to improve; in and around Manchester there were strikes and peaceful demonstrations against low wages, but agitation for political reform, which alarmed the authorities so much more than economic unrest, seemed to have died away. In the spring the law suspending *habeas corpus* was repealed, and most of those imprisoned under it were released. In June the government decided, rather unwisely, to dissolve Parliament and go to the country a year earlier than it need have done. Canning went up to Liverpool to get himself re-elected. It was a 'pretty fatiguing fortnight', but at least there had been nothing that was not 'satisfying and gratifying in the highest degree'.[34] The government as a whole, however, had less cause for satisfaction. When the new Parliament assembled in January 1819, most pundits on both sides of the House agreed that it had lost ground, although their estimate of the loss varied between 10 and 25 votes.

Canning, as usual, attended conscientiously to his parliamentary duties during the session. He defended government policy on most of the contentious (largely financial) issues that arose, and he was a member of the committee appointed to investigate the question of the restoration of cash payments by the Bank of England.* But his interventions in debate were still much fewer than Castlereagh's although the latter had been absent because of illness for part of the session. He did not, apparently, try to fill the gap created by Castlereagh's absence, nor try to remedy the damage caused by the lack of proper management and discipline in the Commons on the government side. It was rumoured that an attempt would be made to strengthen the government by promoting Canning to the Home Secretaryship in place of Sidmouth, and making Peel† Chancellor of the Exchequer instead of Vansittart who was widely considered not to have made the grade. Peel's friends were certainly anxious to see him in high office, although Peel himself, it seems, was not enthusiastic. There is no evidence, however, that Canning showed any active interest, either in preserving the government or promoting his own political future. His real rival

* They had been suspended by Pitt in 1797 as a wartime emergency.
† Peel had resigned as Chief Secretary for Ireland the previous summer.

was still Castlereagh, and Castlereagh's position was virtually impregnable so long as he had the strength to stay the course. Nothing had really happened since Canning's return to England three years earlier, either to improve his political prospects or make him shake off his depressing conviction that he had reached the end of the road at Westminster.

'The truth is,' wrote Canning in the summer of 1817 when he was immersed in arrears of departmental work, 'that any business, however heavy, is trifling compared with the toil and anxiety of [parliamentary] warfare.'[35] He felt like that because, however dispirited, he never really lost his sense of emotional involvement in the debates in the Commons. But he was also an efficient and conscientious departmental minister; and although the President of the Board of Control had only been a regular member of the Cabinet since 1812, he held by no means either the least onerous or the most straightforward of the administrative posts.

When Canning became responsible for Indian affairs, Britain's interest in India was still primarily commercial.[36] The expansion of British military and political control over the past twenty years had been regarded with as much foreboding by the government and by Parliament as by the East India Company itself. It was difficult to understand that if the British were to remain at all in the anarchic, feuding Indian subcontinent, they would have to fight their enemies, govern conquered territory and extend their protection to friendly, but weak, native states. Lord Wellesley, whom Pitt sent out as Governor-General in 1797, believed that Britain should become the dominant power in India and (with the help of his younger brother, Arthur) he made considerable strides towards achieving this. But the directors of the company in London were appalled by the colossal cost of his campaigns and outraged by the scant respect he showed for their authority. The government too lost confidence in his expansionist policies, and in 1805 he resigned and came home. For nearly ten years, Wellesley's successors tried to follow a policy of consolidating the company's position inside the territories it had already acquired, leaving the native princes to work out their own salvation or destruction.

When its Charter was renewed in 1813, the company lost its monopoly of the India trade. But it kept its monopoly of the more lucrative China trade, it retained its right to dispose of patronage and it was confirmed in its political authority under the supervision of the Board of Control. This arrangement suited the government because it gave it a very real measure of control over Indian affairs, while providing it with a scapegoat (the company) if anything went seriously wrong. In the long run it was not to the advantage of the company, which was increasingly forced to act as the government's political and adminis-trative agent in India at the expense of its own trading interests and steadily became more financially dependent on its political masters.

Sustained, however, by the prestige of its long history and its expert knowledge, the company jealously guarded the remains of its inde-pendence. It was housed in a rather grand establishment in Leadenhall Street, with a large, experienced and very able permanent staff, and was run by a Court of Directors, headed by a chairman and two deputies. By contrast, the Board of Control (or India Board) was a much more modest affair, with a very much smaller and, on the whole, less able staff, crammed into far from commodious premises near Whitehall. By Canning's day, the duties of the other members of the Board had become largely a formality. In effect, the President himself was the Board, and he personally approved the official despatches sent by the company to India. The drafts would go backwards and forwards between Whitehall and the City, with both sides making amendments until agreement was reached. It was a slow and cumbersome process, but in practice the delay often did not greatly matter because of the slowness of communications between England and India. The author-ities in London could lay down general policy and deal with personal matters; but the many unforeseen contingencies and crises of Indian life had to be left to the initiative of the men on the spot. When this happened, the company and the Board would between them draw up a judgment of the action taken, which might serve as a precedent and guide for future action.

Clearly, much depended on the personal relations of the chairman of the Court of Directors (and his deputies) and the President of the Board of Control. These had in fact usually been good; there would be a regular weekly conference and a good deal of informal consultation as well. Canning's immediate predecessor, Lord Buckinghamshire, how-ever, chose to regard the company's directors as opponents, rather than allies. He managed to create so much bad blood that eventually the Court of Directors broke off all personal intercourse with him and if he had not died, something fairly drastic would have had to be done to prevent the Indian administration in London from breaking down altogether.

Canning's success at the Board of Control depended, therefore, in the first place, on his ability to restore harmony between the Board and the company. Fortunately, the disastrous propensity which he showed as a politician for creating distrust and making enemies, was as absent from his administrative work as it was from his private personal relations. He quickly reinstituted regular meetings with the Court of Directors. He was polite, tactful and conciliatory. He had the sense to realise, and frankly admit, that he was ignorant of conditions in India and was willing to accept expert advice. When the directors disagreed with his own officials' views on the abstruse question of revenue collection in Bengal, he at once deferred to them. 'I hesitate,' he wrote, 'to disagree with the considered opinion of the court on this topic . . . I wish above all things to avoid controversy in our correspondence'; and he sensibly added that he thought nothing was 'so little useful as reasoning by analogy from Europe to India'. The cordial relations which Canning early established with the directors were maintained, almost unblemished, until his resignation from the Board. At the same time, he increased the efficiency and morale of his own department by improving its organisation, increasing its staff and raising the salaries of the senior officials.

The most momentous crisis of the whole of his period at the India Board confronted Canning when he had scarcely had time to read himself into his new job. It arose, not out of any disagreement with the directors in London, but out of the policies that Lord Moira, who had gone out to India as Governor-General three years earlier, was urging on an equally reluctant government and company in London. Moira had not at the time agreed with Wellesley's expansionist policies, but when he found himself in his shoes, he became an increasingly urgent advocate of his predecessor's views. For some years, bands of fierce freebooters, known as Pindaris, had been pillaging far and wide throughout central India. As early as March 1814, Moira had proposed that the British should put themselves at the head of a confederacy of native states strong enough to restore and maintain law and order. He was sent a dusty answer from London. Before this reply reached him, he wrote again, urging that he should be given authority to act on his own initiative.

This letter arrived on Canning's desk soon after he took over at the Board. Almost all the experts whose advice he immediately sought were strongly opposed to giving Moira his head. The threat from the Pindaris was not denied. But it was feared that if the Governor-General committed his forces to an all-out attempt to suppress them, the Maratha states, straddling a vast area of central India, which

Wellesley had subjugated, would try to take advantage of the situation and a general war would ensue. Since that was the last thing that either the company or the government wanted, the despatch that was finally sent off to Moira on September 16, 1816, was extremely cautious. Canning did, however, give Moira some latitude by adding that 'the principle of protecting ourselves and our allies against specific inroads and to punish the aggressors is fully admitted.' Three days later, it was learned that the Pindaris had carried out a ferocious raid into the British territory of the Northern Circars. Canning immediately wrote again to Moira, giving him an 'explicit assurance' that any measures necessary to repel and pursue the invaders would be approved. But he again warned the Governor-General that his objectives must be limited to crushing the Pindaris.

Moira took full advantage of the latitude he had been reluctantly given and did not pay too much attention to the cautionary strictures which accompanied it. He was a competent general himself and he was served by exceptionally able subordinates. In due course, he crushed the Pindaris, and – as the pessimists had foretold – became involved in war with the Maratha states. He defeated them one after the other and imposed a series of settlements which by the end of 1818 had confirmed Britain as the paramount power in India. The authorities in London had to applaud his military skill, but they were not converted to his policies.

In March 1819, Canning introduced a vote of thanks in the Commons to the Marquess of Hastings (as Moira had by then become) and the army in India for their successful operations against the Pindaris and the Marathas. He began his speech by carefully emphasising that the vote was 'intended merely as a tribute to the military conduct of the campaign and not in any wise as a sanction of the policy of the war.' He deprecated the 'disposition of our Indian empire to stretch its limits wider every day,' and acknowledged Parliament's efforts to check this disposition. 'Would to God,' he added, 'that we could find, or rather that we could long ago have found, the point – the resting-place – at which it was possible to stand. But the finding of that point has not depended upon ourselves alone.'[37]

Hastings, like Wellesley fifteen years earlier, had some excuse for feeling let down. From the point of view of Bengal, Madras or Bombay, it was simply unimaginative and unrealistic of the Board of Control to deplore the steady enlargement of British power and possessions in India. But from the point of view of Canning and his colleagues it was equally unrealistic to contemplate creating an empire in the East. Their horizons were primarily European, their preoccupations overwhelmingly British. Most of them had spent their entire political life trying to prevent the establishment of a French hegemony over Europe. They had been genuinely shocked by Napoleon's apparently insatiable ambition and ruthless methods. They had no desire to embark on empire-building of their own on the other side of the world. In any case, there were much more pressing preoccupations at home. There was economic distress and social unrest and a genuine fear of revolution. When Canning wrote in July, 1819, that although the situation was bad enough in the manufacturing districts, he thought the worst was over, his mind was very far from the problems – and the opportunities – of India.[38] And in this, as in so many other things, he was typical of his generation.

When Parliament rose in July 1819, Canning felt the need for what he described as a frisk on the Continent. He had not had a proper holiday for nearly three years. Moira's campaigns had increased the amount and urgency of the paper work he had to get through and a multitude of red boxes would follow him even when he tried to get away for a break to Welbeck. He was, moreover, like most of his colleagues, beginning to get a good deal of gout; and although to Mr Rush, the American minister, who met him that July at a fancy-dress ball at Carlton House, he seemed to be in very good form, privately he admitted to feeling dead tired. So in the middle of August the Cannings set off for Italy. They took with them Harriet, who was to improve her languages and her manners in the year before she was due to 'come out', Carlo, now aged seven, who, it was hoped, would learn French and Italian without any trouble, and Joan's 21-year-old niece, Lady Harriet Bentinck. They travelled overland to Genoa by way of Rotterdam, Stuttgart and Milan, then down to Naples by sea and towards the end of October were established in Rome. Canning saw all the places he had planned to see on his way back from Lisbon three years earlier, and he told his mother that the sight of so many places, especially Naples and Rome, that he had been longing to see all his life 'affords a satisfaction so lively that I would not have missed it for any consideration – short of actual duty.'[39]

It was not long, however, before Canning was recalled from the ruined grandeur of ancient Rome to the frustrations and misery of industrial Britain. Towards the end of October he received a letter from Lord Liverpool urging him to return as quickly as possible because

Parliament was to meet early, on November 23, to deal with the crisis arising out of what came to be known as the 'massacre of Peterloo'. During a huge but orderly open-air meeting at St Peter's Fields in Manchester on August 16 the watching magistrates had ordered a regiment of hussars to go to the support of the local yeomanry who were trying to arrest Orator Hunt. The hussars charged the crowd and in the ensuing panic eleven people were killed and several hundred wounded.

Peterloo and its aftermath made a profound impression at the time and have been the subject of lively and voluminous controversy ever since. Whigs and Radicals, as well as many ordinary people who did not usually sympathise with either, were genuinely shocked by the magistrates' precipitate action and its tragic consequences. They were also outraged by the complacency with which the government seemed to regard what had happened. The magistrates were promptly and warmly thanked, and when the City of London's Common Council sent a petition of protest to the Regent, it was snubbingly told that it did not know what it was talking about. Early in October, the most extreme Whigs began to organise a series of county meetings at which the speakers emphasised the arbitrary action of the magistrates and the threat to the people's ancient rights of assembly and petitioning. At the Norfolk meeting, Lord Albemarle declared that nothing could prevent 'revolution, anarchy and bloodshed' unless 'men of character, talent and respectability' united to look after the needs of the people.[40]

Lord Liverpool's government and most of the middle and upper classes also feared – but for a different reason – the imminent approach of civil war and revolution. The fatal meeting at St Peter's Fields had been preceded by a recrudescence of activity by the wilder political reformers, and it was perhaps not surprising that Sidmouth, inundated with alarmist reports from all over the country and not of a very doughty disposition anyway, should have been convinced that the country was in greater danger than it had been since George I ascended the throne.[41] More surprisingly, that coolest of cool customers, the Duke of Wellington, believed that a general uprising was going to break out simultaneously in different parts of the country with the object of plundering rich houses. He thought this could not be entirely prevented, but so long as the mob never managed to get the better of the troops, 'the mischief will be confined to plunder and a little *murder*, and will not be irretrievable.'[42]

It was against this alarming background that the government decided to summon Parliament early and push through repressive

GEORGE CANNING

legislation. Considering the state of near-panic in which they were drafted, the notorious Six Acts might have been much worse. One prohibited unauthorised military drilling, another allowed magistrates to search private property for arms and a third speeded up the administration of justice. Two more were designed to stem the flow of libellous and seditious pamphlets; one imposed heavy penalties for seditious libels and the other extended the fourpenny stamp tax on newspapers to pamphlets. The sixth act, which drastically restricted the right of public meeting, was the most controversial. But the government did not insist on again suspending *habeas corpus*, and it was surprisingly ready to accept amendments to its legislation. The Grenvillites, whose connection with the Whigs was on the point of disintegrating, warmly supported the legislation, although they tended to feel that it was not tough enough. The Whigs turned out in force and put up a spirited fight against the government's measures, but although they were united in condemning the Manchester magistrates, they were far from agreed on their attitude towards the crisis that grew out of Peterloo. Most of them probably felt, privately at any rate, that some repressive legislation was necessary. Even Brougham thought that huge open-air public meetings ought to be stopped. This made it difficult for them to attack the government's general policy with much conviction. But they could, and did, effectively attack the details of its legislation.

Canning could not get back to London in time to have much, if any, effect on the government's policy decisions. But he was back in time to defend them in the House of Commons on the second day of the session, after which he succumbed to a violent attack of gout, brought on, he thought, by the fatigues of his hurried journey and the worry of the situation he found when he got home.

Ill-health apart, there is no evidence that he felt any reluctance to support his colleagues. In October, he had had doubts about the wisdom of the Manchester magistrates' proceedings,[43] but none at all about the imperative importance of supporting them now that the damage was done; otherwise they would resign and the whole system of maintaining local law and order through unpaid J.P.s would break down.[44] In the Commons, he defended the magistrates and restated his views on parliamentary reform.[45] He saw no reason to change them. Like his colleagues, he still did not realise that a growing number of working people rejected his claim that the interests of all classes were already properly cared for by Parliament. It did not occur to him, any more than to his colleagues, that if Parliament were more obviously concerned about poverty and unemployment (even if it could not cure them), inflammatory pamphlets and papers might not have such a ready market. He firmly believed that it was the licence of some sections of the Press (he did not condemn it all) that created the unrest, not vice versa, and he opposed an amendment that would have placed a time limit on the operation of the new stamp act. In the committee stage of the other bill to curb the Press, Canning delivered one of his bursts of eloquence in an attempt to refute the criticism made by Sir James Mackintosh, the distinguished Whig lawyer and historian, of the bill's definition of a blasphemous and seditious libel.[46] Wilberforce's friend, Henry Bankes, wrote that 'the speeches of Sir James Mackintosh and Mr Canning . . . were singularly brilliant and entertaining; the advantages, both in splendour of diction and in argument, being decidedly in favour of the latter.' Bankes was bound to prefer Canning's arguments since he himself supported the two Press bills; his only fear was that they might not be strong enough. It did not, indeed, require Canning's eloquence to persuade a large majority of the Commons (and the country) that the Press, in Bankes's rather apocalyptic words, was a 'tremendous engine in the hands of mischievous men' and must therefore be properly controlled.[47]

Towards the end of February 1820, the worst fears of the alarmists seemed to be confirmed by the discovery of a crazy conspiracy to murder all the members of the Cabinet while they were at dinner at Lord Harrowby's.* After this alarm, however, there was a lull in the unrest of recent years. The government naturally put this down to the beneficial effect of the Six Acts, although they were only spasmodically applied. A more likely explanation may have been the improvement in the economic situation. People with work to do and food to eat tended to lose interest in political agitation.

For Lord Liverpool's government, however, if it was not one thing, it was another. On January 29, 1820, George III at last died. Within a few days, the hapless Cabinet was coping with a crisis caused by George IV's determination to get rid of his wife. It found itself caught between the vociferous disapproval of the mob and the near-hysterical anger of the King. For Canning himself it was the beginning of a process which, but for Castlereagh's suicide, would have led him two and a half years later finally to renounce his cherished political ambitions in England and seek what for him would have been the doubtful consolation of ruling Britain's Indian empire.

* It became known as the Cato Street conspiracy because most of the conspirators were arrested at their rendezvous in Cato Street.

CHAPTER XIV

The Indian option
1820-1822

If Canning had not been caught up in the national crisis over Queen Caroline, it seems likely that he would have created a private crisis of his own. He had never lost his yearning to be leader of the House of Commons, and after playing second fiddle to Castlereagh for three years, he yearned more strongly than ever. Early in the New Year of 1820, he told Lord Liverpool that he did not think he could go on as he was much longer. The prime minister agreed that Canning's present position in the Cabinet was far less than his due. He asked Canning whether he would take the Home Office if, as he thought likely, Sidmouth retired when George III died. In time of peace, Liverpool assured Canning, the Home Office was the number two post in the Cabinet. But what Canning wanted above all was the number one post in the Commons. And without mentioning Castlereagh by name, he said as much to Liverpool. He felt, he said, that he had not half the scope which he believed himself to be capable of making use of, and that he was, as it were, defrauded of half the reputation to which he had a right.[1]

It was not any personal dislike or rivalry that moved Canning, but the consciousness of his own exceptional talents and the restless urge to make the greatest possible use of them. But he was a wiser and more controlled man than he had been some dozen years earlier. He had made up his mind that if he could not have what he really wanted, he would keep quiet until he could find some tolerable means of extricating himself from politics altogether. He recurred to the expedient of going to India, which had been a possibility at the back of his mind for several years. Now it seemed more than a possibility, for Hastings, who had been Governor-General since 1813, must be about due to come home – or so Canning believed. So he put it plainly to Liverpool that if he could not be leader of the House as well as Home Secretary, he would prefer to succeed Hastings in India.[2]

Before Liverpool was called upon to deal with what can only be called this ultimatum – although Canning assured him it was nothing of the sort – he was confronted with a far graver problem. George IV's first wish on ascending the throne was to get a divorce. Since 1814 his wife had lived abroad, visiting North Africa, Greece and the Levant, as well as Germany and Italy. She had shown herself to be a remarkably intrepid traveller and an excessively indiscreet woman. In 1818, the Regent, with the approval of Liverpool and Eldon,* had sent a commission to Milan to investigate the reports of the Princess's scandalous conduct, and in particular of her alleged adultery with her handsome Italian attendant, Bartolommeo Pergami. It was on the basis of the report produced by this commission that the King now called on his ministers to rid him of his wife. If they refused, he would, he said, get rid of them.

For Canning, the crisis was personal as well as political. His friendship for Caroline may not have said much for his discrimination, but it was at any rate loyal and disinterested. With the passage of time it had become much less close, and by 1820, Canning can hardly have remained unaffected by the scandalous stories of her conduct abroad, although he could not forget that she had befriended him when he was still a comparatively obscure young politician, and had stood godmother to his eldest son. He realised that Caroline ought to settle for as comfortable an exile as she could get. But if she insisted on returning, he felt he could not be a party to any penal proceedings against her.

For political, if not for personal, reasons Canning's colleagues were just as much against a divorce as he was. They doubted whether they or anyone else could get a divorce bill through both Houses of Parliament, and they knew that if they tried there would be a tremendous public outcry against the King, who was both wildly unpopular and widely criticised for the irregularities of his own private life. The difficulty was to make him see reason. After discussing the problem at eight consecutive meetings, the ministers decided to advise strongly against a divorce and begged the King to be content with a settlement under which Caroline, in return for a generous financial provision, would renounce her royal title and live permanently abroad.

The King eventually agreed to give way about the divorce but forced the ministers to agree to Caroline's exclusion from the Liturgy. 'If she is fit to be introduced to the Almighty,' argued Croker, 'she is fit to be received by men, and if we are to *pray* for her in Church, we may surely bow to her at Court . . .' He claims in his diary that this argument,

---

* But Canning protested to Liverpool when he learnt that the commission had been financed with government money. (Stapleton Mss. Canning to Ellis October 14, 1820)

purveyed to the King by his private secretary, Sir Benjamin Bloomfield, made a profound impression on the royal mind.[3] The ministers, on the other hand, who sat up till past two in the morning discussing the problem of the Liturgy, were probably less concerned with the Almighty than with the inflammatory effect of this concession both on Caroline and on public opinion. But they made it all the same. Canning had at first argued strongly against giving way over the Liturgy, but in the end agreed to do so in the hope that this concession would help to head the King off from a divorce. He also hoped that the settlement extracted from her husband would suffice to head Caroline off from England.

It was not to be. As soon as she heard of George III's death, Caroline determined to return to England to claim her royal rights. The government, fearing it could not survive the popular storm that would blow up if she really returned, armed her principal legal and political adviser, Henry Brougham, with its financially generous proposals and sent him to intercept her and stop her from crossing the Channel. But Brougham mismanaged his mission, and on June 6 Caroline drove in triumph into London in an open carriage, tumultuously applauded all the way. *The Times* went so far as to say that the landing of neither William the Conqueror nor William III had agitated the bosoms of Londoners so much as the arrival of brave Queen Caroline.[4] And when the people were tired of cheering their heroine, they took to breaking the windows and stoning the carriages of the hated ministers of a hated King who between them were supposed to be responsible for her wrongs.

For Canning, the Queen's return blocked the exit he hoped he had found out of his personal quandary. The Cabinet met as soon as it heard of her landing, and decided to lay the evidence it had against her before Parliament. Canning agreed to this, but after the meeting offered Liverpool his resignation. The prime minister, who thought Canning was being too scrupulous and in any case did not want to lose his services, refused to accept it. He told the King afterwards – perhaps with the intention of frightening him a little – that Canning's resignation would have serious consequences for the government and might even lead to its dissolution.[5]

So Canning stayed, and on June 7 made a long speech in the Commons defending the government's policy towards the Queen. Unfortunately, he twice expressed, in warm and glowing terms, his personal regard and affection for her.[6] One cannot tell whether his tributes were deliberate, or whether (perhaps more probably) they were impulsive emotional responses to a tense and highly-fraught atmosphere. In any case, they created a great sensation; what he actually said naturally lost nothing in the telling and the gossips revived the rumours that he had once been Caroline's lover.

On no one did Canning's words make a greater impression than the King. He was so furious that he refused to see Liverpool unless he brought with him an explanation of Canning's speech.[7] On June 11, the prime minister, harassed but loyal to his friend and colleague, wrote a dignified letter to the King in which he declared that he was 'fully satisfied upon inquiry that Mr Canning . . . took a part which, however misrepresented in the daily prints, was honourable to himself, and substantially useful to your Majesty and your Government.' He therefore declined 'being the channel of requiring an explanation from Mr Canning of particular expressions which may have fallen from him in the warmth of speaking.'[8] Next day Liverpool was allowed to see the King but found him in such a state of irritation that he decided to tell Canning who had not been informed about the royal rage. Canning immediately asked for an audience and apparently came away from it under the impression that he had made a satisfactory explanation and apology. His hopeful impression might possibly have turned out to be justified if the strenuous efforts made to hammer out a compromise agreement with Caroline had succeeded. But they broke down because she was determined to vindicate her honour by having her name in the Liturgy. On June 25, the Cabinet gave up and decided to proceed against her by a Bill of Pains and Penalties in the Lords.* In effect, she was to be tried by Parliament on a charge of adultery with Pergami.

Canning at once saw the King and frankly explained his predicament. He entirely approved of all that had been done since the Queen's unfortunate return, but as he had so often acted in the past as her confidential adviser, he could not possibly now put himself in the position of her accuser. He could either retire altogether, or stay where he was but take no part in the Queen's affairs. He himself thought it would be better if he resigned, but he was willing to do whatever the King preferred. After talking the matter over for more than an hour in a perfectly friendly way, the King shook hands and said he would like to think over what had been said. Next day, he told Liverpool he would like Canning to stay on the understanding that he was free to follow his own line about the Queen.[9] From then on, Canning took no further part in the Cabinet's deliberations on this subject. He had, he told Joan cheerfully on July 2, washed his hands of the whole business.[10] But only three days later he was writing to the

* A device for punishing someone by act of Parliament without a legal trial.

prime minister, arguing forcibly against the government's decision to introduce a divorce clause into the bill.[11] He could never refrain from giving Liverpool the benefit of his advice, especially of course when he thought he was going astray.

Canning did, however, decide to remove himself as far as possible from the temptation to interfere by joining Joan who was still in Italy. Before he went he refused an offer from Liverpool to make him Home Secretary on the grounds that this would bring him into too much personal contact with the King.[12] This was tactful, but it is doubtful whether he understood just how violently the King, for all his apparent cordiality, had turned against him. He realised that the King did not believe that he was giving him all his reasons for refusing to take part in the proceedings against the Queen. But he would have been very surprised to learn that according to the version of the interview the King gave Wellington, he had almost confessed his former '*extreme intimacy*' with Caroline. Mrs Arbuthnot, to whom the duke recounted this, was anything but an admirer of Canning, but she wrote in her diary that she did not believe this part of the King's story.[13]

But the King believed it. At least he seems to have convinced himself that publicly in the Commons, if not privately to himself, Canning had virtually confessed to having once been Caroline's lover. Fifteen years earlier he had seemed to discount the rumours about Canning and his wife; and although he had always been rather cool about him, he had never shown any strong personal reluctance to have him among his ministers. Now, however, in the unusually (even for him) wrought-up state to which his wife's return had reduced him, he chose to read a far more lurid interpretation into Canning's words than any reasonable person could make them bear. It was only Liverpool's cajolements and, perhaps, threats of his own resignation, that persuaded him graciously to refuse to let Canning resign. But behind his smiling mask he had conceived a violent and uncharacteristically durable prejudice against him.

The reunion of Canning and his wife must have been rather a sad one, for since their last meeting their eldest son George had died. His stay in Portugal had improved his general health, without doing anything for his hip complaint. But the improvement had not lasted. The old unending search for better doctors and new cures started all over again. In March 1817, Canning took the boy to a surgeon in Chester who claimed to have cured similar cases. But tentative plans for sending him there fell through. In the autumn of that year, he was suffering from recurrent abscesses, and his father, fed up with the doctor who had been treating him with 'plaisters', took him to a Mrs Davies who thought she might be able to do him some good and offered to treat him for a trial period. So George went to her three times a week for a 'fumigation of herbs' and sometimes his father went along too to watch him being 'steamed'. Both father and son were very satisfied with this treatment and after about a month the boy said he felt much better and actually managed to walk fifteen times round the room, without crutches but holding Mrs Davies's hand.[14]

Neither that nor any other treatment, however, was of any permanent use, and when the Cannings went abroad in the summer of 1819, George was too much of an invalid to go with them. The following February Canning, back at Gloucester Lodge, reported to Joan: 'George is poorly – and then well again – in short just as he has been for years.'[15] Ten days later, Canning wrote that his son had been suffering a good deal lately and it was thought he might now have gravel. About a fortnight later, he developed dropsy, and on March 31 he died. His malady, wrote Canning to his mother on the same day, 'was, in effect, nothing else than the breaking up of a frame so weak that the wonder rather is that it should have lasted so long.'[16] The boy was buried in the new churchyard of Kensington Church. Canning sent Joan an account of the simple funeral, adding that he was very glad she had not been there. 'God knows, my own dear love has long ago and to the full discharged all her maternal duties to the poor sufferer – in years of privation and self-banishment; it was my turn to take my part in this painful office; and most thankful am I that I have had to take it in this sad instance, alone.'[17]

Canning rejoined his family in Venice – a place he had always longed to visit. Their windows overlooked the Grand Canal, and his mind was full of Shylock and Portia and Othello. He told his mother he thought he had seen Shylock in the market place. 'But Othello, and all that belonged to the splendour of government, and the feats of armies, is gone. Decay and desertion are sadly perceptible. It must have been a magnificent city in its day.'[18]

On their way home, they stopped at Munich and Canning took Joan and Harriet to dine with the King and Queen of Bavaria at their country palace. They reached Paris early in October, and there Canning determined to stay until Caroline's trial was over. It had begun early in

August and whatever were Brougham's private views on her behaviour, he had been outstandingly successful in discrediting a considerable part of the prosecution's case. By the time the defence had finished its summing-up, it seemed doubtful whether the bill would pass the Lords by a satisfactory majority and even possible that it would not get through the Commons at all. Moreover, popular feeling was still fervently in favour of the Queen.

Canning, who still could not refrain from bombarding Liverpool with epistolary advice, thought that the bill should be completely withdrawn without bringing it to a vote.[19] Although a good many people, including Castlereagh, thought the same, Liverpool optimistically decided to press on. His optimism proved ill-founded. The bill passed its second reading on November 6 by only 28 votes, and three days later, the majority for it on the third reading sank to a mere nine votes. The prime minister immediately decided to drop it.* Charles Arbuthnot thought the government had got out of an awkward situation without 'any shabbiness'.[20] But Eldon, the Lord Chancellor, was not so sure. He thought the bill should either have been passed or rejected, and that to leave such grave charges against the Queen hanging in the air was unjust both to her and the country.[21] Queen and country, however, seemed perfectly satisfied. There were illuminations and wild rejoicings, and a few weeks later Caroline insisted on driving in triumph to St Paul's to give thanks for her deliverance from her enemies.

The chief person not to be pleased by the outcome of the trial was of course the King. When Canning got back to London on November 18, he found his colleagues just emerging from a violent tussle with their royal master. Understandably enough, he wanted Caroline's financial provision to be settled immediately. But the ministers, who thought it would be madness to raise the matter while public opinion was so inflamed, were determined to prorogue Parliament for two months in the hope that the country would by then have come to its senses. The King, whose language and manner were said to resemble those of a Bedlamite,[22] eventually gave way.

* Liverpool had hoped for a majority of 50 on the second reading. But the ministers were not disheartened because so many of the peers who had voted against the bill had virtually admitted the Queen's guilt. Charles Arbuthnot thought Lord Grenville had 'damned' her when he said that if what had been proved against her was not enough, no case of adultery could henceforth be proved 'except upon ocular demonstration'. (BM. Add. Mss. 38742 November 6, 1820)

Canning was not spared his share of the royal wrath by his attempt at neutrality. In any case, it had been compromised by his friends in the Lords* who, in many people's opinion, had done him a very bad turn by voting against the second reading of the bill.[23] Morley had even openly canvassed against it. The King, who knew they were Canning's friends, thought he had put them up to it and was furious. Canning had in fact done no such thing and was extremely annoyed by Morley's indiscreet behaviour.[24] At a private audience with the King, he apparently managed to clear himself of this charge. But the root cause of the royal antipathy remained. 'Mr Canning,' wrote the King, 'had strongly manifested by his conduct, what everybody here believed, almost an open avowal of a criminal intercourse with the Pcess . . .' What confidence, he asked, could he have 'in a mind tainted with dishonour, and disturbed by the apprehension of guilt?'[25]

The King's views about Canning's feelings of guilt must have been strengthened by his conduct during the next few weeks. The ministers had managed to postpone the discussion of the Queen's affairs in Parliament, but they themselves could hardly avoid discussing them, especially as she was not slow to stake her claims. Liverpool, supported by most of the Cabinet, was convinced that after all that had been revealed during her trial about her behaviour, it was quite impossible to restore her name to the Liturgy. But Canning felt equally strongly that since Caroline had in effect been acquitted, by far the wisest and fairest course would be to grant her everything she could claim. If the government did this, she would soon be packing her bags to return to Feraro, and the popular outcry in her favour, which was stirred up by the feeling that she had been unjustly treated, would die away. 'As it is,' he wrote on November 28, 'they [the ministers] have just broken off the thorn at the skin, and left the little point of it rankling in the wound.'[26]

But Canning's views did not prevail, and he eventually told Liverpool that as the government seemed determined to treat the Queen as if she had been found guilty, he really must resign. He had told Charles Ellis when he was still in Paris that he *should* have resigned the moment he found his colleagues going along a road on which he could not accompany them.[27] When he found himself diverging from them a second time on the same delicate issue, he may well have felt that a clean break was better than another equivocal compromise. 'So long as I could be neutral,' he told his mother, 'that was the position that became me. When neutrality is no longer compatible with office, I must abandon

* Portland, Stafford, Morley, Granville and Amherst.

one or the other, and I prefer, without hesitation, the abandonment of office.'[28]

It was of course put about by those who disliked Canning that his real reason for resigning was that he thought the government was about to sink and he had better find a more seaworthy craft. It is certainly true that he did not think highly either of his colleagues' past performance or their future prospects, although he did not disagree with them on grounds of general policy. He can be criticised for not sticking by them at a difficult time, but there is no evidence that he expected to advance his own political fortunes by his resignation, or had any notion of linking up with some of the Whigs.

It seems more likely that Canning was moved by political apathy rather than by political ambition. At the beginning of 1820, as we have seen, he told Liverpool that he felt he had reached a dead end in politics. The events of the year can only have strengthened that conviction. He may have felt that he had little to lose by doing what he believed to be right. On the other hand, he certainly realised that by jumping off the ladder of power, he risked never getting a foothold on it again. Moreover he had come to enjoy his work at the India Board, which, when leaving it, he nostalgically described as the pleasantest office in the government.[29] Like most people in his position, he was pushed this way and that by conflicting considerations and emotions; he was, he told Huskisson on December 12, quite 'knocked up with worry'.[30] But on the same day he told Joan that his decision to resign was definitely taken. 'It is an unavoidable one, but it is a fearful one – for I take it purely to avoid evil – not in the hope of good. My position in the House of Commons would have been intolerable; but what will be the result of my moving from it – unless total and permanent exclusion from power, I do not know. However, my judgment and conscience are alike convinced that I have done right – the rest must follow as it may.'[31]

Canning's resignation had been so widely expected that when it actually happened it created very little stir. The King, predictably, received it coldly but civilly and made no attempt to persuade him to stay. From most of his Cabinet colleagues his parting was more cordial. Sidmouth and Castlereagh, who had had a great deal to put up with from him in the past, were particularly friendly. Sidmouth declared that 'the loss to the King's service and to your colleagues will be irreparable; and let me add that I shall feel it deeply; for your kind, cordial and honourable conduct has made a strong and lasting impression on my mind.'[32] Castlereagh wrote that he could not presume to question Canning's decision, but 'as the individual member of the Government who must feel your loss the most seriously, both in the House of Commons and in the business of the Foreign Office, I will not refrain from expressing my disappointment.' And he added in his stilted but patently sincere way: 'Allow me at the same time most cordially to thank you for the uniform attention with which you have followed up, and the kindness with which you have assisted me, in the business of the department for the conduct of which I am more immediately responsible.'[33]

At the last Cabinet meeting which Canning attended, Castlereagh produced a draft despatch for his colleagues' comments. To the general surprise, Canning took as much trouble suggesting changes and improvements as if he had not, as everyone knew, been on the point of leaving them. Castlereagh took his criticisms in very good part and in the end asked him to take the draft away and look it over. So Canning spent three hours putting it into better shape and Castlereagh, when he saw it, declared it to be greatly improved.[34] There was always a streak of the schoolmaster in Canning; he enjoyed correcting other people's exercises. All the same, it was a graceful way to bow out.

Canning and Liverpool remained on excellent terms. Apart from genuine ties of friendship, the prime minister wanted Canning back in the Cabinet as soon as possible. He realised that, without him, Castlereagh was very poorly supported on the front bench in the Commons. Vansittart, the Chancellor of the Exchequer, hardly ever uttered except on financial matters, while Bragge-Bathurst (Chancellor of the Duchy of Lancaster), Wellesley-Pole (Master of the Mint) and Frederick Robinson (President of the Board of Trade) were all lightweights in debate. Liverpool tried to tempt Peel back into office with an offer of the India Board and a seat in the Cabinet. But Peel, who disliked the government's handling of the Queen's affairs, preferred to remain aloof. So Liverpool, not wishing to appear desperate for help, got Bragge-Bathurst to stand in at the Board of Control and decided to soldier on for the time being without reinforcements.

In the middle of January, Canning escaped from the impending parliamentary battles to rejoin Joan and Harriet in Paris. There he lived a life of unaccustomed idleness, sharing with Joan the pleasant duty of chaperoning Harriet in the evenings, and in the mornings sometimes taking a kind of busman's holiday listening to the debates in the Chamber of Deputies.[35] Meanwhile in the House of Commons, the ministers were resisting the opposition's efforts to make political capital out of their treatment of the Queen. By the middle of February, the Whigs had shot their bolt and the ministers, rather to their surprise, had emerged more or less unscathed. They might be weak in Parliament and unpopular in the country, but to the independent country gentlemen in the Commons, they were at least a lesser evil than their opponents. The comment of Mme Lieven, the wife of the Russian ambassador, that 'these Whigs have plenty of brains and not a shadow of common sense', reflected a widespread feeling.[36] Moreover, the tide was beginning to turn against Caroline; she was becoming a bore. Even Canning, reflecting on the unsatisfactory state of her affairs from his Parisian vantage point, determined not to get roped in as her adviser ever again.[37]

He was in no hurry to return to London. But at the end of February William Plunket successfully carried (by six votes) a motion which allowed him to introduce a Catholic emancipation bill. It was the first majority for a pro-Catholic motion since 1813 and Canning could hardly turn his back on a cause which had always meant so much to him. He was back in London in time to speak in support of the second reading of Plunket's bill on March 16. His tactics were not to mix in every detail of the debate, 'but wait for the opportunities, when there is a great difficulty to be met, or a considerable impression to be made.'[38] His opportunity came in the committee stage, when an amendment was introduced to exclude the Catholics from sitting in Parliament. It was the success of a similar amendment which had caused Canning to abandon his bill in 1813. This time the Speaker himself spoke in favour of the amendment. Canning rose immediately after him and eloquently ridiculed those who feared that the admission of even as many as a hundred Roman Catholic M.P.s could overturn either the established church or the state.[39] The amendment was defeated by twelve votes, and on April 2 the bill passed its third reading by a majority of nineteen. Predictably, with Liverpool, Sidmouth and Eldon all speaking strongly against it, the bill was thrown out in the Lords. But for the pro-Catholics, who had been disappointed so often, it was tremendously encouraging at least to have got the Commons to accept, not just the principle of emancipation, but a concrete measure for putting principle into practice.

For Canning, however, parliamentary triumphs no longer meant what they once did; he was too worried by the problem of his own future. The day after the Catholic bill passed the Commons, he poured out his unhappiness, uncertainty and uneasiness in a long letter to Joan. 'But in truth,' he wrote, 'I am sick of the whole thing. I have nothing to gain in Parly reputation – the last three weeks have placed that at the pinnacle. All to come is risk, rather than gain. And what does the reputation of being the first speaker in the House of Commons do for me? Nothing. It only leads people to believe that *fine speaking* is not necessary for carrying on the affairs of the Government ... but that business can go on very well without it. And so it can. And the more it goes on without me the better. I am weary – and at 51 or thereabouts I cannot afford, either in the common or the moral sense of the word, to hazard new experiments, and new combinations, as I would with the possibility of 20 years before me. The next stage – whatever it be – must be decisive for life – and if it is to be as barren of advantage as all former steps have been I shall have done little for the comfort of old age, and of that of those whom I ought to have thought of long ago rather than of my own etiquette and points of honour.' He was still haunted by the fatal wrong turning he had taken nearly a dozen years earlier. And he went on, passionately and jerkily, as if he were talking instead of writing to his wife: 'These thoughts come upon me at all times and seasons – and often most unseasonably – even in the middle of the debate in the House of Commons I ask myself what is all this good for? Luckily' (he added honestly) 'I have yet enough of vigour, and of the taste for the applause in me, to forget everything, while I am actually speaking, except the subject and the glory of success.'[40]

Canning ended this revealing outburst by complaining that the Tories assumed that he would take *any* office in order to support them; but they were mistaken, he wrote, if they thought he would be content to play second fiddle to the end of his days. This was hardly fair on Liverpool. Moreover, in his more sanguine moments Canning was prepared to overlook the supposed humiliation of having to play second fiddle. About three weeks later, he had a long and apparently satisfactory discussion with Liverpool about how to strengthen the government.[41] But back in Paris, his old despondency returned and at the end of May, 1821, he was telling Huskisson that he did not think the changes proposed by Liverpool would satisfy either the country or Parliament. It did not matter to him personally, for he was heartily weary and wished that his course was run.[42] Soon after he had brought Joan and Harriet back to London early in June, it began to appear that, whatever his own changeable feelings, his course at Westminster was indeed run.

Liverpool had run into difficulties with his plans for strengthening the government by bringing in Canning, Peel and the Grenvillites, who were ready to abandon their increasingly unsatisfactory liaison with the Whigs. He should not have found it too difficult, for the Home Secretary, Sidmouth, now old and tired, was increasingly anxious to retire and the Board of Control was waiting for a permanent President. Trouble arose, not out of any issue of principle, but because of the personal pretensions and prejudices of those involved. Castlereagh was jealous of Peel being made Chancellor of the Exchequer in place of the politically ineffective Vansittart; and Peel would not take the Board of Control, partly for health reasons and partly because he did not think it good enough. Liverpool was more successful in persuading Melville, the First Lord of the Admiralty, to let himself be 'kicked upstairs' (Melville's phrase) to the Home Office, so that Canning could have the Admiralty.

But when Liverpool formally explained these proposals to the King on June 10, he was met by outraged objections to the inclusion of Canning. The prime minister, feeling that he had done quite enough for the King's feelings by not suggesting Canning for the Home Office, indignantly departed without giving way. His relations with his royal master were already at a very low ebb. The King found him personally uncongenial and thoroughly irritating. He nursed a strong grudge against him because of the fiasco of the Queen's trial; and in April Liverpool had made himself still more unpopular by refusing to give a vacant canonry at Windsor to an obscure young clergyman whose only claim was that he was tutor to the children of the King's latest favourite, Lady Conyngham. The King openly abused Liverpool, graciously entertained some of the Whig leaders at Brighton, and frequently talked of changing his ministers. Wellington* tended to dismiss such talk as mere love of talking nonsense and making people believe that the prime minister was a kind of *maître d'hôtel*, liable to instant dismissal by his master.[43] Liverpool, understandably, could not treat the King's threats so nonchalantly and throughout the year he had been alternating between a wish to strengthen his ministry and a desire to throw in his hand altogether. In the middle of June, desperate private grief over the

* The Duke of Wellington had joined the Cabinet in January 1819 as Master-General of the Ordnance.

death of his wife made him still more distraught and consequently even less willing to compromise with the King.

Instead, Liverpool convinced himself that a constitutional issue was at stake: the King was claiming the right to exclude a minister from his government indefinitely for purely personal reasons. 'Excluding a man,' wrote Liverpool on June 16, 'at the time his services are wanted, and when there is an opening for him, is to all intents and purposes *proscription* – and upon such a principle I cannot agree to remain at the head of the government.'[44] If they gave way to the King, they would be acknowledging that they governed simply by his whim. Liverpool's colleagues sympathised with him, but did not consider the situation as dramatically dire as he did. They had the instinctive Tory reluctance to put too much pressure on the sovereign, and hoped that with a little judicious temporising, the King, a notoriously volatile character, could be brought round. Moreover, they did not share Liverpool's personal friendship for Canning; on the contrary, behind all the surface cordiality, many of them distrusted and disliked him. Wellington took a coolly practical view of the situation. Although he perhaps distrusted Canning more than most and felt Liverpool was making altogether too much of a fuss, he thought the King would do well to give way. Canning, he explained to Bloomfield, the King's secretary, would strengthen the government more than anyone else because of his 'parliamentary talents', but if he were left out in the cold, he would collect round him all the discontented M.P.s, all the 'young philosophers', and would soon be dangerously powerful. In short, the only way of both making him really useful and depriving him of the power to make mischief was to bring him into the Cabinet.[45]

The ministers did not tell Canning of the King's attitude towards him, but eventually he heard through the public grapevine and on June 22 begged Liverpool not to make an issue of him. Since, he wrote, he himself agreed that it was impossible for him to go to the Home Office for the moment, he had no right to be surprised if the King felt that even the occasional contacts arising out of his position at the Admiralty would be very unpleasing.[46] Next day Canning wrote again in a further attempt to persuade Liverpool to give way. He pointed out that his friend Huskisson, then in a junior office, was very anxious for promotion and in particular for the India Board. Huskisson had been prepared to give way to Peel or Robinson, but could hardly be expected to waive his claims for a 'stranger' (presumably the Grenvillite, Charles Wynn, whom Liverpool had in mind for the post). Clearly, wrote Canning, it would not be possible for him to enter the government by one door while Huskisson was going out by another; and he suggested that if his own name were withdrawn, Liverpool could recast his arrangements so as to do justice to Huskisson, while also gratifying the King.[47]

Canning was a proud as well as an ambitious man. Later he told Liverpool that he certainly did not object to his letter of the 22nd being shown to the King. 'In such case,' he wrote, 'it was for my honour that the King should know that nothing was further from my wish than that I should be pressed upon His Majesty.'[48] It seemed a perfect let-out for Liverpool. But instead of taking it, he wrote again to the King emphasising the great importance of securing Canning's services. His obvious anxiety to have Canning back apparently only strengthened the King's resolve not to agree.* Eventually, as Sidmouth was willing to postpone his retirement, Liverpool agreed – in the stiffest and tartest manner – to declare a truce, at least until after the coronation and the King's projected visit to Ireland.

But as the summer wore on, the situation seemed to get worse rather than better. On July 19, the King was crowned, while his wretched Queen knocked vainly on the locked doors of the Abbey. Shortly afterwards a fresh row broke out between the King and Liverpool, when the latter refused to appoint Lord Conyngham to an important post in the royal household. On August 7, while the King was on his way to Ireland, the Queen died after a short illness. There was rioting while her coffin passed through London and the King was furiously angry with Liverpool for bungling the funeral arrangements. Sidmouth, who was with the King in Ireland, reported that there were 'evident symptoms of a great storm hanging over us'.[49] But the storm passed over without breaking. The King returned from Ireland in mid-September and before the end of the month was off again on a visit to Hanover. When Liverpool called at Carlton House, the King refused to receive him, although he had already given audience to other members of the Cabinet.

Liverpool did not, as the King may have hoped, let himself be snubbed into resigning voluntarily. On the other hand, he was ready to listen to his colleagues' suggestions that he should be more conciliatory. Wellington assured him that they all wanted Canning to rejoin the Cabinet, but he doubted whether they would be prepared to resign if they could not have him. Nor did he think that the govern-

* According to Wellington, the King at one point admitted that he objected to Canning because Liverpool was so anxious to have him. But this clearly was only part of the reason. (Brock, *Liverpool*, p. 136)

ment's supporters as a whole would approve of such a course. 'There is no doubt that Mr Canning is not very popular with them.' He advised Liverpool to remember his duty. If, he pointed out, they all decided no longer to put up with the 'many inconveniences and evils resulting from the King's habits and character', they would abandon the country to Whigs, Radicals and 'irretrievable ruin'.[50] Meanwhile, Castlereagh, who had accompanied the King to Hanover, was trying his hand as a conciliator. He was so far successful that when the King returned from Hanover, he was ready for a formal reconciliation with Liverpool. It duly took place on November 13. A month later Castlereagh reported that he had found the King 'in the most perfect good humour with his Government'.[51]

This new harmony was largely due to an agreement between the King and Castlereagh that Canning should have a Cabinet post which did not bring him into personal contact with the King on the definite understanding that he would go to India as soon as Hastings retired.[52] The compromise may have helped to reconcile the King and his prime minister, but it did not settle Canning's future. On the contrary, it now became the subject of negotiations and manœuvres that were as obscure and confused at the time as they remain in retrospect.

In the first place, no one knew whether Hastings really did want to resign. From hints dropped in his letters, the directors of the East India Company were convinced that he did, and in September Canning agreed to their suggestion that they should put forward his name as the new Governor-General. But their conviction was shaken by Hastings's confidential agent in London, Colonel Doyle, who hotly denied that he wanted to come home. Doyle admitted that he had Hastings's letter of resignation in his pocket, but he was convinced it had been written under a misapprehension and was determined not to part with it without further instructions from India.[53]

To add to the confusion, Canning himself seems to have misunderstood exactly where he stood in relation to the King and his colleagues. He does not appear to have been told of the bargain reached by the King and Castlereagh in Hanover. At any rate he left a meeting with Liverpool on November 14 under the definite impression that if the India job was not available after all, Liverpool could and would get him into the Cabinet, either at the Admiralty or the Home Office, and he could still have the refusal of India later when it did fall vacant.[54] Liverpool always tended to retreat into obscurity when he had anything awkward or unpleasant to impart, and it seems likely that he simply funked telling Canning that the King would only have him in the Cabinet on sufferance and on a temporary basis. The King was indeed so determined to get rid of Canning that when he gave an audience to Doyle, he managed to persuade him that he ought to hand in Hastings's resignation after all. So when Canning saw Liverpool again a few days later, he was amazed to find that the only question under discussion was not what post he should have in the Cabinet, but whether or not he should go to India.[55]

Faced unexpectedly with such a momentous choice, Canning's heart failed him. 'I must think well and deeply before I decide,' he wrote to Huskisson, 'and then decide once and for all.'[56] If the King was really determined to exclude him indefinitely he felt he might as well go to India and at least have the satisfaction of making things easier for Liverpool. But when it came to the point it was very difficult to leave Westminster, however unsatisfactory it had become. And because of Liverpool's reluctance to tell him the cruel, unvarnished truth, he failed to grasp how determined the King was to exclude him from his counsels.

Looked at from a purely personal point of view, the decision whether or not to go to India was perhaps even more difficult. If he went, there would be the problem of his beloved daughter, Harriet. Should they leave her behind with Joan's relations, or exile her to Bengal throughout her most marriageable years? 'If there were no Harriet in the world,' he wrote, 'the decision would be easy – but with such a Harriet and just *now*, what to do?'[57] On the other hand, Canning was financially in very low water. Joan's extended stay abroad with Harriet had been largely an economy measure which, before her return in June, had made it possible to reduce the Gloucester Lodge establishment to one manservant and a gardener. To go to India as Governor-General was a recognised way of restoring one's finances. Hastings had gone largely for that reason, and Canning was strongly tempted to follow his example. In 1821, when he had no official salary, his income amounted to only £2,200, of which £980 came from a farm in Lincolnshire and £360 from his small Irish estate – both precarious and fluctuating sources of income. He paid out a total of £700 a year in insurance premiums and interest on a loan, which left him with a maximum income of £1,500 and very much less if there was a sharp drop in his income from Ireland and Lincolnshire. Gloucester Lodge represented an asset, variously estimated at between £4,000 and £6,000.

LORD LIVERPOOL
by Lawrence

GLOUCESTER LODGE

A watercolour by T. H. Shepheard

Of Joan's original fortune of £75,000,* only £12,000 remained in the funds. Of the remainder, £10,000 had been spent at the time of their marriage on buying and furnishing South Hill, paying off Canning's debts, and so on; £10,000 had gone on procuring a seat in Parliament in 1802, 1806 and 1807; £33,000 went on buying land in Lincolnshire; and the remaining £10,000, which Canning could not account for, had presumably been gradually spent on current expenses over the years. By 1821 he was rather appalled at the way in which he had let his wife's fortune slip through his fingers, as well as by his failure to make any provision for his children. His salary as Governor-General would be nominally £25,000, but worth £30,000 because of the rate of exchange at which it was paid, and he was told that he would be able to remit half of it to England each year. After half a dozen years in India, he would be a long way towards repairing the family fortunes.[58] From a financial point of view, the case for going to India was very strong.

But while he was trying to make up his mind, yet another misunderstanding cropped up to complicate the situation further. He learnt that Hastings was under the impression that, while he was President of the Board of Control, he had deliberately tried to make trouble between Hastings and the directors so that he could succeed to Hastings's job.[59] This was untrue. Canning had always assumed that if he went to India it would be when it suited Hastings to come home. Hastings had only his own imprudence and negligence to blame for the disagreeable letters he received from Leadenhall Street. Far from trying to make matters worse, Canning had tried to smooth them over. But when he learnt what Hastings was alleging about him, he rather naturally felt that he could not possibly agree to step into his shoes until he had had a chance to put the record straight in a personal interview.[60] Hostile critics alleged that he was just trying to shuffle out of going to India. But Lord Harrowby thought that Canning, through no fault of his own, was in a most awkward and embarrassing situation.[61] Harrowby was nearer the mark, although Canning, still a prey to conflicting emotions and considerations, was probably not sorry to gain some time before he had finally to make up his mind.

Time, however, was not on his side. Towards the end of November, Liverpool, convinced that he could not overcome the royal prejudice against Canning, decided to go ahead without him. On November 26, he and Peel went down to Brighton to describe their proposals to the

* It is usually said to have amounted to £100,000 but Canning put it at £75,000 in a letter to Joan written early in 1822, which discusses their financial situation.

King. Peel would go to the Home Office instead of Sidmouth who would remain in the Cabinet without office; Wellesley would go to Ireland as Lord-Lieutenant; and the Grenvillites would be brought into the ministry, although it was not yet clear exactly how.* Canning seems to have found it difficult to realise that the door to office at home was inexorably closing in his face, and when he did, he tried hard to put his foot in it.

By the end of the year, further letters from Hastings made it quite plain that he really did want to come home. The directors again offered his post to Canning who this time refused. Early in the New Year he told Huskisson that his name had not been mentioned again and he believed himself to be 'clear of India'.[62] A few days later he suggested to Liverpool that if Peel was willing, as he apparently might be, to postpone his accession to the Cabinet, he himself might take the Home Department. He could hardly believe, he wrote, that if he made it clear that he would remain in the House of Commons and not go to India, the King would continue to exclude him from office; and he was sure that if he and the King were obliged to do business together, all former unpleasantness would soon be forgotten. But if, he added, Peel became the Home Secretary, 'the door is closed against me for ever.'[63]

It was all wishful thinking, the desperate throw of a man who, whatever the splendour and material rewards of ruling in the East, could not bear to abandon the chance of high office at home. A few days later, Peel received his seals of office, and Canning, brought down to earth again, wrote: 'I see no imaginable combination of things through which I can ever again be engaged in a political negotiation.'[64]

But the Indian option was still open, and as the weeks passed the pressure to take it became increasingly strong. There were his own unsolved financial problems. There were the directors of the company who were extremely anxious that Hastings's successor should be someone they knew and liked. And there were his former colleagues who could not think of anyone else to send to India. More important, rightly or wrongly, they feared for the stability of their government if Canning remained, without office, in the Commons. 'I must say,' Liverpool wrote to Bathurst on December 23, 'that I hold the keeping

---

* The new arrangements took some time to complete. Early in December, Castlereagh urged Liverpool not to leave the Grenvillites 'loose' in the Commons, but to 'make love in your best manner to whichever of these charmers may come within your reach.' By the following February, Liverpool had enticed Charles Wynn with the Board of Control, and Buckingham, the head of the Grenville family, with a dukedom. (Yonge, *Liverpool*, III, p. 162, December 6, 1821)

the situation of Governor-General open for Canning as a question of VITAL *importance*. We shall find the greatest inconvenience in his being here for any time out of office, and yet his return to office now is rendered nearly impracticable, even if the King's objections could be over-ruled.'65

With the apparently final extinction of Canning's political ambitions in England, the only factors weighing in the other side of the scale were Hastings's illusions about his behaviour at the India Board and the reluctance of Joan and Harriet to be exiled to India. The latter weighed heavily, but not enough to tip the scales. In the middle of March, Reid, the chairman of the Court of Directors, pressed Canning to make up his mind. Three days later, Canning asked Doyle for firm assurances that Hastings really did have urgent personal reasons for wanting to come home. Doyle gave satisfactory assurances and next day Canning told Reid he would go to India.66 'The die is cast,' he wrote to his mother. 'The decision is an awful one. Many conflicting considerations held it long in suspense. But at length, that of what I owe to my family, has turned the balance – though (as naturally may be expected) against their wishes.'67

Canning was elected Governor-General by a unanimous vote of the Court of Directors – a distinction which only Cornwallis had previously enjoyed. As his appointment was nominally by the company, not the Crown, he did not have to resign his seat in Parliament at once and he decided to see out the session and set out for Bengal in the autumn. He found it difficult to 'emancipate' himself from the Commons, however time-consuming and unprofitable he might like to say it was. Before Parliament rose he spoke for what he believed would be the last time on the two great reform issues of the day, one of which he strongly opposed and the other equally strongly supported. On April 25 he spoke against Lord John Russell's parliamentary reform motion, and a few days later he moved for leave to bring in a measure of Catholic emancipation.

He was determined to make one more effort for a cause which he had so much at heart. Arguing, with a wealth of historical example, that a valid distinction could be drawn between excluding Roman Catholics from the Commons and from the House of Lords, he proposed to bring in a bill that would admit Roman Catholics to the Lords.68 Peel replied with an extremely able speech which showed that he too had done his homework in the history books. Privately, Peel described the bill as 'extraordinary and objectionable'.69 From the Protestant point of view, it certainly was objectionable, because if passed, it would clearly be the thin end of the wedge. By May 17, as Canning had confidently expected, it was safely through the Commons. He did not despair of complete success. But the Lords, influenced no doubt by Liverpool's argument that it would be most mischievous to grant this concession and then refuse any more, threw the bill out by more than forty votes. Canning, it seemed, had shot his last bolt against the Protestants and once again had missed his mark.

Parliament rose for the summer recess on August 6, 1822. Less than a week later Castlereagh, suddenly prostrated by an overwhelming physical and mental collapse, took his own life.

Inevitably, while sharing the general sense of shock, Canning wondered what effect, if any, the tragedy would have on his own future. His first reaction was that if he were asked to succeed Castlereagh as Foreign Secretary, he would only accept if he were offered the lead in the Commons as well. But by now he was by no means certain that he wanted even Castlereagh's 'whole inheritance'. Since January, when he had been forced to come to terms with his exclusion from office at home, he had taught himself to make the most of the unquestionable financial advantage of going to India. His efforts had been so successful that by now the certainty of financial loss, if he stayed in England, tended to weigh more with him than the chance of a political comeback. He had convinced himself that with the return of peace the Foreign Office was no longer the stepping-stone to fame and power that it had been ten years earlier. Moreover the Foreign Secretary's salary – supposing he were offered the post – had recently been cut from £6,000 to £5,400. Canning reckoned that he would need at least another £5,000 (which he had not got) if he were to support the position properly. So 'public glory' would be accompanied by 'private ruin'.[70] He had even managed to persuade himself that to go to India would help his long-term political prospects – although in the past he had always argued that if he fell out of the race now, he would be out for good. The only argument he could find in favour of staying in England was that it would be better for Harriet.[71]

With these thoughts filling his head, Canning waited for the government to make clear its intentions (if any) towards him. Meanwhile he could only assume that he was going to India as planned and carry on with his programme of farewell visits. By August 19, accompanied by Carlo, he was staying at Storrs, the country home on the shores of Lake Windermere of Colonel Bolton, the well-known Liverpool Tory. 'The beauty of the place,' he wrote to Joan, 'and of the country is beyond describing – and the quiet of the scene is strangely contrasted with the busy thoughts and anxieties which it is impossible to keep from stirring within one.'[72] But outwardly he maintained an unruffled front, making his farewells and straining his digestion at a formidable series of grand dinners just as if there were no doubt at all about his imminent departure for India. 'This is, of *course*,' he wrote, 'the tone which I must maintain throughout.'[73]

He was due to speak at a big farewell dinner at Liverpool on August 30, and with the papers full of rumours about his return to office and a bevy of reporters arriving from London to cover his speech, the prospect filled him with uncharacteristic embarrassment. When the chairman referred to hopes that Mr Canning might yet be detained in England, the company burst into enthusiastic applause. Canning responded by slipping into his speech a brief statement that he had received no offer from the government and did not know whether he would accept it if it came. Lord George Bentinck (Joan's nephew) reported afterwards that 'certainly an orator never sat down and left his audience under such a charm . . .'*

A week later, on his way south, Canning was still as much in the dark as ever.† He persuaded himself that he might be offered the lead in the Commons plus the thoroughly uncongenial post of Chancellor of the Exchequer, and fretted about how he could decently decline an offer which on public grounds he ought to accept. On September 8, in a mood of bitter frustration, he wrote to Huskisson: 'I have heard nothing. I know nothing. And I care nothing – except that, if possible, there should be nothing for me to hear.'[74]

It does not seem to have occurred to him that there might still be royal opposition to his return to office. He was not aware that shortly

* Of one member of the audience at least this was certainly true. Young Carlo was brought in to listen to his father's speech and sat looking up into his face 'with his little eyes glittering, and his face beaming with anxiety and wonder'. (Harewood Mss. 26, August 31, 1822)

† Between Warrington and Northwich, Canning had a lucky escape when '*smash* went the perch of the chaise and down came I and George [Bentinck] and Carlo with a bump which, however, luckily did us no injury beyond *squnching* over us a whole vintage of grapes which had been put into the chaise for Carlo's provender.' Fortunately, Mr Egerton, the county member for Cheshire, happened to ride by and bore them off to eat their dinner and spend the night in great luxury at his country home. Canning reported afterwards to Joan that Carlo was 'as happy as a prince' and had had a fishing and rowing party with Mr Egerton's sons next morning – 'so that if we were to have any mishap at all, we could not have had one with pleasanter consequences.' (Harewood Mss. 26)

after Castlereagh's death the King, who was on a visit to Edinburgh, wrote to Liverpool insisting that Canning must still go to India and that there must be no delay in his departure. Liverpool sent an evasive reply and decided to take no action until the King's return at the beginning of September. By that time most of the Cabinet had realised that Canning would have to be brought back into the government. The ministers, who a short time before had feared for the stability of their administration if he were not bundled off to India, were now afraid that they would be forced out of office if they could not prevail on him to stay. Canning's claim to succeed Castlereagh was overwhelmingly strong in terms of seniority, similarity of views and outstanding ability. There could be no doubt that the government would be immensely strengthened by having a man of his experience, forcefulness and debating skill managing the House of Commons. However much some members of the Cabinet might distrust his brilliance and fear his dominating personality, they realised that if they passed him over, they would risk losing the votes of many of their supporters in the Commons. They would also lose the support of the Grenvillites, who let it be known that they would feel free to withdraw their support if Liverpool let slip this opportunity of strengthening the government.

Liverpool had no intention of doing anything of the sort. He dealt without much difficulty with the minority in the Cabinet – Eldon, Sidmouth and Melville – who opposed bringing in Canning, largely because of his strongly pro-Catholic views. But the King seemed almost prepared to drive the government to resignation rather than accept him. The situation was saved by the Duke of Wellington, who although forced to take to his bed with a severe illness, sent a message which the King admitted had had more effect on him than anything else that had been said to him. 'If,' he wrote to the duke, 'I could get over that which is so *intimately connected* with my *private honour* all might be well, but how, my friend, is that to be effected?'[75]

Two days later, on September 7, Wellington was well enough to tell him. After paying tribute very handsomely to the 'ability, zeal and fidelity' with which he was sure Canning would serve his royal master, he tactfully suggested that a king's honour consisted of 'acts of mercy and grace', and that his honour would be most safe if he extended his grace and favour to Mr Canning.[76] This argument seems to have done the trick. Next day the King told Liverpool that he would accept Canning, although it was the greatest sacrifice of his personal feelings that he had ever made.[77]

Early on the morning of September 9, Charles Arbuthnot delivered a letter from Liverpool to Canning at Gloucester Lodge. When he learned that Canning was in Birmingham, he left the letter* with Joan and wrote at once to Canning asking him to return to London as quickly as possible. Canning saw Liverpool on the 11th and was told that the whole of Castlereagh's inheritance was his for the taking. In spite of his fears, it seems unlikely that he would have been offered anything less once the principle of his admission to the Cabinet had been conceded. Peel made it clear that he thought Canning should be leader in the Commons and seemed quite content to stay where he was at the Home Office.[78] Wellington had rejected the King's suggestion that he himself should go to the Foreign Office and was strongly of the opinion that if they were going to have Canning at all, they had better give him the greatest possible scope.[79]

Canning, for his part, hesitated, partly because of all the conflicting feelings that had perplexed him for the past month, and partly because he was shown the King's letter to Liverpool and was incensed by its lofty reference to the royal power of extending grace and favour to a subject who had incurred royal displeasure. Since, in his view, there was nothing to forgive, there should be no talk of forgiveness. It was, he thought, like being given a ticket for Almacks and finding 'Admit the rogue' written across the back.

Two days later, however, he made up his mind to accept, although he could not refrain from sending the King a remarkably haughty letter.[80] Nor, in spite of the heartfelt rejoicing of Joan and Harriet, was he immediately convinced that he had made the right choice. 'I would rather,' he wrote to a friend, 'have been an absolute sovereign than a buffetted Minister, but the fates have decreed otherwise, and the call of public duty, however unwelcome, must be obeyed.'[81] And to his

* Professor Temperley doubted whether Liverpool intended at first to offer Canning both the lead in the Commons and the Foreign Office. But, as Professor Aspinall has pointed out, the evidence for this is slim and unconvincing. It rests on a statement made by Joan to Canning's private secretary, A. G. Stapleton, in 1828 when she was still in a thoroughly embittered frame of mind as a result of her husband's death. She alleged that Liverpool's letter was 'vague and unsatisfactory' and hinted that in her view it did not offer the 'whole inheritance'. She was speaking from memory, having failed to discover the text of the letter. It has never been found since. Before leaving Birmingham on the 10th, Canning told Joan to send the letter to Kingston where he could pick it up on his way to Liverpool's house at Richmond. In the event, he saw Liverpool, not at Richmond, but at the prime minister's town house. Whether he had by then received the letter which he had asked Joan to send to Kingston, we have no means of knowing. (Temperley, EHR Vol. 45, pp. 211/12) (Aspinall EHR, Vol. 78, p. 531 ff. Harewood Mss. 26)

mother he wrote: 'I would that the offer had not come. The sacrifice of personal interest which I make to public duty is enormous – beyond what perhaps any man (or king) had a right to ask, but what, when asked, I know not how to refuse.'[82] He was right about the 'buffetting' he was going to receive. But he was quite wrong to imagine that the Foreign Office in 1822 would not give him just as many openings for power and fame as it would have done ten years earlier.

CHAPTER XV

Congress Europe
1822-1824

Shortly after he had taken over at the Foreign Office, Canning told Charles Bagot that he found himself with 'a very different sort of "world to bustle in" than that which I should have found in 1812. For fame it is "a squeezed orange", but for public good there *is* something to do, and I will try – but it must be cautiously – to do it.'[1] In this subdued, cautious and rather disillusioned frame of mind Canning accepted Castlereagh's heritage.

It was not an easy one. At the Congress of Vienna in 1814-15 the victorious allies had fixed the frontiers of Europe and agreed to preserve peace by maintaining the territorial status quo. Castlereagh had been impressed by the advantages of the congress system as a civilised and effective way of settling international problems. He steered clear of the Russian emperor's so-called Holy Alliance, which did not in fact commit anyone to anything except a profusion of high-flown sentiments. But he did sign a Quadruple Alliance with Russia, Austria and Prussia, which bound the signatories, not only to prevent the return of Napoleon to France, but also to hold periodic consultations on their 'general interests'. The difficulty was to agree about what exactly this commitment involved. Was it, as Castlereagh thought, confined to defending existing frontiers? Or should it, as Alexander maintained, be extended to preserve existing institutions?

The congress system worked well enough at Aix-la-Chapelle in 1818 when it was largely confined to tidying up the loose ends left by the Napoleonic wars and restoring France to her place among the great powers. But Castlereagh only just managed to argue the Tsar out of his grandiose schemes for guaranteeing monarchs against revolution by means of an international army. Revolution was in the air. In 1819 there were disturbances in many German states, and between the beginning of 1820 and the spring of the following year, unrest erupted into revolution in Spain, Portugal, Naples, Piedmont and Greece. The revolts varied considerably in their nature and aims. They were rarely genuinely popular, but they were certainly inspired by a deep dissatisfaction with the existing order, and conservatives like Alexander and the Austrian Chancellor, Count Metternich, firmly believed them to be the work of Jacobins and probably part of an international conspiracy into the bargain.

So when Alexander heard that Ferdinand VII of Spain had been forced to accept an ultra-democratic constitution, he at once proposed an international congress on the affairs of Spain. Castlereagh disapproved of the European liberals scarcely less than Alexander or Metternich, but he knew that to confer on the internal affairs of a country would be to extend the congress system further than any British government would either wish or be able to venture. The British public was deeply suspicious of the Holy Allies whom *The Times* indignantly described as sitting in a kind of 'panopticon from which they observe and watch all that passes from Sicily to Siberia'.[2] In his famous state paper of May 5, 1820, Castlereagh flatly declared that the Quadruple Alliance had never been intended to be a 'union for the government of the world or for the superintendence of the internal affairs of other states'. He admitted that it might widen the original scope of its discussions, but it could not take account of every possible danger. Britain, he pointed out, was a constitutional state, and autocratic and constitutional states could not be expected always to think alike. 'We shall be found in our place when actual danger menaces the system of Europe; but this country cannot and will not act upon abstract and speculative principles of precaution.'[3] Changing from the general to the particular, he insisted that the revolt in Spain did not constitute a danger to the rest of Europe. With a bad grace, the British case was accepted and, for the time being, the Spaniards were left to their own devices.

Castlereagh's state paper was an attempt to define the limits of Britain's co-operation with the continental powers. During the remaining two years of his life he tried to preserve these limitations without forfeiting his good relations with his allies. The Neapolitan revolt in July 1820 need not have been a divisive issue. The British government (including Canning) recognised that the Austrians had special interests and treaty rights in Italy. But Metternich wanted Russian, as well as British, moral support and he could not get this without giving way to the Tsar's addiction to congresses and controversial public declarations. The conference held at Troppau in October 1820 (at which both Britain and France were represented only by observers) produced a protocol signed by Russia, Prussia and Austria which resoundingly reaffirmed the signatories' right to overthrow any revolutionary government, 'if need be by arms', if they considered it a danger to other states. Such sentiments were bound to be anathema to the British, who took great pride in the fact that their constitution was the outcome of a successful revolution and Castlereagh protested vehemently, both privately and publicly, against them.

Metternich had in fact been pushed further than he really wished to go, and the outbreak of the Greek revolt in April 1821, gave him an opportunity to collaborate once again with Castlereagh. Both were alarmed by Alexander's threat to go to war with the Turks on behalf of his Greek co-religionists, for if the Tsar's huge armies overran the ramshackle Ottoman Empire, the European balance of power would be seriously disturbed. They agreed to do their best to restrain Alexander, and they were so far successful that in February 1822 he agreed to submit the Greek question to a meeting of his allies. It was, it is true, a return to the congress system. But it was in a good cause – the preservation, not of despotic régimes, but of European peace – and if he had lived, Castlereagh would himself have attended the congress which met at Verona that autumn.

On September 16, 1822, *The Times* declared that 'Mr Canning is indeed a fit agent or associate for the Holy Alliance – he is the sworn antagonist of every reform in church and state.' *The Times* was misled by its almost pathological dislike of Canning. He had nothing in common with the autocratic monarchs of St Petersburg, Vienna and Berlin who seemed to think they had a kind of divine right to keep the world set for ever in the mould they had constructed for it in 1815.

With his predecessor at the Foreign Office, however, Canning had much in common in spite of their wide differences in style, temperament and experience. Before he died, Castlereagh foresaw the possibility of a 'separation' between Britain and her continental allies. If he had lived, his policy would in principle not have been greatly different from the policy that Canning was to follow. But the spirit, emphasis and probably the consequences would have been different.

Canning had never worked, chatted and dined with the members of what might be called the Vienna club. He was an outsider and in some ways this was of course a grave disadvantage. Metternich and Alexander had known and trusted Castlereagh. They did not like what they had heard about his successor and they never really trusted him. On the other hand, being an outsider made it easier for Canning to accept and make use of the rift that the policy of the continental powers was creating between themselves and England. Castlereagh would have regarded the separation as a painful necessity to be managed as discreetly as possible. To Canning it was regrettable but not particularly painful, and he saw that it could be turned to England's advantage. Soon after taking office, he wrote: 'for *Europe*, I shall be desirous *now* and *then* to read *England*.'[4]

Canning believed passionately in England's greatness, but he did not think she could or should stand isolated and alone. 'The situation which she holds,' he declared in a public speech at Plymouth in October 1823, 'forbids an exclusive selfishness; her prosperity must contribute to the prosperity of other nations and her stability to the safety of the world.' That was perhaps a rather high-flown way of putting it. His policy was in fact based on a careful, pragmatic – even opportunist – calculation of what would best preserve peace and promote England's prestige and prosperity. He had believed that it was in England's interest to free Europe from an overmighty France. But he did not believe it was in her interest to intervene in the post-1815 ideological struggle. To his pragmatic mind, it was foolish to make an international issue out of abstract principles. In any case, England was not involved because, in his view, she had long ago reached a satisfactory compromise between the contending principles of monarchy and democracy. It was not the British government's business, nor was it competent, to dictate to other countries what kind of compromise would suit them. 'Let us not,' he urged the Commons in March 1821, 'in the foolish spirit of romance, suppose that we alone could regenerate Europe . . . The price at which political liberty is to be valued and the cost at which it is to be obtained, constitute the nicest balance and one which only those immediately interested in the calculation are competent to decide.'[5] England should intervene only to uphold specific treaty obligations or if the struggle of ideas boiled over and threatened the peace of Europe. In other words, internal change was inevitable and must be accepted, but treaty obligations and the territorial balance were sacred and must be upheld.

In the same speech Canning dramatically declared that he saw the principles of liberty in operation on the Continent and would be the last to restrain them. These were striking words from a lifelong conservative. But they did not mean that Canning had changed his views or that he had the slightest sympathy for the impracticable, ultra-democratic constitution that Ferdinand of Spain had been forced to accept. In his opinion it bore no relation to the British constitution which was unique and not for export. He had spent his life fighting change, as represented by French Jacobins, and foreign domination as represented by French armies. But if a choice now had to be made, he believed that the pretensions of the absolute monarchs were a greater evil than the extravagant ideas of some liberals. Change, as England had shown, could be beneficent; but the claim of the European despots to interfere – as Canning put it – on 'the general principle of setting things to rights whenever they thought them wrong,'[6] was a standing threat to all.

The Congress of Verona, preceded by a preliminary meeting at Vienna and attended by two emperors, three kings and a galaxy of lesser luminaries, was the last of the post-1815 congresses. It was also the least successful. One of the great powers openly repudiated the principle of intervention to crush revolution wherever it might erupt, and the others barely managed to paper over their differences about how the principle should be applied.

Canning did not go to Verona. When he took over the Foreign Office Wellington had already been asked to take Castlereagh's place at the congress and had been given the instructions which Castlereagh drew up for his own guidance shortly before his death. But by the time Wellington set out in the middle of September, Castlereagh's instructions had been overtaken by a new crisis in Spain where no stable settlement had emerged out of the revolution two years earlier. The victorious liberals were divided, unrealistic and inefficient, and Ferdinand was bent on regaining absolute power. He refused to compromise with the moderates who were prepared to revise the excessively democratic constitution. In July 1822, his intrigues led to a counter-revolutionary coup which failed, leaving Ferdinand virtually a captive and the democratic extremists in the ascendant.

Ferdinand's predicament greatly increased the pressure on the ultra-royalist government of France to intervene in Spain. The French were still sore from the humiliation of defeat. The desire for some assertion of national independence was strong, and what better excuse than to rescue a Bourbon prince and restore him to his throne? There was also the danger that if revolutionary principles triumphed in Spain, they might spread across the Pyrenees to France.

When Wellington reached Paris on his way to the congress, he learnt – apparently for the first time – that a large French army had already been posted along the Pyrenean frontier, allegedly as a *cordon sanitaire* against the yellow fever rampant in Spain. He was told by the Comte de Villèle, the head of the French government, that France was considering a military intervention in support of the King of Spain. No final decision had been taken, and Villèle admitted that he himself had doubts. But if the French did invade Spain, he said, it would be in defence of their national interests and they wanted only moral support from their allies.

Moral support was, of course, the last thing that any British government could give to a French invasion of Spain. But Canning foresaw that it would certainly be forthcoming from France's continental allies and that they might want to give material support as well. The British government, he told Wellington on September 27, believed that any intervention 'by force or by menace' in Spain would be so objectionable in principle and so utterly useless in practice, that it wished Wellington 'at once frankly and peremptorily to declare, that to any such interference, come what may, His Majesty will not be a party.'[7] Canning disclaimed any wish to quarrel with the continental powers, but if he had to disagree with them, he would not be squeamish about it.

Ironically, it was not British lack of enthusiasm for intervening in Spain, but Russian over-enthusiasm, that at first threatened the harmony of the congress. Wellington found the Tsar greatly worked up over the danger that Spain – 'the headquarters of revolution and of Jacobinism' – represented for the whole of Europe and especially for France. He urged that an allied (largely Russian) force should be sent to Spain. Alternatively he was ready to march an army of 150,000 men through Germany and station it in Piedmont, where it would be ready to help the French, either in Spain, or in France if the French Jacobins made trouble there.[8]

Alexander's bellicose plans caused general alarm. It was suspected that his underlying motive was to find some employment for his huge armies which he might otherwise decide to turn against the Ottoman Empire. Metternich, feeling that anything would be better than having Russian troops (who were regarded as little short of barbarians) tramping through Germany and settling down in Piedmont, joined forces with Wellington to argue Alexander into a more peaceable frame of mind.

Inevitably, however, in the end it was Wellington who was the odd man out. He alone, to the surprise and consternation of his colleagues, flatly refused to promise the French any support – diplomatic, moral or military – if they went to war with Spain. Alexander and Metternich fought hard to avert an open rift in the anti-revolutionary front. 'We have passed but a stormy week,' Wellington wrote philosophically to Canning on November 5.[9] But he was unmoved by the storms and openly disapproved of the diplomatic missiles which the other powers were preparing to launch against Madrid. At the end of November he started for home, declaring that his colleagues were completely in the wrong, and (according to Metternich) *'mécontent de nous tous'*.[10] The feeling, presumably, was mutual.

Canning, however, was warm in his praise and thanks. 'I verily believe,' he wrote while Wellington was still at Verona, 'that, if we escape the Spanish war, it will be owing exclusively to your experience of one; and that any other negotiator than yourself would have reasoned *politically* and *morally* against it, to no purpose.'[11] Wellington had, it is true, made an international crusade against Spain less likely. But the threat of a unilateral French crusade remained. The French were divided and undecided. Villèle was still anxious to keep the peace, but the war party grew stronger every day. Both, however, were determined to use the Spanish crisis to increase French influence and prestige. So when the Russians, Austrians and Prussians decided to withdraw their ambassadors from Madrid, the French government refused to fall into line. Instead, it formally and publicly dissociated itself from its allies' diplomatic protest, while indicating that it reserved the right to take whatever action it thought necessary if the Spaniards did not mend their ways.[12] The language was oblique but the threat was plain, and it was not well-received by the Spaniards. If, however, they refused to compromise, would the French carry their self-assertion to the point of invading and occupying Spain?

Canning was determined to prevent this if he could. To have French armies occupying the Peninsula barely ten years after Wellington had driven them out, would be a damaging blow to British prestige. He did not believe that the Spanish liberals were a serious danger to any other country except their own. He thought it reasonable, however, that they should give assurances to France that their revolutionary movement would be 'as little turbulent within, and as little obnoxious without, as possible,'[13] and (like most Spaniards) he saw that the Spanish constitution would have to be revised if the country was to achieve any stability at all. In January 1823, he tried to push the touchy Spaniards in this direction. Lord Fitzroy Somerset was sent to Madrid on behalf of Wellington, who was a Spanish grandee, with instructions to make tactful suggestions for strengthening the executive. Canning also instructed Sir William à Court, the British minister in Madrid, to offer British good offices, urge the Spaniards to make some conciliatory proposals and emphatically assure them that the British government would not go to war on their behalf.[14]

In Paris the British ambassador, Sir Charles Stuart, was instructed to urge the French not to go to war against Spain. He was to assure them that the most enlightened Spaniards *did* want to reform their constitution. But how could they be expected to do so 'on the demand of a foreign power, made under the menace of foreign war, as the penalty of refusal?'[15] Canning also wrote a series of eloquent personal appeals to Chateaubriand, the French foreign minister. But Chateaubriand, who was strongly in favour of restoring France's glory by a successful war, replied with elegant nothings. Canning's last appeal to him reached Paris on January 28, 1823. On the same day, Louis XVIII opened the French parliament with a speech which revealed just how far the French had already gone along the road to war. He declared that the French minister in Madrid had been recalled and that a hundred thousand French soldiers were ready to restore a Bourbon prince to his throne. As if that were not provocative enough, he added that peace could still be secured if Ferdinand was 'free to give to his people the institutions they cannot hold but from him.'[16]

This blunt affirmation of the ultra-legitimist creed was greeted with great indignation by the British press and public. *The Times* described the French king's speech as the most important document to be published since 'Bonaparte's iniquitous career' had ended. 'We sincerely participate,' it pompously added, 'with the British nation in the indignation – we might rather say the horror – which this composition will excite.'[17] Canning indignantly asked Mme Lieven, the Russian ambassadress: 'How do you expect us to support, or even tolerate, such a doctrine, when our form of government is rooted in the very opposite principle?'[18] To Monsieur, Louis XVIII's brother and heir, whom he had known as an exile in England, Canning sent a polite but urgent private appeal to prevent a French invasion of Spain.[19]

When Parliament reassembled on February 4, the Speech from the Throne deplored any intervention in Spain's internal affairs and (on Canning's insistence) omitted any pledge of British neutrality. Creevey, the Whig diarist, gleefully described it as a 'regular spat on the face to the villains of Verona.'[20] Brougham was sufficiently impressed to abandon his intention of moving an amendment and, for the first time in his life, spoke in support of the Address. The vehemence and unanimity of feeling in the Commons greatly strengthened Canning's hand in negotiating with the French, and he persevered in his efforts to avert war. 'We are working, working, working,' wrote Planta from the Foreign Office on February 26, 'as hard, or a little harder, than we

Air "_Scots wha hae_."

"Spain awaked from slavery's trance—
"Spain who spurned the yoke of France,
"Saw Napoleon's hordes advance
        "Flushed with victory,
"Spain in native valour strong
"Backward drove th'invading throng
"Bold her sons and this their song
        "Death or liberty!

"Proud Iberia, gallant land,
"Reared the pile by freedom planned,
"Fired the torch by freedom fanned
        "Scorned to bend her knee!
"Urged by foreign despots, Gaul
"Flies to arms, and venturing all,
"Forced to fight, but fights to fall,
        "Leagued 'gainst liberty!

"Shall (forbid it, Heaven!) the men
"Who, from mountain, rock, and glen,
"Baffled France as France was then,
        "Now defeated be?
"Shall they break their patriot vow,
"Who master'd strength to weakness bow,
"Yield to France, as France is now?
        "No—they shall be free!

"Britons you whose patriot train,
"Oft has spurned oppressions reign—
"You whose hearts beat high for Spain,
        "Pledge one cup with me.
"Soon may Spain, in justice strong,
"Backward drive th'invader's throng
"Bold her sons, and this their song—
        "Death or liberty!"

This song was sung at a dinner given at the London Tavern on March 7, 1826
to the Spanish and Portuguese ambassadors

THE CATHOLIC ASSOCIATION or PADDY — coming it STRONG —! *Feb 1825*

An example of popular anti-Catholic and anti-Irish feeling. Canning on the platform is portrayed as willing to give
the Irish whatever they want, although in fact he supported the Bill for the suppression of the Catholic Association.

possibly can.'[21] Canning still had a faint hope that the strength of British opinion might make the French draw back, especially if the Spaniards would make some compromise proposals, and he went on urging à Court in Madrid to press for concessions. But the Spaniards obstinately refused to modify their constitution, and on March 15 the Duc d'Angoulême left Paris to take command of the French army in the south. War, it was clear, could no longer be averted.

Up to this point Canning had left the French to make their own guesses about his government's reaction to an invasion of Spain. He may have delicately implied that public feeling might push it further than it wished to go, but he never threatened war because he believed it could be only an empty threat. A purely maritime war would be ineffective, and England was neither prepared for a land war nor could she afford the expense of one. If Russia and Prussia came to France's aid, Hanover and Portugal would be at risk. It was believed (quite wrongly, as it turned out) that if left to herself France might get disastrously bogged down in Spain. Finally, most of the Cabinet, in particular Wellington, were opposed to war, and thought that Canning's behaviour had already been too warlike. So at the end of March, when all hope of peace was gone, Canning instructed Stuart to inform Chateaubriand that provided France did not occupy Spain permanently, or seize any of Spain's ex-colonies, or invade Portugal, England would remain neutral in the coming conflict.[22] All that could be done for the Spaniards was to lift the existing ban on the sale of arms to them.*

On April 14 Canning told the House of Commons that the French had finally gone to war with Spain eight days earlier and the British government had decided to remain neutral. In other words, he had to confess to a resounding diplomatic defeat. He defended himself by laying before the House a copious selection of diplomatic correspondence to demonstrate that everything possible had been done to prevent the war. But now that it had come, the only sensible course was strict neutrality. The whole tone of his speech was highly critical of France and sympathetic towards Spain – he 'earnestly hoped and trusted that she would come triumphantly out of this struggle.'[23]

Such a wish coming from a Tory minister made a deep impression both at home and abroad. Brougham complimented Canning on his

* In the Anglo-Spanish peace treaty of 1814, Britain had agreed to ban the sale of arms to the Spanish colonies in South America which were in revolt. In 1818, the embargo was extended to Spain as well in order to preserve British neutrality in the conflict between Spain and her ex-colonies. For the same reason, the ban was also lifted from the South Americans in 1823.

liberal sentiments, but on the Continent, according to Charles Bagot, who was then British envoy in St Petersburg, they made 'a devil of a sensation.'[24] Bagot was told by Count Nesselrode, the Russian foreign minister, that the Tsar deeply regretted Canning's wish that Spain would triumph, which he felt (fairly enough) was not quite consistent with the unequivocal neutrality expressed elsewhere in his speech. The Austrian, Russian and Prussian ministers in London privately uttered 'general regrets and lamentations' to Canning, which he did not feel obliged to pass on to his Cabinet colleagues. But none of them made a formal protest. Canning thought afterwards that they all believed he would be defeated in Parliament anyway.[25]

For Canning's diplomatic failure provided the opposition with plenty of ammunition, and his pro-Spanish sentiments did not deter them from firing it. On April 14 Brougham attacked him sharply for having been duped by the French and declared that he never knew a minister to cut a worse figure than Canning had done that night. On the 24th a motion of censure was introduced in the Lords. But although Grey painted a lurid picture of what would happen to Britain's free institutions if the despots were allowed to overrun the Continent, a pro-government amendment was passed by 94 votes. Four days later, when a similar censure motion was introduced in the Commons, Mr Stuart-Wortley moved an amendment expressing pleasure that England was not involved in war. That after all was the heart of the matter. Could Spain have been saved without going to war, and did the Whigs, or the people of England, really want that? The debate continued for three days and Canning spoke at the end. Before he went down to the House, he sent Wilberforce an urgent plea to attend the debate. 'I am upon my trial tonight. Come and hear me!'[26]

Canning based his defence squarely upon Castlereagh's state paper of May 5, 1820. The government's primary aim had been 'to keep within reasonable bounds that predominating *areopagitical* spirit, which the memorandum of the British Cabinet of May 1820, describes as "beyond the sphere of the original conception and understood principles of the alliance." ' He rejected at length the criticism frequently made by opposition speakers that the government should never have tried to persuade the Spaniards to modify their constitution. Britain was not interested in Spain's political experiments, but only in preventing war. 'Good God!' he exclaimed, 'when it is remembered how many evils are comprised into that little word "war" – is it possible for any man to hesitate in urging every expedient that could avert it, without sacrificing the honour of the party to which his advice was tendered?' He denied that the situation was comparable to 1808. Then we were at war anyway and the Spaniards were united against France; now we were at peace and the Spaniards were divided. 'I was – I still am – an enthusiast for national independence; but I am not, I hope I never shall be, an enthusiast in favour of revolution. And yet how fearfully are these two considerations intermingled, in the present contest between France and Spain. This is no war for territory, or for commercial advantages. It is unhappily a war of principle.' The British, who had fought this fight already, had no need to intervene on the Continent, but from their essentially neutral position they could try to enlighten, reconcile and save others 'by our example in all cases, by our exertions where we can usefully interpose.'[27]

Mrs Arbuthnot, who although a Tory was one of Canning's most waspish critics, wrote afterwards that '. . . so complete was Mr Canning's defence and so fine the speech that he made that Mr Brougham, who answered him, could make no sort of impression and was hardly listened to . . .'[28] Brougham, realising the mood of the House, tried to get the censure motion withdrawn. But Canning insisted that every man should stand up and be counted. The result was a vote of 372 for Stuart-Wortley's amendment, with only 20 against.

'I wish,' wrote Canning to Bagot, 'you had seen the *ultrageous* faces – ultra in either extreme – at the first interview that I had with them after the 30th of April.' He was referring to the Russian, Austrian and Prussian envoys in London. 'Since that time, I have had pretty much my own way; and I believe you may now consider my politics as those of the Government as well as of the country.'[29]

Canning's estimate of his political position in the middle of 1823 was wildly optimistic. He had plenty of enemies – and very few friends – in high places, and it is unlikely that he would have survived their persistent efforts to get rid of him over the next two years if he had not enjoyed almost unprecedented popularity in the country as a whole. To many ordinary Englishmen, it had seemed during the years after Waterloo that their country had poured out its blood and treasure to overthrow one despot only to make it easier for other despots in central and eastern Europe to extend their influence and control. Castlereagh had understood the limits of Britain's co-operation with her continental allies, but he had lacked both the inclination and the ability to make a popular issue out of her differences with them. Canning had both and he was convinced that without popular support the government would have little influence abroad: '. . . our influence, if it is to be maintained abroad, must be secure in the sources of our strength at home; and the sources of that strength are in the sympathy between the people and the Government; in the union of the public sentiment with the public counsels; in the reciprocal confidence and co-operation of the House of Commons and the Crown.'[30]

When Canning spoke in Parliament on the Spanish crisis, people were impressed not so much by his diplomatic failure as by the way he had stood up to the continental despots; not by his inability to prevent war but by his success in keeping Britain out of it. With his eloquent praise of Britain's 'mixed' constitution, he reinforced his countrymen's insular complacency; with his repeated advocacy of non-interference in other countries' affairs, he appealed to their innate preference for minding their own business. The *Morning Chronicle* declared that after hearing Mr Canning's 'plain unvarnished tale,' every Englishman 'will feel elated that the Government of his country has acted so highly honourable and magnanimous a part in this important crisis.' Canning's tale carried conviction because he produced evidence of its truth. He not only laid before Parliament extensive extracts from his recent – some of it very recent – diplomatic correspondence; he also repeated in public to the Commons, sometimes in the same phrases, what he had been urging privately in Paris and Madrid. A Foreign Secretary who revealed his secret diplomacy thus openly was a surprising and popular phenomenon.

In those days, parliamentary debates were read eagerly by those who read the newspapers at all. On big occasions, *The Times* would strip its front page of its customary advertisements to provide more space for the debates. Canning's parliamentary speeches, therefore, reached a much wider public than those who actually listened to them. But as M.P. for Liverpool he had discovered the advantages and attractions of public speaking, and as Foreign Secretary, he used every opportunity he got to explain his policies directly to the public. Perhaps the most famous of these speeches was the one he made in October 1823, when he was presented with the freedom of the borough of Plymouth. Popular feeling was greatly stirred up on behalf of the Spaniards whose resistance to the French invaders had completely collapsed. At the presentation ceremony in Plymouth, the corporation spokesman, Sir William Elford, went full swing into the subject of Spanish politics and was enthusiastically cheered. Canning felt he could not shirk this opportunity to give what he thought was 'the right tone upon the issue of the Spanish war; and as the fitting out of the *Superb* had made a great stir and talk of war here,' he also took care to 'preach peace to all the world.'[31] The general theme of his speech had been heard often before. But Canning included a passage for the benefit of his local audience which rang through the country. After justifying his refusal to be drawn into war on behalf of Spain, he added:

'. . . let it not be said that we cultivate peace either because we fear or because we are unprepared for war . . . Our present repose is no more a proof of inability to act than the state of inertness and inactivity in which I have seen those mighty masses that float in the waters above your town is a proof that they are devoid of strength, and incapable of being fitted out for action. You well know, gentlemen, how soon one of those stupendous masses, now reposing on their shadows in perfect stillness – how soon, upon any call of patriotism or of necessity, it would assume the likeness of an animated thing, instinct with life and motion; how soon it would ruffle, as it were, its swelling plumage; how quickly it would put forth all its beauty and its bravery, collect its scattered elements of strength, and waken its dormant thunder . . . Such is England herself; while apparently passive and motionless, she silently concentrates the power to be put forth on an adequate occasion. But God forbid that that occasion should arise!'[32]

The Austrian chargé d'affaires complained that this speech was a 'complete diplomatic manifesto' addressed not to the Corporation of Plymouth but to the world.[33] But on October 30 *The Times*, speaking, as it rightly admitted, from 'no private partialities', described it as 'a happy display of just reasoning and accurate description, enriched by magnificent language and splendid imagery.' The Englishmen of the early 1820s wanted to be reassured about their country's greatness; they also wanted a quiet life. Canning's oratory struck just the right note, and left them with the comfortable feeling that they had the best of both worlds.

In September 1823, Canning's cousin, Stratford, just back from three years as British minister in Washington, found London much improved, the country more prosperous and 'to crown the chapter of marvels a popular Administration'.[34] One thing, of course, followed from the other. The country's new prosperity, which in 1823 even the heavily depressed countryside began to share, took the edge off economic and social discontent and helped to make the government popular.

Canning's 'liberal' foreign policy and the way he presented it also played their part. But Wellington, Eldon and the rest of the powerful High Tory group in the Cabinet were far from grateful. They strongly disapproved of the growing estrangement between Britain and her continental allies, and throughout the early part of 1823 some of them had openly sympathised with French designs against Spain. On February 11, the Vicomte de Marcellus, the French chargé d'affaires in London, reported to Chateaubriand that several ministers had 'expressed to me the hope of seeing our army take the field in Spain and hurry on to Madrid.' And a few days later he reported from 'a good source' that the King saw with joy the rights of legitimacy sustained.[35] This irresponsible and indiscreet behaviour probably made little or no practical difference to the outcome; but it was hardly a good start for a new Foreign Secretary who needed to establish his authority abroad.

It was not only Canning's policy, but his whole style and personality which aroused the hostility of the King and a powerful section of the Cabinet. They realised that in the long run the government needed to carry the country with it. But Canning's open and deliberate efforts to do so appalled them. His habit of explaining his policy in public speeches in different part of the country drew much adverse comment. The King told Liverpool that he must try to correct 'the passion which seems to exist for speech-making out of time and out of proper place.'[36] And the unprecedented profusion of the diplomatic correspondence published by Canning in April dismayed his colleagues who felt afterwards that he had bounced them into flouting diplomatic convention.[37] In March the King confided to Mme Lieven that he did not like Canning any more than he had done. He recognised his talent and believed that he was needed in the Commons, but he was no more capable of conducting foreign policy than Mme Lieven's baby – he did not know the first thing about his job and lacked tact, judgment and decorum.[38]

Such extravagant criticism – if correctly reported – is evidence of the critic's state of mind rather than of the actual state of affairs. The King disliked his Foreign Secretary so much and had accepted him so reluctantly that such outbursts were perhaps inevitable. Less predictable was the sad deterioration in Canning's relations with Wellington. The duke's influence had been crucial in overcoming the King's resistance to accepting Canning as Foreign Secretary. At Verona he had loyally carried out Canning's instructions. But he had been considerably dismayed by the outcome. He began to feel that Canning was too clever by half and he was soon complaining to Mrs Arbuthnot that he had had 'no conception what a man he was'.[39] Since Mrs Arbuthnot disliked Canning and doted on Wellington, she presumably made the most of his grumbles. Her journal at this time describes Canning as 'a sort of volcano', as making a flashy speech now and then but otherwise leaving all at sixes and sevens, and as not having a 'conciliatory way of doing business'.[40]

With those of his colleagues whom he either disliked, like Eldon, or despised, like Westmorland, Canning probably did not always hide his impatience or curb his sarcastic tongue. But he always seems to have treated Wellington with respect and consideration. The duke used to complain that his advice was either ignored or not sought at all. But Canning did try to take account of Wellington's views in the drafting of despatches, and far from not seeking his advice, he asked for more. In February 1823, he good-humouredly reproved him for not volunteering his advice without being asked. 'Now this is not according to our compact,' he wrote. '. . . Be assured that no suggestion of yours can ever be otherwise than most welcome to me; that if I do not always ask for them, it is only because the current business of every day so fully occupies and overflows the day, that I have seldom a moment for *seeking* communication, but that I rely upon your offering it; and, if I had not had that reliance, should have hesitated much more than I did to undertake an office so full of difficulty at a moment so critical as the present. Pray believe in the sincerity of this assurance once for all . . .'[41]

The tone of this letter suggests that Canning was scarcely aware of the change in Wellington's attitude towards him. If he had been, there was little he could have done about it. For although the duke's grievances may have grown in the telling as they went the rounds of London society, they had a real foundation in the fact that he had grave doubts both about Canning's policies and about the way in which he carried them out. Charles Arbuthnot was no doubt reporting correctly when he told Liverpool that the duke thought that Canning 'often decides in haste and then writes in haste, and that what he does write has better sounding phrases than good solid sense.'[42] Wellington was the most famous man in Europe; he was deferred to by monarchs and statesmen; he was fast becoming an institution. But after Verona he may have felt that for once he was not on top of a situation. And Canning was the obvious person to blame – as well, to a smaller extent, as Liverpool, who apparently either would not, or could not, restrain his Foreign Secretary.

It is indeed unlikely that Canning would have survived long in office without the prime minister's loyal support. It was not at all what he had expected. The rather bumbling, indecisive, easily agitated side of Liverpool's character had always exasperated him. In August 1822, while he was still uncertain whether he would be offered the succession to Castlereagh, he told Joan that Liverpool's weakness was 'shockingly apparent' and would be 'one very alarming circumstance' attending office if he were offered it. He went on to describe Liverpool's failings (as he saw them) at length and with picturesque embellishments that could only have been displayed in a letter to his wife. Liverpool, he wrote, 'will neither do nor *let* do; is jealous of his authority, but afraid to use it himself . . . mysterious where he ought to be open . . . selfish – without absolute heartlessness, indeed – but with such nervous intensity of desire to avoid anything that can give him pain, that I am quite sure if one was to drop down in a fit or be shot through the head while in his room, he would (if he could, unobserved) sneak out of the room and get into his carriage, ringing perhaps for Willimot [his private secretary] to take care of one.' Yet after this crushing catalogue of inadequacies, Canning was forced to add that Liverpool alone had the confidence of the country and was the only member of the government 'upon whom *I* could for a moment rely'.[43]

This final judgment at least was right and Canning had not been in office more than a few months before he was rapidly revising his views about Liverpool's supposed weakness and moral cowardice. For the next four years they worked closely and loyally together; only the Catholic question divided them. Indeed, for the King and the ultra Tories in the Cabinet, their co-operation was much too close. Before Canning had been in office a year, they were indignantly alleging that he had unbounded influence over the prime minister and was constantly perverting his judgment. In October 1823, Arbuthnot passed on these allegations to Liverpool in a long and distinctly threatening screed which Wellington helped to draft.[44] Liverpool's reply was dignified and uncompromising. He pointed out that there must be confidence and a good understanding between a prime minister in the Lords and the leader of the House of Commons. He was sure that if these were lacking between him and Canning the government could not stand many months, 'but I am not aware of Canning having *assumed* in a single instance authority or influence in matters which do not belong to him.' Liverpool went on to admit without apology that he and Canning happened to agree more than some of their colleagues on the possible consequence of a successful French invasion of Spain.[45] This was indeed the nub of the matter. The King and the ultra Tories wanted to force Liverpool to withdraw his support from Canning's 'liberal' foreign policy. But Liverpool genuinely sympathised with Canning's views and he made it plain that he would resign rather than desert him.

It was, however, the painful complexities of a ministerial reshuffle that first caused Canning to revise his opinion of the prime minister. The reshuffle was caused by his request – the only one he made – that William Huskisson should be brought into the government with him. Liverpool devised a neat way of achieving this. He persuaded Bragge-Bathurst, who was old and ill, to retire as Chancellor of the Duchy of Lancaster, Vansittart, the Chancellor of the Exchequer, to take this non-departmental seat in the Cabinet plus a peerage, and Frederick Robinson, President of the Board of Trade, to move to the Exchequer. This left the Board of Trade vacant for Huskisson. The only snag was that the King would not have Huskisson in the Cabinet, partly because he was a friend of Canning's and partly because he thought the Cabinet ought to be reduced in size. Huskisson, however, insisted that he could not take Robinson's job without his seat in the Cabinet. Nothing that Liverpool, Wellington or Canning (who spoke with all the bluntness of an exasperated friend)[46] could say would make him budge. 'I cannot conceive,' wrote Liverpool indignantly, 'anything in worse taste than a man endeavouring to *force* himself into a Cabinet against the wishes of the King and his own friends. *Entre nous*, my hope is that the King will object to it.'[47] Surprisingly, however, the King graciously waived his objections. Whereupon Huskisson ungraciously agreed to forego his Cabinet seat for twelve months.*

In self-defence Huskisson said he might have been led away by his feelings – and who was sometimes not? This was very true. Robinson's very competent deputy at the Board of Trade, Thomas Wallace, assured Canning a hundred times that he was 'broken-hearted' at being passed over in favour of Huskisson and insisted on resigning.[48] Huskisson little thought, wrote Canning crossly, 'when he was kicking so sturdily, how other people's feelings were to be tried.'[49] Liverpool tried to mollify Wallace by asking Arbuthnot to let him have his own post of Woods and Forests and go himself to the Board of Trade. Arbuthnot agreed but made it so clear that his feelings had never been so 'cut to pieces'[50] that Canning persuaded Liverpool to drop the idea.†

* In fact Huskisson was able to enter the Cabinet in August 1823, after Liverpool had persuaded Lord Maryborough (Wellesley-Pole) to resign.

† Maryborough resigned as Master of the Mint when he resigned from the Cabinet in August 1823. Wallace was then offered (and accepted) the Mint without Cabinet rank.

337

It was all very wearing. Aspirants to office (unless they were especially tiresome) were treated very tenderly in those days, and Liverpool's agitation at having to cope with so many hurt feelings almost made him ill. Canning was amazed that he had found the nerve to battle on.[51] 'I am very much of your opinion,' he wrote sympathetically to Liverpool on January 18, 1823, 'that if one could have foreseen all the worry and vexation to grow out of this attempt to improve everybody's condition, it would have been a great saving of anxiety to let the whole alone. But we must do as well as we can.'[52]

Canning's most important colleague on the Treasury front bench in the Commons remained aloof from all this nervous wear and tear. Robert Peel, who had become Home Secretary in January 1822, was the only other person, besides Liverpool, on whom Canning thought he might perhaps rely 'if we came to understand each other . . . but it is very *perhaps* indeed.'[53] They probably never really did understand each other, although in their political views they were only seriously divided on the Catholic issue. Their respective partisans tried to set them up as rivals. But there is no direct evidence that they felt more than the normal rivalry of politicians on the same side. Early in 1822, Canning had momentarily dreamed of going to the Home Office rather than India, only to find that Peel had been definitely picked for the post. But shortly afterwards Canning was telling Croker that he found it quite impossible to do justice to Peel's 'frankness and straightforwardness', and to 'feelings for which I own I did not before give him credit, but which I hope I know how to value and to return.'[54] A few months later, this verdict was amply confirmed when Peel, whom the King at first wanted to have the lead in the Commons, loyally supported his colleagues in their battle to overcome the royal opposition to Canning. Yet although the two men were always civil and considerate colleagues, they never became friends, and during the last years of Liverpool's administration, Peel seems to have shared in the distrust and resentment that Canning's intimacy with the prime minister aroused in some members of the Cabinet. In any case, to have the two most important members of the government in the Commons divided on the most important domestic issue – Catholic emancipation – was bound to create strain.

On other issues, however, the Treasury bench generally worked well together. It was stronger than it had been for most of Castlereagh's stint as leader of the House. Robinson was a much abler and more popular Chancellor of the Exchequer than Vansittart had been, and although Huskisson was a poor speaker, his economic expertise and intellectual distinction added weight and authority to the government front bench. Whereas in the Cabinet Canning had to contend with heavy opposition to his 'liberal' foreign policy from the ultra Tory peers, as leader of the House of Commons, he presided over a little team with whose quiet unpretentious reforms (the groundwork of most of which had already been laid) he was entirely in sympathy. Peel's reforms of the criminal law, Huskisson's commercial reforms, and the moves towards free trade in budgetary and colonial policy, were the kind of practical, pragmatic improvements of the existing system of which he approved. He did not budge from his opposition to parliamentary reform, but he ridiculed those who feared that any reform was a step towards Jacobinism.

Canning, of course, was not involved in the domestic reforms of Liverpool's government except as a member of the Cabinet which approved them. Nor was he often actively involved in piloting domestic measures through the Commons. But as leader of the House, he had to arrange its business and brief himself well on what was going forward. And it can be assumed that even if he did not speak as frequently as some of his colleagues, he was always in his place on the Treasury bench unless prevented by official duties or a particularly bad attack of gout. However many despatches he had to write, the Commons always had a compulsive attraction for him. The debates were always a battle, however dull; they drained him of physical and nervous energy, and too often for the good of his reputation, they caused him more or less to lose his temper.

After the debates on Spain and the Catholic issue in April, the rest of the 1823 session was not very interesting. When it was over, Canning told Bagot that it had been 'tedious, rather wearing, however, than harassing . . .'; there had been only one day of 'great violence' and only one debate – that on the Spanish negotiations – which developed into 'a pitched battle'. But yet, he went on, '10 hours a day for 5 days in the week for 7 weeks consecutively is hard work, and such has been the nature of our campaign since Whitsuntide.' He himself had got through it pretty well 'by dint of extreme abstinence'. 'It is quite refreshing,' he concluded, 'to return to the labours of the office.'[55]

By 1823, however, the parliamentary battle really had become much less violent than during the stormy post-Waterloo years. The lessening of economic and social distress reduced the pressure on the Whigs to agitate for parliamentary reform and administrative economy, while the government's pragmatic, piecemeal reforms tended to take the wind out of their sails. Some important Whigs, like Grey, continued to nourish an implacable distrust of Canning. But others, like Brougham and Lord Holland, were genuinely impressed by his openly critical attitude towards the Holy Allies as well as by the gradually more progressive character of the government's domestic policies. They began to realise that the liberal Tories could be potential allies and that in any case it was in the Whigs' interest to widen the growing gap between them and the ultra Tories by refraining as far as possible from attacking them. So Brougham, formerly Canning's most formidable and implacable opponent, sweetened his attacks on his Spanish policy with fulsome praise of his independent attitude towards the European despots. Whig newspapers also sang his praises.

For Canning, the opposition's compliments were not an unmixed blessing. They exacerbated, as Brougham had hoped, his relations with his ultra colleagues who chose to believe that the main motive behind his foreign policy was his desire to curry favour with the opposition. Changing times and circumstances were indeed bringing Canning and the Whigs closer, and with some of them, like Sir James Mackintosh and Lord Holland, he was on very friendly terms. But he never bent his views or his actions to please them; on parliamentary reform he was as far from them as ever. And he deplored the way in which they made a party issue out of Ireland – at this time the most important and time-consuming domestic issue. The Whigs, on the other hand, felt frustrated by the sight of so many prominent pro-Catholics enjoying office but apparently content to let the stalemate over emancipation continue. Many felt that Canning had been a traitor to the Catholic cause because he had not insisted on emancipation as the price for his return to the government. Canning, however, was convinced that public opinion was still far behind parliamentary opinion on the Catholic question. He believed that it would 'make its way' under any government which did not positively oppose it, but that it would not be possible to form an administration that was united in favour of Catholic emancipation and agreed on other questions. In other, blunter, words, he did not believe that a coalition between pro-Catholic Whigs and Tories would work.

When Canning said this in the Commons in April 1823, he precipitated an almighty row.[56] Brougham lost his temper and accused Canning of having abandoned his pro-Catholic beliefs in order to overcome the arch-Protestant Eldon's objections to his return to office. Canning, he said, had exhibited 'the most incredible specimen of monstrous truckling for the purpose of obtaining office which the whole history of political tergiversation could furnish.' Canning jumped to his feet in a flaming passion and said: 'I rise to say that that is false.' There was a dead silence for a few seconds, then – as Creevey laconically reported – 'we had the devil to pay for near an hour.'[57] Canning refused to withdraw the word 'false', and a motion was put that both men should be committed to the custody of the Serjeant-at-Arms. But after strenuous and ingenious peacemaking efforts by friends of both parties, the quarrel was patched up, the motion was withdrawn and the Commons were spared the remarkable and rather shaming sight of the leader of the House and the most prominent member of the opposition being marched off in the custody of the Serjeant-at-Arms.

The incident caused much adverse comment on Canning's passionate temper. But his friend, Charles Bagot, thought that although he had certainly been in a 'd —— d passion', he had deliberately decided to crush for ever this kind of personal attack.[58] However that may be, the affair did not permanently damage the tentative and spasmodic rapprochement between Canning and Brougham.*

One issue on which all parties were agreed and on which humanitarian feeling in the country as a whole was passionately strong was the slave trade. By the time Canning became Foreign Secretary, all the leading maritime countries had been persuaded to follow the British example and abolish it.† It had been an uphill fight, waged with admirable determination by Castlereagh and Wellington, with Wilberforce exerting his remarkable personal influence behind the scenes. But it was a hollow victory because no government except the British took effective steps to enforce the prohibition on their own nationals. So although the British slave trade had been effectively stamped out by the Royal Navy, the trade as a whole was increasing. Moreover, as Canning indignantly pointed out in a long despatch to Wellington at

* According to a contemporary memoir, shortly after their row Canning and Brougham met by chance when out riding near Lowther castle. They arrived at opposite sides of a locked gate, looked steadily at each other and then burst out laughing; they chatted for a while, then shook hands before parting. (Quoted by New, 272 fr. Charles Knight, *Passages of a Working Life*, II, 198)

† The exception was Portugal, which in the Anglo-Portuguese treaty of 1817 had agreed to abolish the trade entirely, except for what was needed to maintain the supply of labour in the Portuguese colony of Brazil. Canning argued that since Brazil had declared her independence in 1821, the Portuguese could not carry on the slave trade on the excuse that they were protecting their colonial interests. But Portugal did not agree to total abolition until after Canning's death. (Well. Desp. NS. I, p. 381)

Verona on September 30, 1822, the trade had become even more inhumane because of the methods of concealing the nature of their cargo practised by the owners of slave ships. These led to 'the most dreadful sufferings to a cargo of which it hardly ever seems to occur to its remorseless owners that it consists of sentient beings.' Wellington therefore was to press this 'scandal of the civilised world' on the attention of the congress.[59] The duke did his best and afterwards was warmly praised by Canning and Wilberforce for his efforts. But suspicion of Britain's motives and jealousy of her naval superiority and commercial success fatally handicapped his efforts, especially with the French.

Canning had to fall back on trying to enforce existing undertakings by diplomatic pressure from London. The Spanish, Portuguese and Dutch governments had agreed several years earlier to allow the Royal Navy to search and detain slavers flying their flags. But Spanish and Portuguese slave ships still resisted by force British attempts to search them. Canning protested vigorously. He also persuaded the Dutch and Spanish governments to agree to the confiscation of vessels which, although not actually carrying slaves, contained *prima facie* evidence that they were intended for that purpose.* He constantly complained to Madrid about the continuing slave trade to Cuba, and persistently urged the French to insist on more effective action by their own navy against slavers flying the French flag. He pressed the United States to agree to a bilateral convention suppressing the slave trade, and after protracted negotiations one was signed in March 1824.[60] But it never came into force because the United States Senate would not ratify it without amendments concerning the right of search which Canning refused to accept.†

To Wilberforce and his friends, however, the struggle to suppress the slave trade was no longer enough. Fresh supplies of slaves were still smuggled to the British West Indies and well-authenticated reports

* Examples of this *prima facie* evidence that Canning suggested might be found in ships anchored or 'hovering' off the west coast of Africa included much greater supplies of food and drinking water than could be consumed by the crew; spare planks in the hold which could be used to make an extra 'slave deck'; supplies of handcuffs and shackles; and instead of the usual closed hatches, hatches fitted with open gratings. (Memorandum sent by Canning to the British ambassador at the Hague. BFSP, X, p. 126)

† It has been estimated that Canning wrote more than a thousand despatches in his efforts to get the slave trade abolished throughout the world. (Temperley, *Foreign Policy of Canning*, pp. 313/14)

of the appalling treatment meted out to some of them still reached England. It was clear that the evil could only be effectively destroyed by striking at its roots – by abolishing slavery itself. Early in March 1823, Wilberforce published a pamphlet in which he forcefully but moderately argued the case for abolition. The public response was swift and enthusiastic, and on May 15 the Commons debated a motion for the abolition of slavery introduced by the prominent Quaker, Thomas Fowell Buxton.

Buxton's specific proposal was that Parliament should declare the freedom of all slaves born after a certain day. This plan of gradual abolition had already been successfully introduced in the northern part of the United States as well as in several British colonial possessions. Canning, therefore, had the difficult task of agreeing with the principle of the motion, while rejecting its practical wisdom in the particular case of the West Indies. He knew that emancipation would be difficult to enforce if the planters proved recalcitrant and that the slaves might rise in revolt if they learnt that the freedom granted to them by the British Parliament was being wilfully withheld by their masters. So he proposed amendments to Mr Buxton's motion which emphasised the primary importance of improving the condition of the slaves and looked forward to their emancipation as soon as was practicable.[61]

The representatives of the West Indian interest in the Commons could hardly either defend slavery or reject the reprieve for themselves that Canning proposed. Their spokesman, Charles Ellis, was reduced to describing slavery as an unfortunate system in which the planters, through no fault of their own, had become involved. The abolitionists, for their part, had to make up their minds, as the long debate ran its course, whether to go on pressing for the whole cake or to accept the half which Canning offered. In the end, they opted for the half and Canning's amendments were passed without opposition.

The government's cautious approach to abolition was soon justified. Bathurst, the Colonial Secretary, sent the amended abolition motion to the Governors of the West Indian colonies together with a request for an immediate ban on the flogging of females and the use of the whip in the field. In all the colonies the planters were outraged by this direct interference by Westminster in their affairs. In Jamaica there was even talk of secession. In Demerara a Negro revolt was sparked off by rumours that the planters were ignoring the King of England's decree of immediate emancipation. Although the rioters showed remarkable consideration for their masters' lives and property, they were bloodily suppressed and savagely punished. In London rumour swelled the riot to monstrous proportions and opinion turned against the abolitionists, who were condemned as irresponsible fanatics.

The government did not, as it might have done, use the Demerara riots as an excuse to drop the cause of the West Indian slaves; but it proceeded with even more heartsearching and circumspection. The Order-in-Council which Canning introduced in the Commons on March 16, 1824, was a painstaking and comprehensive attempt to protect the slaves from ill-treatment, enlarge their rights and improve their status.[62] It was clearly intended to pave the way to emancipation and the penalties for flouting it were severe. But it was to apply only to Trinidad, St Lucia and Demerara, which were all under direct rule from London. Canning hoped that the colonies with their own legislatures – and the vast majority of the slaves – would eventually enact similar legislation. Wilberforce, on the other hand, had no illusions about the colonial assemblies and bluntly declared that the crux of the matter was whether or not the imperial parliament should insist on abolition in all the colonies. Canning, however, insisted that there was a middle way between perpetual slavery and immediate abolition. 'By gradual measures, producing gradual improvement, not only may the individual slave be set free, but his very status may be ultimately abolished.'

Canning's attitude was not that of a knight in shining armour crusading in a noble cause. It was that of the practical statesman, aware of the vested interests that would doggedly oppose change and acutely conscious that by promising more than it could fulfil the government might easily plunge the colonies into violence and bloodshed. He persuaded the Commons that his approach was the right one and the Order-in-Council was accepted without a division. It was not until 1833 – nearly ten years later and six after Canning's death – that Parliament at last decided that a gradual approach would not do and voted in favour of the total abolition of slavery in the British empire.

CHAPTER XVI

Balancing the Old World with the New
1822-1825

Early in November 1822, Canning told Wellington that he was more and more convinced that 'the American questions are out of all proportion more important to us than the European, and that if we do not seize and turn them to our advantage in time, we shall rue the loss of an opportunity never, never to be recovered.'[1] Mexico, Buenos Aires (Argentina), Chile, Peru and Colombia (New Granada and Venezuela) were all engaged, with varying degrees of success, in establishing their claim to independence from Spanish rule. Canning was determined not only to turn their liberation struggle to Britain's advantage but also to prevent France from inheriting the power and influence in South America which Spain had lost.

The British already enjoyed prestige and goodwill in South America. The Royal Navy had become a well-known presence in the principal ports. Individual British military and naval volunteers, like Lord Cochrane, had played a notable part in the South American wars of liberation. Bolivar once said he would much rather be indebted to England for help than to any other country. Like many South Americans, he admired her political institutions as a successful compromise between the extremes of despotism and democracy. The British also had a large commercial stake in South America. In 1823, some eighty British commercial houses were established in towns scattered throughout the continent. 'The power of England is without a rival in America,' wrote a French agent in Colombia in 1823; 'no fleets but hers to be seen; her merchandises are bought almost exclusively; her commercial agents, her clerks and brokers, are everywhere to be met with.'[2]

Canning believed that Britain's commercial position in South America would be consolidated and her international prestige strengthened if she were the first of the great European powers to recognise the new states. But to the King and the ultra Tories in the Cabinet, recognition would be both a dangerous concession to 'Jacobin' ideas and a further cause of estrangement between Britain and the European powers. They kicked long and hard before they were forced, with extreme reluctance, to accept it. Yet before his death Castlereagh, like Canning, had decided that recognition was inevitable. In 1817 and 1818, when the outcome of the struggle between Spain and her colonies was still in doubt, he used his influence to prevent the other European powers from helping Spain, either with military aid or by economic sanctions against the South Americans. He received little credit for this at the time, but it can be argued that it was at least as great a service as any that Canning rendered the new states. In the Verona instructions which he prepared for himself, Castlereagh stated that recognition of the new South American states had become a matter of time and method rather than of principle.[3] For him recognition was an unavoidable necessity, but not, as for Canning, an opportunity to be turned to his country's advantage.

Although at the Verona congress the Spanish American question was pushed into the background by the crisis over Spain herself, it remained very much in the foreground of Canning's mind, largely for commercial reasons. Because of the general breakdown of law and order in the Caribbean over the past few years, British merchantmen were suffering greatly from the depredations of pirates. They were also being confiscated by the Spanish authorities in the Caribbean on the grounds that they were trading with rebel colonies, although for years Madrid had tacitly tolerated this trade on the understanding that Britain would not recognise the rebel colonies. Since the Spanish government in Madrid either could not or would not prevent these seizures, Canning decided that his own government must apply its own remedy. In October 1822, an additional naval squadron was sent to the West Indies and the British naval commander there was instructed not only to protect British traders, but to go after the pirates – even, if necessary, landing on the Spanish island of Cuba, with or without the local governor's consent, in order to hunt them down.

It was obvious, however, that British commerce in the Caribbean could not be effectively protected without the co-operation of the new local authorities from whose coasts and harbours along the South American mainland many of the pirates operated. This was a powerful argument in favour of some form of British recognition of the new states. Moreover British merchantmen would be less liable to seizure by the Spanish authorities if they could claim they were trading with states duly recognised by their own government, and British interests could be looked after by official consular representatives.

Throughout his first few months at the Foreign Office, Canning strongly urged the case for recognition to his Cabinet colleagues in London, and in letters to Wellington at Verona. It was doubtful, he told Wellington, whether the world would gain either by the re-establishment of Spanish predominance in South America or by the establishment 'of a set of wild buccaneering piratical republics' – or rather, he added, 'whether England would gain, that being in this particular question, above all others the world for which we are bound to provide.'[4] But even with the issue thus squarely placed in a context of national self-interest – which was where Canning thought it ought to be – Wellington was anything but enthusiastic. He considered it a point of honour not to recognise the Spanish colonies in a hurry[5] and assured Canning that at Verona nobody thought or cared anything about the matter except in so far as it provided an excuse to find fault with the British.[6] However, he dutifully presented to the congress a Cabinet memorandum which Canning had persuaded his colleagues to accept. The memorandum was in effect a warning that in order to stamp out the 'intolerable evil' of piracy, the British government might have to grant *de facto* recognition to some of the 'self-created' states of South America.[7] Wellington reported that it had been received without much comment except 'regret that Great Britain should be the protector of Jacobins and insurgents in all parts of the world.'[8]

Apart from their general conviction that revolutions ought not to be allowed to succeed, the powers of central and eastern Europe had little direct interest in the future of South America. The French, on the other hand, had. They were anxious to seize any opportunity that came their way to extend their influence and their commercial stake in the region. They were also violently jealous of the naval and commercial predominance of the British in the area and strongly suspected that they would grab some territory if they could. Canning did his best to allay French suspicions through Sir Charles Stuart, the British am-bassador in Paris. But when Villèle saw Wellington, who stopped in Paris on his way home from Verona, he grew 'excessively warm' about the steps taken by Britain to protect her merchantmen in the Caribbean and assured Wellington that France could not submit to any further extension of Britain's commercial advantages and territory.[9]* When Canning heard about this his reactions were equally warm. 'I confess,' he told the duke, 'I long to tell M de Villèle . . . that we *will* trade with the late Spanish American colonies, whether France likes it or not.'[10] It seemed clear to him, even if it was not to Wellington, that French ambitions would need careful watching.

Meanwhile the Spanish liberals in Madrid had been suitably im-

* He also said that France would provide naval transport if the Spaniards wanted to try to reconquer Mexico or Peru.

pressed by the no nonsense instructions sent to the Royal Navy in the West Indies. They apologised, offered compensation, and agreed not to hinder British trade with South America. In return Canning, as a gesture of goodwill, suspended the new naval instructions. He also went more slowly on the recognition issue. He was beginning to realise just how formidable was the opposition in the Cabinet. And however much he might declare that Spain's domestic troubles were irrelevant to the South American question, he was extremely anxious not to do anything that could be construed as support for the European powers' attempts to interfere with the Spanish liberals. Moreover there were indications that the Spaniards were reconciled to the loss of some at least of their colonies and might be prepared to accept British mediation. If the Spaniards themselves would recognise the independence of their own colonies, the way would be clear for Britain to follow suit and the ultra Tories could not complain. By the beginning of 1823 Canning was hopefully working for this solution of the South American problem.

The French invasion of Spain extinguished his hopes. The Spanish liberals were divided among themselves and had little popular support in the countryside. The Duc d'Angoulême and his troops marched through Spain without meeting any serious opposition and entered Madrid on May 24, 1823. The liberals, taking Ferdinand with them, retreated first to Seville and then to Cadiz, where they attempted a last ditch stand. The city fell on September 30. Ferdinand, released and restored to his throne by the French, rejected all their pleas for moderation, returned to his unregenerate absolutist ways and began a reign of bloody terror against his political enemies.

Predictably, France's easy triumph in Spain strengthened Canning's fears about her intentions in Spanish America. The former had to be accepted because it could not be prevented. But an extension of France's ascendancy in Spain to Spain's former colonies was totally unacceptable – there were no divisions in the Cabinet about that. In the last resort it could be prevented by the Royal Navy. But that would mean war, and Canning always regarded Britain's naval strength as a means of preventing war, not of waging it. In August 1823, therefore, while the Spanish liberals were still holding out in Cadiz, he decided to try to forge a new diplomatic weapon for the containment of the French. He turned to the United States.

In some ways it was a surprising move. There was no love lost between the Americans and the British and a great deal of mutual suspicion. It was, after all, only fifty years since the Americans had finally won their independence, and only ten years since they had again been at war with England. Each country suspected the other of territorial ambitions in Central and South America, and each feared the other's commercial rivalry. Canning's often less than complimentary references to the 'Yankees' in his private correspondence were typical of his countrymen's attitude; while his opposite number in Washington, John Quincy Adams, was even more touchy, stand-offish and suspicious of the British than most Americans. But by 1823, the United States had formally recognised Colombia, Mexico, Buenos Aires and Chile, and reports that Canning was strongly in favour of British recognition of the new states created an unusually friendly feeling towards the British in Washington. Stratford Canning reported before his return to England in the summer of 1823 that even Adams 'had caught something of the soft infection' and had spoken with satisfaction of the 'coincidence of principle' that now seemed to exist between the two governments.[11]

Thus there was some excuse for thinking that any overtures made to the Americans would not fall on stony ground. What Canning had in mind was a public Anglo-American declaration that neither government had any claim to the former Spanish colonies and neither would view with indifference the transfer of any part of them to any other power. In the letter in which he first broached the matter to Mr Rush, the American minister in London, he declared that there had seldom been such an opportunity 'when so small an effort of two friendly governments might produce so unequivocal a good and prevent such extensive calamities.'[12] He believed that this would be the most effective and least offensive way of serving a hands-off notice on France or any other European power with designs on Spain's ex-colonies, and reports that the French intended to summon a congress on Spanish American affairs increased his sense of urgency.

Canning afterwards described his exchanges with Rush as 'soundings'. This may have been partly a cover-up for his extreme disappointment at their failure. But it was true in the sense that although he corresponded with the prime minister about them, he never felt they had reached a stage at which the whole Cabinet had to be formally involved.[13] There is no doubt, however, that he tried very hard to bring them to that stage. While on holiday at Windermere he bombarded Rush with letters and on his return to London flattered and surprised him by insisting that the United States was now too important a commercial and maritime power to leave the future of Spanish America to be settled by the European powers.[14]

Rush was at length sufficiently impressed by Canning's overtures to offer on his own authority to pledge his government not to remain inactive if any of the new states should be attacked by a European power. But he insisted that Britain should recognise them without delay. His point – which later was unequivocally endorsed by his masters in Washington – was that unless the British were firmly committed to recognition they might change their minds and even help the Spaniards to recover their colonies. So great was the American mistrust of the British. Canning was quite unable to shake Rush, even when he offered to promise future recognition. Immediate recognition he knew he could not offer because of the opposition of the King and most of the Cabinet.

By the beginning of October Canning reluctantly decided that he was getting nowhere with Mr Rush and abruptly broke off their exchanges. He made up his mind that if he could not create an Anglo-American diplomatic shield to protect the new South American states from the French, he had better disarm the enemy – and do it without delay. Whether or not he was right in thinking that the French were about to try to regain Spain's colonies for her by force, he certainly believed he was. That autumn Stuart in Paris had sent despatch after despatch all breathing the deepest suspicions of French intentions in South America.

Canning's sense of urgency was not shared by the Duke of Wellington who maintained that there was no firm evidence, apart from newspaper reports which he did not trust, that the French had any intention of interfering in South America.[15] Canning, on the other hand, while admitting that there was no proof, maintained that there were quite enough 'pregnant indications' to justify the British government in making its opposition unmistakably clear before the French irrevocably committed themselves. 'I am morally convinced,' he wrote to Wellington on September 25, 'that if France is suffered to get a sway in Spanish America, not only will our ministry be overturned, and I think deservedly, but the reputation of this country will be irretrievably lowered. I am convinced equally that the French ministry, Villèle particularly, have that object still ... and that we have not many months, perhaps weeks, to lose in thwarting them.' It was, he added, too important a matter for him to decide alone or with two or three colleagues, in view of the divergence of opinion, and he proposed to assemble as many members of the Cabinet as quickly as possible.[16]

In the end, however, a confrontation across the Cabinet table was avoided. Canning and Wellington differed over means, not ends. Wellington, believing that Canning was making an unnecessary fuss, insisted that the French should be warned as politely and delicately as possible. Canning therefore gave up his first plan of sending France a blunt warning Note, and instead invited Polignac, the French ambassador, to a meeting at which each would both explain his government's attitude towards Spanish America, and make an agreed written record of their conversation.

Polignac and Canning met first on October 9, 1823, and the outcome of their discussions was embodied in what came to be known as the Polignac Memorandum. Canning spelled out his government's view that the recognition of Spain's ex-colonies depended on 'time and circumstance'. It would prefer recognition to come first from the mother country, but could not undertake to wait for this indefinitely, and it would consider any foreign interference 'by force or by menace' in Spanish America as a motive for immediate recognition. The crux of Polignac's statement was that he unequivocally disclaimed 'any intention or desire' on the part of France to appropriate any part of Spanish America or to obtain any exclusive advantages there. He also denied that his country had any design of acting against the ex-colonies by force of arms.[17]

It seems clear that in his confrontation with the formidable British Foreign Secretary, Polignac felt obliged to give the assurances which he demanded. Unable afterwards, when faced with Canning's draft of their conversation, to deny what he had said, he could only ask for some textual amendments (which were accepted) and then try to make out that the memorandum was merely a private and informal aide-mémoire. 'You see,' wrote Canning indignantly to Wellington, 'how he would shuffle out of it if he could.'[18] But Polignac's masters in Paris blandly expressed surprise at his shuffling and declared that they had no difficulty in accepting the memorandum as a binding, official document.[19] It did not explicitly state that Britain would use her naval power to prevent any foreign interference in South America. But it was assumed that this was what Canning meant to imply. Villèle, who realised that he meant business, presumably saw no point in refusing to give assurances to refrain from action which could only be taken at the risk (which he was not prepared to take) of war with England.

The Polignac Memorandum was an important diplomatic victory for Canning and was widely acknowledged to be so – even by Metternich who cordially disliked him. Next year, when the European powers were seriously discussing the possibility of helping Spain to reconquer her colonies, Chateaubriand had to remind them that France was pledged not to intervene by force.[20] But although French ambitions in Spanish America had been curbed, they had not been destroyed – and Canning never for a moment believed they had.

Meanwhile the Americans were considering Rush's first reports of Canning's overture, which reached Washington on October 9. Unaware that he had already made other arrangements to block the French, even the Anglophobe Adams could not help feeling gratified by the British Foreign Secretary's attentions. It was a new experience to learn from a European statesman that the United States had an important role to play on the other side of the Atlantic. President Monroe and his two predecessors, Madison and Jefferson, were among those who thought that a favourable response should be made. In the end, however, Adams's profound distrust of the British prevailed. In his view, if the United States had to take a stand against the European powers, she had better take an independent one and not 'come in as a cock-boat in the wake of the British man-of-war.'[21] So Rush was merely given a watching brief and strict instructions not to act on his own initiative.

But the Americans distrusted the Holy Alliance just as much as Canning did. The news that France had completely overthrown the Spanish liberals and restored Ferdinand VII to his throne was received with dismay in Washington. Adams rather contemptuously noted that Calhoun, the Secretary of War, was 'perfectly moonstruck' by the danger to South America that this might portend.[22] Moreover, they were alarmed by the pretensions and doctrines proclaimed by the Russian Tsar. Two years earlier Alexander had issued a *ukase* in which he claimed a Russian monopoly of trade and territory along a vast stretch of the north-west coast of the American continent. This was totally unacceptable to both Britain and the United States.* But while Canning reckoned that it was of small practical importance, the Americans could not take it so lightly, especially in the light of the extreme absolutist, anti-republican doctrines proclaimed by the Russians. Alexander's principles and pretensions probably influenced American policy as least as much as French designs on Spanish America.

The outcome of the long and anxious discussions in the American

* Castlereagh had at once sent a formal protest to St Petersburg.

Cabinet during November 1823 was President Monroe's famous Message to Congress. Canning afterwards said he had very little doubt that Monroe was encouraged to make his declaration by his knowledge that Britain was opposed to any European intervention in the new South American states. This was also Rush's opinion.[23] To a large extent they were probably right. But Canning underestimated the Americans' profound mistrust of British motives and intentions. No doubt his discussions with Rush stimulated the Americans into making their position plain. But it cannot be assumed that Monroe spoke out so boldly simply because of a confident assumption that the Royal Navy would protect the new states. The Americans were very impressed by the British refusal to recognise these states and their mistrust of Britain was greatly strengthened by the arrival of Rush's report that Canning had suddenly turned cold and unfriendly. The possibility that Britain might after all join in a general free-for-all in Spanish America was not ruled out. Adams thought that Canning's real motives had been to secure a pledge from the United States that she would not seize Cuba or any other South American territory. He also pointed out that if Britain could claim to be solely responsible for saving Spanish America from European attack, her influence in the new states would become overwhelmingly preponderant.[24] Thus, for a variety of reasons the Americans felt obliged to assert themselves. But it was a calculated gamble because they were neither prepared (nor able) to protect the new states themselves and they were not certain that the Royal Navy would do so either.

Monroe's Message, which was delivered on December 2, was known to Canning on the 24th and published in the newspapers a few days later. On the whole, it was well, even enthusiastically, received. *The Times* complacently congratulated itself on the fact that the United States had adopted a policy 'so directly British'.[25] The European governments had the same impression, and at first were convinced that the Message must be the result of a secret understanding between Britain and the United States.

But Canning was anything but pleased by parts of the Message, in particular by its announcement that although the United States would not interfere with existing European colonies, there was to be no further colonisation of the American continent by any European power. This was a new doctrine, and a bold one in view of the conflicting British and American claims in Oregon and the still unsettled frontier between the United States and the Russian territory of Alaska. Rush told Canning unofficially (he had received no official instructions) that he thought it was directed principally, if not specially, against the Russian *ukase* of 1821.[26] Canning accepted this but told Rush very firmly that neither the American Message nor the Russian *ukase* could limit Britain's freedom to colonise the unappropriated parts of America.[27] He was not concerned with acquiring more territory but with protecting and encouraging British commerce. It was essential not to let the Russians close the Bering Straits to British shipping. It was still more essential to resist the American claim to the whole coast of Oregon as far north as Alaska which, if conceded, would deprive British traders of any outlet on the Pacific.*

Canning also strongly disapproved of President Monroe's statement that the United States would not tolerate any attempt by the European powers to impose their 'political system' on any of the new states of South America. In other words, Quincy Adams, with his passionate republican principles, wanted to make the American continent a preserve for republics, just as the Holy Alliance wanted to make Europe a preserve for monarchs. Canning deplored both aims equally. He was less worried than Castlereagh had been by the establishment of republics in South America, but he always hoped that they could be leavened by a few monarchies – in Brazil certainly, and perhaps in Mexico – precisely so as to avoid the creation of an ideological gulf between Europe and America. The Monroe Message, on the other hand, seemed deliberately designed to deepen the gulf.

In the short term, however, Canning was not on the whole displeased with the Message. It amounted to a welcome reinforcement of the Polignac Memorandum. He felt that he had now got all that he had hoped to get from a joint Anglo-American declaration. 'Pozzo† may bustle,' he wrote jubilantly, 'and Ferdinand may swear; . . . the Spanish American question is essentially settled.'[28] So it was, although he had

* The boundary between British and Russian territory in North-west America was settled by a convention signed early in 1825. Canning told Bagot, who was then British envoy in St Petersburg, that the draft had been submitted to 'both the furry and the finny tribes' – i.e. the representatives of the Hudson Bay Company and the whaling interests. 'In addition to the claims of science,' he added, 'there is very nice "bobbing for whale" they tell me, *ipsis Behringi in faucibus*, which must be guarded.' (Bagot II, p. 266, July 29, 1824.) The rival British and American claims in Oregon were not settled in Canning's lifetime. Two days before his death in 1827 it was agreed that the temporary condominium set up in 1818 should be continued. In the final settlement of 1846 the 49th parallel, which Canning had always said was the proper southern boundary for Canada, was conceded by the Americans.

† Count Pozzo di Borgo, a Corsican by birth, who was appointed Russian ambassador in Paris in 1814 and remained there for twenty years.

in front of him exactly a year of arduous effort before King and Cabinet could be brought to agree.

Meanwhile Canning was determined that the 'Yankees', with their presidential Message, should not gain a propaganda victory over the British. He launched what by the standards of the time was a remarkable publicity campaign. Copies of the Polignac Memorandum (one of the first documents to be lithographed) were circulated to British diplomats in Europe with instructions to make discreet use of them. Canning pointed out the importance of emphasising the date of the Memorandum, which showed that the British had been considerably more prompt than the Americans in warning off the French from South America.[29] Copies were also given to the consuls who set sail for South America early in 1824. They were told to use them to show 'how early and how anxiously Great Britain declared against any project of bringing back the late Spanish colonies under the dominion of the mother country by foreign aid.'[30] On March 30 Canning laid the Memorandum before Parliament and it was published in the British press. By the middle of the summer it was finding its way into the South American Press where it was received with great enthusiasm. The Chilean authorities even went so far as to describe Canning as the 'Redeemer of Chile'.[31] The fact that the United States had recognised the new states, whereas Britain had not, does not seem to have affected the success of the campaign. What really mattered was that Britain's naval supremacy was unchallenged, and her protection was more effective than anything the United States could offer.

With characteristic over-optimism, Canning assumed that President Monroe's unexpected declaration had effectively clinched his own efforts to cure the European powers of their itch to meddle in South America. The French, backed by their allies, had for some months been pressing Canning to attend a conference on South America. 'The congress,' he wrote on December 31, 'was broken in all its limbs before, but the President's speech gives it the *coup de grâce*.'[32] He sadly over-estimated the importance that Metternich, Villèle or Alexander would attach to the pronouncement of a mere American president.

Although the French no longer had any illusions about Spain's ability to get her colonies back, Villèle and Chateaubriand still toyed with plans for planting Spanish Bourbon princes on South American thrones; Villèle even admitted these 'visionary schemes' to Stuart.[33] They would have liked to recognise the new states, so that they could pick up their share of whatever commercial and political advantages were going. But they were tied to King Ferdinand whose unwillingness to acknowledge current realities was encouraged by Alexander's ultra-legitimist emissaries. 'Spain is a dead body to which we are attached,' wrote Villèle gloomily. 'God grant that the dead may not injure the living.'[34] This pious prayer might be answered if England could be stopped from unilaterally recognising the new states and thereby denied the opportunity of increasing the lead she already enjoyed in South America. If brought to the conference table, the British – it was hopefully assumed – would have to go along with the rest. But if they boycotted a congress, not only would their own freedom of action be unfettered, but the congress's decisions would have very little value. To overcome Canning's well-known dislike of congresses which met to dispose of other people's affairs, it was arranged that Spain herself should invite the other powers to advise her on her South American problems.

But Canning was not so easily fooled. 'It may be very fit,' he wrote to Wellington, 'that the Allied sovereigns should govern the Old World as they list; but they have no business to expect that they shall be suffered to extend their continental rule to the New.'[35] France, in particular, must not be allowed to think that her military occupation of Spain gave her any special voice in the affairs of Spain's former colonies. So he stoutly refused to attend a congress unless the United States was also invited – a condition which he rightly surmised would be too unpalatable for the champions of monarchical rule to stomach.* And not all Chateaubriand's epistolary eloquence could move him.

Metternich and Villèle found it hard to believe that Canning was not playing hard to get simply for the benefit of British public opinion, and they lamented the separation he was creating between England and the Continent. But Canning believed that this separation must be made. In August 1823, he had urged upon Liverpool 'the necessity of carefully reconsidering how we stand towards the Alliance; and framing systematically some decision as to the part which we will, or will not, take in these periodical sessions of legislation for the world.'[36] England had already been the odd one out at two congresses – Laibach and Verona – and he was determined that she should not occupy this ignominious

* There was, of course, in any case, a strong case for inviting the United States. 'It would be strange indeed,' wrote Canning to Wellington, 'that the powers of the European continent, some of whom never had a colony, nor saw a ship in their lives, should sit in judgment upon a great maritime, colonial question, from which the American government should be excluded.' (Well. Desp. NS, II, p. 137)

position again, especially when the subject under discussion affected British interests (above all, commercial interests) so much more closely than rebellions in southern Italy or even a French invasion of Spain. 'To have protested a third time,' he wrote to Bagot in April 1824, 'in the face of the world, and to have been a third time perfectly passive after such protest, would have placed the British Government in a point of view almost ridiculous . . .'[37]

Canning realised, moreover, that there were real differences of principle between England and the European monarchies, just as there were between England and the extreme republicans in Washington. And although the most pragmatic – some would say opportunist – of statesmen, he believed it would be a mistake to try to fudge them over. 'The times,' he wrote in January 1824, 'are really too big for compromise of this sort. If things are prevented from going to extremities, it must be by *our* keeping a distinct middle ground between the two conflicting bigotries and staying the plague both ways.' And, he added, with heavy underlinings, 'This only is sure. *Conference there shall be none*; with us in it.'[38] Nor was there, although to Canning's intense irritation, the European allies went on badgering him to change his mind until well on into the summer.*

Canning had repeatedly made it plain that as far as Britain was concerned recognition of Spain's former colonies was a matter only of time and circumstance. By the beginning of 1824 both seemed increasingly favourable. Only Peru still had to contend with a sizeable force of Spanish royalist troops. Elsewhere an isolated garrison still held out in Mexico, and the island of Chiloe, off Chile, was still in Spanish hands. There was a danger that if Britain did not act quickly, the United States, which had already granted recognition, would seriously undermine Britain's prestige and commercial position in South America. Finally, and above all, there was the growing pressure of parliamentary and public opinion in England. In October 1823, Canning had sent consuls to Buenos Aires, Chile, Peru, Mexico and Colombia. But this did not satisfy British merchants and traders, who kept on petitioning Canning to do more to protect their interests in South America. On June 15, 1824, a leading Whig, Sir James Mackintosh, presented a petition to the Commons from the merchants of London. He described Canning's published despatches as 'models and masterpieces of diplomatic

* A series of conferences on South America were held in Paris by the European allies, but to little purpose.

composition', and using them as his text, forcefully argued the case for recognition.

Canning could only make a cautious and non-committal reply because he knew he must reckon with a hostile King and a divided Cabinet. But he made it clear that since Spain persistently refused to take the initiative, the British government felt free to grant recognition without any further consultation with Madrid.[39] He had tried very hard to get Ferdinand to lead the way. In January 1824, he had offered to mediate between Spain and her ex-colonies, but Ferdinand turned the offer down. In April he secretly offered to give Spain a naval guarantee of Cuba if she would acknowledge the independence of her colonies. In view of the traditional British reluctance to give guarantees, this was a remarkable offer, but early in May it too was rejected. After that Canning made no further attempt to bring the Spaniards round. But, as he told the Commons on June 15, the government must have more reliable and precise information about the new states before it could itself recognise them.

This was not just a delaying tactic. Buenos Aires was the only new state whose internal condition was fairly well known in London through the reports of British diplomats and agents in neighbouring Brazil. Elsewhere, the Foreign Office was largely dependent on newspapers and the reports of merchants and naval officers. The consuls sent to Peru and Chile were told to report on the political situation, but to Mexico and Colombia (which, together with Buenos Aires, were the countries thought most likely to qualify for recognition) Canning had decided nearly a year earlier to send special missions of inquiry. Their history illustrates the cautious deliberation with which he approached the South American question, in spite of his forceful and sometimes rather flamboyant public statements.

The commissioners, each with two colleagues, had set out in October 1823, with instructions to find the answers to four specific questions. Had the government (of Colombia or Mexico) irrevocably opted for independence? Was it in military control and capable of resisting attack from Europe? Was it reasonably stable and did it enjoy popular support? And finally, had it abolished the slave trade? No objection was to be made if either country wanted to go back to Spain. But the mother country must be really independent and in no way subservient to France.[40] This proviso reflects Canning's suspicions of French intentions in South America rather than the realities of the situation there. Neither Colombia nor Mexico had any intention of returning to Spanish rule, although some Mexicans might have accepted a Spanish Bourbon prince as a constitutional monarch.

Mr Lionel Hervey, the diplomat sent to Mexico, arrived at his destination early in 1824 and reported on January 18 that he and his colleagues had been received with 'unbounded marks of respect and attention' and the only question causing them any difficulty was the internal state of the country. But he believed that the government's difficulties were largely the consequence of thirteen years of civil war and its virtual bankruptcy. There was no large pro-Spanish party (as claimed in Madrid) and financial help should go far to set the government firmly on its feet.[41] Canning's reply, dated April 23, began with a mild but stately reproof for the haste with which Hervey had formed his conclusions. 'A fortnight's or three weeks' experience could hardly supply, even to the most active and intelligent observers, sufficient opportunity for estimating justly a state of things so new and so extraordinary.' But in spite of its 'defects and omissions,' Hervey's report satisfied Canning that Mexico was worthy of recognition. He would still, however, have much preferred the Mexicans to make their peace with Spain first and he told Hervey to try to persuade them that British recognition would be 'but of trifling benefit' by comparison with recognition by the mother country.[42] This was not the view of the Mexican leader, General Victoria Guadalupe, who would only grudgingly go so far as to offer Spain some commercial privileges in return for immediate recognition. 'I think,' wrote Hervey, 'we should have found more grace in his eyes if we had acknowledged the independence of Mexico without waiting for Spain, and had taken those commercial privileges for ourselves which we are so anxious to obtain for her.'[43]

Hervey's efforts to persuade the Mexicans – as he quaintly put it – 'to conciliate their debilitated parent' were brought to an abrupt halt later that summer. Convinced that the Mexican government's stability was seriously endangered by its financial difficulties, he had allowed himself to undertake to try to persuade the British government to guarantee a loan to Mexico. Canning, however, was determined not to get mixed up financially or in any other way in the new states' internal affairs. He sent the unfortunate Hervey a stiff rebuke and recalled him to London.[44]

Colonel Hamilton, the chief commissioner sent to Colombia, also got into hot water with the Foreign Secretary, but his offence was not so much excess of zeal as too little.* By August 1824, Planta, on

* Hamilton started off on the wrong foot with Canning. In a private letter

Canning's instructions, was sending him complaints about the 'unsatis-factory meagreness' of his written communications.[45] At the beginning of November, Hamilton's deputy, Colonel Campbell, arrived back in London, bearing a despatch from his chief which did little more than state, with military brevity, that Colombia had, in the opinion of the British commissioners, fulfilled the conditions set by Canning for recognition.[46] This earned a stinging rebuke from Canning who noted 'with considerable surprise and disappointment' the 'total absence' of detailed information about conditions in Colombia. 'If,' he wrote, 'you will compare your report with your Instructions, you cannot but perceive how far short you have fallen of that which was expected of you.'[47]

Hamilton evidently found official despatches rather a bore and preferred to expend his epistolary energies on chatty private letters to Planta. He complained about the cost of living and how badly off he was in spite of all his economies. He described in detail his own hospitality and the meanness of the Colombians in returning it. He deplored the dullness of the local society – 'I can assure you there is as little variety at Bogota as at Oxford or Cambridge.'[48] He was convinced that French agents were thick on the ground and that some were disguised as naturalists. He rhapsodised about the fauna and flora and the natural curiosities – 'We want a few English savans [sic] and naturalists in this country, what a harvest these gentlemen might reap in Colombia in mineralogy, geology, botany, zoology and draw-ings! ! !'[49]

In short, Hamilton was an amiable character who took his official duties rather lightly. Canning learnt 'with extreme astonishment' that he had never even shown Campbell their full instructions and had only informed him of Canning's four specific questions two weeks before his deputy's departure for England.[50] Fortunately, however, Campbell was well able to supply the deficiencies of his chief. He sat down in London and drew up a detailed report, 128 pages long, on the geo-graphy, topography, natural resources, people and politics of Colombia. Even this did not satisfy Canning who demanded further information

---

thanking him for his appointment, he referred to his gratitude to Lord Lowther 'for promoting a result so favourable'. Canning took strong exception to the implication that he had let himself be influenced by the Tory grandee. In an abject apology, Hamilton said his mind had been very agitated by the appointment and he had only meant to express gratitude to Lowther for introducing him to Canning. In fact, Hamilton turned out to be not a very suitable choice. (FO 18/1)

on the number of Spanish royalists remaining in the country and on the political sympathies of the Indian tribes.[51] Eventually, however, his craving for information was satisfied and Colombia's claim to independence was deemed to be valid.

Throughout 1824, while Canning was gradually making up his mind to act alone on the South American question and was waiting for the information that would allow him to come to a firm decision, he was also contending with the worst problem of all: the obstinate refusal of the King, Wellington and an influential group in the Cabinet to accept the inevitability of recognition.

Of all contemporary politicians, perhaps the two least suited to persuade George IV to accept a policy he instinctively disliked were Liverpool and Canning. The prime minister was indispensable, but that did not make him any the less irritating to his royal master. And for Canning, the King seems to have felt an almost pathological dislike; he could, if he wished, hide it, but behind Canning's back it betrayed him into conduct that was shocking even by the rather fluid contemporary standards of how a king should behave towards his ministers.

The incident of the Lord Mayor's banquet in April 1824 illustrates how difficult it was for Canning to do anything right in the King's eyes. The Lord Mayor, Alderman Waithman, was a linen-draper of pronounced anti-Tory views who had earned the King's undying hatred by stirring up the crowds at Queen Caroline's funeral. His inaugural banquet in November 1823 had been boycotted by ministers, but the opposition had turned up in force. Both Liverpool and Canning thought it unwise for the government not to be represented at these dinners, because there was then nothing to prevent them from being turned into Whig demonstrations. Canning also had a particular reason for accepting his invitation to the Easter banquet. Missions from Colombia, Mexico and Brazil were in London and if they attended the banquet, it would be politically embarrassing to have them fêted by all the Whig leaders in the absence of any member of the government while the question of recognition was still undecided.[52]

But when the King learnt that Canning (and Charles Wynn, President of the Board of Control) had been to the Mansion House, his fury knew no bounds. He blew off steam to Lady Conyngham for six hours without ceasing, and his secretary, Sir William Knighton, reported that he had never seen him so 'outrageous'.[53] In a letter of protest to Liverpool, he said that Canning must have known that his presence at the dinner would be highly disagreeable and offensive to him.[54] But this aspect of the matter had, it seems, never occurred to Canning. He himself was not a man to harbour a personal grudge for long; nor would it occur to him to let personal prejudice weigh in the balance against political realities. *'The city* may be a very inconvenient power in the state,' he wrote to Liverpool, 'but *there it is.* You cannot put it aside. You cannot even control it.' But it was good policy to try, and at the Easter banquet he thought he had done pretty well. In addition to the South Americans some Greek deputies had been present, and Canning was 'morally certain' that his presence had been of 'signal use' in preventing their health from being drunk.[55]* Since the Turks would never believe the City was not under the government's influence, this would have gravely jeopardised the diplomatic efforts that Britain was then making in Constantinople on behalf of the Greeks.

Eventually it was all smoothed over. Wellington, who in spite of his dislike of Canning was a fair-minded man, saw the point of his attendance at the banquet and joined with Liverpool in defending him to the King, while Canning himself wrote a suitably contrite apology. More difficult to deal with than this more or less open set-to, were the King's efforts to undermine Canning's policies and position behind his back. As Elector of Hanover, George IV had what amounted to a private diplomatic service of his own. It was run by his Hanoverian adviser in London, Count Munster, and the King used it to try to counteract Canning's efforts to assert England's independence of the Holy Alliance. Castlereagh had usually been allowed to see the Hanoverian correspondence. Canning, of course, was not.

The King also collected round himself a small group of the most important foreign diplomats in London – the Russian ambassador, Count Lieven, and his much more famous wife; the Austrian ambassador, Count Esterhazy, and his witty attaché, Baron Neumann; and Count Munster. Later the French ambassador, Prince Polignac, joined what came to be known as the 'Cottage Coterie'.† The only English

---

* Creevey, who was present, wrote: 'The Greeks were a most unexpected Godsend. The contrast between the vivacity of their faces and those of the Spaniards was particularly striking . . . The handsome Greek who wore his native costume is a merchant of fortune, who has fought in one of his own ships against the Turks, and has given his ships and everything else to the Greek cause . . . from 35 to 40 years of age, incomparably handsome, a perfect dandy in his dress and neatness and with excellent manners for a jolly fellow which he evidently is . . .' (Creevey C & T 191/2)

† So called because it met, usually at weekends, at the 'Cottage' in Windsor Park where the King lived while the Castle was undergoing repair.

people present were Lady Conyngham, Sir William Knighton and, occasionally, Wellington who was sometimes appallingly indiscreet but maintained his independent judgment.* The group amused the King with their clever talk, listened approvingly to his unbridled criticism of Canning and encouraged him to get rid of his obnoxious Foreign Secretary. The Coterie's anti-Canning activities, which began early in 1823, reached a climax in the summer of the next year. On June 12, 1824, the King told Esterhazy that he was only waiting for a good opportunity to get rid of his Foreign Secretary. Wellington did not trouble to hide his dislike of Canning; and it was common knowledge that the Cabinet was bitterly divided over the South American issue. Not altogether surprisingly, the Coterie decided that Canning was on the way out and they would give him a shove. A plot was concocted by the Austrian diplomats and what Neumann called 'la saine partie' in the Cabinet; its aim was to provide Canning's enemies in the government with weapons which they could use to force him out of office. The plot eventually fizzled out and much about it remains obscure. But the King apparently knew of it and referred to it approvingly in a letter to Metternich. Canning, who had a good source of information in Lord Francis Conyngham,† also knew that something was afoot.[56] There was an intrigue, he wrote afterwards, 'to change the politics of this Government by changing *me*'.[57]

But Canning was too powerful and popular to be easily dislodged by the intrigues of foreign diplomats – or, on the other hand, to be allowed by his own colleagues to grow any more powerful. And in the early summer of 1824 it looked as if the country might soon need a new prime minister. Lord Liverpool was in very poor health. The variations in his pulse rate, which was abnormally low, were anxiously noted by the political gossips. Knighton told the King that Liverpool's blood vessels were becoming 'grisly' and he could not live long.[58] The King told Wellington he must step into the breach if Liverpool failed. The duke was reluctantly prepared to do his best, but genuinely felt he lacked the right qualities for the job; in any case he too looked very ill – 'withering and drying up', in Croker's lugubrious phrase.[59]

Naturally, it was suspected that Canning would think his chance had

* He agreed with Canning that England should not get mixed up in a congress on South America and therefore refused to help the Coterie to persuade the King to overrule his Foreign Secretary.

† Lord Francis Conyngham, the son of the King's favourite, Lady Conyngham, had been appointed an Under-Secretary at the Foreign Office by Canning. As a propitiatory gesture towards the King, this was only very temporarily successful; but the young man became devoted to Canning and served him well.

come. Most of the Whigs hoped it had; reckoning that Canning's ultra Tory colleagues would refuse to serve under him, they confidently assumed that they would be invited to join a coalition government and spared no effort to get the message across to Canning. From the opposition benches in the Commons, Lord Althorp declared that the Foreign Secretary had risen so high that there was no situation in Europe or even the world that could now be considered a promotion for him.[60] These and similar scarcely less extravagant encomiums were of course not well-received by Canning's colleagues. Nor were they reassured when he once again emphatically declared in the Commons that he did not believe a coalition between Whigs and liberal Tories would work.[61]

He almost certainly meant what he said. More than most members of his party, he realised that the political scene was changing. But he assumed too readily that with what he called the battle against Jacobinism won, politics would be concerned more with ways and means than with differences of principle. He envisaged not a change in party alignments but a dying down of party strife. 'I think our business,' he wrote to Liverpool in March 1824, 'is to admit the extinction of party feeling rather than to show a determination to keep it alive.'[62] It was a comfortable doctrine for a politician in power, who enjoyed almost unprecedented popular support and whose chief preoccupation was with foreign rather than domestic problems.

Parliament rose early that summer after a session cheerfully described by Canning as 'unexampled in shortness as well as good humour'.[63] Encouraged by the debate on the London merchants' petition, he determined to make the Cabinet budge at least a little on the South American issue. Of all the new states, Buenos Aires, the most important province in the former Spanish Viceroyalty of the Rio de la Plata, seemed the most obvious candidate for recognition. It had been effectively, if not formally, independent since 1810, had a settled government and no pro-Spanish party. Moreover, the volume of its trade with Britain and the number of British merchants settled there were both steadily increasing. On July 23, after strenuous argument, Canning persuaded the Cabinet to submit to the King a memorandum on the whole South American issue. It concluded that while there might be valid reasons, such as lack of information or unsettled conditions, for delaying the recognition of Mexico, Colombia, Chile and Peru, in the case of Buenos Aires, a decisive step could and should be taken.[64] The Cabinet therefore recommended that Woodbine Parish, the British Consul-General in Buenos Aires, should be empowered to negotiate a commercial treaty, which when ratified would amount to diplomatic recognition.

The advice was given and received with a marked lack of enthusiasm, and there was neither any public announcement nor any private intimation to the foreign ambassadors in London. The King 'accepted' the memorandum without 'approving' it, while Wellington argued that the step was neither necessary nor expedient. Woodbine Parish's instructions were, however, sent off all the same on August 23.*

In the middle of September 1824 Canning set out on a short holiday. His plan was to spend about a week with Lord Wellesley in Dublin, join Joan and Harriet at Liverpool, and make a tour which would include visits to Mr Bolton at Windermere and Sir Walter Scott near Edinburgh.

There is no evidence that his aim was anything more than a badly-needed holiday, but it was widely assumed that he had ulterior motives. 'It is Canning's misfortune,' wrote Croker, 'that nobody will believe that he can take the most indifferent step without an ulterior object, nor take his tea without a stratagem.'[65] The prevailing theory was that Canning, assuming that Liverpool's retirement was imminent, was going to Dublin to make takeover plans with his old political ally, Lord Wellesley. The King and his colleagues also feared that a visit by such an eminent pro-Catholic English minister might seriously inflame popular feeling in Ireland, especially if Canning gave way to his much deplored predilection for public speaking. Canning, however, assured both King and prime minister that he would be careful. 'Depend upon my not getting into difficulties,' he wrote soothingly to Liverpool. 'I have inculcated privacy on Wellesley, and he has engaged for it; and I am determined not to go anywhere without him.'[66] He was as good as his word. With the help of the Lord Mayor of Dublin – 'a person of unusually civilised and intelligent understanding' – he managed to avoid all addresses and public entertainments without giving offence to anyone.[67] Even Arbuthnot, who was not one of Canning's admirers, had to admit that he had not put a foot wrong.[68]

---

* On Wellington's insistence, Parish was instructed not to negotiate the treaty unless Buenos Aires had established its authority over the whole confederacy. This proviso caused him to postpone action until January 1825 when a congress of the de la Plata provinces agreed to accept the executive authority of the Buenos Aires government pending the promulgation of a new constitution. (FO 6/8. January 25, 1825)

While he was still in Dublin, the long-expected death of Louis XVIII obliged Canning to cancel the rest of his holiday plans and return to London. He would have liked to lead the mission of condolence to Paris himself because he was anxious to achieve a good understanding with France – 'on which, more than on any other political combination, the permanence of peace depends'[69] – and he was increasingly worried by the French government's failure to start withdrawing its army of occupation from Spain. A personal meeting with Villèle might help to remove much mutual mistrust; Polignac in London and Stuart in Paris were giving him directly opposite accounts of the French minister's intentions. He had also been on sufficiently friendly terms with the new King, Charles X, during his exile in England to hope that he might be able to establish a good understanding with him.[70]

It seemed sensible enough. But the ultra Tories again mistrusted his motives. Wellington firmly believed that nothing but mischief would come of his visit. Even Liverpool did not want him to go because he believed that public opinion was strongly in favour of keeping as separate as possible from the continental powers. Eventually Canning agreed that Granville,* who had just been appointed to succeed Stuart as ambassador in Paris, might as well carry the King of England's condolences to Charles X. But he still wanted to go himself some time soon. Unfortunately his tentative discussions on the subject with the King and Liverpool reached the ears of an indignant Wellington as something firmly fixed and due to begin on a definite date in the middle of October.[71]

The duke's misunderstanding might have been quite easily cleared up if there had not been so many people, including the King, who were only too anxious to make mischief between Canning and his colleagues. In the end, with Liverpool's help, the matter was smoothed over, and Canning abandoned his trip to Paris. But the duke, although he had got his way, still felt sore; he had had, he told Mme Lieven, 'a devil of a letter' from Canning and they were on the worst possible terms.[72] Canning, on the other hand, whose impulsive temper earned him so much dislike, could always snap quickly out of his anger and revert to a sane and balanced view. Wellington, he told Granville, was entitled to every consideration; 'even when one's opinion is not exactly the same, nothing could be so agreeable to the ultras, or so inconvenient

*Lord Granville Leveson-Gower had been made a peer in August 1815 and took the title of Viscount Granville.

to me, as the divergency of our opinions on any question or action, of real or supposed importance.'[73] It was an inconvenience which he often had to suffer.

In this inauspicious atmosphere, the Cabinet met for the first time in more than three months on December 1, 1824. Canning, with Liverpool's support, had decided that a showdown over the new South American states could no longer be avoided. Before the meeting he circulated a memorandum which forcefully and cogently recapitulated all the arguments in favour of recognition. By this time, the continued French occupation of Spain seems to have weighed at least as heavily on his mind as the need to protect British commerce or forestall the growth of the United States' influence in South America. He pointed out that throughout the eighteenth century, it had always been a British aim – though not always a successful one – to prevent Spanish foreign policy from being dictated from Paris. Now, with a French army occupying Spain, Madrid's foreign relations were again bound to be dictated from Paris. 'Surely, then, it is of the utmost importance to the best interests of this country that we should prevent the American dependencies of this power [Spain] from being involved in the same subjection.'[74]

After two days of acrimonious discussions the ultras in the Cabinet were still unshaken. Wellington argued strongly that the longer recognition could be deferred the better. On December 7 he offered to resign but Liverpool politely refused the offer. Meanwhile Canning sent Granville urgent instructions to get a firm commitment from the French to withdraw their troops, at least from Cadiz, by a definite date.[75] Granville reported that the French were polite but stubbornly non-committal.

Granville's report, which reached the Foreign Office on December 9, provided Canning and Liverpool with fresh ammunition. There was much energetic drafting and re-drafting of memoranda by both of them. Canning sent his effort to the prime minister on the 12th with the comment that it was 'one of the toughest jobs I ever had to manage. But I *hope* it will do.'[76] Two days later they presented the Cabinet with a memorandum recommending that Colombia and Mexico should be granted recognition through the negotiation of commercial treaties in the same way as Buenos Aires. They added an ultimatum that they would resign if their advice was not accepted. By this time only Wellington, Eldon, Bathurst and Westmorland were holding out.*

* When Peel, who had held aloof from the controversy, finally came down in

Next day, afraid presumably of the public reaction if Liverpool and Canning resigned on such an issue, they too hauled down their flag.

The Cabinet's recommendation[77] was at once sent to the King at Windsor, and after an audience with him on the 16th, Liverpool reported optimistically that he was not disposed to make serious difficulties.[78] Next day, Canning, physically 'knocked up' but thoroughly delighted with Liverpool's performance, wrote exultantly to Granville, 'the fight has been hard, but it is won. The deed is done. The nail is driven. Spanish America is free, and if we do not mismanage our matters sadly, she is English . . .' And he added, thinking of the few days' holiday he was hoping to get: 'This thing achieved, indeed, it matters not whether I go out of town, or out of office; for it was the one thing needed in the present state of the world. And I would most assuredly have gone out of office if I had been thwarted in it.'[79]

His optimism was rather premature. The Cabinet had been brought round, and Parliament's approval was a foregone conclusion. But contrary to Liverpool's impression, the King was far from reconciled. On the 17th he formally accepted the government's advice, at the same time emphatically disagreeing with it. On the same day he saw Wellington, and the duke's report of the audience made Liverpool and Canning suspect that the King was going to change his mind. So next day they went down to Windsor determined to have it out with their royal master. Canning was set on resigning if the King made any difficulties; he had even meant to take his seals of office with him, but could not get them brought to Gloucester Lodge in time. Liverpool urged him not to be hasty, arguing, as they sat in the coach together, that the King would not dare dismiss him, and if he did what they wanted against his will, they ought to let him console himself with a little grumbling. Surprisingly, however, the King decided to charm, not to grumble, and gave no sign of changing his mind. He merely said he thought they were all wrong, but as he had agreed, he hoped they would carry out their decision in the way least offensive to his allies.[80]

Canning did his best to oblige. Struck down by a violent and extremely painful attack of gout in his right foot, he took to his bed in the Foreign Office and tried to draft a circular despatch that would inform the allies of the British decision with the least damage to their susceptibilities. He sent the draft to Liverpool with a request for suggestions on how to make it still more acceptable to the King. Even

favour of recognition, Wellington's face – according to Canning – was a 'picture'. (Harewood Mss. 27, Canning to Joan, December 19, 1824) though he had reason to suspect that the King was intriguing against him behind his back, Canning still took it for granted that the royal feelings should be carefully considered. He was not surprised, he wrote to Joan, that the King should find the recognition of the new states the most distasteful measure of his reign. 'It sanctions what he conceives to be a revolutionary principle. It cuts him off from his dearly beloved Metternich . . .' And, he added rather ruefully, 'it exposes him to the risk of having a coconut-coloured minister to receive at his levee – a circumstance to which I, *liberal* that I am, do not look forward altogether with indifference.'[81]

But although he could understand the King's feelings, Canning underestimated their strength. Three days after Christmas he heard from Lord Francis Conyngham that the royal mind was still 'terribly sore'.[82] And since a soothing balm was the last thing that any of the Cottage Coterie would dream of providing, the royal mind remained very sore. Wellington, on the other hand, with his usual cool good sense, realised that it might be dangerous to go on kicking against the pricks. In the middle of January he told Esterhazy that he had been mistaken to bring Canning into the government. But since he was now so popular and so widely identified with British interests as most people saw them, he could not be dismissed without the risk of a *coup d' état*. Wellington, therefore, meant to use his influence to bring the King round.[83] Apparently, however, he did not act in time to prevent the King from writing to Liverpool on January 27 and reopening the whole question.[84]

The Cabinet met next day and discussed the situation for four to five hours. Both Canning and Liverpool talked of resigning. Canning was indeed furious; he told his colleagues that the King's attitude was all due to foreign meddling, organised from Vienna with the aim of making the King change his policy by changing part of his government. He had, he said, warned Liverpool what was going on six weeks earlier, and if it went on he would feel obliged to remind the King that *constitutionally* he had no right to see foreign envoys except in the presence of the Foreign Secretary.[85] Canning's vehement arguments, stoutly supported by Liverpool, carried conviction even with those who distrusted him and disliked him. They could not give way to a sovereign who fought his ministers at foreign instigation and with foreign allies. Nor could they risk the uproar that would ensue if Canning in his anger complained of the King's behaviour to the Commons. He was clearly far too furious to be bluffing. If he had been forced to resign, he told Granville later, he would have told the

Commons 'that I was driven from office by the Holy Alliance; and further, that the system, which I found established, of personal communication between the sovereign and the foreign ministers, was one under which no English minister could do his duty. If, after such a denunciation, and the debates which would have followed it, the L[ieven]s and Esterhazy did not find London too hot for them, I know nothing of the present temper of the English nation.'[86]

This dramatic contingency plan never had to be put into operation. After a stormy discussion, Canning's colleagues eventually agreed to send the King a joint reply in which, after admitting that there had been disagreements over Spanish America, they declared they were now unanimously agreed that the decisions they had taken on this subject were irrevocable.[87] Two days later, the King grudgingly capitulated after having been warned by Wellington that further intransigence might expose him to a damaging attack in Parliament. He was of course very angry.* But he was also badly frightened by Wellington's warning, reinforced by Knighton's gloomy talk of Canning's extraordinary popularity. He told Esterhazy that he had been forced to yield because he could not dismiss Liverpool or Canning.[88] He began to make conciliatory noises to Lord Francis Conyngham which he knew would be passed on to the Foreign Office, and by February 10, Canning was triumphantly telling Joan that the King and his cronies were 'routed and down upon their knees'.[89]

Before the King made his final attempt to undo what had already been decided, Canning had already announced the British decision to Spain and the continental powers. The foreign envoys in London were, he reported, 'grumpy', but on the whole took the news better than he had expected. He heard afterwards that Mme Lieven had even admitted that recognition was a great stroke of policy for England and she did not see what harm it could do the European powers; moreover it would open up splendid prospects of increasing civilisation. 'Now this is very well for so ultragious a She ultra as herself and for the confidante of the D. of W.'[90]

The official reaction was one of surprise and outraged anger.† The

---

* In order to avoid making the public announcement of British recognition of the new states himself, the King flatly refused to open Parliament. His excuse was that he had gout and the recent loss of his few remaining good teeth prevented him from using his present set of false ones.

† The Russian, Austrian and Prussian envoys were all instructed to make formal

surprise no doubt was genuine because it had been assumed that Canning would be thrown out by the King and the ultras. The anger varied in its intensity and its cause. The Russian emperor was really furious because of his current obsession with legitimacy and also, presumably, because he was already at odds with Canning over the Greek problem. Metternich never felt tremendously strongly about Spanish America, but he wanted to keep in step with Alexander and he was genuinely incensed by England's decision to act alone. Villèle was angry because privately he would have liked France to do the same.

The Spanish government, as was to be expected, protested immediately, vigorously and at length. It also sent a new ambassador to London with instructions to deliver still more remonstrances. But M de Los Rios, unfortunately for his government, got on very well with Canning, who described him as 'the best-humoured little man that ever was seen' and after two conversations persuaded him that there was no point at all in firing off his protests. De Los Rios ruefully made the best of his situation; 'when I drank a glass of wine with him yesterday,' reported Canning, 'at the Duke of Wellington's, being seated at a great distance from each other at a long dinner table, [and] while the smirk on his face addressed itself to me, he said to those immediately sitting near him, "C'est bin c'est très bien mais cela ne nous rend pas nos Amériques." '[91]

The countries whose loss the Spanish ambassador lamented received the news of British recognition with jubilation. It was first learned unofficially in Bogota early in March from a copy of the *Evening Star* of January 4, which a private traveller had bought just before sailing. The effect of the news was vividly described by Hamilton in one of his chatty letters to Planta. 'All the people of Bogota are half mad with joy . . . Rockets are flying in all directions, bands of music parading the street, and the Colombians galloping about like madmen, exclaiming: "We are now an independent nation!!" ' Hamilton had called at the presidential palace where Señor Gual, the foreign minister, 'got me in his arms, and I really thought at one time he would have suqeezed me inside out.'[92] A treaty of commerce was negotiated with Colombia

---

protests to Canning. In each case he insisted on making a memorandum of what the envoy said and then making him endorse it. 'Does Prince Metternich suppose it possible,' he wrote afterwards to Granville, 'that we can allow the Allies to say to every Court in Europe – "See what a snubbing we gave to the British Government", without taking care to reduce that snubbing to its just value?' But he knew Metternich would be annoyed 'because simultaneous scolding is a part of the assumed jurisdiction of the Holy Alliance'. (A. G. Stapleton, G. C. & T., p. 432)

without difficulty and signed on April 18, 1825. With Buenos Aires, Woodbine Parish had already concluded a treaty on February 2. Only the Mexicans caused difficulties by pitching their commercial demands too high. Canning thought they deserved to be snubbed and duly did so. After this treatment they gave way to all his demands* and a treaty was signed early in 1826.

The first accredited South American envoy to arrive in London was Señor Hurtado from Colombia. In November 1825, Canning presented him at Court. Opponents of recognition had repeatedly declared that the King would never bring himself to receive any South American minister. Yet in fact he made no difficulty about it and his reception of the minister was all that Canning could desire. Señor Hurtado, for his part, made 'a very judicious and proper speech' even though it was rather long 'and in the most unlicensed and arbitrary French which it is possible to imagine.' Altogether it was a most satisfactory occasion. 'And so behold,' wrote Canning exultantly to Granville, 'the New World established, and if we do not throw it away, ours.'[93]

British recognition of Mexico, Colombia and Buenos Aires clearly gave Canning a peculiarly personal sense of satisfaction and achievement. It was not unjustified. Without his drive and persistence and readiness to risk his career, the opposition of the King and the ultra Tories would not have been overcome – not, at any rate, as quickly as it was. Liverpool was a loyal ally, but left to himself he might well have let the matter slide.

But Canning's attitude towards Spanish America was governed much more by commercial considerations and power politics than by dislike of colonial rule as such or by a philanthropic interest in the new states. He saw no objection to Cuba, Spain's most important remaining colonial possession, staying under Spanish rule. Indeed, he preferred that it should do so, because then it was less likely to fall into the hands of either France or the United States.† He privately admitted some time afterwards that for him the most compelling argument in favour of the recognition of the new South American states was the continued French occupation of Spain.[94] Since the French refused to save British face

*Except on one point – the free exercise of the Protestant religion – which the Mexican government felt unable to concede because of the strength of Roman Catholic feeling in the country.

† He would have accepted an independent Cuba, but not a Cuba controlled by either France or the United States.

by even promising to withdraw their troops, it was necessary to re-establish British influence and prestige by diplomatic counter-coup. The new South American states provided an opportunity. England's unilateral recognition of them demonstrated her will and ability to take effective independent action without waiting for the approval of the European powers, who for months had been discussing the Spanish American problem in Paris without getting anywhere. In effect, Canning snubbed the Holy Allies, and at bottom this probably annoyed them much more than the flouting of legitimist principles which worried the King and the ultra Tories in England so much.

Too much, however, can be made of the practical effects of recognition. The negotiation of commercial treaties and the establishment of regular diplomatic relations improved the security and generally strengthened the position of British traders and merchants in Mexico, Colombia and Buenos Aires. But the non-recognition of Chile did not noticeably impede the expansion of British economic interests there. On the other hand, commercial interests in England clearly believed that recognition was important to them and their increasingly urgent pressure made a strong impression on Canning and Liverpool.

Canning himself set great store by recognition as a link between the old world and the new. He believed that it prevented the danger of 'a division of the world into European and American, republican and monarchical, a league of worn-out governments on the one side, and of youthful and striving states, with the United States, on the other.'[95] To him this was a great point gained. But it was not a point of great substance because he greatly exaggerated the danger of the United States attempting to establish some kind of hegemony over the whole continent.*

It can also be argued that Canning exaggerated the importance of British recognition for the South American states themselves. It certainly did not create them, as his more high-flown utterances might lead one to suppose. They already existed as *de facto* independent

* In 1826, Bolivar invited both England and the United States to send observers to a Spanish American congress at Panama. Canning's instructions to the British observer, Edward Dawkins, included a warning that although a league formed by the former colonies of Spain was unobjectionable, 'any project for putting the United States of North America at the head of an American confederacy as against Europe would be highly displeasing to your Government.' He need not have worried. Neither of the North American observers turned up at the congress (one died on the way and the other set out too late) and Dawkins reported that in his opinion the general influence of the United States was not to be feared, although it did exist in Colombia. (Temperley, pp. 179/80)

entities, and they had already been recognised by the United States, Brazil and Portugal. Recognition did not really give them any more security then they already enjoyed because, in the Polignac Memorandum, Canning had in effect undertaken to place British naval power between them and any attempted reconquest from Europe. Nor did it provide them with the commercial and financial lifelines that were essential to their economic growth and prosperity. British trade and money were already pouring into South America; recognition stimulated the flow but did not start it.

The fact remains, however, that the South American themselves felt that to be formally accepted by a great European power was much more significant and desirable than recognition by the United States. England was both more disinterested and more powerful than their northern neighbour. The Chileans, who had hoped for recognition at the same time as Mexico, Columbia and Buenos Aires, were greatly disappointed when Canning decided that they lacked sufficient political stability.* The South Americans believed that British recognition was of the greatest importance to them and that Canning had got it for them. Whether or not they were altogether right about the first point, the second was certainly true.

* Neither Chile nor Peru was ever recognised by Canning. It is not clear exactly why – Spanish resistance in Peru was finally eliminated by the end of 1824 – but presumably he was not satisfied by his agents' reports on the internal state of each country.

CHAPTER XVII

The Eastern Question
1822-1825

'Portugal alone,' wrote Canning on August 17, 1824, 'has given me more trouble, during the last two months, than ought fairly to be spread over half a year from all the Courts of Europe.'[1] Because of French diplomacy and intrigue, the special relationship that had existed between Britain and Portugal for centuries was at risk. To let the French gain control in Lisbon would not only be an intolerable affront to British prestige, it would also pave the way for Portugal's absorption in a French-dominated Spain – or so Canning feared. Portugal, he wrote, 'has been, and always *must* be English so long as Europe and the world remain in anything like their present state.'[2] His problem was to keep Portugal 'English' without breaking the cardinal rule of British policy not to interfere in another country's domestic affairs. He could not solve it with complete success.

The treaty links between England and Portugal stretched back more than 400 years and since the seventeenth century England had guaranteed Portugal against foreign attack in return for commercial privileges. Twice in the eighteenth century British troops had been sent to defend Portugal. In 1808 they went again to liberate the country from Napoleon. But, as Canning had found when he went to Lisbon at the end of 1814, the war left the Portuguese thoroughly disenchanted with their deliverers. It also left them a prey to acute domestic instability. King John,* whom Canning had gone to Lisbon to welcome home, continued to linger indecisively in Brazil and in his absence the country was ruled by a corrupt, incompetent and increasingly unpopular regency.

In 1820, only a few months after the Spaniards had risen in revolt, part of the Portuguese army also rose, overthrew the regency in Lisbon and proclaimed a constitution amid scenes of wild rejoicing. The European powers tended to regard Portugal as a British responsibility and, at this stage, did not attempt to intervene. Castlereagh preached moderation to the revolutionaries in Lisbon and sent urgent messages to King John to come home and save his throne. The king,

* The Prince Regent of Portugal had become King John VI in 1816

although incurably weak and indecisive, was well-meaning and comparatively liberal in his views. He was not unwilling to come if he could be sure of not losing his Brazilian throne as a result. Eventually, he did return, bringing with him most of the contents of the Bank of Brazil and leaving his eldest son, Don Pedro, behind as regent, with instructions to declare Brazil independent if he had no choice, but at all costs to keep her under the House of Braganza. The king arrived in Lisbon in July 1821 and immediately accepted the new constitutional régime.

But King John's return did not bring political stability to Portugal. His wife, who was the sister of the King of Spain, and his second son, Dom Miguel, were determined to restore absolutist rule; the constitutionalists were divided among themselves; the new Assembly behaved with extravagant irresponsibility; and clerical reaction gathered strength. In May 1823, Dom Miguel won over part of the army, removed his father from Lisbon and frightened him into withdrawing the constitution. But King John, indecisive as ever, immediately promised to grant another. He was brought safely back to Lisbon, but Dom Miguel assumed the title of commander-in-chief, arrested liberals and let it be known that he would not allow another constitution to be introduced.

At first Canning was inclined to welcome Dom Miguel's counter-revolution. He had no use for the Portuguese reformers, whom he privately described as 'fierce, rascally, thieving, ignorant ragamuffins' who hated England;[3] his chief concern was that the Portuguese should set their house in order without foreign interference. But instead of settling the struggle for power in Portugal, Dom Miguel had merely increased the likelihood of foreign intervention. In July 1823, Count Palmella, the Portuguese foreign minister, who was anti-Miguel and pro-British, appealed to the British government to send troops to Lisbon to maintain order and overthrow the reactionaries. Canning had already publicly reaffirmed Britain's obligation to defend Portugal if she were invaded by the French army then swarming through Spain. Wellington, who regarded the Portuguese crisis as largely a matter of restoring military discipline, argued strongly that the British also had a duty to help their ancient ally deal with its rebellious subjects and mutinous troops.[4] But Liverpool and Canning argued equally strongly that to send troops would be to intervene in Portugal's internal affairs. In any case there were no troops to send and more could not be raised without summoning Parliament.[5] They would only agree to send a naval squadron to the Tagus in the hope that it would have a beneficial moral effect and at the worst could offer a refuge to King John.

Throughout the autumn and early winter of 1823-4, King John was subjected to increased pressure from the contending Portuguese factions and the foreign envoys in Lisbon. The Russians, Austrians and Prussians, having abandoned their self-denying ordinance on Portugal, pressed him hard to break his promise to grant another constitution. The able and energetic French ambassador, Hyde de Neuville, concentrated on building up the pro-French faction, led by Count Subserra, the minister of war. The new British minister, Sir Edward Thornton, was instructed by Canning to point out to Palmella that since the Portuguese people had been promised a constitution, the wisest course would be to grant one.[6] But Canning was not prepared to back up this advice with an offer to guarantee any new institution, although he uneasily admitted to Liverpool that if they washed their hands of Portugal, she would become incorporated in a continental alliance.[7]

The crisis came the following spring. King John finally decided to summon the ancient Portuguese Cortes. This was hardly a democratic, let alone a revolutionary, step. But Dom Miguel and his reactionary supporters decided to use it as an excuse for a coup. The prince, however, seems to have inherited his father's indecisiveness and his coup went off at half-cock. On April 30, 1824, he put on a show of military force in Lisbon, made some arrests and surrounded the palace. But he gave way when the whole diplomatic corps forced its way into the palace and declared that no violence should be done to the king. Thornton, understandably impressed by 'this most extraordinary scene', solemnly reported next day that Dom Miguel 'had all the air of a guilty young man, confounded at the discovery and defeat of his plots, and abashed at the presence of the assembled ministers of Europe, crowding round his father and his sovereign, and supporting His Majesty's cause with no other than moral force and feeling, derived from the eternal principles of justice and truth.'[8]

But Thornton's satisfaction was premature. King John was free, but so too was Dom Miguel, who recovered his nerve and proceeded to issue orders, make arrests and generally terrorise the people of Lisbon. After several days Palmella decided to take refuge on a British warship. So did Subserra. The minister of war was no lover of constitutions, but by now both he and Hyde de Neuville had realised that their best course was not to replace King John but to dominate him. On his own authority, Hyde de Neuville promised French aid to deal with Dom Miguel and actually ordered the French garrison, across the Spanish border at Badajoz, to march on Lisbon. It was an impressive gesture but fortunately for the cause of international peace, the French commander decided to ignore it.*

It was Thorton, with British warships at hand in the Tagus, who was best placed to turn the crisis to good account, and on May 9 he at last persuaded King John to take refuge on board the British flagship, H.M.S. *Windsor Castle*. That was the end of the affair so far as Dom Miguel was concerned. For the second time he lost his nerve, meekly obeyed his father's command to appear before him, fell on his knees on the *Windsor Castle*'s quarter-deck, agreed to travel abroad and was at once packed off to Vienna. A few days later the king made a triumphant return to dry land amid the salutes of men-of-war and the enthusiastic cheers of his subjects who also loudly cheered the English people and their representative, Sir Edward Thorton.

But Thornton's triumph was short-lived. He had, in Canning's opinion, sadly mismanaged things by allowing Subserra to transfer from the British warship on which he had taken refuge to the *Windsor Castle* where he immediately began to re-establish his influence over the king. Eventually, instead of being forced to retire from office, as Thornton had optimistically forecast and he himself had feared, Subserra became more firmly entrenched and Hyde de Neuville and the pro-French faction with him. Thornton, aware that the tables had somehow been turned on him, tried to retrieve the situation by listening sympathetically to Palmella's fresh appeal for British troops. But when he recommended to Canning that the request should be granted, he got a very dusty answer. Canning replied that he presumed Subserra and de Neuville were responsible for the request; they counted on a refusal which would open the way for the introduction of French troops. But England was publicly pledged not to allow French troops into Portugal. If a British force was sent to prevent this, who could say what might happen next? In any case there were still no British troops to send.

George IV, however, was prepared to send a Hanoverian force to Portugal if necessary. When the news leaked out, early in July, 1824, Mme Lieven rejoiced greatly. 'Bravo,' she wrote, England 'is on our side! What has become of the Ministers' speeches against the principle of intervention and occupation? . . . England is once more linked up with the European system.'⁹ But the French, who were more interested

* On May 24, 1824, Canning wrote to Thornton: 'It would be well if M Hyde de Neuville could be taught to consider the risk to which he exposed the peace of Europe by such unauthorised assumption of authority.' (FO 63/284)

378

in their private duel with England over Portugal than in European ideological solidarity, were less pleased. When, however, Polignac represented to Canning the 'inconvenience' that would arise from the despatch of British troops to Portugal, the Foreign Secretary immediately complained strongly about de Neuville's goings-on in Lisbon. Polignac saw the point and persuaded Villèle officially to disown de Neuville's attempt to bring the Badajoz garrison to Lisbon; in addition, Polignac gave Canning an explicit written assurance that no French troops would be sent to Portugal. This was much more satisfactory than unconvincing verbal assurances. Canning decided to cancel the despatch of Hanoverian troops to Portugal but strengthen the British naval squadron in the Tagus.[10] Wellington, greatly annoyed at this change of plan, privately declared that his life's work was being undone merely because of 'Mr Canning's love of undoing'.[11]

But the Portuguese situation could not be considered satisfactory so long as English influence was in eclipse at Lisbon. Canning's first move to remedy this was to recall Thornton. One cannot help feeling some sympathy for Sir Edward, who was keen and energetic and had at least been largely responsible for Dom Miguel's discomfiture. But he was not in the same class as de Neuville, whom he rather naïvely descibed as 'a virtuous and an honourable man,' and he had failed to prevent Subserra from re-establishing his influence over King John. He also brought Canning's wrath down on his head by attending meetings of the major foreign envoys in Lisbon to advise the Portuguese on various internal matters. Poor Thornton, who probably thought it was his duty to co-operate with the Portuguese and his colleagues in this way, was snubbingly assured by Canning that his conduct was 'wholly out of your province and entirely disapproved by your Court.'[12]

Thornton was succeeded by Sir William à Court, who was hurriedly transferred from Madrid and arrived in Lisbon towards the end of September 1824. Sir William was a much tougher and more adroit diplomat than his predecessor. Moreover he only briefly had to match his wits against Hyde de Neuville, who had also got into trouble with his own government and early in the New Year left for home. Sir William's main task was to establish his own influence over King John (who had become attached to Thornton and was upset by his recall) and – acting on Canning's explicit instructions – persuade him to get rid of Subserra who was by now chief minister. Nothing, wrote Canning rather disingenuously, was further from the government's mind than to dictate to King John his choice of ministers. But since The French ambassador had openly stated in the royal palace that *he* would recognise no minister appointed in place of Subserra, it was high time for the British ambassador to declare frankly how much his government distrusted a minister 'so ostentatiously proclaimed to be the chosen minister of France'.[13]

It was not exactly an easy assignment for à Court. 'You have given me no sinecure here,' he ruefully commented to Canning.[14] But he was persistent and forceful and in the end he got his way. On January 15, 1825, King John summoned him to the palace and told him that his mind was made up and à Court might send word to London by the packet sailing that night. Six days later, he was as good as his word and dismissed the whole ministry.* It was replaced by a new set of not very distinguished but suitably pro-British ministers.

For once, Canning had broken his own strict rule of non-interference in another country's internal affairs. He had to, because to obey it would have conflicted with his view of England's interests. To guarantee King John against foreign aggression did not stop French influence from reigning supreme in Lisbon. Only a pro-British ministry could do that; there was no choice therefore but to instruct the British ambassador to become a maker and breaker of ministries. Canning was determined not to deviate any further than he must from the policy of non-intervention which he believed in and which in any case was the only one that was politically acceptable in England. But it was difficult to draw the line. King John was old and afraid of a coup against his not very strong ministry; he felt the British should give him troops and not just moral support in return for accepting their advice. 'The truth is,' wrote Canning to à Court in his most pontifical vein, 'that the successive military occupations of Piedmont, Naples and Spain have gradually and insensibly wrought a great change in the view of international rights and duties; and have led the greater Powers (for one reason) and the smaller (for another) to look upon the introduction of a foreign force into a country as one of the ordinary resources of a weak Government, and one of the natural good offices of a powerful neighbour, in cases of internal danger or alarm.'[15] So King John's repeated requests for some British troops were politely turned down and he was told that he must make do with the ships of the Royal Navy still stationed in the Tagus.

Canning realised that the distinction between military and naval intervention could seem rather a fine one. He stoutly maintained,

* At first, rather to Canning's dismay, it was proposed to send Subserra as ambassador to London. But in the end he went to Madrid and Palmella came to England.

however, that the principle of non-intervention was 'relaxed', but not 'violated' by the presence of the British ships. The squadron undoubtedly served to protect the person of the King of Portugal, but it was 'not capable of being employed as an instrument of domestic policy, or as an agent in civil dissensions'.[16] It was in fact a compromise, sensible in the circumstances of the moment but, like many compromises contrived to deal with essentially unstable situations, inadequate when the real crisis came.

One important consequence of the reassertion of British influence in Lisbon was a more or less satisfactory settlement of the relationship between Portugal and Brazil. After King John's return to Lisbon in 1821, the new Portuguese Assembly, whose liberal principles did not apparently extend overseas, completely alienated the Brazilians by its high-handed attempts to re-establish a tight control over their affairs. Dom Pedro was left with no choice but to side with the Brazilians or get out. In September 1822, he assumed the title of 'constitutional emperor' and a month later Brazil declared her independence.

When Canning heard the news, he realised there was nothing to be done about it. For nearly fifteen years Brazil had been the seat of the Portuguese monarchy from which Portugal herself had been ruled; it was absurd to expect the Brazilians to revert meekly to a purely colonial status. Canning did not acknowledge any British obligation to help Portugal recover her colony; but, because she was such an old ally, he did accept a moral obligation to help the two countries work out a peaceful separation. He was also firmly, almost obsessively, convinced that it was in the general interest to preserve monarchical institutions in Brazil. Again and again he insisted that the 'conservation of monarchy in one part at least of the great continent of America is an object of vital importance to the Old World.'[17] And he hopefully supposed that the imperial title, which had an elective connotation, was meant to be 'a sort of middle term' which would assert the independence of Brazil while at the same time preserving the throne of the Braganzas.[18]

But in practice a Portuguese-Brazilian settlement proved very hard to get. Neither King John nor Dom Pedro had a free hand. The king was under constant pressure, both from his own subjects and the envoys of the European powers, to take a tough line; and in Brazil, where a considerable party wanted to sever all links with Europe, Dom Pedro's intentions were suspect and he was in no position to make concessions to his father. The Portuguese would not acknowledge that Brazil was in fact already independent; the Brazilians would not negotiate unless they did. When Portuguese commissioners arrived off Rio de Janeiro towards the end of 1823, their ship was seized and they were ignominiously sent back to Lisbon in a packet boat.

Throughout the following year Canning tried hard to mediate between King John and his son, but without success. He brought Portuguese and Brazilian representatives together in London, but their meetings got nowhere. He himself drew up an ingenious compromise plan and sent it to Lisbon. The Portuguese, however, who thought they could do better by surreptitiously appealing to the other European powers, reject it outright. But their appeal came to nothing and early in 1825, when British influence was again becoming predominant in Lisbon, Canning decided to make one more effort to secure a peaceful settlement between King John and his son. In order to save time, he suggested that an experienced British diplomat, Sir Charles Stuart, should go to Rio to negotiate on King John's behalf. It would be, Canning told Granville, a regular mediation asked for by both parties, to which Villèle could not object. Nothing,' he added, with his tongue rather in his cheek, 'ever was more "European." But he will not like it the better I fear.'[19]

Stuart's mission was a double one: first to extract reasonable terms from King John in Lisbon and then to persuade Dom Pedro in Rio to accept them. In a sense, his task was to settle a family quarrel, which threatened to cost the squabbling relatives a large slice of the family inheritance. But it was even more intractable than most family quarrels because neither party could afford to ignore the public reactions to their private dispute. In one of his most distinguished and forceful despatches, Canning instructed Stuart to make it quite clear that if King John would not be reasonable he would forfeit England's support and protection. If he decided to try to retake Brazil by force, the result would probably be a Brazilian fleet off the Tagus rather than a Portuguese army in Rio. Furthermore, Stuart was to leave the Portuguese in no doubt that if he failed in Lisbon, he would still have to go on to Rio to negotiate a new commercial treaty, and the conclusion of this treaty would amount to British recognition of Brazil.[20]

After much havering – he was constantly badgered by the French and Spanish envoys to stand firm – King John eventually conceded enough for Stuart to feel justified in going on to Brazil as the king's plenipotentiary. He arrived at Rio in July 1825, and after several weeks of rather abstruse wrangling over the imperial title and who was ceding sovereignty to whom, a treaty of independence was at last signed on August 29. Predictably, it was not well-received by the Portuguese. But the old King duly ratified it and illuminated Lisbon for three nights in celebration – which showed, commented Canning, 'his good sense and his love of illuminations'.[21]

In the circumstances, Stuart had done well to get a treaty at all. But Canning, who was a perfectionist, was not altogether satisfied. In particular there was no provision in the treaty (as there had been in the plan he had put forward the previous summer) for what was to happen after King John's death – an event which was not likely to be much longer delayed. But in spite of its defects, and its unpopularity in both Rio and Lisbon, the treaty had at least secured a peaceful separation between Portugal and Brazil and preserved the family link between the two countries.* It was a tribute to Canning's patient persistence in the face of 'weakness and vacillation beyond all belief'[22] in Lisbon, and the obstruction, opposition and intrigues of most of the European powers.†

Spain and Portugal and their former colonies in South America were not Canning's only preoccupations as Foreign Secretary. At the other end of Europe the Greeks were fighting for their independence and the Russians were threatening to upset the European balance of power by overwhelming the decrepit Ottoman Empire.

The Greek war of independence had been sparked off early in 1821 by an abortive rising against the Turks in the Principalities of Moldavia and Wallachia. In April the Greeks of the Morea rose and massacred thousands of the local Turkish population. The Turks responded with even worse atrocities. The fighting spread to the Peloponnese and the islands, while throughout Europe there was growing public sympathy

* In 1826 war broke out between Brazil and Buenos Aires over the possession of Montevideo, in spite of British efforts at mediation. Canning was greatly concerned, partly because British commerce on the River Plate was paralysed by the hostilities, and partly because he feared for the survival of Dom Pedro's government which he described as 'the strongest connecting link between the Old World and the New'. The quarrel was settled in 1828 by the establishment of the independent state of Uruguay – a solution which Canning had suggested before his death.

† Stuart went on to negotiate two treaties with Brazil, on behalf of Britain, one dealing with commerce and one with the slave trade. Unfortunately Canning was obliged to disavow both on technical grounds. Stuart, whose relationship with his chief was already strained, was furious and accused him of 'spite'. But Canning had in fact acted on the advice of both the law officers and Huskisson, the President of the Board of Trade.

for the Greek cause. Pamphlets were written, funds raised and in a number of European cities Philhellenic committees were set up.

The public sympathy for the Greeks was not shared by the great powers of Europe. Only in Russia, sympathy for co-religionists and the centuries-old yearning to expand towards Constantinople and the Mediterranean combined to make an explosive mixture which no government could ignore even if it wanted to. The Russians, moreover, had various specific grievances of their own against the Turks: in particular, the continued Turkish military occupation of the Principalities,* and the restrictions placed by the Porte on Russian commerce in the Black Sea. Moreover, Russia had ill defined treaty rights to protect the religious and personal freedom of Christians in parts of the Ottoman Empire, and she readily assumed that these gave her more general rights of interference. Alexander himself was torn between his desire to avenge persecuted fellow Christians and his violent hatred of all rebels, between his vision of himself as a universal peacemaker and his awareness that his huge army was itching to fight someone.

Neither Metternich nor Castlereagh was interested in what happened to the Greeks, but only in preventing the Russians from using their revolt as an excuse to overrun the Ottoman Empire. For once, Castlereagh thought that a European conference might serve a useful purpose, and the Congress of Verona was originally designed by him and Metternich primarily as a device for controlling Alexander and defusing the Greek crisis. In the event, as we have seen, it was diverted to a crisis nearer home, and the Greeks were almost completely ignored.

When Canning went to the Foreign Office, he shared his predecessor's anxiety to prevent a Russo-Turkish war. Like Castlereagh, he had inherited from Pitt a strong belief in the importance of preserving the decaying Ottoman Empire as a bastion against a possible Russian threat both to the British position in India and to Britain's naval supremacy in the Mediterranean. Although one of the most accomplished classical scholars of his day, he did not share the illusions of the Philhellenes about the modern Greeks. 'There in no denying,' he wrote, 'that they are a most rascally set.'[23] On the other hand, he had a greater sympathy for their aspirations than Castlereagh had had. He thought they might hope, if not for independence, at least for some form of autonomy under the suzerainty of the Porte. He wanted a settlement as quickly as possible, both for humanitarian reasons and to prevent

* The Russians had occupied Moldavia and Wallachia between 1806 and 1812 and continued to regard them as a very 'sensitive' area.

the conflict from spreading. But the extent to which he was prepared to intervene at any given moment to help solve the crisis depended entirely on his judgment of whether it would help or hinder his own country's interests and prestige. In other words, he adopted an attitude of tactical opportunism – or, to put it less pejoratively, flexibility – towards the Greek problem, in order to follow a strategic policy that was consistently 'English'.

One constant factor in Canning's policy, however, was a strict neutrality between Greek and Turk, although this was not always apparent to the other powers. When he recognised the Greeks as belligerents in March 1823, Metternich complained that he was acknowledging revolutionaries and Lord Strangford, the British ambassador in Constantinople, was somewhat nonplussed when asked by the Turkish foreign minister whether his government would acknowledge the right of the Americans to recognise Irish rebels as belligerents. It was in fact a purely practical step, which Castlereagh, shortly before his death, had foreseen would have to be taken. Belligerency, Canning argued, was not so much a principle as a fact. The Greeks had acquired 'a certain degree of force and consistency' and 'monstrous consequences' would flow from treating them as pirates. 'Can it be necessary to suggest the advantage to humanity of bringing within the regulated limits of civilised war, a contest which was marked on its outset on both sides, with disgusting barbarities?'[24] In those days it was assumed that war could be civilised. Belligerents (unlike pirates) were obliged to obey the rules and the Royal Navy was present to make sure the Greeks did.*

The activities of the English Philhellenes also threw some doubt on Britain's neutrality, especially among the Turks who found it hard to believe that a government could not control the activities of its subjects. English officers volunteered to go and fight in the Greek cause; Canning did not stop them, but he had them struck off the active list. The most famous of the volunteers was a civilian, Lord Byron. The London Greek Committee, which issued its first circular in March 1823, grew rapidly and attracted some distinguished names, although its fund-raising activities were not conspicuously successful. The oppo-

---

* The British government insisted that the Greeks should withdraw a proclamation in which they announced that they would sink, with their crews, all European ships carrying troops or provisions for the Turks. On the other hand, the Porte complained that British naval officers sometimes intervened on behalf of the Greeks. Canning insisted that they only intervened for humanitarian reasons, not to influence the course of the struggle, and defended their right to do so.

sition M.P., John Cam Hobhouse, who was a member of the committee, wrote that 'they had the satisfaction of knowing that Mr Secretary Canning regarded their efforts with far more favour than those of the Spanish patriots.'[25] This was no doubt true of Canning's private feelings. But he denied any public or official partiality for the Greeks. The government, he wrote in July 1823, had not discouraged pro-Greek activities in England, partly because it lacked effective means to do so, and partly because 'discouragement generally inflames enthusiasm.' But, he added, British neutrality in this quarrel was 'as strict and sincere as in that of Spain'.[26] Only if her neutrality was believed to be genuine, could England hope to play a useful role in tranquillising the Balkans.

When the Verona congress ended, it was still uncertain whether the Russians intended peace or war against the Turks. Alexander himself was believed to want peace, but his offer to send troops to crush the Spanish liberals had been rejected and, as Canning graphically feared, 'in the prurient and tantalised state of the Russian army, some vent must be found.'[27] Diplomatic relations between Russia and Turkey had been broken off in August 1822, and until they were restored there was an acute danger of war and virtually no chance of an agreement on Greece. The Russians insisted that the Turks must accept certain demands before relations could be resumed, and Lord Strangford, the British ambassador in Constantinople, did his best to persuade the Turks to swallow them.

Strangford was an extremely able, if somewhat temperamental, diplomat, and towards the end of 1823 he had made enough progress for Canning to feel justified in pressing Alexander to nominate an envoy to Constantinople. In the middle of January 1824, he heard from Charles Bagot in St Petersburg that the Tsar had at last agreed in principle to the restoration of the Russian mission in Constantinople. Canning jubilantly described this as 'the greatest point gained this many a day,' and he told Bagot that on the morning the new Russian envoy actually left St Petersburg, 'you may get something to drink – what you please – the liquid bubble in the inside of a frozen bottle of usquebaugh if you will – and charge it to the office. I will face out Hume* himself on that article of your extraordinaries.'[28]

In the end, however, Canning was not called on to justify the expenditure of public funds on this exotic drink. The Tsar, who wanted Greece as well as all other outstanding Russo-Turkish problems

* Joseph Hume was a Radical M.P. who was constantly accusing the government of extravagance.

settled before sending a mission to the Porte, produced a memoir on a Greek settlement and invited the European powers to approve it at a congress at St Petersburg.* Metternich disliked the plan which, although it left the Greeks under Turkish suzerainty, was clearly designed to place them firmly within the Russian sphere of influence; but he was prepared to attend a congress in the hope that it could be used to control rather than further Russian ambitions. France and Prussia both approved the memoir – which, commented Canning acidly, 'when a plan consists of many and complicated parts, is absolutely foolish and of very little help.'[29]

Canning himself was very much in two minds how to respond. It was typical of his pragmatic approach to international problems that he should even have considered sending a representative at a time when he was firmly refusing to be drawn into a congress on Spain's former colonies. But while on South America England had nothing to lose and much to gain from taking an independent line, on Greece Canning realised that there was a good deal to be said for joint action. On this problem Russia, not England, was the odd man out, for it was not in the interest of any of the other powers to have the huge Russian empire enlarged still further at the expense of the Turks. If England attended the congress she could not be accused of being obstructive in a crisis which Canning feared could lead to a general war, and she would have a chance of influencing the outcome.

All the same, he found it hard to overcome his aversion to congresses. He strongly suspected that Alexander intended that the St Petersburg congress should give him a free hand on Greece, just as previous congresses had allowed Austria to deal with Naples and France with Spain. He wanted some assurance that the Russians would not, whatever happened, go to war, because he was determined not to risk (as at Verona over France and Spain) the humiliation of protesting ineffectively against the use of force. He also saw no point in holding a congress unless it had a reasonable chance of success – which would not exist unless Russia first put her relations with the Porte on a normal footing. 'Russia *cannot* place the Greeks on the footing of peaceable subjects of the Porte, but she *can* place herself on the footing of a friendly power.'[30] The Russians, however, were reluctant to send a mission to Constantinople until the Turks had evacuated the Princi-

* The Russian memoir proposed to divide Greece into three principalities, with a status similar to that of Moldavia, Wallachia and Serbia, in all of which Russia had a recognised treaty right to protect the Christian inhabitants. The Turks would have an annual tribute and the right to garrison certain fortresses.

palities, while the Turks for their part were unwilling to take this step until Greece had been satisfactorily pacified. Thus, wrote Canning at the end of February 1824, 'the tranquillity and perhaps the existence of the Turkish empire are put to hazard upon the single issue of the next campaign in Greece.'[31]

At the end of April, however, the persistent Strangford at last persuaded the Turks to start withdrawing their troops from the Principalities. Unfortunately, a month later, the Russian plan for Greece was published in a French newspaper. The Turks, of course, were furious, but they were content to expend their wrath on Strangford and, rather surprisingly, the slow evacuation of the Principalities was not halted. The Russians responded by sending a commercial attaché to Constantinople and in August, after much prodding from Bagot, the Tsar publicly nominated M de Ribeaupierre as his minister to Constantinople. Canning, for his part, went so far as to announce that his cousin Stratford would go as special plenipotentiary to the proposed congress on Greece. But as de Ribeaupierre showed no sign of leaving for Constantinople, Canning could not make up his mind to send Stratford off to St Petersburg. 'The Greek problem is full of peril and plague,' he wrote to Liverpool in the middle of October.[32]

A fortnight later his doubts were resolved by the arrival of a letter from the Greek provisional government categorically rejecting the Russian plan. The Greeks had set their hearts on complete independence and were outraged to discover from the French press that the Tsar, whom they regarded as their natural protector, was ready to settle for less. In their disillusionment with Russia, they turned to England, for although she had not yet recognised any of the new South American states, news of Canning's sympathetic attitude towards them had travelled as far as Greece. His sympathy, however, did not stretch to the kind of help the Greeks wanted. As he pointed out in his reply, England could not engage in unprovoked hostilities in a quarrel not her own, especially against a friendly power like Turkey. But she was ready to mediate, and she would not participate in any attempt to force on the Greeks a plan which they had so uncompromisingly rejected.[33]

In short, the Greeks got a polite brush-off. But privately Canning confessed himself to be better pleased with them 'than for anything they have done since Epaminondas or (as Mr Maxwell, the Scotch member, pronounces the other worthy) of Harry Stodgiton, meaning, it was supposed, Aristogeiton.'[34] They had given him a plausible excuse for wriggling out of the St Petersburg congress, since there was no point in discussing the Russian plan if the Greeks as well as the Turks were adamantly hostile; it could only be imposed by force and to that England was resolutely opposed.

Both Alexander and Metternich were extremely put out by the British withdrawal. The first had wanted England's endorsement of his Greek plan, while the second had hoped that she would take on the thankless task of persuading the Tsar not to impose his plan by force. Canning thought it likely that the congress would fail and hoped that he would then be able to intervene to good effect. But would he? The Russian army and people were strongly in favour of a war against Turkey which they assumed would be a walkover. The breakdown of the congress might well be followed by a Russian invasion of the Ottoman Empire which it was Canning's (as well as Metternich's) primary aim to prevent.

In an attempt to mollify and restrain Alexander, Canning sent his cousin Stratford to St Petersburg, not to attend the congress, but to try to explain the British government's point of view. He did not get very far. Alexander, in his wrath, decided that if the English would not talk about Greece around his conference table, they should not talk to him about it at all.* Towards the end of January 1825, Count Lieven in London received instructions to keep his mouth shut on Greece. 'The Emperor of Russia seems to be in a passion,' commented Canning coolly, '. . . he will be damned if he ever talks Greek to us again.'[35] But barely nine months later Alexander was obliged to change his mind.

* Stratford Canning's two months in St Petersburg were not entirely fruitless. He concluded the negotiations that Bagot had begun on British and Russian claims in North-west America, and before he left the Russian foreign minister, Count Nesselrode, did discuss the Greek problem with him. But as he refused to give a pledge against the use of force Stratford refused to consider attending the allied congress on Greece that was then meeting in St Petersburg. (Lane-Poole, I, pp. 363/6)

CHAPTER XVIII

Catholics, Corn and Currency
1825-1826

When Canning announced that England would not attend the St Petersburg conference on Greece, Mme Lieven declared that his decision broke the last bond uniting England to the Continent. 'It means a complete revolution in the political system of Europe; it means the breaking up of the Alliance; in a word, it means that Mr Canning gets his own way . . .'[1] By the beginning of 1825, Canning had insisted on pursuing an 'English' rather than a 'European' policy on Spain, Spanish America, Portugal, Brazil and Greece. In the case of Spain, the outcome had not been glorious. Greece was still something of a cliff-hanger. But elsewhere the policy had paid off. Instead of playing a largely passive role in European politics, as she had done since 1818, England had struck out on a course of her own, and the dividends, in terms of political prestige, were unmistakable. Canning's aim had been to make England an object of fear, rather than of cajolery and contempt.[2] To Wellington this merely meant being rude to the rulers and statesmen he had been accustomed to hobnob with in the years after Waterloo. But – no doubt to some extent for the same reason – with the general public it was immensely popular; and although Wellington assured Mme Lieven that Canning's popularity was a 'false glitter',[3] it frightened the King into giving way over the recognition of Spain's former colonies.

Canning's South American victory marked the beginning of the end of the activities of the Cottage Coterie. Early in March 1825 Esterhazy confessed to Lord Strangford, who told Canning, that the 'Cabal' was now convinced that it was hopeless to try to overturn the Foreign Secretary.[4] Encouraged by this news, Canning pressed home his advantage. Metternich was on a visit to Paris and had been secretly invited by the King to visit him at Windsor. Canning told Granville to let the Austrian Chancellor know that although the British Foreign Secretary was aware of his intrigues, he was still prepared to co-operate with him where they agreed – as on Brazil and Greece – but he did not recommend him to visit England.[5] Canning also used a more unorthodox method of getting his message across. He told Joan, who was visiting the Granvilles, that if she met Metternich she was to let him know that her husband knew about the intrigues against him, 'but that while there is a House of Commons, I defy them.'⁶* It is not known whether Metternich received this message, but he heard enough from Granville and Esterhazy to abandon his visit to England.

Canning knew he was strong enough to triumph over his enemies, foreign and domestic. What he had no reason to expect was a voluntary overture from his royal master. But the King had in fact been gradually coming round to the view that since he could not get rid of Canning, he had better make the best of him. In any case, he was too astute not to grasp that some of the popularity of Canning's policies would rub off on to himself if he supported his Foreign Secretary, and that, contrary to what he had been constantly assured, Canning had not lost him his status among the continental powers, but only changed it from the tail of Europe to the head.⁷ So he decided to send him an olive branch. On April 27, 1825, when Canning was recovering in bed from a severe attack of gout, he was amazed to learn that Sir William Knighton wished to see him for a few minutes to give him a message from the King. The few minutes stretched to nearly three hours, and when Knighton at last went, Canning, 'with a countenance beaming with pleasure', announced to his secretary, Stapleton, that they had had 'a most curious and satisfactory conversation'. After making the most solicitous inquiries about Canning's health, Knighton had assured him at great length that the King was now perfectly satisfied that his fears about the conduct of foreign policy had been unfounded. Knighton also expressed his belief that gatherings of the Cottage Coterie were no longer of any political importance, and finally offered his own services to Canning in any way that might be helpful.⁸

This interview marked a turning-point in Canning's relationship with the King. Henceforward, although occasionally still guilty of small duplicities towards his Foreign Secretary, the King on the whole gave him his full backing.† Equally important, he abandoned his attempt to pursue a separate and all too often contradictory foreign policy through his Hanoverian diplomats. In November 1825, Count

* It was during this visit to Paris that Harriet became engaged to the young Earl of Clanricarde, described by Lady Granville as 'immensely rich, quite good-looking enough, clever and very gentlemanlike'. The progress of the courtship was the subject of much anxious comment in Canning's letters to Joan, intermixed with instructions on what to say to Metternich and Villèle.

† Wellington, who had a long audience with the King a week after Knighton's visit to Canning, found him very civil but 'different'. (Mrs Arbuthnot Journal, I, p. 392)

Munster officially informed them of the new régime in a circular despatch.[9] The following January, when the King was secretly given a letter from the Austrian government, he read it aloud in Canning's presence and asked his Foreign Secretary to advise on the answer. Afterwards Canning told the British ambassador in Vienna to inform Metternich that the British constitution did not allow personal correspondence between the King and other sovereigns on public matters.[10] Canning now saw all the Hanoverian correspondence, which, incidentally, he was vexed to discover often contained much better intelligence than that provided by British diplomats. In return, Canning began to show the King his private letters from abroad. 'I am now upon that footing with HM,' he wrote to Granville on October 13, 'that enables me to approach him with details which on a more distant and merely official footing I should not think myself justified in obtruding upon him.' This meant that Granville must take more trouble with his private letters, in which Canning detected 'a carelessness which I have felt it would not do you good to show – and that as much in the handwriting as in the matter.' And he added, perhaps to soften the reproof: 'All Kings are particular about handwriting.'[11]

The seal was set on the royal conversion to Canningite policies at the Austrian ambassador's farewell audience just before Christmas 1825.* The King unexpectedly revealed that many months before Esterhazy had confessed to him that he was ashamed of the way Canning had been treated. Esterhazy, with tears in his eyes, immediately seized both Canning's hands and assured him that this was quite true. He had at first been very dissatisfied with Canning's refusal to join the St Petersburg conference, but he had soon realised that he was quite right to have nothing to do with such a useless exercise. The conference had in fact broken down some months before, and Canning was quick to improve the occasion by pointing out that in England they could not afford to take any public step which would obviously lead to no good. With this irreproachable sentiment the King concurred, adding grandly: 'When we see our way, and can employ our own influence, we can do anything.' And by way of illustration, he mentioned Brazil, whose separation from Portugal had recently been negotiated by Sir Charles Stuart.[12] Altogether, Canning's official audiences can rarely, if ever, have caused him so much surprise, satisfaction and – one suspects – private amusement.

On a personal level, too, relations between Canning and the King

* In fact Esterhazy remained in London because of a request by the King that he should not be recalled.

improved out of all recognition. Canning had always had a greater tolerance of royal quirks than some of his more aristocratic colleagues and was perfectly willing to let bygones be bygones. Whenever opportunity offered, he made himself useful and agreeable beyond the strict call of duty. On one occasion, when the King was recovering from a severe illness, Canning sat by his bedside to help him, as it were, with his arrears of homework – picking out for him the most important despatches and relieving him of the rest. On another, he found the King in very low spirits because Lord Ponsonby, with whom Lady Conyngham had once been in love, was returning to England from a post in Corfu. Canning tactfully suggested that Ponsonby, who was able as well as extremely handsome, should be appointed to the embassy in faraway Buenos Aires, and promised to arrange that he should proceed to his new post as quickly as possible.*

The King, for his part, went out of his way to be gracious. In the summer of 1826, he invited Canning to one of his weekend parties at the Cottage and made a point of being particularly polite to him under the inwardly disapproving eye of the Duke of Wellington. Shortly before, he had told him that he would like to show some public appreciation of his services. Canning replied that he wanted nothing for himself and 'the circumstances of my family would not justify me in accepting a peerage in the way in which alone I have ever thought of accepting one for them – *not* in my own person.'[13] Presumably he meant that in appropriate circumstances he would have accepted a peerage for his heir; but of his two surviving sons, William was dedicated to a naval career and Carlo was still only a boy. So Canning suggested that the King should grant a peerage to Charles Ellis, whom he regarded as the person nearest to him after his own family. The King was delighted with this suggestion. He thought it showed true goodness of heart in Canning and he liked Ellis because he was a 'perfect gentleman' and because of his 'steady affection' for his friend.[14] So some weeks later an extremely surprised Charles Ellis was informed that the King wished to elevate him to the peerage. After taking twenty-four hours to get over the shock, he accepted the honour and became Lord Seaford. 'It is impossible,' wrote Canning to Granville,

---

* Ponsonby was delighted to be posted to Buenos Aires, but dreadfully disappointed with the place when he got there. 'No eye,' he lamented, 'ever saw so odious a country as this Buenos Aires is . . . I really sigh when I think I may spend my days here . . . this land of mud and putrid carcasses – no horse, no roads, no houses . . . no books, no theatre that can be endured . . . Nothing good but beef.' (Bagot, II, p. 308)

'to describe the kindness of the K[ing] on this occasion. If HM had been at C[hrist] C[hurch] with us, and full of the recollections of those times, he could not have entered more cordially into all my feelings.'[15] According to the conventions of the time, Ellis had acquired his peerage in an acceptable way, although this did not prevent Canning's enemies from waxing very indignant about it. It was indeed, as they said, rather ridiculous, but in asking for it and in giving it the King and Canning had each showed an attractive and endearing side of his character.

With the support of King, prime minister and public opinion, Canning's personal position looked very strong. But it was not as strong as it seemed because its foundations were always liable to crumble. Liverpool could keep his colleagues' mutual antagonisms more or less under control but he could not heal them. On the most important domestic issue of all – the Catholic (or Irish) problem – the Cabinet's differences were openly assumed to be irreconcilable. But the Catholic problem would not conveniently go away just because the government could not agree on how to solve it. On the contrary, it became more inflamed, and consequently more intractable. 'I look upon the session till Easter,' wrote Canning on February 15, 1825, 'as monopolised by the grievances and distractions of Ireland.'[16]

By the beginning of 1825, the government had become seriously worried by the activities of the Catholic Association. Since Daniel O'Connell, the Irish Catholic leader, had launched it in the spring of 1823, the Association had grown greatly in size and influence. Many Catholics joined because they despaired of ever obtaining political equality through Westminster. The Association engaged in furious polemics with the Orange societies, overawed the magistrates and ran its meetings as if they were sessions of the House of Commons. It seemed to be making a bid for political power and might, it was feared, end by demanding complete secession. Wellington foresaw civil war and the King talked of rebellion.

Something had to be done, and the Cabinet agreed, without too much difficulty, to try to bring peace to Ireland by banning both the Catholic Association and the Orange societies. Its decision was strongly attacked by the Whigs, who insisted that immediate emancipation must accompany the banning of the Association, and throughout the protracted debates on the bill, they bitterly accused Canning and the other pro-Catholic Tories of deserting the cause for the sake of power and popularity. Canning described the debates as 'very disagreeable and to me personally very difficult'.[17] But this time, instead of losing his temper as he had done two years earlier, he turned the tables on his persecutors with an extremely effective defence both of the government's policy and his own consistency. The opposition, he triumphantly told Joan afterwards, 'have given me a golden opportunity, which I could never have contrived for myself, of discriminating *my* Catholic policies from theirs, and of acquiring the confidence of the Protestants of England which I wanted before, but of which, since Tuesday's debate, I have received some singular demonstrations.'[18] And to Granville he wrote that he now had 'an intelligible and assured position upon a ground hitherto doubtful and slippery; a position in which . . . I may perhaps hereafter – but at my own time and in my own way – be enabled to do some good to Ireland, and to bring this most intractable question to a pause, if not a final settlement.'[19]

Canning felt so deeply that the future of Ireland depended on granting political equality to all her people, whatever their religion, that he seriously contemplated resigning over this issue. To take this step when he was at the height of his fame and popularity as Foreign Secretary would indeed have been a striking gesture. But would it have done any good? It might possibly have had some effect on public opinion which was exceptionally volatile on this question. But it would not have changed the views of the King or the ultra Protestants in the Cabinet and the House of Lords. Brougham tauntingly asked Canning why, if he could make the King and the ultras change their mind over recognising the new South American states, he could not do likewise over the Catholic question. One reason, of course, was that the opposition in the Cabinet to emancipation, which included both Liverpool and Peel, was stronger than it had been to recognition. But Canning's trump card in carrying recognition had been that he knew, and his opponents knew, that he had the strong backing of public opinion as well as of the House of Commons. This he could not claim on the Catholic issue. And, he asked the Commons: 'What would a minister do with only these benches, and with no England at his back?'[20]

Canning's estimate of the state of public feeling was a major – perhaps the decisive – factor in his calculations. His resignation would either simply gravely weaken the liberal tendencies in the government, leaving the ultras to make all the running – in foreign as well as domestic policies. Or it would break up the government completely, leaving Canning free to form a coalition with the Whigs pledged to carry emancipation. Canning thought the first alternative the most likely and was not attracted by the second. He believed that there was still a 'great inert mass of opposition to the Catholic question' in the country; and that any government which tried to carry the Catholic question before the country was ready, would not only fail, but would light up an anti-Catholic flame which it would be most difficult to quench.[21]

It was only on this tactical issue of dealing 'gently and considerately' with Protestant prejudices that Canning differed from the opposition. When on February 28 Burdett, as a counter-blow to the ban on the Catholic Association, moved that the House should debate the whole Catholic question, Canning supported the motion in a way that can have left the opposition in no doubt that his heart was in the right place. He spoke leaning on a crutch in the throes of a bad attack of gout – 'while I was speaking,' he told Joan, 'gout was painful and foot angry and swelled, but the exertion only *matured* a fit which was coming on at all events . . .' It was well worth the effort, he felt, because there were so many 'loose' votes, and if he had been thought to be holding back, many others would have done the same. He spoke for only twenty to thirty minutes 'but I put at least two hours worth of speakable matter into that space – and tried a new *genre* of speaking, which had prodigious success – such as becomes an elderly gentleman with a stick.'[22] Canning was never given to underestimating his own performance. But on this occasion his judgment was confirmed by no less a critic than Brougham, who said that Canning had contrived to concentrate more force and effect into a small space than he ever remembered having heard in a speech before.[23]

Burdett's motion was passed by a slender majority of thirteen. Its effect was to authorise the introduction of yet another Catholic Relief Bill. It was carefully framed to assuage Protestant fears, and on May 10 it passed its third reading in the Commons by 21 votes. A week later, the Lords threw it out by 48 votes, after Liverpool, in a speech of uncompromising hostility, had gone so far as to declare that if the measure was passed, the Protestant succession would not be worth a farthing.

Liverpool had always been reckoned a moderate Protestant, and the violence of his attack on the bill surprised everyone including, apparently, himself. He was probably suffering from the effects of a protracted personal crisis over the Catholic issue. It was indeed a paradoxical situation. The country as a whole was going through one of its periodic bouts of 'no-popery' near-hysteria. A flood of anti-Catholic petitions descended on Parliament. People eagerly bought up copies (decorated in gold) of a sensational speech by the Duke of York in which he had solemnly warned the Lords against the dangers of giving political power to the Catholics. When the bill was finally thrown out there were public rejoicings and in many towns the church bells were rung. Liverpool, however, was becoming more and more convinced that sooner or later the Catholic claims must be conceded. But instead of concluding, as was widely rumoured, that he had better change sides, he was coming round to the view that he had better go altogether. His distress was increased by Peel, who was finding his position as the only Protestant cabinet minister in the Commons increasingly invidious and embarrassing. On April 29 he told the prime minister that he definitely must resign. Liverpool, in despair, declared that if Peel went, he must go too.

Unknown to the general public the government was apparently about to collapse and if it did, the chances of keeping out the Whigs were minimal. If the King sent for Wellington, it was doubtful whether Canning would serve under him; and who else but Canning or Peel could lead in the Commons? But if, as Liverpool hoped, the King sent for Canning, it was even more unlikely that Wellington and other ultra Tories would serve under him, and he would be forced to turn to the Whigs. When Liverpool, made aware by candid friends of the 'confusion and mischief without end'[24] which his resignation would create, indicated that he would stay if the Home Secretary would stay too, Peel in his turn found himself unable to resist the arguments that he ought to change his mind.

In spite of their disagreements, nobody really wanted to be personally responsible for bringing down the government, although for a few days Canning seemed ready to risk it. On May 18, the day after the Lords threw out the Catholic Relief Bill, he suddenly and unexpectedly told Liverpool that he felt it was impossible for the government to maintain its neutral attitude on the Catholic question and he proposed to summon a Cabinet meeting to discuss it.[25] But when the Cabinet met on the 20th, it received his proposal that it should make up its collective mind with such obvious lack of enthusiasm that a few days later he told his colleagues that he would not press the matter.

It was odd that he should have raised it in the first place. Probably it was an impulsive reaction to Liverpool's speech. Although he later defended in the Commons the prime minister's right to his own opinions, he confessed privately that they were an 'astounding disappointment' to him. On reflection, however, he must have realised that with feeling in the country running strongly against the Catholics, it was the worst possible moment to create a government crisis on this issue. He was convinced, he told the Commons on May 26, that his resignation would hinder, not help, a Catholic settlement.[26] But it did not pass unnoticed that for the first time he publicly declared that he felt himself at liberty to raise the matter in the Cabinet whenever he chose.

In the circumstances, it is perhaps less surprising that Canning should have made a tactical error of judgment in trying to bring the Catholic problem to an issue than that he should have had the good sense to retreat quickly from an untenable position. 'One's mind at full stretch,' he once remarked to Joan, 'with one's body failing one, is a very trying combination.'[27] In the last few years of his life he had to cope with this combination most of the time. During 1825, his old enemy, gout, attacked him with relentless persistence. It prevented him from taking much part in the debates on the Catholic Relief Bill after his initial effort on February 28. By the middle of May he was able to ride a little way but could not use a pen because 'the gout still keeps a small garrison in the foot and one in the hand.'[28] When he spoke in the Commons on May 26 he appeared to be severely indisposed and was at times scarcely audible. By the end of June he still could not walk properly and in July he fell dangerously ill again with some bowel complaint.

One of Canning's friends remarked that his only chance of overcoming his tendency to repeated attacks of gout was to live 'systematically'.[29] If he meant that Canning must learn to work regular hours and relax in between whiles, he was asking the impossible of someone with such a highly strung temperament who was emotionally, as well as intellectually, involved in whatever he was doing and who was incapable of doing things by halves. When the bill banning the Catholic Association was before the Commons, Canning besought Granville to make Villèle understand 'the entire absorption of my whole time and existence' by the debates. 'Monday and Tuesday quite overthrew me,' he went on. 'Make Villèle consider a little . . . what it is to go into the House, as I did on Monday at five in the afternoon, remain there till two in the morning; then to have for sleep, refreshment, and such business as will not stand still, only twelve hours; then a Cabinet from two to four, then to be in the House again at five to nine, to get up to speak for two hours at eleven, and to get to bed not before five.'[30]

Canning had great reserves of nervous energy, but he expended them with reckless prodigality. Just as he never learnt to suffer fools gladly, so he never learnt to treat with philosophic resignation the often tiresome routine business of the House of Commons. At the end of the 1825 session he complained to Granville of 'various petty and vexatious questions which give more trouble than they are worth, and which it is as unpleasant to deal with as if they were of the most vital importance to the existence of the Government.'[31] He did not let his work, whether parliamentary or official, get on top of him, but he let it take too much out of him, and he could not bring himself to shed any of the load. He once admitted to a friend that the two functions of Foreign Secretary and Leader of the House 'are too much for any man – and ought not to be united; though I of course would rather die under them than separate them, or consent to have separation in my person.'[32]

At the end of August 1825, Canning went to stay with Colonel Bolton on the banks of Windermere, where he enjoyed a fortnight of '*comparative* abstraction from hard work'.[33] (It was only 'comparative' because he still kept a close eye on the Foreign Office.) 'If air,' he wrote to Huskisson, 'plenty of exercise, and a temperance amounting to privation, can make me well, and keep me so, I shall return in robust health to my office.'[34]

The visit to Westmorland of the Foreign Secretary, the most famous and popular statesman of the day, stimulated considerable local celebrations. On his arrival at Kendal, Canning was received at the King's Arms by the mayor and all the local dignitaries. He was entertained to a cold collation (at which he himself drank only soda water) and presented with an address to which, according to the local paper, he replied 'in a most beautiful manner'. The house party at Storrs included three of the best-known literary figures of the day – Walter Scott, William Wordsworth and Robert Southey. The celebrations included a grand procession of boats on the lake, with Canning and Scott (each wearing a white hat) sitting with Wordsworth in their host's barge. The procession was accompanied by 'the roar of cannon, the sound of bells, and the harmonious strains of two bands of music'. It must have been a gratifying and stimulating occasion for the guest of honour. But in spite of all the lighthearted junketing Scott did not fail to observe that Canning's health had changed greatly for the worse.[35]

While Canning was still on holiday at Storrs, the date of the dissolution of Parliament was added to the list of issues on which the members of the government disagreed. Parliament's seven-year life cycle would in any case end the following year. The problem was whether it would not be politically expedient to cut it short that autumn. The Protestants in the Cabinet wanted to take advantage of the current anti-Catholic feeling in the country to try to get a House of Commons less firmly in favour of emancipation. Wellington argued that they could not go on indefinitely with the two Houses of Parliament so strongly committed to opposite sides of the question. This was true enough, but the pro-Catholics naturally did not feel that a more Protestant Commons was the right way to break the deadlock. On the other hand, apart from the Catholic issue, there was much to be said for getting the elections over while the country was enjoying the effects of an excellent harvest, especially as there were signs that a new financial and economic crisis was imminent. In the end, it was agreed that Parliament should be allowed to run its full course, but that neither the Catholic question nor the corn laws (the other explosive issue) should be raised during its final session.

The temporary truce on the Catholic question was kept, but the plan to shelve contentious economic issues broke down. Before the end of 1825, the economic and financial crisis which Huskisson and others had seen approaching in the autumn, had burst upon the government. For nearly two years the country had been riding on the crest of a wave of prosperity. Money had been plentiful, credit easy and the frenzy of speculation was stimulated to crazy lengths by the government's recognition of the new South American states. 'Everybody,' wrote Mme Lieven in January 1825, 'from the lady to the footman, is risking pin-money or wages in these enterprises. Huge fortunes have been made in a week.'[36] Inevitably, the boom collapsed. Over-confidence was succeeded by blind panic. There was a run on the banks and in December 1825 more than seventy were forced to close their doors.

The emergency measures taken by the government in collaboration with the Bank of England were prompt, bold and almost entirely successful. But the aftermath of the crisis dominated the short parliamentary session of 1826. As part of a much-needed reform of the banking system, Liverpool proposed to abolish the issue of paper money in small denominations by the country banks. This was bitterly opposed by many country gentlemen, city merchants and country bankers who usually supported the government. On February 10, 1826, Canning asked Liverpool whether he really was determined to carry the measure and take the consequences, for 'the perfect consciousness of the truth that such is the determination is necessary to govern my language.'[37] Liverpool was determined, and Canning duly made a powerful speech in support of the bill. But without the help of the opposition, it would almost certainly have been lost. 'It is but just to the Opposition,' wrote Canning afterwards, '. . . to say that their cordial support helped very much to discourage a combination of our *friends*.'[38]

About a fortnight later, the government again looked like foundering on the rock of Lord Liverpool's economic principles. It was under strong pressure, especially from the City, to oil the country's economic wheels by an issue of Exchequer bills. Canning tended to feel that, although objectionable in principle, it might for once be necessary to give way because nothing else seemed capable of restoring confidence. 'My opinion,' he wrote, ' – perhaps from not understanding the matter so well, or from not rating anything of the sort so highly – was by no means so strong as his [Liverpool's]; indeed was, at first, in the opposite direction.'[39] But Liverpool felt that since the business community had only itself to blame for its present troubles, it would be quite wrong for the government to bail it out. So strong were his *laissez-faire* convictions – one might almost say morals – that on February 28, when the Commons was due to debate a petition for an issue of Exchequer bills, he told Canning to make it clear that he would rather resign than implement such a measure.

Canning was considerably taken back. But he loyally carried out his instructions, much to the consternation of many government supporters in the Commons.[40] Rather surprisingly, the opposition failed to seize a golden opportunity to force a vote against the government; and after some days of agitated and acrimonious negotiation between Liverpool and the Bank of England, an expedient was devised by which the Bank was able to release some funds to the public in a way that satisfied Liverpool's scruples. Peel and Huskisson thought he was right to have them. But Canning, whose enemies often accused him of exercising an undue influence over the prime minister, was prepared to support him to the point of resignation, not out of conviction, but out of loyalty. It would, he wrote afterwards, 'have been a mighty foolish kind of death'.[41]

Early in March, Canning reported to Wellington, who was abroad, that on the whole the economic situation was improving, but there was still much suffering and he feared there would be more before the crisis was weathered.[42] His fears were justified. During the next two months, unemployment and starvation caused severe distress and unrest in the manufacturing districts, especially in Lancashire. The liberal wing of the government realised that something more than repression was called for. By the mid-1820s, although agriculture had largely recovered from its postwar depression and had achieved a considerable measure of stability and prosperity, it was failing to provide an adequate and steady supply of cheap bread for the rapidly increasing industrial population. Under the corn laws of 1814 and 1822, corn could only be imported when the price of domestic supplies rose above 80s. a quarter. There might be the most acute distress when the price stood at 79s., but the government could do nothing whatever to relieve it so long as the price did not rise another shilling.

Liberal Tories like Liverpool, Huskisson and Canning were convinced that sooner or later this would have to be changed. But the landed interest was very strong, both in the Cabinet and in Parliament, and corn was as explosive and divisive a political issue as the Catholic question. Wellington assured Liverpool in the autumn of 1825 that it would not be possible to force through Parliament any alteration of the corn laws 'which shall not be founded upon the principle of securing to the landed interest the same advantages as they enjoy at present.'[43] Liverpool feared he was right. But by the following May his hand had been forced by the prevailing distress and he himself proposed two temporary measures to relieve the shortage. One was to release up to 300,000 quarters of wheat stored in warehouses on to the market at a reduced duty; the other was to grant the government a temporary discretionary power to import 500,000 quarters of wheat at a low duty.

That staunch Whig, Thomas Creevey, declared that Liverpool's proposals were certainly 'the boldest thing that ever was attempted by a Government – after deprecating any discussion on the Corn Laws during the present session, to try at the end to carry a Corn Law of their own by a *coup-de-main*, and to hold out the landed grandees as the enemies of the manufacturing population if they oppose it . . .'[44] But the landowners, who were reported to be in a terrible commotion, did oppose the measures. However much they might profess to lament the plight of the working classes, they were determined that it should not be relieved at their expense. They did not object so much to the release of the bonded wheat; indeed, it was not easy to do so when, as Canning pointed out, most of it was actually stored in districts where there was 'a grinding, pressing, dangerous and destructive distress'.[45] But they did strongly object to the request for a discretionary power to import corn; it aroused ineradicable suspicions that the government intended to tamper with the corn laws – which, indeed, was Liverpool's long-term but not immediate intention. 'I never saw,' wrote Creevey gleefully, 'anything like the fury of both Whig and Tory landholders at Canning's speech; but the Tories much the most violent of the two.' It was considered, he added, as 'a breaking down of the corn laws'.[46] But with the help of the Whigs both bills were passed, and by surprisingly large majorities. 'Our party,' lamented the Tory Mrs Arbuthnot, 'as a party, is entirely broken up.'[47]

Domestic issues had proved as divisive as foreign ones, and when M.P.s dispersed after the dissolution of Parliament in May 1826, the gap between the liberal and ultra Tories had conspicuously widened. The ultras felt obliged to make the best of Liverpool; but they had never had any inhibitions about criticising that parvenu, Huskisson. Canning, on the other hand, felt a great respect for his intellectual ability. He stoutly defended Huskisson's liberalising measures in the Commons, and for this reason, and because of his eminence and popularity, he became associated with them in the public mind. He was indeed becoming increasingly impatient of those (mostly in his own party) who made a virtue of being old-fashioned and ascribed the country's economic difficulties to 'hasty and sudden innovations in trade'.[48] On one occasion, in an impassioned defence of Huskisson for his moves towards a free trade system, he denounced those who equated improvement with Jacobinism. 'These persons,' he declared, 'seem to imagine that, under no possible circumstances, can an honest man endeavour to keep his country upon a line with the progress of political knowledge, and to adapt its course to the varying circumstances of the world.' And he ended with a warning that 'they who resist indiscriminately all improvement as innovation, may find themselves compelled at last to submit to innovations, although they are not improvements.'[49]

It was hardly surprising that many Whigs, who had little sympathy for the pretensions and prejudices of the grandees in their own party, should have approved of a politician who spoke in these terms, and should have felt moved to support a government of which he was such a prominent member. 'We are certainly,' Tierney told the Commons in April 1826, 'to all intents and purposes, a branch of his majesty's government.' The measures are ours, he added, but the emoluments belong to the gentlemen in office.[50] How much longer, he and his listeners may have wondered, before the emoluments were shared?

CHAPTER XIX

'Let us fly to the aid of Portugal'
1825-1826

The four power conference on Greece, which met in St Petersburg early in 1825, was a bitter disappointment to Alexander. His allies stubbornly refused to authorise him to use force against Turkey and after some months he suspended the meetings in disgust. Canning, it seemed, was right in believing that Metternich merely intended to 'amuse' the Tsar while the Greek revolt was being stamped out. To make matters worse, during a visit to Paris that spring Metternich openly preened himself on his skill in managing the Tsar. When these 'astonishing indiscretions' – as Mme Lieven called them – reached Alexander's ears, his disillusionment with the Austrian Chancellor was complete.[1] In the middle of August Russian diplomats in Europe were officially notified of their emperor's breach with Metternich.

But having given himself a free hand over Greece, Alexander hesitated to make use of it. Instead, he began to think it was time to 'talk Greek' with England again in spite of his strong suspicion that the English Foreign Secretary was no better than a Jacobin. That summer Mme Lieven returned to Russia for some weeks. Alexander took advantage of her visit to brief himself about the views of the British government and finally sent her back with secret instructions to her husband to work for a rapprochement between England and Russia so that between them they could settle the Eastern question.[2] What precisely he had in mind was not clear, and Count Lieven understandably obeyed the 'living despatch', represented by his wife, with caution. But in two long talks with Canning at the end of October, he did make it clear that Russia had broken with Austria and France on the Greek question and that he himself felt free to talk about it again.

Alexander's intentions towards Greece never were made clear because on December 1 he died suddenly at Taganrog in the Crimea. Very little was known about the new Tsar, Nicholas I, whose accession was as much a surprise to himself as to everyone else.* But the omens

* The Grand-duke Constantine had renounced the throne in 1822. But Alexander had kept his abdication secret, even from Nicholas, thus causing several weeks of confusion in December 1825.

were not encouraging. It was known that he wished to follow his brother's policies, and many people (including Canning) assumed that the unpredictable Alexander had suddenly gone to the Crimea in order to prepare for war against the Turks. Moreover Nicholas was forced to start his reign by putting down a palace revolt. Presumably he would be tempted to establish himself on his throne by giving way to the popular demand for a war against the infidel Turks, which could easily develop into a general European conflict. Austria and France would rush in to seize a share of the disintegrating Ottoman Empire and England would be left as the Turks' only friend.

The news of Alexander's death reached England on December 18. Canning was stimulated rather than dismayed by the dangers and uncertainties of the new situation. At any rate it might be hoped that the principles of the Holy Alliance would wither away now that their inventor and leading exponent was dead. His first concern was to send someone to St Petersburg who could win the new Tsar's confidence and dissuade him from war. The best person was obviously the Duke of Wellington. Nothing would be more likely to flatter the young Tsar than to be sent Europe's most famous general to congratulate him on his accession; and no one could give him a more impressive warning against the folly of war. Moreover with such a high-powered emissary in St Petersburg, it might be possible to make some progress towards solving the Greek problem. In September Canning had told some Greek delegates, who had come to London in search of an English prince for a still rather hypothetical Greek throne, that although England must remain neutral in their fight for independence, she would try to help them by promoting a fair compromise with the Turks.[3] Wellington was, it is true, strongly pro-Turk and had little use for the Greeks. But he understood as well as Canning that the Greek revolt must be stopped from developing into a general war and he had lost all his illusions about the congress system as a means of maintaining order and peace.[4] 'I hope,' wrote Canning, 'to save Greece through the agency of the Russian name upon the fears of Turkey, without a war, which the Duke of Wellington is the fittest man to deprecate.'[5] Wellington accepted the mission without hesitation although he had been ill and the King, for that reason, was very reluctant to let him go. He was, the duke told Canning, as well able and willing to undertake a long journey as ever he was.[6] Canning's private comment was that 'the selection of *another* person would have done his health more prejudice than all the frosts and thaws of the hyperborean regions can do it.'[7]

Count Lieven was so astonished and gratified when Canning told him that Wellington was to go to St Petersburg that he could not refrain from shedding tears of pleasure.[8] The appointment, he felt, showed that Canning really was interested in working with Russia. From this point on the understanding and co-operation between Canning and the Lievens grew steadily stronger. Canning had always got on well with Lieven and counted himself lucky to have no worse a representative from the Russian court. With the formidable Mme Lieven, hitherto one of his severest critics, he had had little contact. He set out to remedy this by paying her social calls – to the intense curiosity of the rest of the diplomatic corps – and by the spring of 1826 they were having regular *tête-à-têtes* every Sunday. His French was halting, but after the first quarter of an hour, when he had got into his stride, everything went swimmingly; and his way of expressing himself was both so highly individual and so precise that Mme Lieven had to admit that it was a pleasure to listen to him.[9]

While Canning, in consultation with Lieven, was mulling over the precise brief on Greece that Wellington was to carry to St Petersburg, a new hazard appeared about to threaten the hard-pressed Greeks in the Morea. In 1824 the Sultan, feeling unable to crush them himself – although they had gone a long way towards destroying themselves by their internal feuding – called on his vassal, Mehemet Ali, the Pasha of Egypt, to do so for him. Mehemet Ali entrusted the task to his son, Ibrahim Pasha, an able and ferocious soldier, who landed in the Peloponnese in January 1825 and by the end of the year had captured and devastated most of the Morea. Missolonghi was the only important remaining centre of resistance. It was rumoured that Ibrahim had still worse in store for the Greeks. According to a report received by the Russian government, he was planning to carry the whole Greek population of the Morea into slavery in North Africa and replace them by Mohammedan colonisers.

When Canning was shown this report by Lieven in the autumn of 1825, he could not at first believe a plan 'so monstrous and extravagant'. But after Stratford Canning, whom his cousin had appointed British envoy to the Porte in October, had picked up similar reports on his way to Constantinople through the Greek Archipelago, the possibility that such a plan existed could no longer be ignored. The atrocities committed by both sides since the Greeks first rose in revolt had shocked European observers and troubled the consciences of the statesmen who could not agree on how to end the war. But a forced transfer of population would give the conflict what Canning called a new 'character of barbarism and *barbarization*'.[10] He was genuinely shocked. But he also realised that Ibrahim's plan gave Britain humanitarian grounds for intervening on behalf of the Greeks which could hardly be criticised. Moreover a definite British commitment to restrain Turkish excesses in the Morea might help Wellington to persuade Nicholas to hold his hand while Stratford was trying to persuade the Turks to accept English mediation.

Instructions were therefore sent to Stratford Canning to tell the Porte 'in the most distinct terms' that Britain would 'not permit the execution of a system of depopulation which exceeds the permitted violences of war, and transgresses the conventional restraints of civilisation.' He was to emphasise that it was Britain's 'fixed determination' to prevent the establishment of a new Barbary state in Europe and that she could certainly do this by interposing her naval forces between the Morea and Egypt.[11] At the same time the commander of the British naval forces in the Mediterranean was told to send a reliable officer to warn Ibrahim that he would be forcibly prevented from carrying off the Greeks of the Morea. In the middle of March, a British naval officer, Captain Spencer, had two interviews with Ibrahim in his camp outside Missolonghi, but failed to get him either to admit or deny any depopulation plan. When Stratford Canning arrived at Constantinople towards the end of February, his inquiries were equally fruitless. The mystery of Ibrahim's intentions was never solved; if he really had contemplated a transfer of populations, he did not attempt to carry it out. The incident, however, shows that by now Canning was prepared in certain circumstances to use the Royal Navy to protect the Greeks, even though – as he frankly admitted – this would involve a breach of neutrality.

But there was no question of helping the Greeks to avoid a straightforward military defeat, and by the beginning of 1826 this looked more than likely. Early in January, while Stratford Canning was on his way to Constantinople, he was intercepted off Hydra by Prince Alexander Mavrocordatos, the leader of the pro-English faction among the Greeks, who asked for the British government's mediation. Officially, the Greeks were still demanding full independence, but Mavrocordatos indicated that they were now prepared to settle for less. Canning was greatly encouraged when news of this meeting reached him in the middle of February, 1826. He now knew for certain that at any rate the Greeks wanted British mediation and were prepared to compromise. It might seem unlikely that the victorious Turks would be equally amenable but Canning optimistically hoped that fear of Russia would have a salutary effect. Wellington had set off for St Petersburg with instructions to urge the Tsar to give his full backing to a British offer of mediation,[12]* and Canning immediately sent him a report of the Hydra meeting in the hope that it would strengthen his hand.

But when Wellington arrived in St Petersburg at the beginning of March he was surprised to find the new Tsar showing an ostentatious lack of interest in the fate of the Greeks. Nicholas seemed much more preoccupied with his own grievances against the Porte and alarmed the duke by brandishing a tough ultimatum which he was about to despatch to Constantinople. Wellington, knowing that his first priority was to keep the peace, concentrated on trying to make the Russian ultimatum more acceptable to the Porte. Indeed, he became so involved with the ultimatum that he rather lost sight of the Greeks. But as soon as the Russians had actually sent it off, they began to consult him on the Greek problem. With the active, and perhaps crucial, assistance of Count Lieven, who had been summoned back to St Petersburg, the negotiation of an agreement went ahead and was comparatively swift and painless. Turkey was to be offered mediation over Greece, either by England alone, or by England and Russia jointly, with the aim of establishing an autonomous Greece under Turkish suzerainty.† Both signatories disclaimed any territorial or commercial designs of their own on Greece, and agreed that Austria, France and Prussia should be invited to accede to the Protocol and join Russia in guaranteeing whatever settlement was reached. Wellington's instructions did not allow him to offer a British guarantee as well.[13]

The Protocol was signed on April 4, 1826. It was the first diplomatic document in which the Greeks were mentioned and therefore in a sense given international recognition. Shortly afterwards Missolonghi was at last forced to capitulate, and at the end of the month the Greek Assembly, meeting in confusion and despair at Epidauros, officially recognised that it could no longer hold out for full independence. The terms offered by the Greeks at Epidauros were similar in substance to those which – unknown to them – had recently been laid down in the St Petersburg Protocol, which in turn were based on Stratford Canning's unofficial meeting with Mavrocordatos off Hydra. In detail the Protocol

* If the Tsar refused, Wellington was to ask him to press a joint Russo-British mediation on the Turks. If the Turks turned this down, he was not to admit that this gave Russia a right to invade Turkey, but he could promise British naval intervention if Ibrahim tried to depopulate the Morea.

† The Greeks were to have full self-government and freedom of conscience, but the Turks were to receive tribute and to have some share in nominating officials.

was less favourable to the Greeks than their own terms. Canning, however, thought it gave 'everything short of that absolute independence which the Greeks can never hope to win, and which the Porte can never be compelled to yield, except after a long and bloody struggle and through a series of successes to the Greek arms, such as, at present, it would be vain to anticipate.'[14]

In the wider field of European great power diplomacy, the implications of the Protocol were considerable – perhaps more considerable than Wellington himself at first realised. In his correspondence with Canning, his references to the Protocol were distinctly casual, and when he got home and began to realise the significance of what he had done, he seemed anxious to play it down. So indeed did all the conservatives, whether in the English Cabinet or in Europe. They were affronted by a Protocol which, in effect, threatened the integrity of the Ottoman Empire and lined up England and Russia on the side of the rebellious Greeks. The European powers were annoyed at being kept in the dark and Metternich was furious that the heir of the author of the principles of the Holy Alliance should have signed an agreement – the Austrian Chancellor described it as an 'abortion' – which broke up the solid anti-liberal front which had dominated Europe for the past ten years.*

Canning himself summed up his feelings about the new understanding with Russia in a letter to his cousin Stratford: 'I am not *quite* satisfied with the prospect of our co-operation; but it was worth the trial; and it affords the only *chance* of bringing things to a conclusion in the East without war.'[15] Peace was his aim, both on general and national grounds. In spite of the activities of Lord Cochrane and other individual Philhellenes, he was convinced that the British people as a whole did not want to go to war on behalf of the Greeks and certainly not in alliance with the Russians; they simply wanted the problem quietly settled 'without coming within a hundred miles of *war* . . .' Nor did the British government want war. Corn, currency and the Catholics were, Canning told Granville in June 1826, three good reasons against it; and in addition the fact that 'we have about 100 millions of Mohammedan and other unchristian subjects in Asia' would make it 'foolish and frantic' to embark on a 'war of the Mitre against the Turban'.[16]

The snag about the Protocol, which presumably gave rise to

---

* Nicholas's realignment was not a mere flash in the pan occasioned by the particular problem of Greece. For the remaining fifteen months of Canning's life, Russia either supported England or at least refused to co-operate with Metternich in opposing her.

Canning's doubts about it, was that if the Turks ignored it – and there was no obvious reason why they should not – the Tsar would be more likely to go to war over Greece and it would be that much more difficult for Britain to keep out of the conflict. Nicholas was still an unknown quantity. He had made a show of taking Wellington into his confidence and had assured him that if he did invade the Ottoman Empire he would not keep a single village for himself. But when the duke's conscientious exposition of the Tsar's confidences had been exposed to Canning's ruthlessly precise and logical analysis, it appeared both confused and contradictory, conveying 'neither a satisfactory assurance of peace nor a clear exposition of the motives and objects of a war.'[17]*

Early in May, however, the prospect of war receded somewhat when the Turks accepted Nicholas's ultimatum and sent delegates to the frontier town of Akkerman to discuss all outstanding questions with the exception of Greece. The talks dragged on for several months, but eventually in October the Turks gave way to all the Russian demands. On Greece, however, the Porte would not budge. Stratford's offer of mediation was disdainfully rejected and for most of the summer he was forced to sit it out in Constantinople, the unwilling and horrified spectator of the Sultan's bloody suppression of a revolt of his janissaries.

Meanwhile Canning was gradually coming to realise that although he owed a great deal of his success as Foreign Secretary to his refusal to let England tag along behind the continental powers, the Greek problem could be more safely and effectively dealt with in co-operation with them than alone. If the Protocol were to fulfil its aims (as Canning saw them) of putting pressure on the Porte and restraining the Tsar, it would obviously help to bring in France, Austria and Prussia as soon as possible. After a long talk with Lieven† on August 6, Canning told Liverpool that for the first time he saw a way of executing the Protocol that was 'at once efficient and harmless; sure (I mean) to be harmless and with a very considerable chance of being efficient.'[18] By harmless he presumably meant without risk of war. Of Liverpool's support he could be sure, but the ultras in the Cabinet had not lost their old distrust of him; they thought he was much too pro-Greek and was reading too much into the Protocol. 'We must proceed in this Greek

* The despatch in which Canning made this analysis infuriated Wellington so much that Canning eventually agreed to withdraw it from the official files. Bathurst thought it was not written in a very 'courtly style'.

† Lieven was rewarded for his services over the Protocol with the title of prince. He got back to London early in August.

business with caution and good heed,' wrote Canning to Granville, 'for I have considerable *difficulty* in my way; not the least of which arises with the signer of the Protocol himself. I see my way, however, and will get through to the end, but it must be, as old Lord Chatham used to say, *gradatim*.'[19]

In September 1826, Canning paid the visit to the Granvilles in Paris which he had wanted to pay two years earlier. This time he went with the King's blessing and nobody tried to stop him, although he had reason to believe that Wellington was very angry.[20] Joan accompanied her husband on what was ostensibly a private visit to friends, although there was in fact very little that was private about it. The whole of Parisian society, from the king down, was anxious to meet and entertain the famous English Foreign Secretary. Lady Granville found it hard work giving dinners and soirées for Canning at the rate of 18 to 25 people every day.[21] The Russian ambassador, Pozzo di Borgo, formerly the most assiduous of anti-British intriguers, went out of his way to be polite, even to the extent of having his dining-room redecorated before entertaining Canning. The King of France invited the Cannings to a private play at St Cloud in honour of the birthday of the Duc de Bordeaux – 'the first act of gaiety which Charles X has committed there,' commented Canning rather irreverently.[22]

The French king also received Canning in a long private audience, and bent the rigid protocol of his court to invite him to dine *en famille* at the Tuileries. Only two other non-royalties – Wellington and Metternich – had received a similar invitation and neither of them was a commoner. Canning explained, almost apologetically, to George IV that he did not regard his own invitation as a personal honour. The Duke of Wellington had been invited because he stood 'on grounds of his own, common to no other individual in Europe, or the world.' But there was no reason why any distinction accorded to the foreign minister of the Emperor of Austria (Metternich) should not be 'communicable equally to the individual (however personally unworthy) who holds the same office under your Majesty.'[23]

Canning, it must be admitted, seldom missed an opportunity of flattering his royal master. But no one doubted that he had really gone to Paris on official business rather than for private pleasure. 'I hope,' he had written to Stratford before he set out, 'to do some good while at Paris on two or three points of pending interest.'[24] Greece, the French occupation of Spain and the disturbed state of Portugal since King

411

John's death in March were the principal items on his agenda. Over Greece, he found the French almost embarrassingly co-operative. Charles X, who was a fervent Philhellene, spoke of coercing the Porte with a show of Russian and Austrian military might on the one side and French and English naval strength on the other. He even offered to place the French navy in the Mediterranean under the command of a British admiral. Canning was relieved to find that Charles's 'warlike propensities' were not shared by Villèle.[25] In any case nothing definite could be done about Greece until the outcome of the Akkerman talks was known.

On the continued French occupation of Spain, Canning's talks were less satisfactory. His inability to get the French troops out of the Peninsula, in spite of constant prodding, was probably at the root of his intense distrust of French policies, whether in Europe or America. (The previous summer he had become acutely suspicious of the French government's intentions towards Cuba and had extracted a pledge that it would not land any troops there.) Even if he had wanted to, he could hardly let the Spanish question drop because it was one of the few remaining sticks with which the opposition could – and did – beat him. In March 1825, Villèle had told Granville that the last French soldier would have left Spain by the following New Year. On the strength of this pledge Canning had assured Parliament that the French intended to evacuate Spain as quickly as possible.[26] Eighteen months later, the French army of occupation in Spain was smaller, but it was still there.

In his talks with Canning, Villèle profusely lamented this unfortunate fact. He may well have meant what he said. The occupation of Spain was very expensive and there was little to show for it. Ferdinand VII was still on his throne but he had conspicuously failed to put his house in order. The evacuation of the troops was opposed chiefly by the ultras in France, and above all by Ferdinand himself, who insisted that without the French army his kingdom would lapse into confusion and civil war. But in spite of Ferdinand's protests – so Villèle assured Canning – the French government would have withdrawn its troops from Spain if it had not feared that the distracted state of Portugal was about to set the whole Peninsula ablaze.[27]

'The events of a series of years,' wrote Canning to the British ambassador in Lisbon on August 30, 1826, 'and treaties of ancient obligation give to England a preponderance in the affairs of Portugal which – whether useful or prejudicial to England herself – she has not the choice of abandoning. The responsibility of this situation is as great as its duties are occasionally burdensome.'[28] The Portuguese crisis of 1826 began with the death of old King John on March 10. Its primary cause, however, was not a disputed succession, but the bitter war of ideas that European ultras and liberals had been waging for the past ten years and nowhere more bitterly than in the Iberian Peninsula; and as in most ideological controversies the protagonists – or most of them – were impervious to the virtues of moderation, compromise and good sense.

King John's eldest son, Dom Pedro, realised that he could not expect to be King of Portugal as well as Emperor of Brazil; the most he could hope for was to keep Portugal within the Braganza family. He decided, therefore, to renounce the Crown in favour of his eldest daughter, Donna Maria, a child of eight, and confirm his sister, the Infanta Isabella, whom King John had appointed Regent just before his death, in her office. He also proposed that his brother, Dom Miguel, who had been living in exile in Vienna since his abortive coup against his father two years earlier, should in due course marry his niece, the new queen. In political terms this was a prudent proposal, since Miguel was probably too ambitious and had too large a following in Portugal to accept his permanent exclusion from power. What really set the cat among the pigeons was Pedro's totally unexpected decision to grant Portugal a constitution as part and parcel of the new settlement.

According to Lord Ponsonby, the Emperor of Brazil hated liberty as much as Sir Toby Belch hated water, but he was 'vain of his political science of which he knows as much as his bosom friend his pimp.'* There was some truth in this flippant comment. Pedro believed that he had given peace and stability to Brazil by granting her a constitution and apparently thought he could now bestow the same blessings on Portugal by the same means. What he forgot was that his brother was a dyed-in-the-wool absolutist, that a number of Portuguese were equally reactionary and that Ferdinand of Spain would almost certainly take fright at having a constitutional régime established in neighbouring

---

* Ponsonby was instructed by Canning to visit Rio de Janeiro on his way to take up his post as British envoy in Buenos Aires in order to try and mediate between Brazil and Buenos Aires in their quarrel over Montevideo. In the letter quoted above to Charles Bagot he went on to describe how one morning the emperor and his pimp, who was also his private secretary, sat down to breakfast with Benjamin Constant's book and by dinner time had produced a constitution. 'I believe,' added Ponsonby, 'after all that this Constitution of such facile parturition is very much better than the elaborate production of herds of French philosophers ... in consequence of certain alterations introduced into it by the Emperor and the Pimp ...' (Bagot II, p. 310)

Portugal. Liberalism was a contagious moral disease which could not safely be tolerated on one's frontiers.

The other European powers, and in particular Austria, were not so much frightened as outraged by Dom Pedro's parting present to the Portuguese people. A prince who gave away constitutions was a traitor to the established system. Metternich even went so far as to affirm that Pedro's gift threatened the social order with death and destruction.[29] They forgot that their original complaint against the various post-1815 constitutions was that they emanated not from the monarch but from the people; and that as champions of absolutism it hardly became them to complain if a monarch chose to use his unfettered prerogatives to grant a constitution. This point, however, did not escape Canning. 'It will indeed be singular,' he wrote to Sir William à Court at Lisbon, 'if after having put down the constitutional systems (however little worth maintaining) of Naples and Spain, not for their worthlessness, but simply and declaredly because they were not *octroyés* by the sovereign, the same powers should now combine against the Constitutional Charter of Portugal which (whatever else its merits) is decidedly and unquestionably the emanation of the grace and free will of the lawful sovereign of Portugal.'[30] In less stately language he rammed the point home in his private interviews with the foreign ambassadors in London. In fact he teased them unmercifully and Esterhazy reported stuffily to Metternich that Mr Canning's arguments in favour of absolute power were not of course to be taken seriously; he only used them from that 'spirit of derision by which this Minister is sometimes led away.'[31]

Although Canning could not resist making fun of Esterhazy, he was in fact extremely vexed by the news from Rio. He had no use for impracticable paper constitutions and feared that Dom Pedro's effort would bring discord rather than peace to Portugal.* But the damage was done. And since most Portuguese and the Regency Council appeared to accept the constitution, Canning declared that nobody else had the right to say them nay. At the same time, however, he warned the Portuguese not to try to make trouble in Spain by spreading pro-liberal propaganda. With this the other powers had to be content. They were not prepared to risk a confrontation with England over Portugal;

---

* Canning's vexation was increased by the fact that Pedro had dragooned Sir Charles Stuart, who was still in Rio, into bringing the new constitution back to Lisbon. Canning did not blame Stuart, who had been most unwilling to accept the commission, but he found it difficult to persuade Metternich that the British had not instigated Pedro into granting the constitution.

and after all, since the absolutist Dom Miguel's supporters were still active, the Portuguese constitutional experiment, if left strictly alone, was perhaps just as likely to come to grief as to succeed.

But Ferdinand of Spain refused to refrain from surreptitiously fishing in the troubled Portuguese waters, in spite of frequent warnings from Frederick Lamb, the British envoy in Madrid, that this was a dangerous pastime. Many weeks before the astonishing news of Dom Pedro's constitution reached Europe, Canning instructed Lamb to complain about reports of Spain's 'meddling disposition' towards Portugal. (There were reports that a Spanish agent had been sent to Vienna to persuade Dom Miguel to go to Lisbon and try to seize power.[32]) 'His Majesty's Government,' he wrote on April 22, 'will feel itself bound to consider any attempt on the part of Spain to disturb the tranquillity of Portugal as an act of aggression against England herself.'[33] He could hardly have been more blunt. But Ferdinand was not likely to take kindly to the admonitions of the only great European power who had recognised his ex-colonies and who was still badgering him to recognise them himself. He leaned on the physical support of the French army of occupation and the moral support of the other continental powers.

Early in August groups of pro-Miguel deserters from the Portuguese army began to cross the frontier into Spain. They were welcomed by the Spanish authorities, who gave them food and shelter and allowed them to keep their arms. To harbour deserters from a neighbouring country was not only contrary to the accepted rules of neutrality, but was also a breach of a specific Portuguese-Spanish treaty. When about the same time some Spanish deserters crossed into Portugal, the Portuguese authorities acted correctly in disarming them and sending them back. They would have been justified in entering Spanish territory in pursuit of their own men. But on Canning's advice they contented themselves with demanding that the Miguelists should be disarmed, separated from their officers and dispersed into the interior of Spain.

When Canning arrived in Paris in the middle of September, the situation along the Spanish-Portuguese frontier was becoming increasingly tense. The Portuguese deserters were openly taking oaths of loyalty to Dom Miguel, and in Madrid Frederick Lamb's insistent demands that they should be disarmed and dispersed fell on deaf ears. Lamb got no help and a good deal of hindrance from his diplomatic colleagues; they either remained passive or, in the case of de Moustiers, the French ambassador, who belonged to the extreme ultra party in France, actively encouraged the Spanish king to be intransigent. 'It is inconceivable, though true,' wrote Lamb on October 2, 'that in their eagerness to blow up their neighbour's house, it is overlooked, both by the Spanish Government and the French ambassador, that their own is undermined.' He meant that a civil war in Portugal might easily spark off a similar conflict between absolutists and liberals in Spain. Overcome by the futility of his own efforts to avert a disaster, he concluded dismally: 'You must totally throw out of your mind the idea that anything can be done through me.'[34]

Although Canning did not share the despair of his man in Madrid, he was greatly concerned about the situation that was developing in Lisbon. To the more extreme Portuguese liberals, their government's restraint was simply deplorable weakness, and it was pretty clear that if the Miguelist deserters were not disarmed and dispersed before the new Cortes met on October 19, the deputies' critical speechifying might well dangerously inflame public opinion and undermine the government's stability.* Canning felt very keenly that since the British had urged moderation in Lisbon, it was up to them to protect the Regency Council from the consequences of following their advice.

The other powers could not of course be expected to share this strong sense of moral obligation to Portugal. But by the beginning of October Canning, who was still in Paris, had convinced Villèle and Pozzo di Borgo that it was in everybody's interest to deal swiftly with a crisis which might easily develop into a general threat to European peace. On October 3, without waiting to get the approval of his own government, he instructed Lamb to make a final demand for the disarming and dispersal of the deserters and, if it was not granted, to leave Madrid, ostensibly on leave of absence.[35] Canning believed that by threatening to take this first step towards a complete rupture of relations Lamb would frighten the Spaniards into giving way; and he calculated that with luck and a fast messenger Lamb could get the news of his success to Lisbon before the Cortes met. At the same time Villèle sent peremptory instructions to de Moustiers to give Lamb his most energetic support. Four days later it was learned in Paris that Ferdinand had at last promised to deal with the Portuguese deserters. He must have done so before Lamb received Canning's latest instruc-

* Canning primed à Court with arguments that could be used to persuade the Regency to restrict public access to the debates. Although in practice, he wrote, the public was now usually admitted to the British Parliament, in theory its debates were still private. If the two Portuguese assemblies allowed the same laxity before they were as settled and mature as the British Parliament, they would become like the assemblies of revolutionary France, 'the echoes of clubs and the slaves of their own galleries'. (FO 63/306, September 9, 1826)

tions and his motives for changing his mind – if indeed he had genuinely done so – were obscure; but at least, as Canning cheerfully commented in a report to the King, he had given them a 'little breathing time'.[36]

After his arrival in Paris, Canning had suggested to Liverpool (presumably not seriously) that perhaps the Foreign Office should be moved there during the summer – 'one is so much nearer every field of diplomatic action.'[37] The French government got its despatches from Lisbon and Madrid by telegraph, which in the case of Lisbon could give it more than a week's start over the British whose ambassador sent his despatches by sea. When Canning was in Paris, the French ministers immediately passed on to him any important telegraphic news from Lisbon and Madrid. He was also in closer touch by overland messenger with Lamb and à Court than he would have been in London. The need for speed at this particular time was not in fact as great as Canning thought it was. But he could not know that the Spanish king was about to give way, nor that the opening of the Portuguese Cortes was to be postponed until the end of the month. So far as he could see at the time, the situation was very critical and it was lucky that he was on the spot in Paris to deal with it.[38]

Wellington's reactions were very different. Acutely worried about the possibility of war in the Peninsula, he was convinced that the Foreign Secretary's presence in Paris made it more not less likely. He disliked Canning personally, mistook his forcefulness for recklessness and profoundly mistrusted his whole conduct of foreign affairs. Although Canning and Liverpool showed him every consideration and consulted him as much as possible, he felt – perhaps inevitably – that he was left out. He complained that he knew nothing of Portugal except what he read in the newspapers and was not shown the official despatches. 'I really do not understand what he would have,' wrote Canning in some exasperation to Liverpool, since the duke was sent the despatches after the King and the prime minister.[39] To Wellington himself he wrote soothingly that they must try to find a better system of circulating the despatches.[40]

With Wellington in this touchy frame of mind it was hardly surprising that he should have been utterly outraged by Canning's instructions to Lamb to threaten to leave Madrid. A step had been taken, he protested to Liverpool, without the rest of the Cabinet knowing anything about it, 'which will be considered as a signal of war throughout Europe. I am certain,' he added, 'that Mr Canning would not

417

consent to such a proceeding by any other man.'[41] Liverpool may well have privately agreed about that, but he stoutly denied that Lamb's instructions might have precipitated war, pointing out that they had been fully approved by Villèle and Pozzo as the only way of inducing the King of Spain to give way.[42]

Before Canning returned to London towards the end of October, he was given another, less controversial, opportunity of demonstrating the advantages that could flow from holidaying in Paris. All this time, while Dom Miguel's supporters were congregating menacingly along the Spanish-Portuguese frontier, the prince's own intentions remained obscure. Metternich declared that the prince was free to do as he pleased. But Canning knew he would in fact do what the Austrian government pleased, and throughout the autumn he subjected Metternich to a barrage of pressing inquiries about Dom Miguel's intentions. Eventually the Austrian Chancellor gave way. On October 19, Canning learnt that Miguel had taken the oath but that Metternich had been concealing the fact as long as he could.

The messenger from Sir Henry Wellesley, the British ambassador in Vienna, who brought this news, also brought the official notification of Miguel's oath-taking for the Portuguese government. Canning was extremely indignant at Metternich's delaying tactics which he believed were aimed at stirring up trouble for the Portuguese Regency. Realising the importance of getting the news to Lisbon before the new Cortes, in which the extreme liberals were strongly represented, met on October 30, he sent it on within the hour. His messenger, travelling by way of Madrid and showing remarkable endurance, rode into Lisbon at 7 o'clock on the morning of the 30th – just in time for Dom Miguel's acceptance of the constitution to be inserted in the speech with which the Infanta Isabella opened the Cortes. If it had met under the impression that the prince was implacably hostile to the constitution, the consequences, in Canning's opinion, might have been fatal to the peace of both Spain and Portugal. 'Whatever,' he complacently observed, 'were Prince Metternich's motives for wishing to expose those kingdoms to such a trial – that object has been happily disappointed.'[43]

With his usual optimism, Canning was so encouraged by the auspicious opening of the Portuguese Cortes that in the middle of November he told à Court to offer to reduce the size of the British naval force in the Tagus; it would, he thought, be a sign of proper deference to the new constitutional authorities who ought not to have to function under the guns of a foreign naval force, however friendly.[44] It was a well-meant but completely unrealistic suggestion. In Lisbon the government still looked to the British warships for protection and a possible refuge (in October some marines had been temporarily landed to protect the royal palace); in Vienna Metternich announced that Miguel had only taken the constitutional oath with reservations; while in Madrid Ferdinand stubbornly refused to give formal recognition to the Portuguese Regency and Lamb could make no headway in his efforts to get the Spanish government to carry out its undertakings. Throughout November his despatches grew increasingly indignant and despondent. Whether the fault lay with the authorities in Madrid, who failed to give the necessary orders, or with the local military authorities, who failed to do what they were told, the result was the same. The Miguelists, equipped and supported by the Spanish, remained deployed along the whole frontier and on November 22 began what could only be described as a regular invasion, advancing into Portugal in the north and the south simultaneously.

Reports of the invasion of northern Portugal first reached London by way of the French telegraph on December 3. On the same day, Palmella, the Portuguese ambassador, formally appealed for British help to defend his country. The reports from Portugal were not altogether to be trusted, and Canning was very much in two minds what to do. His first reaction was that prompt and decisive action might bring Spain to her senses, especially as the French at last showed signs of losing patience with Ferdinand. Parliament was in session, having been summoned unusually early to deal with the corn question; there was still time to secure its approval for sending military aid to Portugal before it rose for the Christmas recess in about ten days' time. If they hesitated, Villèle would assume they were not serious and would probably decide it was safer to side with the ultra factions in France and Spain. 'This moment is ours,' wrote Canning urgently to Liverpool, 'if we use it, we shall settle the dispute; but if we miss it I foresee a series of growing difficulties, and the very war, which we wish to avoid, in the distance.'[45] But Liverpool – perhaps because he happened to be ill – was full of doubts and indecision, and Canning had to content himself with sending instructions to Lamb to withdraw immediately from Madrid.

Two days later, on the 5th, Canning heard from Lamb that the Spanish government disclaimed all responsibility for the invasion and was profusely promising measures of redress and prevention. He was greatly relieved and at once told Lamb to stay in Madrid. In spite of his brave words to Liverpool, he was well aware of the risks involved in sending troops to help the Portuguese repel an invasion backed by Spain while Spain herself was occupied by a French army. 'Is it possible,' he wrote to Granville on the 6th, 'that Villèle should not now see the endless embarrassment in which that [French] army [in Spain] involves him and us, and all the world?' Would not the French at least threaten to withdraw it in order to force Ferdinand to accept the Portuguese constitution?[46]

Immediately after sending off this appeal, Canning, like Liverpool, was forced to take to his bed. Having tried unsuccessfully to bully his incipient illness by going on as if nothing was the matter, he had succumbed to a violent pain in his chest. The pain yielded to the usual treatment of bleeding and blistering, but the combined effect of the complaint and the remedies was to leave him extremely weak. On December 8, however, stimulated by more despatches from Lamb which this time were far from encouraging, he again unburdened himself to Granville. He could not, he wrote, even pretend to believe the Spanish assurances. But he would much rather that France dealt with the troubles of the Peninsula than forced England to do so. 'The recall of the French army from Spain would be a hundred-fold more efficacious than the sending of troops from here to Portugal.' And, he added significantly, it would be 'more beneficial in its consequences.'[47] In other words, it would remove a major bone of contention between England and France – and, moreover, one for which Canning had an especially personal sense of responsibility.

But it was not to be as he wished. Late the same evening he learned for the first time, in a despatch from à Court, that the Miguelists were also invading Portugal in the south and had captured a town on the road to Lisbon. He could no longer doubt that a concerted attempt, backed by Spain, was being made to overthrow the constitutional régime in Lisbon. There was no longer any excuse for hesitating. That same night Canning told Liverpool that 'we have not an hour to lose in doing our duty by Portugal.'[48]

Next day, Saturday, December 9, the Cabinet met and drew up a royal Message for submission to Parliament. For once there was no disagreement. On Sunday the Message was approved by the King; on Monday it was formally presented to Parliament; and on Tuesday, the 12th, it was debated and approved by both Houses. By that time the first of a corps of 5,000 troops were already on the march to their ports of embarkation.

Canning was still far from well and when he formally presented the King's Message to the Commons, his voice was so feeble that he could scarcely be heard. Next day, however, he summoned all his physical and emotional reserves for what was to be, if not a great parliamentary battle, at any rate a great parliamentary occasion. 'He made great efforts,' wrote one listener, 'and was crowned with great success.'[49] He defended the government against the opposition's complaints that it had taken too long to go to Portugal's help. He convincingly demonstrated that it had now no other choice. He insisted that they were not making war against Spain, but only defending Portugal.* He disclaimed any wish to interfere in Portugal's internal affairs and once again expressed his conviction that England ought to remain neutral in the struggle of political opinions that agitated so many countries. Nearly four years earlier, he had used this argument to justify his refusal to go to war on behalf of the Spanish liberals. Now, when her treaty obligations obliged England to defend Portugal's liberals, he skilfully used the same argument to flatter his fellow countrymen and reconcile them to a course of which no one could foresee the outcome. England, he said, had a giant's strength and the consciousness of this gave her confidence and security. But, he added, 'our business is not to seek opportunities of displaying it, but to content ourselves with letting the professors of violent and exaggerated doctrines on both sides feel that it is not their interest to convert an umpire into an adversary.'

Canning had always been acutely conscious of the uncontrollable nature of what he called 'wars of opinion'. He would, he now told the Commons, have put up with almost anything 'rather than let slip the furies of war, the leash of which we hold in our hands – not knowing whom they may reach, or how far their ravages may be carried.' But since it was a matter of national honour there was no choice; and in perhaps the most brilliant peroration of his career, he exhorted the Commons: 'Let us fly to the aid of Portugal, by whomsoever attacked, because it is our duty to do so; and let us cease our interference where that duty ends. We go to Portugal, not to rule, not to dictate, not to prescribe constitutions, but to defend and to preserve the independence of an ally. We go to plant the standard of England on the well-known heights of Lisbon. Where that standard is planted, foreign dominion shall not come.'[50]

* On December 11, he told Lamb that he must not leave Madrid without definite instructions to do so, because his departure now would be almost tantamount to a declaration of war. (FO 72/313)

No speaker to that most critical of assemblies could have wanted a more appreciative audience, although it was said that he was cheered more by the opposition than by his own side. Two Whigs who suggested that the country could not afford to go to war were received with obvious disapproval. Brougham extravagantly praised the Foreign Secretary and made (according to Croker) 'a most tedious repetition of what Canning had said so much better.'[51] But two opposition members, Sir Robert Wilson and Mr Baring, while supporting the decision to aid Portugal, could not refrain from taunting Canning for failing to prevent the French occupation of Spain and then tolerating it for so long. This was, of course, hitting Canning below the belt and, in his reply to the debate, he launched into a passionate – and presumably impromptu – defence of his Spanish policy. He admitted that the occupation was an affront to England's pride, but denied that it called for her military intervention. He pointed out to the Commons that their ancestors had feared Spain because of the huge power she derived from her vast empire. Without that empire she was a harmless and valueless prize. So when France occupied Spain, it was no longer necessary to redress the balance of power by military means. 'No,' declared Canning, 'I looked another way – I sought materials of compensation in another hemisphere. Contemplating Spain, such as our ancestors had known her, I resolved that if France had Spain, it should not be Spain "with the Indies." I called the New World into existence to redress the balance of the Old.'[52]

In this famous boast Canning was presumably harking back, at any rate in his own mind, to his determination two years earlier to recognise the new South American states as a riposte to the French occupation of Spain. To that extent, he was justified in calling it afterwards 'an obvious but unsuspected truth'.[53] But in every other respect it was just a splendid piece of bombast, an exercise in rhetorical sleight of hand which could not possibly stand up to close examination. It infuriated his enemies and confirmed them in their view that he was an intolerably arrogant and clever charlatan. But it went down extremely well with the general public who were not bothered by his personal presumption, but delighted to discover that they had after all got the better of the French. Canning was probably right in claiming that his declaration had 'been more grateful to English ears and to English feelings ten thousand times, than would have been the most satisfactory announcement' of a French withdrawal from Spain.[54] It was not for nothing that his greatest political asset had become his unrivalled ability to play upon and gauge the popular mood.

The reaction of more dispassionate and informed opinion in England to the despatch of military aid to Portugal was summed up by Lord Sidmouth. Britain, he wrote, might possibly get involved in a civil war in Portugal; 'but, be that as it may, our course is an honourable one, our motive is good faith, and our object the defence of an ally.'[55] But abroad these impeccably proper motives were not so apparent. To Metternich they weighed little against his ineradicable distrust of Canning and the fact that England was not merely defending an ally, but upholding a constitution. Not only was one sentence in Canning's speech – 'May God prosper this attempt at constitutional liberty in Portugal' – enough to wipe out all his measured warnings against the danger of getting involved in a 'war of opinion', but these warnings were misinterpreted as giving encouragement to revolutionaries. Canning, wrote Metternich, 'gains the revolutionary party and goes to moral war with us.'[56] In Paris, on the other hand, it was principally Canning's forthright references to the French occupation of Spain that created such a 'prodigious uproar' that Lady Granville confessed to some nervousness at appearing in public.[57]

Canning did his best to allay the storm. The strain of the debate brought back all the 'rheumatics' he had been 'bleeding and blistering away during the preceding week' and he had to take to his bed the day after the debate. But he forced himself to get up that evening to go to a dinner given by the Austrian ambassador. 'It would,' he told Granville, 'have been a heinous omission not to go there, as Esterhazy takes the Message* as an act of hostility to his Court.' (He had, he added, expected 'to be quite knocked up by this sacrifice to propriety', but he now felt 'marvellously well'.[58]) He also carefully went over the official version of his speech, which was intended for the consumption of foreign governments, especially that of France, and – as he reported to the King – 'studiously softened down every strong expression which (uttered in the heat of public speaking) might possibly appear to bear hard on France.'[59]

The French ministers had of course seen the original version of the speech, and Canning's stream of explanatory letters to Granville suggests that, in spite of his recurrent bouts of suspicion about the French, he was genuinely anxious not to damage the frail foundations of a better relationship which he had recently laid in Paris. He was now on friendly personal terms with Villèle who, he realised, had to contend with both liberal and ultra (especially the latter) factions. Moreover, he did not want to damage the chances of French co-operation over

* The royal Message to Parliament on sending troops to Portugal.

Greece. But to Canning's great relief, the French behaved very well. In the French parliament, the foreign minister, Damas, handsomely defended the British government's conduct towards Portugal and condemned that of Spain. 'I am really at a loss for words,' wrote Canning to Granville, 'to express my admiration of the frankness, *loyauté*, good faith, good temper, and I may add, good sense of that [Damas's] speech.'[60]

Meanwhile Canning was anxiously wondering whether the news that British troops were on the way would arrive in time to impose restraint in Madrid and stability in Lisbon. The Portuguese army was in poor shape to repel the intruders; and in Lisbon the Regent Isabella's moderate government was being violently denounced by the ultra liberals in the Cortes and the mob in the streets of the city. Sir William à Court reported that the mob had assaulted the Minister for War in his carriage.[61] 'The intelligence from Lisbon,' wrote Canning to Liverpool on the 21st, 'is alarming but not desperate. By this time, I trust, they are aware of our determination.'[62]

The news in fact reached Sir William à Court on the 18th, and in a despatch written next day he found it difficult to describe the joy and enthusiasm with which it had been received. 'The gloom and despondency which hung over all for the last fortnight seemed at once to disperse and hope and confidence to revive as if by magic.'[63] On Christmas Day, when the sails of the British troopships were first sighted, the banks of the Tagus were lined with cheering crowds. 'We are perfectly tranquil now,' wrote à Court. 'England has spoken, and some of her troops have already arrived.'[64] In Madrid the news made an equally gratifying impression. 'The certainty of the early arrival of our troops at Lisbon,' wrote Lamb complacently on the 23rd, 'gave me a very different tone from any I had hitherto held.'[65] The Spanish king hurriedly promised to withdraw support from the Miguelists and recognise the Infanta Isabella's government. Although one would not have thought Ferdinand's promises worth a great deal, Canning triumphantly reported to Bathurst that the Spanish government's conduct was 'MORE *satisfactory* than that which Lamb would have been authorised to take as *satisfaction*. I hope and believe that all is well over.'[66]

Canning's optimism was not entirely unjustified. After some further back-sliding by the incorrigible Ferdinand, Spain did abandon her attempt to overthrow Portugal's constitution by force. And by the end of January, 1827, the Portuguese army, encouraged by the arrival of British troops, had defeated and expelled the Miguelist intruders. But

John Bull in the guise of a British officer goes to the rescue of Portugal, his country's ancient ally

[Robert Cruikshank, December 1826]

Saint George, George IV and George Canning attack a wounded dragon with seven heads representing the seven ministers who resigned when Canning was made premier

the internal stability of the new régime continued to be undermined by military plots, political dissensions between liberals and ultras and the unhelpful behaviour of the House of Braganza. Dom Miguel claimed that he should take over as Regent on his approaching 25th birthday, while in Rio Dom Pedro behaved suspiciously as if he meant to hang on to his Portuguese crown after all.

In Downing Street, the brief euphoria over the successful and bloodless outcome of the despatch of troops to Portugal was succeeded by anxiety over how and when to get them out again. No one wanted them to get embroiled in Portugal's internal affairs, and Liverpool was in favour of withdrawing them as soon as possible. But Canning felt they might have a stabilising effect and was reluctant to pull them out too quickly. Moreover, he had always been determined that the presence of a British force in Portugal should be used to remove an existing 'disparagement' to England – the French occupation of Spain. Villèle, he believed, wanted to withdraw if he could overcome the opposition of the French ultras, and the British withdrawal from Portugal, if properly timed, could make it easier for him to do this.[67]

For most of the last six months of Canning's life the affairs of the Peninsula had to take second place to more pressing problems at home and abroad. But almost literally until the day of his death he was worrying over the potential danger that a disturbed and divided Portugal represented to the country that was bound to defend her against external attack.

Portugal was the main preoccupation of the Foreign Office towards the end of 1826 just as Greece had been towards the end of the previous year, South America in 1824 and the French occupation of Spain in 1823. But most of these – and other – issues were simmering most of the time. While Canning was dealing with the developing Portuguese crisis in the late summer and autumn of 1826, he was also trying, among other things, to build a Greek settlement on the foundation laid by the Anglo-Russian Protocol. He was trying (unsuccessfully in the end) to prevent the bitter quarrel between Brazil and Buenos Aires over Montevideo from developing into war. He was keeping an eye on Bolivar's congress of South American states at Panama, and the possible designs of Mexico and Colombia on Cuba. And he was worrying about the hazard to British commercial expansion represented by the United States' claims in Oregon.*

* After seeing some Chinese manufactures imported into Mexico, he became very

No issue which concerned British commitments and prestige, or affected British interests, political or commercial, escaped Canning's meticulous scrutiny. Whether it was of major or minor importance, he briefed himself conscientiously and wrote voluminous instructions in which he tried to cover every possible contingency. Castlereagh had also been a hard-working Foreign Secretary, but the amount of paperwork to and from the Foreign Office increased sharply under his successor; the number of out-going despatches rose from 1,659 in 1821 to nearly 3,850 in 1826. Canning's mind worked exceptionally fast and he wrote with as much fluency and force as he spoke in the House of Commons. It was said that he hated to dictate because no one could write fast enough, and there are various stories of him dictating two (according to one version, three) despatches on different subjects to different secretaries at the same time.[68] His despatches were elegant, lucid and stately. Sometimes he allowed himself a touch of lofty irony, sometimes he expressed himself with disdainful anger. But everything he wrote in his official capacity was characterised by a strong sense of the dignity and greatness of the country he represented.* He was proud of his compositions, but when he had to show them to the Cabinet, submitted gracefully to the criticism of his colleagues.

Canning increased the staff of the Foreign Office from 28 to 36, not including several private secretaries, of whom the most important was his personal secretary, A. G. Stapleton. He was fortunate to have Joseph Planta as his permanent Under-Secretary. Planta, who had worked in the Foreign Office all his life, was an excellent deputy –

---

enthused about the potentialities of a trans-Pacific trade link, once the East India Company's monopoly of the China trade expired in 1836. 'I should not like,' he wrote to Liverpool on July 7, 1826, 'to leave my name affixed to an instrument by which England would have foregone the advantage of an immense direct intercourse between China and what may be, if we resolve not to yield them up, her boundless establishments on the N.W. coast of America.' (Off. Corr. II, 74)

* Canning's famous 'rhyming despatch' was characteristic of his love of practical jokes, but entirely untypical of his approach to his official correspondence. When Charles Bagot was in the Hague in February, 1826, he received what purported to be an important despatch in a cipher which (as Canning probably knew) he did not possess. In great agitation he confessed his inability to decipher the despatch and hoped this would 'not be productive of any public inconvenience'. But when he had at last received the right cipher and could unravel the despatch, he discovered it was only a lighthearted verse on the recent imposition of a 20 per cent levy on Dutch shipping of which he had already been officially informed. 'You have fretted me to fiddlesticks,' he wrote crossly to Canning, 'and I have a great mind not to give you the satisfaction of ever knowing how completely your mystification of me has succeeded.' (Bagot, II, pp. 320/5)

efficient, amiable, popular with the foreign diplomats and devoted to his chief. But all the young men who served as joint Under-Secretaries – Lord Francis Conyngham, Lord Howard de Walden (Charles Ellis's son) and Lord Clanricarde (Canning's son-in-law) – were lightweights, although they were loyal and anxious to please. The Foreign Office clerks were a mixed bunch; too many owed their job to string-pulling rather than to their own industry.

Neither the diplomatic missions abroad nor the heterogeneous collection of consuls were much more satisfactory. Canning was served by some outstandingly able and dedicated ambassadors, but the missions themselves were largely staffed by unpaid attachés who tended to be less interested in their work than in seeing the world and amusing themselves. Canning called it a bad system but despaired of changing it. 'If this be a burden,' he told Sir Henry Wellesley, the British ambassador in Vienna, when sending him one young sprig of the aristocracy as attaché, 'it is not my fault. I find the system established and cannot break it up. My determination is not to extend it; and to diminish it where I can.'[69] With Huskisson's help, however, he was able to introduce some useful, though limited, reforms into the consular service.

Although the machinery through which he had to work was often amateurish and inadequate, Canning's attitude to the conduct of diplomacy was essentially professional. Heads of missions abroad found that nothing escaped his critical eye or censorious pen. Sir Edward Thornton once had the misfortune to omit a page of one of his despatches, thereby making it largely unintelligible; Canning did not fail to point this out, at the same time commenting critically on the ambassador's 'slovenly penmanship'. Granville, who was an able diplomat but tended to be insufficiently energetic for Canning's taste, was reproved not only for his handwriting but for the brevity of his despatches. Since he was a close friend, his excuse that he was always being interrupted by dinner was demolished very gently. 'The perpetual recurrence of dinner,' wrote Canning, 'is exceedingly distressing. But did it not ever enter your mind that you might evade the force of that not unexpected impediment, by beginning to write at a time of day when it does not usually present itself? Try that device.'[70]

But what Canning would not tolerate, either in his friends or anyone else, were blunders, misjudgments or plain failure to obey instructions. The offender might have acted through excess of zeal and with the best of intentions; it made no difference if Canning did not approve. Sir Edward Thornton was obviously well-meaning, keen and conscientious, but he was brusquely recalled from Lisbon in 1824 after making what Canning regarded as several serious blunders.[71] When Henry Vaughan in Washington made suggestions to the Americans on Cuba of which Canning disapproved, he was immediately disavowed and plainly told that he had taken too much upon himself.[72] When Bagot was in St Petersburg in 1824 he also overstepped his brief. Canning sent him a stiff official rebuke, but in a private letter apologised to his friend for having 'to *snub* and *snouch* you in your old age (the old age of your embassy) for disobedience of your instructions.' Bagot accepted the rebuke philosophically. 'I take my *snouching*,' he wrote, 'as all diplomatic snouchings should be taken, in meekness and repentance.'[73]

But those who were not personal friends of Canning did not always take their reprimands in such good part, especially if they happened to have rather prima donna-ish tendencies. Sir Charles Stuart was furious when Canning disavowed the commercial and slave trade treaties he had negotiated with Brazil. So was Lord Strangford who in December 1825, when ambassador in St Petersburg, was very smartly rapped over the knuckles for disobeying his instructions on the Greek issue.* Canning was equally angry with Strangford and closed the matter by curtly telling him that his instructions were 'comprised in a few short words, *to be quiet*.'[74] Privately, he lamented to Granville: 'O! that people would learn that doing nothing is often a *measure*, and full as important a one as the most diligent activity; and that clever people could reconcile it and themselves to own that they have no instructions when they really have none.'[75]

Those who worked under Canning in London also found him an exacting chief. They also found him irritable, especially if he had gout. 'You are aware,' wrote young Conyngham to Sir William Knighton, 'how irritable such an attack always makes a person, more especially Mr C. who is never over cool in his mind.'[76] Yet Conyngham, like most of the Foreign Office staff, was devoted to Canning and counted it a privilege to work for him. He became so upset when telling him that he would have to resign because he was getting married that he finished up by throwing himself into his chief's arms and weeping on his shoulder like a child.[77] Canning solved the problem of reconciling the claims of matrimony with the long hours worked by a Foreign Under-Secretary by bringing in Lord Howard de Walden to help out.

For although Canning might get cross and be hard to please, he was also extremely good-natured, kind and fair-minded. He always took

---

* Strangford strongly resented this important issue being entrusted to the Duke of Wellington.

the trouble to show his appreciation of those, whether in the Office or serving abroad, whom he thought had done well. Sidmouth's nephew, Henry Addington, for instance, who served for two years as chargé d'affaires in Washington, wrote very warmly of Canning's 'invariably just, and friendly and liberal' attitude towards him when he returned to London.[78] And when the handsome Lord Ponsonby learnt that the Foreign Secretary approved of his conduct in Buenos Aires, he thought it was the most gratifying news he had ever heard in his life. 'I am extremely proud,' he wrote to Charles Bagot, 'as every man must be of being approved of by a person of his singular acquirements and unequalled abilities, but I am also delighted to have been able to show the zeal with which I am actuated to serve him who has been so kind to me and for whom I took such a very strong fancy personally.'[79] It perhaps says as much for Ponsonby as for Canning that in the thoroughly uncongenial surroundings of Buenos Aires he could still pay such a warm and obviously sincere tribute to the man who had sent him there.

In July 1825, the Cannings sold their villa at Brompton and moved into Downing Street. Gloucester Lodge, set among trees and lawns, with its elegant suite of drawing-rooms and well-stocked library, was in many ways an eminently suitable place for the official entertaining that was expected of a Foreign Secretary. Canning did not enjoy this kind of formal entertaining, but he recognised that it was part of the job and he liked to do it in style.* Gloucester Lodge, he felt, was too far out for the diplomatic corps to be expected to come in inclement weather, and also, presumably, he himself preferred to be closer to the Office. During the parliamentary recess he would escape from London, but he never escaped from the Foreign Office boxes. They followed him everywhere – whether he was staying at Windermere or with Joan's in-laws at Welbeck, whether he was keeping Lord Liverpool company at Bath or enjoying the sea air at Charles Ellis's house at Seaford. Lord Dudley, who became Foreign Secretary during Canning's brief premiership, described once meeting him at a country house

---

* Early in September 1822, when discussing in a letter to Joan what would be involved if he succeeded Castlereagh as Foreign Secretary, he wrote: 'I will not underlive any of my predecessors, though a gaol, when I go out, may be the consequence. I know C. Ellis has a favourite theory that one may plead poverty, and give crusts and water twice a year. That I *will not do*. I would plead poverty and retire into Wales, with all my heart, but a great station, not lived up to, is of all things the most miserable and unsatisfactory.' (EHR, Vol. 78, p. 538, quoted by Aspinall. Harewood Mss.)

where he had gone 'for what he was pleased to call his holidays. He had his secretaries about him soon after eight, had despatches ready before breakfast, then wrote all day till six. At tea-time he established himself in a corner of the drawing-room to write his private letters – and this every day – only now and then with the exception of a ride, and even during that he talked eagerly and fully upon public affairs or any other subject that happened to present itself.'[80]

Canning was a brilliant and ready talker in congenial company and when the conversation interested him. But at the small, informal dinner parties that he himself gave, he often seemed more interested in drawing out his guests than in holding forth himself. The conversation was as likely to turn on literary as political subjects. Canning, whose mind was stored with classical learning, was also very well-read in the literature of his own country and loved to discuss his favourite authors, such as Swift and Dryden, or some literary problem, such as the authorship of the Junius letters. But he never enjoyed the frivolous chat of the great London drawing-rooms. He once told his mother that the polite world was a *terra incognita* to him – which was not all that much of an exaggeration. He never learned to make small talk and tended to be as shy and reserved at a formal royal or diplomatic dinner as he was among his mother's friends at Bath. 'You have no idea,' he once wrote to her, 'how I dread strangers – how little I can make conversation and how little I should like to be thought *proud* because I cannot talk common talk – which, right or wrong, I cannot.'[81]

But he was far from stuffy, nor was he invariably serious-minded. He never lost his weakness for practical jokes or his enjoyment of parlour games,* and his sense of humour rarely deserted him. He saw the funny side of anything with unrivalled quickness and if a comic idea crossed his mind in the middle of a serious discussion, he would burst out laughing. When he was invited to spend the evening at Windsor, he would sometimes catch Mme Lieven's eye with a look which meant 'Did you see the joke?'[82] Wilberforce once described one of Canning's speeches in the Commons as 'invincibly comic' and when he got home could not describe it for laughing. Afterwards he wrote: 'Canning's drollery of voice and manner were inimitable; there is a

* At a dinner party given by Mr Planta in 1823 Canning suggested that they should play Twenty Questions. He himself was one of the 'askers' and a fellow guest afterwards described how at the end of the questions he found the answer. 'He sat silent for a minute or two; then, rolling his rich eye about, and with a countenance a little anxious, and in an accent by no means over-confident, he exclaimed, "I think it must be the wand of the Lord High Steward." And it was – even so.' (Rush. Court of London, 1819–25, p. 372)

lighting up of his features, and a comic play about the mouth, when the full fun of the approaching witticism strikes his own mind, which prepares you for the burst which is to follow.'[83]

But too often he lapsed into ridicule which hurt and sarcasm which angered and alienated those at whom it was aimed. Sometimes he employed the weapon of ridicule deliberately in what he believed was a good cause. But sometimes his tongue and his imagination simply ran away with him and he seems to have been unaware of how much he was wounding others and damaging himself. Yet he was a naturally sensitive man, and neither his experience of the world nor the rough and tumble of politics ever blunted his feelings or hardened his emotions.* He was visibly moved when referring to any kindness which he felt had been shown to him. He was perceptive about other people and instinctively considerate, especially to those who were ill-placed to look after themselves or who had been hardly treated by fate. When Castlereagh died, Lord Clanwilliam, his adopted son, felt obliged out of loyalty to resign as Foreign Under-Secretary. When Canning learnt that his predecessor had intended to send Clanwilliam as minister to Berlin, he determined that he would do the same for 'the only person to whom he could for Castlereagh's sake be kind'; and when he met Clanwilliam he could not refrain from tears when pressing him to accept Berlin or some other diplomatic post.[84] Clanwilliam did agree to go to Berlin and later Canning told Henry Wellesley that he never would have done for a friend of his own what he had done for Clanwilliam. 'I considered myself therein as executing the testamentary disposition of my predecessor in favour of the child of his adoption, and of one whose existence was totally changed by my succession to the Foreign Office.'[85] Unfortunately, it is not by such private acts of sensitive kindness that a public man's reputation is made.

* When Wilberforce went with Canning to hear a famous preacher, he was surprised to observe that Canning was 'quite melted into tears' by the sermon. 'I should have thought,' wrote Wilberforce, 'he had been too much hardened in debate to show such signs of feeling.' (*Life*, IV, pp. 324/5)

CHAPTER XX

The Premiership
1827

In October 1826, Croker noted that the political sky looked very cloudy.[1] It was an understatement. There was, it is true, no significant change in the balance between government and opposition in the new House of Commons elected that summer. But the real opposition now came from behind the Treasury bench, not from the have-nots across the gangway. As Palmerston commented in disgust, it came from 'the stupid old Tory party, who bawl out the memory and praises of Pitt while they are opposing all the measures and principles which he held most important.'[2] Inside the Cabinet, dissension had tended to shift from foreign to domestic issues, but the split between liberals and ultras was just as deep and bitter.

There was a feeling that things could not go on as they were. Canning, noting Wellington's 'extraordinary fretfulness' and frequent references to the approach of critical times, was inclined to suspect that the duke and Eldon were anticipating 'some convulsion' in the government, and might even be contemplating bringing one on.[3] The prime minister, dogged by persistent ill-health, was extremely pessimistic about his government's prospects. In the middle of December, Robinson, preoccupied by worry over a sick wife, suggested that he should exchange the Chancellorship of the Exchequer for some less demanding office and retire to the Lords. Liverpool, who was just recovering from an acute bout of illness, replied bluntly that the government was hanging by a thread and a Cabinet reshuffle would certainly prove fatal. At the same time he admitted – rather inconsistently – that he was contemplating resigning himself before it was too late to enjoy the pleasures of retirement.[4]

Corn and Catholics had been the most discussed issues during the general election and – apart from the threatening Portuguese crisis – they were the government's chief preoccupation afterwards. An exceptionally hot dry summer had destroyed or damaged much of the harvest and at the beginning of September the government felt obliged to relax the restrictions on the import of foreign oats and rye. It was because the ministers needed to indemnify themselves for this breach of the law that the new Parliament was summoned exceptionally early, in the middle of November, and thus happened to be in session to give prompt approval to the despatch of troops to Portugal. 'How fortunate,' wrote Canning, 'that we were obliged to meet – much against our will – for corn!'[5]

But it was clear that some more satisfactory way of ensuring the country's food supply must be found, whether the landowners liked it or not. Canning did not consider himself an expert on this and had no strong feelings about what exactly should be done. But he did feel very strongly that this must not be allowed to be an issue – as the Catholic question had perforce become – on which the Cabinet could afford the luxury of either private or public disagreement. He must insist, he told Liverpool, that the Cabinet should take a decision on corn and 'that it shall be an understood compact among the members of the Govt that their individual language out of doors shall conform to the decision of the majority – not of the minority – within. In matters relating to my own department the contrary practice has been inconvenient enough in former times. Now it does not signify. But in a question so vital as that of corn, an apparent discrepancy between the members of the Govt (after a measure had been once agreed upon) would be disgraceful and ruinous.'[6] The letter reflects the accumulated resentment of years.

In his less emphatic way, Liverpool was equally determined to revise the corn laws, and he and Huskisson worked out a plan for a sliding scale of duties on foreign corn that would begin to operate when the home price reached 60s. a quarter. It was to be introduced as soon as possible after Parliament reassembled on February 8 after the Christmas recess. Liverpool knew that it would provoke a violent storm; and since Huskisson was regarded with the deepest dislike and distrust by the landed interest, the prime minister decided that he and Canning must introduce it themselves in the two Houses.

But death and disease played havoc with Liverpool's plans. On January 5, 1827, the Duke of York died. He was buried late one evening in St George's Chapel, Windsor. Unfortunately the funeral arrangements were bungled. After the members of the Cabinet, the royal dukes and the other dignitaries had assembled in the chapel there was a delay of nearly two hours before the coffin was brought in. It was a bitterly cold night and since, for some unaccountable reason, the matting in the aisle had been removed, there was nothing but the cold damp stones to stand on during the long wait. 'I presume,' wrote Canning to Wellington afterwards, '. . . that Mr Mash, or whoever filched the cloth or the matting from under our feet in the aisle, had bets or insurances against the lives of the Cabinet.'[7] The only fatality was the Bishop of Lincoln, but several of the mourners, including Wellington, the Duke of Montrose and Canning were seriously ill afterwards.

A notable absentee from the funeral was Lord Liverpool, who had escaped this hazardous duty because he was convalescing at Bath from the severe illness which had struck him down before Christmas. Canning, who was not immediately affected by his bleak vigil, set off for Bath next morning, accompanied by his private secretary, Augustus Stapleton. On the way he told his companion that Liverpool intended to retire at the end of the session and talked over the likely consequences. According to Stapleton's account, Canning never doubted that he himself would be the next prime minister.[8] When they got to Bath, however, they found Liverpool much restored in health and in excellent spirits. The three of them went riding and at dinner Canning and Liverpool entertained the young man – and themselves – with stories of the fun and games of their youth. Any idea of retiring seemed to have passed right out of the prime minister's mind.

By this time the cold caught in St George's Chapel was beginning to 'mature' and when Canning rejoined Joan at the house they had recently bought in Brighton, he was seriously ill. According to Stapleton, his illness 'assumed every variety of form of which cold and rheumatism are capable,'[9] but his worst symptom was bouts of agonising rheumatic pains in the head which kept on recurring in spite of vapour baths and frequent doses of the strongest form of bark (quinine). By the middle of February, however, he was sufficiently recovered to send Granville a lighthearted description of the Brighton scene. 'The map of Brighton,' he wrote, 'is a curious one at the present moment. H.My is laid up at the Pavilion and I at the eastern extremity of the cliff. Constant interchanges of enquiries and good offices pass between us, in the shape of supplies of whey and fruit on His Majesty's part, which on mine have been amply compensated by Mme de Bouche's unexpected quadruped.* On the other side of the Pavilion are encamped the Lievens and Palmellas waiting with no small solicitude for one or other recovery in order that either business or society may begin. I hope that my rheumatics will get the start of the King's gout and then I shall be able to receive the ambassadors at a conference before the King entertains them at the Pavilion.'[10]

In the meantime, while convalescing, Canning tried to concentrate

* A wild pig sent as a present to the Cannings. The King was known to be very partial to wild pig.

434

on the details of the new Corn Bill which he hoped to be able to introduce in the Commons on February 26. He wrote to Huskisson asking him to come down to Brighton to give him a thorough briefing on the 17th. At 10.30 on the same Saturday morning, Lord Liverpool was found lying unconscious on the floor of his study in his London home. In his hand he clutched a letter from Stapleton containing yet another discouraging bulletin on Canning's fluctuating state of health.

The burden of coping with this tragic emergency fell on the sensible and competent Peel. He immediately sent a messenger to the King at Brighton. He also informed Wellington and wrote to ask Joan Canning to tell her husband as soon as she thought he was fit to hear the news. She told him that same evening. Next day, Peel went down to Brighton where he found the King reasonably calm in spite of a severe attack of gout in both feet, one knee and one hand. Later Peel called on Canning and they decided that it would be best to advise the King to carry on as usual for the time being.

When Canning was able to visit the Pavilion himself four days later he found that their advice to do nothing had – not surprisingly – put the King into a surprisingly equable frame of mind. Liverpool had more or less recovered consciousness but he was paralysed down the right side. Even if he did not die it seemed most unlikely that he would be able to resume public life. But it would be 'highly indelicate', the King told Canning, to assume at this stage that the prime minister would not fully recover. Moreover, he added, it would be a great satisfaction to all of them when Liverpool was able to learn that no move to fill his place had been made or even considered.[11] No doubt it would be. But for once kindliness was convenient as well as worthy; for it must have been clear to the King that the choice of a successor to Liverpool, if it had to be made, would be neither easy nor painless.

In fact, of course, the pretence of business as usual deceived nobody, although the ministers did their best to be convincing. Canning made his first appearance in the Commons since the Christmas holidays on March 1 when he at last introduced the new Corn Bill. Hobhouse thought he made a feeble speech and looked very ill.[12] Canning, however, thought he had thrown the 'bumpkins' into confusion and disagreement over how to oppose the measure.[13] He turned out to be right. The bill was criticised by some for making any change at all and by others for not making change enough. But on April 3 it passed its second reading by a substantial majority of 165, and on the 12th it was read a third time without a division.

The other major issue – the Catholic question – fared less well. The strength of the popular 'no-popery' prejudice in England had helped to increase the number of committed Protestants in the new House of Commons. But in Ireland the elections had stimulated the Roman Catholic majority to assert their claim to political equality with increased determination; the Catholic voters, obeying their clergy and their political leaders rather than their landlords, had refused to elect candidates opposed to emancipation. With the situation in Ireland deteriorating so obviously, Sir Francis Burdett and other leading pro-Catholics in the Commons believed they had a fair chance of success. Some Whigs were in favour of delay because of the government crisis, but Canning encouraged Burdett to go ahead.

Burdett's resolution in support of the Catholic claims was debated on March 5 and 6. The well-worn arguments could still produce an apparently inexhaustible flow of oratory and passion. Much of the heat was generated on the Treasury bench and directed at other members of the government. Peel attacked Plunket, the Irish Attorney-General, while Canning lashed out with furious sarcasm at Copley, the Master of the Rolls.* It was an unedifying spectacle, although the Whigs enjoyed it. In the end the motion was lost by four votes. The result, it was generally agreed, was largely due to the accidental absence or illness of several pro-Catholics; it could easily have gone the other way and probably would do so next time. To many observers, it seemed clear that the expedient of a Cabinet in a state of armed neutrality on the most important issue of the day would hardly last much longer. But it seemed no more possible to form a government united either for or against this issue than it had been fifteen years earlier.

By this time no one doubted that Liverpool, whether he lived or died, would have to be replaced, and the problem of his successor was the most absorbing subject of conversation. Canning was by no means alone in assuming that he himself would be the King's choice. As leader of the House of Commons he was the recognised number two in the government. In terms of age and experience he was senior to

* Sir John Copley, a moderate Protestant, had the misfortune to crib most of his speech from a pamphlet originally addressed to Canning by Dr Philpotts, an argumentative clergyman who had already unsuccessfully tried to involve him in a private controversy over the Athanasian creed. Canning recognised the source of Copley's speech and was excessively irritated. Copley was very put out by Canning's vehemence and said afterwards that he had not had the slightest intention of offending him. Canning afterwards apologised.

Peel. His brilliance and ability were acknowledged to be unrivalled, however much some might distrust and resent them. His great handicap was that he was committed to the Catholic cause. His friends had hoped that an unequivocal victory in the Catholic debate would neutralise that disadvantage. His enemies rejoiced at the Catholic defeat (however accidental) and assumed that it would justify an entirely Protestant government from which what a Canning sympathiser ironically called the 'dreadful liberal taint' would be completely eradicated.[14]

A number of peers began to campaign actively against Canning. Early in March the Duke of Rutland wrote ingratiatingly to Mrs Arbuthnot suggesting that she should use her influence with her 'excellent and highly talented friend the Duke of Wellington' to prevail on him in effect to put himself at the head of the Protestant party.[15] The Duke of Buckingham who, although pro-Catholic, had good reason to suppose that his unassuaged yearning for high office would not be satisfied in a Canning ministry, prodded Wellington to keep Canning out of the premiership.[16] Lord Lowther told Knighton, who was close to the King, that many wise men thought Wellington was the fittest man to be first minister. The Duke of Newcastle intrigued more openly, and with Lord Mansfield's help, set about forming 'an Association for supporting the King in appointing a Protestant Administration'. Mansfield reckoned they could count on the support of about sixty peers. Towards the end of March Newcastle went down to Windsor and urged the King to appoint a Protestant administration. He not only offered him the support of many influential peers if he did, but threatened him with their opposition if he did not. The King assured Newcastle that he was Protestant heart and soul, but he diverted the conversation rather snubbingly to the subject of his tailor and afterwards complained that the duke had spoken in a 'very unbecoming manner'.[17] He objected to moral blackmail as much as anyone.

In spite of these pressures, the King continued to do nothing, although this was daily becoming more difficult. Embarrassing references to the government's headless state were beginning to be made in both Houses of Parliament and the excuse that Liverpool might recover enough to resume office was wearing increasingly thin. On March 22 Wellington saw the King at Windsor and next day the Cabinet met in the confident expectation that he would have brought back some interesting news. But Wellington had learned nothing at all about the King's political intentions and the Cabinet was reduced to discussing the details of the Corn Bill. A few days later, however, Lady Liverpool sent word to the King that her husband had been able to indicate his wish to resign. There was no further excuse for delay.

So Wellington and Canning were summoned to Windsor and on March 28 the King discussed the political situation with each of them separately. He told Canning that he wished to keep his present Cabinet on its present basis with a Protestant peer as prime minister. Canning at first suggested that the King should form a ministry that represented his own opinions. The King replied that this could not be done. Canning knew perfectly well that it could not, but he may have felt that if he was to arrive at the premiership only by a process of elimination, he was entitled to have the different steps in the process clearly delineated. The King made it clear that although he could not do without Canning in his government, he could not have a pro-Catholic premier for fear of being accused of abandoning his Protestant principles. Canning replied that he, for his part, could not possibly change his attitude on the Catholic question without disgracing himself. On this subject he could give no pledges but must remain as 'free as air'. Moreover if the Catholic issue was to remain an open one, with every minister free to take his own line, he did not see why he should allow himself to be excluded from the highest office simply because of his pro-Catholic opinions. He went on to tell the King plainly that he must either have the 'substantive power of First Minister' or resign. In other words, the office of First Lord of the Treasury must be filled either by himself or by some peer who would be, and would be known to be, simply a figurehead.[18] The audience ended in a polite deadlock.

Whether the King's feelings on the Catholic question were really as strong as he made out may be doubted. They were certainly not as uncompromising as those of his father or brother, the Duke of York. Many people at the time thought that what he minded about most was his own ease and comfort. It did not of course contribute to either to let the crisis drag on so long. The King may have been genuinely unable to make up his mind; or he may have felt that if he had to take Canning in the end, there was no harm in first demonstrating the lack of a suitable alternative. At any rate his next move was to suggest to Canning and Peel that the Cabinet should choose a premier for him. He had got away with this evasion of responsibility in 1812 when the Cabinet had chosen Liverpool to succeed the murdered Perceval. But this time Canning and Peel decided, as a matter of constitutional principle, that it would not do.[19] On March 31 they firmly put the ball back in the King's court and there it remained for the next ten days.

By this time the opposition was beginning to think that the political interregnum had lasted long enough. On March 30 Tierney proposed that the Commons should grant no further supplies until a new ministry had been formed. It was, he said, undoubtedly the King's privilege to choose his own minister; but it was equally undoubtedly the privilege of the Commons to stop supplies until it knew to whom they were to be entrusted. The opposition cheered loudly when he hinted at the possibility of Canning becoming prime minister, but the response from the government benches was distinctly half-hearted. Canning told the House that a definite decision to replace Liverpool had been taken within the last few days, but in response to further prodding from Tierney he could give no assurance that the new ministry would be announced before Parliament rose for the Easter recess.[20] The opposition motion was comfortably defeated. But it was a humiliating exchange for the minister who had never doubted that he had the best right to succeed Liverpool and it was observed that Canning found it hard to hide his chagrin.[21]

For nearly a week Canning, Peel and Wellington had no further communication with the King but a good deal of discussion among themselves. Peel's position was quite straightforward. He was willing to go on serving as Home Secretary under another Protestant peer if one of sufficient character, prestige and ability could be found. He did not aim at the premiership for himself because he did not think that Canning, who was unquestionably his senior, could be expected to serve under him and he did not believe that the government could stand without Canning. But he himself could not serve under Canning because they disagreed on the Catholic question. It was his only objection but it seemed to him insuperable. The office of prime minister carried with it great influence and prestige; whoever held it had patronage to dispose of and the last word on innumerable appointments. If the premier was pro-Catholic, he was bound in the long run to give a pro-Catholic tendency to his administration, even though officially it remained neutral. Moreover, as the minister responsible for Ireland, Peel would either have to endorse this tendency or fall out with the prime minister.[22]

Peel first told Canning that he could not serve under him as early as March 29 and nothing that Canning could say or suggest would make him budge. He was offered the Foreign Secretaryship and later, on the King's suggestion, a peerage and the leadership of the Lords. But with implacable rectitude he decided that a change of office would be only a paltry subterfuge. Canning was bitterly disappointed. He was consoled by the knowledge that Peel had no other objection to serving under him and by the absence of any shade of personal estrangement between them. 'In truth,' he wrote to Peel, 'so far as you and I are concerned, the fault is in circumstances which neither of us could control, not in ourselves.'[23]

Canning's relationship with Peel had a solid foundation of mutual respect and esteem which allowed them to disagree without rancour. With Wellington it was different. There was no real basis for an understanding, let alone an agreement – even to disagree. Their exchanges at this time were marked by mutual suspicion and, on the duke's side, by his profound dislike and distrust of Canning. He recognised that the government could not do without him, but he could not bring himself to accept his claim to be prime minister. He had convinced himself that Canning was intriguing with the opposition and made no secret to his friends of his strong reluctance to serve under him. Canning for his part had apparently got wind of the approaches that were being made to Wellington by the Protestant peers and suspected him of encouraging them. On April 3 the two men had a two-hour talk during which Canning told the duke what he had said to the King on March 28 and suggested that Robinson might be called to the Lords and made First Lord of the Treasury – in effect a 'dummy' prime minister. Wellington, on his side, seems to have successfully scotched the rumours that he was intriguing with the Protestant peers, for Canning reported to Knighton afterwards that 'everything that was in doubt between us has been cleared up satisfactorily.'[24] Yet two days later, after another interview with the duke, he was angrily telling Knighton that, contrary to his previous belief, he now thought that Wellington wanted the premiership himself.[25]

Canning's second thoughts were almost certainly less correct than his first. It was widely believed that Wellington had disqualified himself for the premiership when he agreed to succeed the Duke of York as commander-in-chief; to have the country's highest military and civilian posts in the same hands was considered incompatible with the country's 'free constitution'. Wellington himself told Croker that he agreed with this view. In any case, he was not attracted by the premiership, and he never responded to any of the suggestions that he should put himself forward. All the same, his position was not so completely unambiguous as Peel's. He did not find it necessary to stop his friends from discussing the pros and cons of his candidature; and he would not have denied that if the King actually commanded him to step into the breach (as he did a year later) he would feel bound to obey.

But when the King at last emerged from his rural seclusion at

The RATS at the CORN !!!

[July 1827]

Canning is portrayed bringing in his temporary Corn Bill after his original measure had been wrecked by Wellington's amendment. The Duke plunges his sword into Canning's sack so that some of the corn pours out in the direction of a circle of rats

After Canning's death John Bull, on the deck of the *Britannia*, encouraged by the Captain – George IV – in the cabin below, warns off a boarding party led by Eldon and Wellington

Windsor on April 5, he was still not ready to issue his commands to anyone. After his return, Greville wrote that 'London was alive with reports; and the *on dit* of the day, repeated with every variety of circumstance and with the usual positiveness of entire ignorance, would fill a volume.'[26] What actually happened can be more briefly told. The King held a series of consultations with Canning, Peel, Eldon and others, but no solution emerged that would allow him to retain the services of the most powerful member of the House of Commons without having to take a pro-Catholic premier. At last, on the 9th, he commanded Peel to go to Canning with the suggestion that they should all serve under Wellington. Peel can hardly have hoped to succeed. With the duke as First Lord of the Treasury, Canning would not have had the 'substantive power' of prime minister on which he insisted. Pride, principle and the intimations of Whig support that he had received may not have been the only factors behind his inflexibility. His health was still very precarious and he may well have felt that it was not worth risking a complete physical breakdown for anything less than the prize at which he had aimed for more than twenty years.

Peel and Canning tried to think of another suitable peer for premier, but since one would not have a pro-Catholic and the other refused to consider a Protestant, Peel was obliged to report to the King next day that his mission had been a total failure. Two hours later the King sent for Canning and told him to try to assemble a new administration formed on the same principles as that of Lord Liverpool. Although the King did not actually say so, Canning assumed that if he could form a government, he himself was to head it.

It was a victory but hardly a triumph. And within a few days it seemed to have turned into something not far short of a humiliation. Canning knew that he would lose Peel and he must have been virtually certain that Wellington would also go – although he cannot have been prepared for the manner of his going. He wrote at once to tell the duke he had been asked to prepare a plan for a new administration and expressed the hope that Wellington would continue to be a member of it. The duke replied by asking who was to be the head of the new ministry. Canning took umbrage and replied stiffly that it was so generally understood that the King usually entrusted the formation of an administration to the person he intended to place at the head of it that it had not occurred to him to state that the King did not intend to depart from his usual practice. He added that he had shown the duke's letter and his reply to the King.[27] Wellington was furious at what he called the 'tone' of this letter. He claimed that Canning had rebuked and insulted him and had covered himself 'with His Majesty's sacred name and protection'. He immediately resigned not only from the Cabinet but as commander-in-chief as well.

Apparently Wellington really was uncertain whether Canning intended to head the government himself or make a 'dummy' peer First Lord of the Treasury; he had after all suggested this possibility to Wellington on April 3. In 1812 when first Wellesley and then Moira had been asked by the Prince Regent to try to form a ministry, neither of them considered that he had been chosen to head the new government.* Moreover Canning's letters were certainly brusque, uninformative and lacked any trace of cordiality. This may have been the unintentional effect of the extreme pressure under which he was working. Wellington, however, concluded that Canning did not really want him in his Cabinet. Although the two men were not on good terms, this was probably not true. Canning was well aware of the value of having the duke's unique prestige supporting his government. He had always tried – not always, it must be admitted, very successfully – to show him special consideration. 'I agree,' he had written to Liverpool the previous November, 'that nothing could be more inexpedient than to get into any direct controversy with him [Wellington].'[28] Now, when it could hardly be more inexpedient, he had done just that.

Even if Canning had felt that it was useless to try to keep Wellington, it was a mistake to give someone with such a strong sense of public duty an excuse to resign on personal rather than political grounds. There was an exchange of justificatory letters early in May, but Canning completely failed to remove Wellington's sense of personal grievance.[29] The duke's resignation as commander-in-chief was quite unforeseen – no doubt by himself as much as by everyone else. It was widely regretted as an unnecessary and unjustifiable act of pique, and he would probably have liked to withdraw it. In the middle of May he told Colchester that if the King asked him to do so, he did not see how as a soldier he could refuse.[30] Yet when a week later the King did ask him he did refuse. The royal letter was accompanied by a friendly little note from Canning.[31] But what Wellington wanted before he could bring himself to back down, was not an olive branch but an abject apology. The breach was never healed.

The resignations of Wellington and Peel were only the beginning of the rot; by the 12th Westmorland, Bexley,† Melville, Eldon and

---

* Lord Westmorland also seems to have been uncertain at first whether the King intended Canning to be prime minister. (A. G. Stapleton, *Pol. Life*, III, p. 329)

† Nicholas Vansittart had been made Lord Bexley in 1823.

Bathurst had all resigned. Moreover, the departure of the big fish in the Cabinet was quickly followed by a shoal of resignations by the smaller fry. It was reckoned that the grand total came to 41 on the 13th.[32] The departure of Eldon was not unexpected, both because he was a fanatical Protestant and because he was well on into his seventies and intended to retire soon anyway. But Canning had not apparently foreseen that so many others would jib at a pro-Catholic premier. Lord Bexley had at first agreed to stay but changed his mind when he heard that Peel, the leading Protestant in the Commons, was going. Melville, who was pro-Catholic, resigned for no better reason than that so many of his colleagues had done so, and his condescending assurance that he did not wish to 'unnecessarily accelerate' his retirement only added to Canning's disgust. 'This is the basest of all,' he wrote to Knighton, 'for *here* is no reason *pretended* except that of prudent speculation. I'll "accelerate" him!'[33]

How far personal mistrust of Canning influenced the resigning ministers it is hard to say. They might well, however, have been less reluctant to serve under a pro-Catholic premier if he had been a less dominating and forceful person. Inevitably, so many virtually simultaneous resignations aroused suspicion that they had been concerted beforehand. This was indignantly denied. Indeed, far from 'caballing', the Protestant ministers seem to have indulged in a kind of implicit conspiracy of silence during the last stages of the interregnum.

One important result of the resignations was that they infuriated the King and placed his hitherto wavering support squarely behind Canning. (Eldon, who was the only one with the temerity – and courtesy – to go to the King himself with his resignation, was thoroughly abused for his pains.) On the morning of the 12th the King received Canning in bed and – according to one version – immediately assured him that if he was not frightened he himself was not, and if Canning named an entirely pro-Catholic Cabinet, he would accept it.[34] According to a second version the King at first expressed some doubt as to whether his new premier could find enough support. Canning answered that he could count on help from the Whigs and then said: 'Sir, your father broke the domination of the Whigs. I hope your Majesty will not endure that of the Tories.' To which the King replied: 'No, I'll be damned if I do.'[35] Since Parliament was due to rise that day for the Easter recess and, if Canning was to take office as prime minister, a new parliamentary writ would have to be moved for him that afternoon, the King immediately gave him his hand to kiss. A few hours later Canning appeared in the Commons as First Lord of the Treasury and Prime Minister.

Canning had lost the support of half the Cabinet and a large part of the Tory party primarily because he was loyal to a cause that still had to contend with a mass of popular prejudice in England. He was also a committed opponent of parliamentary reform. Yet his appointment as premier was received with the greatest enthusiasm throughout the country. His personal magnetism, together with his reputation as a supporter of liberal policies at home (in particular the new Corn Bill) and abroad, ensured that he would be the popular favourite in any contest with the ultra Tories. *The Times*, which for years had bitterly criticised him, declared that the ultras' personal hatred of Canning was mixed with dislike of 'the popular measures now in progress, of which Mr Canning was only the author more than Lord Liverpool and the other members of the late Administration, inasmuch as he possessed more talents and a clearer elocution to carry them into effect.'[36] Among the 'Seven Sages', as the *Morning Chronicle* ironically dubbed the resigning ministers, Eldon and Wellington were especially vehemently attacked, while the King, praised on all sides for standing up to them, basked in unaccustomed popular approval.

It was all very gratifying but it did not prevent the political pundits from prophesying that Canning could not survive. Robinson, the Chancellor of the Exchequer, never a very determined man, found the situation most distressing, but – to his credit – could not bring himself to desert the supposedly sinking ship. Canning himself does not seem to have shared the general gloom. He realised that he would have to turn to the Whigs, but he set to with determination to exhaust the resources of his own side first. He immediately 'accelerated' Melville's departure from the Admiralty by announcing that he would be succeeded by the Duke of Clarence with the title of Lord High Admiral. Not everyone thought it wise to bring in the heir-presumptive; but on the whole it was regarded as something of a coup and a significant demonstration of royal support.

Lord Bexley, who had been Chancellor of the Duchy of Lancaster, was prevailed on to change his mind yet again after the King had sent for him and lectured him for three hours after church on Good Friday. Bexley was not in himself much of an asset (although he perhaps did not deserve Lord Howard de Walden's description of him as 'a little hypocritical evangelical sneaking fox').[37] But he was a Protestant and

Canning badly needed some in a Cabinet that was supposed to be, like its predecessor, neutral on the Catholic issue. Two other Protestants were secured. One was Sir John Copley, the distinctly mediocre lawyer, who had not been too wounded by Canning's sarcasm in the Catholic debate to spurn the glittering prize of the Lord Chancellorship and the title of Lord Lyndhurst. The other was the Marquess of Anglesey, the gallant soldier who had lost a leg at Waterloo and who now conquered his fear of speaking in the Lords sufficiently to take – appropriately enough – Wellington's place as Master-General of Ordnance. To please the King, Canning also made great efforts to replace Peel at the Home Office by another Protestant. The office was hawked round to Bathurst, Manners-Sutton (the Speaker), Thomas Wallace (the economic expert who had resigned as Master of the Mint) and Lord Farnborough, but all turned it down, although Manners-Sutton and Wallace were both offered a peerage for good measure. Canning even had difficulty in finding a temporary Home Secretary. But just when he was in 'absolute despair',[38] his friend, William Sturges Bourne, agreed to stand in.

Canning had varying success with his personal friends. He wanted Granville to go to the Foreign Office temporarily until – as he apparently intended – he could go back there himself. But Granville was so appalled at the prospect of speaking in the Lords (having completely dried up during a previous attempt) that Canning let him off.* He managed to persuade another friend, Lord Dudley (formerly J. W. Ward), to go there instead; but, as everyone knew, he himself still really ran the country's foreign policy. He even had to fall back on his wife's relations; Joan managed to persuade her brother-in-law, the Duke of Portland, to lend the prestige of his name to the Cabinet by temporarily taking the Privy Seal; she assured him that the office had 'absolutely nothing in the way of business belonging to it' and he need not even go to the Cabinet meetings if he did not want to.[39]

Lord Palmerston, on the other hand, who had been Secretary at War since 1809, was delighted to be brought into the Cabinet for the first time. Three other former members of Liverpool's administration, who were already in the Cabinet, stayed put: Lord Harrowby as Lord

---

* 'I could not,' wrote Granville pathetically to Canning, 'even undertake to make a speech in explanation of, or in defence of, the foreign policy of the Government, because I know from experience that such is my nervousness and painful embarrassment when I attempt to speak, that there is always a great chance of every idea which I had arranged in my head as the substance of my speech escaping my recollection, at the moment when I found myself upon my legs (as was the case when I last spoke in the House of Lords), and I cannot wish the disgrace of a positive *breakdown*.' (Aspinall FCM, p. 97, April 17, 1827)

President of the Council, Charles Wynn at the Board of Control and William Huskisson at the Board of Trade. Huskisson's reforms, especially the Corn Bill, had been, and still were, under very strong attack; he was determined to remain at a 'post so threatened, if for no other reason, because it is threatened'.⁴⁰ A less doughty fighter, Frederick Robinson, seemed the best available choice to take the lead in the House of Lords. Canning took the Chancellorship of the Exchequer himself for the time being, and Robinson went to the Lords as Viscount Goderich and Secretary for War and Colonies. He accepted his elevation with deep foreboding.

The new Cabinet did indeed lack strength and talent, and the government as a whole, even with the votes of those who habitually backed the King's ministers, lacked assured parliamentary support. Canning had no choice but to turn to the Whigs, although there was a tendency in those days to condemn coalitions as opportunistic and rather disreputable; it was assumed that one, if not both, of the parties must have abandoned at least some of its principles. But by now the liberal Tories had far more in common with the moderate Whigs than with their ultra colleagues. For some years, those old enemies, Brougham and Canning, had exchanged compliments across the floor of the House of Commons, and the Whig rank and file had been disappointed by Canning's unmistakable hints that he would not consider joining forces with them. His enemies, however, found no difficulty in convincing themselves that he had been treacherously negotiating with the Whigs before Liverpool's seizure. The story is inherently improbable and no evidence has ever been unearthed to corroborate it. Canning was certainly in friendly collaboration with some of the Whig leaders over their support on specific issues. He believed that the old party labels were losing their meaning, but he knew that old party loyalties – and prejudices – still ran deep. Moreover, while he realised that the King's antipathy to the Whigs would be extremely hard to overcome, he was apparently unaware of the depth of the ultra Tories' aversion to himself.

After Liverpool's collapse it did not take most of the Whigs long to make up their minds that they wanted Canning to be the next premier, that he would need their support against the ultra Tories and that they must not make too many difficulties about the terms on which they gave it. The opposition press began openly and eagerly to urge the formation of a Whig-Canningite coalition. A group of moderate Whigs decided that they ought to support Canning even if he could give them neither office nor a definite pledge to carry Catholic emancipation. They took care to report their conclusions to a friend of Canning's, E. J. Littleton, who duly passed them on. They were, he wrote, quoting the words of his informant, 'so satisfied of your sincerity, they were persuaded you *would do anything consistent* with the safety of your principles to advance your own power.'[41] Brougham also let it be known that he was enthusiastically in favour of a coalition and – knowing that the King loathed him because of his championship of Queen Caroline – magnanimously disclaimed any interest in office for himself.[42] Meanwhile Canning was in touch with the Marquess of Lansdowne who the previous year had become, with Grey's full agreement, the acknowledged leader of the moderate Whigs. He was anxious to discover whether the Whigs would allow him time to remove the King's prejudices on the Catholic question gradually. Lansdowne replied that he would be satisfied if Canning promised not to shelve it altogether. He also gave an assurance that the Whigs would not insist on coming in *en bloc* but would be content to take office as individuals.[43]

Some Whigs thought that Lansdowne ought to be more demanding. 'He [Canning] is at your mercy,' wrote Ellenborough on April 13. 'Use your power generously but use it firmly and insist upon the First Lord of the Treasury being a Whig.'[44] But Lansdowne showed no inclination to push himself forward, while Canning went on coolly playing his hand as if he still held plenty of trumps. At first he did no more than approach two individual Whigs, offering the Privy Seal to his friend, Lord Carlisle, and the office of Lord Chamberlain to the Duke of Devonshire. Both referred the offers to their leader, Lansdowne. On the 14th, Canning sent Carlisle to tell Lansdowne, in effect, that he was indeed anxious for the Whig party's support, but could make no formal offer until he had discovered what help he could get from his own.[45]

Five days later, having thoroughly examined the extent – or rather paucity – of the Tory resources available to him, Canning was ready to open negotiations with Lansdowne. During a long meeting at Carlisle's house he described in detail the negotiations that had taken place since Liverpool's illness. Lansdowne was clearly impressed. Nothing, he told Sir Robert Wilson, 'could be more candid and honourable than Mr Canning's exposé and deportment.'[46] But the 'bill of fare', as Canning called it, which he set down on the same day, was not particularly generous; it included the Home Office, the Privy Seal, one other Cabinet post, the office of Lord Chamberlain and one of the law offices.[47] Nor did Canning show any willingness to modify his terms.

The Cabinet must be allowed to remain divided on the Catholic question; and neither parliamentary reform nor the repeal of the Test and Corporation Acts were to be brought forward or supported. Thus far Lansdowne was reluctantly prepared to acquiesce. But he insisted that the composition of the Irish government should be entirely pro-Catholic. The King, on the other hand, finding himself obliged to accept an English Cabinet that was far more pro-Catholic than he had bargained for, had told Canning that it must be balanced by a predominantly Protestant government in Dublin. Canning found the stipulation not unreasonable and insisted on respecting it. On this issue the talks broke down scarcely more than twenty-four hours after they had begun.

Only a few Whigs, led by Lord Grey, openly rejoiced at the failure of the negotiations. Grey was possessed by an ineradicable dislike and distrust of Canning which he expressed in terms of violent personal abuse that thoroughly shocked his fellow Whigs. With aristocratic disdain, he declared that the son of an actress was incapacitated *de facto* for the premiership of England.[48] 'I am no defender of the life and character of Canning,' wrote James Abercromby, a moderate and level-headed Whig, 'but I should scorn to depreciate him or any other man by vilifying his parentage and reproaching him with the frailties of his mother.'[49] Abercromby thought that Grey was moved solely by personal feelings and not at all by public principle. This was not quite fair. Grey was genuinely convinced that the time had come to make the Catholic question a government issue, and he thought it wrong that the great Whig party should come into power as an appendage to a group of Tories. Other Whigs shared these more respectable misgivings. They felt that Lansdowne owed it to the party to press at least for the lead of the House of Lords and he had not done so. They were worried by rumours spread by the ultra Tories that Canning had sold his Catholic principles to the King in return for the premiership. The rumours were false, but Canning was well aware that he could not press the King too hard on the Catholic question.

Most of the Whigs, however, were furious with Lansdowne for giving up so easily. It was not only that after so many long years in the wilderness they were looking forward to the pleasures and profit of office, although of course that played a part. They were also genuinely appalled that a golden opportunity to get rid of the Protestant ultra Tories had apparently been let slip. 'We ought to consider Eldon and Wellington as our natural enemies,' wrote Abercromby, 'and ought to support anybody who will keep them out – we owe at least as much as that to the man who has broken and ousted such a band of intolerant, selfish and prejudiced politicians.'[50] Even Holland, who was full of doubts and reservations about joining Canning, admitted that the exclusion of 'the ultra Tory intolerants' was *prima facie* evidence in favour of any government.[51]

By the time the Lansdowne-Canning talks had broken down, many other Whigs had emerged from anxious and prolonged heartsearchings with the same conclusions. Even those who felt too deeply committed to parliamentary reform to serve under Canning themselves, thought that moderate Whigs could join him without violating their principles and ought to do so. As a political issue, parliamentary reform was temporarily dormant. The demand for it had been blunted by the Liverpool government's liberal economic policies and attempt to reform the corn laws. It was Ireland, trembling – as many thought – on the brink of civil war, that preoccupied the minds of responsible opposition politicians. And a Canning ministry, known to be sympathetic to the Irish Catholics' demand for political equality, might at least tranquillise them by giving them hope for the future. When the coalition was at last formed, Lord Duncannon, the Whig whip, wrote apologetically that 'connected as I am with Ireland, I could not forgo the opportunity of *the chance even* of saving Ireland.'[52]

Lansdowne already knew when he set out for his country house in Wiltshire on April 21 that the breakdown of his talks with Canning had thrown the Whig party into an uproar. The previous night, Brougham had organised a meeting of thirty to forty rebellious Whigs at Brooks's. The dissidents had come out strongly in favour of a coalition with Canning and attempted to reopen negotiations through Lord Dudley. More conventional Whigs, who thought that Brougham had no business to hustle the Whig grandees in this way, made their views known more discreetly but equally firmly. Lansdowne, in fact, was deluged by letters advocating a union with Canning, while the opposition press went overboard in favour of a coalition.

Lansdowne himself, who lacked all personal ambition, was probably not sorry for an excuse to withdraw from party politics which – as he had complained to Holland – 'are now so much mixed with personal pique and passion as to have become very disagreeable to say the least of it . . .'[53] But he also had a strong sense of duty and as he was by no means sure that he was doing the right thing he left the Duke of Devonshire free to reopen negotiations. The duke, who declared that he was sick of the absurd way in which the wretched Whigs always cut their own throats, applied himself energetically to the task of bringing them to their senses. After further consultations with Canning and a number of leading Whigs, he posted down to Wiltshire on the 23rd and persuaded Lansdowne to modify his insistence on an all-Catholic Irish government. The Whig leader agreed not to insist that the pro-Catholic Lord Wellesley, who was due to retire as Lord Lieutenant at the end of the year, should be succeeded by another Catholic, provided that the key post of Irish Secretary, which in the previous government had been held by the Protestant Henry Goulburn, should be given to a Catholic.

Devonshire immediately hurried back to London with these new terms. Canning, however, decided that Lansdowne's insistence on a pro-Catholic Secretary in Dublin was unacceptable. 'After the confiding and generous manner,' he wrote, 'in which the King has sanctioned the proposed distribution of Cabinet offices, I could not bring myself to submit to His Majesty any limitation of his royal discretion upon a point (and the only one) which His Majesty has specially reserved.'54 Out of deference to the King, Canning refused to concede the point. In fact it turned out to be rather an academic one, because he was quite unable to find another Protestant to succeed Goulburn (who had resigned) and had no choice but to appoint a pro-Catholic, William Lamb. The King accepted Lamb without fuss because he happened to like him very much.

Lansdowne no longer had any excuse for resisting the urgent requests of his friends to return to London. He arrived on April 26 and the same evening, accompanied by Devonshire, called on Canning and together they came to an understanding. Lansdowne agreed to advise his friends to support the government and join it if invited. He himself would support it, but would not enter the Cabinet until the permanent composition of the Irish government had been settled. It was agreed that Devonshire who, although a Whig, was personally very acceptable to the King, should take office at once as Lord Chamberlain, that James Scarlett, the Whig lawyer, should become Attorney-General, and that a few minor offices should be allotted to Whigs.

The new ministerial arrangements were officially gazetted on April 30. *The Times* hopefully described them as 'a remedy for the unnatural state into which the public men of England had been latterly distributed, where friends were separated and enemies crammed together.'55 But the Duke of Bedford, an arch-Whig, scornfully dismissed them as 'one of Canning's jokes'.56 It was certainly not an impressive team. The stop-gap ministers, like Sturges Bourne, Dudley and Portland, were lightweights, and the connection with the Whigs seemed too exiguous to count for much. Altogether, there was a depressing air of fragility and impermanence about the ministry. The King advised Canning to cultivate the Lowther interest. 'The more you can strengthen yourself by the Tory party,' he wrote rather wistfully on May 1, 'the greater security I feel in the stability and permanency of my present government.'[57]

But matters had gone too far for the government to hope to gain strength from anyone except the Whigs. And early in May Scarlett wrote to Lansdowne urging him to give 'some more distinct outward and visible sign of a union between you and the Government than the mere support by speaking and voting in Parliament.'[58] A few days later, Canning formally approached Lansdowne, and on the 16th it was agreed that three Whigs should enter the Cabinet: Lansdowne without portfolio; Carlisle as first Commissioner of Woods and Forests; and Tierney as Master of the Mint. Although it was another two months before Lansdowne agreed to take the Home Office and Carlisle was given the infinitely more prestigious office of Lord Privy Seal, the accession of even three Whigs to the Cabinet helped to give the government a more solid and permanent aspect than it had hitherto possessed.*

Rows within parties, like family rows, are particularly bitter. The protracted political crisis in the spring of 1827 produced a split in both the two great political parties (even the tiny Radical party was divided) and contemporary observers can hardly have been surprised, although they were clearly rather shocked, by the extreme violence of party feeling. 'There is so much confusion,' wrote Lady Cowper on May 1, 'and splitting among families and parties that it is quite a service of danger to talk politics at all, and yet it is impossible to talk of anything else.'[59] The ultra Tories had supposed that Canning could not survive without them and were furious when they found he could. Lady Cowper was being shrewd as well as mildly malicious when she suggested that the Tories had been in office so long that they regarded taking away their places like taking away their private property.[60]

The confusion and bitterness of politics were reflected in Parliament

---

* The Duke of Portland and Sturges Bourne both remained in the Cabinet, the first without portfolio and the second in Carlisle's former post – '. . . Sturgeon Burgeon,' reported Binning flippantly, 'falls soft, and gladly, from his present eminence [the Home Office] into the rural lap of Woods and Forests . . .' (Bagot, II, p. 407, July 12, 1827)

when it reassembled on May 1 after the Easter recess. The House of Commons, crowded to capacity with members and spectators, provided the remarkable spectacle of such staunch Whigs as Henry Brougham, George Tierney and Sir Robert Wilson (not to mention the well-known Radical, Sir Francis Burdett) sitting on the government benches behind a Tory prime minister. The sight was indeed too much for many Whigs; a large and influential group led by Lord Althorp, who five years later piloted the Reform Bill through the Commons, decided that they would rather stay where they were and support the government only when they thought fit.

Among the Tories, Peel made a courteous personal statement on his reasons for resigning which was acknowledged with equal courtesy by Canning. But on the third day, Peel scornfully attacked Brougham for apparently abandoning his principles on such issues as parliamentary reform, and announced that he could not support the government unless he had a clearer idea of the principles on which it was based. The ultra Tories directed their fire against Canning himself. He met their challenge head-on, declaring that he intended to oppose parliamentary reform until the end of his life in the House of Commons 'under whatever shape it may appear.' He would also oppose the repeal of the Test Act because he believed that Parliament should concern itself with remedying practical, not theoretical, grievances and that to meddle with the Test Act might prejudice the Catholic question.[61]* His defiant speech was well received and Canning believed that it had brought over many wavering Tories.[62] A few nights later Peel declared that he was now satisfied with the government's position, and would not indulge in 'factious' opposition. But the ultras, led by Sir Thomas Lethbridge, had no such scruples and pursued their campaign against Canning with a ruthless disregard for the rules of parliamentary procedure.†

Canning had refused to try to conciliate the doubtful Whigs by modifying or disguising his opposition to parliamentary reform. But many of them were so impressed by the extreme hostility shown towards him by the ultra Tories that they were won over all the same. Althorp still had serious private doubts about Canning personally, but he realised that he was the lesser of two evils and on May 7 led a consider-

* In practice, dissenters who infringed the Test and Corporation Acts were protected by annual acts of indemnity. Both Acts were formally repealed in 1828.

† In a private letter on May 5, Canning scornfully described 'this brawling opposition' as 'a fire of straw; and the eyes of bystanders are already grievously offended by it.' (Harewood Mss. 117. To Sir William à Court)

able group of Whigs across to the government benches. He told the House that after the discussions of the past week it was impossible not to see that 'we must choose between a government actuated by liberal and enlightened principles and one of Toryism in its most odious forms.' He would, he added, be worse than a madman if he refused to support the government because he did not agree with it on certain issues when there was so much else on which they did agree.[63]

This was satisfactory for Canning as far as it went, but the issue of parliamentary reform was only temporarily quiescent and there were signs that the battle for it would be joined sooner rather than later. Some of the manufacturing towns were pressing for representation and even those people who considered a general reform too revolutionary tended to be sympathetic to reform in individual cases. On May 28 Lord John Russell moved that the borough of Penrhyn, which a Commons committee had found guilty of gross corruption, should be disfranchised and its seat transferred to Manchester. Canning opposed, not because he denied the corruption, but because he did not think it sufficiently extensive to justify disfranchisement which would penalise innocent and guilty voters alike.[64] His Whig supporters, however, voted for disfranchisement, and their action, together with the accidental absence of many Tories at the annual Pitt dinner, gave Russell a decisive victory. It was not a ministerial vote and Canning, maintaining that it was simply a judicial question, professed not to care about his defeat.[65] But it was a disturbing demonstration of his inability to control the votes of his coalition partners.

A few days later the government suffered a much more serious setback in the Lords when it was defeated on an amendment to the Corn Bill introduced by the Duke of Wellington. The duke, who had approved the bill when a member of Liverpool's Cabinet, merely intended to improve it and had very properly consulted Huskisson before introducing his amendment. Unfortunately the technical issues it raised were both obscure and complicated and Huskisson's reply – as he himself later admitted – was so carelessly drafted that Wellington misunderstood its meaning. The amendment he finally introduced after taking account – as he thought – of Huskisson's advice would have permanently prohibited the release of warehoused corn unless the average price amounted to 66s. a quarter.[66] This would have undermined the sliding scale principle which was the crux of the reform the bill was intended to make; it would also, in effect, have killed the measure because it would infringe the financial prerogatives of the

453

Commons who would certainly throw it out when it was returned to them. Goderich therefore opposed the amendment. It was carried all the same by four votes.

At first Canning and Lansdowne were confident that they could reverse what the Whig leader icily described as this 'strange proceeding in the House of Lords.'[67] Royal displeasure should have a salutary effect. The King was so angry that three peers who had voted for the amendment felt obliged to resign their posts in the royal household. But in spite of ostentatious royal backing, the combination of those who hated the new Corn Bill and those who hated the new government was still strong enough to confirm Wellington's amendment by a majority of eleven votes. Next day Goderich announced that the government would drop the bill.

Canning's first reaction was to drop the corn issue altogether and let the odium and unpopularity fall on those responsible for carrying Wellington's amendment. Grey's emotional diatribe against the government for abandoning the bill suggests that he was not unaware of this danger. But Canning's more worthy second thoughts recognised that it would not do to play party politics with the people's main source of food. In any case, the government could not hope to escape blame if it failed to guard against a scarcity. So on June 18 he brought in a temporary bill which would allow the existing stocks of warehoused corn to be released on the terms of the bill which had failed. This should prevent prices from rising too high before the next harvest, which promised to be abundant, and next session the whole question would have to be gone into again. Canning believed that the bill would be acceptable to the Lords unless they were 'absolutely mad with faction'.[68] The Lords, in fact, were somewhat chastened and the bill passed quickly and with negligible opposition through both Houses.

The struggle over the Corn Bill was not a reliable indicator of Canning's strength in the Lords because, on this issue, so many peers had already pledged themselves to vote against it before Liverpool's collapse. But there was undoubtedly much personal prejudice against Canning in the upper house. When Creevey asked Althorp whether it was 'the question of *corn* that made the great opposition in the Lords', he was told: 'No, it was the question of *Canning* and only that; for you know no one can have any confidence in him.'[69] Canning himself thought that in a division on purely party lines, he might lose in the Lords, but would have an 'immense majority' in the Commons.[70] Since there was no purely party division during the summer session of

1827, his optimistic assumption was never tested.* But he could have been right. The dissident Tories in the Commons lacked organisation and credible leadership. Most of the Whigs supported him and he could count on increasing support from the independent members who tended to support the government of the day. Moreover, he was steadily growing more popular at Court. The King had always found Liverpool uncongenial and he had been deeply affronted by the efforts of the great Tory peers to impose their own choice of prime minister on him. Canning, on the other hand, made himself agreeable and had a pleasant way of conducting business. After his death, the King said that one of his many agreeable qualities as prime minister was that he never kept anything back from him.

As coalition partners, however, the Whigs were not proving very satisfactory. They ignored Treasury notes and would only obey the summons of their own Whip, Lord Duncannon. Moreover, they soon became disgruntled over their meagre share of office and patronage; in addition to their three Cabinet seats, they had only got some half-dozen other places. 'Malignant' Whigs, like Grey, unsparingly criticised them for selling the great Whig party at a shockingly cheap price. Inevitably, they were stung by these gibes as well as by their natural acquisitiveness into agitating for more. Brougham, in particular, in spite of his lofty professions of disinterestedness, found it hard to stifle his yearning for office; on one occasion, the importunities of his friends on his behalf drove Canning to exclaim: 'Damn him, he can have my place.'[71] Naturally, the government's enemies made the most of every sign of tension, while its supporters tried to look on the bright side. But even Tierney, one of the three Whigs in the Cabinet, was said to have despondently confessed: 'We cannot go on, the coach must all be unpacked and repacked again.'[72]

A few days after Parliament rose for the summer recess the Anglo-Russian Protocol on Greece, which Wellington had signed fifteen months earlier, was converted into the tripartite Treaty of London between England, Russia and France. When the news reached Stratford Canning in Constantinople, he commented dryly that the treaty was good but it should have come sooner. By that time he was in a state

* The budget which Canning introduced on June 1 was – as he frankly confessed – a holding operation designed to carry the country's finances over until he had had time to study what economies and reforms were possible and necessary. It was passed without a division.

verging on despair. Early in the year he had again approached the Porte on the Greek question, but had fared no better than before, even though this time he had Russian support and the Turks knew about the Anglo-Russian Protocol. But the Protocol had no teeth and Stratford realised that nothing short of force would make any impression on the Turks, especially as the struggle was going badly for the Greeks.

There were better reasons for the long delay in coming to the aid of the Greeks than Stratford realised. Canning and Lieven had hoped that the Turks might be intimidated by a show of Christian solidarity if the five great powers could be persuaded to withdraw their missions simultaneously from the Porte. But the plan fell through because neither Austria nor Prussia would co-operate. Metternich's reply was evasive rather than flatly negative. His aim, Canning believed, was 'to gain time, in the hope that the period for doing anything effectual might pass by.'[73] The Prussians, who took their cue from the Austrians, made the excuse that they were too remote from Greece to get involved. Canning, who thoroughly despised the Prussians, commented acidly that it was a pity they had not realised this some years earlier and spared the rest of Europe their innumerable and interminable exhortations on the claims of Greece to Christian assistance.[74]

Charles X's Philhellenic enthusiasm helped to make the French much more co-operative, but it did not remove all difficulties. After Canning's return from Paris in October 1826, they agreed to accede to the Protocol, but for the sake of their *amour propre* wanted it to be renegotiated as a full-blown treaty. To this Canning had no objection. But the negotiations, which began in earnest in January 1827, must have added considerably to the strains imposed on him by the political crisis and his own ill-health. The first draft was produced by Damas, the French foreign minister. It was amended by the British and Russian ambassadors in Paris, and sent to London. Lieven, who was under pressure from his government, was anxious for quick results. A few days after Liverpool's collapse, he told Canning that he had received full powers to sign a treaty and that Nicholas insisted it should contain a secret clause committing the signatories to coerce the Turks, if necessary, into accepting an armistice. It was clear that the Russian emperor, who had been engaged in reorganising his army and navy, was ready to go it alone against the Turks and probably sooner rather than later.

But so long as the political crisis in England remained unsettled, Canning lacked both the time and the authority to conclude a treaty. Lieven continued to press him all the same. On March 22 they agreed on the final draft. But it was three weeks before Canning was appointed premier and more than another month before the draft had been approved by the new Cabinet. It was then the turn of the French to cause delay. Now that they were actually being asked to commit themselves, they began to have cold feet and regret the absence of Austria and Prussia. Damas agreed to sign if the treaty was first submitted to his other continental allies. Canning and Lieven would have welcomed Metternich's signature but they were determined not to let the French give him a chance to hold the treaty up indefinitely. In the end Metternich, followed obediently by the Prussians, refused to join in, the French gave way and the tripartite treaty was signed in London on July 6.[75]

The three powers agreed to mediate between the Turks and the Greeks as soon as both had accepted an armistice. The mediation was to be based, as in the Protocol, on Greek autonomy under Turkish suzerainty. Earlier, Canning had suggested that the allies should threaten to recognise the *de facto* independence of the liberated parts of Greece if the Turks would not accept an armistice. That was too revolutionary for Nicholas, but in a secret clause it was agreed to establish consular relations with the Greeks if the Turks were recalcitrant. Although the Greeks were so hard-pressed militarily, Canning seems to have become increasingly convinced that they would ultimately achieve their independence; he insisted that they should be described in the treaty as 'Greeks' and not as Ottoman 'subjects'. He also insisted that the collective guarantee included in the treaty should be confined to Greece and should be optional. He found it very hard to overcome his rooted distrust of binding commitments – perhaps because Portugal had been such a troublesome one – but he was willing to discuss joining in a Greek guarantee later.

The nub of the treaty was the secret clause which committed the allies to employ force if necessary to end the fighting. In practical terms, this meant using their naval power to prevent further troops and supplies from being sent to Ibrahim from Egypt. There was no Russian naval squadron in the Mediterranean at that time and Lord Bathurst thought it a great mistake to give Nicholas an excuse to bring one in to do a job which could be done equally well by the British and French navies.[76] But the Russian emperor had prepared his fleet and it seems most unlikely that he would not have sent it anyway. It was much better to be able to control its activities by making it part of an allied fleet.

What was much more dubious was whether the allied naval squadrons could carry out their assignment without getting involved in hostilities with the Turks or Egyptians. Canning must have been aware of this although he professed to be satisfied with the treaty.* He never lived to see the outcome. Less than three months after his death, on October 20, 1827, a general engagement between the Allied and the Turkish navies was brought on by a single incident and by the end of the day virtually the whole Turkish fleet had been wiped out. The news of the battle of Navarino was received with mixed feelings in official circles in England where Codrington received as much blame for exceeding his instructions as praise for winning a spectacular victory. But the Greeks, who realised that after Navarino their freedom was assured, rejoiced greatly. What Canning's reactions would have been, we cannot know. But it is tempting to think that privately, at any rate, he would have rejoiced with the Greeks. They for their part certainly believed that without his diplomatic efforts, the battle of Navarino could never have taken place.

On July 13 Canning told Granville that having dealt with Greece he must now take up the still unsettled problem of Spain and Portugal. 'But,' he added, 'I must take a few days rest between for I am quite knocked up.'[77] He had indeed been carrying a tremendous load of work and responsibility and he pushed himself very hard. He was prime minister, leader of the House and Chancellor of the Exchequer – although John Herries, a Joint Secretary to the Treasury, complained that all the work was left to him.[78] He was also still deeply involved in the Foreign Office. In addition, the task of filling all the minor offices in the new government had been tiresome and time-consuming. Yet in spite of it all, he was exhilarated by the achievement of his life-long ambition. Observers were struck by the gleam in his eye, however pale his countenance. Many years later, a young journalist, who had watched him enter the Commons for the first time as prime minister, recalled 'his radiant face as he rapidly mounted the old staircase'.[79] He could still rise to an occasion.

On the other hand, he was less and less able to shrug off the things

* Canning tried to prevent Codrington from being put to the test by sending a certain Major Cradock on a secret mission to Cairo to try to persuade Mehemet Ali not to let the Porte drag him into a dangerous confrontation with the European powers. Cradock was an old acquaintance of the Pasha and it was hoped he would have some influence with him. Unfortunately, he did not have enough. Mehemet Ali listened to him but could not bring himself to break with the Porte. (Temperley, pp. 401/2)

that went wrong. He was mortified by the hostility and controversy that surrounded his political success. The Tory press published vicious personal attacks on him and even on his mother, who had died that spring. It fretted him that he could not answer his enemies in the House of Lords. The Duke of Newcastle called him 'the most profligate minister that had ever been placed in power,'[80] and although the adjective was used 'in a political sense' he could not get it out of his mind. He was even more upset by a weighty and comprehensive attack by Grey on his policies and career and seriously considered asking for a peerage so that he could answer it. His irritability was already notorious and under the stress and overwork of his last parliamentary session it became still more difficult to control.* 'He cannot be blamed,' wrote his friend Binning, 'for it is the effect of his serious illness upon his nerves, which must have been cruelly played upon by the grievous provocation he has received. But . . . it is a matter for much regret, as in these times one word out of joint plays the devil.'[81] Binning hoped that if Canning could recruit his strength during the summer recess he would be less liable to the 'strong impulses of excited feeling' which damaged his reputation as much as they exhausted his nervous energy.

In all the speculation about the prospects of the new ministry, the most important and unpredictable factor, on which it was recognised that everything else hinged, was Canning's health. Most of those who commented on his appearance during the last months of his life thought he looked a very sick man. At Windsor, in the middle of June, he was reported to look 'dreadfully ill'.[82] A month later, a doctor, who saw him for the first time when summoned to attend a meeting of the Privy Council, asked: 'Who is that gentleman with such a fine eye and who is so near his end?' His own doctors remained hopeful and his friends optimistic; it was hoped that a good rest would put him right.

Canning himself thought that that was all he needed, and on July 20 he left Downing Street for Chiswick House which the Duke of Devonshire had lent him. Within a week he had caught another chill, and when Sidmouth's nephew, Henry Addington, dined at Chiswick, he was struck by his host's 'ghastliness of feature and dejection of air'.

* But the Foreign Secretary, Lord Dudley, who saw Canning almost every day during the last three months of his life, never found him irritable during the private transaction of business; '. . . never did I hear from him an unkind, peevish or even impatient word. He was quicker than lightning, and even to the very last gay and playful, so that it was very agreeable to do business with him, the more so as he was always inclined . . . to disguise [his] immense superiority . . .' (Dudley, *Letters to Ivy*, p. 326)

He urged him to follow the example of Huskisson who had also been ill and was taking a complete holiday. Canning replied that he could not just yet, but added, 'cheerfully and rather playfully', that he hoped for one in September.[83]

On July 30 he paid his last visit to Windsor. According to one report, when the King told him that he looked very ill, he replied that he did not know what was the matter with him but he was ill all over.[84] Next day he forced himself to go up to London to the Foreign Office, returning to Chiswick the same afternoon. That evening he seemed very languid and scarcely had strength to get up off the sofa to go to bed. He never came out of his room again.

When Stapleton saw Canning next morning, after the doctor had administered a blister, he was very cheerful, although troubled by a pain in his side. He insisted on finishing a paper on Portugal which he had begun to dictate some days earlier. Next day, August 2, Sir William Knighton called. He was so alarmed by Canning's appearance that he insisted on going immediately to London to fetch two more doctors. After he had gone, Canning spent three hours going through Treasury business with Herries. Afterwards he confessed he was tired but was anxious all the same to go over his paper on Portugal. Stapleton, however, persuaded him to rest, and after signing two Treasury warrants he lay down and tried to sleep. Just over an hour later he was seized with the most violent pain in the side. Next day the doctors admitted that he was in great and imminent danger.

There was little they could do for him. He was apparently suffering from an inflammation of the liver and the lungs and his general condition was so weak that he was unfit to undergo what passed in those days for medical remedies. He suffered agonising pain; on the 5th he told Stapleton that if all the pain he had suffered throughout his life were collected together it would not amount to one hundredth part of the pain he had undergone over the past three days. In between the bouts of pain, he was perfectly lucid; but for most of the time he was either unconscious or delirious. He was obsessed with Portugal; he tried hard to tell Stapleton what was on his mind but could not express himself coherently.

During the morning of Sunday the 5th, he suggested that Harriet should read the prayers for the day to him. But he began to wander in his mind and it was not done. That evening he said to Knighton: 'This may be hard upon me, but it is still harder upon the King.' Yet those about him were never sure whether he really realised that he was dying, and they did not tell him in case it made him worse. Nor did they ask him whether he had any parting words for his country in case it should excite him.* His last whispered words were to his wife. She was carried fainting from the room and was still unconscious when he died some hours later. It was about ten or twelve minutes before four on the morning of August 8. He died so peacefully that those watching him could not tell the precise moment of his death.

Canning's funeral took place the following week in Westminster Abbey. He was buried within a few inches of the grave of his mentor and friend William Pitt. The chief mourner was his youngest son, Carlo, a boy of fifteen, who was to become Governor-General of India, and thirty-five years later was buried in the same corner of the Abbey.† Carlo was supported on his right by the Duke of Clarence, and on his left by another of the King's brothers, the Duke of Sussex, and by his uncle, the Duke of Portland. Behind them came Canning's son-in-law, Clanricarde, and his private secretary, Augustus Stapleton. His relations, Cabinet colleagues, doctors, secretaries and a few intimate friends made up the rest of the procession of mourners.

The funeral was intended to be private, but the immense popular interest turned it into a public, even a national, event. There were nearly 800 people inside the Abbey and the road to it from Canning's house in Downing Street, where his body had been taken, was made almost impassable by the dense throng. The crowd was quiet and respectful – which was not always the case in those days at the funerals of the great. *The Times* commented next day: 'The loss of such a man at such a time was well calculated to draw forth the strongest expressions of deep regret among all classes of his fellow-subjects. That regret was exhibited in the conduct of the assembled multitude of yesterday more strongly and intensely than, we believe, was witnessed at the death of any subject within the memory of the oldest person now living.'[85]

That Canning should have succumbed to ill-health and overwork only three months after reaching the summit of his ambition was widely felt – even by those who liked to moralise on the transitoriness

---

* Some alleged dying words were recorded by his friend Morley. But Stapleton afterwards told Huskisson that 'there were no parting words by way of legacy to his country.' Stapleton was there all the time and would be the last person to hide any dying pronouncement by his master. This account of Canning's death is taken largely from the diary Stapleton kept at the time. (G. C. & T., pp. 602–4)

† Canning's second son, William, by now naval captain, was serving abroad at the time. He was drowned the following year in a bathing accident.

of earthly hopes – to be a shocking personal tragedy. But to many it also seemed little short of a national tragedy. Canning's name had become so firmly associated in the public mind with progressive policies at home and the maintenance of peace abroad that his death aroused widespread feelings of depression and even dismay, especially among the commercial and manufacturing classes. The *Scotsman* commented that the events of the past few months had proved that for five years Mr Canning had been struggling with his colleagues for sounder policies both foreign and domestic. 'The veil, it may be said, has been rent, which concealed the brighter and better side of his character.' In the political world, all those with progressive leanings shared the *Scotsman*'s sense of having lost the one politician who had both the power and the inclination to carry through policies under which, as *The Times* put it, 'the poor man's food would have been increased and the national expenses economised.' Byron's friend, John Cam Hobhouse, a politician of radical outlook, was overwhelmed when he learnt that Canning was dying and although he hardly knew him, felt that he would have given his right arm to save him. He found that almost everyone he met shared his sense of sadness and loss.[86]

Abroad the news of Canning's death created almost as much stir as in England. The first reports to reach Paris caused a fall on the stock exchange and were at first dismissed as a deliberate falsehood designed to depress the funds. In every country the news dismayed liberals and encouraged reactionaries. Huskisson, who was holidaying in Austria at the time, found that in every place through which he passed on his return journey the people seemed to feel as if mankind had lost a benefactor. Metternich, on the other hand, rejoiced greatly that a merciful providence had delivered Europe from this 'malevolent meteor'. Yet even he could not avoid paying an involuntary tribute to his old enemy. 'It is an immense event,' he wrote of Canning's death, 'for the man was a whole revolution in himself alone.'[87] It was a curious and paradoxical comment on the life of a man whose deepest instinct was probably his sense of the need to preserve – and renovate – existing institutions.

In England, the public disquiet at Canning's death was relieved by signs that the King approved his policies and did not intend to bring back the ultra Tories. He immediately sent for the two ministers who had been most closely associated with Canning in public and private life – Goderich and Sturges Bourne – and asked the former to take over as prime minister. A few days later it was approvingly noted in the press that the King had with his own hand directed the Treasury to give a vacant commissionership of the Customs to Augustus Stapleton 'as a mark of respect for Mr Canning's memory'. He also – although this would not have been publicly known – immediately offered Canning's widow a peerage.*

The new ministry was very largely identical with the old one. But within a few months it had foundered because of Goderich's lack of leadership and of nerve. The King prevailed on Wellington to step into the breach and after the formation of his ministry in January 1828 the Canningites began to disintegrate as a distinct group in Parliament. Some, in particular Huskisson, agreed to serve under Wellington, some decided to support him without taking office, some preferred to remain independent. The dispersal of the group was accompanied by much bitterness which – it is sad to relate – Joan Canning helped to stir up; she could not forgive those of her husband's friends and followers who agreed to serve under the ultra Tory who had made his dislike of him so unmistakably plain. The resignation of Huskisson and his supporters after only a few months failed to heal the divisions within the group.

Eighteen months after Canning's death, Catholic emancipation – the reform for which he had striven unsuccessfully all his political life – was brought in by Wellington, who understood the writing on the wall in Ireland and forced the measure on the King and his Protestant colleagues. Three years later, parliamentary reform, which Canning had always stubbornly opposed, was achieved under his most implacable Whig opponent, Lord Grey. Fifteen years later again, Peel split the Tory party, but demonstrated his own enlightened statesmanship, by carrying the total repeal of the corn laws whose reform had been one of Canning's last preoccupations.

Several of Canning's friends thought that if he had been alive in 1832 he would not have opposed the Reform Bill. If he had been convinced that the alternative was likely to be the overthrow of the existing political system, he probably would not have done so. He was essentially a pragmatist and a realist, not a theorist or idealist. 'We must look at things as they are,' he once wrote, 'and not as we would wish them to be.'[88] Nor was he a creative thinker or innovator. Like most of his contemporaries he only dimly understood the great economic and social changes that were taking place during his lifetime. But he had a greater awareness of the need to respond to the pressures for

---

* Joan hesitated to accept at first for financial reasons. But after a few months she decided she must accept for her husband's sake and was made a Viscountess. In 1828 Parliament granted an annual pension of £3,000 to Canning's family.

change than a great many of the governing classes. When discussing the opposition of the Lords to a reform of the corn laws shortly before he died, he exclaimed with some vehemence: 'They ought to see that we are on the brink of a great struggle between property and population. Such a struggle is only to be averted by the mildest and most liberal legislation.'[89] After his death, one of his closest friends, Lord Granville, summed up his attitude towards change: 'Canning was anti-revolutionary, but he sought to avoid revolution, not by stubborn resistance to all movement and reformation, but by rendering the acts of the Government conformable to the spirit of the times.'[90]

Canning was always a dedicated House of Commons man. As an orator he was not in the same class as Chatham, William Pitt or Charles James Fox. After 1806, however, he became outstanding, with only Brougham and perhaps Plunket as serious rivals. His great set pieces would both move and entertain the House, while his extraordinary quickness of mind and command of language made him an exceptionally formidable opponent in debate. But he became much more aware than his fellow politicians of the wider audience beyond Westminster which read his speeches in the newspapers and perhaps occasionally heard him speak at a public meeting at Liverpool or some other great town. He became very conscious of what he called, without ever exactly defining it, public opinion. He once said that since 1688 it had grown from a pigmy to a giant and become a power 'which watches over and governs, and controls, not only the actions, but the words of every public man.'[91] He accepted the power of public opinion to bar the Catholics from full political equality. He resisted it when he thought to give way would be more harmful – as over parliamentary reform or for some time over Greece. But he could and did enlist it to good purpose on behalf of most of his foreign policy objectives, wielding it as a weapon in his duels with the continental powers, especially over Spain and the new South American states. He explained his policies to the British people in his speeches and they approved because he stood up to the continental despots and made their country's influence felt without risking war. He brought pressure to bear on governments by publishing his despatches and making his position plain to the whole world, not just to the diplomats behind closed doors. This open diplomacy and apparent playing to the gallery appalled his conservative colleagues to whom popularity was something to be evaded rather than courted. It infuriated Metternich; but although he would never have dreamt of bothering about public opinion in his own country, the Austrian Chancellor seems to have acknowledged that in England, with its constitution and free parliament, it was something which foreign statesmen would be wise not to antagonise.

On issues of public policy, both domestic and foreign, Canning's attitudes were more controversial at the time than (with the exception of parliamentary reform) they seem in retrospect. It was in his political tactics and in the pursuit of his own career that his judgment sometimes went lamentably astray. There was his violent campaign against Addington after Pitt's resignation, in which he did far more damage to himself than to his intended victim. In 1809 there was his shortsighted inability to swallow his dissatisfaction with Castlereagh's performance as War Secretary. Above all, there was his disastrous (for him) refusal in 1812 to accept Castlereagh's generous offer of the Foreign Secretaryship because he could not have the lead in the Commons as well. Most of his mistakes can be traced to his over-reaching ambition. He strove for power, not for the sake of material rewards or personal prestige, but because he knew that he possessed great talents and wanted to use them to 'do some good' – by which he meant to expand his country's influence and prestige (but not territory) without war, increase its commercial wealth and compose its domestic discords. But his ambition and his obvious brilliance made him disliked and distrusted more than most politicians, just as his personal charm – his humanity, kindness, gaiety and sheer vitality – earned him more affection and devotion from his friends and subordinates than most men enjoy.

Yet although he was a person about whom few did not feel strongly, either one way or the other, his aims and policies were essentially cautious and middle-of-the-road. Towards the end of his life, in a speech in the House of Commons, he summed up the guidelines of his political conduct in the following terms:

'I consider it to be the duty of a British statesman, in internal as well as external affairs, to hold a middle course between extremes; avoiding alike extravagancies of despotism, or the licentiousness of unbridled freedom – reconciling power with liberty; not adopting hasty or ill-advised experiments, or pursuing any airy and unsubstantial theories; but not rejecting, nevertheless, the application of sound and wholesome knowledge to practical affairs, and pressing, with sobriety and caution, into the service of his country, any generous and liberal principles whose excess, indeed, may be dangerous, but whose foundation is in truth . . .'[92]

It is perhaps surprising to find such a sober, commonsense approach in a man who combined outstanding intellectual distinction with a passionate emotional involvement in what he was doing – or trying to do. Such an approach did not appeal to either the Eldons or the Cobbetts of Canning's day. But to most of his countrymen, who saw the signs of economic and social change all round them but had not forgotten the excesses of the French Revolution, it was what they wanted to hear.

Abbreviations

Aspinall FCM. A. Aspinall, *The Formation of Canning's Ministry*. (Camden, 3rd Series, LIX, 1937)

Bagot J. Bagot, *George Canning and his Friends*, 2 vols. (1909)

B.M. Add. Mss. British Museum Additional Manuscripts

Festing G. Festing, *John Hookham Frere and his Friends* (1899)

George III *The Later Correspondence of George III*, 5 Vols. Ed. by A. Aspinall

George IV *The Letters of George IV*, 3 Vols. Ed. by A. Aspinall

G.L.G. *Private Correspondence of Lord Granville Leveson-Gower 1781-1821*, 2 Vols. (1916)

Marshall Dorothy Marshall, *The Rise of George Canning* (1938)

P.R.O. Public Record Office

A. G. Stapleton. G.C. & T. A. G. Stapleton, *George Canning and his Times* (1859)

A. G. Stapleton. Pol. Life. A. G. Stapleton, *Political Life of George Canning* 3 Vols. (1831)

Temperley *The Foreign Policy of George Canning 1822-27* (1925)

Webster Sir Charles Webster, *Britain and the Independence of Latin America. 1812-30.* Select Documents from the Foreign Office Archives. 2 Vols. (1938)

References

CHAPTER I

1. Harewood Mss. 1. April 11, 1770.
2. Lane-Poole. *The Life of Stratford Canning.* I pp. 2–4.
3. Harewood Mss. 1.
4. Notes and Queries. Vol. 157 (Sept. 14 and 21, 1929) pp. 183–5 & 201–3.
5. Harewood Mss. 2. Nov. 19, 1780.
6. Harewood Mss. 2. Sept. 29, 1782.
7. *Ibid.* Oct. 19, 1782.
8. 'Some Letters of George Canning' by Rev. J. Raven. *Anglo-Saxon Review.* Vol. III pp. 48/9. G. Canning to H. J. Rickman. Sept. 27, 1786.
9. *Ibid.*
10. Harewood Mss. 2. Feb. 3, 1787.
11. *Ibid.* August 7, 1787.
12. Harewood Mss. 13. Canning to Mr Leigh. March 23, 1796.
13. Harewood Mss. 2. May 28, 1783.
14. *Ibid.* May 23, 1785.
15. *Anglo-Saxon Review.* Vol. III pp. 51/2. Sept. 6, 1787.
16. Harewood Mss. 2. Sept. 4, 1784.
17. *Anglo-Saxon Review.* Vol. III p. 52. Sept. 13, 1787.
18. Harewood Mss. 12. Nov. 24, 1787.
19. J. F. Newton. *The Early Days of George Canning* (1828).
20. *Ibid.*
21. Harewood Mss. 12. Sept. 26, 1788
22. Harewood Mss. 2. Canning to his Mother. Dec. 27, 1789.
23. Harewood Mss. 12. Canning to Mr Leigh. Dec. 18, 1789.
24. D. Marshall. *Early Life of George Canning.* p. 23. Dec. 31, 1789.
25. Marshall. p. 19. Nov. 23, 1790.
26. *The Private Correspondence of Granville Leveson-Gower.* Vol. I pp. 73 & 76.
27. Harewood Mss. 2. August 1790.
28. Marshall p. 24. Sept. 7, 1789.
29. Harewood Mss. 2. August 10, 1785.
30. Harewood Mss. 12. to Mr Leigh. Sept. 26, 1788.
31. Harewood Mss. 2. June 13, 1791.
32. Marshall p. 28. to Bessy Canning. June 26, 1791.
33. Harewood Mss. 12. to Mr Leigh. August 1791.
34. *Anglo-Saxon Review.* Vol. III p. 52. Sept. 13, 1787.
35. Marshall p. 27. to Bessy Canning. May 17, 1790.
36. *Ibid.* pp. 27/8. June 26, 1791.

37. Marshall. p. 26.
38. A. G. Stapleton. *George Canning and his Times.* p. 7. to Boringdon. Dec. 13, 1792.
39. J. Bagot. *George Canning and his Friends.* I p. 37. to John Sneyd. Dec. 12, 1792.
40. A. G. Stapleton. *G.C. & T.* p. 9. to Boringdon. Dec. 13, 1792.
41. Bagot. *George Canning and his Friends.* I p. 38. to Sneyd. Dec. 12, 1792.
42. Marshall p. 33.
43. Harewood Mss. 30. July 28, 1792.
44. Marshall. pp. 34-37.
45. Marshall. p. 41. to Leveson-Gower. Dec. 2, 1792.
46. Bagot. I p. 36. to Sneyd. Dec. 12, 1792.
47. Bagot. I. *Ibid.*
48. *Ibid.* p. 30. to Bootle Wilbraham. Dec. 4, 1792.
49. G. Festing. *John Hookham Frere and his Friends.* p. 28. to Frere.
50. *Ibid.* to Mr Leigh. April 27, 1793.
51. Harewood Mss. 30. June 21, 1793.
52. Bagot. I p. 44. to Bootle Wilbraham. August 12, 1793.
53. Harewood Mss. 12. to Mr Leigh. July 9, 1793.

CHAPTER II

1. Harewood Mss. Canning's Journal.
2. Marshall. p. 49 (Canning's Journal).
3. *Ibid.* p. 124 (Canning's Journal).
4. Harewood Mss. Canning's Journal.
5. Fox Correspondence. III pp. 61/2. to Lord Holland, Dec. 1793.
6. Derry. *William Pitt.* p. 100.
7. Marshall. p. 50 (Canning's Journal).
8. *Ibid.* p. 54 (Canning's Journal)
9. A. G. Stapleton. *G.C. & T.* p. 17. Canning to Boringdon. March 20, 1794.
10. Marshall. p. 59 (Canning's Journal).
11. *Ibid.* p. 56 (Canning's Journal).
12. *Ibid.* p. 59 (Canning's Journal).
13. Parliamentary History 1792-4. Vol. 30, 1317 ff.
14. Harewood Mss. 12. Feb. 3, 1794.
15. Bagot. I p. 47. Canning to Sneyd. Feb. 22, 1794.
16. Harewood Mss. Canning's Journal.
17. Harewood Mss. 12. April 3, 1794.
18. Fox Correspondence. III p. 71. to Holland. March 18, 1794.
19. Marshall. pp. 69/70 (Canning's Journal).
20. Harewood Mss. Canning's Journal.

21. *Ibid.*
22. Parl. Hist. 31. 1009 ff.
23. Harewood Mss. 13. Jan. 14, 1795.
24. G.L.G. I p. 79. Feb. 5, 1794.
25. Harewood Mss. 12. April 24, 1794.
26. *Ibid.* Canning's Journal.
27. *Ibid.*
28. Marshall. pp. 105/6 (Canning's Journal).
29. Marshall. pp. 101–110.
30. Harewood Mss. 13 to Mr Leigh. Oct. 31, 1795.
31. *Ibid.* Dec. 10, 1795.
32. *Ibid.* Dec. 24, 1795.

CHAPTER III

1. Harewood Mss. Canning to Mr Leigh. Dec. 24, 1795.
2. Bagot. I p. 59. Canning to Sneyd. Jan. 10, 1796.
3. Minto (Sir Gilbert Elliot). III p. 253. June 10, 1802.
4. Windham Papers. I p. 136.
5. Harewood Mss. 13. to Mr Leigh. Dec. 14, 1795.
6. Holland Rose. *Pitt and the Great War*. pp. 276/7.
7. Matheson C. *Life of Henry Dundas*. p. 226.
8. Marshall. pp. 159/60. Jan. 16, 1796.
9. Harewood Mss. 13. Canning to Mr Leigh. Feb. 22, 1796.
10. A. G. Stapleton. *G.C. & T.* pp. 37/8. August 21, 1796.
11. *Ibid.* pp. 38/9.
12. Bagot. I p. 62. George Ellis to Sneyd. 1796.
13. Harewood Mss. 14. Oct. 4, 1796.
14. A. G. Stapleton. *G.C. & T.* p. 38. August 21, 1796.
15. Harewood Mss. 14. Canning to Mr Leigh. Oct. 7, 1796.
16. *Ibid.*
17. Bagot. I p. 62. George Ellis to Sneyd. 1796.
18. Harewood Mss. 14. Canning to Mr Leigh. Nov. 9, 1796.
19. Malmesbury Diaries. III p. 269. Oct. 23, 1796.
20. Marshall. p. 163. Nov. 7, 1796.
21. Malmesbury Diaries. III p. 322. Malmesbury to Canning. Nov. 27, 1796.
22. Harewood Mss. 13. Feb. 25, 1797.
23. *Ibid.*
24. Windham Papers. II p. 53. May 12, 1797.
25. Dropmore Papers. III p. 327. June 1, 1797.
26. Harewood Mss. 14. July 1, 1797.
27. *Ibid.* July 15, 1797.
28. Malmesbury Diaries. III p. 463. August 14, 1797.

29. *Ibid.* p. 517. Malmesbury to Canning. August 29, 1797.
30. Harewood Mss. 14. Canning to Mr Leigh. Sept. 29, 1797.
31. Dropmore Papers. III p. 334. July 20, 1797.
32. Malmesbury Diaries. III p. 416. to Malmesbury. July 20, 1797.
33. Harewood Mss. 14. to Mr Leigh. July 24, 1797.
34. *Ibid.*
35. *Ibid.* to Mr Leigh. Sept. 5, 1797.
36. *Ibid.* July 24, 1797.
37. *Ibid.* August 1, 1797.
38. G.L.G. I p. 257. Sept. 10, 1799.

CHAPTER IV

1. Holland. *Memoirs of the Whig Party.* I p. 82.
2. Harewood Mss. 62. Oct. 19, 1797.
3. Farington Diary. I p. 226. Dec. 28, 1797.
4. *Ibid.* p. 222. Nov. 25, 1797.
5. *Anti-Jacobin.* No. 1. Nov. 20, 1797. Prospectus (Vol. I pp. 1–9).
6. *Ibid.* No. 2. Nov. 27, 1797 (Vol. I pp. 71/2).
7. Bagot. I p. 136. Nov. 14, 1797.
8. Draper Hill. *Mr Gillray* (1965). p. 68.
9. *Anti-Jacobin.* No. 36. July 9, 1798 (Vol. II p. 615 ff.).
10. *Anti-Jacobin.* No. 15. Feb. 19, 1798 (Vol. I p. 524 ff.); No. 16. Feb. 26, 1798 (Vol. I p. 558 ff.); No. 21. April 2, 1798 (Vol. II p. 97 ff.).
11. Harewood Mss. 62. Feb. 27, 1798.
12. *Ibid.*
13. Harewood Mss. 30. Feb. 6, 1798.
14. *Ibid.* May 21, 1798.
15. J. H. Frere. *Works.* I p. 40. n2.
16. Harewood Mss. 15. Sept. 5, 1798.
17. Canning *Speeches.* Ed. Therry. Vol. I p. 54 ff.
18. Matheson. *Life of Henry Dundas.* p. 282 ff.
19. Harewood Mss. 15. April 16, 1799.
20. Cornwallis Correspondence. III p. 102. June 8, 1799.
21. B.M. Add. Mss. 37844. Oct. 23, 1799.
22. Parl. Hist. XXXIV. 537 ff.
23. Harewood Mss. 15. May 25, 1799.
24. *Ibid.* June 6, 1799.

CHAPTER V

1. G.L.G. I pp. 250/55. August 22, 1799.
2. Festing p. 31.
3. G.L.G. I p. 253.
4. Marshall. p. 210.
5. Harewood Mss. 15. August 26, 1799.
6. *Ibid.* Sept. 2, 1799.
7. *Ibid.*
8. *Ibid.* Sept. 9, 1799.
9. *Ibid.* Sept. 30, 1799.
10. G.L.G. I pp. 253/4. August 22, 1799.
11. Marshall. p. 206.
12. Marshall. p. 214.
13. Harewood Mss. 30. Sept. 18, 1799.
14. Bagot. I p. 155. Sept. 17, 1799.
15. Marshall. pp. 215/16.
16. *George III.* Vol. 3, p. 316n.
17. Harewood Mss. 15. March 8, 1800.
18. *Ibid.* April 18, 1800.
19. *Ibid.* May 6, 1800.
20. *Ibid.* May 10, 1800.
21. B.M. Add. Mss. 47841 to E. Bootle Wilbraham. May 23, 1800.
22. Harewood Mss. 15. July 8, 1800.
23. Festing p. 31.
24. G.L.G. I p. 279. May 12, 1800.
25. Wellesley Papers. I p. 142. August 28, 1801.
26. Harewood Mss. 15. April 8, 1800.
27. *Ibid.* May 28, 1800.
28. Lady Holland. *Journal.* II p. 98.
29. Lane-Poole. I p. 14.
30. G.L.G. I p. 228.
31. Malmesbury Diaries. IV pp. 367/8.
32. Marshall. pp. 90/1.
33. Harewood Mss. 14. Sept. 5, 1797.
34. G.L.G. I pp. 230/1.
35. *Ibid.* I pp. 272/3.
36. Marshall. pp. 91/6 (Canning's Journal).
37. Lady Holland. *Journal.* I p. 218.
38. Marshall. pp. 117/18 (Canning's Journal) and Harewood Mss. 15.
39. Harewood Mss. Canning's Journal.
40. Harewood Mss. 62. Canning to C. Ellis. Jan. 26, 1798.

41. Harewood Mss. 15.
42. *Ibid.*
43. *Ibid.* June 18, 1799.
44. *Ibid.* June 22, 1799.
45. Marshall. p. 195.
46. G.L.G. I p. 255. August 22, 1799.
47. Harewood Mss. 15. Feb. 5, 1800.
48. Harewood Mss. 30. Sept. 14, 1800.
49. Harewood Mss. Canning's Journal.
50. Harewood Mss. 15. to Mr Leigh. April 19, 1800.
51. G.L.G. I p. 163. July 9, 1797.
52. A. G. Stapleton. *G.C. & T.* p. 61. Nov. 28, 1799.
53. *Ibid.* p. 58. Nov. 23, 1799.
54. Harewood Mss. 30.
55. *Ibib.* March 18, 1798.
56. *Ibid.* Nov. 20 and 22, 1800.
57. B.M. Add. Mss. 38833.
58. Harewood Mss. 63. to Lady Malmesbury.

CHAPTER VI

1. Harewood Mss. 15. to Mr Leigh. Feb. 7, 1801.
2. Minto. III p. 201. Feb. 8, 1801.
3. Bagot. I p. 180. to Sneyd. Feb. 14, 1801.
4. *Ibid.*
5. G.L.G. I p. 296. Feb. 19 and 20, 1801.
6. *Ibid.* March 5, 1801.
7. Harewood Mss. 30. Feb. 15, 1801.
8. Harewood Mss. 15. to Mr Leigh. Feb. 27, 1801.
9. Festing. pp. 44/5.
10. Harewood Mss. 15. to Mr Leigh. June 15, 1801.
11. B.M. Add. Mss. 38833. to Frere. August 10, 1801.
12. Festing. p. 53.
13. Festing. p. 52 and B.M. Add. Mss. 38833.
14. Harewood Mss. 15. July 6, 1801.
15. Festing. pp. 55/6.
16. B.M. Add. Mss. 38833. Nov. 7, 1801.
17. Festing. p. 54. August 17, 1801.
18. Festing. p. 50.
19. Festing. p. 58.
20. Harewood Mss. 15. August 30, 1801.
21. A. G. Stapleton. *G.C. & T.* p. 67. Oct. 29, 1801.
22. Harewood Mss. 30. Oct. 1, 1801.

23. Dropmore. VII p. 48. Oct. 4, 1801.
24. Granville Mss. PRO 30/29. 8/2. Oct. 14, 1801.
25. Harewood Mss. 30. Oct. 21 and 26, 1801.
26. B.M. Add. Mss. 38833. Canning to Frere. Nov. 13 and Dec. 14, 1801, June 1, 1802.
27. Festing. p. 62. Nov. 7, 1801.
28. Granville Mss. PRO 30/29. 8/2.
29. Granville Mss. PRO 30/29. 8/2.
30. Festing. pp. 70/71.
31. G.L.G. I p. 338. April 6, 1802.
32. Minto. III p. 249. May 15, 1802.
33. Bagot. I p. 188. to Sneyd. Feb. 10, 1802.
34. Canning *Speeches*. II pp. 1–40.
35. Harewood Mss. 15.
36. Granville Mss. PRO 30/29. 8/2.
37. Festing. p. 77.
38. Minto. III p. 250. May 29, 1802.
39. Harewood Mss. 15. to Mr Leigh. June 1, 1802.
40. Festing. p. 84. July 26, 1802.
41. Festing. p. 89.
42. Malmesbury Diaries. IV p. 103 ff.
43. Dropmore. VII p. 128. to Pitt. Nov. 16, 1802.
44. Ward Plumer Memoirs. I p. 91. Nov. 24, 1802.
45. Malmesbury Diaries. IV p. 126. Nov. 26, 1802.
46. B.M. Add. Mss. 42773. Dec. 2, 1802.
47. George Rose. *Diaries & Correspondence*. I p. 466.
48. Canning *Speeches*. II p. 44 ff.
49. Malmesbury Diaries. IV pp. 144–6.
50. Fox Correspondence. III p. 376. to Charles Grey. Nov. 29, 1802.
51. Malmesbury Diaries. IV p. 150. Dec. 14, 1802.

CHAPTER VII

1. Dropmore. VII p. 140. Jan. 30, 1803.
2. Colchester. *Diaries & Correspondence*. I p. 423. May 27, 1803.
3. Harewood Mss. 28. Canning to Joan. April 19, 1803.
4. *Ibid.* May 17, 1803.
5. Harewood Mss. 15. Canning to Mr Leigh. May 24, 1803.
6. Harewood Mss. 28. Canning to Joan. May 26, 1803.
7. *George III*. 4. p. 104.
8. Minto. III p. 289. June 4, 1803.
9. Harewood Mss. 15. Canning to Mr Leigh. June 8, 1803.
10. Wilberforce. *Life*. III pp. 142/3.

11. Moorman. *W. Wordsworth*. Vol. I p. 602.
12. Granville Mss. PRO 30/29. 8/3. Sept. 5, 1803.
13. Harewood Mss. 30. Nov. 15, 1803.
14. Granville Mss. PRO 30/29. 8/3. Nov. 17, 1803.
15. B.M. Add. Mss. 38833. Canning to Frere. Nov. 23, 1803.
16. P.R.O. Dacres Adams Mss. Dec. 1, 1803.
17. Buckingham. George III Memoirs. III p. 342. Grenville to Buckingham. Jan. 10, 1804.
18. Harewood Mss. 30.
19. *Ibid.*
20. Malmesbury Diaries. IV p. 291.
21. Marshall. pp. 261/2.
22. Fox Correspondence. III p. 464. Fox to Grey. April 13, 1804.
23. Minto. III p. 314. March 27, 1804.
24. Marshall. p. 263.
25. Harewood Mss. 19. Canning to Joan. April 16, 1804.
26. Marshall. pp. 264/5.
27. Harewood Mss. 19. May 1, 1804.
28. Derry. *William Pitt*. p. 145.
29. Marshall. p. 272.
30. Dudley. *Letters to Ivy*. p. 23. May 18, 1804.
31. Harewood Mss. 30.
32. Marshall. pp. 269/70.
33. Harewood Mss. 19. May 13, 1804.
34. Auckland. Journal and Correspondence. IV p. 196. Sheffield to Auckland. May 17, 1804.
35. Harewood Mss. 19. June 19, 1804.
36. Minto. III p. 348. Minto to his wife. June 19, 1804.
37. George III. 4, p. 197, n3. June 20, 1804.
38. Marshall. p. 275.
39. *Ibid.* p. 278.
40. Stanhope. *Life of Pitt*. IV pp. 244/8.
41. Harewood Mss. 30. Pitt to Canning. Jan. 6, 1805.
42. Granville Mss. PRO 30/29. 8/3. Canning to Leveson-Gower. Jan. 11, 1805.
43. Harewood Mss. 15. Feb. 16, 1805.
44. Matheson. *Dundas*. p. 350.
45. Malmesbury Diaries. IV p. 347.
46. Harewood Mss. 15.
47. Harewood Mss. 15. April 27, 1805.
48. Dropmore. VII p. 278. Buckingham to Grenville. June 13, 1805.
49. Harewood Mss. 15. Canning to Mrs Leigh. June 15, 1805.
50. G.L.G. II p. 82. June 13, 1805.
51. Harewood Mss. 20.

52. Marshall. p. 287.
53. *Ibid*. pp. 287–94.
54. Holland Rose. *Pitt and Napoleon*. p. 328. Nov. 7, 1805.
55. Marshall. p. 295.
56. Harewood Mss. 15. Canning to Mr Leigh. Nov. 11, 1805.
57. Harewood Mss. 30. Nov. 7, 1805.
58. Dropmore. VII p. 318. Nov. 29, 1805.
59. Holland Rose. *Pitt and Napoleon*. pp. 329/32. Nov. 29, 1805.
60. Marshall pp. 295/6.
61. G.L.G. II p. 172. Jan. 29, 1806.
62. Stanhope. *Life of Pitt*. IV pp. 364/5. Dec. 31, 1805.
63. Dropmore. VII p. 325. Jan. 6, 1806.
64. Stanhope. *Life of Pitt*. IV p. 372.
65. Harewood Mss. 29D. Jan. 13, 1806.
66. Marshall. p. 298.
67. G.L.G. II p. 162. Lady Bessborough to G.L.G. Jan. 23, 1806.
68. Marshall. p. 298.

CHAPTER VIII

1. Harewood Mss. 21. March 10, 1806.
2. G.L.G. II p. 178. Feb. 6, 1806.
3. Rose, George. *Diaries & Correspondence*. II p. 263.
4. Harewood Mss. 21. Canning to Joan. March 11 and 27, June 5, 1806.
5. Lonsdale Papers p. 180. Essex to Lowther. March 18, 1806.
6. Harewood Mss. 21. March 4, 1806.
7. *Ibid*. May 15, 1806.
8. *Ibid*. May 7, 1806.
9. Gray. *S. Perceval* p. 61.
10. Harewood Mss. Canning to Joan. June 11, 1806.
11. *Ibid*. June 10, 19, 20, July 5, 1806.
12. Dropmore. VIII p. 213. July 2, 1806.
13. B.M. Add. Mss. 42773. Canning to Rose. August 9, 1806.
14. Harewood Mss. 76. Canning to Rose. August 14, 1806.
15. A. G. Stapleton. *G.C. & T.* p. 97. Canning to Boringdon. August 29, 1806.
16. G.L.G. II p. 222. Lady Bessborough to G.L.G. Oct. 28, 1806.
17. A. G. Stapleton. *G.C. & T.* p. 103. Canning to Boringdon. Sept. 24, 1806.
18. *George III*. 4. p. XXXVII.
19. Harewood Mss. 15. Canning to Mrs Leigh. Sept. 4, 1805.
20. Lady Holland *Journal*. II p. 235.
21. Harewood Mss. 17. Jan. 13 and 30, Feb. 16, 1807.

477

22. B.M. Add. Mss. 49174. S. Perceval to Melville. Jan. 19, 1807.
23. *George III.* 4, p. 517 or 8.
24. Gray. *S. Perceval.* p. 70.
25. Harewood Mss. 22. Canning to Joan. Feb. 7, 1807.
26. *Ibid.* March 6, 1807.
27. *Ibid.* March 20, 1807.
28. *George III.* 4, p. XI (Harewood Mss.).
29. *Ibid.* p. XXXVIII.
30. Harewood Mss. 22. Canning to Joan. March 22, 1807.
31. *Ibid.*
32. Rose. II p. 165.
33. Harewood Mss. 22. March 25, 1807.
34. *Ibid.*
35. Harewood Mss. 17. March 25, 1807.
36. Gray. *S. Perceval.* p. 96.
37. Canning *Speeches.* II p. 277.
38. Romilly. *Memoirs.* II p. 200. Malmesbury Diaries. IV p. 382.
39. *George III.* 4, p. 572. April 25, 1807.
40. Harewood Mss. 17. Canning to Mr Leigh. June 27, 1807.
41. Gray. *S. Perceval.* p. 140.
42. *George III.* 4, p. 599 n3.

CHAPTER IX

1. Harewood Mss. 22. April 21, 1807.
2. Malmesbury Letters. II p. 25.
3. Bagot. I pp. 238/41.
4. Sherwig. *Guineas and Gunpowder.* p. 188.
5. *Ibid.* p. 187.
6. Paget Papers. II pp. 290/3. Canning to Paget. May 16, 1807.
7. *Ibid.* p. 309. Paget to Canning (undated, probably July 30, 1807).
8. Holland Rose. Trans. R.H.S. Vol. XX 1906 p. 63.
9. F.O. 65/69. June 30, 1807.
10. F.O. 65/69. July 21, 1807.
11. *Ibid.*
12. F.O. 65/70.
13. F.O. 78/56.
14. F.O. 65/70. August 2, 17, 1807.
15. Granville Mss. PRO 30/29. 8/4. June 9, 1807.
16. *George III.* 4, p. 604.
17. *Ibid.* p. 606.
18. Jackson Diaries. II pp. 187/8. F. J. Jackson to G. Jackson. July 18, 1807.

19. Holland Rose. Trans. RHS. Vol. XX 1906 p. 69.
20. A. N. Ryan. EHR. 1953. Vol. 68 p. 50.
21. *George III*. 4, p. 607. July 18, 1807.
22. Granville Mss. PRO 30/29. 8/4. Canning to Leveson-Gower. (Added as a postscript dated July 22, to a letter written on the 21st.)
23. Gray. *S. Perceval*. p. 164.
24. Harewood Mss. 24. July 31, 1807.
25. *Ibid*. August 1, 1807.
26. *Ibid*. August 14, 1807.
27. A. G. Stapleton. *G.C. & T*. p. 127.
28. Granville Mss. PRO 30/29. 8/4. Canning to Leveson-Gower. August 25, 1807.
29. *George III*. 4, p. 607 n2.
30. Malmesbury Letters. II p. 46. Captain Bowles to Fitzharris. Sept. 6, 1807.
31. Harewood Mss. 17. Sept. 15, 1807.
32. B.M. Add. Mss. 42773. Canning to Rose. Sept. 24, 1807.
33. *The Times*. Sept. 17 and 19, 1807.
34. Gray. *S. Perceval*. pp. 166/7.
35. Wilberforce. *Life*. III pp. 344/5. Sept. 19, 1807. Diary.
36. Dropmore. IX pp. 144/5. Nov. 15, 1807.
37. G.L.G. II p. 315. Lady Bessborough to G.L.G. Dec. 20, 1807.
38. Jackson. *Diaries*. II p. 218. F. J. Jackson to G. Jackson. Sept. 26, 1807.
39. Parl. Deb. X p. 284/5.
40. Windham Papers. II p. 334. Windham to Capt. Lukin. Sept. 5, 1807.
41. *The Times*. Sept. 30, 1807.
42. Harewood Mss. 32. Canning to Castlereagh. Sept. 19, 1807.
43. Castlereagh. Letters & Despatches. 2nd Series. VI pp. 182–6. Sept. 22, 1807.
44. Harewood Mss. 32. Canning to Castlereagh. Oct. 1, 1807.
45. Jackson. *Diaries*. II p. 222. Oct. 1, 1807.
46. B.M. Add. Mss. 48219. Canning to Boringdon. Sept. 30, 1807.
47. *George III*. 4, pp. 628–30.
48. *Ibid*. p. 631.
49. F.O. 65/70. Sept. 27, 1807.
50. *George III*. 4, pp. 653/4. Dec. 2, 1807.
51. *Ibid*. p. 629 n1. Canning to Boringdon. Dec. 4, 1807.
52. Harewood Mss. 22. August 26, 1807.
53. F.O. 63/56. Nov. 2, 1807.
54. *Ibid*. Nov. 9, 1807.
55. *Ibid*. Strangford to Canning. Nov. 20, 1807.
56. *Ibid*. Nov. 30, 1807.
57. *Ibid*.
58. Harewood Mss. 17. Canning to Mr Leigh. Dec. 19, 1807.
59. Paget Papers. II p. 374. Paget to Canning. Oct. 22, 1807.

60. *Ibid.* p. 363. Paget to Uxbridge. Sept. 25, 1807.
61. Gray. *S. Perceval.* pp. 167–71.
62. Parl. Deb. X 692, 708, 1182.
63. Granville Mss. PRO 30/29. 8/4. Oct. 2, 1807.
64. *George III.* 4, p. 652. Nov. 20, 1807.
65. Parl. Deb. X 801 ff.
66. *George III.* 5, p. 27. March 1, 1808.
67. Roberts. *The Whig Party. 1807–1812.* p. 110 (Grey to Whitbread).
68. Parl. Deb. X 252 ff.
69. *George III.* 5, p. 15 n2.
70. *Ibid.*
71. Parl. Deb. X 385 ff and 736 ff.
72. Glenbervie. *Journal.* II pp. 17/8.
73. Parl. Deb. X 388.
74. Harewood Mss. 32. Feb. 23, 1808.
75. Parl. Deb. X 755.
76. Wellington Supplementary Despatches. V p. 447. to Richmond. June 6, 1808.
77. Parl. Deb. XI 156
78. Wellington Supp. Despatches. V p. 419. to Richmond.
79. *George III.* 5, p. 80 n2. Whitbread to Grey. May 26, 1808.
80. *Ibid.* pp. 74/5 n2. Canning to Richmond. May 27, 1808.
81. Wellington Supp. Despatches. V p. 447. to Richmond. June 6, 1808.
82. *George III.* 5, p. 94 n3. Tierney to Grey. July 12, 1808.
83. *Ibid.* p. 65. Castlereagh to the King. April 17, 1808.
84. Raymond Carr. EHR. January, 1945. Vol. 60 p. 59.
85. Moore Diary. II p. 206. May 20, 1808.
86. *Ibid.* p. 220. June 25, 1808.
87. *Ibid.* p. 223. June 25, 1808.

CHAPTER X

1. *George III.* 5, p. 84. Canning to the King. June 8, 1808.
2. R. Coupland. *Wilberforce.* p. 292.
3. Dropmore. IX p. 212. Auckland to Grenville. August 7, 1808.
4. Farington. *Diary.* V p. 84.
5. Gray. *S. Perceval.* pp. 179/80.
6. Harewood Mss. 31. August 4, 1808.
7. Coupland. *Wilberforce.* p. 292.
8. Parl. Deb. XI 886 ff.
9. *Ibid.* 890/1.
10. Harewood Mss. 32.
11. Sherwig. *Guineas and Gunpowder.* p. 198.

12. Fortescue. *History of the British Army*. VI pp. 193/4.
13. Malmesbury. *Letters*. II p. 78. Ross to Malmesbury. Sept. 16, 1808.
14. *The Times*. August 31, 1808.
15. *Ibid*. Sept. 3, 1808.
16. *Political Register*. Sept. 10, 1808.
17. *George III*. 5, p. 121. Sept. 4, 1808.
18. Castlereagh. VI pp. 423/4. Sept. 4, 1808.
19. *Ibid*. p. 423. Sept. 4, 1808.
20. Gray. *S. Perceval*. p. 182.
21. Harewood Mss. 31. Sept. 17, 1808.
22. Bathurst Papers p. 75. Sept. 16, 1808.
23. Gray. *S. Perceval*. p. 183.
24. Castlereagh. VI p. 439. Sept. 17, 1808.
25. S. Walpole. *S. Perceval*. I pp. 300/1. Sept. 27, 1808.
26. Harewood Mss. 31. Canning to Chatham. Sept. 17, 1808.
27. Harewood Mss. 32. Canning to Portland. Sept. 17, 1808.
28. Longford. *Wellington: The Years of the Sword*. p. 157.
29. S. Walpole. *S. Perceval*. I pp. 300/1. to Perceval. Sept. 27, 1808.
30. *George III*. 5, p. 133-6. Sept. 28, 1808.
31. Parl. Deb. XII 969 ff.
32. *George III*. 5, p. 207 n1. W. Fremantle to Grenville. Feb. 22, 1808.
33. *George III*. 5, p. 143. Oct. 22, 1808.
34. Parl. Deb. XII 102/3.
35. Moore. *Diary*. II p. 283.
36. *Ibid*. p. 374.
37. *Ibid*. p. 287.
38. Oman. *Sir John Moore*. p. 599.
39. *George III*. 5, p. 210. Feb. 25, 1809.
40. Parl. Deb. XII 1096 ff.
41. Oman. *Sir John Moore*. pp. 545/6.
42. F.O. 72/71. April 19, 1809.
43. *Ibid*. May 1, 1809.
44. F.O. 72/70. Dec. 9, 1808.
45. Harewood Mss. 32. Dec. 30 and 31, 1808.
46. *Annual Register*. 1809. p. 577.
47. F.O. 72/71. April 19, 1809.
48. Harewood Mss. 31. June 9, 1809.
49. *Ibid*. July 6, 1809.
50. Castlereagh. VII pp. 83/4.
51. Harewood Mss. 31. June 23, 1809 and F.O. 72/75. June 27, 1809.
52. *George III*. 5, pp. 302/3.
53. Colchester. II p. 180.
54. *Ibid*. p. 179.
55. *Annual Register*. 1809. p. 577.

56. *George III.* 5, p. 264 n.
57. *Ibid.*
58. Harewood Mss. 33. Canning to Portland. May 5, 1809.
59. *Ibid.*
60. Twiss. *Eldon.* II p. 80. May 26, 1809.
61. *Annual Register.* 1809. p. 576 ff.
62. Harewood Mss. 33. June 27, 1809.
63. *Ibid.* June 27, 1809 (2nd letter).
64. Granville Mss. PRO 30/29. 8/4. Portland to Canning. June 28, 1809.
65. *George III.* 5, p. XXIV and pp. 310/11.
66. Bathurst Papers p. 97.
67. *George III.* 5, p. XXIV.
68. *Ibid.* p. XXV.
69. *Ibid.* p. XXV.
70. *Ibid.* pp. 320/1.
71. Gray. *S. Perceval.* p. 223.
72. S. Walpole. *S. Perceval.* I pp. 362/3. August 31, 1809.
73. *Ibid.* pp. 363/4.
74. Harewood Mss. 23. Sept. 1, 1809.
75. Harewood Mss. 33. Sept. 2, 1809.
76. Bathurst Papers p. 101. Camden to Bathurst. Sept. 8, 1809.
77. *George III.* 5, pp. 340/2.
78. *Ibid.* pp. 342/9.
79. *Ibid.* p. XXXI.
80. S. Walpole. *S. Perceval.* II p. 21.
81. Harewood Mss. 23.
82. Rose. II pp. 372/8.
83. Harewood Mss. 34. Sept. 18, 1809.
84. *George III.* 5, p. XXXII.
85. *Annual Register.* 1089. p. 862.
86. Harewood Mss. 34. Canning to Sir J. Bankes. Dec. 2, 1809.
87. *George III.* 5, pp. 368/9 n1.
88. Harewood Mss. 34. C. Ellis's account of duel.
89. Harewood Mss. 17. Sept. 21, 1809.
90. Gray. *S. Perceval.* p. 242.
91. Twiss. *Eldon.* II p. 104 to his brother. Oct. 4, 1809.
92. Holland. *Further Memoirs.* p. 35.
93. Wilberforce. *Life.* III p. 431.
94. *George III.* 5, p. XXXIV.
95. B.M. Add. Mss. 38737. Canning to Huskisson. Oct. 13, 1809.
96. Holland. *Further Memoirs.* pp. 35/6.
97. Bathurst Papers p. 102.
98. *George III.* 5, p. 389 n.
99. Rose. II pp. 378/9.

100. Ward Plumer. I p. 280.
101. Bathurst Papers. p. 118.
102. Twiss. *Eldon.* pp. 90/1.
103. Malmesbury. *Letters.* II p. 183 to his son, Fitzharris. Nov. 17, 1809.
104. Dudley. *Letters to Ivy.* p. 87.

CHAPTER XI

1. *George III.* 5, p. 369.
2. B.M. Add. Mss. 37295. Oct. 30, 1809.
3. Jackson. *Bath Archives.* I p. 145. July 1810.
4. Ziegler. *Addington.* p. 288.
5. Gray. *S. Perceval.* p. 258.
6. Harewood Mss. 24. Jan. 25, 1810.
7. *George III.* 5, p. XVIII.
8. Creevey. I p. 123. Parl. Deb. XV 80 ff.
9. *George III.* 5, p. 505n.
10. Harewood Mss. 24. Feb. 3, 1810.
11. *George III.* 5, p. 554n.
12. Harewood Mss. 24. April 7, 1810.
13. *George III.* 5, p. XLVII.
14. Harewood Mss. 24. Canning to Joan. August 28, 1810.
15. *Ibid.*
16. B.M. Add. Mss. 37299. Sept. 11, 1810.
17. Granville Mss. PRO 30/29. 8/5.
18. Ward Plumer. I pp. 308/9. Parl. Deb. XVIII 663 ff.
19. Granville Mss. PRO 30/29. 8/5.
20. Holland. *Further Memoirs.* p. 85.
21. Harewood Mss. 7. Feb. 11, 1811.
22. Parl. Deb. XIX 224 ff.
23. *Ibid.* 1076 ff.
24. Horner Francis. *Memoirs.* II p. 86. May 10, 1811.
25. Bagot. I p. 372.
26. Ward Plumer. I p. 441.
27. Harewood Mss. 25. Feb. 22, 1812.
28. Parl. Deb. XXI 1135 ff.
29. Harewood Mss. 25. Canning to Joan. Feb. 29, 1812.
30. Parl. Deb. XXI 1139 ff.
31. Wilberforce. *Life.* IV p. 17.
32. Ward Plumer. I p. 448.
33. Harewood Mss. 25. Canning to Joan. March 5, 1812.
34. *Ibid.*

35. Colchester. II p. 380. May 12, 1812.
36. Harewood Mss. 7. Canning to his mother. May 16, 1812.
37. Wilberforce. *Life*. IV p. 27.
38. Dropmore. X p. 233. April 1, 1812.
39. Parl. Deb. XXIII. Appendix p. X. May 18, 1812.
40. Dropmore. X p. 261. May 20, 1812.
41. *Ibid*. p. 263. to Grenville. May 21, 1812.
42. B.M. Add. Mss. 38243. May 23, 1812.
43. *Ibid*.
44. Bathurst Papers. pp. 175/6. May 27, 1812.
45. B.M. Add. Mss. 37297.
46. Dropmore. X pp. 276/7. June 1, 1812.
47. Creevey. *Life and Times*. p. 56 to Creevey. June 3, 1812.
48. Bathurst Papers. p. 178. June 7, 1812.
49. Roberts. *Whig Party 1807–1812*. p. 412 (Arbuthnot to Huskisson. June 2, 1812).
50. *Ibid*. pp. 414/15.
51. *Ibid*. p. 401.
52. Buckingham. *Regency Memoirs*. I p. 357.
53. Wilberforce. *Life*. IV pp. 33/4.
54. Parl. Deb. XXII 1012 ff.
55. Parl. Deb. XXIII 633 ff.
56. Wilberforce. *Life*. IV p. 100. Feb. 11, 1813.
57. Malmesbury Letters. II pp. 311/12. Ross to Malmesbury. Sept. 3, 1812.
58. A. G. Stapleton. *G.C. & T.* p. 208.
59. Malmesbury Letters. II p. 312. Ross to Malmesbury. Sept. 3, 1812.
60. Arbuthnot Correspondence. pp. 7/8. July 18, 1812.
61. B.M. Add. Mss. 38738 and Yonge. I pp. 405/6. July 19, 1812 (2 letters).
62. Yonge. *Liverpool*. I pp. 407/10. July 22, 1812.
63. B.M. Add. Mss. 38738. Arbuthnot to Huskisson. July 26, 1812.
64. *Ibid*. July 24, 1812.
65. Yonge. I pp. 417/18. July 26, 1812.
66. B.M. Add. Mss. 38738. Arbuthnot to Huskisson. July 26, 1812.
67. Harewood Mss. 69. July 27, 1812.
68. B.M. Add. Mss. 38738. July 27, 1812.
69. Yonge. I p. 421. July 27, 1812.
70. G.L.G. II p. 437. Lady Bessborough to G.L.G.
71. *Ibid*. p. 443.
72. Dropmore. X p. 290.
73. B.M. Add. Mss. 38738.
74. Huskisson Papers. pp. 79/80.
75. Wilberforce. *Life*. IV p. 41.
76. A. G. Stapleton. *Political Life of G. Canning*. I p. 292.
77. Leveson-Gower. II p. 443. Lady Bessborough to G.L.G.

78. Wilberforce. *Life.* IV p. 37 ff.
79. Granville Mss. PRO 30/29. 8/5. August 3, 1812.
80. Harewood Mss. 8.

CHAPTER XII

1. Granville Mss. PRO 30/29. 8/5.
2. Huskisson Papers p. 88.
3. Holland. *Further Memoirs.* p. 46.
4. B.M. Add. Mss. 37297. Canning to Wellesley. Oct. 19, 1812.
5. Creevey. *Life and Times.* pp. 61/2.
6. Brougham. *Life and Times.* II p. 62.
7. *The Times.* Oct. 16, 1812.
8. Creevey. *Life and Times.* p. 61.
9. Creevey Papers. I p. 171.
10. New. *H. Brougham.* p. 78.
11. Wellesley Papers. II p. 121. Oct. 17, 1812.
12. Lane-Poole. I p. 186.
13. *Political Register.* Nov. 14, 1812.
14. Harewood Mss. 7. Nov. 9, 1812.
15. Croker Papers. I p. 46. Peel to Croker. Oct. 30, 1812.
16. Colchester. II p. 417. Jan. 30, 1813.
17. Wellesley Papers p. 127. Nov. 19, 1812.
18. Parl. Deb. XXIV 61 ff. Nov. 30, 1812.
19. Harewood Mss. 8. Canning to his mother. May 1, 1813.
20. Aspinall. *Essays for Lewis Namier.* p. 236.
21. Parl. Deb. XXVI 88 ff.
22. Harewood Mss. 8. Canning to his mother. May 1, 1813.
23. *Ibid.* May 29, 1813.
24. Ward Plumer. I pp. 363/4. Jan. 25, 1811.
25. *George III.* 5, pp. 520/1 n3.
26. Aspinall. Trans. RHS. 4th Series. Vol. XVII p. 190. to Leveson-Gower.
27. Huskisson Papers p. 91. July 24, 1813.
28. Aspinall. Trans. RHS. 4th Series. Vol. XVII pp. 193/4.
29. Buckingham. *Regency Memoirs.* II pp. 36/7. Horner to Grenville. July 22, 1813.
30. Dudley. *Letters to Ivy.* p. 215.
31. Buckingham. *Regency Memoirs.* II p. 38. Grenville to Horner. July 25, 1813.
32. Granville Mss. PRO 30/29. 8/5. Canning to Leveson-Gower. July 30, 1813.
33. Colchester. II p. 453.
34. Granville Mss. PRO 30/29. 8/5. August 9, 1813.

35. Bagot. I p. 400. Sept. 2, 1813.
36. Granville Mss. PRO 30/29. 8/5.
37. *Ibid.* Nov. 30, 1813.
38. Parl. Deb. XXVII 144 ff. Nov. 17, 1813.
39. Harewood Mss. 8.
40. Granville Mss. PRO 30/29. 8/5. June 26, 1814.
41. Harewood Mss. 8.
42. B.M. Add. Mss. 38193.
43. Harewood Mss. 25. Canning to Joan. July 14, 1814.
44. Aspinall. Trans. RHS. 4th Series. XVII p. 194 ff.
45. Granville Mss. PRO 30/29. 8/5. Oct. 8, 1814.
46. Lady G. Leveson-Gower. *Letters.* I p. 50. Lady G.L.G. to Lady Morpeth. Nov. 9, 1814.
47. Harewood Mss. 8. Canning to his mother. Nov. 29, 1814.
48. Harewood Mss. 8. Canning to his mother. Dec. 9, 1814.
49. B.M. Add. Mss. 38193. Dec. 29, 1814.
50. *Ibid.* Jan. 30, 1815.
51. B.M. Add. Mss. 38740. Canning to Huskisson. Jan. 9, 1815.
52. B.M. Add. Mss. 38193. Canning to Liverpool. Jan. 14, 1815.
53. *Ibid.* Dec. 29, 1814.
54. B.M. Add. Mss. 38740. Canning to Huskisson. April 15, 1815.
55. F.O. 63/185.
56. *Ibid.* May 1, 1815.
57. B.M. Add. Mss. 38193. April 26, 1815.
58. B.M. Add. Mss. 38740. Canning to Huskisson. April 15, 1815.
59. Bagot. II p. 6. July 14, 1815.
60. Parl. Deb. XXXVI 178 ff. May 6, 1817.
61. Bagot. II p. 45.
62. Harewood Mss. 9. May 10, 1817.
63. Bagot. II p. 45 to Bagot. May 7, 1817.
64. Parl. Deb. XXXVI 221/2.

CHAPTER XIII

1. Yonge. II pp. 253/5. Feb. 13, 1816.
2. B.M. Add. Mss. 38741 to Huskisson.
3. Yonge. II p. 255. March 8, 1816.
4. *Ibid.* p. 270. March 21, 1816.
5. B.M. Add. Mss. 38741. March 22, 1816.
6. A. G. Stapleton. *G.C. & T.* p. 333.
7. *Ibid.* pp. 357/8.
8. Harewood Mss. 17. Nov. 11, 1816.
9. *Ibid.* to Mr Leigh. Dec. 1816.

10. Wilberforce. *Life.* IV p. 316.
11. Bamford. *Passages in the Life of a Radical.* I p. 106.
12. Parl. Deb. XXXV 134. Jan. 29, 1817.
13. Harewood Mss. 9. May 16, 1819.
14. Parl. Deb. XVII 161. May 21, 1810.
15. *Ibid.* XXI 882. Feb. 22, 1812.
16. *Ibid.* XVI 776/7. May 1, 1810.
17. *Ibid.* XXXX 543/4. May 18, 1819.
18. *Ibid.* XXXVIII 1170/1. June 2, 1818.
19. A. G. Stapleton. *G.C. & T.* p. 344.
20. Parl. Deb. XXXV 845/6. March 3, 1817.
21. *Ibid.* 380. Feb. 17, 1817.
22. Harewood Mss. 8. Dec. 3, 1816.
23. *Ibid.* March 1, 1817.
24. Harewood Mss. 9. Jan. 31, 1818.
25. Parl. Deb. XXXVII 382. Feb. 11, 1818.
26. *Ibid.* XXXV 1114 ff. March 14, 1817.
27. Bamford. I p. 26.
28. Bagot. II p. 56. to Bagot. July 31, 1817.
29. Harewood Mss. 9. July 12, 1817.
30. Parl. Deb. XXXVI 1423 ff.
31. Rush. *A Residence at the Court of London.* p. 235.
32. Harewood Mss. 26. Nov. 29, 1817.
33. *Ibid.* Sept. 28, 1817.
34. B.M. Add. Mss. 38741. July 5, 1818.
35. Harewood Mss. 9. Canning to his mother. July 19, 1817.
36. The following pages are greatly indebted to C. H. Philips. *The East India Company 1784-1834.*
37. Parl. Deb. XXXIX 865 ff.
38. Harewood Mss. 9. July 10, 1819.
39. *Ibid.* Oct. 13, 1819.
40. Austen Mitchell. *The Whigs in Opposition 1815-1830.* p. 130.
41. Ziegler. *Addington.* p. 377.
42. Wellington Despatches Correspondence and Memoranda, new series. I p. 80. Oct. 21, 1819.
43. B.M. Add. Mss. 38568 to Liverpool. Oct. 25, 1819.
44. *Ibid.* 38741 to Huskisson.
45. Parl. Deb. XXXXI 192 ff. Nov. 24, 1819.
46. *Ibid.* 1544 ff. Dec. 23, 1819.
47. Colchester. III p. 104. Banesk to Colchester. Dec. 31, 1819.

CHAPTER XIV

1. Harewood Mss. 26 to Joan. Jan. 28, 1820.
2. *Ibid.*
3. Croker. I p. 159.
4. New. *Brougham.* p. 242.
5. *George IV.* 2, p. 345, n.
6. Parl. Deb. new series. I 950 ff.
7. *George IV.* 2, p. 344. Bloomfield(?) to Liverpool. June 10, 1820.
8. *George IV.* 2, p. 345 n.
9. A. G. Stapleton. *G.C. & T.* pp. 290/2.
10. Harewood Mss. 26.
11. A. G. Stapleton. *G.C. & T.* pp. 293/4. July 5, 1820.
12. *Ibid.* pp. 294/5. July 30, 1820.
13. Mrs Arbuthnot. *Journal.* I p. 25.
14. Harewood Mss. 26 to Joan. Oct. and Nov. 1817.
15. *Ibid.* Feb. 9, 1820.
16. Harewood Mss. 9. March 31, 1820.
17. *Ibid.* 26. April 6, 1820.
18. *Ibid.* 9. August 28, 1820.
19. A. G. Stapleton. *G.C. & T.* pp. 300–7.
20. B.M. Add. Mss. 38742 to Huskisson. Nov. 7, 1820.
21. Twiss. *Eldon.* II pp. 399/40.
22. Mrs Arbuthnot. I p. 53.
23. B.M. Add. Mss. 38742. Arbuthnot to Huskisson. Nov. 17, 1820.
24. *George IV.* 2, p. 388 n.
25. *Ibid.* p. 391.
26. Harewood Mss. 26. to Joan. Nov. 28, 1820.
27. Stapleton Mss. Oct. 14, 1820.
28. Harewood Mss. 9. Dec. 6, 1820.
29. Harewood Mss. 26. to Joan. Jan. 12, 1821.
30. B.M. Add. Mss. 38742. Dec. 12, 1820.
31. Harewood Mss. 26. Dec. 12, 1820.
32. A. G. Stapleton. *G.C. & T.* p. 318. Dec. 12, 1820.
33. *Ibid.* p. 319. Dec. 19, 1820.
34. Harewood Mss. 26. to Joan. Dec. 20, 1820.
35. Bagot. II p. 110. to Bagot. Feb. 21, 1821.
36. Lieven, Princess. *Letters to Metternich.* p. 110. Jan. 28, 1821.
37. B.M. Add. Mss. 38742 to Huskisson. Feb. 22, 1821.
38. Harewood Mss. 10. March 24, 1821.
39. Parl. Deb. new series. IV 1454 ff.
40. Harewood Mss. 26. April 3, 1821.
41. Brock. *Liverpool.* p. 133.

42. B.M. Add. Mss. 38742. May 29, 1821.
43. Mrs Arbuthnot. I p. 79.
44. Yonge. III p. 146 to Arbuthnot. June 15, 1821.
45. Brock. *Liverpool*. p. 140.
46. E. J. Stapleton. *Official Correspondence of G. Canning*. I p. 24.
47. *Ibid*. p. 25.
48. BM. Add. Mss. 38568. July 3, 1821.
49. Arbuthnot Corr. p. 26. Liverpool to Arbuthnot. August 28, 1821.
50. Wellington Desp. N.S. I pp. 192–6. Oct. 26, 1821.
51. Arbuthnot Corr. p. 28. to Arbuthnot. Dec. 13, 1821.
52. *George IV*. 2, p. 466. King to Londonderry. Oct. 12, 1821.
53. A. G. Stapleton. *G.C. & T*. p. 325. Canning to Morley. Dec. 12, 1821.
54. Harewood Mss. 26. to Joan. Nov. 14 and 15, 1821.
55. B.M. Add. Mss. 38743. C. Ellis to Huskisson. Nov. 20, 1821.
56. *Ibid*. Nov. 16, 1821.
57. Harewood Mss. 17. to Mrs Leigh. Dec. 21, 1821.
58. Harewood Mss. to Joan, undated, but probably early 1822.
59. *George IV*. 2, p. 409. Hastings to Bloomfield. Feb. 4, 1821.
60. *Ibid*. pp. 472/3. Canning to Liverpool. Nov. 28, 1821.
61. Bathurst Papers. p. 523. to Bathurst. Nov. 26, 1821.
62. B.M. Add. Mss. 38743. Jan. 5, 1821.
63. Brock. pp. 147/8.
64. B.M. Add. Mss. 38743 to Huskisson. Jan. 15, 1822.
65. Bathurst Papers. p. 527.
66. B.M. Add. Mss. 38411. Reid to Canning. March 14; Canning to Doyle. March 17; Doyle to Canning. March 18; Canning to Reid. March 19, 1822.
67. Harewood Mss. 10. March 22, 1822.
68. Parl. Deb. N.S. VII 211 ff.
69. Gash. *Mr Secretary Peel*. p. 299.
70. Harewood Mss. 10. to his mother. Sept. 21, 1822.
71. Harewood Mss. 26. to Joan. Sept. 3, 1822.
72. Harewood Mss. 26. August 19, 1822.
73. *Ibid*. August 24, 1822.
74. B.M. Add. Mss. 38743. Sept. 8, 1822.
75. Wellington Desp. N.S. I p. 273. Sept. 5, 1822.
76. *Ibid*. pp. 274/6.
77. Yonge. III p. 199. Sept. 8, 1822.
78. Arbuthnot Corr. p. 31. Arbuthnot to his wife. Sept. 2, 1822.
79. Wellington Desp. N.S. I pp. 277/8. Sept. 7, 1822.
80. Yonge. III p. 201/2.
81. Harewood Mss. 76. Canning to Hammond. Sept. 14, 1822.
82. Harewood Mss. 10. Sept. 14, 1822.

CHAPTER XV

1. Bagot. II p. 138. Nov. 5, 1822.
2. *The Times.* Oct. 14, 1822.
3. Webster. *Foreign Policy of Castlereagh.* p. 240.
4. Bagot. II p. 138. Nov. 5, 1822.
5. Parl. Deb. N.S. IV 1375. March 20, 1821.
6. A. G. Stapleton. *Pol. Life.* II p. 304.
7. Wellington Desp. N.S. I p. 304. Sept. 27, 1822.
8. *Ibid.* Wellington to Canning p. 343. Oct. 4, 1822 and p. 457. Oct. 20, 1822.
9. *Ibid.* p. 492.
10. Temperley. *The Foreign Policy of Canning.* p. 68.
11. Well. Desp. N.S. I p. 536. Nov. 15, 1822.
12. Temperley. pp. 69/71.
13. A. G. Stapleton. *G.C. & T.* p. 386. to à Court. Dec. 29, 1822.
14. British and Foreign State Papers. X p. 54. Feb. 9, 1823.
15. Stapleton. *Pol. Life.* I pp. 244/5. Jan. 26, 1823.
16. Temperley. pp. 77/8.
17. *The Times.* Jan. 30, 1823.
18. Lieven. *Letters.* p. 232. Jan. 31, 1823.
19. E. J. Stapleton. Off. Corr. I pp. 71/6. Feb. 1, 1823.
20. Creevey Papers. II p. 62. Feb. 4/5, 1823.
21. Bagot. II p. 156.
22. Temperley. p. 83.
23. Parl. Deb. N.S. VIII 872 ff.
24. Bagot. II p. 169. to Binning. May 15, 1823.
25. *Ibid.* pp. 179/80. to Bagot. July 14, 1823.
26. Wilberforce. *Life.* V p. 176. April 30, 1823.
27. Parl. Deb. N.S. VIII 1520 ff.
28. Mrs Arbuthnot. I p. 231. May 1, 1823.
29. Bagot. II p. 180. July 14, 1823.
30. A. G. Stapleton. *G.C. & T.* pp. 377/8. to Henry Wellesley. Sept. 16, 1823.
31. Harewood Mss. 70. to Liverpool.
32. Bagot. II p. 234 (footnote).
33. Harewood Mss. 136. Planta to Canning. Nov. 7, 1823.
34. Bagot. II p. 200. to Bagot. Sept. 19, 1823.
35. Temperley. EHR. April 1923. Vol. 38 p. 210.
36. *George IV.* 3, p. 39. Nov. 6, 1823.
37. Lieven Letters. pp. 258/9. April 24, 1823.
38. *Ibid.* pp. 241/2. March 5, 1823.

39. Mrs Arbuthnot. I p. 213. Feb. 7, 1823.
40. *Ibid.* p. 198 (Nov. 24, 1822) pp. 238 and 237 (May 30, 1823).
41. Wellington Desp. N.S. II p. 34. Feb. 11, 1823.
42. Brock. p. 239. Dec. 23, 1822.
43. Aspinall. EHR. July 1963. Vol. 78 p. 533 (Harewood Mss.).
44. Arbuthnot Corr. pp. 46/57. Oct. 7(?), 1823.
45. *Ibid.* Oct. 8, 1823.
46. B.M. Add. Mss. 38743. Oct. 23, 1822. Add. Mss. 38744. Jan. 13, 1823.
47. Arbuthnot Corr. p. 37 to Arbuthnot. Dec. 30, 1822.
48. Harewood Mss. 70. Canning to Liverpool. Jan. 18, 1823.
49. Arbuthnot Corr. p. 38 to Arbuthnot. Jan. 10, 1823.
50. Huskisson Papers. p. 159. to Huskisson. Jan. 15, 1823.
51. *Ibid.* p. 152. to Huskisson. Jan. 3, 1823.
52. Harewood Mss. 70. Jan. 18, 1823.
53. Aspinall. EHR. July 1963. Vol. 78 p. 533 (Harewood Mss.).
54. Parker. *Peel.* I p. 331. April 3, 1822.
55. Bagot. II pp. 178/9. July 14, 1823.
56. Parl. Deb. N.S. VIII 1079 ff.
57. Creevey Papers. II p. 68. April 18, 1823.
58. Bagot. II p. 168. to Binning. May 15, 1823.
59. Wellington Desp. N.S. I pp. 322–9.
60. BFSP. XII p. 838 ff.
61. Parl. Deb. N.S. IX 265 ff.
62. Parl. Deb. N.S. X 1091 ff.

CHAPTER XVI

1. Wellington Desp. N.S. I p. 511. to Wellington. Nov. 8, 1822.
2. Humphreys. Trans. RHS. 5th series. No. 16 (1966) p. 146.
3. Bartlett. *Castlereagh.* p. 150.
4. Wellington Desp. N.S. I p. 465. Oct. 29, 1822.
5. *Ibid.* p. 516 to Canning. Nov. 10, 1822.
6. *Ibid.* pp. 544/5. Nov. 19, 1822.
7. Webster. *Britain and the Independence of Latin America 1812-1830.* II pp. 76/8.
8. *Ibid.* p. 78. to Canning. Nov. 26, 1822.
9. Wellington Desp. N.S. I p. 640. to Canning. Dec. 10, 1822.
10. *Ibid.* p. 650. Dec. 13, 1822.
11. Dexter Perkins. *A History of the Monroe Doctrine.* p. 36.
12. Temperley. p. 111. August 20, 1823.
13. Harewood Mss. 70. to Liverpool. August 26 and 30, 1823.
14. Rush. *The Court of London 1819-25.* pp. 376 ff.
15. Wellington Desp. N.S. II p. 134. Sept 23, 1823.

16. *Ibid.* p. 140
17. Temperley. pp. 115/17.
18. Wellington Desp. N.S. II p. 154. Oct. 21, 1823.
19. Webster. II p. 127. Stuart to Canning. Nov. 15, 1823.
20. Temperley. p. 119.
21. Adams, J. Q. Memoirs. VI p. 179.
22. *Ibid.* VI p. 186.
23. Bagot. II pp. 216/17. Jan. 22, 1824.
24. Adams, J. Q. Memoirs. VI p. 188 and p. 208.
25. *The Times.* Jan. 6, 1824.
26. Bagot. II p. 209. Canning to Bagot. Jan. 9, 1824.
27. Temperley. pp. 127/8.
28. A. G. Stapleton. *G.C. & T.* p. 394. to à Court, Dec. 31, 1823.
29. Webster. I p. 23.
30. F.O. 18/3. Planta to Colonel Hamilton. Feb. 6, 1824.
31. Webster. I p. 356. C. Nugent to Canning. July 30, 1824.
32. A. G. Stapleton. *G.C. & T.* p. 395. Canning to à Court.
33. Webster. II p. 122. Stuart to Canning. Nov. 3, 1823.
34. Webster. I p. 22.
35. Wellington Desp. N.S. II p. 137. Sept. 24, 1823.
36. Harewood Mss. 70. August 26, 1823.
37. F.O. 65/141.
38. Bagot. II p. 222. to Bagot. Jan. 22, 1824.
39. Parl. Deb. N.S. XI 1344 ff.
40. Webster. I pp. 433/6. to Hervey. Oct. 10, 1823.
41. *Ibid.* pp. 442–5.
42. *Ibid.* pp. 446/50.
43. *Ibid.* pp. 453/4. to Canning. July 9, 1824.
44. *Ibid.* pp. 455/7. July 20, 1824.
45. F.O. 18/3. July 30 and August 19, 1824.
46. Webster. I p. 379. to Canning. July 5, 1824.
47. *Ibid.* p. 381. Nov. 8, 1824.
48. F.O. 18/3. Sept. 9, 1823.
49. *Ibid.* April 10, 1824.
50. Webster. I p. 381. Nov. 8, 1824.
51. F.O. 18/3. Nov. 8, 1824.
52. E. J. Stapleton. Off. Corr. I pp. 147/8. Canning to Liverpool. March 3 1824.
53. Mrs Arbuthnot. I p. 306. April 29, 1824.
54. Yonge. III p. 280. May 1, 1824.
55. *George IV.* 3, pp. 74/5. May 5, 1824.
56. Temperley. EHR. April 1923. Vol. 38 pp. 215/16.
57. E. J. Stapleton. Off. Corr. I p. 258 to Granville. March 11, 1825.
58. Mrs Arbuthnot. I p. 321. June 10, 1824.

59. Croker. I p. 266. May 10, 1824.
60. Parl. Deb. N.S. XI 663.
61. *Ibid.* 715 ff.
62. E. J. Stapleton. Off. Corr. I p. 148. March 3, 1824.
63. Bagot. II p. 241 to Bagot. May 29, 1824.
64. A. G. Stapleton. *G.C. & T.* pp. 397/400.
65. Croker. I p. 268.
66. E. J. Stapleton. Off. Corr. I p. 160. Sept. 11, 1824.
67. *Ibid.* p. 163. to Liverpool. Sept. 18, 1824.
68. B.M. Add. Mss. 38746. to Huskisson. Sept. 29, 1824.
69. A. G. Stapleton. *G.C. & T.* p. 404. to Granville. Nov. 15, 1824.
70. E. J. Stapleton. Off. Corr. I p. 162. to Liverpool. Sept. 18, 1824.
71. Wellington Desp. N.S. II pp. 313/14. Wellington to Canning. Oct. 5, 1824.
72. Lieven Letters. p. 336. Nov. 2, 1824.
73. E. J. Stapleton. Off. Corr. I p. 181. Oct. 25, 1824.
74. Wellington Desp. N.S. II pp. 354/8.
75. A. G. Stapleton. *G.C. & T.* p. 488. Dec. 6, 1824.
76. Harewood Mss. 71.
77. A. G. Stapleton. *G.C. & T.* pp. 407/11.
78. Wellington Desp. N.S. II p. 368 to Wellington.
79. A. G. Stapleton. *G.C. & T.* pp. 411/12. Dec. 17, 1824.
80. Harewood Mss. 27. to Joan. Dec. 19, 1824.
81. *Ibid.*
82. *Ibid.* to Joan. Dec. 28, 1824.
83. Temperley. EHR. April, 1923. Vol. 38 pp. 220/21.
84. Wellington Desp. N.S. II pp. 401/2.
85. Harewood Mss. 27. to Joan. Jan. 28, 1825.
86. E. J. Stapleton. Off. Corr. I p. 258. March 11, 1825.
87. Wellington Desp. N.S. II pp. 402/4.
88. Temperley. EHR. April 1923. Vol. 38 p. 221.
89. Harewood Mss. 27.
90. *Ibid.* Jan. 3 and 6, 1825.
91. F.O. 352/10 to Stratford Canning. Feb. 23, 1825.
92. Webster. I pp. 385/6. March 8, 1825.
93. A. G. Stapleton. *G.C. & T.* p. 447. Nov. 21, 1825.
94. E. J. Stapleton. Off. Corr. II p. 244 to Granville. Jan. 2, 1827.
95. Festing. p. 268. to J. H. Frere. Jan. 8, 1825.

CHAPTER XVII

1. E. J. Stapleton. Off. Corr. I p. 153. to Granville. August 17, 1824.
2. A. G. Stapleton. *G.C. & T.* p. 509. to Granville. Jan. 21, 1825.

3. Bagot. II p. 183 to Bagot. July 14, 1823.
4. Wellington Desp. N.S. II pp. 110/2. July 31, 1823, pp. 113/5, August 3, 1823.
5. *Ibid.* pp. 112/3. August 1 and 2, 1823.
6. F.O. 63/269. August 5, 1823.
7. Harewood Mss. 70. Nov. 10, 1823.
8. F.O. 63/286. May 1, 1824.
9. Lieven Letters. p. 320. July 4, 1824.
10. Temperley. p. 203 and F.O./304. July 6, 16 and 18, 1824. Canning to Stuart.
11. Mrs Arbuthnot. I p. 328.
12. Temperley. p. 204. July 19, 1824.
13. F.O. 63/294 to Thornton. Jan. 1, 1825.
14. A. G. Stapleton. *G.C. & T.* p. 504. Dec. 18, 1824.
15. F.O. 63/295. August 23, 1825.
16. *Ibid.* Sept. 21, 1825.
17. Webster. II p. 242.
18. *Ibid.* p. 236.
19. E. J. Stapleton. Off. Corr. I p. 237. Jan. 17, 1825.
20. Webster. I p. 262.
21. E. J. Stapleton. Off. Corr. I p. 337. to Liverpool. Nov. 27, 1825.
22. *Ibid.* p. 237. to Granville. Jan. 17, 1825.
23. Temperley. p. 329.
24. Wellington Desp. N.S. II p. 534. to Stratford Canning. Oct. 12, 1825.
25. Broughton. *Recollections of a Long Life.* III p. 34.
26. Bagot. II p. 181 to Bagot. July 14, 1823.
27. *Ibid.* p. 198 to Bagot. August 20, 1823.
28. *Ibid.* p. 215. Jan. 22, 1824.
29. Wellington Desp. N.S. II p. 323. to Liverpool. Oct. 17, 1824.
30. F.O. 65/141. to Bagot. Jan. 15, 1824.
31. F.O. 78/120. to Strangford. Feb. 24, 1824.
32. Wellington Desp. N.S. II p. 323.
33. B.F.S.P. XII pp. 899/903.
34. A. G. Stapleton. *G.C. & T.* p. 458. to Granville. Nov. 15, 1824.
35. E. J. Stapleton. Off. Corr. I p. 234. to Granville. Jan. 17, 1825.

CHAPTER XVIII

1. Lieven Letters. p. 338. Nov. 24, 1824.
2. A. J. Stapleton. *G.C. & T.* p. 439. Canning to Knighton. April 27, 1825.
3. Lieven Letters. p. 343. Feb. 4, 1825.
4. Harewood Mss. 27. Canning to Joan. March 11, 1825.

5. E. J. Stapleton. Off. Corr. I p. 259. March 11, 1825.
6. Harewood Mss. 27. March 11, 1825.
7. A. G. Stapleton. *G.C. & T.* p. 466. Canning to Granville. Oct. 31, 1825.
8. A. G. Stapleton. *G.C. & T.* pp. 437–44. Memorandum dictated by Canning. April 27, 1825.
9. Temperley. pp. 250/1.
10. Harewood Mss. 110. to H. Wellesley. Jan. 9, 1826.
11. E. J. Stapleton. Off. Corr. I p. 298.
12. A. G. Stapleton. *G.C. & T.* pp. 448–52. Memorandum by Canning. Dec. 21, 1825.
13. Bagot. II p. 351 to Charles Ellis. May 27, 1826.
14. *George IV.* 3, p. 143 n4.
15. Temperley. p. 255.
16. E. J. Stapleton. Off. Corr. I p. 241. to Granville.
17. *Ibid.* p. 250. to Granville. Feb. 22, 1825.
18. Harewood Mss. 27. Feb. 22, 1827.
19. E. J. Stapleton. Off. Corr. I p. 250. to Granville. Feb. 22, 1825.
20. Parl. Deb. N.S. XII 75 ff.
21. *Ibid.* 463 ff.
22. Harewood Mss. 27. March 4, 1825.
23. A. G. Stapleton. *Pol. Life.* II p. 152.
24. Arbuthnot Corr. p. 76. Arbuthnot to Liverpool. May 13, 1825.
25. E. J. Stapleton. Off. Corr. I p. 269. May 18, 1825.
26. Parl. Deb. N.S. XIII 888 ff.
27. Harewood Mss. 27.
28. Harewood Mss. 71. to Liverpool. May 6, 1825.
29. Bagot. II p. 283. Binning to Bagot. May 27, 1825.
30. E. J. Stapleton. Off. Corr. I pp. 246/7. Feb. 18, 1825.
31. *Ibid.* p. 278. June 28, 1825.
32. Festing. p. 260. to Frere. August 7, 1823.
33. Bagot. II p. 289. to Bagot. August 27, 1827.
34. B.M. Add. Mss. 38747. August 24, 1825.
35. Bagot. II p. 288.
36. Lieven Letters. p. 343. Jan. 27, 1825.
37. Harewood Mss. 72.
38. Wellington Desp. N.S. III p. 116. to Wellington. Feb. 17, 1826.
39. Granville Mss. PRO 30/29. 8/10. to Granville. March 26, 1826.
40. Croker. I p. 314. Croker to Wellington. March 20, 1826.
41. Granville Mss. PRO 30/29. 8/10. to Granville. March 26, 1826.
42. Wellington Desp. III p. 147 to Wellington. March 4, 1826.
43. *Ibid.* II p. 500. Sept. 19, 1825.
44. Creevey Papers. II p. 100. May 3, 1826.
45. Parl. Deb. N.S. XV 796.
46. Creevey Papers. II pp. 100/1. May 5, 1826.

47. Mrs Arbuthnot. II p. 26.
48. Arbuthnot Corr. p. 74. Arbuthnot to Wellington. April 25, 1825.
49. Parl. Deb. N.S. XIV 854/5.
50. *Ibid.* XV 145.

CHAPTER XIX

1. Lieven Diary. p. 85.
2. *Ibid.* p. 88 ff.
3. Wellington Desp. N.S. II p. 507 ff.
4. *Ibid.* III pp. 115/6. Wellington to Bathurst. Feb. 17, 1826.
5. A. G. Stapleton. *G.C. & T.* pp. 471/2 to Granville. Jan. 13, 1826.
6. Wellington Desp. N.S. III p. 56. Jan. 1, 1826.
7. A. G. Stapleton. *G.C. & T.* p. 471 to Granville. Jan. 13, 1826.
8. A. G. Stapleton. *Ibid.*
9. Lieven Letters. p. 363. March 28, 1826.
10. F.O. 352/13 (Pt. 1). to Stratford Canning. Jan. 9, 1826.
11. Wellington Desp. N.S. III pp. 104/7. Feb. 10, 1826.
12. *Ibid.* pp. 85/93.
13. Temperley. pp. 586/7.
14. F.O. 7/191 to H. Wellesley. May 4, 1826.
15. F.O. 352/13 (Pt. 1). July 3, 1826.
16. Granville Mss. PRO 30/29. 8/10. to Granville. June 2, 1826.
17. Wellington Desp. N.S. III pp. 290/6. April 11, 1826.
18. Harewood Mss. 72.
19. A. G. Stapleton. *G.C. & T.* p. 477. August 7, 1826.
20. *Ibid.* p. 528 to Liverpool. Oct. 16, 1826.
21. Lady Granville. Letters. I p. 397.
22. A. G. Stapleton. *G.C. & T.* p. 517 to Liverpool Sept. 29, 1826.
23. *George IV.* 3, pp. 175/6. Oct. 20, 1826.
24. F.O. 352/13 (Pt. 1). Sept. 6, 1826.
25. *George IV.* 3, p. 159 (Sept. 22, 1826) and p. 165 (Oct. 1, 1826).
26. A. G. Stapleton. *G.C. & T.* pp. 490/1. to Granville. April 29 and July 1, 1825.
27. *George IV.* 3, p. 166. Canning to King. Oct. 1, 1826.
28. F.O. 63/306.
29. Temperley. p. 367.
30. F.O. 63/305. June 28, 1826.
31. Temperley. p. 369.
32. F.O. 73/312. April 14, 1826.
33. *Ibid.* April 22, 1826.
34. F.O. 72/317.
35. F.O. 72/313.

496

36. *George IV*. 3, p. 172. Oct. 9, 1826.
37. E. J. Stapleton. Off. Corr. II p. 134. Sept. 20, 1826.
38. A. G. Stapleton. *G.C. & T.* p. 522. to Liverpool. Oct. 5, 1826.
39. *Ibid.* p. 528. Oct. 16, 1826.
40. Wellington Desp. N.S. III p. 431. Oct. 20, 1826.
41. *Ibid.* pp. 417/18. Oct. 11, 1826.
42. *Ibid.* p. 422. Oct. 15, 1826.
43. *George IV*. 3, p. 181 to the King. Nov. 13, 1826.
44. F.O. 63/306. Nov. 15, 1826.
45. Wellington Desp. N.S. III p. 474. Dec. 3. 1826.
46. A. G. Stapleton. *G.C. & T.* p. 541.
47. *Ibid.* pp. 542/3.
48. *Ibid.* p. 542.
49. Broughton. III p. 159.
50. Parl. Deb. N.S. XVI 350/69.
51. Croker. I p. 322.
52. Parl. Deb. N.S. XVI 390/7.
53. A. G. Stapleton. *G.C. & T.* pp. 546/7. to Granville. Dec. 14, 1826.
54. *Ibid.* p. 547.
55. Colchester. III p. 454.
56. Temperley. p. 384.
57. Lady Granville. Letters. I p. 400.
58. A. G. Stapleton. *G.C. & T.* p. 545. Dec. 14, 1826.
59. Stapleton Mss.
60. A. G. Stapleton. *G.C. & T.* p. 548. Dec. 22, 1826.
61. F.O. 63/310. Dec. 9, 1826.
62. Harewood Mss. 72.
63. F.O. 63/310.
64. Temperley. p. 388.
65. F.O. 72/318.
66. Bathurst Papers. p. 629. Feb. 1, 1827.
67. Yonge. III pp. 443/7 to Liverpool. Feb. 5, 1827.
68. For example A. G. Stapleton. *G.C. & T.* p. 607.
69. Harewood Mss. 110. August 19, 1823.
70. E. J. Stapleton. Off. Corr. I p. 218. Dec. 31, 1824.
71. Temperley. pp. 203/5.
72. *Ibid.* p. 175.
73. Bagot. II p. 266. July 29, 1824 and p. 268. August 1824.
74. Temperley. p. 291.
75. Granville Mss. PRO 30/29. 8/9. Jan. 3, 1826.
76. *George IV*. 3, p. 51. Dec. 13, 1823.
77. Harewood Mss. 27. Canning to Joan. April 1824.
78. Aspinall. *The Formation of Canning's Ministry*. p. 279.
79. Bagot. II p. 309. Oct. 26, 1826.

80. Dudley. *Letters to Ivy*. p. 327.
81. Harewood Mss. 8. Oct. 1813.
82. Lieven Letters. p. 372. June 14, 1826.
83. Wilberforce. *Life*. V p. 217. March 19, 1824.
84. Bagot. II p. 148.
85. Harewood Mss. 110. August 19, 1823.

CHAPTER XX

1. Croker Papers. I p. 321.
2. Bulwer. *Palmerston*. I p. 171.
3. A. G. Stapleton. *G.C. & T.* p. 528. to Liverpool. Oct. 16, 1826.
4. Yonge. III pp. 438/9. Dec. 16, 1826.
5. A. G. Stapleton. *G.C. & T.* p. 548. to Granville. Dec. 19, 1826.
6. Harewood Mss. 72. August 24, 1826.
7. Well. Desp. N.S. III p. 574. Jan. 29, 1827.
8. A. G. Stapleton. *G.C. & T.* p. 579.
9. E. J. Stapleton. Off Corr. II p. 258. A. G. Stapleton to Huskisson. Feb. 10, 1827.
10. Granville Mss. PRO 30/29, 8/12. Feb. 16, 1827.
11. Parker. *Peel*. I p. 450. Canning to Peel. Feb. 23, 1827.
12. Broughton. III p. 173.
13. *George IV*. 3, p. 204. to Knighton. March 3, 1827.
14. Aspinall. FCM. p. 38. F. Cathcart to Bagot. March 9, 1827.
15. *Ibid*. p. 32. March 5, 1827.
16. *Ibid*. pp. 10/11. Feb. 21, 1827.
17. Colchester. III pp. 472/3 and Well. Desp. N.S. III p. 634.
18. A. G. Stapleton. *G.C. & T.* pp. 582/6. Memorandum dictated by Canning.
19. Parker. *Peel*. I pp. 457/8.
20. Parl. Deb. N.S. XVII 157/71.
21. Aspinall. FCM. p. 49 (Hobhouse's Diary).
22. Parker. *Peel*. I pp. 460/2. Peel to Eldon. April 9, 1827.
23. Parker. *Peel*. I pp. 464/5. April 15, 1827.
24. A. G. Stapleton. *G.C. & T.* p. 588. April 3, 1827.
25. *Ibid*. pp. 588/9. April 5, 1827.
26. Greville. I p. 92. April 13, 1827.
27. Well. Desp. N.S. III pp. 636/7.
28. Harewood Mss. 72. Nov. 20, 1826.
29. A. G. Stapleton. *Pol. Life*. III p. 369 ff.
30. Colchester. III p. 502.
31. Well. Desp. N.S. IV p. 35. May 21, 1827.
32. Aspinall. FCM. p. XXXIX.

33. *Ibid.* p. 66. April 12, 1827.
34. Aspinall. FCM. p. 67 (Viscount Sandon's memorandum). April 12, 1827.
35. Greville. III pp. 137/8 (Sept. 23, 1834).
36. *The Times.* April 14, 1827.
37. Aspinall. FCM. p. 129. to Bagot. April 19, 1827.
38. Harewood Mss. 74. to Bexley. April 27, 1827.
39. Aspinall. FCM. p. 155. April 21, 1827.
40. *Ibid.* p. 111 to John Gladstone. April 18, 1827.
41. Aspinall. EHR. 1927. Vol. 42 pp. 202/3.
42. E. J. Stapleton. Off. Corr. II p. 301. Brougham to Sir R. Wilson. March 26, 1827.
43. Aspinall. EHR. 1927. Vol. 42 p. 205.
44. Aspinall. FCM. p. 76. April 13, 1827.
45. *Ibid.* p. 80. Carlisle to Holland. April 14, 1827.
46. Sir Robert Wilson's *Narrative.* p. 22.
47. Aspinall. FCM. to Carlisle. April 19, 1827.
48. Wilson *Narrative.* p. 17.
49. Aspinall. FCM. p. 106. to Althorp. April 1827.
50. Aspinall. FCM. p. 105. April 1827.
51. *Ibid.* p. 81. to Carlisle. April 14, 1827.
52. Aspinall. EHR. 1927. Vol. 42 p. 221.
53. Aspinall. FCM. p. 74. April 13, 1827.
54. *Ibid.* pp. 170/1. to Lansdowne. April 24, 1827.
55. *The Times.* April 30, 1827.
56. Aspinall. FCM. p. 214. to Holland. May 5, 1827.
57. Harewood Mss. 103A. May 1, 1827.
58. Aspinall. FCM. p. 216.
59. *Ibid.* p. 206 to F. Lamb. May 1, 1827.
60. *Ibid.* p. 218. May 8, 1827.
61. Parl. Deb. N.S. XVII 539 ff.
62. *George IV.* 3, p. 227. to the King. May 3, 1827.
63. Parl. Deb. N.S. XVII 583 ff.
64. *Ibid.* 1049 ff.
65. Aspinall. FCM. p. 239. Seaford to Granville. June 5, 1827.
66. W. D. Jones. *Prosperity Robinson.* pp. 147/8.
67. Aspinall. FCM. p. 236. to Canning. June 4, 1827.
68. Granville Mss. PRO 30/29/8/12. to Granville. June 19, 1827.
69. Creevey Papers. II p. 121. June 19, 1827.
70. Wellesley Papers. II p. 158. to Wellesley. May 22, 1827.
71. Aspinall. FCM. p. LIII.
72. Aspinall. EHR. 1927. Vol. 42 p. 226.
73. F.O. 78/151. to Stratford Canning. Feb. 19, 1827.
74. *Ibid.*
75. Temperley. pp. 595/606.

76. Arbuthnot Corr. p. 88. to Arbuthnot. July 4, 1827.
77. Temperley. p. 403.
78. Aspinall. FCM. pp. 262/3. to R. Herries. July 16, 1827.
79. Temperley. pp. 437/8.
80. Parl. Deb. N.S. XVII 707. May 10, 1827.
81. Bagot. II pp. 407/8. to Bagot. July 12, 1827.
82. Greville. I p. 99.
83. Aspinall. FCM. p. 279. to Stratford Canning. August 9, 1827.
84. Greville. I p. 103.
85. *The Times.* August 17, 1827.
86. Broughton. III pp. 212/3.
87. Temperley. p. 446.
88. Webster. II p. 520. to Rufus King (United States minister). August 7, 1825.
89. A. G. Stapleton. *G.C. & T.* p. 350.
90. Aspinall. Trans. RHS. 4th series. 17 p. 218, n3. to Haddington. Jan. 8, 1829.
91. Parl. Deb. XXXV 683. Feb. 25, 1817.
92. Parl. Deb. N.S. XIV 854/5. Feb. 24, 1826.

Select Bibliography

Manuscript Sources

British Museum Additional Manuscripts. Canning, Huskisson, Liverpool, Morley, Perceval, Rose, Wellesley, Windham Mss.

Leeds City Libraries, Archives Department. Harewood and Stapleton Mss.

Public Record Office. Foreign Office Papers. Granville Mss. Dacres Adams Mss.

Published Sources

Adams, E. D. *The Influence of Grenville on Pitt's Foreign Policy 1787–1798.* Washington 1904.

Adams, John Quincy. *Memoirs 1795–1848.* Vol. VI. ed. C. F. Adams. Philadelphia 1875.

Anti-Jacobin The. 4th Edition. Revised and Corrected. 2 Vols. London 1799.

Anti-Jacobin, Poetry of the, edited by Charles Edmonds. 3rd edition. London 1890.

Arbuthbot, Charles. *Correspondence,* 1808–1850. ed. A. Aspinall. Royal Hist. Soc. Camden, 3rd series, Vol. 65 (1941).

Arbuthnot, Harriet Mrs. *Journal 1820–32.* ed. F. Bamford and the Duke of Wellington. 2 Vols. London 1950.

Aspinall, A. *Lord Brougham and the Whig Party.* London 1927.

Politics and the Press, c. 1780–1850. London 1949.

'The Formation of Canning's Ministry, February to August, 1827', Royal Hist. Soc. Camden. 3rd series. Vol. 59 (1937).

'The Canningite Party', *Trans. Royal Hist. Soc.* 4th series. Vol. 17.

'The Coalition Ministries of 1827. I. Canning's Ministry.' *English Historical Review.* Vol. 42. April 1927.

'Canning's Return to Office in September 1822'. *Eng. Hist. Review.* Vol. 78. July 1963.

Auckland, Lord (William Eden). *Journal and Correspondence.* 4 Vols. London 1861–62.

Bagot, J. F. *George Canning and his Friends.* 2 Vols. London 1909.

Barnes, D. G. *George III and William Pitt 1783–1806.* Stanford (O.U.P.) 1939.

Bartlett, C. J. *Castlereagh.* London 1966.

Bathurst Mss. Historical Manuscripts Commission. London 1923.

Briggs, Asa. *The Age of Improvement.* London 1959.

British and Foreign State Papers, Calendar of. London.

SELECT BIBLIOGRAPHY

Brock, W. R. *Lord Liverpool and Liberal Toryism 1820–1827.* Cambridge 1941.
Broughton, Lord (John Cam Hobhouse). *Recollections of a Long Life.* Vol. 3, 1822–29. London 1910.
Bryant, Arthur. *The Napoleonic Wars.* 3 Vols. London 1942–50.
Buckingham & Chandos, Duke of. *Memoirs of the Court & Cabinets of George III.* 4 Vols. London 1853–55.
Memoirs of the Court of England during the Regency 1811–20. 2 Vols. London 1856.
Memoirs of the Court of George IV 1820–30. 2 Vols. London 1859.
Cambridge History of British Foreign Policy. Vols. 1 & 2. Cambridge 1922–23.
The New Cambridge Modern History. Vol. 9, 1793–1830. Cambridge 1965.
Canning, George. *Speeches.* ed. R. Therry. 6 Vols. London 1828.
Carr, Raymond. 'Gustavus IV and the British Government 1804–9'. *Eng. Hist. Review.* Vol. 60. January 1945.
Castlereagh, Viscount. *Correspondence, Despatches and other Papers.* 2nd series. Vols. 6 & 7. London 1851.
Colchester, Lord (Charles Abbot). *Diary & Correspondence.* 3 Vols. London 1861.
Coquelle, P. *Napoleon and England 1803–1813.* trans. G. D. Knox. London 1904.
Coupland, R. *Wilberforce.* London 1923.
Creevey, Thomas. *The Creevey Papers.* ed. Sir H. Maxwell. 2 Vols. London 1903.
Creevey's Life & Times. ed. J. Gore. London 1934.
Croker, J. W. *Correspondence & Diaries.* ed. L. J. Jennings. 3 Vols. London 1884.
Davis, H. W. L. *The Age of Grey and Peel.* Oxford 1929.
'Brougham, Lord Grey and Canning 1815–30'. *Eng. Hist. Review.* Vol. 38, Oct. 1923.
Derry, J. W. *William Pitt.* London 1962.
Dropmore Papers. The Mss. of J. B. Fortescue at Dropmore. 10 Vols. Hist. Mss. Comm. 1892–1927.
Dudley, Earl of (J. W. Ward). *Letters to Ivy from the first Earl of Dudley,* by S. H. Romilly. London 1905.
Farington, Joseph. *The Farington Diary.* 8 Vols. London 1922–8.
Feiling, Keith. *The Second Tory Party 1714–1832.* London 1938.
Festing, G. *John Hookham Frere & his Friends.* London 1899.
Foord, A. S. *His Majesty's Opposition 1714–1830.* Oxford 1964.
Fortescue, J. W. *History of the British Army.* Vols. 4–6. London 1906–10.
Fox, Charles J. *Memorials and Correspondence of.* Vols. 3 & 4. ed. Lord John Russell. London 1854 & 1857.
Fulford, R. *Samuel Whitbread.* London 1967.
The Trial of Queen Caroline. London 1967.
Gash, N. *Mr Secretary Peel: the Life of Sir Robert Peel to 1830.* London 1961.

George III. *The Later Correspondence of George III*. ed. by A. Aspinall. Vols. 2–5. Cambridge 1963–70.

George IV. *Letters 1812–1831*. ed. A. Aspinall. Cambridge 1938. 3 Vols.

Glenbervie, Lord (Sylvester Douglas). *Diaries*. ed. F. Bickley. 2 Vols. London 1928.

Granville Leveson-Gower, Lord (Earl Granville). *Private Correspondence*. ed. Castalia, Countess Granville. 2 Vols. London 1916.

Granville, Harriet, Countess. *Letters Vol. I 1810–27*. ed. Hon. F. Leveson-Gower. London 1894.

Gray, Denis. *Spencer Perceval. The Evangelical Prime Minister 1762–1812*. Manchester 1963.

Greville, C. C. F. *Memoirs*. ed. H. Reeve. Vol. 1. London 1874.

Hill, Draper. *Mr Gillray. The Caricaturist*. London 1965.

Holland, Lord. *Memoirs of the Whig Party*. 2 Vols. London 1852–54.
Further Memoirs of the Whig Party 1807–21. ed. Lord Stavordale. London 1905.

Holland, Lady. *Journal 1791–1811*. ed. Earl of Ilchester. 2 Vols. London 1908.

Horner, Francis. *Memoirs & Correspondence*. 2 Vols. London 1843.

Humphreys, R. A. *Tradition and Revolt in Latin America*. London 1965.
'Anglo-American Rivalries & Spanish American Emancipation.' *Trans. Royal Hist. Soc.* 5th series. No. 16.

Huskisson, W. *The Huskisson Papers*. ed. Lewis Melville. London 1931.

Jackson, Sir George. *Diaries & Letters*. 2 Vols. London 1872.
The Bath Archives. 2 Vols. London 1873.

Jones, W. D. *Prosperity Robinson. The Life of Viscount Goderich 1782–1859*. London 1967.

Lane-Poole, S. *The Life of Stratford Canning*. Vol. 1. London 1888.

Lieven, Princess. *Private Letters to Prince Metternich 1820–26*. ed. P. Quennell. London 1937.
Unpublished Diary, Political Sketches & Some Letters. ed. H. Temperley. London 1925.

Longford, Elizabeth. *Wellington. The Years of the Sword*. London 1969.

Lonsdale, Earl of. Papers. Hist. Mss. Comm. 1893.

Machin, G. I. T. 'The Catholic Emancipation Crisis of 1825'. *Eng. Hist. Review*. Vol. 78, July 1963.

Mackesy, Piers. *The War in the Mediterranean. 1803–10*. London 1957.

Malmesbury, Earl of. *Diaries & Correspondence*. Vols. 2–4. London 1844.
Letters. 2 Vols. London 1870.

Marshall, Dorothy. *The Rise of George Canning*. London 1938.

Matheson, Cyril. *The Life of Henry Dundas, 1st Viscount Melville*. London 1933.

Minto, Earl of (Sir Gilbert Elliot). *Life & Letters*. Vols. 2 & 3. London 1874.

Mitchell, Austin. *The Whigs in Opposition 1815–1830*. Oxford 1967.

Moore, Sir John. *Diary*. ed. Major-General Sir J. F. Maurice. Vol. 2. London 1904.

New, Chester W. *Life of Henry Brougham to 1830*. Oxford 1961.

Newton, J. F. *The Early Days of George Canning*. London 1828.

O'Gorman, F. *The Whig Party and the French Revolution*. London 1967.

Oman, Carola. *Sir John Moore*. London 1953.

Oman, Sir Charles. *A History of the Peninsular War*. Vols. 1 & 2. London 1902.

Paget, Sir Arthur. *The Paget Papers*. ed. Sir Augustus Paget. Vol. 2 (1801–7). London 1896.

Pares, Richard. *King George and the Politicians*. Oxford 1953.

Parker, C. S. *Sir Robert Peel*. Vol. 1. London 1891.

Parliamentary History (1794–1803), continued as *Parliamentary Debates* (1803–20) and *Parliamentary Debates*, new series, 1820–27.

Perkins, Dexter. *A History of the Monroe Doctrine*. London 1960.

Petrie, Sir Charles. *George Canning*. London 1930.

Lord Liverpool and his Times. London 1954.

Philips, C. H. *The East India Company 1784–1834*. London 1961.

Plunket, Lord. *Life, Letters & Speeches*. Vol. 2. London 1867.

Reid, Loren. *Charles James Fox*. London 1969.

Roberts, Michael. *The Whig Party 1807–12*. London 1939.

Rolo, P. J. V. *George Canning*. London 1965.

Rose, George. *Diaries & Correspondence*. 2 Vols. London 1860.

Rose, Holland. *William Pitt and the Great War*. London 1911.

Pitt and Napoleon. Essays and Letters. London 1912.

'Canning and Denmark in 1807'. *Eng. Hist. Review*. Vol. 11, Jan. 1896.

'Canning and the Secret Intelligence from Tilsit'. *Trans. Royal Hist. Soc.* Vol. 20. 1906.

'Canning and the Spanish Patriots'. *American Hist. Review*. Vol. 12, Oct. 1906.

Rush, Richard. *Residence at the Court of London. 1817–1825*. London 1872.

The Court of London. 1819–1825. London 1873.

Ryan, A. N. 'The Causes of the British Attack upon Copenhagen 1807'. *Eng. Hist. Review*. No. 68, Jan. 1953.

Seton-Watson, R. W. *Britain in Europe 1793–1914*. Cambridge 1937.

Sherwig, J. M. *Guineas & Gunpowder. British Foreign Aid in the Wars with France, 1793–1815*. Harvard 1969.

Stanhope, Earl of. *Life of Pitt*. 4 Vols. London 1861–62.

Stapleton, A. G. *George Canning and his Times*. London 1859.

Political Life of George Canning. 1822–1827. 3 Vols. London 1831.

Stapleton, E. J. *Some Official Correspondence of George Canning 1820–1827*. 2 Vols. London 1887.

Temperley, H. *The Foreign Policy of Canning 1822–1827*. London 1925.

'Canning, Wellington & George IV'. *Eng. Hist. Review*. Vol. 38, April 1923.

'French Designs on Spanish America, 1820–1825'. *Eng. Hist. Review*. Vol. 40, Jan. 1925.

Twiss, H. *Life of Lord Eldon*. 3 Vols. London 1844.

Walpole, Spencer. *Life of Spencer Perceval*. 2 Vols. London 1844.

Ward, R. Plumer. *Memoirs of the Political & Literary Life of*, by Edmund Phipps. London. 2 Vols. 1850.

Watson, Steven. *The Reign of George III 1760–1815*. Oxford 1960.

Webster, Sir Charles. *The Foreign Policy of Castlereagh 1815–1822*. London 1925.

Britain and the Independence of Latin America 1812–1830. Select Documents from the Foreign Office Archives. Oxford 1938.

Wellesley, Marquess. *The Wellesley Papers*. by the editor of *The Windham Papers*. 2 Vols. London 1914.

Wellington, Duke of. *Supplementary Despatches* V. Civil Correspondence, 1807–9. London 1860.

Despatches Correspondence & Memoranda. new series. 1819–28. 4 Vols. London 1867–68.

White, R. J. *Waterloo to Peterloo*. London 1957.

Wilberforce, William. *Life of*, by his sons, Robert W. and Samuel W. 5 Vols. London 1838.

Wilson, Sir Robert. *Narrative of the Formation of Canning's Ministry*. London 1828.

Windham, William. *Diary*. 1784–1810. ed. Mrs Henry Baring. London 1866. *The Windham Papers*. Vol. 2. London 1913.

Woodhouse, C. M. *The Philhellenes*. London 1969.

Woodward, E. L. *The Age of Reform 1815–1870*. Oxford 1938.

Yonge, C. D. *Life & Administration of the 2nd Earl of Liverpool*. 3 Vols. London 1968.

Ziegler, Philip. *Addington*. London 1965.

Index

Bentinck, Lord George, 317
Bentinck, Lady Harriet, 292
Bentinck, Lady Mary, 74
Bernadotte, Marshal Jean, 173
Bernstorff, Count Christian, 174
Bernstorff, Count Joachim, 174
Bessborough, Lady, 129n, 148, 255
  on Fox's death, 149n; on G.C., 90, 133;
  on Greville's ministry, 143
Bexley, Lord, see Vansittart
Binning, Lord (later 9th Earl of Hadding-
  ton) (1780-1858), 265, 451n, 459
Binning, Lady, 265
Bloomfield, Sir Benjamin, 1st Baron, 298,
  309
Bolivar, Simon, 345, 373n, 425
Bolton, Colonel, 316, 399
Bonaparte, Jerome (King of Westphalia),
  167
Bonaparte, Joseph (King of Naples (1806)
  and Spain (1808)), 161, 191, 200
Bonaparte, Louis (King of Holland), 161,
  167, 187
Bonaparte, Napoleon, see Napoleon
Bond, Nathaniel, 133
Bordeaux, Duc de, 411
Boringdon, Lord, 1st Earl of Morley
  (1772-1840), 18, 20, 83, 85, 96, 160, 269,
  303, 461n
  on G.C., 159
  See also Canning, George, letters
Borrowes, Mr, 17
Braganza, House of, 376ff, 413-25 passim
Bragge, Charles, see Bathurst, Charles
  Bragge
Brand, Thomas, 20th Baron Dacre, 157-8
Brazil, 180-2, 213, 341n, 354, 358, 361, 374,
  428; King John in, 375-6; declares inde-
  pendence (1822), 381; G.C.'s policy for,
  390, 392; and Montevideo, 413n, 425
Britain: at war with France (1793-1801),
  27-8, 31-2, 44-5, 49-51, 59, 94; peace with
  France (1801), 102-5; renewal of war with
  France (1803), 116-17; at war with Russia
  (1807), 180; habeas corpus suspended in
  (1794), 38, (1817) 281, 285, 287; and
  Anglo-Russian Protocol (1826), 408-11,
  425, 455-6; and Treaty of London (1827),
  455-7; sends military aid to Portugal
  (1826), 420-1, 423n, 424-5, 433; economic
  and social problems in, (1795) 41-2, (1797)
  51, 59, (1801) 94, (1811) 242, (1816-17)
  279-82, (1819) 292, (1823) 333, (1825)
  400-3
Foreign Office, 44, 47, 417, 426-9

and Parliamentary reform, 279-84, 339,
  449, 453
Royal Navy, 59, 65, 103, 112, 116, 122,
  126-7, 169-70, 184-5; and slave trade,
  341-2; and South America, 345-8, 351,
  353, 355, 374; in Tagus, 376-81; and
  Greece, 385 and n, 407, 408n, 458-9
South American trade, 345-9, 357, 364,
  367, 373-4, 383n
Brodrick, William, 228
Brougham, Henry (Baron Brougham and
  Vaux) (1778-1868), 245, 252, 259-61, 285-
  6, 294, 298, 302, 449, 464; relations with
  G.C., 328-31, 340, 341 and n, 422, 446-7,
  452, 455
Brunswick, Charles William Ferdinand,
  Duke of, 27
Buckingham, George Nugent Temple
  Grenville, 1st Marquess of (1753-1813),
  137, 250
Buckingham, Richard Temple Chandos
  Grenville, 2nd Marquess of, 1st Duke of
  Buckingham and Chandos (1776-1839),
  314n, 437
Buckinghamshire, Earl of, see Hobart
Buenos Aires, 345, 349, 357-8, 364, 365n,
  367, 372-4, 383n; and Montevideo 413n,
  425; Lord Ponsonby on, 393n, 429
Burdett, Sir Francis (1770-1844), 236-7,
  247, 275, 279-80, 285, 436, 452
Burke, Edmund, 23-4, 26, 28, 33, 36, 50,
  69, 283
Burney, Dr, 39
Burney, Fanny, 47
Burrard, General Sir Harry (1755-1813),
  198-9, 205-6
Buxton, Thomas Fowell, 343
Byron, Lord, 385, 462

Cadiz, 213, 214n, 367
Calhoun, John C., 352
Camden, John Jeffreys Pratt, 2nd Earl,
  1st Marquess (Viscount Bayham) (1759-
  1840), 34, 155n, 217, 219-21, 224, 228-9
Campbell, Colonel, 360
Canning, Bessy, 16, 20
Canning, Charles George, eldest son of
  G.C. (1801-20), 98-100, 150-1, 232-3, 246,
  268-70, 274, 278, 286; death of, 300-1;
  G.C. on, 151, 233, 270
Canning, Charles John (Carlo), son of
  G.C. (1812-62), 266, 292, 316, 317n, 393,
  461
Canning, George, father of G.C. (1736-71),
  11-13

INDEX

CANNING, GEORGE, [*contd.*]
Portugal, Prussia, Russia, Spain, Sweden, Turkey
America (South), see separate entries, South America, Brazil, Buenos Aires, Chile, Colombia, Cuba, Mexico, Montevideo, Peru
'New World' and 'Old' Speech (Dec. 1826), 422
America (North), see separate entries, United States of America, Oregon
Foreign Office, 44, 47, 426-9
India (G.C.'s policy for, 1816-20), 288-92
Slave Trade, see separate entry
LETTERS
– to Boringdon (later Morley), 47-8, 90, 173, 180, 278
– to Frere, 92, 99-100, 104, 108, 110, and n
– to Mrs Hunn (mother), 13-14, 30-1, 241, 256-7, 262, 267-8, 275, 282, 284, 286, 292, 301, 303, 315, 320
– to Huskisson, 278
– to Joan: (1803-6) 117, 118n, 123-5, 128, 134-6, 138, 140-1; (1806-7) 142, 144-5, 147n, 153-4, 156; (1807-8) 160, 172-3, 180; (1808-9) 223, 225-7; (1809-12) 232-3, 235-6, 238-9, 245; (1812-16) 264-5; (1820-22) 299, 301, 304, 307, 317; (1822-25) 369-70, 429n; (1823-26) 398
– to Leighs: (1794-5) 30, 35, 38; (1796-7) 48, 51, 53, 56; (1799-1800) 74-9, 87-8; (1801-2) 99, 101, 108; (1805-6) 131, 132-3, 134n; (1806-7) 146n, 151, 157, 175, 227, 278
– to Leveson-Gower (later Granville), (1796-7) 47, 50; (1799-1800) 72-3, 76, 87; (1801-2) 105, 108; (1803-6) 120, 138; (1807) 173; (1810-12) 240-1, 254n, 256; (1812-14) 258, 266-8, 270; (1825) 371n, 372, 428; (1827) 458
– to Liverpool, 270
– to Pitt, 120, 139
– to Lady Hester Stanhope, 130, 131
– to Wellesley, 261
– to Wilberforce, 256

Canning, Colonel George (later Lord Garvagh) (1778-1840), 260n, 264
Canning, Harriet (G.C.'s daughter, b. 1804, m. Lord Clanricarde), 123, 151, 232-3, 292, 301, 305, 307, 312, 315-16, 319, 460; engagement of, 391n
Canning, Joan (*née* Scott), 72-9, 92, 96, 110, 243, 315, 429, 445; birth of Charles George, 98-100; miscarriages, 105, 110;

birth of second son and daughter, 123 and n; with family at Hinckley, 150, 201-2, 226, 232, 267; birth of Carlo, 266; in Lisbon, 271-4; in Paris (1816), 278; in Italy (1819), 292, 300; in Paris with Harriet (1821), 305, 312; in London (1821-2), 307, 319; and G.C.'s warning to Metternich (1823), 390-1, 319; in Paris with G.C. (1826), 411; in Brighton with G.C. (1827), 434-5; and G.C.'s death, 461, 463 and n
wealth of, 312-13
on Liverpool's letter (1822), 319n
See also under Canning, George, letters
Canning, Mary Ann (*née* Costello), *see* Hunn
Canning, Mehitabel (Hetty), 16, 19, 26, 83-4
Canning, Stratford (G.C.'s grandfather), 11-12
Canning, Mrs Stratford (G.C.'s grandmother), 16
Canning, Stratford (G.C.'s uncle), 12-13, 16, 22
Canning, Stratford (Viscount Stratford de Redcliffe) (1786-1880), 84, 261, 333; in St Petersburg, 389 and n; in Constantinople, 407, 409-11, 455-6
on G.C., 80
Canning, William Pitt (G.C.'s second son) (1802-28), 123n, 151, 233, 268, 393, 461n
Canning, Willy, 84
Canninge, George, 11
Canningites, 234, 264-6, 463
Canynges, Thomas, 11
Cape of Good Hope, 45
Cape Town, 103
Carlisle, 5th Earl of, 40, 62
Carlisle, 6th Earl of, *see* Morpeth
Carnot, Lazare, 32
Caribbean, piracy in, 346-7
Caroline, Princess of Wales (1786-1821), 87-8, 153 and n, 241, 263, 295, 296-303, 305-6, 308, 447; death of, 310, 361
as godmother to George (G.C.'s son), 100
Cartwright, Major John, 279-80
Castlereagh, Robert Stewart, Viscount, 2nd Marquess of Londonderry (1769-1822), 91, 96, 110n, 118n, 124 and n, 135n, 139-40, 281, 285-8, 465; as Pittite, 142-3, 146-8, 152, 155; as Secretary for War and Colonies, 155n, 157, 159, 162-5, 170-1, 177, 184, 189-93, 196-224 *passim*, 217, 238; duel with G.C., 226-31; as Foreign Secretary, 245, 247-8, 252-6, 264, 272, 296, 302, 304-5, 308, 311, 336, 362,

510

INDEX

Vimeiro, Battle of (1808), 199-201
Volunteer Consolidation Bill (1804), 122
Volunteers, 119

Wagram, Battle of (1809), 215-16
Waithman, Alderman, 361
Walcheren expedition, 216-17, 220-2, 229, 235-7
Walker, Adam, 27 and n
Wallace, Thomas (later Baron Wallace), 337 and n, 445
Wallachia, 163, 383-4, 387n
Walmoden, Count, 214
Walpole, Horace, 62n
Walpole, Sir Robert, 246
Ward, J. W. see Dudley
Ward (later Plumer-Ward), Robert, 245, 246
Wardle, Gwyllym, 229 and n
Waterloo, Battle of (1815), 273, 331
Wellesley, Sir Arthur, see Wellington
Wellesley, Sir Henry (1773-1847), 226, 269, 418, 427, 431
Wellesley, Marchioness, 221 and n
Wellesley, Richard Colley, 1st Marquess (1760-1842), 120n, 147-8, 156 and n, 210 and n, 221-5, 234 and n, 235, 237-9, 244-50 passim, 261-2, 265, 290-1, 314, 365, 442, 450
Wellesley-Pole, William, 1st Baron Maryborough, later 3rd Earl of Mornington (1763-1845), 160, 234, 238, 265, 305, 337n
Wellington, Arthur Wellesley, Duke of (1769-1852), 79, 147, 174, 178, 189-91, 193, 219n, 265, 271-3, 293, 308 and n, 336, 345, 401, 432, 434, 444-5, 463; Peninsular campaigns of, 198-205, 215-16, 223, 236-7, 242, 256, 263, 266-7; at Congress of Verona (1822), 325-7, 334, 342, 346-7; and South America, 350-1, 356 and n, 365, 367, 369-71; and Portugal, (1823-4) 376, 379, (1826) 417; mission to St Petersburg (1826), 405-10, 428n, 455 and Catholic emancipation, 400; and Corn Laws, 402, 453-4; and G.C., 300, 318-19, 334-6, 362-3, 366, 390, 393, 411, 417-18, 437-42; and George IV, 363, 391n; and slave trade, 341-2
West, Benjamin, 43
West Indies, 38, 45, 70-1, 107, 342-4, 346, 348

Westmorland, John Fane, 10th Earl of (1759-1841), 155n, 217, 220, 335, 367, 442
Westphalia, 167, 215
Whig Party, 36, 65, 114, 121, 148, 157-9, 178, 187-8, 205, 209-10, 225, 265, 306, 361; and Catholic question, 190, 251, 436; and French Revolution, 89; Friends of the People, 24, 28; and G.C., 16, 19, 22-6, 31, 83, 241-2, 244-5, 262-3, 339-41, 364, 403, 443-55; and George IV (Prince Regent), 96, 239-41, 244, 249-50, 308; Lansdowne Whigs, 18, 447; and Peterloo, 293-4; Portland Whigs, 36 and n, 39, 68, 155 and n; quarrel between Burke and Fox, 24
Whitbread, Samuel (1764-1815), 132-3, 187-8, 190, 244-5, 247, 249, 263, 270
Whitworth, Sir Charles, Earl Whitworth, 116
Wickham, William, 45
Wilberforce, William (1759-1833), 42, 51, 69-71, 107, 113, 119, 152, 175, 240, 241n, 246, 295, 330; condemns Melville, 132; and slave trade, 341-2, 344 on G.C., 81, 228, 250, 253, 256, 431n; on industrial unrest, 247, 281; on Sheridan, 196; on Spanish deputies, 195
William, Prince of Orange, 73n
Wilkes, John, 11
Wilson, Mr (Treasurer of the Navy's office), 132n
Wilson, Sir Robert, 179-80, 422, 447, 452
Windham, William (1750-1810), 36 and n, 51-2, 69, 87, 95, 114, 121, 148, 176, 190, 283
Wolfe, General, 43
Woolwich, army mutiny at, 51
Wordsworth, 200n, 201, 399; on Volunteers, 119
Worsley, Sir Richard, 28, 49
Wright (bookseller), 58-9, 63n
Wynn, Charles (1775-1850), 309, 314n, 361, 445

Yarmouth, Francis, Earl of, 3rd Marquess of Hertford, 226-7
York, Frederick, Duke of (1763-1827), 31, 156, 198-9, 217-18, 229n, 249, 433, 438, 440
Yorke, Charles Philip (1764-1834), 135 and n, 143